DERIVATIVES

AN INTRODUCTION

ROBERT A. STRONG

UNIVERSITY OF MAINE

SOUTH-WESTERN
THOMSON LEARNING™

Australia · Canada · Mexico · Singapore · Spain · United Kingdom · United States

Derivatives: An Introduction, by Robert A. Strong

Vice President/Publisher: Jack W. Calhoun
Senior Acquisitions Editor: Michael B. Mercier
Senior Developmental Editor: Susanna C. Smart
Marketing Manager: Julie Lindsay
Production Editor: Robert Dreas
Manufacturing Coordinator: Sandee Milewski
Media Production Editor: Mark Sears
Media Technology Editor: Vicky True
Media Development Editor: Kristen Meere
Design Project Manager and Internal Design: Rik Moore
Cover Design: Meighan Depke Design
Cover Photographer: Tony Stone Images
Production House: Publishers' Design and Production Services, Inc.
Printer: R.R. Donnelley & Sons Company, Crawfordsville Manufacturing Division

Printed in the United States of America
1   2   3   4   5   04   03   02   01

For more information contact South-Western, 5101 Madison Road, Cincinnati, Ohio, 45227 or find us on the Internet at http://www.swcollege.com

For permission to use material from this text or product, contact us by
- **telephone: 1-800-730-2214**
- **fax: 1-800-730-2215**
- **web: http://www.thomsonrights.com**

Library of Congress Cataloging-in-Publication Data

Strong, Robert A.
    Derivatives: An Introduction / Robert A. Strong.
        p.   cm.
    Includes bibliographical references and index
    ISBN 0-324-04174-8
    1. Derivative securities.   I. Title
HG6024.A3 S78 2001
332.63'2—dc21   2001042656

To Kristen and her discovery
of mango as a color.

Brief Contents

Contents

Preface

Ten years ago university courses on futures and options were relatively uncommon. When such a course existed, it was often a special topics elective. Today, understanding derivatives is essential to all finance students, regardless of whether they anticipate a career in investments, corporate finance, or banking.

Although most universities now have an undergraduate derivatives course, many instructors have not yet found a book with coverage that is both adequate *and* accessible. I was one of those instructors, and have responded to this need by writing *Derivatives: An Introduction* with an approach that is attractive to my students, and will be to many instructors, as well.

THE PHILOSOPHY OF THE TEXT

The phrase "derivative assets" has to a large extent replaced its predecessor, "futures and options." This reflects the growing importance of the swaps market, of engineered derivative products, and of exchange-traded hybrid securities such as futures options. *Derivatives: An Introduction* provides a broad introduction to the options, futures, swaps, and interest rate options markets and also provides the *intuition* needed to understand the fundamental mathematics of pricing.

In addition, coverage of innovative derivative products such as exotic options, weather derivatives, catastrophe futures, and volatility spreads has not been neglected. I cover these concepts—without delving into their pricing or valuation—and conclude with a contemporary issues chapter that discusses the latest developments in the field.

This book presents a good balance of theory and practice. It is important for a student of the derivatives market to understand how arbitrage arguments lead to rational option pricing, why the cost of carry is crucial to futures pricing, and how a swap dealer determines the fixed rate on an interest rate swap. These are enjoyable topics to teach, and motivated finance students can find them fascinating. At the same time, it is equally important to understand how the end-user makes intelligent use of these products as risk management tools. I have included a variety of application examples from the perspective of both the speculator and the hedger.

One feature of the book that students find interesting is the *Trading Strategy* box. Most chapters have one or two of these. Each provides an example of how someone finds a way to accomplish some objective—speculative, income generation, or risk management—by clever use of derivative products. Some of these exemplify trading practices not commonly found in an academic textbook, but widely used in practice. These examples reinforce either text coverage in the chapter where they appear, or concepts covered earlier in the book.

Additionally, *Derivatives Today* boxes appear throughout the text and serve a similar purpose. They describe a contemporary event, some aspect of a derivative product, or something unusual about the marketplace.

Finally, a useful self-assessment tool is provided at the end of each chapter. *Self Tests* allow students to test their understanding of chapter material with short quizzes; answers are provided at the end of the text.

AUDIENCE

The coverage is appropriate for most undergraduate derivatives courses and for application-oriented MBA courses. Students taking this course should have basic familiarity with stocks and bonds and with time value of money principles. Many students will have had a prior investments course, although that is not a prerequisite.

SUPPLEMENTAL MATERIALS

An *Instructor's Manual* is available to adopters, either in hard copy or downloadable from the text Web site. The manual includes answers and solutions to end-of-chapter materials, as well as a test bank.

The *text Web site*, at *http://strong.swcollege.com*, contains the Instructor's Manual, PowerPoint slides, a link to the CBOE, and links to useful items on the South-Western Finance Resource Center — FinanceLinks Online, Finance in the News, Wall Street Analyst Reports, Thomson Investment Network, and more.

PowerPoint slides, prepared by Oliver Schnusenberg of St. Joseph's University, will be useful teaching tools for instructors, and a study aid for students.

A *Study Guide*, prepared by Raj Kohli of Indiana University, South Bend, contains for each chapter an expanded outline, list of important formulas, self-test questions in multiple choice and true-false formats, problems, creative thinking questions, and answers to all items.

The *CBOE* (Chicago Board Options Exchange) has an excellent Web site with very helpful material for both the beginner and the expert. You can link to the CBOE at the text Web site under Student Resources, or go to it directly at *www.cboe.com*. The "Learning Center" and "Trading Center" sections are especially relevant to the classroom study on which you are about to embark. The Learning Center is a product of the CBOE's Options Institute, the exchange's educational arm. Here you will find a good overview of option strategies, profit and loss diagrams, and pricing considerations. This book makes frequent use of the Options Calculator found in the Trading Center. Become familiar with it early; it will save you a great deal of time and let you explore a wide variety of "what if" questions. As you read the book, use the Self Tests at the end of each chapter and explore the analytical tools from the CBOE; you will develop a solid understanding of the role derivatives play in our economic system.

ACKNOWLEDGMENTS

This project benefited from careful reviews by a number of my colleagues. They made excellent topical suggestions, caught errors in logic or math, and contributed substantially to the quality of the final product. These reviewers are:

Rick Borgman
University of Maine

Margaret Smoller
Wayne State University

Theodore F. Byrley,
Buffalo State College

Tie Su
University of Miami

Anurag Gupta
Case Western Reserve University

Andrew McKenzie
University of Arkansas

Michael Alderson
St. Louis University

Kevin McNew
University of Maryland

Oscar Varela
University of New Orleans

John A. Clark
University of Missouri–Kansas City

Frank T. Griggs
Grand Valley State University

Raj Kohli
Indiana University–South Bend

David Rystrom
Western Washington University

Francis E. Laatsch
Bowling Green State University

Joseph McCarthy
Bryant College

Clark L. Maxam
Montana State University

D. K. Malhotra
Philadelphia University

M. Nimalendran
University of Florida

Arlyn R. Rubash
Bradley Universtiy

Rakesh Bharti
Southern Illinois University

I want to especially thank two of my students, Alfred Doyle and Cate Wnek, and also Alexander Nikolaev, who painstakingly checked all the mathematics. They found a number of mistakes that others had missed. We have fixed these, thereby reducing the number of headaches in the classroom when the book is in use. I also want to thank Jim Bittman of the CBOE Options Institute for clearing up some questions I had and Sheldon Natenberg, an experienced options trader and one of the best instructors around, for providing me with numerous examples to help illustrate options in practice. Thanks also to Paul Stephens, Director of Institutional Marketing at the CBOE, for his support of options education at the University of Maine Business School.

As usual, it was a pleasure to work with the folks at South-Western. Julie Lindsay is a very creative marketing professional who knows how to get her field force to sell books. Dennis Hanseman and Bob Dreas tried to keep me on schedule to get the project done according to plan. This marks the third book I have done with the editorial assistance of Mike Mercier and Susan Smart, and I would be pleased to do three more with either of them. The whole South-Western team has been extremely professional and helpful in the conception and completion of this project.

Robert A. Strong
University of Maine

ABOUT THE AUTHOR

DR. ROBERT A. STRONG, CFA

Bob Strong is University of Maine Foundation Professor of Investment Education and Professor of Finance at the University of Maine.

His Bachelor of Science degree in engineering is from the United States Military Academy at West Point, his Master of Science degree in business administration from Boston University, and his Ph.D. in finance from Penn State University. He has also been a visiting professor of finance at Maine Maritime Academy and at Harvard University, where he was Deputy Director of the Summer Economics Program from 1997–1999. He is a Chartered Financial Analyst.

Dr. Strong's consulting focuses on risk management and asset valuation. Among the organizations for which he has consulted are Eastern Maine Healthcare, Bangor Hydro Electric Company, Maine Public Service Company, Energy Atlantic, the Maine State Police, the Maine Forest Service, Irving Oil, and the National Broadcasting Corporation. He has been a conference speaker for the Chicago Board Options Exchange, the Chicago Board of Trade, and the American Stock Exchange.

His current research interests center on investor asset allocation. He has published in journals ranging from the *Journal of Finance* and the *Journal of Portfolio Management* to the trade journals *Pensions and Investments* and *Futures*. His third book, *Practical Investment Management, 2nd edition*, was published in 2000.

Dr. Strong is immediate past president of the Northeast Business and Economics Association; an honorary captain in the Maine State Police; a member of the Board of Directors of the Maine Chapter of the Boston Security Analysts Society, Whitehorse, Inc., Bangor Savings Bank, Bangor Savings Bank Foundation, Eastern Maine Charities, Acclaim Systems, Inc., and is Chairman of the Board of Livada Securities.

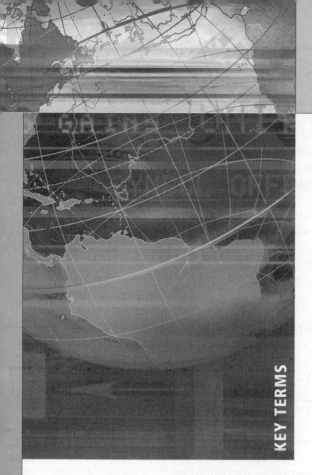

Introduction

It is a gloomy moment in history. Not for many years has there been so much grave and deep apprehension. Never has the future seemed so incalculable as now . . . the political cauldron seethes and bubbles. It's a solemn moment, and no one can feel the indifference. And yet, the very haste to be rich, which is the occasion of so much widespread calamity, has also tended to destroy the moral forces with which we are to resist and subdue the calamity!

Harper's Weekly
October 10, 1857

INTRODUCTION

The passage above from *Harper's Weekly* is a century and a half old, yet those words could easily be inserted into today's newspapers. There is worldwide interest in the financial markets and their influence on our quality of life. There is pervasive curiosity about the "strange" collection of assets known as **derivatives**.

A course on derivatives starts out on an awkward foot when someone asks the logical question, "What exactly is a derivative?" Unfortunately, there is no universally satisfactory answer to the question. When an expert is unable to give a quick answer to this question, decision makers can become suspicious of these things called derivatives, whatever they are, and decline to approve them as portfolio components or risk management tools.

One pioneer in the business calls the term "derivative" unfortunate and describes its spread as a public relations nightmare. Another executive says that from reading newspapers and listening to the news, it seems that a good definition for a derivative is "anything that results in a large loss." Others refer to the "dreaded D word." Piggybacking on the connotation of the term, one announcer for the British Broadcasting Corporation, reporting on the outbreak of mad cow disease, referred to hamburger as a "beef derivative." Whether the announcer intended the connotation or not, for much of the listening audience the term *derivative* undoubtedly conjured up notions of unusual risk and potential disaster.

Of late, each time a market participant suffers a large, newsworthy loss, the term "derivatives" is used almost as if it were an explanation.

> Frank N. Newman
> Acting Secretary of the Treasury
> Congressional Testimony, January 5, 1995

The bankruptcy of Orange County, California in 1994 probably did more than anything else to bring the term to America's kitchen table. In fact, in our history books Orange County and the unwise use of derivatives are probably going to be perpetually linked. However, from the perspective of someone schooled in derivatives, *Orange County had nothing to do with derivatives*.[1] The county treasurer, Robert Citron, was engaging in leveraged transactions (known as reverse repurchase agreements) with government securities. While not familiar to the public, repurchase agreements are *not* derivatives. He was essentially speculating with borrowed money and prices moved against him.

The futures and options markets are very useful, perhaps even essential parts of our financial system. Still, they have a long history of being misunderstood. To professionals in the field, it is a disturbing fact that many people who offer advice about the relative merits of futures and options products are ill equipped to do so. You cannot understand these products by casual contact, by a conversation on a golf course, or by reading a few magazine articles. Derivatives require serious study if they are to be used properly. Two major objectives of this book are to illustrate their economic function and to inform the potential user so that an intelligent decision might be made regarding the role of these products in a particular portfolio.

There is no universally satisfactory definition of the word "derivative."

---

[1]Mary Shapiro, Chairman of the Commodity Futures Trading Commission, stated before a Congressional committee on January 5, 1995: "The losses recently suffered by the Orange County Investment Fund appear not to have been related to the use of derivatives but instead by the use of leveraged transactions in government securities."

What many critics of equity derivatives fail to realize is that the markets for these instruments have become so large not because of slick sales campaigns but because they are providing economic value to their users. By enabling pension funds and other institutional investors to hedge and adjust positions quickly and inexpensively, these instruments have come to play an important role in portfolio management.

> Alan Greenspan
> Congressional Testimony, May 19, 1988

TYPES OF DERIVATIVES

This book looks at three broad categories of derivatives: *options, futures contracts,* and *swaps* (Figure 1–1).

OPTIONS

Three broad categories of derivatives are options, futures, and swaps.

An **option** is the right to either buy or sell something, at a set price, within a set period of time. The right to buy is a **call option**, while the right to sell is a **put option**. It is important to note that an option is the *right* to do something. This means you can exercise your option *if you wish,* but you do not have to do so.

FUTURES CONTRACTS

An option is different from a **futures contract** in that futures involve a *promise* to exchange a product for cash by a set delivery date. Someone who buys an option contract can abandon the option if they wish, whereas someone who enters into a futures contract does not have this prerogative. As the name suggests, the *futures* market deals with transactions that will be made in the future. A person who buys a December U.S. Treasury bond futures contract promises to pay a certain price for Treasury bonds in December. If you buy the T-bonds today, you purchase them in the *cash,* or **spot market**.[2]

Futures involve marking to market; forwards do not.

A futures contract involves a process known as **marking to market**. This means that there are no paper gains or losses; money actually moves between accounts each day as prices move up and down. A **forward contract** is functionally similar to a futures contract in some ways, but different in certain important ways, too. With a forward contract, there is an agreement (a promise) to exchange goods in the future, but with no marking to market along the way. Also, a forward contract is not marketable. This means you cannot sell your part of a forward contract to someone else. The interest rates associated with forward rate agreements are critical if you are to understand the price and value of an interest rate swap, as we will see in Chapter 14. Swaps are the third broad category of derivatives.

---

[2]That is, you buy them "on the spot."

The two major types of swaps are interest rate swaps and foreign currency swaps.

SWAPS

The third broad category of derivative products includes **swaps**. As the name implies, these are arrangements in which one party trades something with another party. The swaps market is huge, with trillions of dollars outstanding in swap agreements.

There are two major types of swaps. In an **interest rate swap**, one firm pays a *fixed* interest rate on a sum of money and, from some other firm, receives a *floating* interest rate on the same sum. Swaps are enormously popular with corporate treasurers as risk management tools and as a convenient means of lowering corporate borrowing costs.

The other type of swap is a **foreign currency swap**. In this arrangement, two firms initially trade one currency for another, perhaps U.S. dollars for Japanese yen. Subsequently, the two firms exchange interest payments, one based on a Japanese interest rate and the other based on a U.S. interest rate. Finally, at the termination of the arrangement, the two firms re-exchange the dollars and the yen.

PRODUCT CHARACTERISTICS

Both options and futures contracts exist on a wide variety of assets. The **underlying asset** is that which you have the right to buy or sell (with options) or to buy or deliver (with futures). We can buy or sell options on individual stocks, on market indexes, on metals, interest rates, or on futures contracts. Futures contracts trade on familiar products such as wheat, live cattle, gold, heating oil, foreign currency, U.S. Treasury bonds, and stock market indexes. They also trade on more abstract things such as the weather, electricity prices, credit, and fertilizer.

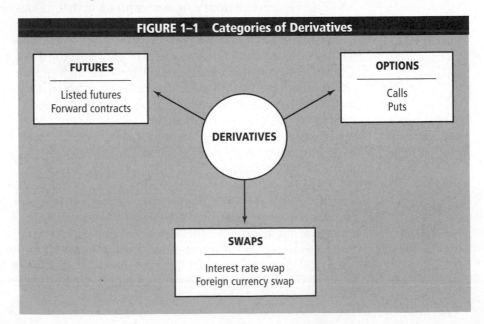

FIGURE 1–1   Categories of Derivatives

Some derivatives trade on an organized exchange such as the Chicago Board Options Exchange or the Chicago Board of Trade. These are **listed derivatives** because they are listed on an exchange. Many customized products trade off the exchange and are individually negotiated between two parties. These are over-the-counter, or **OTC derivatives**.

Options are securities; futures contracts are not.

Legally, options are securities, and are therefore regulated by the Securities and Exchange Commission (SEC). Futures contracts, in contrast, are legally not securities; they are contracts. Because they are not securities they fall outside the regulatory purview of the SEC. Their regulatory body is the Commodity Futures Trading Commission, or CFTC.

PARTICIPANTS IN THE DERIVATIVES WORLD

The main theme of this book is the many ways in which both individuals and institutions can use derivative products to reduce the risk they bear or to enhance their anticipated portfolio return. With futures and options, two especially important groups of market participants are *hedgers* and *speculators* (Figure 1–2). Without attracting both types of players a particular derivative product is likely to be unsuccessful.

HEDGING

If someone bears an economic risk and uses these markets to reduce that risk, the person is a **hedger**. Normally, the hedger understands the market well and makes an informed decision regarding if, when, and how much to hedge.

While the word may be new, almost everyone is familiar with the hedging concept. Homeowners hedge when they buy fire insurance on their houses. Car owners hedge by buying collision insurance. In similar fashion, you can acquire "insurance" on a portfolio to provide some protection against an adverse event in the marketplace.

In legal circles, the courts are looking with increasing displeasure on managers who fail to properly manage risk. In a landmark case, the Indiana Court of Appeals in *Brane v. Roth*[3] found the directors of an agricultural cooperative liable for more than $400,000 in grain sale losses that might have been avoided had the cooperative hedged the inventory. The essence of the ruling is that hedging is a prudent business practice and a prudent manager has a legal duty to understand and use the futures market hedging mechanism.

SPECULATION

A person or firm who accepts the risk the hedger does not want is a **speculator**. Speculators accept the risk because they believe the potential return outweighs the risk. Insurance companies accept the risk of a house fire or auto accident because when they spread this risk out over thousands of policies, they believe the insurance premium will compensate them adequately for the risk they choose to bear.

---

[3]*Brane v. Roth*, 590 NE 2nd 587 (Ind. Ct. App. 1992).

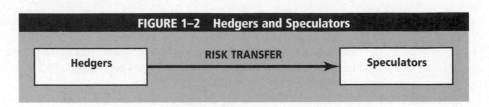

FIGURE 1–2   Hedgers and Speculators

| Hedgers | RISK TRANSFER → | Speculators |

Speculation is not the primary function of the derivatives markets.

The futures and options markets are widely associated with speculation, and the press gleefully reports on instances of speculation gone bad, such as the tale of Nick Leeson's unbridled foray into Japanese stock index futures and the subsequent downfall of the Barings Bank. Speculation, however, is not the primary purpose of these markets. Rather, they permit the transfer of risk between market participants as they desire, and this contributes to our national economic welfare.

ARBITRAGE

Finance is sometimes called the study of arbitrage. **Arbitrage** is the existence of a riskless profit. A $5 bill lying on the sidewalk is arbitrage. The first person who sees it will gladly pick it up and pocket it. We don't see a $5 bill on the sidewalk very often, but that is not because they are never there. They just aren't there very long.

Minor arbitrage opportunities often arise but are quickly eliminated.

Arbitrage opportunities routinely present themselves in the financial marketplace, but they are quickly exploited and eliminated. Persons actively engaged in seeking out minor pricing discrepancies are called *arbitrageurs*. These people help keep prices in the marketplace efficient. An efficient market is one in which there are few free lunches; securities are priced in accordance with their perceived level of risk and their potential return.

This book illustrates that certain relationships must prevail among the various security, option, futures, and interest rate complexes. When a price temporarily moves out of line with its counterparts, arbitrageurs are there to pick up the profit by engaging in a series of transactions to lock in a sure profit regardless of the direc-

DERIVATIVES TODAY

SPECULATION

The late Professor Merton Miller (Nobel Laureate from the University of Chicago) tells a story of a conversation he had with the treasurer of a Chicago oil company. In the aftermath of the Persian Gulf War, the price of oil dropped sharply and the value of the firm's oil inventory declined substantially. Merton told the man that it "served him right for speculating on oil prices."

"But we didn't speculate," the man said. "We didn't use the futures market at all."

Merton replied, "That's the point; by not hedging your inventory, you gambled that the price of oil would not drop. You guessed wrong, and you lost."

If you do not hedge, you are a de facto speculator.

SOURCE: Conversation between the author and Merton Miller, February 7, 1992, North Miami Beach, Florida.

tion prices subsequently take. We will take an especially close look at arbitrage when we investigate option pricing in Chapters 5 and 6 and again when we consider interest rate swaps in Chapter 13. Option pricing theory is based on arbitrage arguments, and the theory's offspring (such as delta, gamma, and theta) are principal players in risk management and financial engineering applications. Widespread, persistent arbitrage would defeat most of these uses of derivatives and turn the market into a gambler's playground rather than a useful economic arena.

USES OF DERIVATIVES

Three broad uses of derivative assets are risk management, income generation, and financial engineering.

RISK MANAGEMENT

The hedger's primary motivation is risk management. Faced with an unacceptable level of risk, the hedger may choose to reduce or eliminate it.

Consider risk management in the stock market. Someone who is **bullish** believes prices are going to rise, while someone who is **bearish** believes just the opposite. "Bullish" and "bearish" are not, however, two faces on the same coin. There are different degrees to one's market attitude. Rather than an on-off switch, our attitude toward the stock market is more like a continuous dial that we can adjust to any position we wish. Derivatives facilitate this fine-tuning of the portfolio. We can tailor our risk exposure to any point we wish along a bullish/bearish continuum (Figure 1–3).

Derivative assets also permit movement along this continuum at a moment's notice. A quick telephone call or Internet hookup to your broker, adding new positions or closing out existing ones, can shift your location on the line. In fact, the passage of time will cause some portfolio components to move spontaneously along the line without the portfolio manager doing anything. This means that portfolios employing derivatives need periodic "maintenance" if it is necessary to keep their characteristics constant.

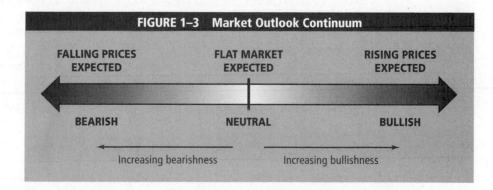

FIGURE 1–3   Market Outlook Continuum

FALLING PRICES EXPECTED	FLAT MARKET EXPECTED	RISING PRICES EXPECTED
BEARISH	NEUTRAL	BULLISH

Increasing bearishness   Increasing bullishness

INCOME GENERATION

The most common use of derivatives by individual investors is the writing of a **covered call**. We will look at this popular strategy in detail in Chapter 3. This involves giving someone the right to purchase your stock at a set price in exchange for an up-front fee that is yours to keep no matter what happens. This fee is called the option *premium* and it can serve to substantially increase a portfolio's ability to throw off cash. Microsoft, for instance, pays no dividends. A public library might hold 1,000 shares of Microsoft in its endowment fund in the hope of future stock price appreciation. If the library were to suddenly run into a cash shortfall, one convenient way of immediately generating some income without having to liquidate part of the investment portfolio is to write covered calls. The income from this 1,000-share holding could easily be several thousand dollars.

Writing calls to generate income is especially popular during a flat period in the market or when prices are trending downward. Continuously writing calls, however, is a suboptimal strategy because you miss out on the periodic home runs the market hits. We will look at how an investment manager can logically evaluate the merits of covered call writing at a given point in time.

FINANCIAL ENGINEERING

The relatively new field of **financial engineering** refers to the practice of using derivatives as building blocks in the creation of some specialized product. A financial engineer selects from the wide array of puts, calls, futures, and other derivatives in the same way that a cook selects ingredients from the spice rack or a chemist mixes compounds in the laboratory.

> Derivatives are neutral products; they are neither inherently risky nor safe.

Financial engineers know that derivatives are *neutral products*; they are neither inherently risky nor safe. We can enjoy watching a toddler feed herself with a spoon, but our reaction changes quickly if the toddler tries to put that same spoon in an electrical outlet. We teach the kid that you can put the spoon in your mouth, but not in the outlet. From the toddler's perspective, it seems contradictory that something else, like an appliance plug, you *can* put in the outlet but *not* in your mouth.

The same analogy can apply with derivatives. As we will see in Chapter 2, someone who creates and sells (or *writes*) a Microsoft call option has theoretically unlimited risk if they do not have any MSFT stock. If they *do* have MSFT stock, however, the risk of the combined "stock and options" position is actually *less* than without the option transaction. Writing the call may dramatically *increase* risk or it might *reduce* risk, depending on the portfolio components with which it is combined.

As I've said on prior occasions, derivatives are something like electricity: dangerous if mishandled, but bearing the potential to do good.

Arthur Leavitt,
Chairman, SEC
Congressional Testimony, January 5, 1995

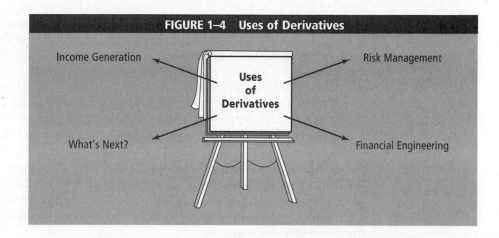

FIGURE 1–4   Uses of Derivatives

Income Generation

Uses
of
Derivatives

Risk Management

What's Next?

Financial Engineering

Chemists understand this concept fully. Table salt is sodium chloride, NaCl, a familiar product that most of us use every day of our lives. In a concentrated form, however, sodium by itself can be highly caustic and cause burns. Similarly, the chlorine in Clorox, if mixed with ammonia, produces deadly poisonous chlorine gas. Financial engineers frequently use derivative products as if they were chemicals, mixing them in a certain way to achieve a desired product. Some recipes may be easy to make, but they may also be an accident waiting to happen. Other recipes, while more expensive or more complicated, are more stable and more reliable. A blasting team is much more comfortable working with modern plastic explosives than with the liquid nitroglycerine that Wild West bank robbers used. The point is that the risk of a derivative product depends on what you do with it (Figure 1–4).

EFFECTIVE STUDY OF DERIVATIVES

Perhaps more so than any other course in a business curriculum, the study of derivatives involves a vocabulary that essentially becomes a new language. You could easily hear an options professional say something like "I'm long 22,000 deltas in Microsoft, I've got negative gamma, hardly any stock, and all of a sudden the near-term at-the-money puts jump from 45% to 88% on the settlement news. My position risk went out of control and I had to cover a bunch of short puts at a ridiculous price." This means nothing to someone who is untrained in the language of the options market. Common option terms like implied volatility, delta hedging, short straddle, near-the-money, and gamma neutrality don't even appear elsewhere in the finance discipline.

People who thoroughly understand the potential uses of options, futures, and swaps are scarce. If you develop fluency in the basic principles of hedging and speculating applications, you will have a marketable talent that makes you stand out in the crowd. All financial institutions can make some productive use of derivative assets. Investment houses use them, and so do asset-liability managers at banks, bank trust officers, endowment fund managers, mortgage officers, pension fund managers, corporate treasurers, foreign exchange managers, multinational corporations, oil companies, ranchers, farmers, and individual investors.

In many respects, derivatives are the fastest game in town. As with a competitive sport, you have to train hard to become above-average, you have to practice, and you have to keep in shape. This book provides your initial training.

At the back of each chapter there is a **Self Test**. This contains fifteen or twenty true-false questions covering the principal topics from the chapter. Answers to the Self Tests are in the back of the book. Completing the Self Test after you read each chapter and then again when you review for exams will be time well-spent. You should also become familiar with the material available at the text website, *http://strong.swcollege.com*.

Appendix

A REVIEW OF STATISTICAL PRINCIPLES USEFUL IN THE STUDY OF DERIVATIVES

1. In statistics, a data point is called an **observation**.
2. An observation whose value does not change is a **constant**. The number of sides of a cube is a constant, as is the number eight and the sum of the interior angles of a triangle. A constant can be represented by a numeral (like 8) or by a symbol (like "x" or π).
3. An observation whose value *does* change is formally a **random variable**, or just a variable.
4. A variable that is counted is **discrete**. The number of strokes you take in a round of golf is a discrete random variable.
5. A variable that is measured is **continuous**. A swimmer's time in the 100-yard freestyle is a continuous random variable.
6. The entire collection of observations of a random variable is a **population**. The weekly stock returns on Home Depot over the firm's entire existence constitute a population.
7. A subset of a population is a **sample**. Weekly stock returns on Home Depot over the past year constitute a sample.
8. A number describing something about a set of variables is a **statistic**.
9. A statistic describing an entire population is a **population statistic**.
10. A statistic describing the characteristics of a sample is a **sample statistic**. The average weekly return on Home Depot over the last 52 weeks is a sample statistic.
11. A population with well-known characteristics is a **distribution**.
12. A distribution in which all the individual random variables are equally likely is a **uniform distribution**. The outcome of the roll of a six-sided die is a uniform distribution.

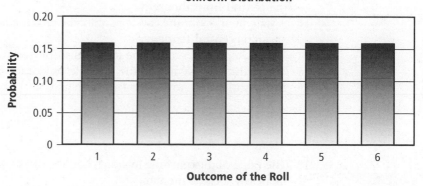

Uniform Distribution

13. The outcome of a roll of two six-sided dice comes from a **triangular distribution**, the name coming from the linear rise and fall of the data.

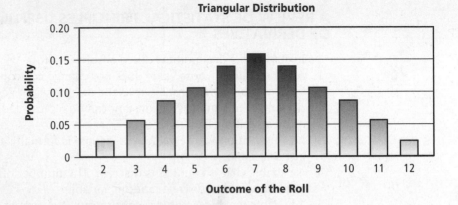

14. If we roll a large number of dice, the outcome of a roll comes from a **normal distribution** with its familiar bell shape.

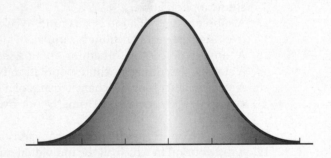

15. Regardless of the distribution from which observations come, if you repeatedly select a large number of them and plot their mean value, the plot will approach a normal distribution as the sample size gets large. This fact is called the **central limit theorem**.
16. A statement about the "average outcome" from a distribution is a statement about its **central tendency**.
17. The most common outcome from a distribution is its **mode**.
18. The arithmetic average of the possible outcomes is the **mean**. A small bar over a variable denotes its mean, such as $\bar{x}$.

$$\bar{x} = \frac{1}{N} \sum_{i=1}^{N} x_i$$

19. The value of the outcome in which half the observations lie above it and half lie below it is the **median**.

20. A distribution where a plot of the values above the mean is a mirror image of a plot of the values below the mean is **symmetric**.
21. The extent to which a distribution is "spread out" from the mean is its **dispersion**.
22. The dispersion of stock returns is often called **volatility**.
23. A distribution that is not symmetric shows **skewness**. A distribution with more dispersion above the mean than below it is skewed to the right. If there is more dispersion below the mean, it is skewed to the left.

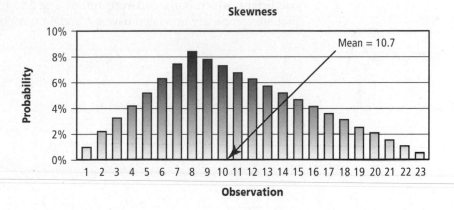

24. An important measure of dispersion with a normal distribution is its **variance**. We solve for the variance by subtracting the mean from each observation, squaring the result, adding all the squared results from each observation, and dividing by the number of observations.

$$\sigma^2 = \frac{1}{N}\sum_{i=1}^{N}(x_i - \bar{x})^2$$

25. The square root of the variance is the **standard deviation**. In option pricing, the standard deviation is called **sigma**.
26. If you subtract the mean from all observations in a normal distribution and divide by their standard deviation the distribution becomes a **standard normal distribution**, with a mean of zero and a standard deviation of one.
27. In a standard normal distribution, about 68% of the observations lie within one standard deviation of the mean, 95% lie within two standard deviations of the mean, and 99.7% lie within three standard deviations of the mean.
28. The **cumulative normal distribution function** N(x) measures the area under a standard normal distribution from the far left (minus infinity) to some point on the x-axis. Because in a standard normal distribution half the area lies to the left of the mean of zero, N(0) = 0.50. About ninety-five percent of the area lies within two standard deviations of zero, so 2.5% lies more than two standard deviations to the left of zero and 2.5% lies more than two standard

deviations to the right of zero. Therefore, N(–2) is about 0.025 and N(2) is about 0.975.

29. If the behavior of one variable has no relationship with the behavior of another variable, the two variables are **independent**.

30. In a study of how variable A is affected by changes in variable B, variable A is a **dependent variable**, while variable B is an **independent variable**. The width of a box is an independent variable. Its volume is a dependent variable, because it depends on other dimensions.

31. The relationship between two variables can be expressed by their **correlation coefficient**, which ranges between minus one and plus one. Two variables that are completely unrelated have a correlation coefficient of zero.

Basic Principles of Stock Options

KEY TERMS you will find in this chapter:

There is an anecdote of Thales the Milesian and his financial device, which involves a principle of universal application, but is attributed to him on account of his reputation for wisdom. He was reproached for his poverty, which was supposed to show that philosophy was of no use. According to the story, he knew by his skill in the stars while it was yet winter that there would be a great harvest of olives in the coming year; so, having a little money, he gave deposits for the use of all the olive presses in Chios and Miletus, which he hired at a low price because no one bid against him. When the harvest time came, and many wanted them all at once and of a sudden, he let them out at any rate which he pleased, and made a quantity of money. Thus, he showed the world that philosophers can easily be rich if they like.

Aristotle

This chapter covers basic principles of stock options that you must master before moving on to more advanced topics. Option traders have a language of their own, and you need to develop fluency in it quickly.

There are five major themes in this chapter:

1. What options are and where they come from;

2. Why options are a good idea;

3. Where and how options trade;

4. Components of the option premium; and

5. Where profits and losses come from with options.

WHAT OPTIONS ARE AND WHERE THEY COME FROM

There are two *types* of options: *call* options and *put* options. Call options are easiest to understand, so we will look at them first.

CALL OPTIONS

Although most people are not familiar with call options, the call option *concept* is something with which they probably *are* familiar. Suppose you are shopping in a department store and find a leather coat on sale for $225. The sale ends today, and you do not have enough money with you to pay for it. You might find the store manager and ask if you could put the coat on 30-day layaway at the sale price. Suppose the manager agrees, provided you pay a $5 nonrefundable layaway processing fee. If you accept these items, the store has created a call option: You have the right (but not the obligation) to buy one coat at a predetermined price ($225) anytime in the next 30 days, when your option expires. The store charged $5 for the option. With any option, the amount you pay for it is the **premium**. The option "premium" is synonymous with the option "price."

The option premium is the amount you pay for the option.

It is important to recognize that you have not *promised* to buy the coat. If you should find an identical coat at a lower price in another store, you can simply abandon your option with the original store and buy the coat in the cheaper location.

A call option gives its owner the right to buy; it is not a promise to buy.

The owner of a **call option** has the *right to buy* within a specified time period. In exchange for this right, the owner of the option pays a premium to the option seller.

The exchanges have historically quoted stock and option prices in fractions of a dollar, such as $50½. At the urging of the Securities and Exchange Commission, the stock exchanges plan eventually to do away with fractions. Since January 29, 2001 all New York Stock Exchange companies have their prices quoted in decimals, such as $50.50. The options exchanges have followed suit. If the underlying stock trades in decimals at its exchange, the option does also.

On the Nasdaq stock market many shares still trade in fractions. Their options also trade in fractions. Both methods of price quotation appear in the examples in this book.

PUT OPTIONS

A call option gives you the right to *buy*; a *put option* gives you the right to *sell*. Put options are conceptually awkward for some people because the right to sell something is not as familiar as the right to buy.

Most households in America receive at least one of the many versions of the L. L. Bean catalog. This company has a lifetime, no-questions-asked money back guarantee policy on the items it sells. This means that if you buy something and six months later decide it isn't right for you, you can return it and get your money back. In essence, L. L. Bean products come with an *embedded put option*. You have the right to "sell" the product to the store for your purchase price, as Figure 2–1 shows. The option is "embedded" because you cannot separate it from the product and sell it separately. Some people will tell you that L. L. Bean goods are expensive. Quality and service aside, the put feature is valuable and the sticker price of the merchandise reflects the put option's value.

Categories of Options

Both puts and calls are based on a set quantity of the **underlying asset**; this is the asset the option gives you the right to buy or sell. An **American option** gives its owner the right to exercise the option anytime prior to option expiration. A **European option** may only be exercised at expiration. The terms have nothing to do with geography; both exercise styles appear throughout the world.

Equity Options. The best-known options are those that give their owner the right to buy or sell shares of stock. These are *stock* options, also commonly called *equity* options. With exchange-traded options, the underlying asset is 100 shares of the stock. A person who buys a call option on the stock of a particular company is purchasing the right to buy *100 shares* of stock; this is an option **contract**. It is not possible to buy or sell "odd lots" of options.

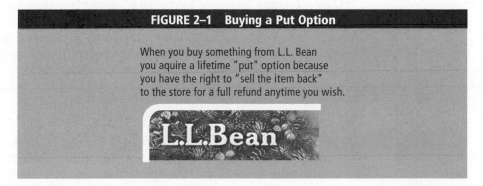

FIGURE 2–1   Buying a Put Option

When you buy something from L.L. Bean you aquire a lifetime "put" option because you have the right to "sell the item back" to the store for a full refund anytime you wish.

Index Options. With an **index option**, the underlying asset is some market measure like the Standard & Poor's 500 stock index. While these are similar to equity options in most respects, one important difference is that they are cash-settled. One especially popular options contract, for instance, is on the S&P 100 index, ticker symbol OEX. It would not be convenient to deliver 100 different stock certificates when an option holder exercises a put or a call. Instead, the *value* of the shares changes hands rather than the shares themselves. We will see more about this later in this book.

Other Options. Equity and index options are the most important option groups, but options trade on other assets as well. Chapter 15 covers futures options (options on futures contracts) in some detail. Other categories include foreign currency and interest rate options.

Standardized Option Characteristics

All options have standardized *expiration dates*. For most options, this is the Saturday following the third Friday of certain designated months. Individual investors typically view the third Friday of the month as the expiration date, because the exchanges are closed to public trading Saturday. Saturday is reserved for bookkeeping operations among the brokerage firms whose clients have dealt in the just-expiring options.

The **striking price** of an option is the predetermined transaction price. These are at multiples of $2.50 or $5, depending on the current stock price. Stocks priced at $25 or below have the lower multiple, while higher-priced stocks have the $5 multiple. Shifts in the price of a stock result in the creation of new striking prices. As a matter of Options Clearing Corporation (OCC) policy, there is usually at least one striking price above and at least one below the current stock price. The consequences of different striking prices will become apparent as the text progresses.

Investors identify a stock option by specifying company, expiration, striking price, and type of option (generally in this order) (see Figure 2–2).

WHERE OPTIONS COME FROM

There is no set number of put and call options on a given underlying security.

If I buy an option, someone has to sell it to me; there must be two parties to the trade. Unlike more familiar securities, such as shares of stock, there is no set number of put or call options. In fact, the number in existence changes every day. Options can be created, and they can be destroyed. This unusual fact is crucial to understanding the options market.

OPENING AND CLOSING TRANSACTIONS

The first trade someone makes in a particular option is an **opening transaction** for that person. When the individual subsequently closes that position out with a second trade, this latter trade is a **closing transaction**. Purchases and sales can

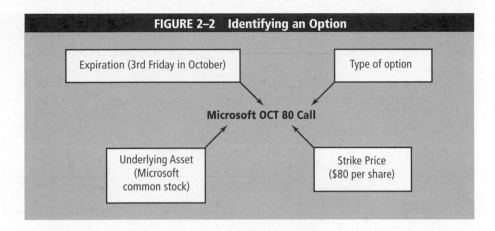

FIGURE 2–2   Identifying an Option

Expiration (3rd Friday in October)

Type of option

Microsoft OCT 80 Call

Underlying Asset
(Microsoft
common stock)

Strike Price
($80 per share)

be either type of transaction. Retail stockbrokers should routinely ask their option customers if a particular trade is *to open* or *to close*.

The owner of an option will ultimately do one of three things with it:

1. sell it to someone else;

2. let it expire; or

3. exercise it.

This is easy to explain using tickets to a university athletic event (Figure 2–3). Suppose you buy two tickets for a *premium* of $12 each. This is analogous to an *opening transaction*. The ticket gives you the right, but not the obligation, to go to the game. If you choose, you can (1) sell your tickets to someone else before the game. Or you could (2) decide to watch the game on television and leave the tickets in your desk drawer where they will "expire" worthless. Finally, you could (3) **exercise** the tickets and go to the game. No matter which of these courses of action you choose, it is analogous to a *closing transaction*. Game day is analogous to the **expiration date**, and when the final gun sounds the tickets are worthless.[1]

Buying something as an opening transaction is perhaps easier to understand than *selling* something as an opening transaction. The university created the tickets and sold them; this was an opening transaction for the university. When someone sells an option as an opening transaction, this is called **writing the option**.

Open interest is a measure of how many options exist at a point in time. Options are created and destroyed depending on how trades are matched up. If an investor writes an option (an opening transaction) and another person buys it as an opening transaction, an option contract is created and open interest goes

> Selling an option as an opening transaction is called writing the option.

---

[1]Note that options are routinely created or canceled in the market, unlike stocks and bonds, which already exist and which are generally fixed in number.

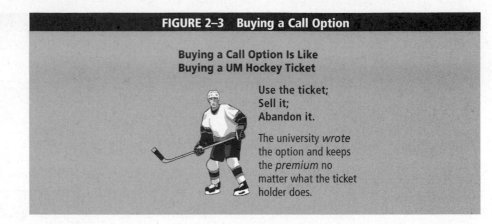

FIGURE 2–3   Buying a Call Option

**Buying a Call Option Is Like
Buying a UM Hockey Ticket**

**Use the ticket;
Sell it;
Abandon it.**

The university *wrote* the option and keeps the *premium* no matter what the ticket holder does.

up. When two closing transactions are matched, open interest goes down. If an opening transaction is matched with a closing transaction, open interest is unchanged.

Open interest is not the same as **volume**, which is a measure of how many trades occurred. A particular option contract may trade many times before its expiration date. There is no necessary connection between volume and open interest. For instance, when someone writes an option he or she creates a contract and open interest goes up by one. The owner of the contract, however, may change several times in the same day. Each trade adds to daily trading volume, but there is still only one contract behind all the trades.

No matter what the owner of an option does, the writer of the option keeps the option premium that he or she received when it was sold. Returning to the athletic event example, the university keeps the $24 you paid for the two tickets, regardless of whether you go to the game or not.[2]

Returning to the L. L. Bean example, the customer acquires the put option that the store *wrote*. Issuing a money-back guarantee is analogous to creating a put option. This is also similar to the collision insurance policy on your car. When you have an accident that totals the car, you have the right to sell it back to the insurance company at its worth (minus the deductible).

The option writer keeps the option premium no matter what happens in the future.

There are many examples of embedded options in other corporate securities. For instance, investors essentially write a call when they buy a callable bond. The issuing firm has the right to buy the bond back by repaying the principal.[3] Homeowners have the right to pay off their home mortgage whenever they wish. Figure 2-4 shows the four basic option positions.

[2]Sport tickets are usually an imperfect example of a call option, as there is no middle outcome between going to the game and not going. In general, the option holder gains or loses depending on some underlying event (such as the stock price going up). One reviewer of this book has a 1964 Philadelphia World Series ticket, which would have given him the option to go to a game if the Phillies made it to the Series that year. They didn't, and the ticket "expired worthless."

[3]This is why callable bonds have a slightly higher interest rate than non-callable bonds. The extra yield is the option premium.

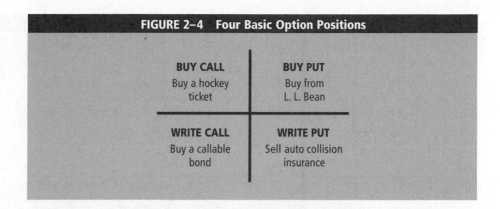

FIGURE 2–4   Four Basic Option Positions

BUY CALL Buy a hockey ticket	**BUY PUT** Buy from L. L. Bean
WRITE CALL Buy a callable bond	**WRITE PUT** Sell auto collision insurance

Exchange-traded options have an important characteristic called **fungibility**. This means that, for a given company, all options of the same type with the same expiration and striking price are identical. The **striking price** of an option is its predetermined transaction price. The striking price is also called the *exercise price*, or just the *strike price*. Fungibility is particularly important to the option writer. I may write an option because the premium is attractive. If market conditions change a week later, I can *buy* an option on the same company with the same contract terms, and this gets me out of the market; writing an option and buying a similar one are two transactions that cancel in my brokerage account. I do not have to buy back the option from the specific person to whom I sold it, because the option is fungible. Note that football tickets, in general, are *not* fungible, because all seats are not equally desirable.

THE ROLE OF THE OPTIONS CLEARING CORPORATION

The **Options Clearing Corporation** (OCC) contributes substantially to the smooth operation of the options market. This organization positions itself between every buyer and seller and acts as a guarantor of all option trades. When someone buys or sells an option, that person is actually buying it from or selling it to the OCC (Figure 2–5). The OCC also regulates the trading activity of members of the various options exchanges, setting minimum capital requirements and providing for the efficient transfer of funds among members as gains or losses occur. The OCC publishes a booklet entitled *Characteristics and Risks of Standardized Options*, which every potential option user receives upon opening an options account.

WHY OPTIONS ARE A GOOD IDEA

Today's financial world is complicated. We face many sources of risk that were not present in the mid-nineteenth century. Today's communication technology provides us almost instantaneous information about events such as the FED inter-

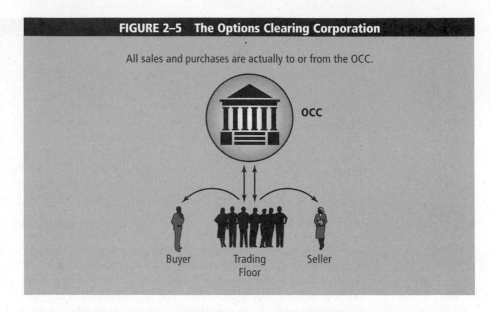

FIGURE 2–5   The Options Clearing Corporation

All sales and purchases are actually to or from the OCC.

OCC

Buyer   Trading   Seller
                 Floor

est rate announcements, corporate mergers, missed earnings, and industrial accidents. Each bit of news can have an impact on investment value.

Experienced investors are seldom 100 percent bullish or 100 percent bearish.[4] Our investment decision trees have many branches and decision nodes. The constant arrival of new information that can affect our investments means that for many people that investment process is dynamic: Positions need to be constantly reassessed and portfolios adjusted. Options make this process much simpler for a variety of market participants.

PORTFOLIO RISK MANAGEMENT

We also continually improve our understanding of the behavior of security prices and the interaction of the security markets. This knowledge makes it possible and prudent for us to fine-tune our investment strategy to deal with the many possible future states of the world.

Stock options are widely used in portfolio risk management. Options are much more convenient (and less expensive) to use than wholesale purchases or sales of shares of stock each time an adjustment is appropriate. This topic will be discussed in considerable detail later in the book.

RISK TRANSFER

Options also provide a means for risk to be transferred from one person to the next. I may own a portfolio of stock and face some potential risk that I find unacceptable. Using options, I can transfer that risk to another market participant who is willing to bear it.

---

[4]A person who is *bullish* believes that prices are going to rise; a *bearish* person believes the opposite.

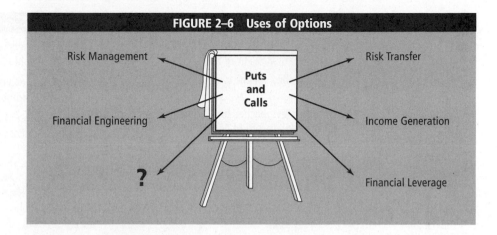

FIGURE 2-6   Uses of Options

FINANCIAL LEVERAGE

Options provide financial leverage, and this is one primary reason many speculators buy them. For example, I may feel that XYZ Corporation, currently selling for $65/share, is an excellent takeover candidate. If I were to buy 100 shares of this stock, it would cost me $6,500. As an alternative, I could speculate on the takeover rumors using a stock option selling for perhaps $300. With this position, I would benefit from a sharp, immediate increase in the stock price, because a rise in the stock price would necessarily cause the option premium to rise as well. However, I would have only a modest amount of money at risk. The worst that could happen to me is that I would lose all $300; if I bought this stock, I could lose much more than that—as much as the entire $6,500—if the stock plummeted.

INCOME GENERATION

Some people use options for generating additional income from their investment portfolio. Options are widely used for this purpose in the portfolios of endowment funds, pension funds, and individual portfolios.

The important point to remember is that options give investors and speculators opportunities to adjust risk or alter income streams that would otherwise not be available.

WHERE AND HOW OPTIONS TRADE

There are several different trading platforms and systems for trading options.

EXCHANGES

In the United States, most options trade on one of five exchanges: the Chicago Board Options Exchange (CBOE), the American Stock Exchange (AMEX), the

Philadelphia Stock Exchange (Philly), the Pacific Stock Exchange (PSE),[5] or the International Securities Exchange.

The International Securities Exchange (ISE) is the first entirely electronic options market in the United States. Open for trading since May 2000, the ISE initially listed options on three stocks. In March 2001 the figure was up to about 200, with plans to expand the list to 600 different companies. The ISE states that its mission is to "create and maintain an efficient, cost effective and liquid market for stock options through the introduction of a new market structure and automated trading systems." The Risk Waters Group named the ISE the 2001 Derivative Exchange of the Year in recognition of the innovations it had made in the derivatives industry.

Well-regulated options exchanges similar to the CBOE exist in Australia, Sao Paulo, Canada, Amsterdam, Hong Kong, Osaka, Manila, Singapore, Sydney, the United Kingdom, and many other countries.

OVER-THE-COUNTER OPTIONS

Besides trading options on the exchanges, it is also possible to enter into "private" option arrangements with brokerage firms or other dealers. Institutions sometimes do this when they need a product with characteristics that are not available in an exchange-traded product. The striking price, life of the option, and premium are negotiated between the parties involved. This is called an **over-the-counter option**. Because the OCC does not get involved with an OTC option, they are subject to counterparty risk. This is the possibility that the other side of the trade (perhaps a large commercial bank or investment house) will be unable to perform as agreed if the option is exercised. If, for instance, my firm buys 100 contracts of a particular OTC option, I assume that if I exercise the option the writer will deliver shares to me as agreed. There is the possibility that the counterparty will be unable to perform in accordance with the option contract.

[5]There was a limited amount of options trading on the New York Stock Exchange until April 1997, when the NYSE sold its options business to the CBOE. The NYSE no longer lists options.

DERIVATIVES TODAY

EXOTIC OPTIONS[6]

As-You-Like-It Option An option in which the owner can decide, by a certain date, whether it is a put or a call.

Asian Option Same as an Average Price Option.

Average Price Option An option whose pay-off depends on the average price of the underlying asset over the life of the option.

Barrier Option An option that is created (an "in" option) or canceled (an "out" option) if a prespecified price level is touched. A "down and in put," for instance, is an option that becomes an ordinary put if the stock price falls to a certain level (the lower barrier). An "up and out call" is an ordinary call that is canceled if the stock price rises to the upper barrier.

Baseball Option A barrier option that is "knocked out" after it touches the relevant barrier for the third time (three strikes and you are out).

Bermuda Option An option that may be exercised only on certain predetermined dates in addition to the final maturity date.

Binary Option An option that pays off either zero or a fixed amount. Also called a digital option.

Chooser Option Same as an as-you-like-it option.

Compound Option An option on an option.

Exchange Option An option giving its owner the right to exchange one asset for another.

Forward Start Option Paid for now, with the option becoming effective at a future date.

Lookback Option An option whose exercise price is the maximum (with a lookback put) or minimum (with a lookback call) over the life of the option. Consequently, the payoff cannot be determined until the end of the option's life.

Because of their unique characteristics, these options are generally *not* fungible. They also might not be liquid; that is, an owner of an over-the-counter option might not be able to sell it quickly at a reasonable price. A **listed option** is traded on an options exchange, and such an option can always be quickly sold.

The Derivatives Today box gives a brief explanation of some of the more common **exotic options**. There is no limit to the number of ways in which you can assemble the terms of an option contract. The important thing to note here is that these exotic options are not gadgets that some marketing department thinks up and tries to sell. They respond to some specific corporate or investment need and usually serve to reduce a risk someone finds unacceptable.

OTHER LISTED OPTIONS

There are two other varieties of options traded at the CBOE. These are *LEAPs* and *FLEX options*. **LEAP** is the acronym for a *Long-term Equity AnticiPation Security*. These are similar to ordinary listed options except they are longer term. All LEAPs expire in January; they may have a life of up to 39 months. Someone might speak of a Microsoft January 2002 or January 2003 LEAP.

[6]For a comprehensive listing of exotic options and other modern financial terms, see the *Dictionary of Financial Risk Management*, by Gary Gastineau and Mark Kritzman. Frank J. Fabozzi Associates, 1996.

Just because options trade on a particular stock does not mean that LEAPs are also available. While the number of LEAPs is increasing, at present they are available on only the most active underlying securities.

A **FLEX option** is fundamentally different from an ordinary listed option in that the terms of the option are flexible. A potential FLEX user can specify a particular expiration date up to three years away, any exercise price,[7] and either American or European style. These have the advantage of user flexibility, while eliminating the counterparty risk associated with an over-the-counter option. In general, a FLEX option trade must be for at least 250 contracts.

TRADING MECHANICS

As with other markets, it is important to understand how an option user interacts with the market to make a trade.

Bid Price and Ask Price

There are actually *two* prices for an option at any given time: a **bid price** and an **ask price**, also called the *offer price*. The bid price is the highest price anyone is willing to pay for a particular option, while the ask price is the lowest price at which anyone is willing to sell. By definition, at any moment there is only one bid price and one ask price, as only one price can be the "highest" or the "lowest."

Types of Orders

When someone wants to place an options order, he or she must specify precisely what the broker is supposed to do, and specifying the type of order facilitates this. *Market orders* and *limit orders* are the two most important types.

A **market order** expresses a wish to buy or sell immediately, at the current price. A **limit order**, in contrast, specifies a particular price (or better) beyond which no trade is desired. A person who wanted to buy 3 Microsoft August 100 calls at the current price would tell the broker, *Buy 3 Microsoft August 100 calls at the market*. The phrase *at the market* shows that the order is a market order.

Another person, in contrast, might say, *Buy 3 Microsoft August 100 calls at $2\frac{1}{2}$, good until canceled*. This indicates a limit order, as a price was specified. Limit orders also require a time limit, which is usually either "for the day" or "good 'til canceled (GTC)." Day orders are canceled at the end of the day if they are not executed.

Individuals and institutions using the options market are subject to a **position limit** on each underlying security. This is the maximum number of contracts that a single party may have outstanding at any one time. These limits are a function of the size of the underlying company and the trading volume in its stock. For large, actively traded companies the position limit is 75,000 contracts on the same side of the market; other stocks have position limits of 60,000, 31,500, 22,500 or 13,500 contracts (Long calls and short puts are on the *same* side of the market; both become more valuable as the underlying asset rises in price. Short calls and long puts are on the *other* side of the market; they become valuable as prices fall).

---

[7]The exercise price can be in dollars or a percentage of the underlying stock price.

OPTION TICKER SYMBOLS

Option ticker symbols have three parts, one each for the underlying security, the expiration month, and the striking price, expressed in that order. A Boeing March 50 call is BACJ:

BA	**C**	**J**
BOEING	EXPIRATION	STRIKING PRICE

The code for the underlying asset is usually the stock ticker symbol if it is three letters or less. Nasdaq securities have a ticker symbol with at least four letters. For these shares, there is a special symbol that you must look up. The Microsoft stock ticker symbol, for instance, is MSFT. The option ticker code is MSQ. A MSFT August 85 *put* would be MSQTQ; an August 85 *call* would be MSQHQ. There are special symbols for LEAPs. Good websites to find option ticker symbols are *www.thomsoninvest.net* or *www.cboe.com*.

EXPIRATION CODES

	JAN	FEB	MAR	APR	MAY	JUN	JUL	AUG	SEP	OCT	NOV	DEC
CALL	A	B	C	D	E	F	G	H	I	J	K	L
PUT	M	N	O	P	Q	R	S	T	U	V	W	X

Striking price codes come from the following table:

A	B	C	D	E	F	G	H	I	J
$ 5	$ 10	$ 15	$ 20	$ 25	$ 30	$ 35	$ 40	$ 45	$ 50
$105	$110	$115	$120	$125	$130	$135	$140	$145	$150
$205	$210	$215	$220	$225	$230	$235	$240	$245	$250

K	L	M	N	O	P	Q	R	S	T
$ 55	$ 60	$ 65	$ 70	$ 75	$ 80	$ 85	$ 90	$ 95	$100
$155	$160	$165	$170	$175	$180	$185	$190	$195	$200
$255	$260	$265	$270	$275	$280	$285	$290	$295	$300

$2½ INTERVAL CODES

U	V	W	X
$7½	$12½	$17½	$22½

Note that striking price codes correspond to more than one number. "A" represents a striking price of $5, $105, or $205. Normally, a single security will have options with only one of these striking prices at a time.

Trading Floor Systems

Under the **specialist system** (used at the Philadelphia and American Stock Exchanges), there is a single individual through whom all orders to buy or sell a particular security must pass. The specialist keeps an *order book* with limit orders[8] from all over the country, and tries to ensure that the market in these securities is maintained in a fair and orderly fashion. If no private individual has placed an order to buy the option you want to sell, the specialist *must* buy the option from you at a reasonable price. This is part of the specialist's job, and it helps contribute to the ease of entry and exit from the marketplace.

Under the **marketmaker system** (used at the CBOE and Pacific Exchange), the specialist's activities are divided among three groups of people: *marketmakers, floor brokers*, and the *order book official*. Instead of a single specialist, competing marketmakers trade in a specific location much like the trading pits discussed in Chapter 8 (Fundamentals of the Futures Market). The number of marketmakers can range from a small handful to sometimes over 500. These people compete against each other for the public's business by attempting to *be there first* with the best price to take your order.

Marketmakers must be quick to react to arriving orders if they want any business. Their bread and butter is buying options at the bid price and then selling at a slightly higher price to someone else as quickly as possible. If, for instance, a particular marketmaker buys 10 option contracts (options on 1,000 shares) at $4 each and sells them 30 seconds later for 4\frac{1}{8}$, there is a profit of $125. The result of this constant competition for the public's business is that you can be confident that you will get a market-determined price for your valuable option.[9]

Marketmakers in a particular option assemble in a specified part of the exchange floor, near an individual called the **Order Book Official**. This person has many duties, but one of particular importance is making sure that small public orders to buy or sell are not ignored and, in fact, *get priority* from the trading **crowd** at the exchange. "Crowd" is the colloquial term used for the people in a trading location. Order Book Officials are employees of the exchange and may not trade for their own account. They are responsible for ensuring that public limit orders get priority from the trading crowd when the limit price is reached. The Order Book Official literally stops the trading among the marketmakers until the requirements of the public limit order book are satisfied. A marketmaker can be censured by the exchange for failure to pay attention to the price information quoted by the Order Book Official or for making a trade with another individual on the exchange floor when a public order was "on the book" at the identical price.

Floor brokers act as agents for the public. They may not trade for their own accounts; instead, they place orders according to the wishes of their customers. An order that an individual placed with a broker at Kidder, Peabody will eventually be transmitted to a floor broker at the appropriate exchange.

---

[8]Market orders do not go in the specialist's book, because they are executed immediately.

[9]This is true, barring another market crash. There were some scattered problems with the specialist and marketmaker systems during the October 19, 1987 market crash.

THE CBOE'S RETAIL AUTOMATIC EXECUTION SYSTEM (RAES)

The Chicago Board Options Exchange uses a system known as the **Retail Automatic Execution System (RAES)** to speed up order execution on relatively small retail customer orders. As long as a trade meets certain criteria, it is guaranteed a fill at the current market bid or offer price. About one third of public customer orders go through RAES.

To be eligible for trading on RAES, orders must generally be for 20 options contracts or less, and with a contract premium of less than $10. A CBOE marketmaker participates in RAES trading by signing on to the system at one of the RAES terminals distributed across the exchange floor.

Trades get assigned to marketmakers via the RAES "wheel." As they sign on, participants are alphabetically ordered in the system. The day's trading begins with the random selection of a letter of the alphabet. Perhaps the letter is "G," and Sandi Greene is the first "G" alphabetically. She gets the first trade, whatever it is, with remaining trades assigned to the marketmakers further down the alphabet until the system "wheels through" back to the G's and Sandi gets another trade. For instance, an XYZ MAR 45 call might currently be bid $2, offered at $2.10. If the first order of the day is to sell eight of these calls, the RAES system will automatically buy eight contracts @ $2 on Sandi Greene's behalf. Marketmakers can periodically check the RAES system to see what trades they have automatically become party to while they were occupied in the trading pit.

SOURCE: CBOE Web Site

THE OPTION PREMIUM

INTRINSIC VALUE AND TIME VALUE

The price of an option is called the *premium*, with two components: *intrinsic value* and *time value*. **Intrinsic value** is the amount that an option is immediately worth, given the relation between the option striking price and the current stock price. For a call option, intrinsic value is equal to stock price minus the striking price; for a put, intrinsic value is striking price minus stock price. By convention, intrinsic value cannot be less than zero. **Time value** is equal to the premium minus the intrinsic value.

An option with no intrinsic value is **out-of-the-money**. An **in-the-money** option *does* have intrinsic value. In the special case where an option's striking price is exactly equal to the price of the underlying security, the option is **at-the-money**. Options that are "almost" at-the-money are **near-the-money**.

OPTION PRICE QUOTATIONS

Table 2–1 is a summary of closing option prices on Microsoft from July 10, 2000. There are numerous different formats for presenting option data. The *Wall Street Journal*, for instance, only lists the most active options in its print version; other

TABLE 2–1　Microsoft Options

CLOSING PRICES FROM JULY 10, 2000
MICROSOFT STOCK CLOSING PRICE = $79^7/_{16}$

STRIKE	EXPIRATION	CALL			PUT		
		VOLUME	LAST	OPEN INTEREST	VOLUME	LAST	OPEN INTEREST
60	AUG	1	21	880	10	$^1/_4$	1116
60	OCT	21	$21^1/_2$	7732	1115	$^5/_8$	245504
65	AUG	6	$16^1/_4$	204	...	...	52392
65	OCT	11	$17^1/_8$	13872	1109	$1^3/_{16}$	83896
70	AUG	52	11	3740	79	$^{13}/_{16}$	14416
70	OCT	148	13	20380	550	$2^3/_{16}$	55788
75	JUL	1447	$5^1/_2$	126556	808	$^{11}/_{16}$	103608
75	AUG	427	$7^1/_4$	6332	302	$1^{13}/_{16}$	22800
75	OCT	165	10	32392	1056	$3^5/_8$	35484
80	JUL	7038	$2^3/_{16}$	236136	3920	$2^3/_8$	118140
80	AUG	805	4	25132	434	4	8568
80	OCT	279	7	47884	148	$5^7/_8$	19564
85	JUL	4207	$^{11}/_{16}$	241916	359	6	56060
85	AUG	1091	$2^1/_4$	43160	54	$6^3/_4$	1736
85	OCT	264	5	61100	6	$8^1/_2$	16396
90	JUL	1185	$^1/_4$	109388	10	$9^3/_4$	10260
90	AUG	653	$1^1/_8$	46632	106	11	720
90	OCT	224	$3^3/_8$	54384	11	$12^1/_8$	10332
95	JUL	59	$^1/_8$	41148	...	...	3780
95	AUG	230	$^9/_{16}$	11756	...	...	36
95	OCT	225	$2^3/_8$	21488	25	$16^1/_4$	1548
100	JUL	176	$^1/_{16}$	96384	...	...	1940
100	AUG	233	$^3/_8$	9900	...	...	420
100	OCT	245	$1^9/_{16}$	46876	...	...	872
105	JUL	3	$^1/_{16}$	47208	...	...	464
105	AUG	5	$^1/_4$	3812	...	...	
105	OCT	650	$1^5/_{16}$	13064	...	...	360
110	AUG	...	...	2620	2	$29^3/_8$	
110	OCT	20	$^{13}/_{16}$	27088	5	$28^7/_8$	268
120	JUL	2	$^1/_{16}$	52256	...	...	224
120	OCT	13	$^7/_{16}$	18176	...	...	8
125	OCT	10	$^5/_{16}$	12560	...	...	
140	OCT	3	$^1/_4$	5688	...	...	

options are available at the *WSJ* website (www.wsj.com). The print version lists options alphabetically, grouped by striking price and expiration. A small letter "p" after the striking price identifies a put, with a blank representing a call option. Every service that reports option prices will show, at a minimum, the option striking price, expiration, and premium. Some (like Table 2–1) are more complete and also show volume and open interest.

This particular format shows striking prices in ascending order, with various expirations for each striking price. Data on call options are in the third, fourth, and fifth columns, with put option data in columns six, seven, and eight. It is easy for the options novice to grab the call premium instead of the put, and vice versa. For instance, Table 2–1 shows the premium for a Microsoft August 75 *call* is $7 $\frac{1}{4}$, while the premium for a Microsoft August 75 *put* is 1^{13}/_{16}$. These are obviously not the same.

The financial pages list the price for an option on a single share. Because "one option" really means an option on 100 shares, an individual who buys one Microsoft August 75 call @ 7\frac{1}{4}$ would actually pay 7\frac{1}{4}$ per share × 100 shares, or $725.

The MSFT AUG 75 call is *in-the-money*, because the right to buy at $75 is valuable when the stock price is 79^{7}/_{16}$. For a call option, *intrinsic value* is the stock price minus the striking price: in this case, 79^{7}/_{16}$ – $75 = 4^{7}/_{16}$. We know the option premium and we know the intrinsic value, so we can solve for the time value: time value = premium – intrinsic value, or 7\frac{1}{4}$ – 4^{7}/_{16}$ = 2^{13}/_{16}$. (Option users quickly develop proficiency with adding and subtracting fractions!)

The MSFT AUG 75 *put* is *out-of-the-money*, because there is no incentive to sell at $75 when the market price of the stock is more than this. Though this option has no intrinsic value, it *does* have time value: 1^{13}/_{16}$. This helps illustrate an important point: Before their expiration, out-of-the-money options *are not worthless*. Their premium is entirely time value.

Stock prices can change every day, and consequently so can the option premium. Even if stock prices do not change, the option premium can still change. The longer the option has until expiration, the more it is worth, because the stock price has more time to fluctuate and therefore has a greater potential to rise or fall. If you look again at the premiums in Table 2–1, you see that for a given striking price, option premiums increase for more distant expirations.

As an option moves closer to expiration, its time value decreases. Option traders refer to this phenomenon as *time value decay*. Everything else being equal (i.e., the stock price does not change), the value of an option will decline over time. This fact makes an option a **wasting asset**, which is an often-misunderstood term. Football tickets are also wasting assets, because there is a time when they cease to have any value. Anyone who has ever observed activity around a football stadium knows that the price scalpers get for tickets begins to decline when kickoff occurs. By the end of the first half, the price has fallen substantially. However, just because something is a wasting asset does not mean that it is not useful.

PROFITS AND LOSSES WITH OPTIONS

UNDERSTANDING THE EXERCISE OF AN OPTION

Options give you the right to buy or sell. As explained earlier, with an American option this right can be exercised anytime prior to the expiration of the option. A European option, on the other hand, can only be exercised at expiration.

Although they can be exercised anytime, there are very few situations in which it is advantageous to exercise an American option early. Doing so essentially amounts to abandoning any time value remaining in the option. Consider the Microsoft Oct 75 call selling for $10, while the underlying stock sells for $79^{7}/$_{16}$. If this option were exercised, stock would be purchased for $4^{7}/$_{16}$ less than its market price. The option has intrinsic value of $4^{7}/$_{16}$. If you exercise it, you recover this intrinsic value, but you would throw away the remaining $5^{9}/$_{16}$ of option premium.

It is normally not prudent to exercise a call option early.

Exercise Procedures

If I decide to exercise any option (put or call), I notify my broker. My brokerage firm, in turn, notifies the Options Clearing Corporation, which selects a contra party to receive the exercise notice. As all trades are through the clearing corporation, neither the option exerciser nor the option writer knows the identity of the opposite party.

The option premium is not a down payment of the purchase of the stock.

The option premium is *not* a down payment on the option terms. A person who exercises a call option with a striking price of $25 must put up $25/share times 100 shares, or $2,500. Remember that the option premium is the option writer's to keep no matter what happens. Similarly, I must either purchase or own 100 shares of stock for each put I want to exercise. The premium I paid for the put does not "count" toward the cost of the stock.

The *writer* of a call option must be prepared to sell 100 shares of the underlying stock to the call owner if the call owner decides to exercise. If the writer owns these shares, the writer delivers the share certificate to the broker, who will deliver it to the Options Clearing Corporation. The OCC will then arrange to have share ownership transferred to the exerciser of the call, collect the striking price proceeds from the exerciser's brokerage account, and also will have the striking price proceeds transferred into the writer's account. If the writer does not own any shares of the stock, then the writer must first purchase the shares in the open market at the current price. The writer of a put option must be prepared to *buy* shares of stock if the put holder decides to exercise the option.

The option holder decides when and if to exercise, not the option writer.

An important point to note from this discussion is the fact that the ball is in the option holder's court; the option writer sits back and waits. The option holder, not the option writer, decides when and if to exercise. Because options are fungible, the option writer can reverse (or offset) a position if it is profitable to do so.

In general, you should not buy an option with the intent of exercising it.

There is another surprising fact of options trading. This is the general rule that people seldom buy an option (American or European) with the intent of exercising it: they anticipate selling the option at a profit rather than exercising it. There is a good reason for this.

Options are not normally exercised until just before they expire, because *early exercise amounts to discarding the remaining time value.* If I exercise a call near the end of its life, I must come up with the money to pay for the stock, which might be inconvenient. I also would have to pay my broker a commission to exercise the call. When I sold the stock, I would pay another commission.

FIGURE 2–7 Four Basic Option Positions		
	CALL	PUT
BUY	RIGHT TO BUY	RIGHT TO SELL
WRITE	OBLIGATION TO SELL	OBLIGATION TO BUY

The same thing is true with puts. Unless I already owned the stock, I would have to buy shares in the open market (paying a commission), and would pay another commission when I exercised the put.

I can recover the value contained in any option by simply selling it. This way I do not have to come up with any more money.

PROFIT AND LOSS DIAGRAMS

A convenient way to envision what happens with option strategies as the value of the underlying security changes is with the use of a *profit and loss diagram*. Profit and loss diagrams are used in this chapter and the next two as an aid in analyzing option positions.[10]

The vertical axis of the diagram reflects profits or losses on option expiration day resulting from a particular strategy, while the horizontal axis reflects the stock price on option expiration day. At expiration, there is no time value left, so the option will sell for its intrinsic value. By convention, the diagrams ignore the effect of commissions you have to pay.

BUYING A CALL OPTION

Figure 2–8 is a profit/loss diagram for a person who *buys* a Microsoft October 80 call for $7. A colloquial term for buying something is "going long." When the option expires, it is worthless if the price of Microsoft stock is $80 or less.

When you buy an option, the most you can lose is the premium you paid when the option was purchased.

Note that the maximum loss is $7. An important point to remember with options is that when you buy an option, the most you can lose is the option premium. You will never be required to put up more money. It is true that you can lose 100 percent of your money, but 100 percent of the option premium amounts to fewer dollars than 100 percent of an investment in 100 shares of stock.

At any price above the striking price of $80, the option will have intrinsic value. The diagram shows that in this situation the option buyer breaks even[11] at a stock price of $87. At this price, the option will be intrinsically worth $87 minus $80, or $7. This is exactly what it cost, and it can be sold for this amount.

Once the stock price goes above the breakeven point of $87 the option holder

---

[10]A related sketch is a *payoff diagram*, which is similar to a profit and loss diagram except that it ignores the initial option premium.

[11]In this and all other examples of profit and loss diagrams, we will ignore the impact of commissions and taxes.

earns a dollar for every dollar rise in the price of the stock. Because the stock price can rise to any level, profits are theoretically unlimited.

It is very important to keep in mind that these *profit and loss diagrams apply to option expiration only*. Before expiration day, an option has time value. Consequently, its premium will be greater than that shown in the typical expiration day diagram; profits and losses will logically differ as well.

WRITING A CALL OPTION

What about the option writer? This person is on the "other side of the market" from the option buyer. Ignoring commissions, the options market is a zero sum game; aggregate gains and losses will always net to zero. If the call buyer makes money, the call writer is going to lose money, and vice versa.

Figure 2–9 shows this situation from the perspective of the person who has *written* the call. A written option is also colloquially called a short option. If I write a call and do not own the underlying shares, that is called writing a **naked call**. Naked calls are also called **uncovered calls**.

The most an option writer can make is the option premium.

You will note that the profit and loss diagram in Figure 2–9 has simply been rotated about the horizontal axis. The option writer's maximum profit is always equal to the option buyer's maximum loss.

The thought-provoking part of Figure 2–9 is the potential for unlimited losses. If the stock price rises sharply from its current level of \$79⁷/₁₆, the naked call writer can lose a lot of money.

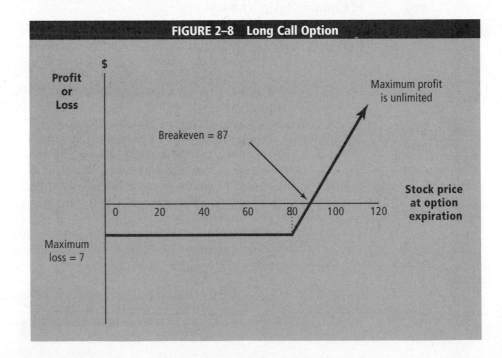

FIGURE 2–8   Long Call Option

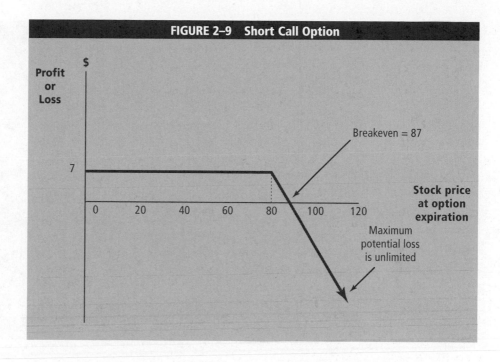

FIGURE 2–9   Short Call Option

BUYING A PUT OPTION

People who buy puts generally do so because they anticipate a decline in the price of the underlying security. Suppose I believe that Microsoft common stock is overpriced and about to fall. From Table 2–1, I see that the premium for a Microsoft OCT 80 put is $5⁷/₈. It costs me 100 times this, or $587.50, to buy such a put. Remember that a principle of option trading is that when someone buys an option, the maximum loss is the option premium. This means my maximum loss from the purchase of this put is $587.50. Figure 2–10 shows the profit/loss possibilities.

The figure shows that the maximum loss will occur at all stock prices at or above the option striking price of $80. If the stock price at option expiration is $90, for instance, my option would be worthless, because it would not make sense to exercise the right to sell at $80 when the market price is $90.

If stock prices fall, then I can benefit from my put. The best thing that could happen to the put buyer is for the stock price to fall to zero. Then the put would permit the sale of 100 shares of worthless stock for $80 per share, for a profit of $8,000 on the stock. My net gain would be $8,000 minus the $587.50 paid for the put, or $7,412.50.

Note that in the diagram the bend in the profit/loss plot occurs at the striking price of $80. This set-up is a general rule with such diagrams and will be particularly helpful with more advanced strategies.

In profit and loss diagrams, any bend(s) in the diagram occurs at the striking price(s).

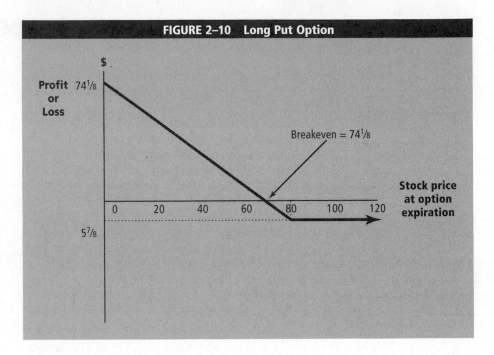

FIGURE 2–10   Long Put Option

WRITING A PUT OPTION

Writing put options is without doubt the least used of the simple option strategies. This is not because writing puts is a bad idea; it is because very few people, brokers included, understand this strategy very well. Put options are conceptually awkward for many people. The right to sell something is not an asset we encounter very often. If I *write* a put and sell it to you, I have created the right for you to sell me something you might not even own. This explanation can easily furrow brows.

If I *own* a put, I have the right to sell. But where did the put come from? It came from the put writer, who is agreeing to buy your shares if you exercise the put. The put holder has the right to sell, while the put writer has the obligation to buy if the put is exercised. The colloquial term "put it to him" probably has its roots in the options market. When I write a put, I may discover that I am obliged to purchase shares of stock because of falling stock prices. The put holder can "put shares in my account" anytime before the option expires. If the put holder chooses to do so, I must pay the striking price for each share I buy.

Suppose I write an OCT 80 put on Microsoft for a premium of $5⅞. The $587.50 is mine to keep no matter what happens. The person who buys the put wants stock prices to go down, because that is how the buyer makes a profit. I, on the other hand, having written the put, want prices to go up, or at least to remain above the striking price. If this happens, the put will expire worthless, and I, as writer, will not have to buy any shares.

A put writer may have to involuntarily purchase shares of stock if the put owner decides to exercise.

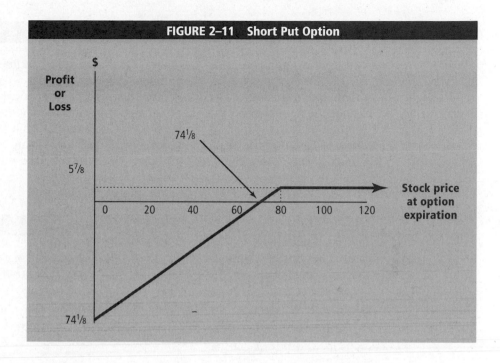

FIGURE 2–11   Short Put Option

Figure 2–11 is a diagram of the profit and loss possibilities. My maximum profit is $5\frac{7}{8}$: this is the option premium I receive for writing the put. The maximum loss occurs if Microsoft stock falls to zero. Here, the holder of the put could exercise the option, and as the put writer, I would be obliged to buy 100 shares at $80 each, even though they are worthless. I still get to keep the $5\frac{7}{8}$ per share premium, though, so my net loss is $74\frac{1}{8}$ per share, or $7,412.50.

A NOTE ON MARGIN REQUIREMENTS[12]

Some option transactions have a **margin requirement**. This is analogous to posting collateral and can be satisfied by a deposit of cash or other securities into your brokerage account. If you *write* an option, the loss associated with an adverse price movement can be large. The margin system is to reduce the likelihood that option writers will be unable to fulfill their obligations under the option terms.

If the posting of margin were not necessary, someone could always generate additional cash by writing more options. Writing more options could always cover losses from unfavorable price movements. If carried to the extreme, this process obviously could bankrupt the OCC system.

---

[12]Margin requirements will be discussed in more detail in Chapter 4.

SUMMARY

There are two types of options: puts and calls. Calls give you the right to buy; puts give you the right to sell. All options have a predetermined buying/selling price called the striking price, and a predetermined expiration date.

In-the-money options have both intrinsic value and time value. Intrinsic value changes every time the value of the underlying security changes, and time value declines as the expiration date approaches.

The first trade an individual makes in a particular option is an opening transaction; when the position is closed out, the trade is a closing transaction. When options are sold as an opening transaction, this is called writing the option.

SELF TEST

T ___ F ___   1. There are three types of options; calls, puts, and vouchers.

T ___ F ___   2. A person who buys a put option has an obligation to sell if the option writer exercises.

T ___ F ___   3. A person who buys a call has the right to buy.

T ___ F ___   4. Having a money-back guarantee is similar to owning a put option.

T ___ F ___   5. With a listed equity option, the underlying asset is normally 50 shares of stock.

T ___ F ___   6. An index option is cash settled.

T ___ F ___   7. The option *striking* price is the same as the option *exercise* price.

T ___ F ___   8. There is no set number of put and call options on a given security.

T ___ F ___   9. Options normally expire on the last business day of the expiration month.

T ___ F ___   10. The option premium is usually greater than the option price.

T ___ F ___   11. Open interest must be less than or equal to option volume.

T ___ F ___   12. Buying an option as an opening transaction is called writing the option.

T ___ F ___   13. An opening transaction with an option may be either a purchase or a sale.

T ___ F ___   14. Exchange traded puts are fungible, while exchange traded calls are not.

T ___ F ___   15. The Options Clearing Corporation solves the credit risk problem for option buyers and sellers.

T ___ F ___   16. Most option trading occurs at the New York Stock Exchange.

T ___ F ___   17. All in-the-money options have positive intrinsic value.

T ___ F ___   18. It is not possible for a JUN 50 GE call and a JUN 50 GE put to both be in-the-money.

T ___ F ___   19. The maximum profit for an option writer is the option premium.

T ___ F ___   20. Writing a call is economically equivalent to buying a put.

PROBLEMS & QUESTIONS

1. In general, does a person who buys a call option want prices to go up or down?
2. True or False: "Buying a call is exactly the same as writing a put." Explain your answer.
3. Why are options considered wasting assets?
4. True or False: "If there are 1,000 people who own Boeing put options, then there have to be 1,000 people who wrote Boeing puts." Explain your answer.
5. Why do most people sell their valuable options rather than exercising them?
6. Explain why it is possible for an options contract to *disappear* without expiring or being exercised.
7. Suppose you are bullish on a stock. What are the relative advantages and disadvantages of (a) buying a call, versus (b) writing a put?
8. Refer to Table 2-1. Give an example of an option that is *near-the-money*.
9. Look at the options listing in a current edition of the *Wall Street Journal* or via the Internet. Why do you think some options have more striking prices listed than others?
10. Would you expect an American option on a particular stock to always sell for at least as much as a European option with the same exercise terms? Why or why not?
11. Comment on the following statement: "An option that is out-of-the-money must have time value prior to expiration."
12. Comment on the following statement: "An option that is in-the-money must have intrinsic value."
13. Comment on the following statement: "Options are nothing more than a side bet on the direction stock prices are going to move."
14. Briefly explain why the following statement is *wrong*: "If you buy an XYZ JUN 25 call option in March, the only way you can make a profit is if the price of XYZ closes above 25 on expiration day in June."
15. True or false: "An at-the-money option has time value equal to its intrinsic value prior to expiration."
16. Briefly explain how it is possible for an out-of-the-money put option on XYZ to sell for *more* than an in-the-money put option on XYZ.
17. True or False: "If I sell an option as an opening transaction, this is called writing the option. But just because I wrote an option does not mean it was an opening transaction."
18. True or False: "The quantity of XYZ call options in existence at any given time is always a constant."
19. Why are typical profit and loss diagrams such as those discussed in this chapter only valid at option expiration?
20. How is the option premium different from a down payment?

The following questions all refer to the Microsoft options in Table 2–1.

21. How much time value is in an AUG 70 call option?
22. What is the intrinsic value of an OCT 70 call?
23. What is the intrinsic value of an OCT 70 put?
24. Suppose you write an AUG 100 call. What is your maximum profit?
25. Suppose you buy an OCT 90 put for the price listed. At expiration, Microsoft stock sells for $71^3/_8$. What is your profit or loss?
26. What is the maximum profit if you buy a JUL 100 call?
27. Construct a profit/loss diagram for the purchase of a JUL 100 call.
28. Construct a profit/loss diagram for the writing of a naked OCT 90 call.
29. Construct a profit/loss diagram for the purchase of an AUG 80 put.

CHAPTER 2 REVIEW

30. Construct a profit/loss diagram for the writing of a JUL 90 put.
31. How much time value is in an AUG 70 call option?
32. What is the intrinsic value of an AUG 90 call?
33. What is the intrinsic value of a JUL 75 put?
34. Suppose you write an AUG 105 call. What is your maximum profit?
35. Suppose you buy an AUG 75 put for the price listed. At expiration, Microsoft stock sells for $83. What is your profit or loss?
36. What is your maximum profit if you buy an OCT 100 call?
37. Construct a profit/loss diagram for the purchase of an OCT 80 call.
38. Construct a profit/loss diagram for the writing of a naked OCT 100 call.

39. Construct a profit/loss diagram for the purchase of an AUG 75 put.
40. Construct a profit/loss diagram for the writing of a JUL 80 put.
41. What is the ticker symbol for a Microsoft OCT 70 call? *(Recall from Box 2–1 that the MSFT option code is MSQ.)*
42. What is the ticker symbol for a JUL 80 put?
43. What is the ticker symbol for an AUG 60 call?
44. What is the ticker symbol for an OCT 140 put?
45. What is the premium for a JUL 90 put?
46. What is the premium for an AUG 70 call?
47. How many MSFT OCT 75 calls exist?

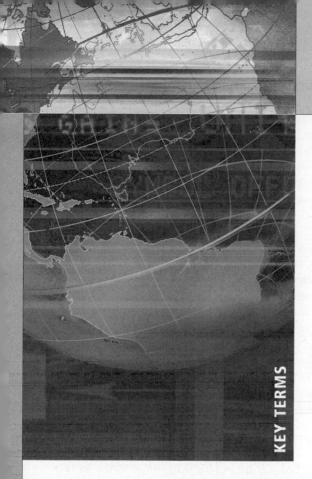

3

Basic Option Strategies: Covered Calls and Protective Puts

The value of a perpetual European put option is zero.

Robert Merton

The previous chapter dealt with basic option principles and terminology. You need to be fluent in them to deal with the concepts in this chapter. Now we look at ways to use options as a portfolio component rather than as a single security. People using options as a portfolio component often do so either to provide insurance against adverse price movements (protective puts) or to generate additional portfolio income (covered calls).

USING OPTIONS AS A HEDGE

A homeowner is uncomfortable bearing the full risk of a house fire. The loss of an uninsured home can be financially devastating, so most homeowners transfer part or all of this risk to an insurance company. The insurance company accepts the risk that the homeowner does not want and receives the homeowner's insurance premium for doing so. The homeowner *hedges* by buying insurance; the insurance company *speculates* that the house will not burn. It is important to note that neither party wants the house to catch fire.

At the end of the policy year, the insurance ends. The insurance company keeps the premium paid by the homeowner, who must then get a new policy (or renew the old one) if he or she wants to continue coverage against economic loss. The fact that the house did not burn does not mean that the insurance was a waste of money; insuring the home provided peace of mind to the family. This is an important point regarding risk management: *money spent on reducing risk is not wasted*. Still, many people subconsciously view the money spent for "unused" insurance as unproductive.

Students often find themselves torn between *hedging* and *speculating* when they begin to study for an exam. Perhaps the class has been provided a list of ten essay questions, of which the instructor will select three to be answered. As a student, you might have a strong suspicion regarding which three will be selected. If you were a fearless (and unwise) speculator, you might study only those three and use the rest of your time to party. Most students would choose to hedge, though, by spending some time reviewing all ten. There are degrees of hedging/speculating that could obviously occur in this example as you allocate your study time to the ten questions. You may study four questions thoroughly and spend less time on the other six. With these thoughts in mind, we now look at how puts and calls can perform this hedging (or insurance) function.

PROTECTIVE PUTS

Someone who owns shares of stock has a **long position** in the security. In the investment business, the term "long" simply means that you own something. It has nothing to do with time span.

Figure 3–1 is a profit and loss diagram for the purchase of Microsoft common stock at $79^7/_{16}$ per share. The maximum loss occurs if the stock declines to zero, while the potential profit is unlimited. Ignoring commissions, dividends, and opportunity costs, the strategy "breaks even" if the stock price is unchanged at a specific future time. In this diagram no options are involved, but you can still note the stock price on option expiration day (the X axis value).

Investors occasionally anticipate a decline in the value of an investment, but cannot conveniently sell it because of tax considerations or other reasons. In such a situation the investor might consider using a **protective put**.[1]

A protective put is not a special kind of put option; it is a descriptive term given to a long stock position combined with a long put position. If someone owns shares of Microsoft and buys a Microsoft put (regardless of striking price or expiration), the put is a protective put.[2]

Figure 3–2 shows the profits and losses associated with various stock prices if someone buys a Microsoft AUG 75 put at the Table 2–1 price of $1^{13}/_{16}$; Figure

The sidenotes:
Hedgers transfer unwanted risk to speculators who are willing to bear it.

Insurance that expires without a claim does not constitute a waste of money.

A protective put is not a special kind of option; it is the simultaneous holding of a long stock position and a put option on that stock.

[1] Robert C. Pozen probably coined this term in an article entitled "The Purchase of Protective Puts by Financial Institutions," *Financial Analysts Journal* (Jul/Aug 1978): 47–60.

[2] The more it is out of the money, though, the less protection the put provides.

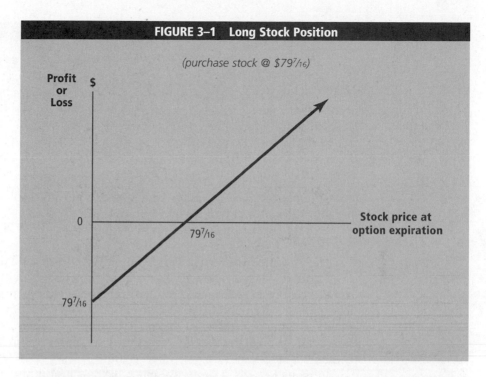

FIGURE 3–1   Long Stock Position

(purchase stock @ $79⁷/₁₆)

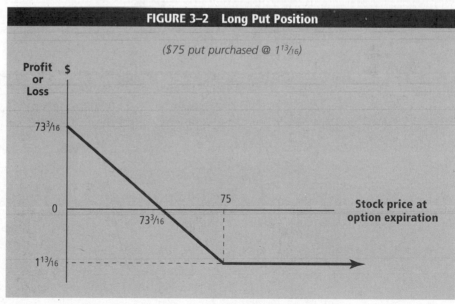

FIGURE 3–2   Long Put Position

($75 put purchased @ 1¹³/₁₆)

TABLE 3–1   Protective Put Worksheet

	STOCK PRICE AT OPTION EXPIRATION								
	0	**15**	**30**	**45**	**60**	**75**	**90**	**105**	**120**
LONG STOCK @ $79⁷/₁₆	−79⁷/₁₆	−64⁷/₁₆	−49⁷/₁₆	−34⁷/₁₆	−19⁷/₁₆	−4⁷/₁₆	10⁹/₁₆	25⁹/₁₆	40⁹/₁₆
LONG $75 PUT @ 1¹³/₁₆	73³/₁₆	58³/₁₆	43³/₁₆	28³/₁₆	13³/₁₆	−1¹³/₁₆	−1¹³/₁₆	−1¹³/₁₆	−1¹³/₁₆
NET		−6¹/₄	−6¹/₄	−6¹/₄	−6¹/₄	−6¹/₄	−6¹/₄	8³/₄	23³/₄	38³/₄

3–1 shows profits and losses for a long position in Microsoft stock. What happens if you graphically add Figures 3–1 and 3–2?

To help in constructing the combined diagram, a profit and loss worksheet like Table 3–1 helps.

The worksheet shows that the maximum loss is $6¹/₄ and that it occurs at all stock prices of $75 or below. The strategy appears to break even at a stock price somewhere between $75 and $90. If you check a few more prices, you will find that the break-even point is $81¹/₄. At this price, the value of the stock has risen $1¹³/₁₆. The put expires out-of-the-money, so it is worthless. At $81¹/₄ the stock rose exactly enough to offset the cost of the put. The maximum gain is unlimited, because the stock can rise to any value. Figure 3–3 shows the combined positions.

In many respects, a protective put is like a collision insurance policy on an automobile. A car is valuable, and its owner suffers if it is damaged in an accident. To protect against this potential for loss, people buy insurance, fully expect-

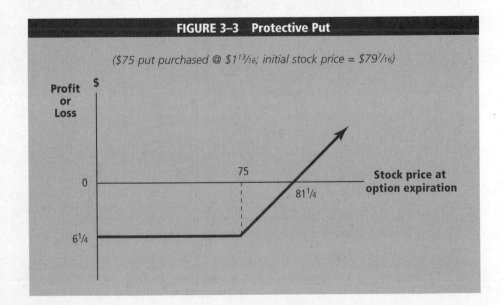

FIGURE 3–3   Protective Put

($75 put purchased @ $1¹³/₁₆; initial stock price = $79⁷/₁₆)

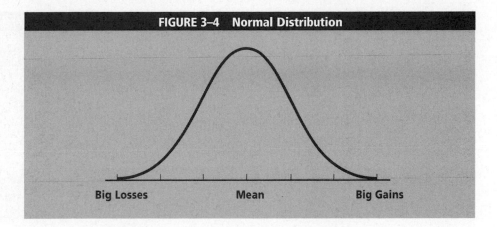

FIGURE 3–4   Normal Distribution

Big Losses   Mean   Big Gains

ing to "lose" all the money they pay for it. A person should not feel discouraged if an accident-free year goes by without the necessity of filing a claim with the insurance company.

When you select an insurance policy, you can choose how much protection you want. If you want coverage for the first dollar of collision damage, the insurance policy is expensive. On the other hand, if you are willing to assume the risk of the first $500 in damage and just buy insurance against a major loss, the insurance premium is much lower. Larger deductibles mean a lower premium, and this is also true in the options market.

Visualize the possible stock returns as a normal distribution "bell curve" like that in Figure 3–4. Large negative returns (those to the far left in the figure) are bad. When someone buys a protective put they are getting insurance against these outcomes.

From the perspective of the protective put buyer, the put premium is what you pay to make these large losses someone else's problem. Once you acquire the put, the striking price puts a lower limit on your maximum possible loss and the return distribution changes to Figure 3–5.

Selecting the striking price for a protective put is analogous to selecting the deductible you want for stock insurance. The more protection you want, the higher the premium you are going to pay. Returning to the example, you might decide to buy a Microsoft AUG 75 put to protect your long stock position of 100 shares. You pay the option premium of $181.25 to the person who wrote the put and hope that the stock continues to rise. In other words, *you fully expect to lose all the money paid for the protective put.* It may seem odd that you would ever buy a security expecting to lose money in your investment, but remember the motivation for buying fire insurance on your home or collision insurance on your car. The situations are similar. Table 3–2 shows analogies between a protective put and an insurance policy.

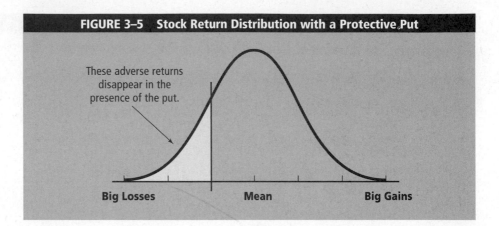

FIGURE 3–5   Stock Return Distribution with a Protective Put

These adverse returns disappear in the presence of the put.

Big Losses   Mean   Big Gains

The shape of Figure 3–3 is generally the same as Figure 2–8 "Buying a Call." This hints at an important result with options. *Certain combinations of securities are equivalent to certain others.* Here, buying a protective put is very similar to the outright purchase of a call option. The term **synthetic option** describes a collection of financial instruments that are equivalent to an option position. A protective put is an example of a synthetic call.

$$\text{long stock} + \text{long put} \approx \text{long call}$$

This does not mean that someone should always buy calls and should never buy stock. Many institutions and individuals need the long-term benefits of a stock portfolio. For these people, put options are a convenient way to obtain temporary "insurance" against declining stock prices. It is fair to say, though, that a person should seriously consider the purchase of a call rather than the *simultaneous* purchase of shares of stock and a put. It will certainly be cheaper in terms of commissions and total dollar outlay. Still, the two positions are different, and you cannot say that one is clearly preferable to the other in every instance.

TABLE 3–2   Protective Puts and Insurance Analogies

INSURANCE POLICY		PUT OPTION
PREMIUM	← →	TIME PREMIUM
VALUE OF ASSET	← →	PRICE OF STOCK
FACE VALUE	← →	STRIKE PRICE
AMOUNT OF DEDUCTIBLE	← →	STOCK PRICE LESS STRIKE PRICE
DURATION	← →	TIME UNTIL EXPIRATION
LIKELIHOOD OF LOSS	← →	VOLATILITY OF STOCK

From "Portfolio Insurance," by Nicholas Hanson, in Institutional Options Update (July/August 1986)

INDEX OPTIONS

Index options are one of the option exchange's best inventions. As the previous chapter indicated, the fact that these are cash-settled enables a portfolio manager or individual investor to alter the risk/return characteristics of the portfolio without actually disturbing the stock in the portfolio. Listed below are a few of the most popular index options.

OPTION	EXCHANGE	TICKER SYMBOL	DESCRIPTION
S&P 100	CBOE	OEX	A CAPITALIZATION-WEIGHTED INDEX OF 100 STOCKS FROM A BROAD RANGE OF INDUSTRIES.
S&P 500	CBOE	SPX	A CAPITALIZATION-WEIGHTED INDEX OF 500 STOCKS FROM A BROAD RANGE OF INDUSTRIES.
DOW JONES INDUSTRIAL AVERAGE	CBOE	DJX	THE 30 STOCKS IN THE DJIA.
NASDAQ 100	CBOE	NDX	A CAPITALIZATION-WEIGHTED INDEX COMPOSED OF 100 OF THE LARGEST NON-FINANCIAL SECURITIES LISTED ON THE NASDAQ STOCK MARKET.
RUSSELL 2000 INDEX	CBOE	RUT	A CAPITALIZATION-WEIGHTED INDEX OF DOMESTIC EQUITIES REPRESENTING THE BOTTOM 2,000 COMPANIES FROM A UNIVERSE OF THE 3,000 LARGEST STOCKS IN THE U.S.

USING CALLS TO HEDGE A SHORT POSITION

The previous section showed how put options can provide a hedge against losses from falling security prices. The same thing can be done with call options to provide a hedge against losses resulting from *rising* security prices.

Investors make money when they sell an asset for more than they pay for it. Normally, they buy something first, and sell it later. Trades do not have to be made in this order. With a **short sale**, the first (or opening) transaction is a sale; the second (or closing) transaction is a purchase. Short sellers borrow shares from their brokers, sell them, hope to buy identical shares in the future at a lower price, and then return the borrowed shares. Closing out a short position is called "covering the short position." Short sellers make a profit if security prices decline.

Chapter 2 illustrates how opposite strategies have profit/loss diagrams that are identical except for their rotation about the horizontal axis. When Figure 3–1 (Long Stock Position) is rotated in this fashion, it becomes the diagram for a short stock position, as in Figure 3–6. Note that with a short sale potential losses are theoretically unlimited. Prices can rise to any level, and the short seller is obliged eventually to replace borrowed shares.

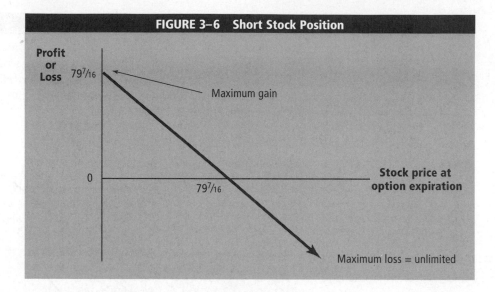

FIGURE 3–6   Short Stock Position

Profit or Loss

$79\frac{7}{16}$ — Maximum gain

0

Stock price at option expiration

$79\frac{7}{16}$

Maximum loss = unlimited

It is useful to compare the profit and loss diagram for a short sale with that of a long put position. Figure 2–10 (Buy a Put) is similar in shape to Figure 3–6 (Short Stock Position), except that *the potential for unlimited losses is eliminated*. In buying a put, the maximum loss is the option premium, yet the profit potential is very similar to the more risky strategy of selling short. Many informed indi-

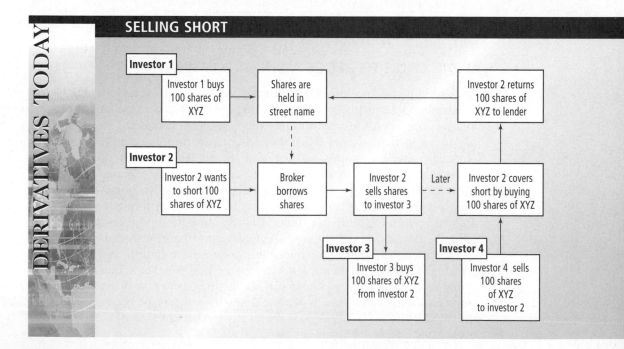

DERIVATIVES TODAY

SELLING SHORT

Investor 1 — Investor 1 buys 100 shares of XYZ — Shares are held in street name — Investor 2 returns 100 shares of XYZ to lender

Investor 2 — Investor 2 wants to short 100 shares of XYZ — Broker borrows shares — Investor 2 sells shares to investor 3 — Later — Investor 2 covers short by buying 100 shares of XYZ

Investor 3 — Investor 3 buys 100 shares of XYZ from investor 2

Investor 4 — Investor 4 sells 100 shares of XYZ to investor 2

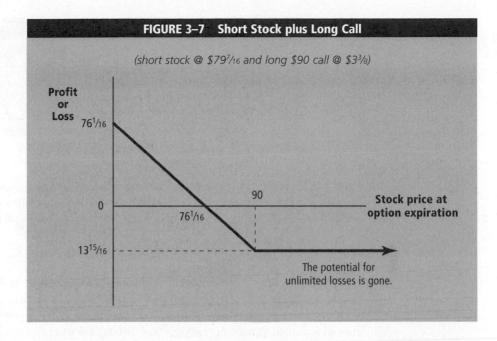

FIGURE 3–7   Short Stock plus Long Call

(short stock @ $79⁷⁄₁₆ and long $90 call @ $3³⁄₈)

Profit or Loss

76¹⁄₁₆

0

76¹⁄₁₆

90

13¹⁵⁄₁₆

Stock price at option expiration

The potential for unlimited losses is gone.

In general, an individual investor should consider buying a put before deciding to sell a stock short.

vidual investors who are bearish find the purchase of a put vastly preferable to a short sale of the stock for this reason.[3] In addition, buying a put requires less capital than the hefty margin requirements necessary to open a short account with a brokerage firm.[4]

Although short positions are dangerous for the typical investor, professional traders, hedge funds, and portfolio managers frequently use them. On the exchange floor, members routinely day trade using short sales, meaning that they close out the short position before the market closes. They avoid margin requirements because the position is not held overnight, and the risk of adverse price movements stemming from overnight news is eliminated. Even for such well-financed people positioned on the front lines of the marketplace, however, the potential for large losses is noteworthy.

One way to hedge this risk is to add a long call position to the short stock position. Combining the profit and loss diagrams for a long call and a short stock position results in a plot like Figure 3–7. This figure comes from a short sale of Microsoft @ $79⁷⁄₁₆ and the purchase of an OCT 90 call @ $3³⁄₈. The important feature of Figure 3–7 is that there is no potential for unlimited losses. The most that the short seller can lose in this situation is $13¹⁵⁄₁₆. While the stock

---

[3]Note, however, that puts have a finite lifetime, while a short position may remain open indefinitely. If the investor's timing is off, the put may expire before the anticipated price movement occurs. Also, there is no premium to recover if you sell short; profits begin as soon as commissions are recouped.

[4]Margin refers to the amount of collateral required to be on deposit with a brokerage firm before an investor is permitted to engage in certain types of security transactions.

TABLE 3–3	**Profit and Loss Worksheet**					
	0	25	50	75	76$^{1}/_{16}$	100
SHORT STOCK @ 79$^{7}/_{16}$	79$^{7}/_{16}$	54$^{7}/_{16}$	29$^{7}/_{16}$	4$^{7}/_{16}$	3$^{3}/_{8}$	−20$^{9}/_{16}$
LONG 90 CALL @ 3$^{3}/_{8}$	−3$^{3}/_{8}$	−3$^{3}/_{8}$	−3$^{3}/_{8}$	−3$^{3}/_{8}$	−3$^{3}/_{8}$	6$^{5}/_{8}$
NET	76$^{1}/_{16}$	51$^{1}/_{16}$	26$^{1}/_{16}$	1$^{1}/_{16}$	0	−13$^{15}/_{16}$

price can keep rising (resulting in increasing losses on the short position), for every dollar the stock rises above $90 the call is worth a dollar more. Here, the dollar gain on the call exactly cancels the dollar loss on the short position.

$$\text{short stock} + \text{long call} \approx \text{long put}$$

Another way to look at a situation like this is via a profit and loss worksheet like that in Table 3–3. This presents the same information as the graph. At a stock price of zero, the speculator gains 79^{7}/_{16}$ on the short stock position. The expiring call is out-of-the-money, so it is worthless, and the premium of 3^{3}/_{8}$ is lost. The net gain is 76^{1}/_{16}$. At a stock price of $90, the option is at-the-money; at any higher stock price the option will be in-the-money. The loss in the short position and the gain in the long call position exactly cancel at any stock price above $90, so the maximum loss on the combined position occurs at $90 and above.

Note that the shape of Figure 3–7 is similar to that of Figure 2–10 (Long Put). If you are simultaneously short stock and long a call on that same stock, your combined position is similar to a long put.

WRITING COVERED CALLS TO PROTECT AGAINST MARKET DOWNTURNS

Sometimes an investor owns stock and writes a call against it, giving someone else the right to buy the shares. Such a call is a **covered call**. A covered call is the same as any other call option, except that you simultaneously are long the stock. Figure 3–8 shows the profit/loss possibilities for an OCT 85 covered call on Microsoft. This graph incorporates the profit and loss diagram for a long position in the stock and a short position in the OCT 85 call.

Option writers get the premium right away, and it is theirs to keep no matter what happens to the stock price. Figure 3–8 shows that if the stock price were to decline, the call premium cushions the loss by $5. Even if the stock were to drop to zero, you keep the option premium, so your net loss is "only" 74^{7}/_{16}$ (rather than 79^{7}/_{16}$ as in Figure 3–1).

Sometimes an investor owns shares of stock and fears a market downturn. That person might consider using covered calls to provide some cushion against losses from a falling market.

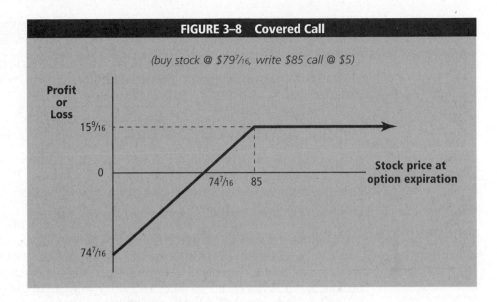

FIGURE 3–8   Covered Call

(buy stock @ 79^{7}/_{16}$, write $85 call @ $5)

In Figure 3–8, the $5 premium received from writing the call means that no actual cash loss occurs until Microsoft falls below the current price (79^{7}/_{16}$) minus the premium received ($5), or 74^{7}/_{16}$. Of course, if the investor's feeling about the market is wrong, and Microsoft rises above $85, there is the risk of the stock being called away unless he or she buys the option back.

While this strategy provides some downside protection, it is not a particularly effective hedge. In general, an individual who needs protection against falling stock prices is better off buying put options.

OPTIONS LINGO: LONG AND SHORT

It is common practice to say that you are "short" an option when you have written it. If you write a put, you have a *short put*. Therefore, a covered call is also a **short call**. Unlike selling stock short, though, you have not borrowed anything. When you buy back a call you have written, you are "covering the call." Conceivably, then, you could "cover" a "covered call." There are really two entirely different meanings to the term "covered."

You can say you "go long," "are long," "went long," or "have a long position," but normally you should not use "long" as a verb. That is, you would not say "I longed the calls." However, you *can* use "short" as a verb: "go short," "went short," "am short," "have a short position," or "shorted the calls" are all common expressions. These semantics may seem awkward, but they are part of the options lingo.

USING OPTIONS TO GENERATE INCOME

Many individual investors use options to generate additional portfolio income. This can be done by writing either puts or calls, although calls are used more often than puts.

WRITING CALLS TO GENERATE INCOME

Writing calls to generate income can be either very conservative or very risky, depending on the composition of the rest of the portfolio. This is an attractive way to generate income, especially with foundations, pension funds, and other portfolios that need to produce periodic cash payments.

Writing covered calls is a very popular activity with individual investors. Brokers find the idea easy to sell to their clients. Suppose today is July 11, 2000 and that you are a stockholder in Microsoft, having bought 300 shares eighteen months ago at $46. Uncertainty continues regarding the company's antitrust litigation, and it is not clear how Microsoft stock will fare in the coming months. Your broker points out that an OCT 90 call on Microsoft sells for $3⅜, or $337.50 on 100 shares. Writing three of these calls results in a credit of $1,012.50 into your account (ignoring commissions). You could use the money to buy another security, to pay off margin debt, or you could take the cash and spend it elsewhere. The worst thing that could happen to you would be for the stock of Microsoft to fall to zero; this, of course, could have happened even if you had not written the options.

If prices advance above the striking price of $90, your stock will be "called away," and you must sell it to the owner of the call option for $90 per share, despite the current stock price. You should not feel too upset about this, though, because you made a good profit. The stock rose[5] from $79⁷⁄₁₆ on July 10th to $90 on the third Friday in October for a per-share gain of $10.5625, plus you keep the $3⅜ premium from writing the option. On 300 shares with three covered call contracts, this is a dollar gain of ($10.5625 + $3.375) × 300 = $4,181.25. This is a gain of about 17½% in three months.

Some people familiar with the options markets are uncomfortable associating the word "income" with the option premium. While it is true that the option writer gets to keep the premium no matter what happens, the premium is really compensation for bearing added risk or for forgoing future price appreciation. It is not income in the sense of cash dividends or bond interest. Still, income is a term commonly associated with the option premium.

The option premium has tax implications, too. The general rule is fairly simple. If you buy an option and it expires worthless, you have a capital loss. If you

Writing covered calls is the most popular use of stock options by both individual and institutional investors.

[5]From your perspective, $90 is the ceiling on the stock price because you will have to sell it for $90 at any market price above that.

write an option and it expires worthless, you have a capital gain. Whether the gain or loss is short-term or long-term depends on whether the option position was outstanding long enough to qualify for long-term treatment.

If an option gets exercised, the option premium alters the purchase or sale price of the underlying stock. For instance, if you pay $2 for a $50 call and exercise it, the IRS considers $52 your purchase price. Now that you own the stock, if you write a $65 call for $3 and the stock gets called away, the IRS considers your selling price to be $68. You have a capital gain of $16, or $1,600 on a contract of 100 shares.

Tax-exempt institutions need not worry about the "unrelated business income" clause in the tax code. (A non-profit firm that generates income from sources unrelated to its charitable purpose may incur a tax liability.) In 1976 President Gerald Ford signed legislation specifically excluding option premiums from unrelated business income. Non-profit firms can write covered calls in their investment portfolio without worrying about losing their tax-exempt status.

As with a protective put, when you write a covered call you change the shape of the possible return distribution. However, instead of getting rid of the bad outcomes, you are selling the good outcomes to someone else. Figure 3–9 shows how you might visualize this.

While writing covered calls is a very popular option activity, there are times when writing calls is not appropriate. One such time is when option premiums are low. This can occur for several reasons, the most important being when

DERIVATIVES TODAY

OPTION OVERWRITING

Late in 1990 the San Diego County Employees' Retirement Association began an overwriting program in an attempt to boost the returns of their fund. The fund began to write S&P 500 index call options against the equity portfolio. They anticipated that the premium income would add about 100 basis points annually to the fund's total return.[6]

By 1994 the program had turned profits of $25 million. 1995 was a banner year for the market, with the S&P 500 rising 37%. The index calls that the fund wrote went substantially in-the-money and the fund had to make large payouts to the option holders. In total, the options program lost 8%, which knocked 3% off the fund's total return. According to the chief investment officer, the program "broke even" over the five years it was in place.

Numerous money management firms, including Loomis Sayles, Oppenheimer, and Analytic/TSA Global Asset Management, were active option overwriting firms during this period. Many of them sustained similar losses when the market rallied sharply. According to a writer in *Institutional Investor*, "In retrospect, the overwriting strategy most managers used was simply wrong for a roaring bull market."

[6]Bensman, Miriam. "The Trouble with Overwriting," Institutional Investor, *April 1997, 149–152.*

WRITING NEAR-TERM AT-THE-MONEY OPTIONS WHEN YOU WANT TO SELL

Britta Katrina is an individual investor holding 500 shares of Alcoa (*AA, NYSE*). She bought the stock at $23, it currently trades at $35¼, and she is thinking about selling it. She does not anticipate a major drop in the stock price but feels it has run out of steam. Britta notices that next month's Alcoa 35 calls are bid at $1½. She writes five of these for this premium, receiving $750 minus trading fees.

If AA remains above $35 she will sell it at that price next month. With the premium income, her effective selling price would be about $36½. If it closes below $35 on option expiration day, her plan is to write another set of one-month calls and wait another month. A point and a half in premium on a $35 stock is 4.3%, which she considers a good return in one month.

volatility in the market is expected to be low. Also, writing very long-term options may not be the best means of generating income. As will be seen in the option pricing material to come, more income is earned by writing a series of short-term options rather than a single long-term option.

Writing Naked Calls

Chapter 2 showed that writing naked calls is risky business because of the potential for unlimited losses. Despite this, there are many market participants who engage in frequent naked call writing as a means of generating income.

In Table 2–1, the premium for a July 95 MSFT call is ⅛, while Microsoft stock is $79⁷⁄₁₆. Recall that these prices are from July 10th, 2000. Looking at the calendar, July option expiration was Friday the 21st, so this option only has about 10

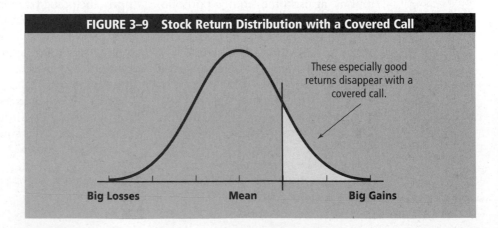

FIGURE 3–9   Stock Return Distribution with a Covered Call

These especially good returns disappear with a covered call.

Big Losses   Mean   Big Gains

days to go. A brokerage firm trading room might feel that it is extremely unlikely that Microsoft stock will rise to $95 per share (a $19\frac{1}{2}$% gain) in 10 days, and the firm may decide to write 100 of these call contracts (options on 10,000 shares). If they can do this at the listed premium of $\frac{1}{8}$, this results in a cash inflow of $0.125/ share × 10,000 shares, or $1,250. The firm receives the money now, and, provided the stock price stays below $95, nothing else happens. If the stock were to rise dramatically, the firm could sustain a large loss. Brokerage firms monitor the market carefully, and if Microsoft stock began to move up, the firm would close its option positions by buying them back, probably at a higher price (and a consequent loss).

Individual investors can write naked options too, but brokerage firms discourage small investors from doing so by enforcing certain minimum account balance requirements before permitting this type of speculative activity.[7]

WRITING PUTS TO GENERATE INCOME

Naked vs. Covered Puts

The previous material indicates that, from a profit and loss perspective, writing puts is similar to writing covered calls. The terms **naked put** and **covered put** are not used very often, and in some circles they might have ambiguous meanings. A naked put usually means a short put by itself, while a covered put usually means the combination of a short put and a short stock position.[8]

One special short put is a **fiduciary put**. This term refers to the situation in which someone writes a put option and simultaneously deposits the striking price into a special escrow account. This ensures that the funds are present to buy the stock in the event the put owner chooses to exercise it. As with a protective put, there is nothing special about the actual option; there just happens to be a cash balance to go with it.

Anytime you write an option you generate income, but you create a contingent liability on your personal balance sheet. When you write a call, you must sell stock if asked to do so. When you write a put, you must buy stock if asked to do so. A naked option position is one where you do not have another related security position that would cushion losses from price movements that adversely affect your short option position. With a covered option position, you *do* have some way of cushioning losses. We have seen that a long stock position cushions losses from a short call, and therefore the call is a covered call. Similarly, a short stock position would cushion losses from a short put, because the shares you get from the exercise of the put could be used to close out the short stock position.

$$\text{short stock} + \text{short put} \approx \text{short call}$$

---

[7]For margin purposes, most brokerage firms treat naked calls as if they were short stock positions.

[8]As the next chapter will show, a short put might also be covered by a long put.

There is an interesting paradox here. Writing covered calls is without doubt the most common option strategy used by small investors; writing *puts* is without doubt the least common. Yet if we compare Figure 3–8 (Writing a Covered Call) with Figure 2–11 (Writing a Put), we see the profit/loss plots have the same general shape.

$$\text{long stock} + \text{short call} \approx \text{short put}$$

In terms of commission costs and capital required, writing puts is certainly cheaper. Ignorance about the merits of this strategy is responsible for its absence from many portfolios.

Writing puts has risk and return characteristics very similar to writing covered calls.

Put overwriting involves being simultaneously long stock and short puts on the same stock.

Put Overwriting

There is another option strategy involving put writing. **Put overwriting** involves owning shares of stock and simultaneously writing a *put* option against these shares. While this strategy is less common than covered call writing, there are many investors who could logically use it.

Because owning shares and writing puts are both bullish strategies, put overwriting must also be a bullish strategy. Remember that anytime an investor writes an option, the largest possible gain is the option premium, but losses can be large if prices move against you.

Suppose an investor simultaneously buys shares of Microsoft at $79^7/_{16}$ and writes an AUG 80 Microsoft put for $4. Table 3–4 is a profit and loss worksheet for this strategy, and Figure 3–10 is the associated profit/loss diagram.

The diagram shows that if prices rise above the option striking price, the put will expire worthless and dollar for dollar profits are enjoyed on the stock rise. If prices fall, however, the position *loses twice* because the stock is depreciating and progressively larger liabilities are being incurred on the short put position. In this diagram the break-even point is $77^{23}/_{32}$. At this price the stock is down $79^7/_{16} - 77^{23}/_{32} = \$1^{23}/_{32}$. You sold the put for $4 and it is now worth $80 – $77^{23}/_{32} = \$2^9/_{32}$ for a gain of $1 $^{23}/_{32}$. The loss on the stock exactly equals the gain on the put.

Put overwriting may be appropriate for a portfolio manager who needs to generate additional income from the portfolio but does not want to write calls for fear of opportunity losses in a bull market. If the portfolio does continue to

TABLE 3–4	Put Overwriting Worksheet					
	0	25	50	75	$77^{23}/_{32}$	100
Buy stock @ $79^7/_{16}$	$-79^7/_{16}$	$-54^7/_{16}$	$-29^7/_{16}$	$-4^7/_{16}$	$-1^{23}/_{32}$	$20^9/_{16}$
Write 80 put @ 4	-76	-51	-26	-1	$1^{23}/_{32}$	4
Net	$-155^7/_{16}$	$-105^7/_{16}$	$-55^7/_{16}$	$-5^7/_{16}$	0	$24^9/_{16}$

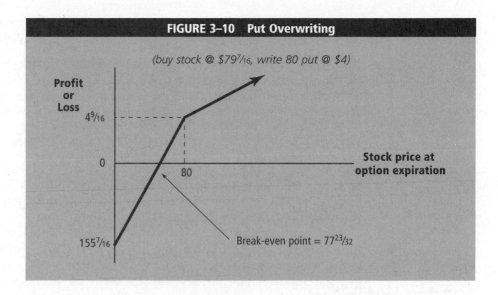

FIGURE 3–10   Put Overwriting

(buy stock @ 79^{7}\!/_{16}$, write 80 put @ $4)

Profit or Loss

Break-even point = $77^{23}\!/_{32}$

Stock price at option expiration

increase in value, the puts will expire worthless, the portfolio will benefit from the premium income received, and the portfolio will remain intact. On the other hand, if stock prices turn down and the portfolio manager does not trade out of the put positions quickly, the overall effect on the portfolio could be disastrous.

TRADING STRATEGY

PUT WRITING AND CORPORATE SHARE REPURCHASE

Corporations periodically buy back their own shares in the marketplace. The firm might believe the shares are undervalued, it may want to reduce its aggregate dividend obligation, or it may need the shares for employee stock option programs. Writing put options is an increasingly popular way to acquire the shares.

Suppose a firm's stock currently trades at $53 and that the firm will repurchase them at $49. The firm might write 100 put contracts with a striking price of $50 for a premium of $1 each. If the stock is below $50 at expiration, the put holders will exercise. The firm buys 10,000 shares @ $50 for an effective price of $49 after considering the option premium. If the stock remains above the striking price, the puts expire worthless and the firm keeps the premium. Interestingly, under the current tax code the premium income is *tax free* to the corporation.[9]

The tax-free nature of this income makes put writing to acquire stock especially attractive to corporate treasurers. According to Robert Gordon, President of Twenty-First Securities Corporation, "It would be crazy to do a corporate repurchase program and not utilize a put writing strategy."[10]

[9]*See IRC § 311(a), 317(b), 1032(a); Revenue Ruling 88-31, 1988-1 C.B. 302, at 305.*

[10]*Quinn, Lawrence Richter. "Can Corporates Really Use Equity Derivatives?", Derivatives Strategy, February 20, 1994, 1–2.*

PROFIT AND LOSS DIAGRAMS WITH SEASONED STOCK POSITIONS

The profit and loss diagrams for covered calls and protective puts earlier in this chapter used the *current* Microsoft stock price as a frame of reference. In practice, the more common situation is when an investor owns shares of stock and then at a later time decides to *add* a protective put or to write a covered call.

ADDING A PUT TO AN EXISTING STOCK POSITION

Consider the earlier investor who acquired MSFT at $46, sees the stock currently @ 79^{7}/_{16}$, and worries about a decline in the stock price. Perhaps this investor buys an AUG 75 put @ 1^{13}/_{16}$. Table 3–5 shows how this action locks in a profit regardless of what happens to the stock.

The worst outcome occurs if the stock falls to $75 or below. For stock prices from $0 to $75 there is a constant profit of 27^{3}/_{16}$. Potential profits remain unlimited as with any long stock position. Figure 3–11 shows the resulting profit and loss diagram. The entire plot lies above the x-axis; there is no possibility of a loss.

TABLE 3–5 Protective Put Worksheet						
	0	25	46	75	79$^{7}/_{16}$	90	100
LONG STOCK @ 46	−46	−21	0	29	33$^{7}/_{16}$	44	54
LONG 75 PUT @ 1$^{13}/_{16}$	73$^{3}/_{16}$	48$^{3}/_{16}$	27$^{3}/_{16}$	−1$^{13}/_{16}$	−1$^{13}/_{16}$	−1$^{13}/_{16}$	−1$^{13}/_{16}$
NET	27$^{3}/_{16}$	27$^{3}/_{16}$	27$^{3}/_{16}$	27$^{3}/_{16}$	31$^{5}/_{8}$	42$^{3}/_{16}$	52$^{3}/_{16}$

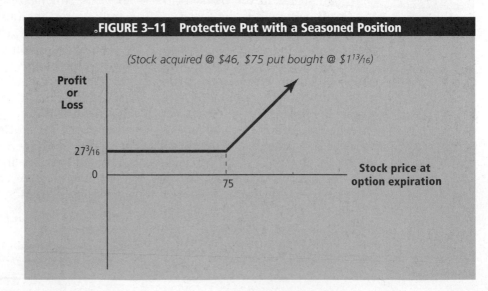

°FIGURE 3–11   Protective Put with a Seasoned Position

(Stock acquired @ $46, $75 put bought @ 1^{13}/_{16}$)

REPLACING AN IN-THE-MONEY COVERED CALL

Robert Alan owns 500 shares of Harley-Davidson (*HDI, NYSE*), currently trading for $37. Last month, in November, he wrote five DEC $35 HDI calls for 1\frac{1}{8}$ each. December expiration is in two days, and Robert has decided he wants to keep the stock. The DEC calls now have essentially no time value, and he sees that he can buy them back for their intrinsic value of $2. This would result in a pre-commission loss of $87.50 per contract, or $437.50. At the same time, he notices that JAN $40 calls are bid at $1. Robert is thinking about writing five of these. This would "pay for" the options he is buying back and allow him to keep the stock another month.

WRITING A CALL AGAINST AN EXISTING STOCK POSITION

The covered call in Figure 3–8 assumes the investor buys MSFT at the current price of 79\frac{7}{16}$ and simultaneously writes an OCT 85 call for $5. Suppose instead that the investor bought the stock much earlier at $46. From the perspective of this earlier stock price, the profit and loss diagram simply shifts upward by 33\frac{7}{16}$, the difference between the original price ($46) and the current price (79\frac{7}{16}$), as Figure 3–12 illustrates.

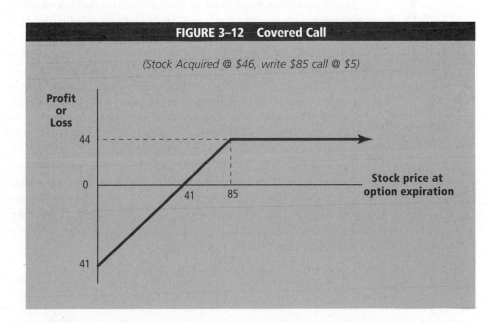

FIGURE 3–12   Covered Call

(Stock Acquired @ $46, write $85 call @ $5)

IMPROVING ON THE MARKET

There are two important strategies that have both hedging and income generation aspects. These methods are neither the best means of hedging nor the best means of generating income, but may serve certain purposes well.

WRITING CALLS TO IMPROVE ON THE MARKET

Occasionally someone decides to sell shares of stock, but is not in any immediate need of the cash proceeds from the sale. This person can sometimes increase the amount they receive from the sale of their stock by writing **deep-in-the-money** calls against their stock position. The phrase *deep-in-the-money* is subjective, with no quantitative definition. This term applies to any option that has "substantial" intrinsic value.

Suppose that on July 10th an institution holds 10,000 shares of Microsoft and decides to move out of the entire position. Table 2–1 shows that the premium for an AUG 60 call on Microsoft is $21; the current market price of Microsoft stock is $79^7/_{16}$. The institution could simply sell their shares outright and receive $79.4375 per share × 10,000 shares, or $794,375. The institution would receive this money, minus trading fees, on the third business day after the sale.

Alternatively, the portfolio manager might consider writing 100 AUG 60 calls on Microsoft. If these could be sold for the indicated price of $21 each, the institution would receive $210,000 in premium income the next day. These calls are in-the-money by a substantial amount. If Microsoft is above $60 per share on expiration Friday, the holder of the call options will exercise them. Then the portfolio manager would have to sell 10,000 shares of Microsoft for $60 each, receiving $600,000. The total received by the institution here is $210,000 + $600,000, or $810,000. This is $15,625 more than would have been received from selling the stock outright.[11]

While this "improving on the market" strategy may look attractive, there are several things to consider before embracing it. First, there is some risk with this strategy that you would not incur if you sold the stock outright. Selling stock results in cash in hand. While it may be unlikely, it is certainly possible that Microsoft could fall below the striking price of $60/share, in which case the options would not be exercised. The $21 option premium received means this improving-on-the-market strategy would "break even" at a stock price of $58^7/_{16}$. At this price, the stock has fallen in value by $21, but you still have the initial option premium. The two amounts exactly cancel each other. If the stock falls below that, you would have fared better had you disposed of your shares in traditional fashion.

---

[11]You would incur trading fees twice here, once for the stock and once for the options, but they would be trivial compared to the gain.

DERIVATIVES TODAY

INSIDER TRADING WITH OPTIONS

Insider information is formally called *material, non-public information*. Information is *material* if public knowledge of it could reasonably be expected to affect security prices. It is *non-public* if the public could not discover this information from publicly available documents or reports.

Security trades made on the basis of inside information are illegal, possibly a felony. The Securities and Exchange Commission routinely investigates unusual trading activity around tender offers and other significant corporate announcements. Persons convicted of inside trading must disgorge profits, may be fined, may be barred from securities trading, and sometimes go to jail.

In January 2001 the SEC brought a federal action against several individuals, accusing them of trading on the basis of inside information regarding Nestle's announcement that it planned to buy Ralston-Purina. In its announcement, the SEC said the case "involves highly profitable purchases of call options and sales of put options in Ralston-Purina stock." The trades occurred between the time merger discussions began in mid-November and their public announcement on January 16th. In its suit, the SEC also stated, "Defendants have already made substantial windfall profits from their illegal trading and, unless enjoined, will be able to continue to do so."

Also, experienced option traders know that you need to be careful about relying on option prices listed in the financial pages. It may not be possible for you to actually trade at the stated premium of $21; the current market price may be less than this. There is also a bid/ask spread to consider, and there may not be much depth to the quotes. Still, there is usually some time value associated with these deep-in-the-money options, and you can often capture it with a strategy like the one described here.

WRITING PUTS TO IMPROVE ON THE MARKET

An institution might write deep-in-the-money calls when it wishes to sell stock. Similarly, an institution might write deep-in-the-money *puts* when it wishes to *buy* stock.

Suppose a bank trust department decides to buy 1,000 shares of Microsoft. Rather than buying the shares outright at $79\frac{7}{16}$ each (for a total investment of $79,437.50), the fund manager could write 10 AUG 90 puts @ $11 and receive total premium income of $11,000. If Microsoft remains below the striking price of $90, the puts will be exercised and the fund manager will be required to buy 1,000 shares at $90 each. The cash outlay would be $90,000 from the exercise minus the premium income of $11,000 for a total of $79,000. In this example, improving on the market by writing these in-the-money puts enables the institution to acquire the stock at an effective price of $79 rather than the current price of $79^{7}/16.

As with selling stock this way, there is some risk involved. If Microsoft rises above the striking price of $90, the puts will not be exercised and the institution will not obtain the shares. Even so, the premium income is the institution's to keep. If MSFT falls below $79 the bank winds up paying more for the stock than if it had just been purchased outright.

SUMMARY

Hedging is the act of transferring unwanted risk to a speculator who is willing to bear it. Options can be used to hedge against losses resulting from adverse price movements, to provide additional portfolio income, or a combination of these two motives.

A protective put is a long put position held in conjunction with a long position in the underlying stock. This is like an insurance policy on stock. The investor selects the deductible, the policy term, and pays a premium for the insurance.

Certain combinations of securities are approximately equivalent to others:

1. long stock + long put ≈ long call
2. short stock + long call ≈ long put
3. long stock + short call ≈ short put
4. short stock + short put ≈ short call

The most common use of stock options by both individuals and institutions is writing covered calls, which is the writing of call options against stock already owned. This strategy has risk and return characteristics similar to that of writing put options, which is a strategy much less frequently used.

Writing puts against a portfolio is called put overwriting. This strategy generates additional portfolio income, but involves substantial added risk if stock prices decline. Writing deep-in-the-money calls can be an effective way to sell stock at a slightly higher than current price. Writing deep-in-the-money puts can be an effective way to buy stock at an effective price below the current market price. Both strategies are often called "improving on the market."

SELF TEST

T ___ F ___ 1. You can use a short call to hedge a short stock position.

T ___ F ___ 2. A naked call is the same as an uncovered call.

T ___ F ___ 3. If someone buys a call that expires in less than one month, the call constitutes a long position.

T ___ F ___ 4. A protective put sells for the same premium as an ordinary put.

T ___ F ___ 5. If someone owns shares of Microsoft and buys a Microsoft put (regardless of striking price), the put is a protective put.

T ___ F ___ 6. Buying a protective put is analogous to buying collision insurance on a car.

T ___ F ___ 7. A person who buys a protective put often fully expects the put to expire worthless.

T ___ F ___ 8. A long stock position plus a short put position is approximately equivalent to a long call position.

T ___ F ___ 9. With a short sale of stock, potential losses are unlimited.

T ___ F ___ 10. A covered call is much less effective than a long put at providing protection against a market downturn.

T ___ F ___ 11. Writing covered calls is the most popular use of stock options by individuals.

T ___ F ___ 12. Potential gains and losses are unlimited with a naked call.

T ___ F ___ 13. The term fiduciary put applies when the put writer deposits the striking price in an escrow account until option expiration.

T ___ F ___ 14. A person who wants to "improve on the market" might write either puts or calls.

T ___ F ___ 15. Regardless of whether one is buying or selling, improving on the market always involves options that are far out-of-the-money.

T ___ F ___ 16. Insider trading rules apply to listed shares of stock but not to listed options.

T ___ F ___ 17. A person can completely hedge a short stock position by writing a put option.

T ___ F ___ 18. A person can completely hedge a long stock position by buying a put option.

T ___ F ___ 19. If you buy a put option, the maximum gain is equal to the striking price of the option.

T ___ F ___ 20. If you buy a put option while holding the underlying stock, your maximum gain equals the stock purchase price minus the put premium minus the option striking price.

PROBLEMS & QUESTIONS

Refer to Table 2–1 as necessary

1. Explain the difference between the terms *covered call* and *covering a call*.
2. Why do many people feel that buying a put is preferable to selling short shares of the underlying stock?
3. Explain the statement from Robert Merton at the beginning of the chapter. Would you agree with a similar statement about American call options?
4. What should a portfolio manager consider before embarking on a put overwriting program during a bear market?
5. Suppose you were the portfolio manager for a church's endowment fund. How would you justify buying protective puts, when you fully expected to lose your entire investment in these options?
6. Suppose you held 10,000 shares of Microsoft in your pension fund. Refer to Table 2–1. Based on current market conditions, select a striking price for a protective put and justify your answer.
7. In question 6, which striking price would you choose for a covered call? Why?
8. Give an example of (a) *hedging* by buying a call, and (b) *speculating* by buying a call.
9. If a short seller wants to generate additional income by writing options, does it matter which type of option is chosen?
10. Compare the risk of writing a covered put with the risk of writing a covered call.
11. If you buy a protective put, you can "cancel" your insurance policy by selling your put. Is it possible for you to cancel your insurance and realize a *profit*?

12. Comment on the relative merits of protecting against a market downturn by (a) buying puts and (b) writing covered calls.

13. Why is writing an in-the-money put more risky than writing an out-of-the-money put?

14. Suppose someone owns 1,000 shares of XYZ (current price: $40) and buys 5 XYZ APR 40 puts and also buys 5 XYZ APR 30 puts. Is this the same as buying 10 XYZ 35 puts?

15. Refer to page 42 and Figure 3–1. What does it mean to say, "ignoring opportunity costs," the strategy breaks even if the stock price is unchanged at a future time?

16. Does the term "improving on the market" imply a pricing inefficiency in the options market?

17. Draw a profit/loss diagram for writing a MSFT OCT 85 put option.

18. Suppose you simultaneously buy 400 shares of MSFT and write two OCT 80 puts. What is your gain or loss if, at option expiration, the common stock of MSFT sells for $74?

19. Draw a profit/loss diagram for the simultaneous purchase of 100 shares of MSFT at $79^{7}/$_{16}$ and the writing of an OCT 80 call at 7.

20. Suppose you bought 200 shares of MSFT at $79^{7}/$_{16}$ and simultaneously bought 2 AUG 75 puts @ $1^{13}/$_{16}$ as a hedge against a declining market. At option expiration, MSFT stock sold for $76. Were your protective puts a good idea?

21. Draw a profit/loss diagram for the simultaneous purchase of 100 shares of MSFT and the writing of an AUG 90 put.

22. Suppose an investor engages in *three* simultaneous transactions: (1) she buys 100 shares of MSFT common stock, (2) she *writes* an OCT 90 put, and (3) she *buys* an OCT 75 put. Does this strategy make any sense?

23. In problem 22, what is her profit or loss if MSFT is unchanged at option expiration?

24. Draw a profit/loss diagram for someone who shorts 100 shares of MSFT and writes one AUG 95 MSFT put. What other option strategy is similar to this?

25. Draw a profit/loss diagram for writing a naked MSFT AUG 75 put option.

26. Suppose you simultaneously buy 300 shares of MSFT and write one OCT 70 put. What is your gain or loss if, at option expiration, the common stock of MSFT sells for $72?

27. Draw a profit/loss diagram for the simultaneous purchase of 100 shares of MSFT at $79^{7}/$_{16}$ and the writing of an AUG 85 call at 2^{1}/$_{4}$.

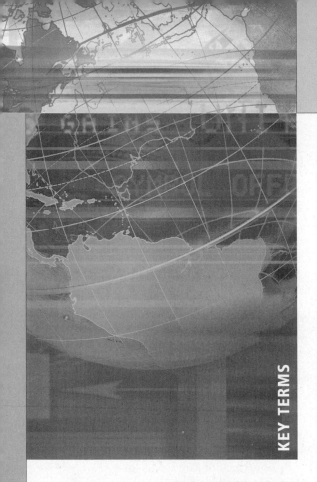

4

Option Combinations and Spreads

KEY TERMS

Risk Not Thy Whole Wad.

Chicago Mercantile Exchange

The previous two chapters focused on fundamental principles of options, showing how options can be used to speculate, to generate income, or to provide protection against adverse price movements. This chapter covers a variety of types of strategies that typically seek a trading profit rather than being motivated by a hedging or income generation objective.

COMBINATIONS

An option combination is a strategy in which you are simultaneously long or short puts and calls.

A **combination** is a strategy in which you are simultaneously long or short options of different types. There are many possible option combinations. This chapter covers the most popular ones.

66

TABLE 4–1 Long Straddle								
STOCK PRICE AT OPTION EXPIRATION								
0	**20**	**50**	**75**	**79⁷/₁₆**	**80**	**90**	**100**	**120**
LONG 80 CALL @ $7 −7	−7	−7	−7	−7	−7	3	13	33
LONG 80 PUT @ $5⁷/₈ 74¹/₈	54¹/₈	24¹/₈	−⁷/₈	−5⁵/₁₆	−5⁷/₈	−5⁷/₈	−5⁷/₈	−5⁷/₈
NET 67¹/₈	47¹/₈	17¹/₈	−7⁷/₈	−12⁵/₁₆	−12⁷/₈	−2⁷/₈	7¹/₈	27¹/₈

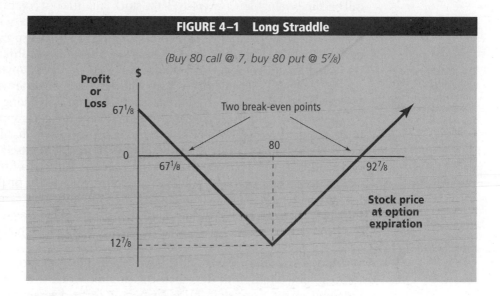

FIGURE 4–1   Long Straddle

Straddles

The **straddle** is the best-known option combination. If you own both a put and a call with the same striking price, the same expiration date, on the same underlying security, you are *long* a straddle.[1] If you are short these options, you have *written* a straddle. Let's look at the motivation behind each of these positions.

Buying a Straddle. It may seem illogical to simultaneously buy a put and a call on the same stock. A long call is bullish, and a long put is bearish. Buying both seems to violate the fundamental need to "take a stand" on the direction of the market.

Suppose a speculator buys an OCT 80 straddle on Microsoft. According to the figures in Table 2–1, it costs $700 to buy the call and $587.50 to buy the put, for a total investment of $1,287.50. Table 4–1 is a profit and loss worksheet for various stock prices at option expiration. A long straddle becomes profitable if prices rise *or* fall, provided they rise or fall substantially. Figure 4–1 shows this.

---

[1]The straddle buyer normally chooses a striking price near the current stock price.

The profit and loss diagram for a long straddle is simply the graphic combination of a long call and a long put. The worst outcome for the straddle buyer is when both options expire worthless. This happens only when they expire at-the-money. In this example, if Microsoft is exactly $80 at October expiration, both options are worthless. At any other price, one (and only one) of the options will have some intrinsic value.

The straddle buyer will still lose money if Microsoft closes near the striking price of $80. In fact, the stock must rise or fall by enough to recover the initial cost of the position, $12\,^7/\!_8$. If the stock rises, the put expires worthless, but the call becomes valuable. Conversely, if the stock falls, the put is valuable, but the call expires worthless. From the diagram, it is apparent that there will be *two* break-even points with the straddle, one corresponding to a price rise and one to a price decline. Each break-even point is $12\,^7/\!_8$ away from the $80 striking price.

> The straddle buyer anticipates a sharp movement in the stock price but does not know in which direction.

When might someone buy a straddle? The answer is anytime a situation develops when it is likely that a stock will move sharply one way or the other. Perhaps a company is involved in takeover talks and is awaiting a Federal Trade Commission decision regarding antitrust rules. If the merger is approved, the stock to be acquired probably will rise sharply. If the merger is disallowed, then the stock might drop just as sharply. Another situation lending itself to the purchase of a straddle is when a court decision is imminent. Perhaps a firm is involved in a class action suit because of alleged corporate negligence or product liability resulting in personal injury claims against the company. If the firm is found liable, the stock will almost certainly lose value. If the firm is exonerated, the uncertainty has been largely resolved and the stock may recover to a higher level.

Writing a Straddle. The straddle buyer wants the stock price to move significantly in one direction or the other. The straddle writer wants just the opposite: little movement in the stock price. Figure 4–2 is the diagram of a short straddle. The maximum gain in this strategy occurs when the options finish at-the-money, and therefore expire worthless. Losses are potentially unlimited on the upside, because the short call is uncovered.

Although the potential profit may seem out of line with the risk of such a strategy, it is popular with speculators. Some experienced option players refer to the expiration "convergence phenomenon," in which it is alleged that stock prices show an unusual tendency to close exactly at a striking price if the stock price was close to that value a few days before option expiration. For example, a stock might close at $24\,^3/\!_4$ Wednesday of expiration week. The convergence phenomenon means that there is a statistically significant likelihood that the stock will move toward the striking price of $25 as expiration approaches. Similarly, if the stock price Wednesday were $25\,^3/\!_8$, the phenomenon predicts a price decline toward $25 from Wednesday to Friday.

Strong and Andrew tested this hypothesis.[2] Using various control groups, they found evidence in support of the convergence phenomenon on the American and

---

[2]Robert A. Strong and William P. Andrew, "Further Evidence of the Influence of Option Expiration on Stock Prices," *Journal of Business Research* (August 1987): 291–302.

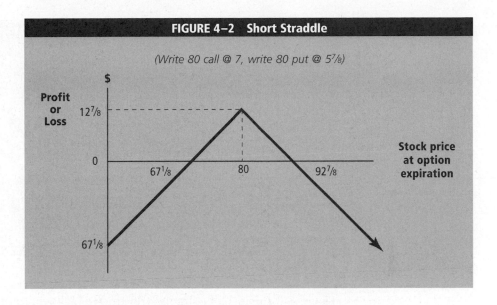

FIGURE 4–2   Short Straddle

(Write 80 call @ 7, write 80 put @ 5⅞)

Philadelphia Stock Exchanges (which use the specialist system), but not on the Chicago Board Options Exchange or the Pacific Stock Exchange (which use the marketmaker system). A possible explanation lies in the hedging activities of the option specialist, who must sometimes involuntarily buy inexpensive options with a little intrinsic value in the last days of an option cycle. Under the market-maker system, where these involuntary purchases may be spread throughout the trading crowd, the need to hedge may be less obvious. In any event, writing strad-dles would be the appropriate strategy if stock prices were biased toward a strik-ing price in the last few days of option trading.

Remember also that just because one speculator is long a straddle it does not mean that someone else is short the straddle. You assemble the straddle by buy-ing both a put and call; these options need not come from the same writer. The call you buy might be from someone writing a covered call, while your long put may be part of someone else's put overwriting program.

Strangles

A strangle differs from a straddle in that the options have different striking prices.

Strangles are very popular with professional option traders. They are similar to straddles, except the puts and calls have different striking prices.

Buying a Strangle. The motivation for buying a strangle is similar to the moti-vation for buying a straddle: the speculator expects a sharp price movement either up or down in the underlying security.

A strangle has two striking prices. With a *long strangle*, the most popular ver-sion involves buying a put with a lower striking price than the call you buy. Done this way, the profit and loss characteristics are similar to those of the long strad-dle, but the maximum loss is smaller.

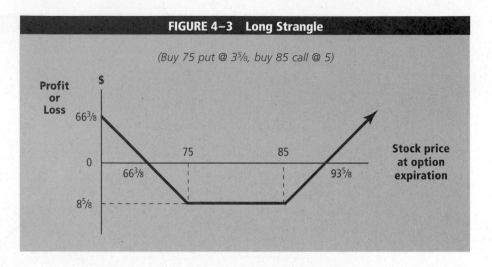

FIGURE 4–3   Long Strangle

(Buy 75 put @ 3⅝, buy 85 call @ 5)

Figure 4–3 shows a long strangle constructed by buying a Microsoft OCT 75 put and buying a Microsoft OCT 85 call. The maximum loss occurs over the price range $75 to $85, because between these values both options expire worthless. Once outside the range, one option has intrinsic value. The position costs $3⅝ + 5 = $8⅝, and to break even, the stock must move enough to leave one option with this much intrinsic value.

Writing a Strangle.   Figure 4–4 shows the short strangle. This is exactly the opposite of the long strangle in Figure 4–3. The plot is just rotated vertically about the x-axis. Because a short strangle involves writing the options, the maximum gain occurs if both options expire worthless, and this happens within the stock price range of $75 to $85.

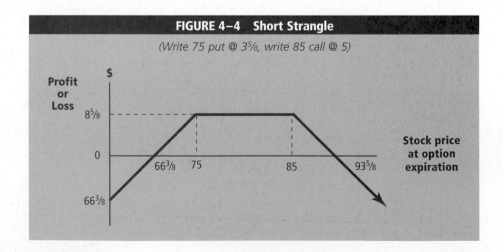

FIGURE 4–4   Short Strangle

(Write 75 put @ 3⅝, write 85 call @ 5)

TABLE 4-2 Long Condor Construction Methods	
CALLS ONLY:	LONG A AND D; SHORT B AND C
PUTS ONLY:	LONG A AND D; SHORT B AND C
BOTH PUTS AND CALLS:	LONG CALL A; SHORT CALL B; SHORT PUT C; LONG PUT D
	OR
	LONG PUT A; SHORT PUT B; SHORT CALL C; LONG CALL D

Note: Normally, $(B - A) = (C - B) = (D - C)$

In the short *straddle*, the maximum profit occurs at a *single point*, the striking price. The short *strangle* involves a slightly reduced maximum profit, but it is earned over a *broader price range*.

The term *strangle* probably originated in April 1978, when stock in International Business Machines was experiencing wide price swings. Many professional option traders routinely write options on active stocks like IBM, and a few of them were wiped out on short IBM strangles during this infamous month.

Condors

A **condor** is a less risky version of the strangle, involving *four* different striking prices.

Buying a Condor. There are several ways to construct a long condor. Suppose we have striking prices A, B, C, and D, where A<B<C<D. Table 4–2 shows four methods. Regardless of the method, a long condor involves buying the outside strike prices (A and D in this example) and writing the middle ones.

The condor buyer hopes that stock prices remain in the B through C range, because this is where maximum profits occur. However, outside this range at least one option will have intrinsic value.[3]

Let's look at an example of a long condor on Microsoft using both puts and calls. Table 4–3 is a worksheet to calculate the profit/loss characteristics. Figure 4–5 shows the characteristic shape.

Writing a Condor. Figure 4–6 is a profit and loss diagram for a short condor position using the options listed in Table 4–3. We get this by reversing the signs from the long condor worksheet. As with all profit and loss diagrams, a quick glance reveals the big picture. In a short condor, you *write* the outside strike prices.

Like the straddle buyer and the strangle buyer, the condor writer makes money when prices move sharply in either direction. The maximum gain is limited to the premium.

---

[3]Commissions have been ignored in these examples. However, with multiple option strategies like condors, commissions can become material, even with the discounted commissions of an online broker. A full service brokerage firm might have a minimum commission of $35 per trade. Establishing a condor involves four trades, or $140. Outside the B to C price range there will be at least one more trade when trading out of the option or options with intrinsic value.

TABLE 4–3   Long Condor Worksheet

	STOCK PRICE AT OPTION EXPIRATION					
	0	75	80	85	90	95
BUY 75 CALL @ 10	−10	−10	−5	0	5	10
WRITE 80 CALL @ 7	7	7	7	2	−3	−8
WRITE 85 PUT @ $8\frac{1}{2}$	$−76\frac{1}{2}$	$−1\frac{1}{2}$	$3\frac{1}{2}$	$8\frac{1}{2}$	$8\frac{1}{2}$	$8\frac{1}{2}$
BUY 90 PUT @ $12\frac{1}{8}$	$77\frac{7}{8}$	$2\frac{7}{8}$	$−2\frac{1}{8}$	$−7\frac{1}{8}$	$−12\frac{1}{8}$	$−12\frac{1}{8}$
NET	$−1\frac{5}{8}$	$−1\frac{5}{8}$	$3\frac{3}{8}$	$3\frac{3}{8}$	$−1\frac{5}{8}$	$−1\frac{5}{8}$

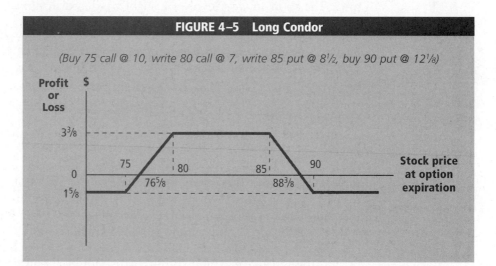

FIGURE 4–5   Long Condor

(Buy 75 call @ 10, write 80 call @ 7, write 85 put @ $8\frac{1}{2}$, buy 90 put @ $12\frac{1}{8}$)

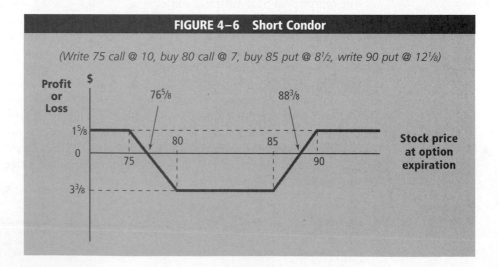

FIGURE 4–6   Short Condor

(Write 75 call @ 10, buy 80 call @ 7, buy 85 put @ $8\frac{1}{2}$, write 90 put @ $12\frac{1}{8}$)

SPREADS

A spread is an option strategy whereby you are simultaneously long and short options of the same type, but with different striking prices and/or expiration dates.

Option **spreads** are strategies in which the player is simultaneously long *and* short options of the *same* type, but with different striking prices or expiration dates. In so doing, the spreader establishes a known maximum profit or loss potential.

TYPES OF SPREADS

In the early days of option trading, the financial press reported option prices using the format of Table 4–4. (This is an extract of Table 2–1.) This is noteworthy because some option spreads get their name from this layout. You still occasionally see this format.

The stock price appears below the company name in the far left column. It appears multiple times, beside each striking price in the next column to the right. The rest of the display is three columns for calls and three columns for puts, with each column corresponding to an expiration month. An ellipsis in a cell indicates the option did not trade the previous day.

Vertical Spreads

In a **vertical spread**, options are selected vertically from the financial pages. This means the spreader selects a single *column* from the listing and chooses two options, one to buy and one to write.

The spreader trades profit potential for reduced cost.

Vertical Spreads with Calls. A person who believes that Microsoft common stock is going to appreciate soon might buy an OCT 85 call option on Microsoft, and simultaneously write an OCT 90 call. If the person felt very sure that prices were going to rise sharply, it would be preferable simply to buy one of the calls, leaving the profit potential open-ended. The spreader, however, trades part of the profit potential for a reduced cost of the position. Let's look in detail at the implications of this strategy.

TABLE 4–4	Old Newspaper Option Listing						
		CALLS			**PUTS**		
MSFT		**JUL**	**AUG**	**OCT**	**JUL**	**AUG**	**OCT**
$79^7/_{16}$	65	...	$16^1/_4$	$17^1/_8$	...	...	$1^3/_{16}$
$79^7/_{16}$	70	...	11	13	...	$^{13}/_{16}$	$2^3/_{16}$
$79^7/_{16}$	75	$5^1/_2$	$7^1/_4$	10	$^{11}/_{16}$	$1^{13}/_{16}$	$3^5/_8$
$79^7/_{16}$	80	$2^3/_{16}$	4	7	$2^3/_8$	4	$5^7/_8$
$79^7/_{16}$	85	$^{11}/_{16}$	$2^1/_4$	5	6	$6^3/_4$	$8^1/_2$
$79^7/_{16}$	90	$^1/_4$	$1^1/_8$	$3^3/_8$	$9^3/_4$	11	$12^1/_8$
$79^7/_{16}$	95	$^1/_8$	$^9/_{16}$	$2^3/_8$	...	...	$16^1/_4$

TABLE 4–5 Vertical Call Bullspread							
	STOCK PRICE AT OPTION EXPIRATION						
	0	85	86	87	88	89	90	100
LONG 85 CALL @ 5	−5	−5	−4	−3	−2	−1	0	10
SHORT 90 CALL @ 3⅜	3⅜	3⅜	3⅜	3⅜	3⅜	3⅜	3⅜	−6⅝
NET	−1⅝	−1⅝	−⅝	⅜	1⅜	2⅜	3⅜	3⅜

Being long the OCT 85 call, the investor has the right to purchase shares of Microsoft at $85. Having written the OCT 90 call, the investor must sell shares of Microsoft at the striking price of $90 if the call is exercised. The short call position means that all profit potential from the long call position is eliminated for stock prices greater than $90. Looking at the situation another way, if the stock rises to $100, the spreader has a profit on the OCT 85 call, but loses on the short OCT 90 call. As stock prices rise above $90, the added loss in the short call exactly cancels the added gain in the long call. With all spreads, the maximum gain and loss occur at the striking prices, so it is not necessary to consider stock prices outside this range. With an 85/90 spread, all you really need to look at are stock prices from $85 to $90.

Buying the OCT 85 requires a cash outlay of $500; writing the OCT 90 brings in $337.50, which reduces the actual cost of the spread to $162.50. This is the maximum loss, which, as Table 4–5 shows, occurs at stock prices of $85 and below. The maximum gain occurs when the stock price is $90 or higher. At prices above this, the spreader will receive an exercise notice on the short 90 call, and therefore will lose any further gains from the long 85 call.

Remember that a fundamental rule of preparing these profit/loss diagrams is that bends in the plot occur at striking prices. A vertical call spread has two striking prices, and therefore has two bends in the diagram.

The strategy depicted in Figure 4–7 commonly is called a **bullspread**, because

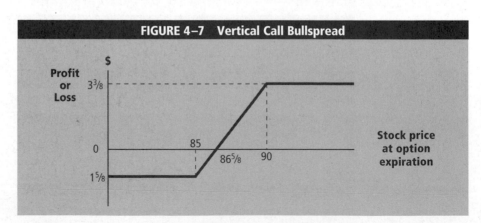

FIGURE 4–7   Vertical Call Bullspread

TABLE 4–6 Bearspread Worksheet							
	STOCK PRICE AT OPTION EXPIRATION						
	0	**85**	**86**	**87**	**88**	**89**	**90**	**100**
SHORT 85 CALL @ 5	5	5	4	3	2	1	0	−10
LONG 90 CALL @ $3\frac{3}{8}$	$-3\frac{3}{8}$	$-3\frac{3}{8}$	$-3\frac{3}{8}$	$-3\frac{3}{8}$	$-3\frac{3}{8}$	$-3\frac{3}{8}$	$-3\frac{3}{8}$	$6\frac{5}{8}$
NET	$1\frac{5}{8}$	$1\frac{5}{8}$	$\frac{5}{8}$	$-\frac{3}{8}$	$-1\frac{3}{8}$	$-2\frac{3}{8}$	$-3\frac{3}{8}$	$-3\frac{3}{8}$

In a bullspread, buy the low striking price and write the high. In a bearspread, buy the high striking price and write the low.

the maximum profit occurs when prices rise. Another type of vertical call spread is a **bearspread**, where just the reverse occurs: the maximum profit occurs with falling prices. In setting up a bullspread, the investor buys the option with the lower striking price and writes the option with the higher striking price. The opposite occurs with a bearspread; buy the option with the higher striking price and write the option with the lower striking price. Table 4–6 and Figure 4–8 show the numbers for a bearspread using MSFT OCT 85/90 calls.

Vertical Spreads with Puts. Individual investors typically set up spreads using call options. You can do them just as easily with puts.

In Table 4–5, the spread uses the OCT 85/90 calls; this requires a net cash outlay of $162.50. An alternative strategy is to set up a similar bullspread using the OCT 85/90 *puts*. This is done the same way as with calls: buy the option with the lower striking price and write the option with the higher one.

A primary difference in these two approaches is that the put spread results in a credit to the spreader's account (meaning money comes in); when this is the case, the spread is a **credit spread**. The call spread results in a debit (meaning money goes out), and is a **debit spread**. Table 4–7 is a worksheet for the put bullspread.

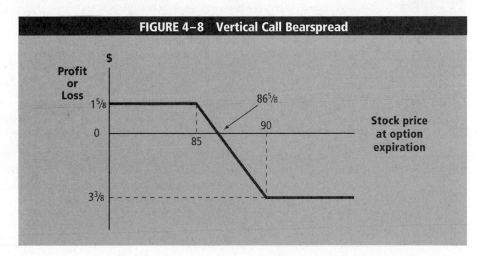

FIGURE 4–8   Vertical Call Bearspread

TABLE 4–7 Vertical Put Bullspread							
	STOCK PRICE AT OPTION EXPIRATION						
	0	85	86	87	88	89	90	100
LONG 85 PUT @ 8$\frac{1}{2}$	76$\frac{1}{2}$	–8$\frac{1}{2}$	–8$\frac{1}{2}$	–8$\frac{1}{2}$	–8$\frac{1}{2}$	–8$\frac{1}{2}$	–8$\frac{1}{2}$	–8$\frac{1}{2}$
SHORT 90 PUT @ 12$\frac{1}{8}$	–77$\frac{7}{8}$	7$\frac{1}{8}$	8$\frac{1}{8}$	9$\frac{1}{8}$	10$\frac{1}{8}$	11$\frac{1}{8}$	12$\frac{1}{8}$	12$\frac{1}{8}$
NET	–1$\frac{3}{8}$	–1$\frac{3}{8}$	–$\frac{3}{8}$	$\frac{5}{8}$	1$\frac{5}{8}$	2$\frac{5}{8}$	3$\frac{5}{8}$	3$\frac{5}{8}$

In this example, the profit and loss payoffs for the put spread are approximately the same as with the call spread, and this is a general characteristic of the two forms of the bullspread. The maximum profit occurs at all stock prices above the higher striking price, while the maximum loss occurs at stock prices below the lower striking price. With vertical spreads, the spreader is concerned only with the range of stock prices between the two striking prices. If the stock price closes outside this range, the spreader incurs either the maximum gain or loss as determined at the extremes of the range.

These examples of vertical spreads use options that are a single striking price apart (85 and 90). This does not have to be the case. I could, for instance, buy the OCT 85 call and write the OCT 95 call. This is still a vertical bullspread, but it involves a different package of risk and return.

CONDORS WITH INDEX OPTIONS

In mid-December, Kirsten Joy believes the broad stock market is likely to remain in a relatively flat trading range over the next month. She would like to use the options market to enhance her portfolio return without taking undue risk. Turning to the market for S&P 100 index options (*OEX*, *CBOE*), she focuses on the following one-month options.[4] The current index level is 668.58.

EXPIRATION	STRIKING PRICE	CALL PREMIUM	PUT PREMIUM
JAN	620	61.70	7.30
JAN	630	53.00	9.50
JAN	730	3.50	63.00
JAN	740	2.20	72.00

Kirsten has figured out that a long condor is a package of two spreads: a bullspread at the lower striking prices and a bearspread at the higher. She also knows that a bullspread with puts and a bearspread with calls both produce a credit to her account. Therefore, she places four orders with her broker: buy the 620 put/write the

[4]These are actual closing values from December 21, 2000, taken from the CBOE website.

CONDORS WITH INDEX OPTIONS (Continued)

630 put (this completes the bullspread), and buy the 740 call/write the 730 call (this completes the bearspread). Assume she is able to make each transaction at the price shown in the table. She then completes a profit and loss worksheet for the condor and finds she can construct it for a credit of $3.50, or $350 per contract. This is her maximum profit, and it occurs at all index levels between 630 and 730. Looking at this another way, she earns the maximum profit if the index does not fall by more than 5.8% or rise by more than 9.2%.

Profit and Loss Worksheet								
INDEX LEVEL AT OPTION EXPIRATION								
	PREMIUM	600	620	630	668.58	730	740	760
LONG 620 PUT	$7.30	$12.70	(7.30)	(7.30)	(7.30)	(7.30)	(7.30)	(7.30)
SHORT 630 PUT	(9.50)	(20.50)	(0.50)	9.50	9.50	9.50	9.50	9.50
SHORT 730 CALL	(3.50)	3.50	3.50	3.50	3.50	3.50	(6.50)	(26.50)
LONG 740 CALL	2.20	(2.20)	(2.20)	(2.20)	(2.20)	(2.20)	(2.20)	17.80
NET	**(3.50)**	(6.50)	(6.50)	3.50	3.50	3.50	(6.50)	(6.50)

The corresponding profit and loss diagram is below.

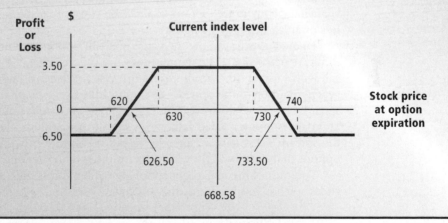

Calendar Spreads

Vertical spreads employ options listed vertically in Table 4–4; with **calendar spreads**, options are chosen *horizontally* from a given row. In fact, people also call these *horizontal spreads* or *time spreads*. Because they are chosen horizontally from the listing, they necessarily involve options with the same striking price. They are also either bullspreads or bearspreads, depending on the options purchased and the options written.

As an example, a speculator might be bullish on Microsoft and buy an OCT

90 call for $3³⁄₈ (refer to Table 4–4). If the speculator believes there is little like-lihood that Microsoft will rise to $90 by option expiration in August, he or she also might choose to write an AUG 90 call for $1¹⁄₈. This latter action results in a cash inflow to the spreader's options account, and provided Microsoft is below $90 per share on the third Friday in August, the option will expire unexercised. The speculator still owns the OCT 90 call and continues to hope for stock price appreciation. With any calendar spread, an element of timing is superimposed on the bullish or bearish attitude toward the underlying stock. A bullish specu-lator will buy a call option with a distant expiration and write one that is near expiration. A bearish speculator will do the opposite.

As an example of a bearish calendar spread, suppose I buy the AUG 80 call and write the OCT 80 call. I expect Microsoft to decline, so I expect to lose all my money on the August option. I expect the expensive option I wrote (the OCT 80) to decline in value, yielding a profit to me. My motivation in buying the cheap call is to reduce risk. If I simply wrote a call when I expected the stock to fall, the call would be uncovered, and we have previously seen that potential losses with naked calls are unlimited.[5] If I am right in my assessment and the stock falls, the call I bought will expire worthless, and I will most likely buy another call in the September or October series to "cover" the call I am short. Calendar spread-ers are concerned with an important option phenomenon called **time decay**. Options are worth more the longer they have until expiration. As time passes, options decline in value if the price of the underlying asset does not change. This is advantageous to the option writer, who hopes that the options expire worth-less or at least decline in value.

Figure 4–9 shows how the value of a call option declines over time if other things remain equal. The figure shows the theoretical value of an 80 and an 85 call with varying times until expiration. When there is a "significant" amount of time remaining in the option's life, time value declines gradually. The value of a spread remains relatively constant if the stock price does not move. As expiration approaches, though, time value begins to drop sharply, and so does the value of the spread. The calendar spreader hopes to capture this time value by writing options that deteriorate in value more rapidly than the long option positions.

You cannot prepare a conventional profit and loss diagram or table for a cal-endar spread. This is because the strategy involves more than one expiration date.

Diagonal Spreads

A **diagonal spread** involves options from different expiration months and with different striking prices: they are chosen diagonally from the option listing. One example would be the purchase of an OCT 90 call and the sale of an AUG 85 call. Diagonal spreads also can be bullish or bearish, but it is less clear what an investor has in mind with certain diagonal spreads. Someone might buy the Microsoft AUG 95 call for $⁹⁄₁₆ and write the OCT 75 call for $10. This would be

---

[5]One inconvenience with calendar spreads involves those situations where you write the option with a more distant expi-ration and buy the near one. For margin purposes, the distant option will probably be considered uncovered by your bro-kerage firm, subjecting you to more strict capital requirements. Margin is discussed later in this chapter.

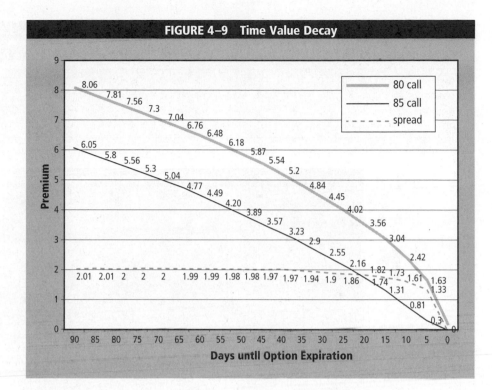

FIGURE 4–9   Time Value Decay

unusual; it seems that the investor wants Microsoft to skyrocket before the August option series expires, then nosedive so that the October option expires worthless. Spreads of this type are uncommon, and should be well conceived before you choose to set one up.

Butterfly Spreads

While all spreads involve added commission costs, butterfly spreads are especially expensive because they involve three commissions when the spread is established and at least one at option expiration.

A **butterfly spread** is a curious strategy that appeals to some people because it can often be constructed for very little cost beyond commissions. As with all spreads, these can be done with either puts or calls. Unlike spreads discussed thus far, you can construct a butterfly spread using puts *and* calls.

As an example, consider the Microsoft October options with striking prices of $75, $80, and $85. For simplicity call these A, B, and C, respectively. There are four ways to build a butterfly spread, as Table 4–8 shows.

TABLE 4–8   Constructing a Butterfly Spread

1. LONG CALL A, SHORT 2 CALLS B, LONG CALL C
2. LONG PUT A, SHORT 2 PUTS B, LONG PUT C
3. LONG PUT A, SHORT PUT B, SHORT CALL B, LONG CALL C
4. LONG CALL A, SHORT CALL B, SHORT PUT B, LONG PUT C

TABLE 4–9   Butterfly Spread Worksheet

	0	75	76	77	78	79	80	81	82	83	84	85	100
LONG ONE 75 CALL @ 10	–10	–10	–9	–8	–7	–6	–5	–4	–3	–2	–1	0	15
SHORT TWO 80 CALLS @ 7	14	14	14	14	14	14	14	12	10	8	6	4	–26
LONG ONE 85 CALL @ 5	–5	–5	–5	–5	–5	–5	–5	–5	–5	–5	–5	–5	10
NET	–1	–1	0	1	2	3	4	3	2	1	0	–1	–1

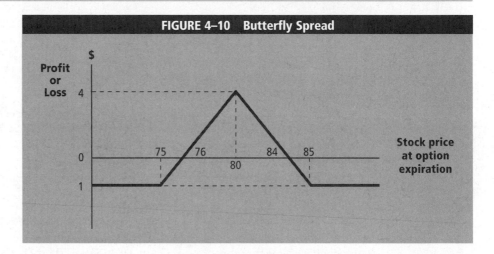

FIGURE 4–10   Butterfly Spread

Using the Microsoft option prices from Table 4–4, we can prepare a worksheet for a long butterfly spread using approach #1 from above. Table 4–9 shows that, with this strategy, very little money is at risk. If prices rise or drop dramatically, losses occur, but the maximum loss is only $1. The largest profit occurs if the middle options are at-the-money when they expire. Figure 4–10 is a profit and loss diagram of this long butterfly spread.

TRADING STRATEGY

ADDING A SHORT CALL TO A SEASONED LONG CALL

Continuing with her adventures in the world of options, Britta Katrina finds that she has a long call position that is now in-the-money by ten points. She paid $2 3/8 for each of five DEC 35 contracts, and they now sell for $11 with 34 days until expiration. The underlying stock is currently $45. She was considering closing out the position and taking her profit of $8 5/8 per contract, but is instead now thinking about writing five of the DEC 45 calls for $2 1/8 each. It seems to her that having bought the 35 calls for $2 3/8, selling the 45 for $2 1/8 effectively reduces her investment to only $25 per contract. Ignoring opportunity costs, this would become her maximum loss, while she stands to gain $975 per contract if the stock remains at $45 or above.

DERIVATIVES TODAY

VOLATILITY SPREADS: LOOKING AHEAD TO OPTION PRICING

The term **volatility spread** applies to a variety of option positions, with changes in the underlying volatility influencing the profitability of the spread. Frequently, the volatility spreader believes there is an inconsistency between the implied volatility* of an option and the likely actual volatility in the future. Straddles, strangles, butterfly and calendar spreads are all examples of volatility spreads.

Volatility spreads are normally market neutral when constructed. They fall into four categories depending on their gamma and vega.[6] (We will investigate these terms in Chapter 7.) The table below shows a method of classifying them.

TABLE A   Volatility Spread Categories

		GAMMA	
		POSITIVE	**NEGATIVE**
VEGA	**POSITIVE**	LONG STRADDLES AND STRANGLES, SHORT BUTTERFLY SPREADS. RISING ACTUAL VOLATILITY HELPS; RISING IMPLIED VOLATILITY HELPS.	LONG CALENDAR SPREADS; RISING ACTUAL VOLATILITY HURTS; RISING IMPLIED VOLATILITY HELPS.
	NEGATIVE	SHORT CALENDAR SPREADS; RISING ACTUAL VOLATILITY HELPS; RISING IMPLIED VOLATILITY HURTS.	SHORT STRADDLES AND STRANGLES, LONG BUTTERFLY SPREADS. RISING ACTUAL VOLATILITY HURTS; RISING IMPLIED VOLATILITY HURTS.

Suppose we have the two options below in Table B. A speculator establishes a long, market neutral calendar spread by purchasing 100 contracts of the six-month option and writing 216 contracts of the one-month option.

TABLE B   Options Data

	S = 50		S = 60	
	PREMIUM	**DELTA**	**PREMIUM**	**DELTA**
30-DAY CALL	$0.52	.205	$5.80	.824
180-DAY CALL	$3.45	.443	$9.31	.717

Initial conditions: K = $55, σ = 35%, R = 5%

Delta is a measure of an option's sensitivity to changes in the stock price.

[6] *I am grateful to Sheldon Natenberg, one of Chicago's best options instructors, for adding to my understanding of this subject.*

As we will see in Chapter 6, implied volatility is a measure of the market's expectation of future volatility. Higher implied volatility means a higher option price.

VOLATILITY SPREADS (Continued)

This position is initially worth $23,268:

Long 100 six-month calls @ $3.45	$34,500
Short 216 one-month calls @ $0.52	(11,232)
Net	**$23,268**

If actual volatility suddenly increases and the stock jumps to $60, the new position value is –$32,180:

Long 100 six-month calls @$9.31	$93,100
Short 216 one-month calls @ $5.80	(125,280)
Net	**($32,180)**

This shows that an increase in *actual* volatility depresses the value of this long calendar spread. Contrast this result with an increase in the *implied* volatility of the options. The table below shows option values at a volatility of 50% rather than the 35% used in Table C.

TABLE C Prices at Different Volatilities		
	PRICE @ 35%	**PRICE @ 50%**
30-DAY CALL	$0.52	$1.20
180-DAY CALL	$3.45	$5.57

Long 100 six-month calls @ $5.57	$55,700
Short 216 one-month calls @ $1.20	(25,920)
Net	**$29,780**

These results indicate that if implied volatility increases, the value of the spread increases, too.

Future volatility is the one unobservable variable in the Black-Scholes model. Many option traders routinely compare the implied volatility of an option to their personal belief regarding the future variability of the underlying asset. When the market's expectations and the trader's diverge, some type of volatility spread may be appropriate.

While this discussion may seem like Greek now, it will make perfect sense in just a few more chapters.

These spreads look attractive, but the potential spreader should recognize that it is difficult to establish any option spread at the exact prices published in the financial pages.

NONSTANDARD SPREADS

The strategies considered so far are well known and constitute a fundamental part of the options game. Market conditions change, and sometimes an investor finds it advisable to alter an existing position by removing part of it or adding to it. Several examples of how this might be done are discussed here.

Ratio Spreads

Ratio spreads involve an unequal number of puts and calls.

A **ratio spread** is a variation on the bullspreads and bearspreads just discussed. Instead of a simple "long one, short one" strategy, ratio spreads involve an unequal number of long and short options. A call bullspread becomes a *call ratio spread* by writing more than one call at the higher striking price.

A person might be inclined to use this type of spread when the market is near the lower striking price, and the investor anticipates a modest rise in prices, but also feels there is potential for a near-term downturn. If prices behave as expected, the extra short option (or options) provide added income and lower the cost of the spread.

A bearspread with puts becomes a *put ratio spread* by the addition of extra short put positions. A bearish speculator might use this strategy if he or she feels there is a significant likelihood of a sharp rise in prices.

Ratio Backspreads

A **backspread** is constructed exactly the opposite as the ratio spreads described above. Backspreads can generate a credit to your account, while ordinary ratio spreads result in a debit. Call bearspreads are transformed into call ratio backspreads by adding to the long call position, and put bullspreads become put ratio backspreads by adding more long puts.

Hedge Wrapper[7]

A hedge wrapper can be used to transform a profitable long position into a riskless profit; the strategy reduces the possibility for further gain from stock price increases.

Suppose an investor owns an appreciated stock for which the outlook continues to be bullish, but with increased risk of a temporary pullback. What can be done? One alternative would be to sell the stock; another would be to buy a protective put. A third would be to create a **hedge wrapper**, which involves writing a covered call and also buying a put.

Assume you bought Microsoft when the stock price was $46 and the current price is $79 7/16. If Microsoft continues to rise, the long stock position appreciates.

[7]My friend Gary Gastineau, author of the excellent *Options Manual* and the fascinating reference book *Dictionary of Financial Risk Management*, points out that hedge wrappers are also called collars, fences, fence spreads, cylinders, spread conversions, conversion spreads, range forwards, tunnel options, and call and floors.

TABLE 4–10	Hedge Wrapper									
	0	**75**	**77**	**79**	**81**	**83**	**85**	**87**	**90**	**100**
STOCK PURCHASED @ $46	−46	29	31	33	35	37	39	41	44	54
LONG 75 PUT @ 3⅝	71³⁄₈	−3⅝	−3⅝	−3⅝	−3⅝	−3⅝	−3⅝	−3⅝	−3⅝	−3⅝
SHORT 90 CALL @ 3³⁄₈	3³⁄₈	3³⁄₈	3³⁄₈	3³⁄₈	3³⁄₈	3³⁄₈	3³⁄₈	3³⁄₈	3³⁄₈	−6⅝
NET	28³⁄₄	28³⁄₄	30³⁄₄	32³⁄₄	34³⁄₄	36³⁄₄	38³⁄₄	40³⁄₄	43³⁄₄	43³⁄₄

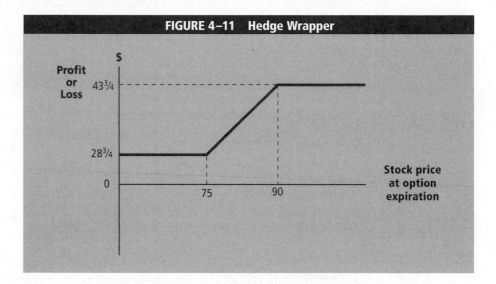

FIGURE 4–11   Hedge Wrapper

If the stock declines, some of the paper profit vanishes. Table 4–10 works out the net effect of an alternative—simultaneously buying an OCT 75 put (for $3⅝) and writing an OCT 90 covered call (for $3³⁄₈).

The table shows that no matter what happens, you have locked in a profit! Buying the put protects the unrealized gains in the stock position.[8] Figure 4–11 shows the combined position.

The maximum profit with a hedge wrapper occurs once the stock price rises to the striking price of the call, while the lowest return occurs if the stock falls to the striking price of the put or below. The fundamental result is that the hedge wrapper transforms the profitable stock position into a certain winner, although with reduced potential for further gain. Note that the hedge wrapper looks like a bull spread.

---

[8]The same thing can happen if you buy a protective put *after* you have a paper gain in the underlying stock.

DERIVATIVES TODAY

THE CBOE OPTIONS TOOLBOX

The Chicago Board Options Exchange has a versatile software package known as the *Options Toolbox* available as a free download at *http://www.cboe.com/education/software.htm*. This package contains a very handy options calculator useful in option pricing as well as a program for showing the profit and loss diagram for any mix of option positions. In addition, you will find a glossary and a basic tutorial on how options work and how people use them. Download your own copy of the toolbox soon, because it will be very helpful in analyzing option strategies or in risk management applications that we will see later in the book.

OTHER STRATEGIES

Combined Call Writing

Suppose an investor is bullish on Microsoft, owns 1,000 shares, and finds it necessary to generate some extra income. The investor could write 10 AUG 75 calls for $7¼ each. This would yield a total of $7,250 in immediate income, but because the calls are currently in-the-money, they stand a good chance of being exercised. Another tactic would be to write 10 AUG 90 calls at $1⅛. This generates $1,125, less income with less chance of exercise.

In **combined call writing**, the investor writes calls using more than one striking price. Consider a portfolio composed of 1,000 shares of Microsoft, 5 short AUG 75 calls, and 5 short AUG 90 calls. Table 4–11 is a profit and loss worksheet for this strategy (based on the current Microsoft stock price).

Figure 4–12 compares this strategy (using two different striking prices) with two more traditional covered call strategies: (a) writing ten in-the-money calls (75 striking price), and (b) writing ten out-of-the-money calls (90 striking price).

TABLE 4–11 Combined Call Writing Worksheet							
	0	**75**	**80**	**85**	**90**	**95**	**100**
Long 1,000							
SHARES @ 79⁷/₁₆	−79,437.50	−4,437.50	562.50	5,562.50	10,562.50	15,562.50	20,562.50
Short 5 75							
CALLS @ 7¼	3,625.00	3,625.00	1,125.00	−2,750.00	−3,875.00	−6,375.00	−8,875.00
Short 5 90							
CALLS @ 1⅛	562.50	562.50	562.50	562.50	562.50	−1,937.50	−4,437.50
Net	−75,250	−250	2,250	3,375	7,250	7,250	7,250

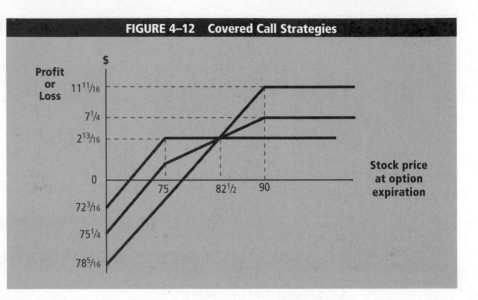

FIGURE 4–12   Covered Call Strategies

A combined write position is a covered call strategy using more than one striking price, and is a compromise between income and the potential for further price appreciation.

The highest gain is possible if you write the calls with the highest striking price. However, this strategy also generates the least income to the portfolio manager. The combined write is a compromise between income and potential for further price appreciation.

CROSS-COMPANY SPREADS

During most of 1986 the common stock of Squibb and Merck (both pharmaceutical companies) sold for approximately the same price. In late summer, rumors in the marketplace caused the price of Merck to fall relative to the price of Squibb. One day the price gap widened to $99⁵⁄₈ for Merck and $114¹⁄₂ for Squibb. Robert Alan felt that a difference of this magnitude was unwarranted; he believed that the price gap was likely to narrow in the near future.

To act on his belief, he considered buying calls on Merck (the low-priced security) and buying puts on Squibb (the higher-priced security). This strategy, however, would require a substantial cash outlay. He decides a better approach would be concurrent spreads on the two companies: a bullspread on Merck and a bearspread on Squibb. This strategy is called a **cross-company spread**. He determined the following price information.

Squibb:	OCT 105 call = $13⅛
	OCT 120 call = $5¾
Merck:	OCT 95 call = $8¼
	OCT 110 call = $2

Because there are two underlying securities, and consequently more than one "stock price at option expiration," it is not possible to construct a typical

CROSS-COMPANY SPREADS (Continued)

profit and loss diagram. He *can* calculate maximum profit and loss figures from the combined positions. Table 4–12 does this.

The table shows that the combined maximum loss from this strategy is $13 $^7/_8$ or $1,387.50 per 100 shares. This occurs if Robert is completely wrong in his assessment of the situation and the spread between the price of MRK and SQB widens rather than narrows. The maximum gain occurs if Merck rises above $110 and Squibb falls below $105. If both securities remain unchanged at option expiration, his combined loss is a modest $375.

TABLE 4–12 Cross Company Spreading			
	STOCK PRICE AT OPTION EXPIRATION		
	$95	**99^5/_8$**	**$110**
MERCK:			
BUY OCT 95 CALL @	8$^1/_4$	−8$^1/_4$	−3$^5/_8$	6$^3/_4$
WRITE OCT 110 CALL @	2	2	2	2
NET COST	6$^1/_4$	−6$^1/_4$	−1$^5/_8$	8$^3/_4$
	105	**114$^1/_2$**	**120**
SQUIBB:			
WRITE OCT 105 CALL @	13$^1/_8$	13$^1/_8$	3$^5/_8$	−1$^7/_8$
BUY OCT 120 CALL @	5$^3/_4$	−5$^3/_4$	−5$^3/_4$	−5$^3/_4$
CREDIT	7$^3/_8$	7$^3/_8$	−2$^1/_8$	−7$^5/_8$
	MAX LOSS	**MAX GAIN**	**RESULT IF STOCK UNCHANGED**
MRK SPREAD	−6$^1/_4$	8$^3/_4$	−1$^5/_8$
SQB SPREAD	−7$^5/_8$	7$^3/_8$	−2$^1/_8$
COMBINED	−13$^7/_8$	16$^1/_8$	−3$^3/_4$

MARGIN CONSIDERATIONS

Posting margin refers to the "extra" cash requirement associated with certain option strategies.

An important consideration in option spreading is the necessity to post **margin** with certain strategies. If you buy an option, the most you can lose is the option premium you paid. If you write an option, you run the risk of losses for more than the option premium received. The requirement to post margin simply means that a speculator in short options must have sufficient equity in his or her brokerage account before the option positions can be assumed.

This is necessary to help ensure the integrity of option contracts. The Options Clearing Corporation interposes itself between the option buyer and seller and guarantees these trades. At the end of every trading day, some accounts have made money and some have lost. From the OCC's perspective, these gains and losses net to zero. On the books of a given brokerage firm, however, the collective gains and losses of its customers *do not* net to zero every day. Brokerage firms are unwilling to assume the entire risk of investor default in the event of unfavorable price movements. Writing a naked call, for instance, can result in catastrophic losses to the writer if stock prices advance sharply. Before writing an uncovered call, an option trader will be required to show an ability to withstand such a loss. Investors do this by depositing and maintaining equity in the option account until they close the option position.

Imagine the situations that could develop if such an escrow account were not required. Investors short on pocket change near the end of the month could merely call their brokers and write some options, generating immediate cash that could be spent for whatever purpose the investors chose. If the initial options ultimately became unprofitable, no problem: simply write more options to generate enough cash to satisfy your cash requirements in closing the unprofitable position. The market wouldn't remain viable very long under these circumstances.

It is important to make a distinction between this use of the term *margin* and the practice of borrowing part of the cost of securities from your stockbroker. An investor in the stock market who buys shares on margin is actually borrowing money and paying interest on it. When you post margin with an option strategy, you *are not* borrowing money, and you pay no interest. This seems unclear to many investors, and may be one reason some attractive option strategies are not used more often.[9] For current margin rules, go to the Institutional section of the CBOE website.

Margin Requirements on Long Puts or Calls

When you buy an option, there is no requirement for you to advance any sum of money other than the option premium and the commission required to make the trade. You simply pay for the option in full; no other cash need be deposited. If the option has at least nine months until expiration, you can borrow up to 25% of the cost of the option position from your brokerage firm. That is, you can buy long-term options partially on margin.

Margin Requirements on Short Puts or Calls

If you write an uncovered call on shares of common stock, the initial margin requirement is the greater of these two amounts:

1. Premium + 0.20 (Stock Price) − (Out-of-Money Amount), or

2. Premium + 0.10 (Stock Price)

---

[9]Option traders on the exchanges often borrow money from their bank to post the margin requirement. In a sense, these people do pay interest on the margin they post.

If the short call is on a broad-based index like the OEX or SPX, the formula changes to 15% of the underlying value rather than 20%.

As an example, suppose you write a company XYZ call with a $125 striking price for a premium of $4^5/_8$ while the stock price is $116. You must deposit the greater of these two:

1. $462.50 + 0.20($11,600) − [($125 − $116)(100)] = $1,882.50, or

2. $462.50 + 0.10($11,600) = $1622.50

Your minimum deposit is therefore $1,882.50.

Under current rules, each account is "marked to market" every day. This means each day additional funds are required or excess funds are released as the relative profitability of a position changes. If you write naked calls and the stock price rises, you must add cash to your account. On the other hand, if the stock price falls, you may be able to withdraw funds from the account.

The computer system your brokerage firm uses will continually monitor the status of your account, and transfer money within your account as needed. If you do not have sufficient funds to meet a margin requirement, your brokerage firm must close out your position.

Brokerage firms are careful about encouraging or even permitting clients to write uncovered options. As we have seen, losses from such a strategy can be substantial. Besides the margin rules discussed here, most brokerage firms have in-house rules on minimum customer account equity requirements before permitting uncovered option writing. A minimum equity requirement of $20,000 is a general rule at many brokerage firms.

A short put on either a common stock or an index requires a margin deposit of 10% of the exercise price.

Margin Requirement on Spreads

Spread requirements are more lenient than those for uncovered options. In general, spreads must be done in a margin account, although with certain spreads there is no margin requirement.[10] To receive the more lenient spread margin, the long option must not expire before the written option. Therefore, certain calendar or diagonal spreads would be treated as separate option positions.

With spreads, the rule is this: You must pay for the long side in full, and you must deposit the amount by which the long put (or short call) exercise price is below the short put (or long call) exercise price. This initial spread requirement must be maintained during the life of the position. This may seem complicated, so let's look at new examples.

Suppose you want to establish the vertical call bullspread evaluated in Table 4–5. These options expire at the same time, so the spread rules are in effect. The short call exercise price is *not* below that of the long call, so the only requirement

---

[10]There were some changes made to the margin requirements of option positions in mid-1999. Certain butterfly and box spreads enjoy less stringent requirements. See *www.cboe.com/margin/index.htm* for details. The publication *Characteristics and Risks of Standardized Options* also covers the margin rules. This is available from any broker or via the CBOE website.

is that the long side be paid for in full. You do this by depositing $1⅝ from your pocket and $3⅜ from the sale of the short option.

Instead of using calls for the bullspread, an investor might choose to use the puts. Suppose someone buys an OCT 80 put on Microsoft and writes an OCT 90 put. The long put exercise price is $10 below that of the short put, so the rules require the investor to put up $1,000. This amount must remain in your account for as long as the spread is in place. If the investor had written the 85 put instead of the 90, the margin requirement would have been 5 points ($500) instead of $1,000, because this is the difference between the striking prices.

A General Margin Rule with Spreads:

- If the spread results in a debit to your account, you must deposit the net cost of the spread.

- If the spread results in a credit to your account, you must deposit the difference between the option striking prices.

Margin Requirements on Covered Calls

There is no margin requirement when writing covered calls, because you can cover any loss in the short option by delivering the shares of stock. Your brokerage firm will, however, restrict your ability to sell your shares of the underlying stock while you have calls written against it unless you are approved for uncovered call writing.

In a call bullspread, the call option that you write is considered covered by the other call option. Although you do not own shares of stock, you own the right to obtain them at an advantageous price if the stock moves up sharply. That is why there are no extra margin requirements on the short call.

EVALUATING SPREADS

What determines a "good" spread? This is a question that option traders continually ponder. If you can predict the future, there is always another strategy that will dominate a profitable spread strategy. A 100 percent bullish speculator should buy calls and write puts; if bearish, he or she should buy puts and write calls.

It is important to remember that to be successful with your speculative activities you *must take a stand* on the direction of the market. You may anticipate an advance or a decline, or you may expect the market to trade in a relatively flat range for a period of time. You cannot cover all the bases in such a way that you make money no matter what happens. Spreads and combinations are bullish, bearish, or neutral. You must decide on your outlook for the market before searching for an appropriate strategy.

The Debit/Credit Issue

If a strategy requires an outlay of funds from your account, it requires a debit. If the strategy generates income, it yields a credit. There are usually several competing option strategies that may serve a particular end, and some will involve a debit and others a credit. Consider bullspreads: they can be done with calls (at a debit) or with puts (at a credit). Tables 4–5 and 4–7 are examples of bullspreads using both types of options. If you were to do the spread using calls, you would have a net cash outlay of $162.50. With puts, your account would be credited with $137.50. In this example, your maximum gain or loss is about the same in either situation. This is not always the case, but the differences will normally be small.

With bearspreads, the spreader writes the option with the lower striking price. This means that a debit balance results from a bearspread with puts and a credit balance from a bearspread with calls. Everything else being equal, one rule of thumb is to use puts for bullspreads and calls for bearspreads.

The Reward/Risk Ratio

Another consideration in looking at spreads is the maximum gain relative to the maximum loss. Gains are good and losses are bad, so we want this ratio to be high.

In Table 4–5, the Microsoft call bullspread has a maximum gain of $337.50 and a maximum loss of $162.50. The reward/risk ratio is then $337.50/$162.5, or 2.08. Table 4–7 is a bullspread using puts, with a reward/risk ratio of 3.625/1.375 , or 2.64, which (everything else being equal) is preferable to the lower ratio.

It is not common to use the reward/risk ratio as a stand-alone decision criterion, but it can provide useful information about a particular spread. A MSFT AUG 65/70 call bullspread, for instance, has a maximum gain of $1/4$ and a maximum loss of $4^3/4$ for a not particularly attractive ratio of 0.05.

The "Movement to Loss" Issue

A third piece of information that can be useful in evaluating spreads is the magnitude of stock price movement that is necessary for a position to become unprofitable. In the AUG 65/70 call spread just described, the reward/risk ratio is low. In order for *any* loss to occur with this strategy, the stock price would have to fall from its current level of $79^7/16$ to $69^3/4$ in the next month. If you consider this ten-point move unlikely, the MSFT spread may be reasonable.

Specify a Limit Price

Spreads involve at least two options: You want to obtain a high price for the options you sell and want to pay a low price for the options you buy. Suppose you want to establish a bullspread like the one pictured in Figure 4–7. In analyzing this strategy, we assumed that you could establish the spread for a net cost of $1^5/8$. However, if you simply give your broker two separate market orders, one to buy a call and a second to sell a different call, you run a significant risk of winding up with a net cost higher than the $1^5/8$ price you extracted from the newspaper or the Internet.

Suppose the actual prices for these options match those in Table 4–13. A market order to buy the OCT 85 call would likely be filled at $5^1/4$; a market order to

TABLE 4–13 Option Bid-Ask Spreads			
	LAST PRICE	BID	ASK
OCT 85 CALL	5	5	$5^{1}/_{4}$
OCT 90 CALL	$3^{3}/_{8}$	$3^{5}/_{16}$	$3^{7}/_{16}$

sell the OCT 90 call would fetch $3^{5}/_{16}$. The cost of the spread is then $5^{1}/_{4} - 3^{5}/_{16} = 1^{15}/_{16}$, $31.25 more than you expected.

You can deal with this kind of uncertainty by specifying a dollar amount for the debit or credit at which you are willing to trade. In the bullspread example in Figure 4–7, you could give your broker an order to establish the spread at $ $1^{3}/_{4}$ debit (the midpoint of the two bid-ask pairs), or, if you were a little more aggressive, $1^{11}/_{16}$. Then the two components of your order are considered simultaneously on the exchange floor, and you can avoid the awkward situation of finding that you didn't complete part of the spread. If your specified price is "away from the market," meaning that you are unable to trade at as good a price as you want, then neither order is executed.

Determining the Appropriate Strategy: Some Final Thoughts

The basic steps in any decision-making process are simple: (1) learn the fundamentals, (2) gather information, (3) evaluate alternatives, and (4) make a decision. You should be at the point now where you can do an above-average job of tackling the first three steps. Making a decision (taking a stand on the market) can be the toughest part. As you consider your involvement with stock options, you might benefit from considering the "Rules for Options Survival," presented in Table 4–14.

TABLE 4–14   Ten Rules for Option Survival for the Beginner
RULE 1: YOU SHOULD SELDOM, IF EVER, GO NAKED.
RULE 2: DON'T PUT ALL YOUR EGGS IN ONE BASKET.
RULE 3: MAKE SOME MONEY DURING QUIETING MARKETS: USE CREDIT SPREADS.
RULE 4: DON'T BE AFRAID TO CASH IN EARLY. YOU DON'T NEED TO HOLD EVERY VALUABLE OPTION UNTIL ITS EXPIRATION.
RULE 5: KNOW WHERE YOU STAND. MONITOR YOUR POSITIONS.
RULE 6: DON'T PRESS YOUR ENTRY. ("DON'T TRY TO GET THE LAST EIGHTH.")
RULE 7: DON'T PLACE MARKET ORDERS.
RULE 8: KNOW THE MARKETS.
RULE 9: USE A BROKERAGE FIRM WHOSE PEOPLE COMPREHEND OPTIONS.
RULE 10: HAVE FUN!
From "How to Survive the First Few Months of Options Trading," by William Degler. *Futures* (August 1986): 52–53.

This chapter and the previous one have illustrated some ways in which options can be combined to suit the particular purpose of an investor or speculator. We have seen how some portfolios of options are equivalent to other collections. Options trading can be exciting and rewarding, but it also can be expensive if you fail to pay attention to basic principles or if you do not respect the risk of your positions. Remember the old Wall Street expression: "There is room in the market for bulls and for bears, but not for hogs." Greed can be your worst enemy.

SUMMARY

Option combinations are strategies in which you are simultaneously long or short options of different types. The best-known combination is a straddle, which is a long call position and a long put position on the same underlying asset, where the two options have the same striking price. Buying straddles is appropriate when you anticipate a major price movement in either direction in the underlying security. Writing straddles is appropriate when you expect little price change.

Other well-known combinations are strangles and condors. Strangles are like straddles except the two options have different striking prices.

A condor is a less risky version of a strangle. There is almost no limit to the number of option combinations that might be constructed on a particular stock.

Options spreads are strategies in which someone is simultaneously long and short options of the same type, but with different striking prices or expiration dates. Spreads are quite popular with individual investors.

There are many different types of spreads. Popular types include vertical spreads, calendar spreads, diagonal spreads, backspreads, butterfly spreads, and ratio spreads.

SELF TEST

T ___ F ___   1. A combination is a strategy in which you are simultaneously long or short options of different types.

T ___ F ___   2. A person who writes a call and also writes a put with the same striking price has a long straddle position.

T ___ F ___   3. A long straddle becomes profitable if the underlying asset moves sharply either up or down.

T ___ F ___   4. There are three breakeven points in the profit and loss diagram of a short straddle.

T ___ F ___   5. A strangle is similar to a straddle except the options have different striking prices.

T ___ F ___   6. Regardless of whether a condor is long or short it requires four separate option positions.

T ___ F ___   7. A spreader often trades profit potential for reduced cost.

T ___ F ___   8. In any bullspread, regardless of whether it is done with puts or with calls, you buy the lower striking price and write the higher.

T ___ F ___   9. Buying a bullspread is equivalent to writing a bearspread.

T ___ F ___   10. A put bullspread is an example of a credit spread.

T ___ F ___   11. Calendar spreads are also sometimes called horizontal spreads.

T ___ F ___   12. Ignoring commissions, butterfly spreads sometimes can be constructed at virtually no cost.

T ___ F ___   13. Ratio spreads involve an unequal number of long and short options.

T ___ F ___   14. A hedge wrapper is a covered call position plus a long put.

T ___ F ___   15. In combined call writing, the investor uses options on more than one company.

T ___ F ___   16. There is no margin requirement when writing a covered call.

T ___ F ___   17. When establishing a spread, the spreader can specify a limit price for the entire trade without regard to the actual prices of the component options.

T ___ F ___   18. Spreads are more popular with institutional investors than with individual investors.

T ___ F ___   19. A speculator who anticipated little price movement in the underlying security could logically write a straddle.

T ___ F ___   20. An investor can sometimes lock in a profit by adding a short call to a seasoned long call position.

PROBLEMS & QUESTIONS

Refer to Table 4–4 as necessary.

1. Suppose an investor feels that a stock price is likely to remain stable over the next few months. What are the advantages and disadvantages of writing a *straddle* versus a *strangle*?

2. In Figure 4–11, the plot of the hedge wrapper is similar to that of a bullspread. How are these two strategies different?

3. An investor who is long 100 shares of a stock might write *two* calls on this stock: one would be covered, the other uncovered. What strategy discussed in this chapter has risk and return characteristics similar to this? (You may want to construct a profit/loss diagram for the "covered call + a naked call" strategy to see what it looks like.)

4. What is the significance of the point in Figure 4–12, where all three plots cross? What stock price corresponds to that point? In a combined write, will there *always* be a common point of intersection for competing strategies such as these?

5. What do you think the quotation at the beginning of the chapter means?

6. "Bullish diagonal spreads should always have the long option position in the most distant expiration month available, and the short side in the closest. This way you only have to buy once, and you can write options three times (one for each expiration) against your long position." Do you agree with that statement?

7. In a call option bullspread, why is the short option position considered covered?

8. Comment on the following statement: "If you own 100 shares of stock and write two calls against it, you have, for all practical purposes, written a straddle."

9. Why must a long straddle always have some intrinsic value if it is not at-the-money?

10. What is the speculator's motivation for a call ratio spread?

11. What is the speculator's motivation for a call ratio backspread?

12. What is the speculator's motivation for a put ratio spread?

13. What is the speculator's motivation for a put ratio backspread?

14. Comment on the following statement: "Hedge wrappers transform risky positions into riskless positions."

15. Using current economic events, make up an example of a cross-company spread.

16. Construct a profit and loss diagram for a MSFT AUG 90/95 call bullspread.

17. Construct a profit and loss diagram for a MSFT AUG 85/90 call bearspread.

18. Construct a profit and loss diagram for a MSFT OCT 65/70 put bullspread.

19. Construct a profit and loss diagram for a MSFT AUG 70/75 put bearspread.

20. Construct a profit and loss diagram for a long condor on MSFT using OCT 70/75/80/85 calls.

21. Construct a profit and loss diagram for a long condor on Microsoft using OCT 65/70/75/80 puts.

22. Construct a long butterfly spread on Microsoft using AUG 75/80/85 calls.

23. In problem 22, what is your profit or loss if, at option expiration, the stock price remains at $79^7/_{16}$?

24. Suppose a speculator establishes a calendar spread by writing a MSFT AUG 80 call and buying a MSFT OCT 80 call. What does the speculator want to happen to the stock price of Microsoft?

25. Repeat problem 24 using puts.

26. Suppose you previously bought 200 shares of Microsoft at $60. Show how you can use the hedge wrapper to lock in a profit.

27. Draw a profit and loss diagram for a long JUL 75/80 strangle on Microsoft.

28. Draw a profit and loss diagram for a long JUL 80/85 strangle on Microsoft. How do the risk/return characteristics of this combination differ from those of the strangle in problem 27?

29. An investor buys 1,000 shares of Microsoft and does a combined write using 5 contracts each of the OCT 90 and 95 calls. Draw a profit and loss diagram.

30. In problem 29, what is the person's profit or loss if, at option expiration, the price of MSFT is $84?

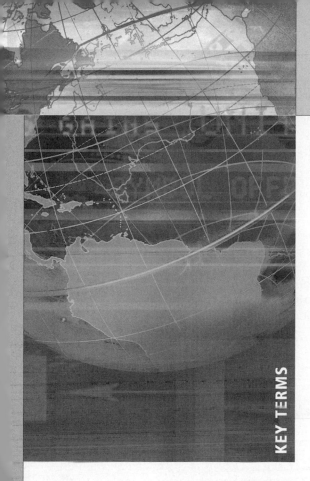

5

Option Pricing

KEY TERMS you will find in this chapter:

arbitrage   law of one price
binomial pricing   put/call parity
financial engineering

*"We sent the first draft of our paper to the **Journal of Political Economy** and promptly got back a rejection letter. We then sent it to the **Review of Economics and Statistics** where it also was rejected.*

Merton Miller and Eugene Fama at the University of Chicago then took an interest in the paper and gave us extensive comments on it. They suggested to the JPE that perhaps the paper was worth more serious consideration. The journal then accepted the paper . . ."

—Fischer Black, on his journal article with
Myron Scholes that gave birth to the Black-
Scholes options pricing model.

Discoveries about option pricing are arguably the single most important development in the field of finance during the last 30 years.

Discoveries about option pricing are arguably the single most important development in the field of finance during the last 30 years. Many professional students of the marketplace spend a good deal of their time investigating the relationship between option prices, economic variables, and psychological phenomena.

This chapter begins with a brief history of option pricing. We then move to some arbitrage arguments showing why an option must sell for a particular price. In the next chapter we extend this to the backbone of modern options pricing, the Black-Scholes model.

THE BLACK-SCHOLES OPTION PRICING MODEL

$$C = SN(d_1) - Ke^{-rt} N(d_2)$$

$$\text{where } d_1 = \frac{\ln\left(\dfrac{S}{K}\right) + \left(r + \dfrac{\sigma^2}{2}\right)t}{\sigma\sqrt{t}} \text{ and } d_2 = d_1 - \sigma\sqrt{t}$$

S = current stock price
K = option striking price
e = base of natural logarithms
r = riskless interest rate
t = time until option expiration
σ = standard deviation of returns on the underlying security
N(·) = cumulative normal distribution function
ln = natural logarithm

A BRIEF HISTORY OF OPTIONS PRICING

THE EARLY WORK[1]

In 1877, Charles Castelli wrote *The Theory of Options in Stocks and Shares*, published in London. This practical, 177-page exposition sought to explain to the public the hedging and speculation aspects of options. Castelli's work was generally unremarkable at the time and, by today's standards, lacks a theoretical base.

Bachelier's work was the first research that sought to value derivative assets.

At the Sorbonne University in France, Louis Bachelier defended his Doctor of Mathematical Sciences dissertation entitled *Théorie de la Spéculation* on March 19, 1900. This 70-page document is now a classic, but sharing Castelli's fate, his research attracted little initial attention. In retrospect, it seems Bachelier's work was the first research that sought to value derivative assets. Bachelier proved that at a given, infinitesimally small instant in time the market price of a security must be in equilibrium with no inherent bias toward a market rise or a market decline.[2]

"The dynamics of the exchange will never be an exact science."
Louis Bachelier

Benoit Mandelbrot, the famous mathematician, feels that Bachelier's chairman, Henri Poincaré, did not understand the importance of Bachelier's work. In fact, *Théorie de la Spéculation* contains the first profit and loss diagrams, which are now standard textbook fare. Fifty years passed before Bachelier's work began to receive the attention it deserved. One person who did notice it was Paul Samuelson, one of the premier economists of the 20th century.

---

[1] I am grateful to Edward J. Sullivan for his generous help in educating me about the early days of option pricing. Peter Bernstein in his book *Capital Ideas* also provides a thorough review of the early days of this history.

[2] As we will see later in this chapter, we now know that an option price is independent of the expected future rate of return on the stock. Bachelier figured this out 100 years ago.

THE MIDDLE YEARS

During the 1950s and 1960s, option pricing research was reborn. In 1955 Samuelson wrote an unpublished paper entitled *Brownian Motion in the Stock Market* that referred to Bachelier's earlier work. The following year he published a paper entitled "Rational Theory of Warrant Pricing." Warrant pricing should logically be very similar to option pricing.[3] Contemporaneously one of Samuelson's M.I.T. students, Richard Kruizenga, completed his dissertation *Put and Call Options: A Theoretical and Market Analysis*, citing Bachelier.

In 1962 A. James Boness finished his Ph.D. dissertation (*A Theory and Measurement of Stock Option Value*) at the University of Chicago, studying under the famous economist Lawrence Fisher. The pricing model he developed constitutes a significant theoretical jump from Bachelier's work and is a precursor to that of Fischer Black and Myron Scholes.

The following year Boness translated Bachelier's dissertation into English: it subsequently appeared in Paul Cootner's now-famous work *The Random Character of Stock Market Prices*, inspiring many research papers and graduate theses.

THE PRESENT

The cornerstone of modern option pricing is the Black-Scholes option pricing model, hereafter BSOPM, developed in 1973. Extensive empirical testing proves this model to be an excellent representation of reality. The BSOPM is really an improved version of the Boness model, with the most substantial changes being the Black-Scholes proof of the risk-free interest rate as the correct discount factor and the absence of assumptions about investors' risk preferences. While there are other pricing models in use today, most are modest variations of Black-Scholes.

Finance's current fast lane involves the pricing of exotic options like those briefly mentioned in Chapter Two. Pricing an "option to buy another option," a barrier option, a lookback option, or any of the other myriad varieties is a substantially more complicated task than pricing plain vanilla puts and calls. Much of the emerging area called **financial engineering** involves building a product with option-like characteristics that is tailored to the needs of a specific customer. The investment firm providing such a product wants to ensure that they have a good idea of what the product is theoretically worth before they quote a price for it. The mathematical complexity of these products is largely responsible for the migration of mathematicians and rocket scientists to Wall Street.

Financial engineering involves building a product with option-like characteristics that is tailored to the needs of a specific customer.

This chapter covers the fundamentals of option pricing logic; the next covers the Black-Scholes option pricing model. Knowing how option prices change as market conditions change is critical for risk managers; we look at this more fully in Chapter 7, where we study the offspring of Black-Scholes: delta, gamma, and theta.

---

[3] Fisher Black was actually working on warrant pricing when he made the first mathematical breakthrough ultimately leading to the Black-Scholes model.

The logic of option pricing stems directly from arbitrage arguments, so let's review that topic first.

ARBITRAGE AND OPTION PRICING

Finance is sometimes called "the study of arbitrage." **Arbitrage** is the existence of a riskless profit. A central precept of the theory of finance is that risk and expected return are generally proportional, so we would not expect to find riskless profit opportunities very often, and if they do appear they should quickly disappear as traders take advantage of them. This is exactly what happens in practice.

It is important to note that finance theory does not say that arbitrage will never appear. Rather, theory states that arbitrage opportunities will be short-lived: the market will quickly act to eliminate the arbitrage and bring prices back into equilibrium.

Finance is sometimes called the study of arbitrage.

FREE LUNCHES

Here is an actual example of an arbitrage situation that occurred on a major university campus some years ago. In the university community, there were two competing bookstores dealing in textbooks. One bookstore was having a sale and offered a particular paperbook title for $10. At the other bookstore, two blocks away, its buy-back offer for that same book was $10.50. The arbitrage did not last long, as the $10 books quickly sold out and were transported to the other store.

Consider another example, this time with the foreign currency market. Suppose you are in a European train station and see the following exchange rates posted for deutsche marks, Australian dollars, and U.S. dollars:

1 DM = $0.62
1 A$ = $0.55
1 DM = A$1.15

This set of exchange rates provides an arbitrage opportunity, as Table 5–1 shows.

TABLE 5–1   Foreign Currency Arbitrage

1. BUY DM 10,000 WITH U.S. DOLLARS: COST = DM 10,000 × $0.62/DM = **$6,200.00**
2. EXCHANGE THE DEUTSCHE MARKS FOR AUSTRALIAN DOLLARS: DM 10,000 × A$1.15/DM = A$ 11,500.00
3. EXCHANGE THE AUSTRALIAN DOLLARS FOR U. S. DOLLARS: A$11,500.00 × $0.55/A$ = **$6,325.00**
4. THIS IS AN ARBITRAGE PROFIT OF $6,325 − $6,200 = **$125**.

Sometimes the apparent mispricing is so small that it is not worth the effort to exploit it. We see this in everyday life. You do not find $5 bills on the sidewalk very often; if you should see one, you would pick it up. You can find pennies, however, on the ground in any parking lot. We have all seen them, and many of us just let them stay there. It is not worth the trouble to pick them up.

Other times an apparent arbitrage opportunity is out of reach because of some impediment to free trade or some other restriction. Imagine that you paid 85 cents to enter a subway station. While awaiting your train you notice two quarters on the floor just outside the gate. To go get them you would have to go back through the turnstile and then deposit another 85-cent token to get back in. Fifty cents lying on the ground is textbook arbitrage, but not if you have to pay 85 cents to get it. You might move quickly into action if the money were a twenty-dollar bill rather than a couple of coins, but even this is not riskless. There are lots of people in a subway station, and you run the risk of having someone else pick up the bill by the time you get to it, in which case you would have wasted the additional token money.

Modern option pricing techniques are based on arbitrage principles. Certain packages of securities are equivalent to other packages. In a well-functioning marketplace, equivalent assets should sell for the same price. Given the required information, we can solve for what an option price must be for arbitrage to be absent. The classic study[4] of arbitrage in option pricing gave birth to the term **put/call parity**, the subject of the next section. This relationship shows that for a given underlying asset the call price, put price, stock price, and interest rate form an interrelated complex, and that given three of the values you can solve for the fourth.

> Equivalent assets should sell for the same price.

THE THEORY OF PUT/CALL PARITY

As Figure 5-1 shows and as we saw in Chapter 3, the shape of the profit/loss diagram for a covered call position is essentially the same as that of a short put. What happens if you combine a covered call with a *long* put? The diagram for a long put is obtained by rotating the short put about the horizontal axis: a long put is exactly the opposite of a short put. With European options and a non-dividend paying stock, an investor who combines a long stock position with a short at-the-money call and a long at-the-money put has a *riskless position*. (See Figure 5–2 and Table 5–2.) The combination of a short put, a short stock position, and a long call also yields a riskless position, and riskless investments should earn the riskless rate of interest, if the riskless position requires you to advance funds.[5]

Suppose an investor borrows money to buy stock, and simultaneously writes a call and buys a put, with both options at-the-money. The investor then holds this position until option expiration. According to Table 5–2, this results in a perfect hedge, because no matter what happens, the future value of the position is

---

[4] Hans Stoll, "The Relationship between Put and Call Option Prices," *Journal of Finance*, December 1969, 801–824.

[5] An "investment" requires you to invest money. A simultaneous long position in stock and short position in the same stock involves no outlay of funds, is therefore not an investment, and does not earn the riskless rate of interest.

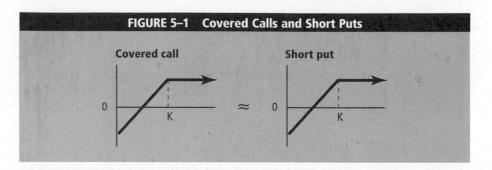

FIGURE 5–1   Covered Calls and Short Puts

Covered call   Short put

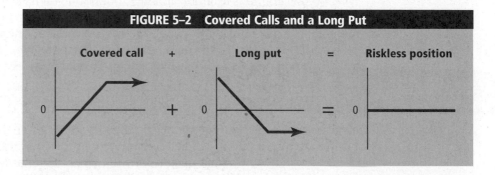

FIGURE 5–2   Covered Calls and a Long Put

Covered call   +   Long put   =   Riskless position

TABLE 5–2   Stock Price at Option Expiration

	0	$25	$50	$75
BUY STOCK @ $50	0	25	50	75
WRITE $50 CALL	0	0	0	(25)
BUY $50 PUT	50	25	0	0
TOTAL	$50	$50	$50	$50

fixed. Because the options are at-the-money, the stock price and striking price are equal. If the stock rises it will be called away at the striking price. If it falls you can sell it at the striking price. Your "stock and options" portfolio will be worth the stock price regardless of what the stock itself does, as Table 5–2 shows.

Because this is the only possible outcome it is riskless, and, in theory at least, a bank should be willing to lend money for this position at r, the riskless rate of interest for the period until expiration. If an investor can establish these three positions and make a profit, arbitrage is present. Arbitrage profits will be exploited and become zero, so the market will adjust such that

$$S - S + C - P - \frac{Sr}{(1+r)} = 0 \qquad (5\text{–}1)$$

THE STOCK REPAIR STRATEGY

Kirsten Joy bought 100 shares of Alcoa (*AA, NYSE*) at $40; it currently trades at $30. The stock no longer appeals to her, and she is inclined to trade out of it but is not happy about having to take the loss. She thinks the stock might recover about half its decline, but does not believe it will be back to $40 anytime soon. At this point, she would just like to get her money back. She remembers attending a CBOE Options Institute class and hearing about a strategy called *stock repair*. This makes sense to her and she decides to use it.

Kirsten finds the following one-month options: $30 call @ $3, $35 call @ $1½. She buys the 30 call and writes two of the 35 calls. In essence, she wrote a 35 covered call and paid $1½ for a 30/35 call bullspread. The table below shows the profit and loss possibilities from the combined position.

| | STOCK PRICE AT OPTION EXPIRATION | | | | | |
POSITION	30	31	32	33	34	35
LONG STOCK	−10	−9	−8	−7	−6	−5
LONG 30 CALL	−3	−2	−1	0	1	2
SHORT TWO 35 CALLS	3	3	3	3	3	3
COMBINED	−10	−8	−6	−4	−2	0

The worksheet shows that, ignoring commissions, she breaks even if Alcoa returns to $35 at option expiration.

or

$$C - P - \frac{Sr}{(1+r)} = 0 \qquad (5\text{--}1a)$$

where C = call premium
       P = put premium
       S = stock price
       r = riskless interest rate

This equation is based on the following logic. After establishing the three positions, there is one cash *inflow* (from writing the call) and two cash *outflows* (paying for the put and paying the interest on the bank loan). The principal of the loan (S) comes in, but I immediately spend it (−S) to buy the stock. The interest on the bank loan is paid in the future: it needs to be discounted to a present value. That is why the interest charge (Sr) is divided by the quantity (1 + r).

I can rearrange the equation as follows.

$$C - P = \frac{Sr}{(1+r)} \qquad (5\text{--}2)$$

Dividing both sides of the equation by the price of the stock (S), we get

$$\frac{C}{S} - \frac{P}{S} = \frac{r}{(1+r)} \approx r \qquad (5\text{-}3)$$

or

$$\frac{C-P}{S} = \frac{r}{(1+r)} \approx r \qquad (5\text{-}3a)$$

The quantity $r/(1 + r)$ is approximately equal to r. Suppose, for instance, the interest rate is 5%. Five percent divided by 1.05 gives 4.76%. On a \$25 stock the difference between the one-year call and put premium, according to equation (5–3a), should be $(4.76\%) \times (\$25) = \$1.19$. On a \$100 stock, however, the difference would be *four times* as much: $(4.76\%) \times (\$100) = \$4.76$.

The point is that relative put and call prices differ by about the riskless rate of interest. In other words, the at-the-money call premium should exceed the put premium, and the difference will be greater as the price of the stock goes up, as interest rates rise, or as the time to option expiration lengthens. A simple example will show the implications of this. First let's expand the list of variables:

> Relative put and call prices differ by an amount corresponding to the riskless rate of interest.

C = call premium   K = option striking price

P = put premium   r = riskless interest rate

S_0 = current stock price   t = time until option expiration

S_1 = stock price at option expiration

> With a non-dividend paying stock, an at-the-money call should sell for more than an at-the-money put.

Suppose we do as before: write the call, buy the put (with the same striking price as the call), and buy stock, but instead of borrowing the current stock value we borrow the *present value* of the *striking price* of the options, discounted from the option expiration date. If the options are at-the-money, the stock price is equal to the option striking price. It is necessary to discount the striking price, because this amount is paid in the future, and dollars today are not the same as dollars tomorrow. This yields a profit/loss contingency table for the combined positions as Table 5-3 shows.

TABLE 5–3   Put-Call Parity Arbitrage Table

		VALUE AT OPTION EXPIRATION		
ACTIVITY	CASH FLOW	IF $S_1 < K$	IF $S_1 > K$	IF $S_1 = K$
WRITE CALL	+ C	0	$K - S_1$	0
+ BUY STOCK	$- S_0$	S_1	S_1	S_1
+ BUY PUT	$- P$	$K - S_1$	0	0
+ BORROW	$+ K/(1 + r)^t$	$- K$	$- K$	$-K = -S_1$
= SUM	$C - P - S_0 + K/(1+r)^t$	0	0	0

Regardless of whether the stock price at option expiration is above or below the exercise price, the net value of the combined positions is zero. This results in the following relationship:

$$C - P - S_0 + \frac{K}{(1+r)^t} = 0.$$

Rearranging terms, we have the **Put/Call Parity** relationship:

$$C - P = S_0 - \frac{K}{(1+r)^t} \tag{5-4}$$

This table shows that call prices, put prices, the stock price, and the riskless interest rate form an interrelated securities complex. If you know the value of three of these components, you can solve for the equilibrium value of the fourth. The relationship assumes that the options can only be exercised at expiration and that the underlying stock does not pay any dividends during the life of the options.

Suppose, for instance, we want to know the no-arbitrage stock price given the following information:

Call price = \$3½   Riskless interest rate = 5%

Put price = \$1   Time until option expiration = 32 days

Striking price = \$75

Rearranging equation (5–4), we have

$$S_0 = C - P + \frac{K}{(1+r)^t}$$

Plugging in the known values,

$$S_0 = \$3.50 - \$1 + \frac{\$75}{(1+0.05)^{32/365}} = \$77.18$$

The equilibrium stock price is about $77^3/_{16}$.

A simple example will show why the put/call parity relationship must be true. Without arbitrage, equivalent financial claims should sell for the same price. This is called the **law of one price**. Suppose we have stock and option prices like those in Table 5–4. No matter what the stock price at option expiration, the activities described yield a profit of \$0.31. Conversely, if the put price is too high relative to the call price, the arbitrageur could write the put, buy the call, sell a share of the stock short, and invest the proceeds from the short sale at the 6 percent interest rate.

The fact that there are 100 options in a contract does not matter; everything can simply be scaled up with no loss of generality. The theory of put-call parity indicates that, *when European options are at-the-money and the stock pays no dividends,*

The law of one price states that equivalent assets should sell for the same price.

TABLE 5–4   Arbitrage via Option Mispricing

INITIAL VALUES:

STOCK PRICE (S_0)	= $50
STRIKING PRICE (K)	= $50
TIME UNTIL EXPIRATION (t)	= 6 MONTHS
T BILL INTEREST RATE (r)	= 6.00%
CALL PREMIUM (C)	= $4¾
PUT PREMIUM (P)	= $3

THEORETICAL PUT VALUE GIVEN THE CALL VALUE:

$$P = \$4.75 - \$50 + \$50/(1.06)^{0.5} = \$3.31$$

THIS MEANS THE ACTUAL CALL PRICE ($4¾) IS *TOO HIGH* OR THAT THE PUT PRICE ($3) IS *too low.*

TO EXPLOIT THE ARBITRAGE:

WRITE 1 CALL @ $4¾
BUY 1 PUT @ $3
BUY 1 SHARE @ $50
BORROW $48.56 @ 6.00% FOR SIX MONTHS

	STOCK PRICE AT OPTION EXPIRATION		
PROFIT/LOSS	**$0**	**$50**	**$100**
FROM CALL	4.75	4.75	(45.25)
FROM PUT	47.00	(3.00)	(3.00)
FROM LOAN	(1.44)	(1.44)	(1.44)
FROM STOCK	(50.00)	0.00	50.00
TOTAL	**$0.31**	**$0.31**	**$0.31**

relative call prices should exceed relative put prices by an amount approximately equal to the riskless rate of interest for the option term times the stock price.

Consider another situation, this time when the options are not at-the-money. In the previous example, suppose the stock price is $47 instead of $50. The $50 call is out-of-the-money, while the $50 put now has intrinsic value of $3. Logically this makes a difference in the pricing of these two options. Suppose the put actually sells for $6. A six-month, $50 call should sell for

$$C = \$6 + \$47 - \$50/(1.06)^{0.5} = \$4.44$$

We can confirm this value by constructing another contingency table. If the prices are in equilibrium there should be no arbitrage profit, which Table 5-5 indicates is the case.

TABLE 5–5 Put/Call Parity Contingency Table			
PROFIT/LOSS	$0	$50	$100
FROM WRITING CALL	4.44	4.44	(45.56)
FROM BUYING PUT	44.00	(6.00)	(6.00)
FROM LOAN	(1.44)	(1.44)	(1.44)
FROM BUYING STOCK	(47.00)	3.00	53.00
TOTAL	$0.00	$0.00	$0.00

We can learn something else about option pricing from the put-call parity relationship. Suppose we have this information:

Stock price (S) = $62⅛   Time until option expiration (t) = 47 days

Striking price (K) = $60

Riskless interest rate (r) = 6.15%

We might ask, what is the minimum price for which a $60 call should sell? Back in Chapter Two when we looked at profit and loss diagrams we saw that an option must always sell for at least its intrinsic value. In this case, the call is in-the-money by $2⅛, so it must sell for at least this amount. In fact, the option must sell for *more* than this.

Rearranging the put-call parity model, the quantity C – P equals the stock price (S_0) minus the present value of the striking price $K/(1+r)^t$. Plugging in our values, C – P = $62.125 – $60/(1.0615)^{47/365}$, or $2.58. The put cannot sell for less than zero, so C must be *at least $2.58*. Although the put is out-of-the-money, it will still have some time value, so the minimum call premium will actually be $2.58 plus the time value of the put. Knowing something about option pricing allows us to refine assumptions from earlier in this book about the minimum value of an option. Another way of looking at this example is to say that this call must have time value of at least $2.58 – $2.125, or about 45 cents.

THE BINOMIAL OPTION PRICING MODEL[6]

Put-call parity shows that given the put price, we can solve for the call price. We do not need the put value to solve for the call value if we know something about the possible future paths the stock price might take. One way to get some intuition into this fact is via **binomial pricing**.

We can learn something about this by creating an imaginary capital market to illustrate rational option pricing. Suppose you can invest in U.S. government

---

[6] Much of the material in this section comes from my article entitled "Wall Street Profits, Arbitrage, and the Pricing of Stock Options," with John Buoncristiani, *Chance*, Summer 2000, 20–24.

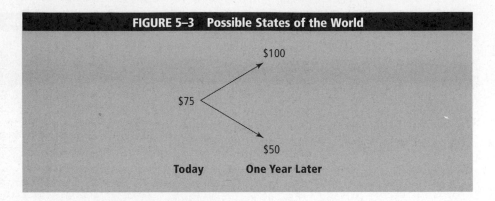

FIGURE 5–3 Possible States of the World

$100

$75

$50

Today   One Year Later

securities and earn 10% over the next year. Stock XYZ currently sells for $75 per share. There are no transaction costs or taxes.

In our hypothetical market there are only two possible states of the world at year-end: either the stock will rise to $100 or it will fall to $50. There are call options for sale that give you the right to buy the stock a year from today at its current price of $75. If the stock rises to $100, the call would be worth $100 – $75 = $25, because it gives its owner the right to buy stock for $25 less than the market price. If the stock falls to $50, the option is unattractive and would expire worthless; no one would choose to pay $75 for stock worth $50. Figure 5–3 illustrates the scenario. For what price should such an option sell?

Returning to pricing our option, one approach to the problem would be to determine the expected value of the stock in one year, from that determine the expected call value, and discount this amount back to a present value. Let's try it. Perhaps an optimistic investor believes there is a 90% chance the stock will rise and a 10% change it will fall. With branch probabilities 0.9 and 0.1, the expected stock price is (0.9 × $100) + (0.1 × $50) = $95. The expected call price is therefore $95 – $75 = $20, with a present value of $20/1.10, or $18.18.

Despite this seemingly logical calculation, such a price presents an arbitrage opportunity to someone who can recognize it, and it could not prevail for long in a well-functioning marketplace. To see why, consider the steps an arbitrageur would quickly implement. First, buy a share of the stock, spending $75. Second, write *two* of these calls at $18.18 each, receiving $36.36. The net investment, then, is $75 – $36.36 or $38.64.

If the stock falls, the options will expire worthless and the portfolio will contain one share of stock worth $50. If the stock rises, the share will be worth $100. The options would be valuable to their owner because each of them permits the purchase of shares worth $100 for only $75. The option holder would exercise this option; the option writer would have to sell two shares for $25 less than their current market value, thereby losing $50. Therefore, the ending portfolio value would be $100 (the value of the stock) minus the $50 loss on the options, or $50. Figure 5–4 shows the possibilities.

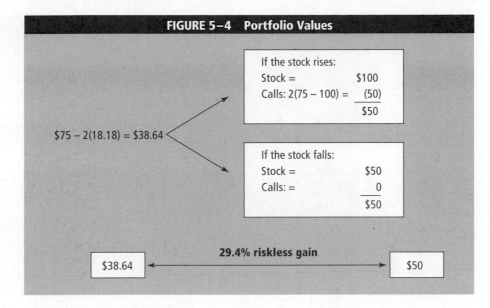

FIGURE 5–4   Portfolio Values

This means regardless of whether the stock follows the upper or the lower branch in Figure 5–3, the portfolio will be worth $50 in one year. Because the initial cash outlay was $38.64, the $50 terminal value translates into a certain one-year gain of 29.4% with no risk. This is inconsistent with a U.S. government riskfree rate of 10%. $18.18 cannot be the correct value for the call option.

Suppose a different investor views XYZ's prospects differently and reverses the probabilities for the two branches: she feels the stock has a 10% chance of appreciating and a 90% chance of falling. Using the prior logic the stock's expected value is $55 and she therefore concludes the option has *no* value because the expected future stock price is less than the price the option entitles you to pay. No one would choose to pay $75 for shares worth $55. The arbitrageur, however, offers to pay $1 apiece for these calls if she will write them. Thinking the arbitrageur has erred in his calculations, she agrees to write two such contracts for $1 each.

Having acquired these two calls, the arbitrageur will then sell one share of the stock short. Selling short involves borrowing a share, selling it, buying a replacement share from someone else at a later time, and replacing the borrowed share. Short sellers are, in essence, selling first and buying second. (They make money when prices decline.) Buying the two calls for $1 each and selling one share short at $75 results in a net cash inflow of $73. As in the prior example, at expiration the portfolio will be worth $50 regardless of the branch traveled. If the stock goes up, the arbitrageur loses $25 on the short position when he purchases shares at $100 to replace those borrowed. However, he profits on each call. The right to buy at $75 is worth $25 when the stock price is $100. Having paid $1, the gain is $24 on each call, or $48 on two of them. The net portfolio gain is 2 × ($25 – $1) – $25 = $23.

If the stock goes down, the calls expire worthless but the arbitrageur makes

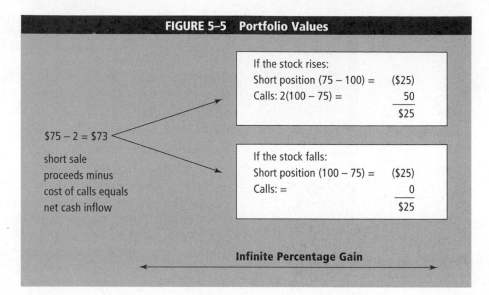

FIGURE 5–5   Portfolio Values

If the stock rises:
Short position (75 – 100) =   ($25)
Calls: 2(100 – 75) =   50
                               $25

If the stock falls:
Short position (100 – 75) =   ($25)
Calls: =   0
                               $25

$75 – 2 = $73

short sale
proceeds minus
cost of calls equals
net cash inflow

Infinite Percentage Gain

$25 on the short sale for a net $23 gain, as before. In this case, the return is infinite, as there was no initial cost to this investment; it began with a net inflow. Clearly $1 is not an equilibrium value for the call, either.

To find out what the call price must be, we can generalize the example and create an arbitrage portfolio as follows. If the stock rises, the call will be worth $25; it will be worth $0 if the stock falls. We can construct a portfolio of stock and options such that the portfolio has the same value regardless of the stock price after one year. One way to do this is to buy one share of stock today and write a quantity of calls we will call N.

If the stock falls, the value of this portfolio will be $50. The share is worth $50 and the calls expire worthless. If the stock rises, the portfolio is worth $100 – $25N. The stock is worth $100 and the options are worth $25 apiece to their owner (or minus $25 to the person who wrote them). When they are exercised the option writer will have to sell $100 stock for $75 per share, losing $25 per share. Figure 5–6 shows the possibilities.

We can solve for N such that the portfolio value in one year must be $50. Setting the two possible values equal, $100 – $25N = $50, and N = 2. This means if we buy one share of stock today and write 2 calls, we know the portfolio will be worth $50 in one year.[7] In other words, the future value is known and riskless. Economic theory requires that an investment with a known future value must earn the riskless rate of interest, which is 10% in this example.

Suppose, for instance, the government promises you $50 in one year (with no risk) and the prevailing one-year riskless rate is 10%. This future payment is

---

[7] Note that this is not a prescribed investment strategy. No one would choose to engage in a strategy that is guaranteed to lose money. We are merely solving for a value that must exist in the absence of arbitrage.

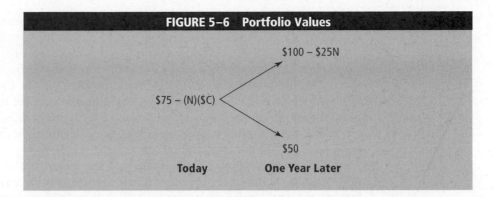

FIGURE 5–6   Portfolio Values

$100 – $25N

$75 – (N)($C)

$50

Today   **One Year Later**

worth $50/1.10 = $45.45 today. If the investment sold for less than this the return would be greater than 10%; if it sold for more the return would be less than 10%. Neither situation is consistent with a riskless rate of 10%. The market will price this future cash flow at $45.45.

Returning to the option example, we know the portfolio will be worth $50 in one year regardless of the path taken. Given the 10% rate, the portfolio must be worth $45.45 today. Therefore, assuming no arbitrage opportunity exists ($75 – 2C) = $45.45. Equivalently, ($75 – 2C)(1.10) = $50.

Solving for C, we find the option must sell for $14.77. This value is independent of the probabilities associated with the two branches! It makes no difference what the probabilities are that the investor assigns to the two branches. At any price above this value a person who buys one share of stock and sells two call options will earn risk-free more than they would by putting money in the bank. Conceptually this means people will be lining up to sell options and their price would be driven down to $14.77. Similarly if the price were lower there would be risk free opportunities to option buyers. This discovery is an epiphany for students of derivatives: the price of an option is independent of the expected return on the stock.

Recall Bachelier's proof that at a given, infinitesimally small instant in time the market price of a security must be in equilibrium with no inherent bias toward a market rise or a market decline. The same is true with the price of an option: the expected rate of return on the underlying stock is irrelevant.

This is admittedly a troubling and seemingly illogical result. Modern option pricing theory makes extensive use of continuous time mathematics and the associated calculus. Calculus is about rates of change, especially how one variable changes when another variable changes by a very small amount. You might get some intuition into why the future rate of return does not matter by considering a more familiar setting: the speed of an automobile.

Suppose you know that at a precise instant in time a car is traveling at *exactly* 45 miles per hour. Now ask yourself this: Is the car speeding up or is it slowing down? Upon reflection you will realize that just knowing the car's speed is an incomplete picture of the situation. The car might be cruising at a constant speed,

The price of an option is independent of the expected return on the stock.

but it could just as easily have been parked and now be accelerating toward 70 miles per hour. It could also be braking to a stop from highway speed. *Regardless of the big picture at some point the vehicle is traveling exactly 45 miles per hour.* Knowing that the car is going 45 miles per hour tells you nothing about its likely future speed. Even a space shuttle, for a very brief instant, travels at 45 miles per hour. The analogy is not perfect, but without going deeply into the mathematics this may give some intuition into why knowing a call option sells for $3 tells you nothing about the future path of the stock price. Therefore, the future path of the stock price should not affect the call price.

Note also that the size of the jump and the length of the time period are unimportant. Actual stock prices can change minute by minute and by very small increments. The Black-Scholes model, which is the principal topic of the next chapter, allows infinitesimally small changes in the stock price in continuous time.

PUT PRICING IN THE PRESENCE OF CALL OPTIONS: FURTHER STUDY

Knowing that this call option must sell for $14.77 we can now turn to its counterpart, the put option, and learn something about its equilibrium price. Suppose the put also sells for $14.77. The arbitrageur, observing that this value is incorrect given the call premium, engages in the transactions shown in Table 5-6.

We see that this series of transactions results in an initial cost of $0.00 and a future portfolio value of $7.50. In other words, we invest no money now but will receive $7.50 in one year. This is the proverbial "free lunch."

In fact, the arbitrageur need not even wait a year for this windfall. The arbitrageur could invest only the discounted value of the striking price, or $75/1.10 = $68.18. Table 5-7 shows this would result in an initial cash flow of $6.82 and a portfolio value at option expiration of $0.

TABLE 5–6   Put-Call Arbitrage

INITIAL STOCK PRICE = $75		PORTFOLIO VALUE AT OPTION EXPIRATION	
ACTIVITY	CASH FLOW	STOCK PRICE = $100	STOCK PRICE = $50
BUY 75 CALL	−$14.77 (PAYMENT)	$25	0 (EXPIRES WORTHLESS)
WRITE 75 PUT	+14.77 (RECEIPT)	0 (EXPIRES WORTHLESS)	−$25
SELL STOCK SHORT	+75.00 (RECEIPT)	−100 (COST TO CLOSE OUT)	−50 (COST TO CLOSE OUT)
INVEST $75 IN T-BILLS	−75.00 (PAYMENT)	82.50 (RECEIPT FROM T-BILL INVESTMENT)	82.50 (RECEIPT FROM T-BILL INVESTMENT)
TOTALS	$0.00 (NET RECEIPT)	$7.50	$7.50

TABLE 5–7 Put-Call Arbitrage			
INITIAL STOCK PRICE = $75		**PORTFOLIO VALUE AT OPTION EXPIRATION**	
ACTIVITY	**CASH FLOW**	**STOCK PRICE = $100**	**STOCK PRICE = $50**
BUY 75 CALL	−$14.77 (PAYMENT)	$25	0 (EXPIRES WORTHLESS)
WRITE 75 PUT	+14.77 (RECEIPT)	0 (EXPIRES WORTHLESS)	−$25
SELL STOCK SHORT	+75.00 (RECEIPT)	−100 (COST TO CLOSE OUT)	−50 (COST TO CLOSE OUT)
INVEST $68.18 IN T-BILLS	−68.18 (PAYMENT)	75.00 (RECEIPT FROM T-BILL INVESTMENT)	75.00 (RECEIPT FROM T-BILL INVESTMENT)
TOTALS	**$6.82** (NET RECEIPT)	**$0.00**	**$0.00**

Table 5–7 shows that with the put and call both selling for $14.77, the arbitrageur could, with no investment and no risk, capture $6.82 today, or, as Table 5–6 shows, capture the future value of this, $6.82(1.10) = $7.50 in one year. Given a call premium of $14.77, the put cannot also sell for this amount in an arbitrage-free market.

In fact, the put must sell for $14.77 − $6.82 = $7.95. This put price would result in an initial cash inflow of $0 in Table 5–7. We would expect something that we know to be worthless at all points in the future to also be worthless today. This brings us back to the put/call parity model: $C − P − S + K/(1+R)^t = 0$.

The call premium, put premium, stock price, and striking price form an inter-related securities complex. If you know all variables but one, you can solve for its arbitrage-free value.

BINOMIAL PUT PRICING

The binomial pricing logic used with call options works equally well with put options. Suppose we have the same situation as before: a current stock price of $75, a striking price of $75, and a one-year later stock price of either $100 or $50,

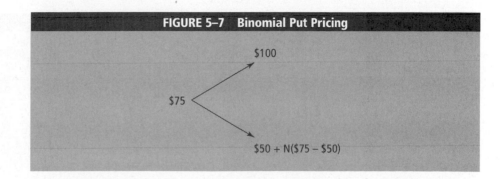

FIGURE 5–7   Binomial Put Pricing

$100

$75

$50 + N($75 − $50)

PATH DEPENDENT OPTIONS

Sometimes the price path of the underlying asset *does* make a difference in the value of the option. Chapter Two identified a few "exotic," non-exchange traded options. Many of these are path dependent, including the lookback option, barrier option, and Asian option. Versions of these may be imbedded in other corporate securities, too.

As an example, in 1982 Manufacturers Hanover issued a 10-year note that required the bondholders to convert to common stock at maturity. The conversion price was the lower of $55.55 or the average closing price of the common stock during the previous thirty days. According to researchers[8] at the Federal Reserve Bank of Atlanta, "By making the conversion price dependent on the average price of the common stock, the company alleviated suspicions among investors that management would fraudulently manipulate the stock price upward just before the conversion date."

[8] Hunter, William C., and David W. Stowe, "Path Dependent Options," *Economic Review*, March/April 1992, 29–34.

as in Figure 5–7. We can combine puts with stock so that the future value of the portfolio is known for certain.

Setting the two portfolio values equal, we find N = 2. This means a portfolio composed of one share of stock and two puts will grow risklessly to $100 after one year. This gives us the equation ($75 + 2P)(1.10) = $100, and P = $7.95. This is exactly the same value we found when we solved for the put premium using put-call parity.

BINOMIAL PRICING WITH ASYMMETRIC BRANCHES

So far the binomial pricing examples have all involved symmetric branches, with the size of the "up" movement equal to the size of the decline. This need not be the case and it makes no difference, because the pricing logic still holds. The only thing we have to do differently is use a quantity of options other than the 2.0 we always have when the branches are symmetric. Figure 5-8 shows the possibilities on another option.

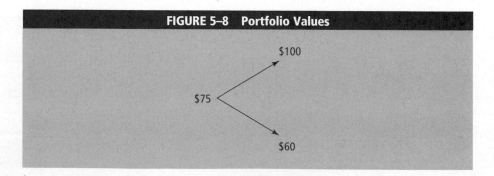

FIGURE 5–8   Portfolio Values

$100

$75

$60

Here we see that the stock will either rise by $25 or fall by $15. Suppose in this example the time period is three months, the annual interest rate is 5.50%, and we want to find the value of a $75 call.

The first step is to determine the number of call options to write in order to create the riskless hedge. Call this number N. If the stock goes up, the portfolio will be worth $100 – $25N. If it goes down, the portfolio will be worth $60. Setting these two values equal, we have $100 – $25N = $60. Solving, we find N = 1.6.

Buying one share and writing 1.6 calls, then, will grow risklessly to $60. Remember that the fractional contract is not a problem here. We could just as easily buy ten shares and write 16 calls. The valuation equation now becomes ($75 – 1.6C)(1.055)$^{.25}$ = $60. Solving, the equilibrium call value (C) is $9.87.

Now let's turn to a slightly more complicated example. This time suppose the branch possibilities are as shown in Figure 5–9, with the striking price remaining at $75, one year until expiration and the interest rate remaining at 5.50%.

If the stock rises to $100, the portfolio will be worth $100 – $25N. If the stock rises to $80, the portfolio value will be $80 – $5N. Note in the latter case that the options will be in-the-money and, therefore, worth $5 apiece. Setting the two possible portfolio values equal, $100 – $25 N = $80 – $5 N. Solving, we find N = 1.0, which means the future portfolio value will be $75 regardless of the path. The valuation equation is then ($75 – C)(1.055) = $75. Solving, C = $3.91.

We know from earlier chapters that calls are worth less the further out of the money they are. What would a $78 call on the stock in Figure 5–9 be worth? Solving for N, we set $100 – $22 N = $78 and find N = 1.0. The valuation equation is ($75 – C)(1.055) = $78, and C = $1.07. This is less than the premium for the $75 call, as expected.

THE EFFECT OF TIME

With options, more time until expiration means more value. Suppose the $78 option in the last example had eighteen months until expiration instead of twelve. All that changes in the valuation equation is the time period:

$$(\$75 - C)(1.055)^{1.5} = \$78$$

Solving, C = $3.02.

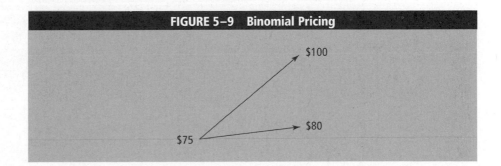

FIGURE 5–9   Binomial Pricing

$100

$80

$75

Now suppose the time until expiration is six months; we would expect the option premium to decline.

$$(\$75 - C)(1.055)^{0.5} = \$78$$

Solving, C = *minus* \$0.94. We know that an option cannot sell for less than zero, so something is wrong here. The problem is that we have introduced arbitrage into our market. We assumed the riskless interest rate is 5.50% per year, and then constructed a portfolio with a known future value of \$78 and a starting stock price of \$75. If the call initially sold for zero, an increase in portfolio value from \$75 to \$78 in six months is an annual interest rate of 8.16% with no risk. If the call sold for more than zero, the rate of return would be even higher. This is inconsistent with a riskless rate of 5.50%, as we assumed.

This example illustrates the fact that you cannot just assume any conditions you want. If your assumed market contains arbitrage, option pricing principles will ferret it out.

THE EFFECT OF VOLATILITY

Perhaps in our hypothetical market there is another firm whose stock also sells for \$75 per share, but this stock is more volatile: in the next year it will either rise to \$110 or fall to \$40 as in Figure 5–10.

Using the same pricing procedure as in the earlier examples, a one-year, \$75 striking price call option on this stock should sell for \$18.54. This is the solution to the equation $(75 - 2C)(1.055) = 40$. Using the put-call parity model, the equilibrium value of the corresponding put is $C - S + K/(1+r)^t$, or \$18.54 – 75 + 71.09 = \$14.63. The higher premium associated with the greater volatility shows why options on Internet stocks sell for a "higher price" than options on similarly priced retail food stores or electric utilities.

You can also get some intuition into why options on volatile assets are expensive by thinking about the pricing of an insurance policy. Drivers with a history

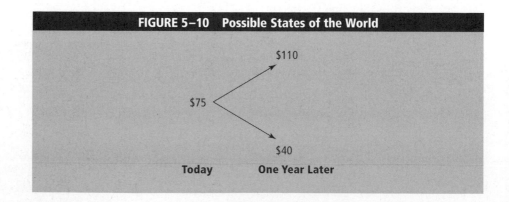

FIGURE 5–10   Possible States of the World

$110

$75

$40

Today   **One Year Later**

of accidents and speeding tickets pay a higher premium than someone with a perfect driving record. Similarly, an insurance policy protecting you against a very remote possibility (like flight insurance) is inexpensive. An Internet stock that routinely moves up or down 5% per day is susceptible to an "accident" and will have expensive options, while a real estate investment trust is likely to be much more stable (and have lower option premiums).

TRADING STRATEGY

LOOKBACK OPTIONS

Because he knows something about options and their pricing, a local electricity company asks Robert Alan to comment on a proposal the company recently received from a Wall Street investment bank. The electric company purchases much of the power it transmits from outside sources on a daily basis. In recent months the price of electricity has been extremely volatile and rising. Consumers are complaining about the high rates, and in some parts of the country (especially California) there are periodic blackouts because there is not enough power to supply everyone's needs.

The investment bank offers to sell the electric company a *lookback call option*. After doing some homework, Robert Alan finds that a lookback call option is essentially a European call option with a striking price equal to the *lowest* price of the underlying asset over a period of time. A lookback put, on the other hand, has a striking price equal to the *maximum* price over the period. The situation is analogous to an ordinary European option where the striking price may change, but only in a direction favorable to the option holder.

The essence of the deal is this. The investment bank will sell the electric company a one-month lookback call on 1,000 megawatt hours. A regional electric cost index is the benchmark price for the "underlying asset." At the end of the thirty-day period the option holder "looks back" in time, and the electric company is able to purchase up to 1,000 megawatts at the minimum level of the index over the past month if it wishes, or it could allow the option to expire worthless. This power can then be used in the coming days to distribute to customers. Because the investment bank does not actually produce power, it sends a check to the electric company to cover the difference between the prevailing electric price and the chosen lookback price.

Robert Alan finds several calculators on the Internet that price exotic options like this, and he discovers the investment bank's option is prohibitively expensive. When he reports to the electric company on his findings, he suggests an alternative: a *partial* call lookback. This is similar to the original option except there is a floor on the minimum price. By limiting the investment bank's downside risk, the option premium becomes much lower. This is what he suggests to the firm.

INTUITION INTO BLACK-SCHOLES

CONTINUOUS TIME AND MULTIPLE PERIODS

The analysis described in the preceding pages is what financial theorists refer to as binomial pricing. The fact that future security prices are not limited to only two values in no way attenuates the usefulness of the model. We can simultaneously make the size of the jumps very small and the time interval very short. There are theoretically an infinite number of future states of the world. By making the jumps infinitely small and the time span infinitely short we move into the world of continuous time calculus and the Black-Scholes model for which its inventors received the Nobel Prize. Figure 5–11 shows how the one-period tree diagrams can be extended to multiple periods and how you might visualize a normal distribution about the range of future states of the world.

The inputs to the Black-Scholes model are the current stock price, the option striking price, the remaining time until option expiration, the interest rate, and the anticipated volatility of the underlying asset. The formula also assumes that the underlying stock price distribution is lognormal.

The pricing logic remains: a riskless investment should earn the riskless rate of interest. If this is not the case, arbitrageurs will quickly transact so as to move prices to their equilibrium relationship. As the earlier example showed, it is not necessary to know the expected rate of return on the stock in order to find the equilibrium value of the right to buy the stock. This is just as true in continuous as in discrete time.

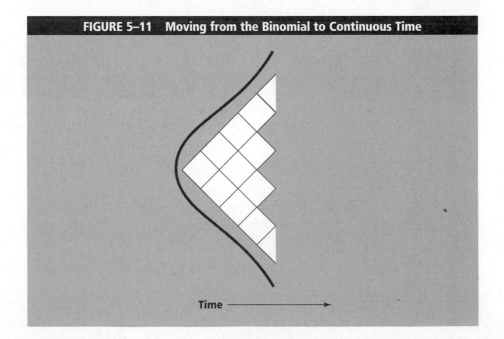

FIGURE 5–11   Moving from the Binomial to Continuous Time

Time ⟶

TABLE 5–8 Possible Ways to Roll a Seven					
1st Die					
1	**2**	**3**	**4**	**5**	**6**
2nd Die					
1					
2	3	4	5	6	7
3	4	5	6	7	8
4	5	6	7	8	9
5	6	7	8	9	10
6	7	8	9	10	11	12

OPTION PRICING AND THE ROLL OF DICE[9]

Suppose we consider an option on a single roll of a pair of ordinary six-sided dice. Because each die has six sides, there are 6 × 6 = 36 possible outcomes, some of which have the same point total. For instance, a 3 on one die and a 4 on the second total seven, the same as a 1 and a 6. In fact, as Table 5–8 shows, there are *six* ways to roll a 7, and this is the most likely result. The table shows that there is only one way to get a two; this comes from a one on each die. Similarly, there is only way to get a 12, that from rolling a pair of sixes.

Table 5–9 summarizes the possible outcomes, the number of ways each might be obtained, and the associated probabilities of each roll value.

Note that the sum of the probabilities is 36/36, or 100%. Figure 5–12 shows the distribution, symmetric about its mean of seven.

Suppose we let the roll of the dice represent the future stock price. (In this age of dot.com speculation and unprecedented Nasdaq volatility, the analogy seems

TABLE 5–9 Outcome Distribution for a Single Roll of a Pair of Dice										
Outcome of Roll	**2**	**3**	**4**	**5**	**6**	**7**	**8**	**9**	**10**	**11**	**12**
# of Possible Ways	1	2	3	4	5	6	5	4	3	2	1
Probability	1/36	2/36	3/36	4/36	5/36	6/36	5/36	4/36	3/36	2/36	1/36

[9] The intuition for this example comes from Dwight Grant, Gautam Vora, and David Weeks, "Teaching Option Valuation: From Simple Discrete Distributions to Black/Scholes Via Monte Carlo Simulation," *Financial Practice and Education,* Fall/Winter 1995, 149–155.

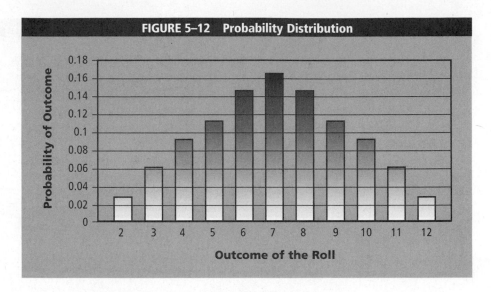

FIGURE 5–12   Probability Distribution

apt.) Now imagine a call option with a striking price equal to the average future stock price of 7. Suppose also that we are on another planet with very low gravity and that it takes the dice a year to settle down once we toss them. The prevailing interest rate is 5% per year. For what price should such a call option sell?

As we saw in the earlier examples with binomial pricing, the expected rate of return on the stock is irrelevant in pricing the option. In the current example, however, we know the probabilities of each future outcome and it is convenient to use them in valuing the call. We are going to roll the dice once; any toss resulting in a score of 8 or more means the option winds up in-the-money at expiration one year from now. With no time left, the option premium will equal its intrinsic value. Any toss of 7 or less results in the option expiring worthless.

Because we know the possible outcomes, we can relate them to their probabilities to determine the value of the call. Discarding the outcomes where the option expires worthless, we are left with a 5/36 probability of getting an 8, a 4/36 probability of a 9, and so on. Exercising the option requires us to pay the exercise price of 7, so we have

$$\left(\frac{5}{36}\times(8-7)\right)+\left(\frac{4}{36}\times(9-7)\right)+\left(\frac{3}{36}\times(10-7)\right)+\left(\frac{2}{36}\times(11-7)\right)+\left(\frac{1}{36}\times(12-7)\right)$$

This represents the expected value of the option one year from now, so we must convert it into a present value. Option pricing theory uses continuous compounding, so with a 5% interest rate over one year, the value of the option is

$$\left[\left(\frac{5}{36}\times(8-7)\right)+\left(\frac{4}{36}\times(9-7)\right)+\left(\frac{3}{36}\times(10-7)\right)+\left(\frac{2}{36}\times(11-7)\right)+\left(\frac{1}{36}\times(12-7)\right)\right]e^{-.05}$$

To get some intuition into the Black-Scholes model that we will look at in the next chapter, let's rearrange terms and use some algebra on this expression. Suppose we separate the striking price from the outcome of the roll as follows:

$$\left[\left(\frac{5}{36}\times 8\right)+\left(\frac{4}{36}\times 9\right)+\left(\frac{3}{36}\times 10\right)+\left(\frac{2}{36}\times 11\right)+\left(\frac{1}{36}\times 12\right)\right]e^{-.05}$$

$$-\left(\frac{5+4+3+2+1}{36}\right)(7)e^{-.05}=0.93$$

Suppose now that we multiply the left term by the expected future stock price and also divide by the expected future stock price. This amounts to multiplication by 1.0, something that algebra always permits.

$$\left[\left(\frac{5}{36}\times 8\right)+\left(\frac{4}{36}\times 9\right)+\left(\frac{3}{36}\times 10\right)+\left(\frac{2}{36}\times 11\right)+\left(\frac{1}{36}\times 12\right)\right]\frac{1}{E(S_1)}e^{-.05}E(S_1)$$

$$-\left(\frac{5+4+3+2+1}{36}\right)(7)e^{-.05}=0.93$$

Finance theory states that the current stock price, S_0, is the present value of the expected future stock price. This means that the expression $e^{-.05}E(S_1)$ equals S_0, or $(0.9512)(7) = \$6.66$. Now let's combine terms, do the math, and restate the equation:

$$\$6.66\times\left(\frac{3.89}{7}\right)-7e^{-.05}\left(\frac{15}{36}\right)=\$0.93$$

$$\text{or } \$6.66\,(0.5557)-7e^{-.05}(0.4167)=\$0.93$$

We can define the values in parentheses as probabilities one and two, respectively. In general terms, then, the equilibrium value of a call option (C) is

$$C = S_0\,(prob_1) - K\,e^{-Rt}\,(prob_2)$$

where K is the striking price and all other variables are as previously defined.

It is worth spending a few minutes here considering the interpretation of these two probability values. They are important in the Black-Scholes model that we will get into in the next chapter. Probability two is the more straightforward of the two. *It is the probability that the option will be in the money at expiration.* In the example we just finished, probability 2 is 15/36. Note from Table 5–8 that 15 of the 36 squares contain a value greater than 7.

Probability one is more complicated. *It is the probability that the option will be in the money, adjusted for the degree in the money, relative to the expected future stock*

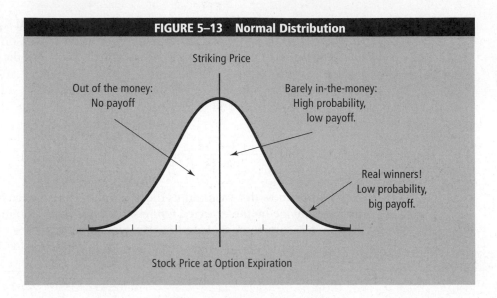

FIGURE 5–13 Normal Distribution

Striking Price

Out of the money:
No payoff

Barely in-the-money:
High probability,
low payoff.

Real winners!
Low probability,
big payoff.

Stock Price at Option Expiration

price. You can get some intuition into this by recognizing that not all the in-the-money outcomes are equally desirable. If I own an option, at expiration I would much rather have it in-the-money by 20 points than by 1 point. While both outcomes are in-the-money, the more deeply in-the-money outcome should get "extra credit" in option valuation. That is exactly what happens with the Black-Scholes model. Figure 5–13 shows the normal distribution curve, pointing out that stock prices in the far right tail are the real winners and, while not as common as outcomes barely in the money, they can contribute significantly to the weighted average return.

SUMMARY

Option pricing is one of the most important developments in the field of finance in the past thirty years. The discovery that there is an unambiguous way to value the right to buy or sell something substantially enriched the fields of corporate finance and investments. The valuation of contingent claims (like options) is largely responsible for the emigration of mathematicians to Wall Street. In finance, arbitrage pricing normally involves the relationship between two or more assets. We may not know the proper value for either security A or security B, but given the value of A, we can sometimes determine what the value of B should be. For example, we now know that put prices, call prices, stock prices, and interest rates form an interrelated securities complex and that one asset does not change price without affecting the others.

SELF TEST

T ___ F ___   1. The first theoretical work on option pricing was published in 1957.

T ___ F ___   2. Finance is sometimes called the study of arbitrage.

T ___ F ___   3. Even small amounts of arbitrage seldom appear in a well-functioning marketplace.

T ___ F ___   4. The law of one price says that equivalent securities should sell for the same price.

T ___ F ___   5. In a break with prior research, modern option pricing techniques are completely unrelated to arbitrage arguments.

T ___ F ___   6. The theory of put/call parity states that after adjusting for the time value of money, the present value of a call option should equal the present value of a put option.

T ___ F ___   7. The profit and loss characteristics of a covered call are generally similar to those of a short put option.

T ___ F ___   8. On a given stock, the difference between the call price and the put price increases as the stock price increases, provided both options have the same striking price.

T ___ F ___   9. If a stock pays no dividends, for a given expiration an at-the-money call should sell for slightly less than an at-the-money put.

T ___ F ___   10. The value of a call option is independent of the expected rate of return on the underlying asset.

T ___ F ___   11. It is possible for a European option to sell for less than its intrinsic value (as measured by the difference between the stock price and the striking price.)

T ___ F ___   12. Under binomial pricing, an increase in time until expiration does not convert into a higher option premium.

T ___ F ___   13. A binomial distribution becomes a normal distribution if there are enough jumps and the jumps are small enough.

T ___ F ___ 14. The value of an option depends on the distribution of future outcomes for the underlying asset.

T ___ F ___ 15. An increase in interest rates, everything else being equal, causes the value of a call option to decline.

PROBLEMS & QUESTIONS

1. Briefly explain the term *arbitrage*.
2. Explain why it is *incorrect* to say that arbitrage *does not occur* in a well-functioning market.
3. In the example contained in Table 5–1, show how you would take advantage of the situation if the Australian dollar sold for seventy-four cents U.S. instead of $0.55.
4. Explain why certain prices may constitute arbitrage to one person, but not to another.
5. Briefly explain the *law of one price*.
6. In the early days of option trading listed puts were not available on most stocks. Using the logic of put-call parity, show how someone could create a synthetic put using shares of stock and call options.
7. In early 2000 interest rates in Japan were very low. What does this portend for at-the-money put and call prices in Japan?
8. Put-call parity, with its assumptions, suggests that at-the-money calls should sell for more than the corresponding put. List *four* reasons why the newspaper price for a put might exceed the value of a call with the same striking price.
9. The discussion on binomial pricing states that the branch probabilities do not matter. Suppose one of the branches had a probability of 100%. How would this influence the option price, if at all?
10. The one-year riskless interest rate is 5.65%. A stock sells for $24^{1/4}$. A three-month $25 call sells for $1. For what price should a three-month $25 put sell?
11. In problem ten, suppose the riskless interest rate rises to 6.15%, the stock falls to $23, and the $25 call premium drops to 50 cents. For

what price should the $25 put sell? Assume there are 86 days until option expiration.
12. Suppose a stock sells for $100. An investor owns three July $95 call contracts, each listed in *The Wall Street Journal* at $8^{1/4}$. The stock then splits two for one. What is the value of the investor's calls immediately after the split?
13. XYZ stock sells for $50. A June $50 call sells for $4^{1/8}$, while a June $50 put sells for $2^{3/4}$. ABC stock sells for $80. On this stock a June $80 call sells for $5. For what price should a June $80 put sell? Neither XYZ nor ABC pay a dividend.
14. A stock sells for $77. The one-year riskless interest rate is 6.25%. A one-month $75 call sells for $4^{1/2}$, while a one-month $75 put sells for $3^{3/8}$. There is arbitrage in these prices. Show how you could take advantage of it.

In problems 15–25, assume the riskless interest rate is 6.50% per year.

15. A stock currently sells for $50. In six months it will either rise to $55 or decline to $45. Find the value of a $50 call.
16. In problem 15, find the value of a call with a striking price of $48.
17. Another stock sells for $85. In one year it will either rise in value to $100 or fall to $70. Find the value of an $85 call.
18. In problem 17, find the value of a $78 call.
19. Another stock sells for $45. In three months it will either rise in value to $50 or fall to $42. Find the value of a $45 call.

20. In problem 19, find the value of a $47 call.
21. Another stock sells for $95. In one year it will either rise to $110 or rise to $97. Find the value of a $100 call.
22. Another stock sells for $50. In one year it will either rise to $55 or fall to $45. Find the value of a $50 put.
23. In problem 22, find the value of a $51 put.
24. In one year, a stock will either be worth $100 or it will be worth $80. A one-year $90 call is worth $4. Find the implied stock price.
25. In one year, a stock will either be worth $72 or it will be worth $56. A six-month $65 call is worth $5. Find the implied stock price.
26. A stock currently sells for $58. In one year the stock price will either be $70 or $48. A one-year $60 call sells for $4½. Find the implied interest rate.

27. Your company's stock sells for $50. After two years the stock price will either be $65 or $35. The riskless interest rate is a constant 6.25%. Your company just awarded you options on 10,000 shares where the option striking price is $50. Determine the value of this award.
28. In problem 27, suppose instead you were to receive options with a striking price of $55. What term would these options have in order to be the same value as the options in problem 27?
29. In the dice problem described in Table 5–9, determine the value of a one-year call where the striking price is 7.5 rather than 7.0.
30. Repeat problem 29 for a six-month option.

CHAPTER 5 REVIEW

Appendix

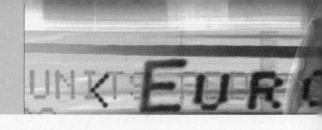

MULTI-PERIOD BINOMIAL OPTION PRICING

Don't be afraid to take a big step if one is indicated. You can't cross a chasm in two small jumps.

> David Lloyd George (1863–1945)
> Prime Minister of Great Britain

Chapter 5 shows how you can use arbitrage arguments to solve for the value of an option in a simple one-period, binomial outcome world. The world of option trading, of course, has more than two possible outcomes and we don't have to wait a year to find out if we make money or not. Prices change in the marketplace minute by minute and option values change accordingly.

We can easily extend the logic of binomial pricing to a multi-period setting. Understanding the recursive method for solving for the option value gives substantial insight into the Black-Scholes option pricing model, the subject of the next chapter. Time spent in getting the Zen of this will make you much more informed. A multi-period binomial option pricing question sometimes appears on Level II of the CFA exam; it is that important.

OPTION PRICING WITH CONTINUOUS COMPOUNDING

In Figure 5–3, we saw that with an annual interest rate of 10%, a $75 at-the-money, one-year call where the stock price either rises by one-third or falls by one-third must be worth $14.77.

The Black-Scholes model assumes that interest compounds continuously.

This result assumes there is no compounding of interest over the one-year period. One of the assumptions of the Black-Scholes model is that interest compounds *continuously*. If this is the case it changes slightly the equilibrium value of the call from the earlier example. Repeating the valuation procedure with continuous compounding, we have

$$(\$75 - 2C)(e^{.10}) = \$50$$

The continuously compounded future value factor for 10% over one year is 1.1052[1]. Solving for C, we get

$$C = \frac{\$75 - \dfrac{\$50}{1.1052}}{2} = \$14.88$$

---

[1] $e^{.10} = 1.1052$.

RISK NEUTRALITY AND IMPLIED BRANCH PROBABILITIES

The Black-Scholes model assumes that investors are *risk-neutral*; they focus on expected return without regard to the dispersion of outcomes around the mean. This is consistent with the Chapter Five results showing that the value of a call option is independent of the expected rate of return on the underlying asset. This has an interesting implication for binomial pricing; it means that while the option price is independent of the probability associated with the two branches, *the option premium contains an implied probability of the stock rising.*[2] We can see this through some algebra.

> The option premium contains an implied probability of the stock rising.

Suppose a risk-neutral investor knows that funds can be invested riskfree over one year at a continuously compounded rate of 10%. After one year, one dollar will be worth $\$1.00 \times e^{.10} = \$1.1052$ for an effective annual return of 10.52%. The risk-neutral investor would be indifferent between investing in the riskless rate of 10.52% and investing in the stock if it also had an expected return of 10.52%. We can determine the branch probabilities that make the stock have such a return.

> The Black-Scholes model assumes investors are risk neutral.

To do so, we need to define the following variables:

$U = 1 +$ percentage increase if the stock goes up

$D = 1 -$ percentage decrease if the stock goes down

$P_{up} =$ probability that the stock goes up

$P_{down} = (1 - P_{up}) =$ probability that the stock goes down

$e^{rt} =$ continuously compounded interest rate factor

The average stock return is the weighted average of the two possible price movements. Setting the average stock return equal to the riskless rate of return in our risk-neutral world, we have

$$(P_{up}\, U) + (P_{down}\, D) = e^{rt} \tag{5A-1}$$

Substituting,

$$(P_{up}\, U) + (1 - P_{up})\, D = e^{rt} \tag{5A-2}$$

Rearranging,

$$P_{up}U + (D - P_{up}D) = e^{rt}$$
$$P_{up}(U - D) + D = e^{rt}$$
$$P_{up} = \frac{e^{rt} - D}{U - D} \tag{5A-3}$$

[2] This is a risk neutral probability.

Equation 5A–3 gives us a direct method for inferring the probability of the stock rising. Because there are only two branches, if we know the probability of one branch we can determine the probability of the other.

In Figure 5–3, the stock either rises 33.33% (U = 1.3333) or falls 33.33% (D = 0.6667). The interest rate factor is 1.1052. Substituting into (5A–3),

$$P_{up} = \frac{1.1052 - 0.6667}{1.3333 - 0.6667} = \frac{0.4385}{0.6666} = 0.6578 = 65.78\%$$

Therefore,

$$P_{down} = 1 - P_{up} = 1 - 0.6578 = 0.3422 = 34.22\%$$

These are the branch probabilities implied in a no-arbitrage, risk neutral equilibrium.

We can now use this information to solve for the equilibrium value of the $75 call option in Figure 5–3. At expiration, a call is worth its intrinsic value, with the caveat that intrinsic value can never be less than zero. If the stock goes up (with probability 65.78%), the call will have intrinsic value of $100 – $75 = $25. If the stock goes down (with probability 34.22%), the call will be worthless. The expected value of the call in one year, therefore, is (0.6578 × $25) + (0.3422 × $0) = $16.45. Discounting this back to a present value, the value of the call today is $16.45/1.1052 = $14.88. This is the same value determined earlier.

EXTENSION TO TWO PERIODS

Suppose now we have *two* periods, each one-year long, with the stock either rising or falling by 33.33% in each period. This gives the two-period lattice shown in Figure 5A–1. What is the equilibrium value of this two-year, $75 European call?

To find out, we work backward from option expiration. Figure 5A–2 shows the branch possibilities. There is only one outcome in which the option winds up in-the-money: this is when the stock advances twice, to point UU. At any other outcome the option expires worthless because the stock price is less than the call striking price.

After two advances the stock price is $133.33, so a $75 call would have intrinsic value of $133.33 – $75 = $58.33. From point U there is a 65.78% probability of taking the upper branch (UU) and a 34.22% probability of taking the lower branch (UD, where the call would expire worthless). (These probabilities are the same as in the previous, one-period example.) The expected value of the call at expiration, then, is (0.6578 × $58.33) + (0.3422 × $0) = $38.37. Discounting at 10% (continuous) for one period, we get $34.72.

At point D the option is worthless because there is no chance it can finish in-the-money. At the end of Period 2, regardless of whether the stock rises or falls, it will be below the option striking price of $75.

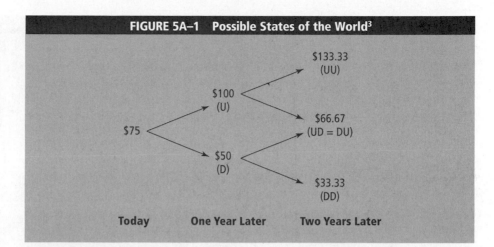

FIGURE 5A–1   Possible States of the World[3]

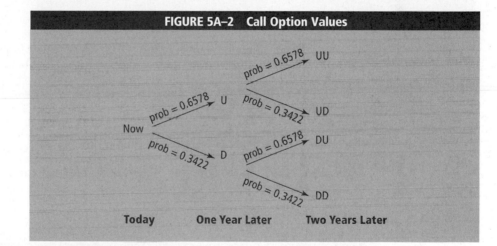

FIGURE 5A–2   Call Option Values

In the same fashion, starting from today we know the probabilities of the stock rising (U) or falling (D) over the next year. The expected value of the call in one year is $(0.6578 \times \$34.72) + (0.3422 \times \$0) = \$22.84$. Discounting at 10% for one period, we get $20.66. This is the equilibrium value of the two-year European call. Figure 5A–3 shows the values at expiration, in one year, and today.

Now let's use the same procedure to value a $60 call. This example is more complicated because there are several ways in which the option can be in-the-money at expiration. In fact, three of the four paths (UU, UD, DU) have terminal stock values greater than $60.

---

[3] The symbols "U" and "D" refer to an "up" path and a "down" path, respectively. "UU" means the path that experiences two up jumps in succession.

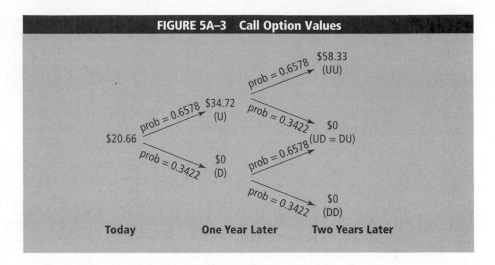

FIGURE 5A–3   Call Option Values

Figure 5A–4 shows the results: with two years until expiration the call is worth $28.44. The indicated values come from the following calculations:

U: [(0.6578 × $73.33) + (0.3422 × $6.67)]/1.1052 = $45.71

D: [(0.6578 × $6.67) + (0.3422 × $0)]/1.1052 = $3.97

Today: [(0.6578 × $45.71) + (0.3422 × $3.97)]/1.1052 = $28.44

You can value a call for any number of periods and for any size time period using this recursive technique.

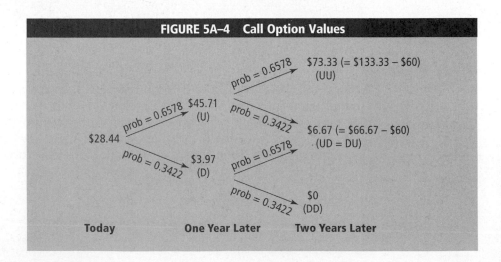

FIGURE 5A–4   Call Option Values

RECOMBINING BINOMIAL TREES

Some binomial trees are *recombining*. In a two-period model this means that the up-down path and the down-up path both lead to the same point, but not necessarily the starting point. Figure 5A–1 shows a tree where the UD and DU paths lead to the same terminal price, a price that happens to be lower than the initial value. A stock that rises by 33% and then falls by 33% does not break even; it loses money, as the figure shows.

In order for a binomial tree to be recombining and return to the initial price, the size of the up jump must be the reciprocal of the size of the down jump (with both jumps in "return relative" percentage terms.[4]) If U is the percentage increase associated with the up jump, then the decrease (D) associated with the down path is 1/U. Suppose, for instance, that U = 1.3333. Then D = 1/U = 1/1.3333 = 0.7500.

Theoretical option pricing is much more complicated if the binomial tree is not recombining. While we can solve simple binomial trees for any kind of jumps, in order to generalize and develop a model for an infinite number of very small periods we need to have a recombining tree. This is also consistent with the risk neutral assumption behind the Black-Scholes model.

ANOTHER EXAMPLE

Let's now use the logic of binomial pricing to solve for the value of a two-year, $60 European call option for the stock in Figure 5A–5. This lattice recombines and returns to the previous price, while the one in Figure 5A–1 does not.

First, we need to solve for the implied probability of the binomial branches. We use equation 5A–3:

$$P_{up} = \frac{e^{rt} - D}{U - D} \tag{5A-3}$$

$$U = 1.3333$$

$$D = \frac{1}{1.3333} = 0.7500$$

$$P_{up} = \frac{1.1052 - 0.7500}{1.3333 - 0.7500} = 0.6089 = 60.89\%$$

$$P_{down} = 1 - P_{up} = 1 - 0.6089 = 0.3911 = 39.11\%$$

Figure 5A–6 shows the results: the call is worth $28.11. The indicated values come from the following calculations:

U: [(0.6089 × $73.33) + (0.3911 × $15.00)]/1.1052 = $45.71

D: [(0.6089 × $15.00) + (0.3911 × $0)]/1.1052 = $8.26

Today: [(0.6089 × $45.71) + (0.3911 × $8.26)]/1.1052 = $28.11

---

[4] A return relative is one plus the return.

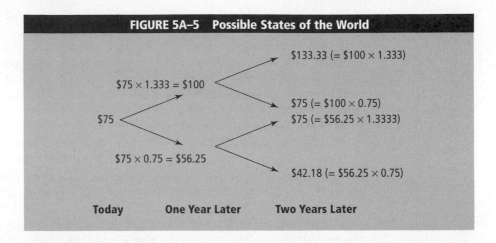

FIGURE 5A–5   Possible States of the World

$75 × 1.333 = $100

$133.33 (= $100 × 1.333)

$75 (= $100 × 0.75)
$75 (= $56.25 × 1.3333)

$75

$75 × 0.75 = $56.25

$42.18 (= $56.25 × 0.75)

Today   One Year Later   Two Years Later

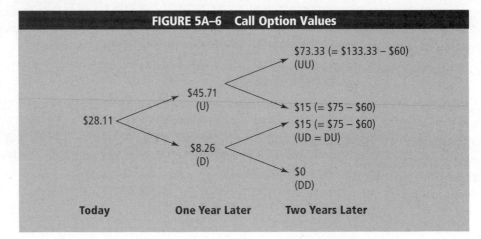

FIGURE 5A–6   Call Option Values

$73.33 (= $133.33 – $60)
(UU)

$45.71
(U)

$15 (= $75 – $60)

$28.11

$15 (= $75 – $60)
(UD = DU)

$8.26
(D)

$0
(DD)

Today   One Year Later   Two Years Later

BINOMIAL PRICING WITH LOGNORMAL RETURNS

In the earlier examples the size of the up and down binomial jumps have been essentially arbitrary. This, of course, is not consistent with a well-functioning market. Security price changes are somehow related to the relative merits of the underlying asset. Another of the assumptions of the Black-Scholes model is that security prices follow a *lognormal distribution*.[5]

---

[5] The behavior of security price returns is a much-studied subject. We know that with a share of stock the price can rise indefinitely while it can only fall 100%. This means that the plot of the return possibilities is actually *skewed to the right*; there are more possible positive outcomes than negative. In other words, the distribution is not symmetric. We also know from empirical studies that with stock returns the tails of the distribution are "fatter" than in a truly normal distribution. Looking at this another way, the high end and the low end of the distribution contain more values than would be expected in a normal distribution. This condition is called *leptokurtosis*. Still, the lognormal assumption does not constitute an especially large departure from reality and is a widely accepted assumption in financial research.

With lognormal returns, you can show mathematically that over a particular period of time the size of the upward movement U equals $e^{\sigma\sqrt{t}}$ where σ = standard deviation of returns per period and t = the time in periods. If the stock price grows at some long-term average periodic rate μ then the probability of an up movement is $P_{up} = \dfrac{e^{\mu t} - D}{U - D}$. However, in our risk neutral world, the expected return on the stock $e^{\mu t}$ equals the expected return on the riskless asset, e^{rt}. Making the substitution gives us equation 5A–3. These results mean that if we know the variance of returns on an asset and the riskless interest rate we can solve for the value of any option on that asset.

As an example, suppose the annual interest rate is 8% and a stock has an annual standard deviation of returns of 0.25. We want to value a one-year, at-the-money $50 call using two six-month periods and the binomial pricing model. In this example, t is half a year, so we determine the following inputs.

$$U = e^{\sigma\sqrt{t}} = e^{(.25)\sqrt{(.5)}} = e^{.1768} = 1.1934$$

$$D = 1/U = 1/1.1934 = 0.8380$$

$$P_{up} = \frac{e^{\mu t} - D}{U - D} = \frac{e^{rt} - D}{U - D} = \frac{e^{(.08)(.5)} - 0.8380}{1.1934 - 0.8379} = 0.5707 = 57.07\%$$

$$P_{down} = 1 - P_{up} = 1 - 0.5707 = 0.4293 = 42.93\%$$

Figure 5A–7 shows the lattice of future stock prices, and Figure 5A–8 shows the corresponding option values.

Because there is only one in-the-money outcome at expiration, you can solve, with continuous compounding, for the value of the call in one step. With continuous compounding,

$$C = \frac{(0.5707)(0.5707)(\$21.21)}{1.0833} = \$6.38$$

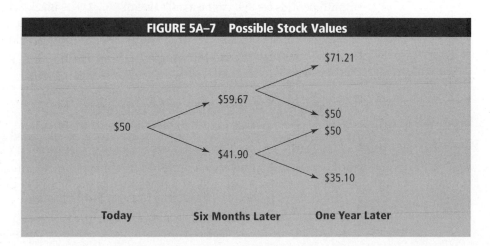

FIGURE 5A–7   Possible Stock Values

$71.21

$59.67

$50

$50

$50

$41.90

$35.10

Today   Six Months Later   One Year Later

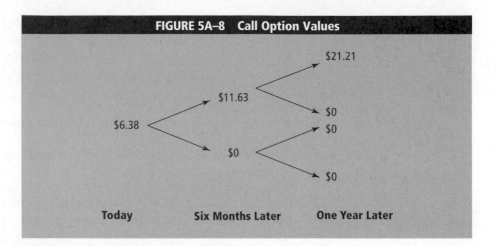

FIGURE 5A–8   Call Option Values

$21.21

$11.63

$6.38

$0

$0

$0

$0

$0

Today   **Six Months Later**   **One Year Later**

Remember that the discounting is continuous. A continuously compounded annual rate of 8% gives a six-month discount factor of $e^{-.08(.5)}$. Now suppose instead of two six-month periods we have four three-month periods. We need to first compute new input parameters:

$$U = e^{\sigma\sqrt{t}} = e^{(.25)\sqrt{(.25)}} = e^{.1250} = 1.1331$$

$$D = 1/U = 1/1.1331 = 0.8825$$

$$P_{up} = \frac{e^{\mu t} - D}{U - D} = \frac{e^{rt} - D}{U - D} = \frac{e^{(.08)(.25)} - 0.8825}{1.1331 - 0.8825} = 0.5495 = 54.95\%^{6}$$

$$P_{down} = 1 - P_{up} = 1 - 0.5495 = 0.4505 = 45.05\%$$

Figure 5A–9 shows the new stock price lattice, and Figure 5A–10 shows the corresponding call option values.

With two six-month periods we found a call value of $6.38. With four three-month periods we determine a call value of $6.72. The Black-Scholes model, using calculus, assumes an *infinite number* of infinitesimally small periods and produces a call value of $6.95.[7] The greater the number of binomial periods, the more accurate the binomial model and the closer the resulting option price will be to the Black-Scholes value.

MULTIPERIOD BINOMIAL PUT PRICING

You can solve for the value of a put using the same binomial pricing logic. Figure 5A–6 shows the value of a two-year $60 call option. To solve for the value of the corresponding put all we need to do is change the terminal intrinsic values, showing them for a put, and work backward just as with call pricing. The branch

---

[6] Note that changing the length of the period also changes the implied branch probabilities.

[7] You can confirm this with the BSOPM file or via the option calculator from the CBOE Option Toolbox.

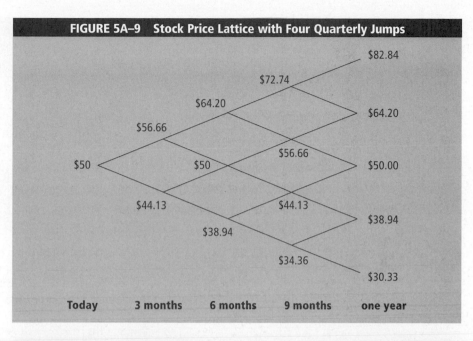

FIGURE 5A–9   Stock Price Lattice with Four Quarterly Jumps

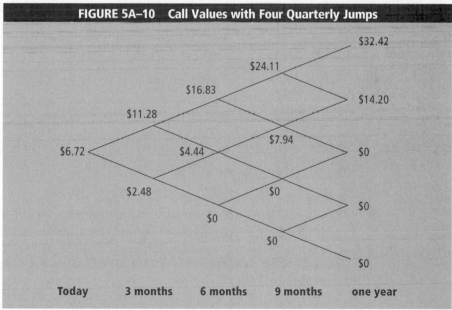

FIGURE 5A–10   Call Values with Four Quarterly Jumps

probabilities do not change. Using the stock prices in Figure 5A–5 we determine the put values in Figure 5A–11:

D: [(0.6089 × $0) + (0.3911 × $17.82)]/1.1052 = $6.31

Today: [(0.6089 × $0) + (0.3911 × $6.31)]/1.1052 = $2.23

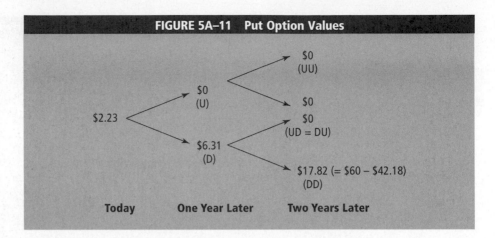

FIGURE 5A–11   Put Option Values

$2.23

$0
(U)

$6.31
(D)

$0
(UU)

$0

$0
(UD = DU)

$17.82 (= $60 − $42.18)
(DD)

Today   **One Year Later**   **Two Years Later**

We find a value of $2.23 for the put. We should get the same answer if we use the put/call parity model with continuous compounding:

$$C - P = S - Ke^{-rt}$$

Rearranging,

$$P = C - S + Ke^{-rt}$$

$$P = \$28.11 - \$75 + \$60\,e^{-(.10)(2)}$$

$$= \$28.11 - \$75 + \$60\,(0.8187) = \$2.23$$

As expected, put/call parity gives the same answer as binomial pricing.

EXPLOITING ARBITRAGE

In the preceding example, with a stock price of $75, a striking price of $60, and an interest rate of 10% we found an equilibrium price of $28.11 for the call and $2.23 for the put. Arbitrage will be present if the options sell for some other price.

Suppose, for instance, the prevailing call price is $29 rather than $28.11. We can lock in the 89-cent differential by constructing a riskless portfolio. Because the call is overvalued, we want to write it. Given the put/call parity formula, if we write the call we need to buy the put, buy the stock, and borrow the present value of the striking price over the two-year period (Table 5A-1).

These activities result in an initial cash inflow of $0.89. Figure 5A–12 shows that regardless of the path the stock takes over the two-year period, the portfolio will be worthless at any terminal point. This is classic arbitrage as we saw earlier in Chapter 5. (It is useful to keep in mind that in any example of this sort, the effect of real-world transaction costs can put the arbitrage out of reach for an ordi-

TABLE 5A–1 Put/Call Parity Arbitrage	
ACTION	**COST**
WRITE 1 CALL	($29.00)
BUY 1 PUT	2.23
BUY 1 SHARE	75.00
BORROW $60e^{-(.10)(2)}$	(49.12)
	($0.89)

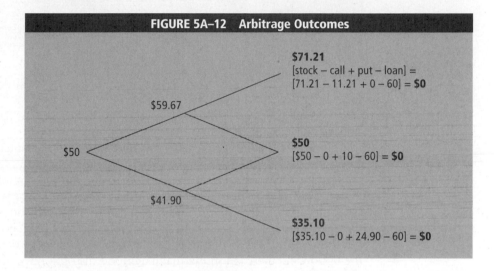

FIGURE 5A–12   Arbitrage Outcomes

$50

$59.67

$41.90

$71.21
[stock – call + put – loan] =
[71.21 – 11.21 + 0 – 60] = **$0**

$50
[$50 – 0 + 10 – 60] = **$0**

$35.10
[$35.10 – 0 + 24.90 – 60] = **$0**

nary retail customer while it remains attractive for an institutional investor or marketmaker.)

AMERICAN VS. EUROPEAN OPTION PRICING

Consider another example based on Figure 5A–5, this time an $80, two-year European put where the current stock price is $75 and the annual interest rate is 8%. Figure 5A–13 shows the value of the put at each node of the tree.

U: [(0.6089 × $0) + (0.3911 × $0)]/1.0833 = $0

D: [(0.6089 × $0) + (0.3911 × $37.82)]/1.0833 = $13.65

Today: [(0.6089 × $0) + (0.3911 × $13.65)]/1.0833 = $4.93

This result provides a good opportunity to get some insight into American versus European option pricing. We just determined the value of a put with an $80 striking price while the stock price was $75. Earlier in this book we saw that

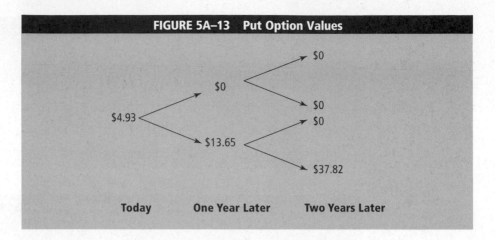

FIGURE 5A–13   Put Option Values

the intrinsic value of a put option is the greater of zero or the striking price minus the stock price. For this put, the intrinsic value is $80 – $75 = $5 yet we solved for an option premium of $4.93. How can this be? In Chapter Two we read that options should not sell for less than their intrinsic value.

The answer is that the basic option relationships in Chapter Two deal with *American* options, those that can be exercised anytime prior to expiration. A *European* option has a limited exercise privilege, being only exercisable at expiration. It seems logical that the option with "more choices" should be worth more than the "one choice only" option, and this is exactly what we find. In this example the $80 put may let you sell stock for $5 more than the stock is currently worth, but it doesn't let you do that now. In fact, you have to wait two years to exercise the option and there is a substantial likelihood the option will finish out-of-the-money.[8]

The key is this: with an American option, the intrinsic value is a sure thing. With a European option the intrinsic value is currently unattainable and may disappear before you can get at it.

---

[8] For the put, the probability of finishing out-of-the-money is the cumulative probability of traveling down the UU, UD, or DU paths. This is (.6089 × .6089) + (.6089 × .3911) + (.3911 × .6089) = .8470, or 84.7%. In other words, there is only a 15.3% chance the option will be worth *anything* at expiration.

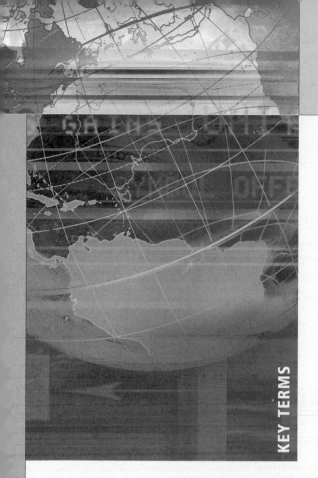

6

The Black-Scholes Option Pricing Model

KEY TERMS you will find in this chapter:

Black-Scholes option pricing model

historical volatility

implied volatility

Merton model

real option

sigma

volatility smile

There exists a passion for comprehension, just as there exists a passion for music. That passion is rather common in children, but gets lost in most people later on. Without this passion there would be neither mathematics nor natural science.

Albert Einstein

The Black-Scholes option pricing model (hereafter BSOPM) has been one of the most important developments in finance in the last thirty years. Because of this model we have a good understanding of the price options should sell for, a fact that has made them more attractive to both individual and institutional investors. Most option analysts use some form of the BSOPM in their decision-making.

THE BLACK-SCHOLES OPTION PRICING MODEL

THE MODEL

We saw this famous model briefly in Chapter 5. Table 6–1 repeats it. This is the basic valuation model for a European call option on a stock that does not pay dividends.

DEVELOPMENT AND ASSUMPTIONS OF THE MODEL

The actual development of the Black-Scholes model is complicated. Its derivation follows steps from physics, from mathematical short cuts, and from arbitrage arguments like those presented in the material on binomial pricing and put/call parity.

Fischer Black had been working on a valuation model for stock warrants, a type of security closely related to call options. After taking a derivative to measure how the discount rate on a warrant varies with time and the stock price, the resulting differential equation reminded him of a heat transfer equation from physics.

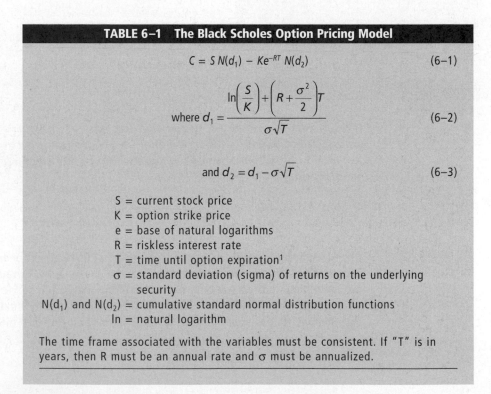

TABLE 6–1   The Black Scholes Option Pricing Model

$$C = S\,N(d_1) - Ke^{-RT}\,N(d_2) \qquad (6\text{–}1)$$

$$\text{where } d_1 = \frac{\ln\left(\dfrac{S}{K}\right) + \left(R + \dfrac{\sigma^2}{2}\right)T}{\sigma\sqrt{T}} \qquad (6\text{–}2)$$

$$\text{and } d_2 = d_1 - \sigma\sqrt{T} \qquad (6\text{–}3)$$

S = current stock price
K = option strike price
e = base of natural logarithms
R = riskless interest rate
T = time until option expiration[1]
σ = standard deviation (sigma) of returns on the underlying security
$N(d_1)$ and $N(d_2)$ = cumulative standard normal distribution functions
ln = natural logarithm

The time frame associated with the variables must be consistent. If "T" is in years, then R must be an annual rate and σ must be annualized.

---

[1] Some authors (including Black and Scholes in their original article) use the expression $(T - t)$ to refer to the time remaining in the option's life. In that usage, the capItal T represents the original life of the option, while the lowercase t indicates how much time has passed since creation of the option. The difference between the two is obviously the time remaining. This book simply uses T to represent time remaining until option expiration.

Myron Scholes joined Fischer Black in working on the problem, and the result is the model used throughout finance today.

While for many option professionals the Black-Scholes model has become a trusted navigational aid, there are some things about the model to keep in mind as you use it. The more you understand about the model, the more adept you will be in options work.

DETERMINANTS OF THE OPTION PREMIUM

We have already seen several factors that influence the option premium. A brief review will be useful.

Market Factors

As shown in the Black-Scholes model, we know six variables that significantly influence the option premium. Because a call option lets you buy at a predetermined striking price, it seems logical that the lower the *striking price* for a given stock, the more the option should be worth. This is exactly what we observe in the financial pages. Table 2–1 shows that as the striking price gets lower for a given company's options, the call option premium goes up.

We have also seen that the more *time* the option has until expiration, the more it is worth. Table 2–1 shows that for both puts and calls, the option premium increases for more distant expirations.

A third factor influencing the call premium is also easy to understand: the current *stock price*. The higher the stock price, the more a given call option is going to be worth. Remember that a primary reason many people buy call options is to benefit from a rise in the price of the stock. If the stock price goes up, so will the value of the call option.

Three other factors influencing the call premium may be less obvious. They are the *volatility* of the underlying stock, the current level of *interest rates* in the economy, and the *dividends* on the underlying security.

In option pricing, a volatility estimate is called *sigma*.

Assets that show price volatility lend themselves to option trading.[2] The greater the price volatility of an asset, the greater its option premium. In the Black-Scholes model, volatility is the annualized standard deviation of returns anticipated in the underlying asset over the remaining term of the option. As elsewhere in finance, what happened in the past is not as important as what is expected to happen in the future. Past volatility can be measured, but future volatility must be estimated. A volatility estimate is called **sigma**, and it is the one variable that cannot be directly observed.

It is possible to look in the financial pages and find options on two different companies where the current stock prices are nearly equal and both companies have, for instance, APR 40 calls. These two options might sell for very different premiums. Because the intrinsic value of an option is a calculated value that does

---

[2] They may also lend themselves to trading in the futures market.

The more volatile a security, the higher its option premium.

not depend on anything other than the current stock price and the option striking price, differences in the premium for these two options must be because of differences in the *time value* of the option. More time means a greater chance of a price change in the underlying asset. Volatility plays a major role in determining time value.

A fifth factor that influences the call option premium is the extent to which the underlying common stock pays *dividends*. This is logical, but speculators often forget it. There is a precise series of events surrounding a corporate dividend announcement. The Board of Directors of the company announces that a certain dollar amount of dividend will be paid on a certain date (the date of payment) to the stockholders as of a certain cut-off date (the date of record). To eliminate uncertainty due to processing time, mail delays, and so forth, in determining exactly who is on the company's shareholder list on the date of record, the brokerage industry uses the *ex-dividend date convention*. The ex-dividend date is two business days before the date of record, and you must buy stock before the ex-dividend date to qualify for the dividend that is about to be paid. People who buy the stock *on* the ex-dividend date do not receive the dividend, and this provides downward pressure on the price of the stock. If it were possible to hold all the other factors influencing stock prices constant, we would expect the value of a share of stock to fall by about the amount of the dividend on the ex-dividend date.

A person who buys a call option does not want the price of the stock to fall, yet the payment of a dividend will necessarily cause the price to fall. The higher the dividend, the more the price will fall. Listed stock options are not adjusted for the payment of a cash dividend. A company that pays a large dividend will have a smaller option premium than a company with a lower dividend, everything else being equal. This is easy to understand if we consider an extreme example where a firm announces its intent to pay a liquidating dividend and go out of business. After payment of this dividend, shares in the firm will be worthless, and so will the associated call options. Anyone who owns these calls and does not exercise them before the last ex-dividend date will lose 100 percent of their investment. Option holders are interested in corporate dividend announcements and in some circumstances will find it profitable to exercise their options before the ex-dividend date.

Listed options are not adjusted for cash dividends.

The sixth factor that influences option premiums is the *risk-free interest rate*. The higher this interest rate, the higher the option premium, everything else being equal. If you review the section on put-call parity you will see why this is the case. A higher "discount rate" applied to the striking price, with all other variables held constant, means that the call premium must rise for the equation to hold.

In sum, the call premium is a positive function of the stock price, time until expiration, expected volatility, and interest rates, and a negative function of the striking price and the dividend.

$$\overset{+\ \ -\ +\ +\ -\ +}{Call\ premium = f(S,\ K,\ T,\ \sigma,\ D,\ R)}$$

DERIVATIVES TODAY

ACCOUNTING FACTORS INFLUENCING THE OPTION PREMIUM

The Options Clearing Corporation adjusts listed options for stock splits and dividends paid in *stock*. The most common event requiring an adjustment is when a firm splits its common stock shares. Two-for-one splits are common; this means that a shareholder who owns 100 shares of stock before the split will own 200 afterward. Similarly, a 4-for-1 split would mean the holder of 100 pre-split shares would have 400 post-split shares. Sometimes the split ratio is not a whole number like 2 or 4. In a 3 for 2 split, the holder of 100 shares would have 150 after the split. Splits of this type are often called *odd-lot generating*, because they result in many people holding shares that are no longer in multiples of 100. Adjustments to the option terms differ depending on whether the split is odd-lot generating.

It is important to recognize that a stock split does not inherently increase the shareholders' wealth. The firm is worth some specific dollar amount, and it does not matter into how many pieces the pie is cut. If you eat one piece of a pie that is cut into four pieces, you have eaten exactly the same amount of pie that you would get had you been given two pieces of a pie cut into eighths. The stock market is not fooled by stock splits. If you own 100 shares of stock worth $50 each and the firm splits 2 for 1, after the split you will have 200 shares worth about $25 each. Your total wealth

has not changed. It remains the same $5,000 that it was before the split.

Suppose you own 1 Microsoft OCT 75 call, and Microsoft then splits two for one. The OCC will dictate the following adjustment to all outstanding options on Microsoft: the striking price would be reduced by the split ratio, and the number of options you own would be increased by the split ratio. You would discover on your monthly brokerage account statement that you now own 2 Microsoft OCT $37\frac{1}{2}$ calls. The dollar amount represented by these two calls is the same as the dollar amount represented by your original single call option.

If Microsoft were to have an odd-lot generating split, say 3 for 2, the adjustment is different. Listed options are only written on multiples of 100 shares; you cannot have an option to buy 50 shares. In this case, the striking price of the option would be reduced by the split ratio (as with the first example). Instead of increasing the number of options you own, the number of shares *covered* by your option would be increased by the split ratio. This means that after the 3 for 2 split you would own 1 Microsoft OCT 50 call[3] giving you the right to buy *150* shares. As before, the dollar amount represented by the call is the same before and after the split.

[3] The new K is $\frac{2}{3} \times \$75$, or $50.

ASSUMPTIONS OF THE BLACK-SCHOLES MODEL

Now that we have seen factors influencing the option premium, let's look at the assumptions of the model and see how much of a departure from reality they constitute.

1. The Stock Pays No Dividends During the Option's Life. The Black-Scholes model assumes that the underlying security pays no dividends during the life of the option. If you try the model on two securities, one with no dividends and another with a 3% dividend yield, the model will predict the same call premium, a result that does not reflect reality. The higher the dividend, the lower the call premium, and the financial pages would most likely not reflect the same premium for these two options.

Many stocks *do* pay dividends, however. This does not mean the BSOPM is useless for these securities. We can make an adjustment to account for the effect of the anticipated dividends over the option's life. One way to do this is to *subtract the discounted value* of a future dividend *from the stock price* used as an input to the model. For instance, if a 50-cent regular quarterly cash dividend will be earned on a $75 stock 90 days from today, you can turn this future value into a present value equivalent, in the same way as in other financial applications. Perhaps the short-term interest rate is 6.10%. The use of the natural logarithm in the BSOPM assumes continuous compounding of interest. We should be consistent in our dividend adjustment, so we will discount the 50 cents continuously as well. Ninety days is 90/365 of a year, or 0.2466. The present value of the dividend payments is then[4] $0.50 $e^{-(.0610)(0.2466)}$ = 0.50×0.985 = $0.49. The adjusted stock price is then $75.00 − $0.49, or $74.51. We would substitute this for S in the list of BSOPM inputs.

An alternative method of adjusting for dividends is the **Merton model**, shown in the Derivatives Today feature on the next page. Both the Merton model and the adjusted stock price heuristic produce similar results. Suppose in this example the option we are considering is an at-the-money $75 call with σ = 30% and 90 days until expiration (90/365 = 0.2466 years). Ignoring dividends, the theoretical Black-Scholes value is $5. With a forthcoming dividend during the option's life, we know the adjusted call premium should be something less than this.

Using the adjusted stock price heuristic, we find a call premium of $4.73:

$$d_1 = \frac{\ln\left(\dfrac{74.51}{75}\right) + \left(0.0610 + \dfrac{0.3^2}{2}\right)0.2466}{0.3\sqrt{0.2466}} = 0.1309$$

$$N(0.1309) = 0.5521$$

$$d_2 = 0.1309 - 0.1490 = -0.0181$$

$$N(-0.0181) = 0.4928$$

$$C = 74.51\,(0.5521) - 75e^{-(.0610)(.2466)}(0.4928) = \underline{\mathbf{\$4.73}}$$

---

[4] It is common practice to discount the dividend from the ex-dividend date rather than from the date of payment. This is because the stock price materially changes on the ex-dividend date. Before that date, the stock comes with the dividend; on that date and after, you are not entitled to the dividend.

THE MERTON MODEL: ADJUSTING FOR DIVIDENDS

Robert Merton, winner of the Nobel Prize in Economics for 1997, developed a simple extension to the Black-Scholes model to account for the payment of cash dividends. The Merton model views the dividends as a continuous stream rather than as discrete payments. Letting d equal this continuous dividend rate,

$$C^* = e^{-dT} SN(d_1^*) - Ke^{-RT} N(d_2^*) \qquad (6\text{-}4)$$

$$\text{where } d_1^* = \frac{\ln\left(\dfrac{S}{K}\right) + \left(R - d + \dfrac{\sigma^2}{2}\right)T}{\sigma\sqrt{T}} \qquad (6\text{-}5)$$

$$\text{and } d_2^* = d_1^* - \sigma\sqrt{T} \qquad (6\text{-}6)$$

The only differences between this model and the classic Black-Scholes model are the slight discounting of the stock price S in Equation 6–4 and reduction of the interest rate R by the dividend yield d in Equation 6–5. Note that if $d = 0$ the Merton model is identical to Black-Scholes.

Using the Merton model,

$$d_1^* = \frac{\ln\left(\dfrac{75}{75}\right) + \left(0.0610 - 0.0267 + \dfrac{.3^2}{2}\right).2466}{.3\sqrt{0.2466}} = 0.1312$$

$$N(0.1312) = 0.5522$$

$$d_2^* = 0.1312 - 0.3\sqrt{0.2466} = -0.0178$$

$$N(-0.0178) = 0.4929$$

$$C = e^{-(0.0267)(0.2466)}75(0.5522) - 75e^{(-0.0610)(0.2466)}(0.4929) = \underline{\$4.73}$$

Dividends paid after option expiration do not affect the option price.

In this instance, the adjusted stock price heuristic and the Merton model give identical answers. When adjusting for dividends, it is important to bear in mind that the only dividends that matter are those that occur over the life of the option. A dividend to be paid after option expiration is immaterial in option pricing.

2. European Exercise Style. Another assumption of the BSOPM is that the option is European style. Unlike American options that can be exercised anytime before their expiration, a European option can only be exercised on the expiration date.

American options are more valuable than European options because the flexibility of exercise is valuable. For ordinary listed options this is not a major pricing consideration, however, because very few calls are ever exercised before the last few days of their life. A person who exercises a call early is essentially throwing away the time value remaining on the call. When you exercise, you recover the intrinsic value, but that is all. Before expiration it makes more sense to simply sell the option, thereby recovering the time value instead of discarding it. Near the expiration date, however, the remaining time value is minuscule and its loss is immaterial.

3. Markets are Efficient. The Black-Scholes option-pricing model also assumes that the stock market is informationally efficient, meaning that people cannot, as a rule, predict the direction of the market or of an individual stock. The theory of put-call parity implies that regardless of whether you are bullish or bearish, you and everyone else will agree on the option premium. You might be absolutely convinced that the market is about to crash, yet theoretically you and the bulls will still agree on the call premium. If this were not so, there would be an arbitrage profit for someone to pick up. As we saw in the section of the last chapter dealing with binomial pricing, the call premium is independent of the expected return on the stock.

Many option traders have trouble with this statement. This assumption does *not* say that everyone is equally ready to buy puts or to buy calls. If you are bullish, you will not be interested in buying puts as a speculation. However, there remains a relationship between the value of puts and calls that we have shown must be true for arbitrage to be absent.[5]

4. No Transaction Costs. Another important assumption of Black-Scholes is that market participants do not have to pay commissions to buy or sell, and do not experience a bid-ask spread. We know this is not true. Even floor traders pay fees that finance the administration and self-regulation of the exchanges. The commissions paid by individual investors are more substantial and can significantly affect the true cost of an option position. All market participants face a positive bid-ask spread, meaning that if you buy a security and immediately sell it, you do so at a loss. These trading fee differentials cause slightly different "effective" option prices for different market participants.

5. Interest Rates Remain Constant. Another assumption is that we have information regarding the interest rate (R) yield curve. It is not necessary that the yield curve be flat, however. Recalling the multi-period binomial pricing model from the Appendix to Chapter Five, we can easily accommodate different interest rates in the various periods. The "risk-free rate" is a common term in finance, but there actually is no such interest rate. It is common to use the discount rate on a U.S. Treasury Bill that has 30 days left until maturity as a proxy for this important interest rate, but even this figure changes daily. During a period of rapidly changing interest rates, the use of a 30-day rate to calculate the value of, for instance, a six-

---

[5] This statement assumes that accurate market information is available; e.g., it is not lunchtime on Black Monday II.

TABLE 6–2   Black-Scholes Assumptions

1. THE STOCK PAYS NO DIVIDENDS DURING THE OPTION'S LIFE
2. EUROPEAN EXERCISE STYLE
3. MARKETS ARE EFFICIENT
4. NO COMMISSIONS
5. INTEREST RATES REMAIN CONSTANT
6. PRICES ARE LOGNORMALLY DISTRIBUTED

---

month option would not be advisable. There are many people who spend much time looking for ways to value options when the parameters of the traditional Black-Scholes model are unknown or are dynamic.

6. *Prices Are Lognormally Distributed.* The model also assumes that the logarithms of the underlying security prices are normally distributed. This is a reasonable assumption for most assets on which options are available.

INTUITION INTO THE BLACK-SCHOLES MODEL

In the throwing dice example of Chapter 5 we saw that the valuation equation has two parts, one giving a "pseudo-probability" weighted expected stock price (an inflow) and another giving the time-value of money adjusted expected payment at exercise (an outflow). In similar fashion we can partition the Black-Scholes model (Figure 6–1).

The value of a call option then, is the difference between the expected benefit from acquiring the stock outright and paying the exercise price on expiration day.

We know that at expiration calls are valuable if the stock price is higher than the option striking price. We also know that the higher the volatility of the underlying security, the greater the likelihood that the security will reach a distant striking price. This is the primary reason that option models are so sensitive to the estimate of volatility used in the model and the reason why many analysts in the securities business make a career of studying volatilities.

FIGURE 6–1   Partitioning the Black-Scholes Model

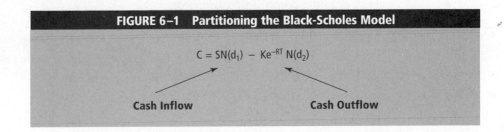

$$C = SN(d_1) - Ke^{-RT} N(d_2)$$

Cash Inflow   Cash Outflow

RHUMBLINE ADVISORS

"On the chilly Monday morning of September 23, 1996, the three most senior executives of RhumbLine Advisors strode nervously into the downtown Boston boardroom of the Massachusetts Pension Reserve Investment Management Board. They were there to explain to the state's overseer of $25 billion in pension funds how RhumbLine had managed to lose $11.8 million for the board's Pension Reserve Investment Trust, or PRIT, on a $230 million enhanced index account designed to carry minimal risk. . . . In addition to PRIT's options-related losses, AT&T Corp.'s pension fund, then the largest in the country, had lost an astonishing $150 million on a pair of accounts with a nominal value of $315 million.

"The SEC's portrayal of (the chief investment officer's) actions at Rhumb-Line is the now-familiar tale of an undersupervised trader who makes some bad bets, then doubles down in a vain effort to win back his losses, only to lose far more. AT&T and PRIT had authorized him to write hedged options contracts on the Standard & Poor's 100, or OEX, and S&P 500, or SPX, indexes that would carry little risk and generate modest premium income to augment an indexing strategy."

"But the SEC says that the clients put strict limits on (the investment officer's) activities, prohibiting him from writing unhedged or in-the-money options and limiting the volume of contracts he could write. When a soaring stock market damaged (his) positions in

1995, the SEC charges, he surreptitiously exceeded both AT&T's and PRIT's trading limits. And in the AT&T account, the SEC alleges, he began writing unhedged, in-the-money options worth hundreds of millions of dollars on volatile technology indexes, hiding the results as the losses mounted."[6]

"The Commission found that the CIO was able to place unauthorized trades because the adviser failed to respond to 'red flags,' and did not have procedures to monitor the CIO's trading or his reporting of performance. The order further notes that the adviser had no policies or procedures designed to detect unauthorized trading in the clients' options accounts, and the adviser's president allowed the CIO to exercise complete control over all aspects of the firm's options trading program, including calculating and reporting the accounts' performance. According to our order, the president relied exclusively on unverified oral reports from the CIO to monitor the program."[7]

Subsequently, both RhumbLine and its CEO settled with the SEC, paying fines, without confirming or denying charges of failure to supervise. The action essentially precludes the former Chief Investment Officer of RhumbLine from further work in the investment advisory business.

[6] Jack Willoughby, "Out of Options," *Institutional Investor*, April 1999, 36–43.

[7] Remarks by Paul F. Roye, Director, Division of Investment Management, U.S. Securities and Exchange Commission, before the Investment Counsel Association of America, Scottsdale, Arizona, April 23, 1999.

CALCULATING BLACK-SCHOLES PRICES FROM HISTORICAL DATA

While most analysts will never have to actually calculate an option price by hand, it is a useful exercise to do it during your training. As stated previously, you do not want any option pricing model to become a black box where you merely input data and take values out. A worked-out example may help prevent that at a later time.

CALL VALUES

To calculate the theoretical value of a call option using the Black-Scholes option pricing model, we need to know the following: the stock price, the option striking price, the time until option expiration, the riskless interest rate, and the volatility of the stock as measured by the standard deviation (or variance) of return on the stock.

Suppose before the market opened on August 24, 2000, we were interested in the theoretical value of a Microsoft OCT 70 call option. Microsoft closed at $70¾ on August 23rd. There were 58 days between August 24, 2000, and the third Friday of October, 2000; Microsoft paid no dividends. Over the Internet, at *http://quote.yahoo.com*, we downloaded the historical Microsoft price information in Table 6–3.

We have the current stock price (70¾), the striking price (70), and the time until expiration (58 days, or 58/365 = 0.1589 year). We still need the interest rate and the stock volatility. The interest rate we can obtain from the "Money Rate" section of the *Wall Street Journal*, or from various Internet sites. Ideally, we want

TABLE 6–3 Microsoft Month-End Stock Prices			
DATE	**CLOSE**	**DATE**	**CLOSE**
Aug-98	47.9688	Aug-99	92.5625
Sep-98	55.0312	Sep-99	90.5625
Oct-98	52.9375	Oct-99	92.5625
Nov-98	61	Nov-99	91.0469
Dec-98	69.3438	Dec-99	116.75
Jan-99	87.5	Jan-00	97.875
Feb-99	75.0625	Feb-00	89.375
Mar-99	89.625	Mar-00	106.25
Apr-99	81.3125	Apr-00	69.75
May-99	80.6875	May-00	62.5625
Jun-99	90.1875	Jun-00	80
Jul-99	85.8125	Jul-00	69.8125

Source: http://quote.yahoo.com

a Treasury bill rate for a maturity that is reasonably close to the remaining life of the option. We find the rate to be 6.10%

Determining the volatility is the most involved part of the exercise. To do this, we might use historical data like those of Table 6–3. It is volatility of *returns* that matter, and the Black-Scholes model assumes the natural logarithms of these returns come from a normal distribution. This means that once we have the returns, we need to take their logarithms and look at the standard deviation of this revised series of numbers. We can prepare a worksheet like Table 6–4 to aid in doing this chore.

We calculate return relatives on a non-dividend paying stock by simply dividing the price for each month by the preceding month's price. We have monthly

TABLE 6–4 Microsoft Stock Return Worksheet			
DATE	CLOSE	RETURN RELATIVE	LN RETURN RELATIVE
AUG-98	47.9688		
SEP-98	55.0312	1.1472	0.1373
OCT-98	52.9375	0.9620	−0.0388
NOV-98	61	1.1523	0.1418
DEC-98	69.3438	1.1368	0.1282
JAN-99	87.5	1.2618	0.2326
FEB-99	75.0625	0.8579	−0.1533
MAR-99	89.625	1.1940	0.1773
APR-99	81.3125	0.9073	−0.0973
MAY-99	80.6875	0.9923	−0.0077
JUN-99	90.1875	1.1177	0.1113
JUL-99	85.8125	0.9515	−0.0497
AUG-99	92.5625	1.0787	0.0757
SEP-99	90.5625	0.9784	−0.0218
OCT-99	92.5625	1.0221	0.0218
NOV-99	91.0469	0.983626199	−0.0165
DEC-99	116.75	1.282306152	0.2487
JAN-00	97.875	0.838329764	−0.1763
FEB-00	89.375	0.913154534	−0.0909
MAR-00	106.25	1.188811189	0.1730
APR-00	69.75	0.656470588	−0.4209
MAY-00	62.5625	0.896953405	−0.1088
JUN-00	80	1.278721279	0.2459
JUL-00	69.8125	0.87265625	−0.1362

VARIANCE OF MONTHLY LOGRETURNS = 0.0268
ANNUAL VARIANCE OF MONTHLY LOGRETURNS = 12 × 0.0268 = 0.3216
ANNUAL STANDARD DEVIATION OF LOGRETURNS* = 0.5671

*Because these are sample returns, we use n–1 weighting in calculating the standard deviation.

price observations for 24 periods, and because it takes two price observations to yield one return, we have 23 monthly returns. The mean of these logreturns is simply the sum of them divided by 23.

Annual variance is different from daily, weekly, or monthly variance.

We could go through the exercise of calculating the variances by hand, but almost certainly the option analyst is going to let a computer spreadsheet software package do that. A computer or a handheld calculator will show that variance of these logreturns is 0.0268. At this point there is an easy mistake to make. Annual variance is different from daily, weekly, or monthly variance. The use of natural logarithms assumes continuous compounding, and the raw stock prices are taken monthly. The estimate of variance from Table 6–4 needs to be multiplied by 12 to convert our monthly estimate into an annual estimate. The annual variance of return is 12×0.0268, or 0.3216. The square root of this is 0.5671, and this is the variable we need for the Black-Scholes OPM. Now we are ready to solve for the value of the call.

$$d_1 = \frac{\ln\left(\dfrac{S}{K}\right) + \left(R + \dfrac{\sigma^2}{2}\right)T}{\sigma\sqrt{T}} \tag{6-2}$$

$$d_2 = d_1 - \sigma\sqrt{T} \tag{6-3}$$

$$d_1 = \frac{\ln\left(\dfrac{70.75}{70}\right) + \left(0.0610 + \dfrac{0.5671^2}{2}\right)0.1589}{0.5671\sqrt{0.1589}}$$

$$= 0.2032$$

$$d_2 = 0.2032 - 0.2261 = -0.0229$$

To get the standard normal values we need a probability table or a spreadsheet program with a preprogrammed standard normal distribution function like the NORMSDIST function in Microsoft Excel. In this example, $N(0.2032)$ is 0.5805 and $N(-0.0229) = 0.4909$.

$$N(0.2032) = 0.5805$$

$$N(-0.0229) = 0.4909$$

$$C = 70.75\,(0.5805) - 70e^{-(.0610)(.1589)}\,(0.4909)$$
$$= \$7.04$$

Based on the input information, these call options should sell for about $7^{1}/_{16}$.

In fact, on August 23rd, the MSFT OCT 70 call closed at $4^{7}/_{8}$. Before concluding the call is severely undervalued and buying as many of them as we can, we should investigate a bit further. One thing we might logically check is whether or not put/call parity seems to be violated.

Rearranging the put/call parity formula to solve for the put value, $P = C - S + Ke^{-RT}$. Substituting, $P = 4.875 - 70.75 + 70e^{-(.061)(.1589)} = \$3.45$. At the market close on the 23rd the OCT 70 put sold for $\$3^1/2$. This is within a nickel of the theoretical value. The market seems to know something we don't.

Microsoft is a very actively traded stock with a deep, highly liquid market for near-term options. The put/call parity relationship holds, yet the call premium is inconsistent with our Black-Scholes calculations. What can be wrong? If we go back and review the input data, there is not much that *can* be wrong. We can observe the stock price, the striking price, the days until expiration, and the fact that Microsoft pays no dividends. All this is unambiguous. The interest rate yield curve was pretty flat in August 2000 so there is not much uncertainty about this variable. In option pricing, the one thing we cannot directly observe is the volatility; we have to estimate this value. We used the past two years of monthly returns to determine sigma, but this may not be what the marketplace is doing.

Further, the volatility that matters is the volatility of the underlying asset *over the option's life*. We cannot observe future stock price behavior; we have to estimate it. The volatility input in the BSOPM is an unobservable statistic. Two analysts, each using a different estimate, will determine a different theoretical option value.

Given that our calculated theoretical value differs significantly from the actual premium we must be using a different estimate of sigma than the rest of the market. Our next task is to determine what estimate the rest of the market *is* using (Derivatives Today below).

ESTIMATING VOLATILITY

In option pricing, the volatility that matters is the future volatility that will occur over the option's life. While we often use historical volatility to get some estimate of future volatility, we need to be very careful when doing so.

The Microsoft example uses volatility based on monthly closing prices from the past two years. An analyst may feel that things have changed so much with Microsoft that the data from two years ago are stale and not indicative of the future. Instead, this particular analyst currently estimates future volatility on Microsoft by using the most recent 32 observations of *daily* data. In a calendar year, taking out Saturdays, Sundays, and holidays, there are about 252 days when the market is open. The analyst annualizes the daily variance by multiplying by 252.

On August 24, 2000, the analyst determines that the daily variance from the previous 32 trading days was 0.000455. (These data also come from a quick *http://quote.yahoo.com* download into an Excel spreadsheet.) Multiplying this by 252, he finds an annual variance of 0.114660. Taking the square root, we have sigma, the Black-Scholes input variable: 0.3386, or **33.86%**.

IMPLIED VOLATILITY

The BSOPM is very sensitive to the volatility of the underlying asset. Professional option traders spend a good deal of time revising estimates of volatility as market conditions change. An important first step in this process is calculating the volatility that is *implied* in the market price of the call using Black-Scholes. In other words, instead of solving for the call premium, *assume the market-determined call premium is correct* and solve for the volatility that makes the equation hold. This value is called the **implied volatility**.

> Implied volatility is the value of sigma that causes the pricing model call premium to equal the actual call premium.

CALCULATING IMPLIED VOLATILITY

In Table 6–1 sigma (the standard deviation estimate) enters the model several times. Unfortunately, sigma cannot be conveniently isolated in the equation such that we can solve for it. We have to solve for sigma using a trial and error, or iterative, process. Taking the other variables (stock price, striking price, interest rate, and time until expiration) as given, we estimate a value for sigma and see what call premium the model gives us. We then compare this premium with the market-determined premium. If the BSOPM gives us a premium that is too high, we know that the implied volatility is lower than our estimate, so we reduce our estimate and try again. We continue revising our estimate until we arrive at a BSOPM call premium that equals the current price. Once we find this value, it is the implied volatility.

The Options Calculator with the CBOE Options Toolbox[8] is a very convenient means of calculating implied volatility. You can also use the BSOPM file available at the website (*http://swcollege.strong.com*) for this textbook. For the MSFT OCT 70 call, we find the implied volatility[9] is 35.75%.

This is quite different from the 57% value calculated from the data in Table 6–4. Perhaps the market does not believe the past two years of monthly return data are representative of likely future volatility. This seems like a reasonable conclusion. In early 2000 Microsoft was doing battle with the U.S. Department of Justice regarding its alleged monopoly position in the computer software business. From March to April 2000 the stock fell about 42%. A jump of this size will significantly influence the calculated standard deviation.

Note that the implied volatility value of 35.75% is much closer to the historical volatility value of 33.85% from the most recent 32 trading days. This is further evidence that, at least for Microsoft, data from the more recent past may be more useful than data from the distant past.

When the market becomes unusually volatile, option premiums increase substantially. As an example, consider the Standard and Poor's 100 index (ticker OEX). This is a broad measure of market activity on which very popular put and

---

[8] *http://www.cboe.com/tools/optcalcu.htm*

[9] This was the value on August 23, 2000. Implied volatility is not a constant, however, and changes daily.

call options trade. One month *before* the stock market crash in October 1987, 30-day, near-the-money calls on this index had an implied annual volatility of 23%. One month *after* the crash, similar calls had an implied annual volatility of 41%. A change in volatility of this magnitude translates into about a 70 percent increase in the premium for a one-month, at-the-money option. In August 2000 implied volatility in the OEX was about 18%.

AN IMPLIED VOLATILITY HEURISTIC

For an exactly at-the-money call option, with sophisticated mathematics you can show that Equation 6–7 will give the correct value of implied volatility.

$$\sigma_{implied} = \frac{0.5(C+P)\sqrt{2\pi / T}}{K / (1+R)^T} \tag{6-7}$$

Suppose an at-the-money call option has sixty days until expiration, a striking price of $50, the riskfree interest rate is 5 percent, and volatility is 0.20. Theoretical Black-Scholes premiums are $1.82 for the call and $1.42 for the put. The volatility implied in these premiums is naturally 0.20, the input value.

Substituting in Equation 6–7, we find the same result:

$$\sigma_{implied} = \frac{0.5(1.82+1.42)\sqrt{2\pi / (60/365)}}{50/(1.05)^{60/365}}$$

$$= \frac{1.62\sqrt{38.22}}{49.60} = 0.20$$

If the stock price does not equal the option striking price Equation 6–7 will not be exact, but it will usually be pretty close. Consider our Microsoft example. The stock price is $70¾ while the actual market prices of the call and put were $4¾ and 3½, respectively. Plugging these values into Equation 6–7, we find

$$\sigma_{implied} = \frac{0.5(4.75+3.50)\sqrt{2\pi / (58/365)}}{70/(1.0610)^{58/365}} = 37.41\%$$

This compares favorably to the actual implied volatility value of 35.75%.

HISTORICAL VERSUS IMPLIED VOLATILITY

The volatility from a past series of prices is an **historical volatility**. This statistic is very useful, and many option traders follow it. It cannot, however, capture recent developments that may portend major changes in market conditions. Implied volatility gives some indication of what the market thinks about likely volatility in the future.

TRADING STRATEGY

CHRISTMAS TREE VOLATILITY SPREAD

Britta Katrina has been following the stock of Ciena (*CIEN, Nasdaq*). Lately, this stock has been very volatile, with the volatility manifesting itself in substantial option premiums. On December 22nd the stock closed at $77, and, using the options calculator from the CBOE Options Toolbox, she finds the implied volatilities/premiums in the table below. She expects implied volatility to decline in the next few days from the current level of about 120% to the 90% range.

OPTION	PREMIUM	IMPLIED VOLATILITY	PREMIUM AT **90%** VOLATILITY
JAN 60 CALL	$20	120%	$18.50
JAN 80 CALL	$9^3/_8$	126%	$6.38
JAN 90 CALL	$5^1/_2$	118%	$3.30

Britta decides to speculate on a decline in volatility by constructing a long call *Christmas tree spread*. This involves being long one call, writing one call with a much higher striking price, and writing another call with an in-between striking price.[10] At current prices, this would cost $20 – $9^3/_8$ – $5^1/_2$ = $5^1/_8$. If she is correct and implied volatility falls to 90% without much passage of time, the value of the spread would be $18.50 – 6.38 – 3.30 = $8.82. This is a 72% increase, before trading fees.

[10] She could also do this with puts by going long a put with a high striking price and selling two different puts with lower striking prices.

Strong and Dickinson explored this topic with a research project ultimately published in the *Financial Analysts Journal*.[11] They considered near-the-money options on the OEX index over the period December 1983—December 1988. The options had an average remaining life of 48 days. The study used regression analysis on current and historical OEX data to predict OEX implied volatility one month later. In other words, given current implied volatility, past measures of implied volatility, and various measures of historical volatility, what is the best regression model to predict implied volatility next month?

Although predictive power increased slightly with the inclusion of more variables, the best regression model[12] needed just two independent variables: last month's implied volatility and historical volatility over the past month. Table 6–5 shows the statistics. The study found "clear evidence of a relation between the standard deviation of returns over the past month and the current level of implied volatility." The most important conclusion was that the current level of implied volatility "appears to contain both an *ex post* component based on actual past volatility and an *ex ante* component based on the market's forecast of future

[11] Robert A. Strong and Amy Dickinson, "Forecasting Better Hedge Ratios," *Financial Analysts Journal*, Jan/Feb 1994, 70–72.

[12] R-squared was 82.79%.

TABLE 6–5   Implied Volatility Regression Models

VARIABLES

H_{10} = HISTORICAL VOLATILITY FROM PAST TEN TRADING DAYS
H_{-1} = HISTORICAL VOLATILITY FROM PAST MONTH
H_{-2} = HISTORICAL VOLATILITY FROM PAST TWO MONTHS
H_{-3} = HISTORICAL VOLATILITY FROM PAST THREE MONTHS
I_{0} = CURRENT LEVEL OF IMPLIED VOLATILITY
I_{-1} = IMPLIED VOLATILITY ONE MONTH AGO
I_{-2} = IMPLIED VOLATILITY TWO MONTHS AGO
I_{-3} = IMPLIED VOLATILITY THREE MONTHS AGO

REGRESSION MODELS FOR IMPLIED VOLATILITY AS A DEPENDENT VARIABLE

R SQUARED	VARIABLE(S) IN MODEL
	ONE INDEPENDENT VARIABLE
11.07%	I_{-3}
23.95	I_{-2}
42.92	H_{-3}
45.36	I_{-1}
49.42	H_{-2}
55.32	H_{10}
67.43	H_{-1}
	TWO INDEPENDENT VARIABLES (BEST MODEL)
82.79	I_{-1}, H_{-1}
	THREE INDEPENDENT VARIABLES (BEST MODEL)
84.97	I_{-1}, H_{-1}, H_{-2}
	FOUR INDEPENDENT VARIABLES (BEST MODEL)
85.40	$I_{-1}, I_{-3}, H_{-1}, H_{-2}$
	FIVE INDEPENDENT VARIABLES (BEST MODEL)
85.49	$I_{-1}, I_{-2}, I_{-3}, H_{-1}, H_{-2}$
	SIX INDEPENDENT VARIABLES (BEST MODEL)
85.57	$I_{-1}, I_{-2}, I_{-3}, H_{-1}, H_{-2}, H_{-3}$
	SEVEN INDEPENDENT VARIABLES
85.61	$I_{-1}, I_{-2}, I_{-3}, H_{-1}, H_{-2}, H_{-3}, H_{10}$

There is evidence that implied volatility contains both an ex-ante and an ex-post components.

variance." This suggests that analysts are wise to look at both historical and implied volatility measures.

PRICING IN VOLATILITY UNITS

Because volatility influences the option premium so profoundly, using dollars to directly compare option premiums on different underlying assets can be a problem. Consider the information in Table 6–6. These call options are all near-the-money, with expirations in October, November, or December. For the equity

TABLE 6–6 Implied Volatility Values (August 25, 2000)				
Underlying Asset	**Closing Value**	**Call Option**	**Premium**	**Implied Volatility (%)**
EQUITY OPTIONS				
Microsoft	$70^5/_8$	OCT 70	6	48.7
General Motors	$71^7/_{16}$	DEC 70	$6^7/_8$	34.7
Delta Air Lines	$49^9/_{16}$	OCT 50	2	25.5
Ciena	$197^{15}/_{16}$	OCT 200	$22^1/_4$	72.3
Home Depot	$50^1/_2$	NOV 50	$4^1/_2$	40.5
Harley-Davidson	49	NOV 50	$3^5/_8$	40.0
Viacom	$69^1/_8$	NOV 70	$6^3/_4$	50.6
Yahoo!	$134^1/_4$	OCT 135	$12^3/_8$	46.1
Cendant	$13^1/_8$	NOV $12^1/_2$	$1^7/_8$	59.2
INDEX OPTIONS				
S&P 100 (OEX)	823.55	OCT 825	$25^1/_4$	17.1
Nasdaq 100 (QQQ)	98.03	OCT 100	$5^5/_8$	39.7
Dow Jones Ind. Avg (DJX)	111.93	OCT 112	$3^1/_8$	27.7

Source: www.cboe.com

options, the premiums range from $1\frac{7}{8}$ for the Cendant NOV $12\frac{1}{2}$ to $22\frac{1}{4}$ for the Ciena OCT 200.

You cannot directly compare the dollar cost of two different options for several reasons. For one thing, options have different degrees of "moneyness." An option that is in-the-money should sell for more than an otherwise equivalent option that is out-of-the-money. Also, a more distant expiration means more time value, so a longer-term option should sell for more than a nearer term one. Finally, the level of the stock price itself makes a difference. An at-the-money option on a $200 stock will sell for considerably more than an at-the-money option on a $20 stock.[13]

Consider the Delta Airlines and Cendant options in Table 6–6. Both have premiums of around $2. An investor who owned both stocks and wrote covered calls against each position might view the respective option premiums as being about equal. There are two problems with this conclusion. First, 100 shares of Cendant only costs $1,312.50, with one call contract bringing in $187.50. One hundred shares of DAL costs $4,956.25, with one call contract bringing in $200. You could buy almost 400 CD for what 100 DAL cost, and 4 CD calls would gar-

---

[13] You can get some intuition into this from put/call parity. Recall that when options are at-the-money, $\frac{C-P}{S}=1-\frac{1}{(1+R)^T}$. The right-hand side remains constant, so as the stock price S increases, C – P must also increase.

ner $750. When you think about the option premium this way it is apparent that the CD option is more expensive, and therefore, a better candidate to write.

The implied volatility statistic tells us this directly. The DAL implied volatility is 25.5%, while that of CD is 59.2%. From this information alone we can conclude that CD options carry more premium than those of DAL. In fact, options users will sometimes denominate their option positions in "sigmas" rather than dollars. You might hear someone say, "Did you see the Ciena OCT 200 calls? They are going for 72%." At any given time we can easily find the volatility of the "average" stock as represented by some market measure. Table 6–6 shows three popular indexes with option users, the OEX (S&P 100), QQQ (Nasdaq 100), and DJX (Dow Jones Industrial Average). Ciena's implied volatility is far more than any of these three measures of the market.

VOLATILITY SMILES

One of the research puzzles in option pricing is the phenomenon known as the **volatility smile**. This is in contradiction to Black-Scholes, which assumes a constant volatility across all strike prices. In fact, you do *not* get the same implied volatility from each of the various striking prices on a given underlying asset. The term "smile" comes from the characteristic curve you get when plotting implied volatility against striking price. Figures 6–3 and 6–4 show August, 2000 volatil-

DERIVATIVES TODAY

THE CBOE VOLATILITY INDEX

It is very helpful to know the average level of implied volatility currently prevailing in the market. One way to do so is to check the CBOE volatility index, ticker VIX, in the financial pages or over the Internet. The value of this index corresponds directly to implied volatility. Figure 6–2 shows the range of this index from September 1995 to May 2001.

FIGURE 6–2   CBOE Volatility Index

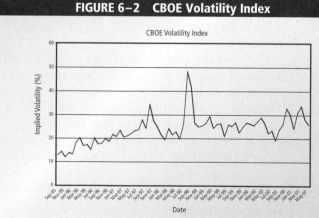

CBOE Volatility Index

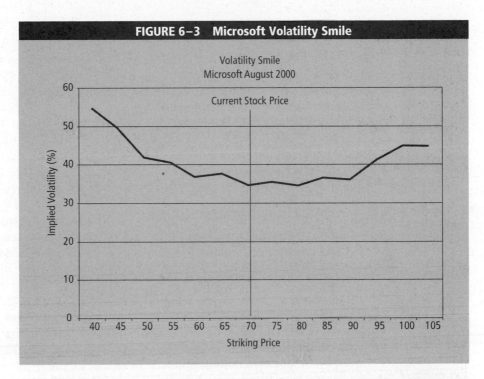

FIGURE 6–3   Microsoft Volatility Smile

Volatility Smile
Microsoft August 2000

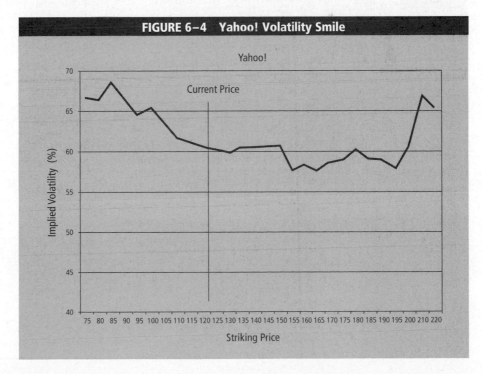

FIGURE 6–4   Yahoo! Volatility Smile

Yahoo!

ROLLING OVER COVERED CALLS[14]

Robert Alan has also been watching the stock of Ciena (*CIEN, Nasdaq*). This fiber optics company had a wild ride during calendar year 2000, moving from about $46 in early January to $180 by March, and over $230 by September. The stock pulled back with the Nasdaq decline in the last quarter of the year, and in late December was below $70. On December 22nd he decided to pull the trigger and buy 100 shares. His trade went off at $67^{19}/$_{32}$. Adding his broker's commission and some minor trading fees, he paid a total of $6,804.63.

While Robert periodically writes calls against stock he owns, he seldom writes the options on the same day he buys the stock. This time, however, he decides to do so; he writes a JAN 77^{1}/$_{2}$ for a premium of $5^{3}/$_{4}$. This option has less than a month to go, is about ten points out of the money, and provides a bit of downside protection. His net receipt from the trade is $529.73.

Mid-day on January 12, 2001, Ciena is trading at $91^{7}/$_{8}$. There is a week left until expiration on January 19th. Robert checks the JAN 77^{1}/$_{2}$ call and finds its ask price to be $14^{3}/$_{8}$. Using the CBOE Options Calculator, he finds that this premium corresponds to an implied volatility of 30%, which he knows from prior investigation is cheap for Ciena. He is thinking about buying this option back and writing a FEB option at a higher striking price if the numbers makes sense. The FEB 95 call is bid at $11^{1}/$_{2}$, corresponding to an implied volatility of 108%. This looks good: buy cheap (30%) and sell expensive (108%). Robert calls his broker to make both trades. He pays a total of $1,482.75 to buy back the JAN call and receives a net of $1,104.71 from the sale of the FEB call.

The stock closed at $88^{7}/$_{8}$ on January 12th. He decides to compare his aggregate option activity with a simple "buy and hold" of the stock.

BUY AND HOLD

CURRENT STOCK PRICE	$8,887.50
PURCHASE PRICE	$6,804.63
GAIN	$2,082.87

OPTIONS ACTIVITY

ACTIVITY	CASH INFLOW	CASH OUTFLOW
BUY 100 CIEN STOCK		$6,804.63
WRITE JAN 77^{1}/$_{2}$ CALL	$ 529.73	
BUY JAN 77^{1}/$_{2}$ CALL		$1,482.75
WRITE FEB 95 CALL	$1,104.71	
TOTAL	$1,634.44	$8,287.38

NET OUTFLOW = $8,287.38 − $1,634.44 = $6,652.94

CURRENT STOCK PRICE	$8,887.50
NET OUTFLOW	$6,652.94
GAIN	$2,234.56

NET ADVANTAGE TO OPTIONS ACTIVITY = $2,234.56 − $2,082.87 = **$151.69**

ROLLING OVER COVERED CALLS (Continued)

As Robert sees it, he is $151.69 ahead at this point. He knows that he still has a short option position in his account and that he has less upside potential because of the call he wrote, but if Ciena stays at $95 or below he will be ahead of the "buy and hold" alternative. If the stock continues to rise he is likely to roll the option over once again.

[14] All figures in this example are real.

ity smiles for Microsoft and Yahoo! While the shape of the smile will vary, you will often find a higher volatility for options that are deep in-the-money or substantially out-of-the-money.

REAL OPTIONS

DERIVATIVES TODAY

A firm might be planning a project potentially involving millions of dollars. If the project is initially successful, the firm would like to have the *option to expand* the scope of the project. It might also benefit from an *option to defer the start* of the project, or an *option to renew*. If the project turns out to be unpromising, it would be nice to have the *option to abandon* the whole thing. These are all examples of **real options**.

Rather than trading on an options exchange, a real option is embedded in some aspect of the business enterprise. A writer in *Forbes* explains real options this way: "When Warner Bros. made Casablanca in 1942 the studio had no idea that television play and later video rentals would produce vast revenue streams running for decades. . . . Video on demand might be a flop, but there is a chance that it will be a bonanza. The value of a share in Viacom or Seagram is in part determined by the value of that particular long-shot option."[15]

Other types of real options include the option to alter the operating scale of a project by expanding, contracting, or temporarily shutting down; the option to switch product mix; and the option to invest in stages.

The theory on real option valuation is still in development. We are not able to price these as accurately as listed options primarily because there is a great deal of subjectivity regarding future event probabilities and potential payouts. The fact remains that something has value if you would rather have it than not have it, and all of the various options described here clearly are something the firm would like to have. There is value there, and analysts know it. Just how much value is not as clear.

[15] Schoenberger, Chana R., "Consider Your Options," *Forbes*, December 25, 2000, 276–278.

USING BLACK-SCHOLES TO SOLVE FOR THE PUT PREMIUM

Having determined the call premium, put/call parity will give us the put premium. It is common practice for option analysts to calculate a theoretical call value using the Black-Scholes OPM, and to use the result to find the arbitrage-free put value.

The Black-Scholes model can be combined with the put/call parity model to yield the put valuation model shown in Table 6–7. Note that interest rates enter the valuation model with a different sign than in the call valuation model. This means that higher interest rates will *reduce* put values, everything else being equal. If the general level of interest rates falls and everything else is held constant, we would expect put values to climb and call values to fall.

Let's calculate a BS put value using the earlier Microsoft data: striking price = $70, a stock price = $70¾, time remaining = 0.1589 year, interest rate = 6.10%, annual standard deviation = 35.75%. Note that this standard deviation is the one implied by the option price, not the one we calculated from historical data.

$$d_1 = \frac{\ln\left(\dfrac{70.75}{70}\right) + \left(0.0610 + \dfrac{0.3575^2}{2}\right)0.1589}{0.3575\sqrt{0.1589}} = 0.2140$$

$$N(-0.2140) = 0.4153$$

$$d_2 = d_1 - \sigma\sqrt{T}$$

$$= 0.2140 - (0.3575)\sqrt{0.1589} = 0.0715$$

$$N(-0.0715) = 0.4715$$

$$P = 70\ e^{-(.0610)(0.1589)}(0.4715) - 70(0.4153) = \$3.62$$

The Black-Scholes put value is about 3⅝. Earlier, we saw that the actual price was 3½.

PROBLEMS USING THE BLACK-SCHOLES MODEL

The Black-Scholes option pricing model does not work well with options that are deep-in-the-money or substantially out-of-the-money. Recall the volatility smile and the fact that Black-Scholes assumes this away. Research also shows that it produces biased values for very low or very high volatility stocks. Both mispricings increase as the time until expiration increases.

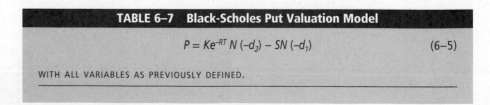

TABLE 6–7   Black-Scholes Put Valuation Model

$$P = Ke^{-RT} N(-d_2) - SN(-d_1) \tag{6-5}$$

WITH ALL VARIABLES AS PREVIOUSLY DEFINED.

Also, under certain circumstances, the model may yield unreasonable values when an option has only a few days of life remaining. The value of either type of option is a strictly decreasing function of time: everything else being equal, the value of an option doesn't go up as time passes. Occasionally the BSOPM will show that the price of a call rises a few cents in the last few days of trading.

For options that are near the money, and usually for options with the next striking price on either side of the stock price, the model works well. The point to remember is that you should always make sure your BSOPM value is reasonable. Do not use it blindly as a black box.

SUMMARY

Research into option pricing shows that there are six important factors determining the value of an option: the stock price, the striking price, the time remaining until the option expires, the volatility of the underlying asset, the dividend paid by the underlying asset, and the level of interest rates.

The Black-Scholes OPM may not yield reasonable values for options that are substantially out-of-the-money, for options that are deep in-the-money, or when there are only a few days remaining until option expiration. In these ex-treme cases it is important to make sure that the indicated option value is reasonable before accepting it.

Sigma cannot be isolated in the Black-Scholes model. By assuming the current option premium is correct, you can solve for the standard deviation that is implied by the current option price. Such a value is an implied volatility. Options users often substitute sigma for dollars in referring to the price of an option.

SELF TEST

T ___ F ___   1. In option pricing, sigma refers to a volatility estimate.

T ___ F ___   2. An option price is influenced more by anticipated future volatility of the underlying asset than by the actual historical volatility.

T ___ F ___   3. Listed options are adjusted for cash, stock, and property dividends.

T ___ F ___   4. A person who is short six call contracts will be short three call contracts if the underlying stock has a two for one stock split.

T ___ F ___   5. The Merton model is a variation of the Black-Scholes model that accounts for dividends on the underlying asset.

T ___ F ___   6. Dividends paid after option expiration do not affect an option's value.

T ___ F ___   7. In general, a European option should sell for more than an American option.

T ___ F ___   8. If you know the riskfree rate, it is not necessary to know the volatility of a stock in order to determine an equilibrium option value.

T ___ F ___   9. Implied volatility is the sigma that comes from an option pricing model if you assume the current option premium is correct.

T ___ F ___   10. Implied volatility is less than or equal to historical volatility.

T ___ F ___   11. There is evidence that implied volatility contains both an ex-ante and an ex-post component.

T ___ F ___   12. The term "volatility smile" refers to the fact that implied volatility is not constant across striking prices.

T ___ F ___   13. The Black-Scholes model does not work well for options that are substantially out-of-the-money.

T ___ F ___ 14. If an option has an unusual striking price such as $43.375 it is probably because the underlying asset recently skipped a cash dividend.

T ___ F ___ 15. An increase in interest rates affects the value of puts and calls differently.

PROBLEMS & QUESTIONS

1. Suppose you look in the newspaper and see that an option has changed price since yesterday, but the stock price has remained the same. Explain three factors that could cause the option premium to change while the stock price remains unchanged.

2. Suppose the general level of interest rates in the economy rises. What affect would this have on call premiums? Why do interest rates matter at all in option pricing?

3. Which is more important, historical volatility or implied volatility, to an options trader, and why?

4. Briefly explain why stock splits do not adversely affect the holder of a stock option.

5. Why do changes in interest rates affect call premiums and put premiums differently?

6. In your own words, explain the "law of one price."

7. Why do dividends adversely affect the value of a call option?

8. Suppose a company *cut* its dividend. Would you expect this to increase the value of a call?

9. Why is the value of a perpetual European put option zero?

10. Suppose you hear someone say, "In calculating historical volatility you get the same answer whether you use logarithms or raw return relatives." Is the person right?

11. Make up an example showing the logical early exercise of a call option.

12. A U.S. government program issues perpetual puts to certain landowners, giving them the right to sell forestland to the federal government at a particular price. Does it make any difference if the options are American or European style?

13. In the Outback Steakhouse "Notice of Annual Meeting of Stockholders to be Held on April 27, 2000," we find the following statement in the section on Director's Compensation:

> "Generally, upon election to the Board, each director who is not an executive officer is granted a one-time stock option to acquire 45,000 shares of Common Stock. The exercise price for such shares is equal to the closing sale price of the Common Stock as reported on the Nasdaq National Market System on the date of grant."

Assume you have been asked to join this Board of Directors and want to estimate the current value of this director perquisite. Show your steps and calculate the value of this employee stock option.

14. When a firm borrows money by issuing bonds, the bondholders effectively acquire the firm (i.e., its assets) and the shareholders obtain an option to buy it back by paying off the debt. The shareholders have in effect obtained a call option on the assets of the firm.

From the following data, you are required to compute the aggregate market value of the firm's bonds, considering the equity to be the call option on the firm's assets:

- Total Assets: $10 million
- Volatility of Asset Value (annual): 25%
- Equity: $4 million
- Zero coupon bonds issued by the firm (face value): $6 million. These bonds are redeemable at face value after two years.
- Risk free rate of return: 5% per year

If the asset volatility increases to 40%, how will the aggregate market value of the firm's bonds be affected?

15. In the fall of 2000 the Nasdaq stock market initiated phase II of its private placement of equity shares. The offering memorandum was dated November 15, 2000. Nasdaq marketmaking firms were able to purchase shares of stock at $13. In addition, Nasdaq offered warrants for $14 apiece, each of which entitled the holder to convert into one share of common stock during four separate tranches as follows:

Tranche 1: One-year exercise period beginning 6/28/2002 at an exercise price of $13/share.

Tranche 2: One-year exercise period beginning 6/30/2003 at an exercise price of $14/share.

Tranche 3: One-year exercise period beginning 6/28/2004 at an exercise price of $15/share.

Tranche 4: One-year exercise period beginning 6/28/2005 at an exercise price of $16/share.

This means that each warrant permitted the purchase of four shares, one during each of the four tranches. Your boss asks you to estimate the volatility implied in the warrant pricing structure. (You recall that Black-Scholes can be used to price warrants the same way it is used to price call options.)

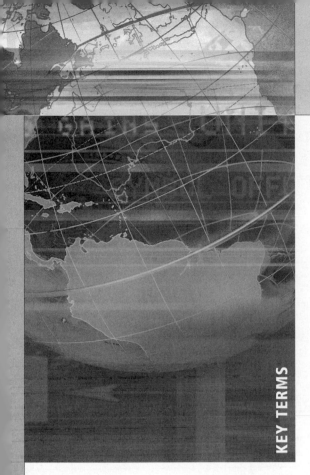

7

Option Greeks

KEY TERMS you will find in this chapter:

delta	position gamma
delta neutrality	position risk
directional market	position theta
gamma	rho
hedge ratio	speed market
kappa	theta
lambda	vega
position delta	

Tactics not mated to strategy lead to consequences unintended.

Gary Kasparov
World Chess Champion

The previous chapter showed how the Black-Scholes option pricing model is useful in determining the value of a put or call option. *Delta*, *gamma*, *theta*, *vega*, and *rho* are partial derivatives of the BSOPM, each with respect to a different variable. Delta, gamma, and theta, in particular, are central to modern portfolio risk management. Delta is the best known and most versatile of these values.

THE PRINCIPAL OPTION PRICING DERIVATIVES

DELTA

When option traders or analysts get together, you will almost certainly hear someone use the term **delta** during the conversation. Delta is an important by-product

167

of the Black-Scholes model, providing particularly useful information to those people who use options in portfolios. There are three common uses of delta.

MEASURE OF OPTION SENSITIVITY

The mathematical definition of delta is the change in option premium expected from a small change in the stock price, *ceteris paribus*. Symbolically, for a call option,

$$\Delta_c = \frac{\partial C}{\partial S} \tag{7-1}$$

where $\frac{\partial C}{\partial S}$ is the partial derivative of the call premium (C) with respect to the stock price (S). Similarly, the put delta is the partial derivative of the put premium (P) with respect to the stock price, or

$$\Delta_p = \frac{\partial P}{\partial S} \tag{7-2}$$

Delta is useful because it indicates the number of shares of stock required to mimic the returns of the option. A call delta of 0.75, for instance, means it will act like 0.75 shares of stock. If the stock price rises by $1, the call option will advance by about 75 cents. A put delta of −0.75 means that the put option will decline by about 75 cents if the stock rises by a dollar. For a European option, the absolute values of the put and call deltas will sum to one. That is,

$$|\Delta_c| + |\Delta_p| = 1.0 \tag{7-3}$$

For European options, the absolute values of the put and call deltas sum to 1.0.

This is not exactly true for an American option, but is still a reasonably accurate heuristic. If, for instance, you know the call delta is 0.545, a good estimate of the put delta is 0.545 − 1.0 = −0.455 regardless of the exercise style.

In the Black-Scholes OPM, determination of the call delta is a simple task: it is exactly equal to $N(d_1)$. For a call[1] option, $0 \leq delta \leq 1.0$ because $N(d_1)$, the area under the normal curve, ranges from 0 to 100%. In the example on page 144, we determined a value of 0.5521 for $N(d_1)$, the option delta. This means that for a very small unit change in the underlying stock price, the option would change about 55% as much.

Figure 7–1 shows how an option's delta changes over time for an at-the-money option, an out-of-the-money option, and an in-the-money option, respectively. For an at-the-money option the decline in delta is approximately linear until the last month or so of the option's life, with delta approaching 0.50 at expiration. The delta of an out-of-the-money option approaches zero as time passes, with delta declining more rapidly as time passes. Less time means less likelihood that the option will wind up in-the-money. The option premium eventually drops to zero and stays there, giving a delta of zero. In-the-money options act more and

---

[1] For a put, $−1.0 \leq delta \leq 0$.

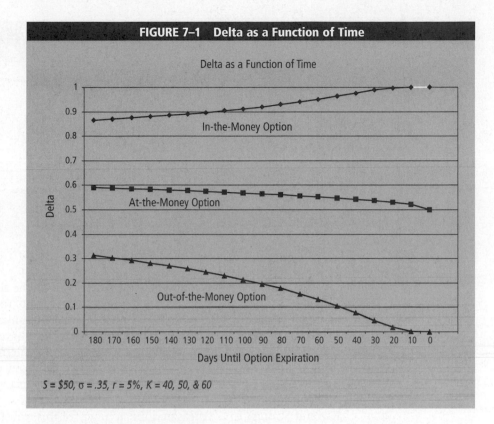

FIGURE 7–1   Delta as a Function of Time

Delta as a Function of Time

$S = \$50, \sigma = .35, r = 5\%, K = 40, 50, \& 60$

more like the stock itself as expiration approaches. Their delta rises as time passes, approaching 1.0 on expiration day.

HEDGE RATIO

Delta is the **hedge ratio**. This value indicates how many units of a particular option are necessary to mimic the returns of the underlying asset. Figure 7–2 shows how delta changes as a call option moves into or out of the money. Suppose a particular call option has a delta of 0.250. A short option position (a written option) has a delta opposite in sign to a long option position. This means that if someone owns 100 shares of the stock, writing *four* of these call contracts would result in a theoretically perfect hedge for small changes in the stock price.[2]

LIKELIHOOD OF BECOMING IN-THE-MONEY

A final use of delta is as a crude measure of the likelihood that a particular option will be in the money on option expiration day. If an option has a delta of 0.45,

[2] The hedge is only perfect for small movements in the stock price. Gamma becomes important for larger changes, as we shall see shortly.

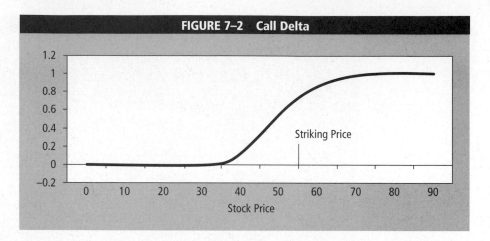

FIGURE 7–2   Call Delta

there is approximately a 45% chance that the stock price will be above the option striking price on expiration day. We saw in the development of the Black-Scholes model that it is actually $N(d_2)$, not $N(d_1)$, that measures the likelihood of exercise of a call.[3] If you want to know the value of $N(d_2)$ you have to calculate it, because this statistic is seldom published or available on the Internet. $N(d_1)$, however, is the delta statistic, and there are numerous convenient sources for this value. The inconvenience of determining $N(d_2)$ probably contributes to the use of delta as a substitute.

Baz and Strong (1997) measured the accuracy of this statistic in a research project published in *Financial Practice and Education*.[4] This heuristic is least accurate for near-the-money, long-term options on volatile stock. In most other circumstances the call delta overstates the probability of option exercise by a few percentage points.

THETA

Theta is a measure of the sensitivity of a call option to the time remaining until its expiration.

$$\Theta_c = \frac{\partial C}{\partial t} \tag{7-4}$$

$$\Theta_p = \frac{\partial P}{\partial t} \tag{7-5}$$

[3] For a put, the likelihood of exercise is $N(-d_2)$.

[4] Jamil Baz and Robert A. Strong, "The Bias in Delta as an Indicator of the Actual Likelihood of Option Exercise," *Financial Practice and Education*, Spring/Summer 1997, 91–94.

Mathematically, theta is greater than zero because more time until expiration means more option time value. We know that everything else being equal, options become less valuable as they approach expiration day. However, because time until expiration can only get shorter, option traders usually think of theta as a negative number. The passage of time hurts the holder of a long option position, so thinking of a long call or a long put as having a negative theta means that theta indicates the decline (i.e., loss) in premium due solely to the passage of time. Conversely, the passage of time is to the benefit of the option writer, so theta is positive for a short call or short put and represents a gain to the option writer. Equations 7–6 and 7–7 show how to calculate theta for a call and a put.

$$\Theta_c = -\frac{S\sigma e^{-.5(d_1)^2}}{2\sqrt{2\pi t}} - rKe^{-rt}N(d_2) \tag{7-6}$$

$$\Theta_p = -\frac{S\sigma e^{-.5(d_1)^2}}{2\sqrt{2\pi t}} + rKe^{-rt}N(d_2) \tag{7-7}$$

These equations determine theta *per year*. It is more convenient to know theta *per day*, as this value indicates how the option price changes with the passage of a single day and is easier to interpret. With a volatility of 0.25 and a riskfree rate of 5%, a 90-day, at-the-money option with a striking price of $45 has a theoretical value of $2.49 and a theta of –5.58. This means it will lose $5.58 in time value over the course of a year. This is not especially helpful information because the option premium is less than half this amount and it expires in three months. Dividing the $5.58 by 365 gives about $0.015, and this result *is* meaningful. This means that at present the option will lose about two cents in time value if you hold it for a day. Hold it for ten days and it will lose about fifteen cents.

Recall the discussion of time value decay in Chapter Four. Time value begins to deteriorate more rapidly as expiration approaches. For this option, theta is $0.03 with 29 days to go, $0.04 with ten days left, and $0.06 at the beginning of expiration week.[5]

GAMMA

Gamma is the second derivative of the option premium with respect to the stock price and the first derivative of delta with respect to the stock price. Gamma is sometimes called *curvature*.

$$\Gamma_c = \frac{\partial^2 C}{\partial S^2} = \frac{\partial \Delta_c}{\partial S} \tag{7-8}$$

---

[5] Determined via the options calculator on the CBOE Options Toolbox.

$$\Gamma_p = \frac{\partial^2 P}{\partial S^2} = \frac{\partial \Delta_p}{\partial S} \tag{7-9}$$

As calls become further in-the-money, they act increasingly like the stock itself. Consider the limiting case of a call option with a striking price of zero, where the underlying stock does not pay dividends. Such a security should behave almost exactly like the stock because it would be an equivalent claim.[6] For options that are out-of-the-money, option prices are much less sensitive to changes in the underlying stock. This means that an option's delta *changes* as the underlying stock price changes. If you recall the variables that go into the determination of $N(d_1)$ in the BSOPM, this relationship makes sense; the value of delta changes when the stock price changes.

Delta changes as the stock price changes.

One use of gamma is a measure of how often option portfolios need to be adjusted as stock prices change and time passes. Options with gammas near zero have deltas that are not particularly sensitive to changes in the stock price, and consequently are more robust. Equation (7–10) shows how to calculate gamma.

$$\Gamma_c = \Gamma_p = \frac{e^{-.5(d_1)^2}}{S\sigma\sqrt{2\pi t}} \tag{7-10}$$

For a given striking price and expiration, the call gamma equals the put gamma.

Gamma is at a maximum when an option is at-the-money and near expiration. Note that for a given striking price and expiration, the call gamma equals the put gamma.

SIGN RELATIONSHIPS

You should memorize the signs for delta, gamma, and theta of the basic option positions in Table 7–1.

The sign of gamma is always opposite to the sign of theta.

The easiest way to remember the sign of gamma is to recognize that, for a given option position, the sign of gamma is always opposite to the sign of theta.

A positive gamma comes from long option positions. A portfolio with a positive gamma becomes more bullish as the underlying price rises (i.e., delta increases) or more bearish as the price declines (delta declines). Negative gammas, conversely, come from short options.

TABLE 7–1　Sign Relationships

	DELTA	THETA	GAMMA
LONG CALL	+	−	+
LONG PUT	−	−	+
SHORT CALL	−	+	−
SHORT PUT	+	+	−

[6] This ignores trivial matters such as voting rights.

DERIVATIVES TODAY

MONITORING THE LEVERAGE RATIO

Bernie Schaeffer, Chairman of Schaeffer's Investment Research and author of *The Option Advisor*, believes that most option speculators "swing for the fences" by selecting options with *too little delta* and *too much leverage*. As we have seen, delta is a measure of how much the price of an option changes with a $1 change in the price of the underlying asset. You can measure an option's leverage by its *leverage ratio*:

$$\text{leverage ratio} = \frac{\text{stock price} \times \text{option delta}}{\text{option price}} \tag{7-11}$$

The equation indicates that leverage is largest when you have a high stock price and an inexpensive option. Schaeffer states that "I've found that when the leverage ratio is much above 10, there is usually not enough time before option expiration for the stock to move above the strike price in any but the rarest circumstances."[7] In essence, the novice option trader's penchant for buying cheap, out-of-the-money options simultaneously puts little money at risk but carries a high likelihood they will expire worthless. Instead, Schaeffer believes options with a leverage ratio in the 3 to 10 range provide the best balance of risk and potential reward.

[7] Bernie Schaeffer, "Out of the Money and Out of the Park," *Bloomberg Personal Finance*, September 1999, 28–29.

OTHER DERIVATIVES

Delta, gamma, and theta are by far the most important of the derivatives of the BSOPM. There are others, however, and an option professional should be familiar with them, even if they seldom influence decisions.

VEGA

Vega is the first partial derivative of the BSOPM with respect to the volatility of the underlying asset. All long options have positive vega.

$$vega_c = \frac{\partial C}{\partial \sigma} \tag{7-12}$$

$$vega_p = \frac{\partial P}{\partial \sigma} \tag{7-13}$$

To my knowledge no one knows where the term *vega* originated. Vega is Alpha in the constellation Lyra, and is one of the twenty brightest stars. Vega is not a Greek letter (though many options folks think it is), and finance people have always had a penchant for Greek letters. Perhaps for this reason, vega is also called **kappa**, or sometimes **lambda**, both of which *are* Greek letters.

Vega is positive for both long calls and long puts. The higher the anticipated volatility of the underlying asset, the higher of the value of the option, everything else being equal. If an option has a vega of 0.30, it will gain 0.30 percent in value for each percentage point increase in the anticipated volatility of the underlying asset. Vega is the same for puts and calls.

Equation 7–14 shows the formula for vega:

$$vega = \frac{S\sqrt{t}e^{-.5(d_1^2)}}{\sqrt{2\pi}}$$
(7–14)

RHO

Rho is the first partial derivative of the BSOPM with respect to the riskfree interest rate. Equations 7–15 and 7–16 show the mathematics.

$$\rho_c = Kte^{-rt} N(d_2)$$
(7–15)

$$\rho_p = -Kte^{-rt} N(-d_2)$$
(7–16)

Rho is the least important of the derivatives. Unless an option has an exceptionally long life, changes in interest rates affect the premium only modestly. As shown by the math in Chapter 6, rho is positive for call options and negative for puts.

Figure 7–3 shows how these various option derivatives vary with the stock price/striking price relationship.

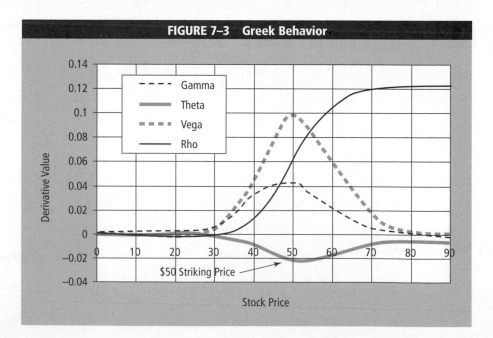

FIGURE 7–3 Greek Behavior

THE GREEKS OF VEGA

There are two derivatives measuring how vega changes. *Vomma* is a measure of how sensitive vega is to changes in implied volatility. The term vomma comes from "volatility of gamma." *Vanna* measures the sensitivity of vega to changes in the price of the underlying asset.[8] These may be important in sophisticated options applications, but are of little importance to the typical option user.

OTHERS

It is also possible to take a derivative of the BSOPM with respect to the striking price, or of the modified BSOPM with respect to a dividend yield. In practice, these statistics are not useful and are very seldom calculated.

POSITION DERIVATIVES

Often a portfolio contains a few different options in addition to shares of the underlying stock. A manager might, for instance, write calls to provide income and also buy puts for downside protection. Regardless of whether the options positions are old or new, each portfolio component has its own delta, theta, and gamma. The sum of the deltas for a particular security is the **position delta**. Similarly, the sum of the gammas is the **position gamma** and the sum of the thetas is the **position theta**.[9]

AN EXAMPLE

Figure 7–4 illustrates the position derivative concept. Here we see a portfolio containing 10,000 shares of stock, with 100 call option contracts written against them, combined with 50 protective puts. The resulting position delta of 7,320 suggests that the total portfolio is equivalent in market risk to 7,320 shares of stock, or 73.2 percent of the risk of the unoptioned portfolio. The position theta of 70 means that if all other variables remain unchanged, the passage of one day will result in an increase of $70 in the value of the portfolio. This is because the decline in the value of the options written will exceed the decline in time value of the puts purchased. Remember the option writer wants time to pass, while the option buyer wants the clock to run slow. The meaning of a position gamma of −180 is less obvious; we will elaborate on this later.

CAVEATS ABOUT POSITION DERIVATIVES

Position derivatives change continuously.

Option derivatives are dynamic; they change with the passage of time or any other of the underlying variables. This means that position derivatives change continuously. A bullish portfolio ($\Delta > 0$) can suddenly become bearish ($\Delta < 0$) if stock

---

[8] For more information on these derivatives, see "Vomma, Vomma, Hey!" by Tim Owens, *Futures and OTC World*, May 1998, 22–25.

[9] The term *position delta* is not generally used to refer to the sum of the deltas on different assets. That is, you would not normally combine deltas on Microsoft and General Motors options.

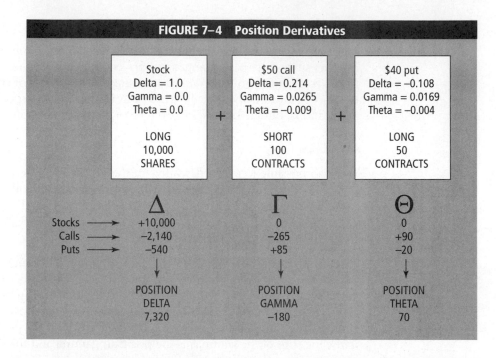

FIGURE 7–4 Position Derivatives

prices change sufficiently. The need to monitor position derivatives is especially important when many different option positions are in the same portfolio.

DELTA NEUTRALITY

We have previously seen that as the price of the underlying security changes, options on the security do not all change in value by the same percentage. Delta measures the extent to which an option premium will change for a given small change in the price of the underlying security.

Certain option strategies are predicated on initial **delta neutrality** of the options portfolio, meaning the combined deltas of the options involved net out to zero. Delta neutrality is an important issue to institutional traders who establish large positions using straddles, strangles, and ratio spreads.[10] A delta neutral strategy is a pure volatility play.

A speculator who buys a straddle, for instance, makes money if the price of the underlying asset moves sharply up or down. A straddle is a neutral strategy: it is neither bullish nor bearish. It is unlikely, however, that the deltas of the put and of the call making up the straddle are equal in absolute value. Consequently, a given percentage rise in the value of the underlying asset will not yield precisely the same result as an equal percentage decline. This means that unless you "weight" the relative proportion of the two types of options appropriately, your

---

[10] Theoretical option pricing models, in fact, assume you are market direction neutral.

straddle position may *not* actually be neutral; it may be unintentionally slightly bullish or bearish. A quick example will help illustrate the situation.

CALCULATING DELTA HEDGE RATIOS

Suppose a stock currently trades at $44, the annual volatility of the stock is estimated at 15 percent, Treasury bills yield 6%, and an options trader decides to write six-month strangles using $40 puts and $50 calls. The two options will have different deltas, so the trader will not write an equal number of puts and calls. To find the proper number to use, it is necessary to calculate the deltas of each option and consider their ratio.

Delta for a call is $N(d_1)$ from the Black-Scholes option pricing model; for a put, delta is $N(d_1) - 1$. Equation 7–17 shows the formula for d_1:

$$d_1 = \frac{\ln\left(\frac{S}{K}\right) + \left[r + \frac{\sigma^2}{2}\right]t}{\sigma\sqrt{t}} \qquad (7\text{--}17)$$

We can now calculate each delta.

$50 call:

$$d_1 = \frac{\ln\left(\frac{44}{50}\right) + \left[0.06 + \frac{0.15^2}{2}\right]0.5}{0.15\sqrt{0.5}} = -0.87$$

$$N(-0.87) = 0.19$$

$40 put:

$$d_1 = \frac{\ln\left(\frac{44}{40}\right) + \left[0.06 + \frac{.15^2}{2}\right]0.5}{0.15\sqrt{0.5}} = -1.23$$

$$N(-1.23) - 1 = -0.11$$

The ratio of these two deltas is $-0.11/0.19 = -0.58$. This means that delta neutrality is achieved by writing 0.58 calls for each put. One approximately delta neutral combination would be to write 26 put contracts and 15 call contracts. To check this simply observe that

$$(-26)(100)(-0.11) + (-15)(100)(0.19) = 1.00$$

This is not materially different from zero.

WHY DELTA NEUTRALITY MATTERS

Neutral option strategies should be established such that they are approximately delta neutral.

The reason for maintaining delta neutrality is simple: strategies calling for delta neutrality are strategies in which you are *neutral about the future prospects for the market*. You do not want to have either a bullish or a bearish position.

Consider another example. In the previous strangle, the position contained $40 puts and $50 calls. Suppose you built the strangle with 100 options of each type. If we use the Black-Scholes model to estimate the prices of the options, we find that the $50 calls would sell for $0.47 each and the $40 puts would sell for $0.26. Writing 100 contracts of each of these would generate immediate income of ($47 × 100) + ($26 × 100) = $7,300.

Now suppose the stock *rises* by 2% to $44.88. The BSOPM prices are $0.18 for the puts and $0.66 for the calls, for a total value of ($18 × 100) + ($66 × 100) = $8,400. Because you wrote the options, your position has *deteriorated* by $1,100. (After you write options, you want their value to decline.)

If, instead, the stock *falls* by 2% to $43.12 the predicted BSOPM prices are $0.37 for the puts and $0.32 for the calls, for a total value of ($37 × 100) + ($32 × 100) = $6,900. In this case the position declines by $400.

Notice that a 2% rise in the stock price did not result in the same dollar change in your portfolio value as a 2% fall. The reason for this is that the original position, short 100 calls and short 100 puts, was not *delta neutral*. For this short strangle, the position delta is

$$(\# \text{ calls} \times \text{call delta}) + (\# \text{ puts} \times \text{put delta})$$

$$= (-100) \times (100) \times (0.190) + (-100) \times (100) \times (-0.110)$$

$$= -800$$

Thus, being short 100 $40 puts and 100 $50 calls is a bearish position, because the position delta is less than zero. We note that when the stock rises by 2%, the dollar change in the value of the portfolio is larger than the dollar change if the stock falls by a similar percentage.

Options, of course, can only be written on multiples of 100 shares. This means that it may not be possible to achieve exact delta neutrality. For institutional investors or arbitrageurs, you can come very close. For these XYZ options, one approximately delta neutral combination is 75 calls and 132 puts. The position delta is $(75 \times 19.0) + (132 \times (-11.0)) = -27$.

Had we written puts and calls in these quantities, we would have received $(75 \times \$47) + (132 \times \$26) = \$6,957$. A 2% rise in the stock price would have caused the option portfolio value to change to $(75 \times \$66) + (132 \times \$18) = \$7,326$. A 2% fall would result in a value of $(75 \times \$32) + (132 \times \$37) = \$7,284$. The dollar changes are not exactly equal, but they are closer than when 100 options each were written.

A gamma near zero means that the option position is robust to changes in market factors.

An option's delta changes as its expiration date approaches, the stock price changes, volatility estimates are revised, or interest rates change. The sophisticated option trader will revise option positions continually if it is necessary to maintain a delta neutral position. Closing a few contracts each day as necessary to keep the position even usually does this. The nearer *gamma* is to zero, the less often this needs to be done.

TWO MARKETS: DIRECTIONAL AND SPEED

Our attitudes toward "the market" usually start with whether we are bullish or bearish. This is the **directional market**. In options applications, however, there is another consideration: how quickly we expect the anticipated move to occur. This is the **speed market**.[11]

DIRECTIONAL MARKET

Delta measures exposure in the directional market. A bullish investor wants to have a positive position delta, because a rise in the value of the underlying asset will result in an increase in the value of the option position. A long position in the underlying asset has a positive delta, as do long calls and short puts. A bearish speculator wants a negative position delta. Negative deltas come from short positions in the underlying asset, from long puts, and from short calls.

SPEED MARKET

The speed market is not a concern to the stock investor, but it can be important to the option speculator. Writing calls and buying puts, for instance, are both bearish strategies; they have negative deltas. If you anticipate a major decline in the value of a particular stock, however, you would stand to earn larger profits from buying puts than from writing calls, because your maximum profit from writing calls is limited to the option premium.

In a fast market, profits are greatest with positive gammas. In a slow market, profits are greatest with negative gammas.

Similarly, in a rapidly advancing market you would benefit from either owning calls or writing puts. Again, your maximum profit is limited to the option income if you write puts. In a *fast, up* market you want to buy calls; in a *fast, down* market you want to buy puts. Notice that both strategies have positive gammas. This is the fundamental rule: In fast markets you want positive gammas. By the same logic, in slow markets you want negative gammas.

COMBINING DIRECTIONAL AND SPEED MARKETS

Ideally, you establish an option position within a framework that considers both the anticipated direction of the market and its speed. Suppose, for instance, that someone is bullish on the market but does not expect a sudden move. Rather, he or she expects gradually increasing prices for the foreseeable future. This person is bullish, so the appropriate directional stand is a positive delta. A slow market means gamma should be negative. What option strategies fit this bill?

Table 7–1 shows that positive deltas come from long calls and short puts, and that negative gammas come from short calls and short puts. So writing puts

---

[11] In this context "speed" refers to how quickly the price of the underlying asset will change. "Speed" can also refer to the *third* derivative of the option premium with respect to the underlying asset. This is not the sense intended here.

TABLE 7–2 Directional and Speed Markets

		Directional Market: Down $\Delta<0$	Directional Market: Neutral $\Delta=0$	Directional Market: Up $\Delta>0$
Speed Market	Slow $\Gamma<0$	Write calls	Write straddles	Write puts
Speed Market	Neutral $\Gamma=0$	Write calls; buy puts	Spreads	Buy calls; write puts
Speed Market	Fast $\Gamma>0$	Buy puts	Buy straddles	Buy calls

may be the most appropriate strategy. Table 7–2 shows the appropriate strategy under the various scenarios.

While a table like Table 7–2 is useful, it should not be taken as gospel. Writing options involves potentially significant risk, and this fact should always be considered before embarking on such a strategy. Simply buying options will not always generate a profit, either. One can choose from many different striking prices and expiration dates, and their relative merits may vary considerably.

Dynamic Hedging

Portfolios need periodic tune-ups.

Delta depends on all the variables that determine the option premium. A consequence of this is that delta frequently changes. Consequently, a position delta also will change as interest rates change, as stock prices change, as volatility expectations change, or as portfolio components change. This means that portfolios need periodic tune-ups (Figure 7–5).

Suppose a portfolio contains 10,000 shares of a particular stock, selling for \$55 per share. Interest rates are 5%, volatility is 0.24, and a \$50 put expires in 88 days. Such a put has a delta of –0.167. Suppose you combine 150 of these put contracts with the stock to provide some protection against a fall in the stock price. After buying these puts the position delta becomes

$$(10{,}000 \times 1.0) + (15{,}000 \times -0.167) = 7{,}495$$

The following day, the stock falls to \$53. The new Black-Scholes delta for the put is –0.256, so the position delta has changed to

$$(10{,}000 \times 1.0) + (15{,}000 \times -0.256) = 6{,}160$$

Overnight, the portfolio has become substantially less bullish because of the changing delta of the put. If the manager wanted to maintain the original delta

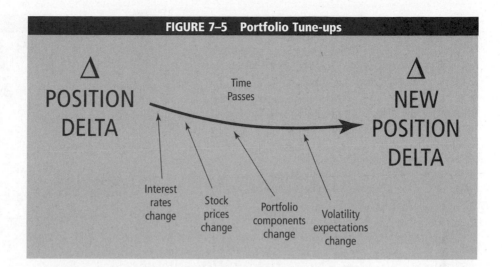

FIGURE 7–5   Portfolio Tune-ups

Δ POSITION DELTA → Δ NEW POSITION DELTA

Time Passes

Interest rates change

Stock prices change

Portfolio components change

Volatility expectations change

exposure of about 7,500, it would be necessary to sell some of the puts, as this would remove negative deltas from the portfolio. The number of puts to sell equals the amount of delta we want to eliminate divided by the delta of one option: $(7{,}500 - 6{,}160)/0.256 = 5{,}234$. Selling about 52 put contracts would maintain the original market exposure.

MINIMIZING THE COST OF DELTA ADJUSTMENTS

Writing options generates income, but involves potentially large losses if prices move adversely. Purchasing options requires a cash outlay, which is a disadvantage, but also results in a known and limited maximum loss to the option buyer. It is possible (and common practice) to adjust a portfolio's delta by using *both* puts and calls to minimize the cash requirements associated with the adjustment.

Suppose that in July a portfolio contains 10,000 shares of this stock and that the portfolio manager decides to reduce the market exposure by half, to a position delta of 5,000. Tax or investment policy considerations make the outright sale of the stock impractical. Assume we have the information shown in Table 7–3.

TABLE 7–3   Initial Conditions

STOCK PRICE = $33
DAYS UNTIL SEPTEMBER EXPIRATION = 66
RISKFREE INTEREST RATE = 5%
IMPLIED VOLATILITY = 0.31
PREMIUM OF SEP 35 CALL = $1.06
DELTA OF SEP 35 CALL = 0.377
PREMIUM OF SEP 30 PUT = $0.50
DELTA OF SEP 30 PUT = −0.196

TABLE 7–4   Simultaneous Equations

LET   C = NUMBER OF CALLS
          P = NUMBER OF PUTS

EQUATION 1: STOCK DELTA − CALL DELTA + PUT DELTA = 5,000
$$10,000 - 0.377C + (-0.196P) = 5,000 \tag{1}$$

EQUATION 2: PRICE OF PUTS − INCOME FROM CALLS = 0
$$\$0.50P - \$1.06C = \$0 \tag{2}$$

SOLVE FOR P IN TERMS OF C IN EQUATION (2)

$$0.50P = 1.06C \tag{3}$$
$$P = 1.06C/0.50$$
$$P = 2.12C \tag{4}$$

SUBSTITUTE EQUATION (4) INTO EQUATION (1):
$$5,000 - 0.377C - 0.196(2.12C) = 0 \tag{5}$$
$$5,000 - 0.377C - 0.416C = 0 \tag{6}$$
$$5,000 - 0.793C = 0 \tag{7}$$
$$5,000 = 0.793C \tag{8}$$
$$C = 5,000/0.793 = 6,305.17 \tag{9}$$

SUBSTITUTE FOR C IN EQUATION (4):

$$P = 2.12(6,305.17) = 13,366.96 \tag{10}$$

ROUND TO WHOLE CONTRACTS:

| P = 134 CONTRACTS |
| C = 63 CONTRACTS |

We can set up a series of simultaneous equations to achieve the position delta we want and have a net cash outlay of zero. The portfolio manager decides to write calls in sufficient quantity to pay for the needed puts. Table 7–4 shows the necessary steps.

Table 7–5 shows the resulting position delta and net position cost. The position delta of 4,998.5 is close to the target figure of 5,000; the income from writing the calls is within $22 of the cost of the puts.

POSITION RISK

Position risk is an important, but often overlooked, aspect of the riskiness of portfolio management with options. Suppose an options speculator holds the positions shown in Table 7–6.

This aggregate portfolio has a position delta of −155, so it is slightly bearish. This does not mean, however, that the speculator wants the market to fall pre-

TABLE 7–5   Position Delta and Position Cost

POSITION DELTA

$$10,000 \text{ shares of stock} \times \frac{1.0 \text{ delta}}{\text{share}} = \quad 10,000$$

$$63 \text{ call contracts} \times \frac{-0.377 \text{ deltas}}{\text{call}} \times \frac{100 \text{ calls}}{\text{contract}} = \quad -2,375.1$$

$$134 \text{ put contracts} \times \frac{-0.196 \text{ deltas}}{\text{put}} \times \frac{100 \text{ puts}}{\text{contract}} = \quad -2,626.4$$

POSITION DELTA = **4,998.5**

COST OF POSITION

$$\text{Cost of puts: } 134 \text{ contracts} \times \frac{\$0.50}{\text{put}} \times \frac{100 \text{ puts}}{\text{contract}} = \quad \$6,700$$

$$\text{Income from calls: } 63 \text{ contracts} \times \frac{\$1.06}{\text{call}} \times \frac{100 \text{ calls}}{\text{contract}} = \quad (\$6,678)$$

NET COST   **$22**

TABLE 7–6 Position Risk				
OPTION	**CONTRACTS**	**POSITION DELTA**	**POSITION GAMMA**	**POSITION THETA**
35 CALL	−15	−1203.0	−33.6	+13.5
40 CALL	+15	615.0	47.1	−15.0
45 CALL	−5	−60.0	−8.1	2.5
CALL TOTAL	−5	−648.0	5.4	1.0
30 PUT	10	−18.0	3.6	−1.0
35 PUT	−20	396.0	−44.8	20.0
40 PUT	15	−885.0	47.1	−10.0
PUT TOTAL	5	−507.0	5.9	9.0
STOCK	10	1000.0	0.0	0.0
GRAND TOTAL		−155.0	11.3	10.0

Initial conditions: $\sigma = 0.22$, $S = 38$, $r = 5\%$, $t = 116$ days

cipitously. Delta is a first derivative, and first derivatives become less useful as the magnitude of the change in variables increases.

Consider first what happens if the market advances very sharply via a "market crash in reverse." All the puts will go to zero, because the stock price rises above the put striking prices. You are short twenty calls and long fifteen others, for a net call holding of short five contracts. Also, you are long 10 lots of stock, or 1000 shares. The calls will be exercised, leaving you with 500 shares of stock. During a major advance, this is an acceptable position.

What if the market crashes? The calls will go to zero, and you will be left with a net put position of five long contracts. These will provide protection against 500 of your shares, but the other 500 will be unprotected. This is no good. Despite your position delta being negative, you will be hurt if the market free falls. Table 7–7 shows the portfolio value at various stock prices. (These are Black-Scholes theoretical prices with the assumption that prices change instantaneously with no passage of time.)

Figure 7–6 shows the general form of the profit and loss relationship. Assuming the options are all priced exactly as they should be according to the Black-Scholes model, the initial situation has zero profit at a stock price of $38. The negative position delta means that profits accrue if prices fall, so the curve moves into profitable territory if the stock price declines. If the stock price declines too far, however, the curve will turn down, indicating that large losses are possible.

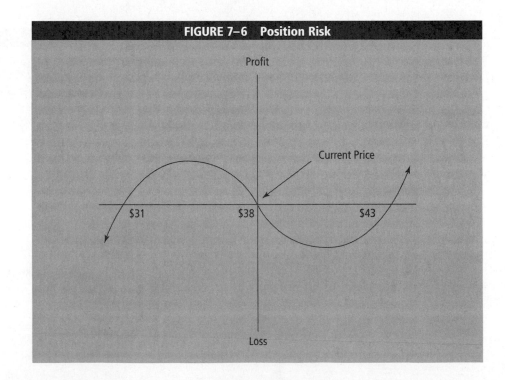

FIGURE 7–6   Position Risk

TABLE 7-7 Theoretical Portfolio Impact at Various Stock Prices

POSITION	0	30	32	33	34	36	38	40	42	50
SHORT 15 $35 CALLS	0	−390	−1,050	−1,560	−2,205	−3,930	−6,135	−8,700	−11,475	−22,500
LONG 15 $40 CALLS	0	30	135	225	390	960	1,950	3,435	5,370	16,005
SHORT 5 $45 CALLS	0	0	−5	−5	−15	−50	−130	−300	−590	−3,100
LONG 10 $30 PUTS	30,000	1,250	600	390	250	90	30	10	0	0
SHORT 20 $35 PUTS	−70,000	−9,460	−6,320	−5,000	−3,860	−2,160	−1,100	−520	−220	0
LONG 15 $40 PUTS	60,000	15,000	12,000	10,500	9,000	6,030	4,020	2,505	1,455	90
OPTION PORTFOLIO VALUE	20,000	6,430	5,360	4,550	3,560	940	−1,365	−3,570	−5,460	−9,505
GAIN OR LOSS ON OPTIONS	21,365	7,795	6,725	5,915	4,925	2,305	0	−2,205	−4,095	−8,140
GAIN OR LOSS ON 1000 SHARES OF STOCK	−38,000	−8,000	−6,000	−5,000	−4,000	−2,000	0	2,000	4,000	12,000
AGGREGATE PROFIT OR LOSS	−16,635	−205	725	915	925	305	0	−205	−95	3,860

Assumptions: r = 5%, σ = 0.22, t = 116, S = $38

On the upside, losses occur if the stock price advances a modest amount, but if it really runs up then the position delta turns positive and profits accrue to the position.[12]

The point behind the position risk idea is that option derivatives are not particularly useful for major movements in the price of the underlying asset. An option expert needs to be aware of the doomsday scenario associated with any position.

---

[12] Some traders use a heuristic stating that, away from the extremes where the stock falls to zero or rises infinitely, the "intermediate" maximum profits occur if the underlying asset changes by a percentage amount approximately equal to the position delta divided by the position gamma. In this example, the figure is $-155.0/11.3 = -13.7\%$. A 13.7% decline from the current stock price of $38 gives a new stock price of $32.8. Table 7–7 and Figure 7–4 show that the intermediate maximum profit is around this point. The percentage amount is a non-exact rule of thumb, but a useful one.

SUMMARY

Delta is a measure of how the price of an option changes in response to small changes in the value of the underlying asset. Many options strategies are based on delta neutrality, meaning that options are combined in unequal numbers such that the weighted average of their deltas is zero. Over-the-counter option dealers sell a number of delta neutral products. Straddles and strangles are important delta-neutral option packages. Delta changes with the passage of time, necessitating frequent adjustments to maintain delta neutrality.

Theta is a measure of how the value of an option changes with the passage of time. Long option positions have a negative theta, because options are wasting assets. Short option positions have a positive theta, as the passage of time is beneficial to the option writer, who wants the option to expire worthless.

Gamma is a measure of how delta changes as the price of the underlying asset changes. Negative gammas are potentially consequential, because a major market movement can seriously hurt an option position with a negative gamma. Gamma is always opposite in sign to theta.

The sum of the deltas in a portfolio is the position delta. Similarly, one can calculate the portfolio position theta or position gamma.

All option derivatives can change rapidly as the underlying conditions change. For this reason, it is necessary to "tune up" option positions as time passes and the value of the underlying asset changes.

First derivatives are most accurate for relatively small movements in the underlying asset. Option traders, therefore, are especially concerned with position risk, which is a measure of the consequences of a "doomsday" move, where the market advances or declines sharply. A sensitivity analysis shows the consequences of large movements in the underlying asset, something that delta might miss.

Vega and rho are relatively unimportant derivatives of the BSOPM that seldom influence managerial decisions.

SELF TEST

T ___ F ___ 1. Delta is a measure of how an option price changes with a small change in the price of the underlying asset.

T ___ F ___ 2. With a European option, for a given striking price and expiration the absolute values of the call delta and the put delta sum to 1.0.

T ___ F ___ 3. Call deltas range from minus one to zero.

T ___ F ___ 4. If an option is substantially in-the-money, delta measures the approximate likelihood that the option will be in-the-money at expiration.

T ___ F ___ 5. By convention, the theta of a long option position is negative.

T ___ F ___ 6. Gamma measures how delta changes as the underlying asset price changes.

T ___ F ___ 7. In practice, delta is opposite in sign to theta for a given option.

T ___ F ___ 8. Vega is also called epsilon or chi.

CHAPTER 7 REVIEW

T ___ F ___   9. You can increase the position delta of an options portfolio by purchasing calls or by writing puts.

T ___ F ___   10. A portfolio that is delta neutral has an equal number of call and put contracts.

T ___ F ___   11. Gamma is a measure of the directional market for the underlying asset.

T ___ F ___   12. Negative gamma can hurt you in a fast market.

T ___ F ___   13. The delta of an in-the-money call approaches 1.0 as expiration approaches.

T ___ F ___   14. The delta of an out-of-the-money put approaches zero as expiration approaches.

T ___ F ___   15. A portfolio with a positive position delta can be hurt by a dramatic increase in the price of the underlying asset.

PROBLEMS & QUESTIONS

1. What are the three definitions of delta?
2. As time passes, does the delta of an in-the-money call rise or fall? Why?
3. Suppose that a call option has a striking price of zero. What would its delta be?
4. Why are some strategies (like straddles) constructed to be delta neutral by many professional option traders?
5. Suppose you establish a delta neutral straddle that is exactly at-the-money. As time passes (and assuming everything else remains unchanged), will the position delta change? If so, in what direction?
6. How is delta useful in determining the potential profitability of an options strategy?
7. A long option position, by convention, has a negative theta. More time, however, means more option value. Doesn't this mean that theta should be positive, because premium goes up as time goes up?
8. Suppose you construct a bull spread with calls using one option at each striking price. Is the resulting position delta positive, negative, or indeterminable?
9. Refer to Figure 7–1. Why do you think that the delta of an in-the-money call *rises* over time while the delta of an out-of-the-money call *falls*?

10. Why is it not possible for the delta of a call option to be greater than one or less than zero? Explain this using intuition rather than mathematics.
11. Why is delta neutrality an important issue with some option strategies?
12. Why is a gamma near zero often desirable?
13. Why is a negative gamma generally undesirable?
14. Does the concept of the delta neutrality have any meaning for an option *spreader*?
15. Is there any added risk associated with establishing delta neutrality?
16. Suppose interest rates rise. Will an option's delta change if the stock price remains unchanged?
17. Why is gamma neutrality a convenience for an options portfolio manager?
18. Explain the difference between the *directional* market and the *speed* market.
19. Suppose you are bullish but expect a slow market. What strategy is particularly appropriate?
20. Briefly explain the idea of position risk.
21. Are any of the BSOPM derivatives more important than the others? If so, why?

Note: Use the following information for the remaining problems:

$$t = 100 \text{ days} \qquad r = 5\% \qquad S = \$45 \qquad \sigma = .26$$

22. Calculate the delta of a $45 call option.
23. Suppose you own 5,000 shares of stock. How many $45 calls would you need to write to be approximately delta neutral?
24. If you write 15 $50 calls while holding 5,000 shares of stock, what percentage of the market risk of the position have you eliminated?
25. You are asked to determine the number of $45 calls and $45 puts that must be purchased to have a delta neutral straddle that costs about $4,000. Find the number of contracts of each type of option that satisfies these requirements.
26. Use your answer to problem 25, and assume the following: twenty days have passed, and the stock price has changed to $48. What must you do to return to delta neutrality?

27. Suppose you own 10,000 shares of this stock. You want to write $50 calls and buy $45 puts to be delta neutral and have as little cash outflow as possible. Solve this using simultaneous equations.
28. Using the initial data at the start of this problem section, find the position delta, position gamma, and position theta of the following portfolio.

    Short 15 $40 calls   Long 10 $40 puts
    Short 25 $45 calls   Long 50 $35 puts

29. Suppose an investor owns 4,000 shares of this stock. How many $40 puts are necessary to hedge half the position?
30. Refer to the portfolio in problem 29. Suppose the portfolio also contains 800 shares of stock. Comment on the position risk of the portfolio.

31. A financial institution has the following portfolio of over-the-counter options on Yen:

TYPE	POSITION	DELTA	GAMMA	VEGA
CALL	−1000	0.5	2.2	1.8
CALL	−500	0.8	0.6	0.2
PUT	−2000	0.4	1.3	0.7
CALL	−500	0.7	1.8	1.4

A traded option is available which has a delta of 0.6, a gamma of 1.5, and a vega of 0.8.
a. What position in the traded option and in Yen would make the portfolio both gamma neutral and delta neutral?
b. What position in the traded option and in Yen would make the portfolio both vega neutral and delta neutral?

8

Fundamentals of the Futures Market

KEY TERMS you will find in this chapter:

Acapulco trade	intracommodity spread
arbitrage	inverted market
backwardation	limit order
basis	long hedge
broker	market order
cash price	market variation call
clearing corporation	mark to market
Commodity Futures Trading Commission	normal backwardation
contango market	open interest
crack	open outcry
crush	out trade
daily price limit	pit
day trader	position trader
deck	price discovery
delivery month	price risk
expectations hypothesis	processor
forward contract	scalper
full carrying charge market	short hedge
futures commission merchant	speculator
futures contract	spot price
good faith deposit	stop order
hedger	stop price
intercommodity spread	Tapioca City
intermarket spread	Unmatched Trade Notice

As near as I can learn, and from the best information I have been able to obtain on the Chicago Board of Trade, at least 95% of the sales of the Board are of this fictitious character, where no property is actually owned, no property sold or delivered, or expected to be delivered but simply wagers or bets as to what that property may be worth at a designated time in the future. . . . Wheat and cotton have become as much gambling tools as chips on the farobank table. The property of the wheat grower and the cotton grower is treated as though it were a "stake" put on the gambling table at Monte Carlo. The producer of wheat is compelled to see the stocks in his barn dealt with like the peas of a thimblerigger, or the cards of a three-card-monte man. Between the grain-producer and loaf eater, there has stepped in a "parasite" between them robbing them both.

Senator William D. Washburn (D-Minn),
before Congress, July 11, 1892

TABLE 8–1 Chicago Board of Trade Selected Commodity Symbols			

GRAINS

S	SOYBEANS
BO	SOYBEAN OIL
SM	SOYBEAN MEAL
W	WHEAT
C	CORN
O	OATS
RR	ROUGH RICE

FINANCIALS

US	30-YEAR U.S. TREASURY BONDS
TY	10-YEAR U.S. TREASURY NOTES
FV	5-YEAR U.S. TREASURY NOTES
TU	2-YEAR U.S. TREASURY NOTES
FF	30-DAY FEDERAL FUNDS
MB	LONG-TERM MUNICIPAL BOND INDEX
BX	30-YEAR BOND INFLATION INDEX
II	10-YEAR NOTE INFLATION INDEX
BI	5-YEAR NOTE INFLATION INDEX

STOCK INDICES

DJ	CBOT DJIA

METALS

AG	1000-OUNCE SILVER
SV	5000-OUNCE SILVER
KI	KILO GOLD
GH	100-OUNCE GOLD

CORN YIELD INSURANCE

CA	IOWA CORN YIELD INSURANCE
YG	ILLINOIS CORN YIELD INSURANCE
YH	INDIANA CORN YIELD INSURANCE
YI	NEBRASKA CORN YIELD INSURANCE
YJ	OHIO CORN YIELD INSURANCE
YC	U.S. CORN YIELD INSURANCE

Source: Chicago Board of Trade

The futures market is a very useful, and very misunderstood, part of our economic system. It enables farmers, businesses, financial institutions, and the managers of investment portfolios to lessen price risk, the risk of loss because of uncertainty over the future price of a commodity or financial asset. As with options, the two major market participants are the hedger and the speculator, with the former transferring some price risk to the latter.

Futures contracts trade on a variety of assets, including grains, petroleum products, precious metals, and cattle, among others. Table 8–1 lists some of them and their trading symbols. Financial futures, like those traded on Treasury bonds, stock indexes, and foreign currencies, are an extremely popular and fast-growing segment of the futures market. While this chapter introduces them, the primary discussion of financial futures is in Chapters 9 through 12. First we look at the role of futures markets in the financial system. Then we will see how the trading system functions, followed by an overview of futures contract pricing.

THE CONCEPT OF FUTURES CONTRACTS

THE FUTURES PROMISE

A futures contract is a legally binding agreement to buy or sell something in the future. Futures contracts are promises; the person who initially sells the contract promises to deliver a quantity of a standardized commodity to a designated delivery point during a certain month called the **delivery month**. The other party to the trade promises to pay a predetermined price for the goods upon delivery.

The Chicago Board of Trade originated in 1848 to provide a centralized place where buyers and sellers of agricultural goods could meet in an orderly market. By 1865 standardized futures contracts traded and procedures were in place to ensure performance on the contracts. Today there are at least 85 futures exchanges worldwide.

A futures contract is a promise to buy or to deliver a certain quantity of a standardized good by a specific date.

Futures Compared to Options

There are some analogies between futures contracts and options contracts. Both involve a predetermined price and contract duration. But an option is precisely that: an *option*. The person holding the option has the *right*, but not the obligation, to exercise the put or the call. If an option has no value at its expiration, the option holder will normally allow it to expire unexercised. With futures contracts, a trade *must* occur if the contract is held until its delivery deadline. Futures contracts do not "expire" unexercised. One party has promised to deliver a commodity that another party has promised to buy.[1]

Futures Compared to Forwards

A futures contract is more similar to a forward contract than to an options contract. Forwards are different from futures in two principal respects: they are not marketable and they are not marked to market. A **forward contract** is an agreement between a business and a financial institution, usually a bank, to exchange something at a set price in the future. Most forward contracts involve foreign currency. A business may anticipate receiving foreign currency in the future or know that it will have to pay in foreign currency and want to eliminate the price risk associated with exchange rate changes. A firm doing business with a German firm might, for instance, arrange with its bank to buy DM100,000 at $0.6903 in 97 days.

Forward contracts are not marketable and are not marked to market.

Once a firm enters into such a forward contract there is no convenient way to trade out of it. Canceling the trade requires mutual agreement between the two parties involved. This is unlike futures where either side can quickly transfer their half of the promise to someone else. Because there is no marking to market, forwards also require no good faith deposit. The two parties exchange assets at the agreed upon date with no intervening cash flows. Other differences between futures and forwards stem from the fact that with forwards the quantity and quality of the underlying asset, and the delivery time and delivery place are all negotiable, while they are standardized with futures.

---

[1] As we will see, it is also possible for one or both parties to the trade to transfer their half of the promise to someone else via an offsetting trade.

Futures Regulation

Legally, futures are not securities; they are contracts. As a consequence, they are not under the jurisdiction of the Securities and Exchange Commission. In 1974 Congress passed the Commodity Exchange Act establishing the **Commodity Futures Trading Commission** (CFTC) to ensure a fair futures market. The CFTC performs much the same function with futures as the SEC does with shares of stock. There is also a self-regulatory organization, the National Futures Association (formed in 1982), that enforces financial and membership requirements. It also provides customer protection and grievance procedures. Any organization that deals with the public must belong to the NFA and abide by its rules.

Trading Mechanics

Suppose a speculator purchases a July soybean contract at the Chicago Board of Trade. The purchase price might be $6.22 per bushel. This contract calls for the delivery of 5,000 bushels of No. 2 yellow soybeans to a specially designated regular warehouse at an approved delivery point by the last business day in July. Upon delivery, the purchaser of the contract must pay $6.22 for each of the 5,000 bushels, or a total of $31,100. If the current price (called either the **spot price** or the **cash price**) for soybeans is greater than $6.22, the purchaser of the contract will profit. A spot price of $6.33, for instance, results in profit of 11 cents on each of 5,000 bushels, or $550. On the other hand, if the spot price were only $6.15, the buyer would lose $0.07 per bushel, or $350.

Alternatively, a speculator may anticipate that long-term interest rates are going to rise. This means that the price of U.S. Treasury bonds will fall. One contract of Treasury bonds calls for delivery of $100,000 face value of bonds that have at least 15 years until their maturity. Because the speculator thinks the price of the bonds will fall, he or she might sell a futures contract at a price of 93, thereby promising to deliver $100,000 face value of these bonds at a price of 93% of par, or $93,000. If the value of the bonds subsequently drops to 92.5% of par, the speculator gains 0.5% of $100,000, or $500.

An important idea to keep in mind with futures is that the purpose of the contracts is not to provide a means for the transfer of goods. Stated another way, property rights to real or financial assets cannot be transferred with futures contracts. They do, however, enable people to reduce some risks they assume in their businesses.

Most futures contracts are eliminated before the delivery month. This is analogous to the exercise of stock options. People who buy puts or calls do not usually intend to exercise them; they sell their valuable options on or before expiration day. A speculator who is long a corn futures contract does not want to take delivery of 5,000 bushels of the commodity. It also may be that a farmer who has hedged by selling a contract prefers to sell the wheat locally rather than transport it to an approved delivery point. In either case making an offsetting trade, or "trading out" of the contract can satisfy the contract obligation. The speculator with a long position would sell a contract, thereby canceling the long position. The

Property rights cannot be transferred with futures contracts.

hedger with a short position would buy. Both individuals would be out of the market after these trades.

WHY WE HAVE FUTURES CONTRACTS

Perhaps no other part of the financial marketplace has received as much scrutiny as the futures market. Unlike other markets where tangible items change hands (stock certificates, diamonds, real estate), the participants in the futures market deal in promises. A trader can buy or sell thousands of bushels of wheat or tons of soybean meal and have absolutely no intention of ever growing the commodity or taking delivery of it. In fact, fewer than 2% of the commodities underlying all futures contracts are ever actually delivered! The quantity of a commodity as represented by the total number of futures contracts sometimes exceeds the available supply worldwide. These facts give a clue why would-be market reformers frequently attack the commodity markets.

Let's look at an example of how the futures market benefits a specific group of people: college students. Many graduating seniors buy a class ring, often made of gold. Students typically order rings months before graduation. When ordering, buyers want a firm price quotation from the manufacturer; they do not want to hear that "it depends on the price of gold when we make your ring." A company like Jostens or Balfour can lock in the price they have to pay for gold by appropriate trades in the futures market. Because the firm wants gold, they *buy* contracts, promising to pay a set price for the gold when it is delivered. This would be a **long hedge**. A gold mining company, on the other hand, would *sell* contracts, promising to deliver the gold. This would be a **short hedge**.

Assume a futures trade in gold occurs at a price of $275.50 per ounce, with delivery set for December. There are 100 troy ounces[2] of gold in one contract. This means that the mining company will deliver 100 ounces and receive $27,550 for them, regardless of the price of gold at delivery time. The suppliers of gold know their ultimate selling price, and the manufacturers of the rings know their major material cost. If these two companies were not able to lock in the future price of gold, the price to the consumer would be higher to account for the added price risk faced by both the miner and the manufacturer.

Unfortunately, there are still influential people who share the views Senator Washburn expressed in the quotation at the beginning of this chapter. They are in the minority. The commodity exchanges are continually adding new products, and the number of people and organizations who find useful opportunities with futures is increasing. The basic function of the commodity futures market is to transfer risk from a business (the hedger) to someone who is willing to bear it (the speculator). The speculator assumes this risk because of the opportunity for profit. We will discuss these people in greater detail later.

I'm not a gambler. I'm not in a crapshoot . . . I'm a speculator. Here's the difference. In gambling, you create the risk. In speculating, you assume the risk.

Lee Stern
Former owner of the Chicago Sting Soccer Team and member of the CBOT

---

[2] A troy ounce weighs 9.7 percent more than a standard (avoirdupois) ounce.

ENSURING THE PROMISE IS KEPT

A reasonable question is "What happens if someone won't pay for the commodity as promised or if a particular farmer is unable to deliver the goods?" If it were possible to back out of the trade without fulfilling your part of the promise, the futures exchanges would die a quick death. People would lose confidence in the system, and it would not be attractive to either hedgers or speculators. Eliminating this uncertainty is the role of the **Clearing Corporation**.

The Clearing Corporation ensures the integrity of each futures contract by interposing itself between each buyer and seller.

Each exchange has a clearing corporation that performs a critical duty: ensuring the integrity of the futures contract. Although trades in the pit occur between two specific individuals, the trades actually become sales to or by the Clearing Corporation. In essence, the Clearing Corporation becomes a party to every trade.[3]

Futures contracts are promises, and promises must be kept. A professional trader's account may fluctuate in value by more than a million dollars daily. Misfortune or incompetence sometimes forces a member into bankruptcy, yet the member's positions still are promises with other exchange members.

The Clearing Corporation assumes the responsibility for those positions when a member is in financial distress. If this were not so, the integrity of the trading system would break down, and members would tend to trade only with other members who were financially strong. In such a situation it is likely that prices at the exchange would become less competitive.

You cannot overstate the value of a sound clearing system at a commodities exchange. The Chicago Mercantile Exchange publishes a short document entitled "The Financial Safeguard System of the Chicago Mercantile Exchange." One section of this paper deals with financial integrity of the marketplace and reads in part as follows:

The accounts of individual members and non-member customers doing business through the facilities of the CME must be carried and guaranteed by a clearing member. In every matched transaction executed through the Exchange's facilities, the Clearing House is substituted as the buyer for the seller and the seller for the buyer. The Clearing House is an operating division of the Exchange and all rights, obligations and/or liabilities of the Clearing House are rights, obligations, and/or liabilities of the CME. Clearing members assume full financial and performance responsibility for all transactions executed through them and positions they carry. The Clearing House, dealing exclusively with clearing members, holds each clearing member accountable for every position it carries regardless of whether the position is being carried for the account of an individual member, for the account of a non-member customer or for the clearing member's own account. Conversely, as the contra side to every position, the Clearing House is held accountable to the clearing members for performance on all open positions.

---

[3] This is the same function performed by the Options Clearing Corporation.

TABLE 8–2 Selected Good Faith Deposit Requirements			
(DATA AS OF 23 MARCH 2001)			
CONTRACT	SIZE	APPROXIMATE VALUE	INITIAL MARGIN PER CONTRACT
SOYBEANS	5,000 BUSHELS	$24,000	$945
GOLD	100 TROY OUNCES	$27,000	$1,418
TREASURY BONDS	$100,000 PAR	$103,000	$2,025
S&P 500 INDEX	$250 × INDEX	$320,000	$21,563
HEATING OIL	42,000 GALLONS	$38,000	$3,375

All margins are posted on the exchange websites and are subject to frequent changes.

Because of the possibility that the collective members of the Clearing Corporation might have to absorb large losses due to the default of one or more members, stringent financial conditions are a condition of membership. The exchanges strictly enforce these requirements.

Good faith deposits (or performance bonds) are required from every member on every contract to help ensure that members have the financial capacity to meet their obligations should market prices not go their way. In practice, the good faith deposit is usually called a margin deposit, or margin requirement. As with the margin requirement on certain stock option spreads, this use of the term *margin* does not imply that someone is borrowing money or paying interest. Table 8–2 lists some representative initial margin requirements.

Let us turn now to a discussion of how a futures contract originates on the exchanges.

The clearing corporation guarantees the integrity of the contracts trading within the jurisdiction and bylaws of the exchange.

MARKET MECHANICS

TYPES OF ORDERS

A broker in commodity futures is technically a **futures commission merchant (FCM)**. It is important that there be no misunderstanding between the FCM and the individual who places an order. When placing an order, the client should specify the type of order, because each type involves different responsibilities and instructions. The simplest order is a **market order**. This instructs the broker to execute a client's order at the best possible price at the earliest opportunity. For instance, the price board may show the last price for soybeans at 530 ($5.30 per bushel), and the broker may observe that this commodity is trading at "9½ to ¾." This means that there are bids to purchase soybeans at 529½ and that there are sellers of soybeans at 529¾. A client placing a market order to buy is instructing the broker to buy at the best available price, so the broker would likely buy at 529³/₄. The broker could offer to pay 531 and be certain of attracting attention in the pit and getting the order filled, but this would not be in the client's best interest and would be inappropriate broker behavior.

With a **limit order**, the client specifies a time and a price. For instance, the order might be to sell five December soybeans at 540, good until canceled.[4] Here the client will accept a selling price of $5.40 per bushel or more, but no less. "Good until canceled" indicates that this is an open order, and that the broker is to execute the order whenever a price of 540 or better can be obtained, even if that price does not occur until weeks from now. Instead of a good-until-canceled instruction, the client might have specified "for the day." This means that if the order cannot be filled during trading hours today, the order is canceled, and the client would have to enter a new order to sell the commodity at a later date.

A third, very useful type of order is a **stop order**. A stop order becomes a market order when the **stop price** is touched during trading action. Stop orders, when executed, close out an existing commodity position. A stop order to buy would be placed by someone with an existing short position; a stop order to sell would be placed by persons with a long position.

With a "buy stop," the stop price is below the current price. With a "sell stop," the stop price is above.

A person using a stop order to buy might be a short seller who wants protection against large losses due to rising commodity prices. A stop order to buy three September soybean futures at 533 means that if the price of soybeans advances to $5.33 per bushel, the broker is to buy three contracts at the best available price (which may be higher than 533).

Another speculator might place a stop order to sell at 528. This would mean that if the price of September soybeans falls to $5.28, then "sell my soybeans and get me out of the market." This person could be minimizing losses or protecting an existing profit. Note that a person with a long position always places the stop price below the current price, while a person with a short position does the opposite.

Protecting profits is a very important use of a stop order, although few individuals make use of stop orders for this purpose. Suppose someone bought five September soybean contracts at 520 and they now trade at 530. Each contract is 5,000 bushels; when beans advance 10 cents per bushel, the owner of five contracts has a profit of $2,500 in their account. To protect most of this profit, the speculator might have a stop order at 528. If prices fall to this level, the speculator will automatically trade out of the market and most of the profit will be preserved. If, instead, soybeans rise to 533, the stop price can be moved, perhaps to 531, thus helping to protect another $750 in profits. Moving a stop price up behind a rising commodity leaves your profit potential untouched but reduces your downside risk.

A person using a stop order is not certain of trading exactly at the stop price.

It is important to remember that stop orders become *market* orders when the asset trades at the stop price. Unlike a limit order, where the person placing the

---

[4] Often abbreviated GTC, which stands for good 'til canceled.

order knows that a trade, if it occurs, will be at a certain price or better, the person using a stop order is *not certain* of trading at the stop price. When the stop is touched, this gives your broker instructions to trade out of the contract immediately at the going price, which may be more or less than the stop price. In a fast market, prices can change very quickly, so the price realized via the stop order may be substantially different than the stop price.

AMBIENCE OF THE MARKETPLACE

The visitor to a commodity exchange is often struck by the apparent confusion in the exchange. Trades occur by **open outcry** of the floor traders, meaning that traders verbally call out buy and sell orders. There is no standing in line or computerized order entry; traders stand in a sunken area called the **pit** and bark their offers to buy or sell at certain prices to others within the trading circle.

Besides spoken offers, traders use a series of hand signals to signal their wishes concerning quantity, price, and whether they wish to buy or to sell. Figure 8–1 shows some of these signals for Treasury bond futures.

Only members of the exchange are allowed in the trading pit itself. There are over 3,600 members of the Chicago Board of Trade, of whom 1,402 are full members with the right to trade in any of the commodities at the exchange. There are also associate members and other membership interests that allow trading in certain products. The price of a full membership varies and can fluctuate widely. As an example, a full membership at the Chicago Board of Trade sold for $530,000 on October 6, 1987. The first sale of a seat after the market crashed on October 19th was on October 29th at a price of $321,000. On May 22, 2000 a seat sold for $540,000. Eleven months later (April 20, 2001) a seat sold for $325,000.

Many newcomers to the exchange choose to lease a membership from someone while trying to develop the expertise and capital to warrant getting their own membership. At the Chicago Mercantile Exchange, in June 2000 it cost about $3,000 per month to lease a seat.[5]

Next to each trading pit is a raised structure called a *pulpit*, where representatives of the exchange's Market Report Department enter all price changes into the price reporting system. The walls surrounding the trading area display a massive electronic wallboard reflecting price information about the commodities being traded. Current prices, as well as the two previous prices, are shown, with the high and low prices at which a particular contract has traded during its life. This wallboard also powers a network of price information to which investors and brokerage firms subscribe around the world.

Hundreds of order desks, where telecommunications personnel from member firms receive orders from clients and relay order confirmations, line the perimeter of the exchange. Most telephone clerks tape their conversations to pro-

---

[5] Exchanges sometimes impose restrictions on seat leasing. The Chicago Board of Trade, for instance, stopped this practice during 1991 and 1992.

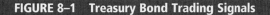

FIGURE 8–1   Treasury Bond Trading Signals

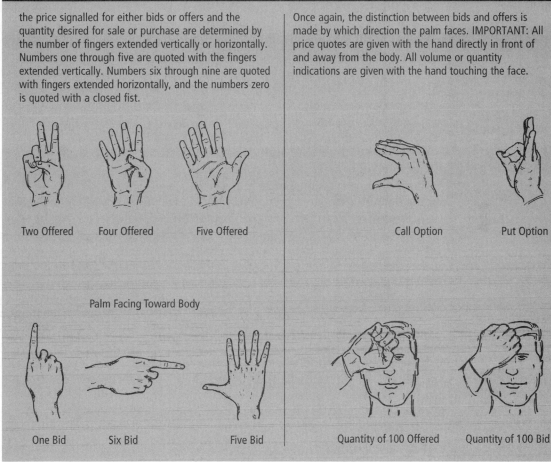

the price signalled for either bids or offers and the quantity desired for sale or purchase are determined by the number of fingers extended vertically or horizontally. Numbers one through five are quoted with the fingers extended vertically. Numbers six through nine are quoted with fingers extended horizontally, and the numbers zero is quoted with a closed fist.

Once again, the distinction between bids and offers is made by which direction the palm faces. IMPORTANT: All price quotes are given with the hand directly in front of and away from the body. All volume or quantity indications are given with the hand touching the face.

Two Offered   Four Offered   Five Offered   Call Option   Put Option

Palm Facing Toward Body

One Bid   Six Bid   Five Bid   Quantity of 100 Offered   Quantity of 100 Bid

Source: Chicago Board of Trade

tect themselves against alleged order errors. There are approximately 1,200 workstations at the Chicago Mercantile Exchange, and 153,600 telephone lines.

At one time the Chicago Board of Trade contained more computer screens than any other building in the world except NASA headquarters. There is so much activity within the building that in the history of the exchange it has seldom been necessary to turn on the heat!

Visitors to any of the exchanges will note the colorful display of trading jackets worn by people on the trading floor. Exchange policy requires every employee to wear either a business suit or a trading jacket. The Chicago Mercantile Exchange provides red jackets to any member who desires one, and for a nominal fee will provide a freshly laundered one every Wednesday. At all exchanges, brokers from a particular firm have the option of wearing some distinctive jacket color to make it easier for their messenger and clerical people to locate them. At the Chicago Board of Trade, all messenger people wear yellow jackets, royal blue signifies a telecommunications person, price reporting supervisors wear tan, and price reporters wear dark brown jackets.

For certain commodities, there are designated areas within the pit for the trading of a particular delivery month. The pit itself is either octagonal or polygonal, with steps descending into the center. The edge of the pit is approximately waist high to an observer outside. Each trader in the pit wears a large badge containing a two- or three-letter (up to four at the Merc) personal identification code and an indication of which firm he or she works for (or clears trades through—more on this later).

As in most professions, there is a parochial lingo with which people on the trading floor quickly become familiar. On days when there is little trading activity, people say you can "see through the pit." An unusually large trade by someone who normally trades just a few contracts at a time is called an **Acapulco trade**, presumably because if you are successful with the trade it will finance your trip to an exotic place. When traders incorrectly assess the market and lose all their trading capital, they have "busted out," or gone to **Tapioca City**. A sudden rush of pit activity for no apparent reason is called a "fire drill." A big price move is a "lights out" move. Traders riding a winning streak joke about establishing an "O'Hare Spread," referring to O'Hare airport. The O'Hare spread is "Sell Chicago, Buy Mexico."

The trading floor will occasionally observe a moment of silence from 11:00 A.M. until 11:01 A.M. This will happen when a long-time member of the exchange dies, or when there is a national or world disaster (such as the Challenger space shuttle explosion or the Chernobyl nuclear power plant accident).

CREATION OF A CONTRACT

Suppose trader ZZZ buys five contracts of September Treasury Bonds from Dan Hennebry at $77^{31}/_{32}$. The trading unit for Treasury bonds is $100,000 par value of U.S. Treasury bonds that have a maturity of at least fifteen years. The price of $77^{31}/_{32}$ means $77^{31}/_{32}$ *percent of par*, or $77,968.75. A price change of $^1/_{32}$ would be the equivalent of $31.25. The two traders confirm their trade verbally and with the hand signals appropriate to the U.S. Treasury bond pit. Each of them then fills out a card recording this information. (See Figure 8–2 for an example.) One side of the card is blue for recording purchases. The other side, for sales, is red. Each commodity has a symbol, and each delivery month has a letter code. On Dan Hennebry's card, we see his notation that he sold five contracts of September U.S. Treasury bonds (ticker symbol US) at a price of $77^{31}/_{32}$ to trader ZZZ at firm OOO. The letter A is circled and written in at the far right of the card. This is the time block at which the trade occurred. The first thirty minutes of trading is Block A, the second thirty minutes block B, and so on until the close of trading. Normally a trader will either circle the letter or write it in, but not both. The time

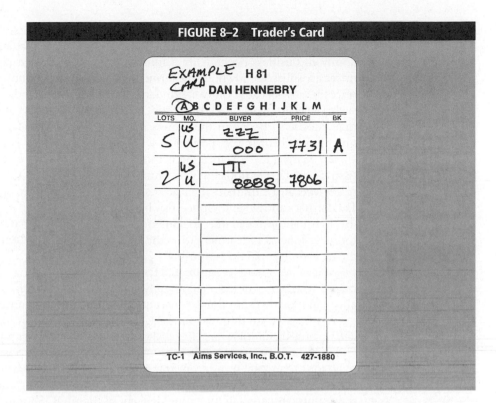

FIGURE 8–2   Trader's Card

block helps to ensure that orders are correctly matched during the clearing process. This card also shows a second, independent trade to TTT for two contracts of September T-Bonds at a price of $78^6/_{32}$.

At the conclusion of trading, each trader submits their cards (called their **deck**) to their clearinghouse, where all the cards are matched up and errors identified. The role of the clearing operation is crucial to a well-functioning exchange, and is discussed shortly. First, let's look at the principal players in the futures market.

MARKET PARTICIPANTS

There need to be two types of participants in order for a futures market to be successful: hedgers and speculators. Without hedgers the market would not exist, and there would be no economic function performed by speculators.

HEDGERS

Hedgers transfer price risk to speculators who are willing to bear it.

In the context of the futures market, a hedger is someone engaged in a business activity where there is an unacceptable level of price risk. For instance, a farmer must decide each winter what crops to put in the ground in the spring. The farmer knows about such things as crop rotation but still may face a decision between soybeans and wheat, for instance. To a large extent, the welfare of the farmer's family or business depends on a future price of the chosen commodity. If the prices are subsequently high, the farmer will earn a fair profit on the crop. Should prices be low because of overabundance or reduced demand, prices may fall to such a level that operating costs cannot be recovered. To reduce this risk, the farmer may choose to hedge in the futures market. Farmers transfer the risk they are unwilling to bear to the speculators who are willing to bear it.

In March, for instance, September soybeans might be selling for $5.80. Assume the farmer finds this price attractive, because it provides for a reasonable profit level and eliminates the price risk associated with growing the commodity. The farmer can hedge the price risk by promising to sell all or part of the crop through the futures market to someone who is willing to pay $5.80 per bushel for it. As long as the farmer grows the crop and delivers it, he or she will receive the agreed-upon $5.80 per bushel.

It is important to recognize that the farmer cannot eliminate the risk of a poor crop through the futures market; only price risk can be eliminated. Crop insurance can provide protection against such an event, but the futures market cannot.

With agricultural futures the hedger normally goes short in the futures market, because the farmer wants to deliver something. The farmer promises to deliver, with the speculator going long (promising to pay). It is also possible for a hedger to go long to protect some economic interest. Consider the earlier example of the class ring manufacturer who must quote prices to upcoming graduates all across the country in early fall for spring delivery of the rings. Should the price of gold rise dramatically after the price quotation on the rings, the manufacturer could see the entire profit eroded. The manufacturer going long sufficient gold contracts to guarantee a supply of gold at reasonable prices could hedge this risk. This is a **long hedge** or a **buying hedge**.

The futures market provides no protection against crop failure.

PROCESSORS

Another market participant is a cousin to the hedger, but is important enough to consider separately. Some people earn their living by transforming certain commodities into another form. A good example is the soybean **processor** who buys soybeans and crushes them into soybean meal and soybean oil. In their natural form soybeans are not particularly useful. Before they can be fed to animals or used as flour they must be ground into meal. The oil from crushing beans is used in salad dressings and in industrial applications.

A common activity of the soybean processor is putting on a **crush**. When the processor discovers a profit margin that is acceptable, this profit can be locked in by appropriate activities in the futures market. Consider the following example.

The processor knows this information:

1. 1 bushel of soybeans weighs 60 pounds; each bushel produces 47 lb of meal, 11 lb of oil, and 2 lb of water.

2. 1 futures contract of soybeans is 5,000 bushels, priced in cents/bu.

   1 futures contract of soy meal is 100 tons, priced in $/ton.

   1 futures contract of soy oil is 60,000 pounds, priced in cents/lb

3. The morning's *Wall Street Journal* lists these prices for the three commodities:

   May beans   654¾

   July soy oil   19.96

   July soy meal   196

The primary statistic the processor wants to learn is the profit margin implied in these prices. Because the processor uses beans as a raw material and sells oil and meal as finished products, "putting on a crush" involves buying beans, selling oil, and selling meal in the futures market. Table 8–3 shows the steps.

The processor must decide if $0.2541 per bushel is enough profit to cover the other costs of processing, such as electricity, labor, etc. If so, then the processor can lock in this profit by this crush. The last step is to figure out how many contracts of each type of commodity need to be bought or sold. Suppose the processor's crushing capacity is 100,000 bushes of beans. Table 8–4 shows the resulting calculations.

Because fractional contracts of futures are not allowed, it is not possible for the processor to hedge perfectly. In general, the processor does not want to promise to deliver more than will be produced, so he or she will probably round down. This means that after the processing is complete, there will be a small amount of soy meal and soy oil to be sold in the cash market.

TABLE 8–3   Putting on a Crush: The Profit Margin

ONE BUSHEL OF BEANS COSTS $6.5475 (FROM PRICES ABOVE).

$$\text{Meal} = \frac{\$196}{\text{ton}} \times \frac{1\ \text{ton}}{2{,}000\ \text{lb}} \times \frac{47\ \text{lb}}{\text{bu}} = \$4.6060\,/\,\text{bu}$$

$$\text{Oil} = \frac{\$0.1996}{\text{lb}} \times \frac{11\ \text{lb}}{\text{bu}} = \$2.1956\,/\,\text{bu}$$

REVENUE FROM GOODS SOLD:

FROM MEAL	$4.6060	
FROM OIL	$2.1956	
		$6.8016

COST OF RAW MATERIALS PURCHASED:

SOYBEANS	−$6.5475
GROSS PROFIT:	$0.2541

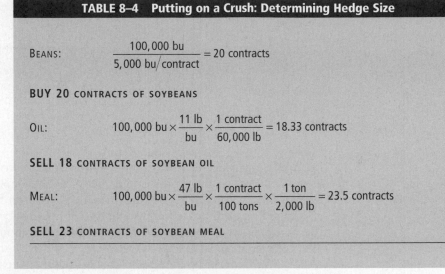

TABLE 8–4   Putting on a Crush: Determining Hedge Size

BEANS: $\dfrac{100,000 \text{ bu}}{5,000 \text{ bu/contract}} = 20 \text{ contracts}$

BUY 20 CONTRACTS OF SOYBEANS

OIL: $100,000 \text{ bu} \times \dfrac{11 \text{ lb}}{\text{bu}} \times \dfrac{1 \text{ contract}}{60,000 \text{ lb}} = 18.33 \text{ contracts}$

SELL 18 CONTRACTS OF SOYBEAN OIL

MEAL: $100,000 \text{ bu} \times \dfrac{47 \text{ lb}}{\text{bu}} \times \dfrac{1 \text{ contract}}{100 \text{ tons}} \times \dfrac{1 \text{ ton}}{2,000 \text{ lb}} = 23.5 \text{ contracts}$

SELL 23 CONTRACTS OF SOYBEAN MEAL

Oil refiners engage in a similar activity called a **crack**. This strategy involves the purchase of crude oil, and the sale of futures contracts in gasoline and #2 heating oil. Precisely the same principles apply in determining a profit margin and locking it in.

SPECULATORS

In order for the hedgers to eliminate an unacceptable price risk, they must find someone who is willing to bear that risk in their place. This person is the *speculator*. The speculator has no economic activity requiring use of futures contracts, but rather finds attractive investment opportunities in the futures market and takes positions in futures in hopes of making a profit rather than protecting one.

In some respects, speculators perform the same role as insurance companies.

You can think of the speculator performing the same role that insurance companies perform when they sell policies. The person who buys insurance is unwilling to bear the full risk of economic loss should an accident occur and so chooses to transfer that risk to the insurance company. The insurance company is willing to bear the risk because it feels there is a profit to be made by providing this coverage in exchange for the insurance premium.[6] One pricing theory holds that the hedger does, in fact, pay a premium for such "insurance"; this theory will be examined later, in the section on pricing fundamentals.[7]

---

[6] While this analogy may be helpful, you should not carry it too far. Insurance companies operate on the basis of the law of large numbers and the statistical probability of certain events occurring. An individual speculator in a futures contract is dealing with one outcome, not an averaging of many.

[7] A pricing theory called *normal backwardation* shows that the hedger does, in fact, pay a premium for the insurance function the speculator performs.

As stated above, the speculator normally goes long. As with other types of securities, it is conceptually easier for most investors to envision price rises rather than declines, but speculators may also go short if they feel that current prices are too high. Speculators might promise to deliver 5,000 bushels of wheat at $4.00 for September delivery if they feel wheat will not sell for that much at delivery time. Most speculators cannot conveniently deliver wheat because they do not grow it; this does not matter, though, because any speculator can quickly exit the market by buying a September wheat contract to cancel the position. The difference in price on the two trades will be the speculator's profit or loss.

Speculators are sometimes classified as either **position traders** or **day traders**. A position trader is someone who routinely maintains futures positions overnight, and sometimes keeps a contract open for weeks. Day traders close out all their positions before trading closes for the day, taking whatever profits or losses they have incurred.

SCALPERS

Scalpers are individuals who trade for their own account, making a living by buying and selling contracts in the pit. Studies have shown that the most successful trades made by a scalper are those where the time between the purchase and sale of the contract is less than 30 seconds! Scalpers may buy and sell the same contract often during a single trading day. The value of their account can change dramatically on days with wide price swings.

In Figure 8–2, we saw that Hennebry sold 5 contracts of September Treasury bonds to ZZZ. Hennebry is a scalper, and what he wants to do after this trade is buy 5 contracts at a lower price as quickly as he can. Perhaps a customer phones his broker and places a market order to sell 5 September Treasury bond contracts. When this order reaches the pit, the scalpers will all attempt to provide the other side of the trade at a favorable price. Suppose Hennebry gets this trade, and that he buys the 5 contracts at $77^{29}/_{32}$. Having sold five contracts earlier at $77^{31}/_{32}$, this is a gain of $^2/_{32}$ on each of five contracts, so the total dollar profit he just made is

$$\frac{2}{32}\% \times \frac{\$100,000}{\text{contract}} \times 5 \text{ contracts} = \$312.50.$$

Three hundred bucks for a minute's work isn't bad!

Scalpers are also called *locals*, meaning that they are "part of the neighborhood" and someone with whom it is desirable to maintain good relations. Although the business of commodity trading for a living is treacherous, locals place a high emphasis on integrity and accuracy, and these traders will sometimes help each other out of a jam in the pit. Doing so usually involves one or more other locals incurring small opportunity losses through lost trades or channeling business to a trader who has had a bad day. The trader in trouble gets a tick[8] here and a tick there, and hopefully recovers from an otherwise catastrophic loss.

---

[8] A tick is the smallest permissible price change in a particular contract.

Scalpers play a crucial role in the economic functioning of the futures markets. By their active trading with each other, they help keep prices continuous and accurate, which is the hallmark of the U.S. financial system. The futures market would be much less liquid without the scalpers.

THE CLEARING PROCESS

Integrity, honesty, and accuracy are crucial features of a viable trading system. At the Chicago Board of Trade, more than one million contracts change hands each day, with a total dollar value in the billions. Large sums of money are made and lost each minute in the trading pits; it is imperative that a mechanism be in place to ensure that traders keep their promises, even when large wealth transfers occur. Making sure promises are kept is the role of the clearing process.

Each trader in the pit prepares trading cards on his or her transactions. The clearing process begins with attempts to match up the cards describing a particular trade. In Figure 8–2, we saw Hennebry's trade of five September U.S. Treasury bond contracts at $77^{31}/_{32}$ to buyer ZZZ of firm OOO. Somewhere in the system there should also be a card from ZZZ showing a purchase from Hennebry with similar terms. When these two cards are matched, a futures contract exists. Besides matching trades, the clearing process performs other functions: guaranteeing trades, supervising the accounting for performance bonds, handling intramarket settlements, establishing settlement prices, and providing for delivery. We now examine each of these functions in greater detail.

MATCHING TRADES

It is the responsibility of each trader on the floor to ensure that his or her deck promptly enters the clearing process. Every trade must be cleared by or through a member firm of the Board of Trade Clearing Corporation. Scalpers make arrangements with a member firm to process their decks each day. Scalpers normally use only one clearinghouse, and the name of this organization will be displayed on their trading jackets. This name will be the "firm name" entered on trading cards by parties to the scalper's trades.

Brokers are people in the pits who are members of the exchange trading for their own account and for whatever public accounts they choose to accept. They also can be hired by brokerage houses such as Merrill Lynch to handle the firm's transactions on the exchange floor. Brokers also fill out trading cards, but it is common practice for them to submit their cards periodically while trading rather than turning in a deck at the end of the day.

Although affiliated with the Board of Trade, the Clearing Corporation is an independent organization with its own officers and rules. Some members of the Board of the Trade are also members of the Clearing Corporation. These people can clear their own trades, and, for a fee, will sometimes clear trades for nonmembers. Scalpers might pay $1.50 per trade to a member firm for clearing their trades. All trades must go through the clearing process.

After a Clearing Corporation member receives trading cards, the information on them is edited and checked by computer. Cards with missing information are returned to the clearing member for correction. The information on valid cards is stored in computer memory. Once all cards have been edited and fed to the computer, the computer attempts to match cards for all trades that occurred on the exchange that day.

Sometimes it is not possible to match all trades exactly. These mismatches, called **out trades**, result in an **Unmatched Trade Notice** being sent to each clearing member. It is the responsibility of the traders themselves to reconcile their out trades and arrive at a solution to the mismatch. A "price out," where the two traders wrote down different prices for a given trade, sometimes occurs when one person writes down a price that is away from the market, or far away from the current trading range. A contract might trade between $5.97 and $6.01 during time block C on a given day. Writing a price of $5.01 rather than $6.01 would result in an out trade that is easily reconciled by the two participants to the trade. Where the error is not obvious, such as a price of $5.97 and a potential match with a price of $5.98, the two traders often compromise by splitting the difference.

Another mismatch is the "house out," where an incorrect member firm is listed on the trading card. This is normally easy to rectify because there will likely be two trades that do match except for the firm. A "quantity out" occurs when the number of contracts in a particular trade is in dispute. A trader may think he bought eight contracts, while the seller sold eighteen. "Strike out" and "time out" occur primarily with futures options, when errors occur with either the striking price or the delivery month. The worst out trade is the "sides out," when both cards show the same side of the market, i.e., both indicate buy or both indicate sell. These are difficult to reconcile but do not happen very often.

Despite the reason for the Unmatched Trade Notice, it is the trader's individual responsibility to resolve the error. On the rare occasions when this cannot be done, the dispute may be taken to arbitration with the Clearing Corporation.

At the Chicago Board of Trade, out trades account for 1 or 2 percent of daily volume. It is estimated that floor brokers lose between 10 percent and 17 percent of gross billings to out trades. A preliminary run is completed at the Chicago Board of Trade by 5 P.M. each trading day. The clearinghouse distributes a listing of unmatched trades to each firm with apparent out trades from this preliminary run. Many entries on the listing are simply clerical errors. Firms have until 8 P.M. to make corrections. Large firms, which clear for many scalpers, sometimes have preliminary run listings several inches thick. Trade checkers attempt to resolve mismatches by checking order cards and calling clearing clerks in other firms. Any mistakes discovered are submitted to the clearinghouse, and another computer run then occurs. According to the market report department at the Chicago Board of Trade, about 90 percent of out trades are cleared by the second computer run. The remainder must be cleared the following morning by an individual trader involved before the trader begins trading for the day. The exchanges employ out trade clerks to help in the process of reconciling trades. This job is a stressful one, since out trades are no fun, and the parties involved are not always in the best of moods. Price disputes are frequently settled by simply splitting the difference.

After resolving all out trades, the computer prints a daily Trade Register showing a complete record of each clearing member's trades for the day. Within a Register are subsidiary accounts for each customer clearing through the firm. These accounts show all positions in each commodity and delivery month, much like other types of brokerage statements.

ACCOUNTING SUPERVISION

The performance bonds deposited by the member firms remain with the Clearing Corporation until each firm closes out its positions by either making an offsetting trade or by delivery of the commodity. When successful delivery occurs, good faith deposits are returned to both parties, payment for the commodity is received from the buyer and remitted to the seller, and the warehouse receipt for the goods is delivered to the buyer.

On a daily basis, the accounting problem is formidable, even when no deliveries occur. Unlike most other types of investment accounts, futures contracts are **marked to the market** every day, meaning that funds are transferred from one account to another based on unrealized (or paper) gains and losses. For instance, if the initial deposit in a member's account is $2,000 on a purchase of a soybean contract at $6.00 per bushel, a decline in the price of the soybeans to $5.99 would result in a $50 loss, and the member's account would show only $1,950 remaining from the $2,000 deposit. After each trading day the Clearing Corporation makes these transfers and prepares a summary of positions and cash in the account for each member.

Table 8–5 presents a hypothetical series of transactions in the soybean commodity futures market showing the handling of the various transactions. The example begins with soybeans selling at $5.30 per bushel. When someone initially establishes a futures position, the trade that does so is called an opening transaction, just as in the options market. Each opening transaction creates half a futures contract. Each closing transaction eliminates half a futures contract. Closing transactions can occur by either delivery of the commodity or by an offsetting trade. A short seller, for instance, can get out of the market by buying an identical contract or by delivering the promised commodity. Table 8–6 shows how open interest varies in the example from Table 8–5 and how the cash at the clearinghouse exactly works out by contract delivery.

Open interest is a measure of how many futures contracts in a given commodity exist at a particular time. This is the same idea as exists with stock options. There is no set number of option or futures contracts. When someone writes an option, they create a new contract. Similarly, when someone decides to go short a futures contract, they have created a new contract. The number of futures "promises" can increase or decrease every day, depending on the relative proportion of opening and closing transactions.

TABLE 8-5 Sample Futures Transactions

		TRADING ACCOUNT BALANCES						
		SPECULATORS				HEDGERS		
		A	B	C	D	A	B	C
Day 1	Hedger A decides to sell 1 contract at 530. This is an opening transaction, requiring a hedger's margin of $1,000. Speculator A buys this contract, also as an opening transaction, and deposits speculative margin of $2,000. The settlement price at the end of the day is 527. Accounts are marked to market.	$2,000 $1,850				$1,000 $1,150		
Day 2	Speculator A takes his loss and gets out of the market by an offsetting transaction. He sells his contract at 527. Speculator B buys the contract from Speculator A and deposits margin of $2,000. Hedger B sells two contracts (opening transaction) at 528 and deposits $2,000. Speculator C sells one contract (opening transaction) at 528 and deposits $2,000. Speculator D buys three contracts (opening transaction) from Hedger B and Speculator C, depositing $6,000. Settlement price at the end of the day is 531. Accounts are marked to market.	Takes $1,850 home	$2,000 $2,200	$2,000 $1,850	$6,000 $6,450	$950	$2,000 $1,700	
Day 3	Speculator B decides to take his profit and sells his contract at 533 (closing transaction). Speculator C elects to get out of the market and buys the contract from Speculator B (closing transaction). The settlement price at the end of the day is 532. Accounts are marked to market.		Takes $2,300 home	Takes $1,750 home	$6,600	$900	$1,600	
Day 4	Hedger C buys 3 contracts at 534 (opening transaction) and deposits $3,000. Speculator D sells 3 contracts (closing transaction) to Hedger C. The settlement price at the end of the day is 535. Accounts are marked to market.				Takes $6,900 home	$750	$1,300	$3,000 $3,150
Day 5	Hedger B delivers 2 contracts, receiving $5.28 per bushel and also getting the $2,000 margin back. Hedger C receives 2 contracts from Hedger B and pays $5.34 per bushel for them. Hedger C also gets $2,000 margin back. Hedger A delivers 1 contract, receiving $5.30 per bushel and getting $1,000 margin back. Hedger C receives the remaining contract from Hedger A, paying $5.34 per bushel and recovering the other $1,000 of the good faith deposit.					Takes $27,500 home	Takes $54,800 home Pays $51,400 net	Pays $25,700 net

		OPEN INTEREST (CUMULATIVE)	CASH RECEIVED	CASH PAID	CASH ON HAND
TABLE 8–6 Cash with the Clearing House					
DAY 1	HEDGER A	+½	$1,000		$1,000
	SPECULATOR A	+½	$2,000		$3,000
		1			
DAY 2	SPECULATOR A	−½		$1,850	$1,150
	SPECULATOR B	+½	$2,000		$3,150
	HEDGER B	+1	$2,000		$5,150
	SPECULATOR C	+½	$2,000		$7,150
	SPECULATOR D	+1½	$6,000		$13,150
		4			
DAY 3	SPECULATOR B	−½		$2,300	$10,850
	SPECULATOR C	−½		$1,750	$9,100
		3			
DAY 4	HEDGER C	+1½	$3,000		$12,100
	SPECULATOR D	−1½		$6,900	$5,200
		3			
DAY 5	HEDGER B	−1		$54,800	−$49,600
	HEDGER C	−1	$51,400		$1,800
	HEDGER A	−½		$27,500	−$25,700
	HEDGER C	−½	$25,700		0
		0			

At the end of Day 5, all positions have been eliminated (open interest is zero) and the Clearing House has disbursed all cash.

Open interest increases by one every time two opening transactions are matched and decreases by one every time two closing transactions are matched. If a trade involves a closing transaction by one participant and an opening transaction by the other, then open interest will not change: the number of "promises" remains unchanged, although the players may change. This is a consequence of the fungibility of futures contracts. If Delta Dick owes $10 to Gabby Gamma, and Gabby Gamma owes $10 to Thaddeus Theta, then Gabby Gamma does not need to be in the picture: the Clearing Corporation can close her out and instruct Delta Dick to pay Thaddeus Theta. The clearinghouse maintains information about open interest and publishes these figures in the financial pages daily. Large open interest figures are desirable to ensure a competitive market.

Open interest is different from trading volume. A single futures contract might be traded often during its life. A bank that hedges interest rate risk by buying T-bond futures might keep this position for several months. But the speculators who take the other side of this trade might exchange their half of the promise 100 times before the delivery date.

Figure 8–3 shows soybean prices from Friday, June 16, 2000. The two columns on the far right indicate that volume and open interest can be substantially different. A tick in soybean futures is $\frac{1}{8}$ of a cent. The newspaper shows prices in pennies and eighths. A price of 5046, for instance, means \$5.04⁶/₈, or \$5.0475 per bushel.

When people leave the market by an offsetting trade, their profit or loss comes from the gains or losses that have been posted to their account each day after trading. In Day 1 of Table 8–5, we see Speculator A buy a contract at \$5.30 per bushel. Instead of advancing, the price of soybeans went down the following day. This speculator chose to take his lumps and get out of the market. The broker was able to sell his contract at \$5.27. This \$0.03 per bushel loss is incurred on each of the 5000 bushels represented by a single soybean contract, so the speculator loses \$150. Although the initial good faith deposit was \$2,000, only \$1,850 goes back home.

Another important point is illustrated by the activities on Day 5. Hedger C receives 10,000 bushels of beans from Hedger B. When Hedger B entered the market, he sold beans for 528. Hedger C, however, agreed to pay 534. Because Hedger C pays more than Hedger B receives does not mean there is something wrong with the market or that there is a "parasite," to use Senator Washburn's words. All market participants perform exactly as promised, and by the end of Day 5 we see that everything nets out exactly to zero. Open interest is also zero after the last closing transaction occurs.

INTRAMARKET SETTLEMENT

On rare occasions, commodity prices move so much in a single day that good faith deposits for many members are seriously eroded even before the day ends.

FIGURE 8–3 Soybean Futures Prices June 16, 2000							
DELIVERY MONTH	OPEN	HIGH	LOW	SETTLE	CHANGE	VOLUME	OPEN INTEREST
JUL 2000	5144	5144	5040	5046	−52	32004	46746
AUG 2000	5070	5074	5004	5012	4	7889	19480
SEP 2000	4980	4994	4950	4960	44	3960	15487
NOV 2000	5020	5042	4994	5006	56	22629	62655
JAN 2001	5110	5130	5084	5100	54	1005	6305
MAR 2001	5204	5204	5160	5180	54	1015	4987
MAY 2001	5240	5270	5230	5230	44	15	6202
JULY 2001	5290	5330	5280	5290	40	53	4187
NOV 2001	5380	5400	5330	5330	30	37	1371

Data from Bridge FutureSource.

When deemed necessary, the President of the Clearing Corporation may call on members to deposit more funds into their account during the day. This is a **market variation call**, and these funds must be deposited within one hour from the time of the call. The procedure also helps to ensure the integrity of commodity futures contracts.

SETTLEMENT PRICES

In the commodity pits it is difficult to tell precisely what the last trade was when the bell rings to signal the end of the trading day. This is understandable given the open outcry system, where other people in the pit do not always see every trade that occurs. Because all commodity accounts are marked to market daily, a final price is necessary so that funds can be transferred among accounts. The settlement price is analogous to the closing price on the stock exchanges, and it is this figure that will appear in the morning's financial pages. While procedures vary slightly from commodity to commodity, the settlement price is normally an average of the high and low prices during the last minute or so of trading. Establishment of the official settlement price is another of the Clearing Corporation's functions.

The prices of some futures contracts are constrained by daily price limit restrictions.

Unlike the prices established on stock and option exchanges, many commodity futures prices are constrained by a **daily price limit**. This means that the price of a contract is not allowed to move by more than a predetermined amount each trading day. For instance, if the daily price limit for soybeans is 30 cents, this means that today's settlement price cannot be more than 30 cents higher or 30 cents lower than yesterday's settlement price. Commodities are said to be *limit up* or *limit down* when a big move occurs. Sometimes it may take several days for prices to work their way to a new equilibrium price.

DELIVERY

Although the Clearing Corporation interposes itself between every buyer and seller, it never takes or makes delivery of any commodity. It does, however, provide the framework that ensures accurate delivery. Let's look at the delivery procedure for a grain contract at the Chicago Board of Trade.

When a seller decides to deliver, a *Notice of Intention to Deliver* is filed with the Clearing Corporation. This shows the seller's intention to deliver the commodity on the next business day. Delivery can occur anytime during the delivery month, and the first business day before the first day of the delivery month is called *First Notice Day*.

On the day prior to first notice day, each member with long positions in his or her account must submit a *Long Position Report* to the Clearing Corporation. This document shows all the members' long positions and their date of purchase. This document also must be updated each day during the delivery month. The due date for this report is *position day*. On the next day, *intention day*, the Clearing Corporation may assign delivery to the member with the oldest long position in the particular commodity. The price of the delivered commodity is adjusted for quality differentials and any other associated costs such as temporary storage or transportation.

As a rule, speculators and their brokers do not like to handle deliveries. Given that delivery can occur anytime in the delivery month, speculators tend to move out of the market in the few days prior to first notice day.

Delivery procedures vary somewhat among the exchanges, and are quite different when financial futures are involved. At the Chicago Mercantile Exchange, for instance, both buyers *and* sellers of its Treasury bill contract may initiate delivery, and delivery must occur on a single, predetermined day of the delivery month.

PRINCIPLES OF FUTURES CONTRACT PRICING

In considering what makes a futures contract valuable and what makes the price of the contract fluctuate from day to day, it is important to remember the basic fundamental that a futures contract is a promise to exchange certain goods at a future date. You must keep your part of the promise unless you get someone to take the promise off your hands (i.e., you make a closing transaction). The promised goods are valuable now, and their value in the future may be more or less than their current worth. Prices of commodities change for many reasons, such as new weather forecasts, the availability of substitute commodities, psychological factors, and changes in storage or insurance costs. These factors include shifts in demand for a commodity, changes in the supply of the commodity, or both.

There are general principles of futures pricing applicable to all contracts. Specific examples of pricing with financial futures appear in Chapters 9 through 12.

There are three main theories of futures pricing:

1. the expectations hypothesis,

2. normal backwardation, and

3. a full carrying charge market.

THE EXPECTATIONS HYPOTHESIS

Remember Senator Washburn's comments about these "fictitious contracts." Of course, the contracts are very real, with brokerage houses and the Clearing Corporation to enforce compliance with the terms of the contract. Because the contract calls for delivery of a specified good in the future, it seems likely that one of the major determinants of the futures contract value is the current value of the commodity in the cash market. This is exactly what we find.

The simplest generalization about this relationship is the **expectations hypothesis**. This states that the futures price for a commodity is what the marketplace expects the cash price to be when the delivery month arrives. Under this hypothesis, if September soybeans are selling in the futures market for $5 per bushel, this means the marketplace expects soybeans to sell for $5 in September. There is considerable evidence that the expectations hypothesis is a good predictor. This is a very important fact for the user of the futures market, because it provides an important source of information about what the future is likely to bring. **Price discovery**, in fact, is an important function that futures perform. If I want to know what people expect the price of heating oil to be this fall, I can look in the *Wall Street Journal* for the price of a heating oil futures contract and know that this figure is a reliable estimate based on current information. (Remember that the price for the retail customer would be somewhat higher than the price that a wholesale distributor would pay.)

For instance, an investor may be interested in learning consensus estimates of the price of gold or German deutsche marks a year from now. According to the expectations hypothesis, the best place to look for an estimate is in the financial pages. You simply need to see what a futures contract with a delivery month one year hence settled at yesterday.

We have previously seen that there needs to be a relationship between the price of a commodity in the cash market and the price of that commodity in the futures market. There is a definite relationship between the cash price of a commodity, the various storage costs associated with the commodity, and the futures price. In a well-functioning marketplace, arbitrage opportunities will not appear often; when they do they are quickly eliminated as people exploit them.

Consider the situation in which in June, cash corn sells for $2 per bushel, the local grain elevator charges 5 cents per bushel per month to store the grain, and an August futures contract sells for $2.15. If these prices were accurate, an arbitrage opportunity would be there for the taking. Simply buy corn in the cash market, sell a futures contract promising to deliver the corn in two months for $2.15 per bushel, store the corn in the elevator for two months, and then arrange for delivery. You would have a little more than $2.10 invested in the corn ($2 cost plus 10 cents storage costs plus a small amount of interest to finance the purchase) and you would receive $2.15 from the Clearing Corporation when you deliver. You have made about 5 cents per bushel profit, without taking any risk.

NORMAL BACKWARDATION

All participants in the futures market are very concerned with the idea of **basis**. Basis is the difference between the future price of a commodity and the current cash price. Normally, the futures price exceeds the cash price; this is a **contango** market. If the futures price is less than the cash price, this is called **backwardation**, or an **inverted market**. As the gap between the futures price and the cash price narrows, we say that the basis has strengthened; basis weakens if the gap gets wider.

Remember that investors do not like risk and that they will only take a risk if they think they will be properly rewarded for bearing the risk. If the futures price is what people think the cash price will be at delivery time, then why would any-one be interested in speculating? It seems that the hedger can get rid of his or her price risk without any cost and that the speculator agrees to take the risk off the hedger's back for nothing. This seems improbable in real life.

Normal backwardation suggests the futures price is a downward biased estimate of the future cash price.

The idea of **normal backwardation** is attributed to the famous economist John Maynard Keynes. Like much of good economics, the idea is simple and very logical. A hedger who uses the futures market is essentially buying insurance. Lock-ing in a future price that is acceptable eliminates price risk. When we obtain insur-ance we pay for it, because the insurance company could not remain in business if it offered this protection for nothing. Keynes argues that this means that the futures price must be a downward biased estimate of the future cash price. In other words, at delivery the cash price will likely be somewhat higher than the price predicated by the futures market. This is because the speculator must be rewarded for taking the risk that the hedger was unwilling to bear. The hedger might really believe that the cash price of soybeans in September will be about $5.04, but might also be perfectly willing to take $5 per bushel for certain. Though this is less than the anticipated price, the risk that the soybean market might col-lapse to $4.75 or less is unacceptable. The peace of mind that $5 per bushel brings is valuable.

The speculator, on the other hand, has access to the same information as the hedger, and might agree that $5.04 is a good bet for the cash price of beans in September. Remember that one contract of soybeans is 5,000 bushels, so if the speculator can promise to pay $5 per bushel and turn around and sell it for $5.04, this is a $200 gain per contract. The high leverage associated with futures con-tracts can make this an impressive rate of return when annualized. On the other hand, prices could take a dive and result in big losses for the speculator (but not for the hedged farmer).

The concept of normal backwardation does not really mean that the expec-tations hypothesis is wrong. Keynes agrees that the futures market provides use-ful information about the future. With the logic of normal backwardation, though, we may be able to fine-tune our estimate of future cash market prices.

A FULL CARRYING CHARGE MARKET

You can buy commodities in the cash market and store them for later consump-tion. As we have seen, the person who performs the storage function gets a fee for this service. It is necessary to keep grains dry, to protect them against fire, to keep the rat population to a minimum, and to provide insurance on the stored commodities. Insurance is necessary to protect against loss of the goods due to tornadoes, floods, fire, and even explosion. Every few years we read of spectacu-lar blow-ups of a grain elevator. The dust and fine seed particles that can get sus-pended in the air during filling and storage will, under certain circumstances, ignite with a vengeance. A **full carrying charge market** occurs when futures prices reflect the cost of storing and financing the commodity until the delivery month.

In a world of certainty, the futures price F is equal to the current spot price S_t plus the carrying charges C until the delivery month:

To calculate basis, subtract the cash price from the futures price.

$$F = S_t + C \qquad (8-1)$$

Although we do not live in a world of certainty, the difference in price between a futures price and the cash price is often quite close to the carrying costs between the two points in time. In such a market, this has important implications for the speculator. Suppose in early September we see prices as follows and that it costs $2^1/_2$ cents per month to store soybeans:

Cash price for soybeans:		$4.85
Futures prices:	Nov:	$4.90
	Jan:	$4.95
	Mar:	$5.00

The speculator might be trying to decide between the January and March delivery months. If the speculator wants to go long (thinking that soybean prices will increase), it is wise to buy the near delivery month (January). To go short (anticipating a downturn in prices), it is best to sell the far delivery month (March). Let's see why.

Arbitrage exists if someone can buy a commodity, store it at a known cost, and get someone to promise to buy it later at a price that exceeds the cost of storage. In a full carrying change market like in this example, the basis must either stay the same or strengthen; it cannot weaken because that would produce an arbitrage situation. In other words, the difference between an January and a March contract could become less than 5 cents, but it should never be more.[9] If it were more, then you could buy January, sell March, pay a nickel storage for two months, and still be ahead without having taken any risk.

Although there is never certainty in any investment situation, in a full carrying charge market the bullish speculator who buys the near contract can be very confident of one of two things. If the price of soybeans does go up, then January soybeans should rise by more than March beans. If soybean prices fall, then January soybeans should fall less than March beans. In either case, the speculator is better off buying the near delivery month.

The logic holds true in reverse for the speculator who is bearish: go short the far contract, because it will either fall in value more or rise in value less than the near delivery month.[10]

---

[9] This assumes that monthly storage costs remain constant. The example also assumes that the arbitrageur can deliver the corn in the right grade as required.

[10] This relationship is less obvious with financial futures. The interest rate yield curve is seldom flat, and this means that the cost of carry varies according to the time span covered. The shape of the yield curve can change in such a fashion that the strategy described above was, in fact, not the best when viewed after the fact.

RECONCILING THE THREE THEORIES

The three theories of futures pricing are actually quite compatible. The differences in them are somewhat like the chicken and the egg question, in that it may not be easy to decide which comes first. The expectations hypothesis says that a futures price is simply the expected cash price at the delivery date of the futures contract. People know about storage costs and other costs of carry (insurance, interest, etc.), and we would not expect these costs to surprise the market when they are incurred. It therefore seems logical that people would "expect" the futures price to be partially determined by these costs.

The essence of normal backwardation is that the hedger is willing to take a bit less than the actual expected futures cash price for the peace of mind that comes with insurance. Because the hedger is really obtaining price insurance with futures, it is logical that there be some cost to the insurance. The hedger might expect a higher price, but be willing to accept a lower price to reduce risk. In a full carrying charge market, the futures price reflects the actual cost of storing a commodity until delivery time. This is consistent with the expectations theory.

SPREADING WITH COMMODITY FUTURES

We have previously seen how the risk and return relationship of a stock option position can be altered by the inclusion of one or more other option positions in the portfolio. The same general result is true with futures contracts. Futures spreading is a type of speculation and involves taking offsetting positions in two related commodities or in the same commodity. As with options, futures spreads have less risk than an outright long or short position.[11] Also, there may be special margin requirements with commodity spreads, meaning that the speculator has to put up a smaller good faith deposit than would be true on two trades made individually.

INTERCOMMODITY SPREADS

An **intercommodity spread** is a long and short position in two related commodities, perhaps corn and live cattle. A speculator might feel that the price of corn is too low relative to the price of live cattle, and that this differential should correct itself in the near future. So, the speculator might sell live cattle (anticipating a price decline) and buy corn (anticipating a price rise). This type of spread is risky, because there is no assurance that your hunch will be correct. It is entirely possible that corn could decline while live cattle prices increased further, in which case you would lose on both investments. For this reason, there is not always a special margin treatment for an intercommodity spread.

---

[11] This is not always true with spreads in the futures market, particularly with old year/new year or intercommodity spreads.

INTERMARKET SPREADS

With an **intermarket spread**, a speculator takes opposite positions in two different markets. Wheat trades on both the Chicago Board of Trade and on the Kansas City Board of Trade. Any difference in price between these two locations should be based primarily on transportation expenses or other administrative costs.

Some international investment houses routinely spread gold in the cash market between major financial centers. It may be possible to buy gold in Zurich at $250 an ounce and simultaneously sell it in London at $255. If this $5 difference is sufficient to overcome shipping costs, then a person who bought Zurich gold and sold London gold would realize a profit.

INTRACOMMODITY SPREADS

An **intracommodity spread** is also called an *intermonth spread*; it involves taking different positions in different delivery months, but in the same commodity. For instance, a speculator who is bullish on wheat might buy September and sell December. These spreads are rather common because they involve a low margin requirement and substantially reduced risk.

An important consideration with these spreads is the difference between a "same crop" spread and a "new crop/old crop" spread. A spread using November and January soybeans would be a same crop spread, because these beans were harvested during the same crop year. Buying July 2000 beans and selling November 2000 beans would be a new crop/old crop spread, and much more risky because the conditions affecting the price of soybeans may be very different next year.

One final thought on commodity spreads involves the extent to which your losses are known or limited. Suppose that in March a speculator reads that September meal sells for $174.60 and that December meal sells for $179.60. The speculator, being bullish, buys a September contract and sells a December contract.

Suppose that in August soy meal has risen (as the speculator had hoped), and that current futures prices are $184.60 for the September contract and $194.60 for the December contract. If the speculator were to close out these two contracts at this point in August, the combined positions would show a loss, even though commodity prices moved in the anticipated direction. On the long side, the contract price rose by $10 per ton, while on the short side the price rose by $15 per ton. Since the speculator was short the December contract, this $15 price rise really translated into a $15/ton loss. Combining this with the $10 per ton gain on the long side yields a net loss of $5 per ton. With 100 tons in a soy meal contract, this means that the combined positions lost $500 even through prices advanced. The reason for this is that the basis on the short position changed adversely relative to the basis on the long position.[12]

---

[12] This is not something we have to worry about with bull spreads using stock options.

WHY SPREAD IN THE FIRST PLACE?

It should be obvious that there can be huge gains and losses in the futures market. Some people, including professional commodity traders, are uncomfortable with the magnitude of loss that could occur from a "lights-out" move. Acapulco is very nice, but we need to remember that Tapioca City is out there somewhere.

Many people choose to trade the basis rather than simply go long or short a particular futures contract and hope that prices move your way. I may expect the basis to strengthen or to weaken, but in either event my maximum loss is likely to be much less than with a single futures position. Playing the basis involves more than one contract, and this is by definition a spread. Most intracommodity spreads are basis plays.

Intercommodity spreads are not necessarily risk-reducing strategies. In the example earlier, where a speculator sold live cattle and bought corn, it is certainly possible that both contracts could move adversely. Such a spread is closer to two separate speculative positions than to a spread in the stock option sense.

Intermarket spreads are really arbitrage plays based on discrepancies in transportation costs or other administrative costs. When arbitrage is spotted, a spread is the way to take advantage of it: buy in the cheap location and sell where it is dear.

SUMMARY

Futures contracts are promises to buy or to deliver a certain quantity of a carefully defined commodity by a certain date. Futures contracts enable farmers, bankers, or anyone else with economic interests in a particular commodity to hedge price risk. The futures market cannot provide protection against crop failure or against making bad investments.

To ensure the integrity of the contract, all trades are actually sales to or purchases from the Clearing Corporation. Both hedgers and speculators post a good faith deposit to show their capacity to sustain any losses that might accrue to them.

There are three main theories of futures pricing: the expectations hypothesis, the concept of normal backwardation, and the concept of a full carrying charge market. Rather than competing philosophies, these three theories are different perspectives on the fundamental result that futures prices are primarily determined by today's cash price, by the cost of storing and transporting commodities, and by expectations about how the cash price is likely to change in the future.

SELF TEST

T ___ F ___   1. Futures markets typically work best when there are relatively few speculators.

T ___ F ___   2. Rather than having an expiration date like an option, a futures contract has a delivery date.

T ___ F ___   3. A forward contract is more similar to a futures contract than to an options contract.

T ___ F ___   4. The Securities and Exchange Commission regulates commodities trading.

T ___ F ___   5. Property rights cannot be transferred with futures contracts.

T ___ F ___   6. A business that needs a particular commodity in the near future could logically use a short hedge to get it.

T ___ F ___   7. All participants in the futures market must post a good faith deposit on which they may earn interest.

T ___ F ___   8. In the marketmaker system at the futures exchanges, trades occur by open outcry.

T ___ F ___   9. If a trader has an out trade, he or she receives an unmatched trade notice.

T ___ F ___   10. The futures market is not designed to provide protection against crop failure.

T ___ F ___   11. "Putting on a crush" involves buying soybeans and selling soybean oil and meal.

T ___ F ___   12. In some respects, speculators perform the same function as insurance companies.

T ___ F ___   13. Scalpers provide liquidity to the market.

T ___ F ___   14. Futures contracts are marked to market weekly.

T ___ F ___   15. Open interest is a measure of how many contracts traded on a particular day.

T ___ F ___ 16. A trader who receives a market variation call has one hour to put money into his or her account.

T ___ F ___ 17. If a futures contract is "limit up," trading essentially stops for the day.

T ___ F ___ 18. The concept of normal backwardation suggests that the future cash price will be slightly higher than predicted by the expectations hypothesis.

T ___ F ___ 19. Basis is the difference between the futures price and the cash price.

T ___ F ___ 20. Unlike options, a futures spread is usually riskier than a single futures position.

PROBLEMS & QUESTIONS

1. How it is possible for the trading volume in a particular futures contract to exceed the open interest in the commodity?

2. Why is a delivery mechanism essential to a well-functioning futures market?

3. Do you think that daily prices limits make sense?

4. Under current rules, hedgers must post a smaller good faith deposit than speculators. Do you feel this is a reasonable rule?

5. Explain how it is possible for a hedger to *benefit* from a narrowing basis in a particular commodity.

6. Why is it that your maximum losses and gains are *not* predetermined with a commodity spread (as they are with most option spreads)?

7. "Closing all futures exchanges would probably be inflationary because of the added risk the producers would have to bear." Do you agree?

8. Suppose you were on a commission that was evaluating several proposals for new futures contracts. What would you want to know before you could make a decision on whether the proposals should be approved?

9. Do you think it would be possible for futures contracts to trade via the *specialist* system? Why or why not?

10. Commodities whose prices are particularly volatile lend themselves to futures trading. Lettuce is usually considered to be the grocery store commodity whose price is most uncertain. One day it is 47 cents a head, the next day it is 99 cents. Some people argue that futures contracts will never work for *perishable* commodities like lettuce. Do you agree?

11. A farmer anticipates having 50,000 bushels of wheat ready for harvest in September. What would be the implications of hedging by (a) selling 8 contracts, (b) selling 10 contracts, and (c) selling 12 contracts of September wheat?

12. Give examples of someone who might profitably use a *long hedge* in (a) corn, (b) gold, and (c) soybeans.

13. Briefly explain why prices for futures contracts on grains are generally higher for more distant delivery months.

14. "Individual speculators tend to lose money on their purchases of futures contracts." Do you agree?

Refer to Figure 8–3 as needed. Assume that today is June 17, 2000.

15. Suppose two weeks ago a speculator purchased 4 contracts of September soybeans at

CHAPTER 8 REVIEW

4912. What is the person's gain or loss as of the date of this newspaper?

16. Suppose a farmer anticipates harvesting 50,000 bushels of soybeans in September. How much money would the farmer receive from hedging by selling 8 contracts of September soybeans at the Chicago Board of Trade (using the settlement price shown in today's paper)?
    (a) today and
    (b) at delivery?

17. Refer to a current *Wall Street Journal*. Assume a soybean processor has a 100,000 bushel capacity. Calculate the processor's profit margin according to the *WSJ* prices and put on a crush for October delivery. Assume it takes one month to complete the processing operation.

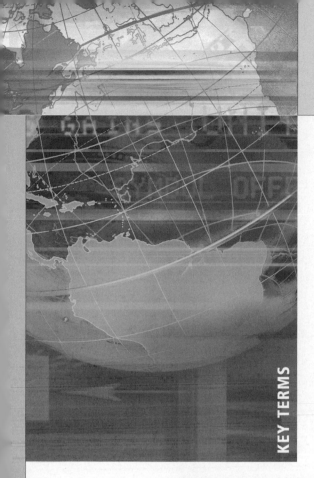

9

Stock Index Futures

Risk Comes from Not Knowing What You Are Doing.

Warren Buffett

The variety of assets on which futures contracts trade continues to grow. There have been proposals for new commodity contracts before the exchanges and other regulatory bodies almost continuously since 1985. The fastest-growing segment of the futures market is in financial futures. In 1972, physical commodities such as agricultural products, lumber, and metals comprised over 95 percent of all futures volume. Today, these combined contracts amount to only about one-third of total futures volume. This chapter and the next two review a representative from each of the three principal subgroups of the financial futures: stock index futures, foreign exchange futures, and interest rate futures.

STOCK INDEXES AND THEIR FUTURES CONTRACTS

The first thing to understand about an index futures contract is the nature of the underlying asset. What is the *stock index* that people promise to deliver or to buy? Someone can hold a handful of soybeans or corn, but what about the Standard

TABLE 9–1   Stock Index Futures Contracts

CONTRACT AND TICKER SYMBOL	EXCHANGE*	FUTURES DESCRIPTION
S&P 500 (SP)	CME	$250 × S&P 500 INDEX
S&P 500 BARRA GROWTH INDEX (SG)	CME	$250 × S&P 500/BARRA GROWTH INDEX
S&P 500 BARRA VALUE INDEX (SU)	CME	$250 × S&P 500/BARRA VALUE INDEX
E-MINI S&P 500 (ES)	CME	$50 × S&P 500 INDEX
GOLDMAN SACHS COMMODITY INDEX (GI)	CME	$250 × GOLDMAN SACHS COMMODITY INDEX
NASDAQ 100 (ND)	CME	$100 × NASDAQ 100 INDEX
E-MINI NASDAQ (NQ)	CME	$20 × NASDAQ 100 INDEX
NIKKEI 225 STOCK AVERAGE (NK)	CME	$5 × NIKKEI STOCK INDEX
RUSSELL 2000 STOCK PRICE INDEX (RL)	CME	$500 × RUSSELL 2000
S&P MIDCAP 400 (MD)	CME	$500 × S&P MIDCAP STOCK PRICE INDEX
DOW JONES INDUSTRIAL AVERAGE (DJ)	CBOT	$10 × DJIA
DOW JONES TRANSPORTATION AVERAGE (DQ)	CBOT	$20 × DJTA
DOW JONES UTILITY AVERAGE (DR)	CBOT	$200 × DJUA
DOW JONES COMPOSITE AVERAGE (DE)	CBOT	$20 × DOW JONES COMPOSITE AVERAGE
NYSE COMPOSITE (SMALL) (YS)	NYBOT	$250 × NYSE COMPOSITE
NYSE COMPOSITE (REGULAR) (YX)	NYBOT	$500 × NYSE COMPOSITE
NYSE COMPOSITE (LARGE) (YL)	NYBOT	$1000 × NYSE COMPOSITE
FINANCIAL TIMES STOCK EXCHANGE 100 (UKX)	LIFFE	£10 × FTSE 100

*CME = Chicago Mercantile Exchange; CBOT = Chicago Board of Trade; NYBOT = New York Board of Trade; LIFFE = London International Financial Futures and Options Exchange

& Poor's 500 index? How can someone "buy" or "sell" a stock index? These are reasonable questions that are asked somewhere in the United States every day by banks, retirement funds, and individual investors who are learning the potential role these contracts have in their portfolios.

STOCK INDEXES

Table 9–1 lists many of the major stock index futures contracts. The examples to follow focus on the best known and most popular stock index contract: the S&P 500 futures contract.

Standard and Poor's began publishing the S&P 500 index in 1917; it was originally proposed as a standard against which portfolio managers and investment advisors might be judged. Initially there were only 200 stocks in the index, with expansion to 500 in 1957. Of the five hundred companies, 400 are industrial firms (including technology), 40 are public utilities, 40 are financial companies, and 20 are transportation firms.[1] The capital stock of these 500 companies adds up to about 80 percent of the total value of securities traded on the New York Stock Exchange. The S&P 500 index is currently one of the Commerce Department's leading indicators, representing about 90% of all U.S. stock index futures trading.

The S&P 500 index represents about 90% of all U.S. stock index futures trading.

[1] These figures sometimes vary slightly.

This index is **capitalization-weighted**; each of the 500 share prices gets multiplied by the number of outstanding shares in that particular firm. Standard and Poor's calculates the index by adding these figures and dividing by the index **divisor**.

Table 9–2 shows an example of a simple capitalization-weighted index formed from three firms. The divisor adjusts for changes in the companies making

TABLE 9–2   Capitalization-Weighted Index

DAY 1

Stock	Shares Outstanding	Closing Share Price	Shares × Price
A	1,000,000	$10	$10,000,000
B	5,000,000	$22	110,000,000
C	10,000,000	$15	150,000,000
		Total	$270,000,000

Suppose the initial divisor is arbitrarily set at 2,700,000. The index is then

$$\text{Index} = \frac{270,000,000}{2,700,000} = 100.00$$

DAY 2

Stock	Shares Outstanding	Closing Share Price	Shares × Price
A	1,000,000	$11	$11,000,000
B	5,000,000	$20	100,000,000
C	10,000,000	$16	160,000,000
		Total	$271,000,000

$$\text{Index} = \frac{271,000,000}{2,700,000} = 100.37$$

DAY 3
STOCK B SPLITS TWO FOR ONE

Stock	Shares Outstanding	Closing Share Price	Shares × Price
A	1,000,000	$12	$12,000,000
B	10,000,000	$11	110,000,000
C	10,000,000	$14	140,000,000
		Total	$262,000,000

$$\text{Index} = \frac{262,000,000}{2,700,000} = 97.04$$

THE INTERNATIONAL TOP TEN

CONTRACTS

Rank	Contract	Exchange	YTD 1999	YTD 2000	% Change
1	Euro-BUND	EUREX, Frankfurt	76,247,074	105,736,279	38.7
2	KOSPI 200 Options	KSE, Korea	49,559,447	96,153,236	94.0
3	3-Month Eurodollar	CME, US	66,461,643	72,920,253	9.7
4	CAC 40 Index Options	MONEP, France	44,815,306	54,795,638	22.3
5	U.S. T-Bonds	CBOT, US	66,009,074	45,006,113	(31.8)
6	Euro-BOBL	EUREX, Frankfurt	26,035,579	42,061,463	61.6
7	3-Month Euribor	LIFFE, UK	23,098,425	38,689,860	67.5
8	Euro-Notional Bond	MATIF, France	4,820,098	33,049,313	585.7
9	Ten Year T-Notes	CBOT, US	23,816,671	31,270,050	31.3
10	Euro-SCHATZ	EUREX, Frankfurt	9,079,741	26,927,236	196.6

EUREX = European Exchange
KSE = Korean Stock Exchange
CME = Chicago Mercantile Exchange
MONEP = Marche des Options Negociables de Paris

CBOT = Chicago Board of Trade
LIFFE = London Int'l Financial Futures and Options Exchange
MATIF = Marche a Terme International de France

EXCHANGES

Rank	Exchange	YTD 1999	YTD 2000	% Change
1	EUREX, Germany and Switzerland	244,704,231	302,195,689	23.5
2	CBOE, US	151,479,686	218,830,197	44.5
3	CBOT, US	183,557,866	163,206,990	(11.1)
4	Paris Bourse, France	121,912,687	156,061,159	28.0
5	CME, US	138,107,837	151,287,452	9.5
6	AMEX, US	77,939,236	133,635,868	71.5
7	KSE, Korea	61,547,200	107,116,085	74.0
8	LIFFE, UK	86,262,012	86,409,383	0.0
9	PSX, US	44,719,771	71,026,330	58.8
10	NYMEX, US	72,409,969	69,862,629	(3.5)

AMEX = American Stock Exchange
PSX = Philadelphia Stock Exchange

NYMEX = New York Mercantile Exchange

Source: Futures Industry, *Oct/Nov 2000.*

up the index, for spin-offs, mergers, and similar events that would cloud comparison of the index over time. If, for instance, Standard & Poor's replaced a $50 stock (100 million shares outstanding) with a $30 stock (50 million shares outstanding), this action replaces $5 billion in capitalization with $1.5 billion. Without an adjustment it would appear that the market declined, when this is not the case. S&P adjusts the divisor to offset this effect. Note that with a capitalization-weighted index a stock split does not change the divisor.

STOCK INDEX FUTURES CONTRACTS

The previous chapter covered basic futures principles: the role of the hedger, the importance of the speculator, standardization of the underlying commodity, and the delivery procedure. Stock index futures contracts are similar in every respect to a traditional agricultural contract *except* for the matter of delivery; index futures *settle in cash* rather than by delivery of the underlying asset. As with other futures contracts, a stock index future is a promise to buy or sell the standardized units of a specific index at a fixed price at a predetermined future date.

THE S&P 500 STOCK INDEX FUTURES CONTRACT

Table 9–3 lists the characteristics of the S&P 500 stock index futures contract. Unlike most other commodity contracts, there is no actual delivery mechanism at expiration of the contract. All contracts terminate with **cash settlement**. It is

---

TABLE 9–3   The S&P 500 Stock Index Futures Contract

- CONTRACT SIZE = $250 × INDEX LEVEL
- MINIMUM PRICE CHANGE = 0.10 (OR $25)
- PERFORMANCE BONDS (MARGIN):
    - SPECULATOR:*
        - INITIAL = $23,438
        - MAINTENANCE = $18,750
    - HEDGER:*
        - INITIAL = $18,750
        - MAINTENANCE = $18,750
- CONTRACTS ARE MARKED TO MARKET THROUGHOUT THE TRADING DAY.
- THE CONTRACT DOES NOT EARN DIVIDENDS.
- TRADING HOURS: 9:30 A.M.–4:15 P.M.
- SETTLEMENT MONTHS: MARCH, JUNE, SEPTEMBER, AND DECEMBER. THE LAST TRADING DAY IS THE THURSDAY PRIOR TO THE THIRD FRIDAY OF THE CONTRACT MONTH.
- TICKER SYMBOLS: FUTURES (SP), CASH (SPX)
- FINAL TRADING DAY: THURSDAY BEFORE THE 3RD FRIDAY OF THE CONTRACT MONTH.
- THE FUTURES ARE NICKNAMED SPUS (PRONOUNCED *SPOOZ*) IN THE TRADING PIT.

*Performance bonds are subject to frequent change.

not practical to have speculators or hedgers deliver 500 different stock certificates in fulfillment of the contract. At delivery time we know the value of the index, and it is much more convenient to credit or debit accounts with accrued gains or losses. What you actually deliver is the *dollar difference* between the original trade price and the final price of the index at termination of the contract.

If someone holds a contract until its last day, there are special procedures for the final debit or credit to traders' accounts. The last day of trading for the S&P 500 contract is the Thursday before the third Friday of the trading month. The next morning (Friday) the exchange determines a *Special Opening Quotation* for the index, calculated to the nearest 0.01, based on the official opening prices of the 500 stocks making up the S&P 500 index, even if the opening of trading for some of the stocks is delayed because of an order imbalance, corporate announcement, or something else. This is in contrast to the normal opening value for the index, which uses the last sales price for a stock if its trading is halted.

> There is no delivery mechanism with stock index futures; all closing contracts are settled in cash.

PRICING OF STOCK INDEX FUTURES

Because the S&P 500 index is a function of the price of the underlying cash index, the same factors affect it and the stock market. As Figure 9–1 shows, the *futures* value depends on four elements:[2]

- the level of the spot index itself;
- the dividend yield on the 500 stocks in the index;
- the current level of interest rates;
- the time until final contract cash settlement.

In finance, most pricing relationships center on arbitrage arguments: equivalent securities should sell for the same price. An institution could have a long position in all 500 securities comprising the SPX index. A more convenient alternative might be to have a long position in the futures contracts. While these positions are similar, they are not equivalent. A major difference lies in the fact that stocks pay dividends while the futures contracts do not. We know from elementary investment principles that on ex-dividend dates stock prices tend to fall by about the amount of the dividend earned. If everything else remains constant, an investor will not turn down a dividend. Holding stocks, you get dividends; while holding futures, you do not. This preference shows up as a pricing differential in the futures price/underlying asset relationship. In recent years the dividend yield on the S&P 500 index ranged between 1% and 3%.

> Stocks pay dividends; futures contracts do not.

Also, you earn nothing on a stock purchase unless it appreciates or pays dividends. In fact, you incur an opportunity cost because you could have earned the Treasury bill interest rate. If you buy a futures contract you must post a good faith deposit, but you can do this with interest-earning U.S. Treasury bills. Satisfying the margin requirement this way, the futures trader earns interest while speculat-

---

[2] Note that this list of factors is a partial list of the factors determining an option premium.

S&P 500 FUTURES CONTRACT DAILY PRICE LIMITS

% Decline	Rules for S&P 500 Stock Index Futures Contract
2.5%	Down only. Once a limit offer has been established, trading can occur at or above this limit for 10 minutes or until 2:30 p.m. Chicago time (CT). Trading will halt for two minutes if the primary futures contract is limit offer at the end of the 10 minutes or at 2:30 p.m. CT. Before 2:30 p.m. CT, trading will resume with the 5% limit in effect; after 2:30 p.m. CT, the 10% limit will be in effect.
5%	Down only. Once a limit offer has been established, trading can occur at or above this limit for 10 minutes or until 2:30 p.m. (CT). Trading will halt for two minutes if the primary futures contract is limit offer at the end of the 10 minutes or at 2:30 p.m. CT (or 45 minutes before the close of an abbreviated trading session). Trading will resume with the 10% limit in effect.
10%	Down only. Prior to 1:30 p.m. CT, trading can occur at or above this limit. If the primary futures is limit offer and the NYSE has declared a trading halt (due to a 10% decline in the DJIA), trading will halt.* Trading will resume with the 15% limit in effect when 50% (capitalization weights) of the underlying S&P 500 stocks reopen. After 1:30 p.m. CT, trading can occur at or above this limit for 10 minutes. Trading will halt for two minutes if the primary futures is limit offer at the end of 10 minutes. Trading will resume with the 15%-point limit in effect.
15%	Down only. Once a limit offer has been established, trading can occur at or above this limit for 10 minutes. Trading will halt for two minutes if the primary futures is limit offer at the end of 10 minutes. Trading will resume with the 20%-point limit in effect.
20%	Down only. Once a limit offer has been established, trading can occur at or above this limit. If the primary futures is limit offer and the NYSE has declared a trading halt (due to a 20%-point decline in the DJIA), trading will halt. Trading will resume with the 20%-point limit in effect when 50% (capitalization weights) of the underlying S&P 500 stocks reopen.

*New York Stock Exchange Trading Halt Rules

Dow Jones Industrial Average % Decline	Action
10%	If the DJIA declines 10% prior to 1:00 p.m. CT, the NYSE will declare a one-hour trading halt. If the DJIA declines 10% between 1:00 p.m. and 1:30 p.m. CT, the NYSE will declare a half-hour trading halt. After 1:30 p.m. CT, the 10% limit is not in effect.
20%	If the DJIA declines 20% prior to 12:00 p.m. CT, the NYSE will declare a two-hour trading halt. If the DJIA declines 20% after 1:00 p.m. CT, the NYSE will declare a trading halt and will not reopen.
30%	If the DJIA declines 30%, the NYSE will declare a trading halt and will not reopen.

Source: Chicago Mercantile Exchange.

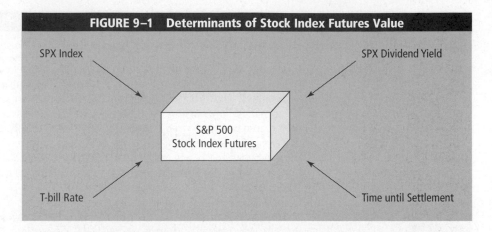

FIGURE 9–1   Determinants of Stock Index Futures Value

SPX Index

SPX Dividend Yield

S&P 500
Stock Index Futures

T-bill Rate

Time until Settlement

TABLE 9–4   Stock Index Futures Information

AUGUST 15, 2000

CURRENT LEVEL OF THE CASH INDEX (S)	= 1484.43
T-BILL YIELD (R)	= 6.07%
S&P 500 DIVIDEND YIELD (D)	= 1.06%
DAYS UNTIL DECEMBER SETTLEMENT	= 121 = 0.33 YEARS (T)

The futures price should equal the index plus a differential based on the short-term interest rate minus the dividend yield.

ing on the general level of the stock market. No interest accrues from holding stock, and the futures price also reflects this difference. The gist of this comparison is that the futures price should equal the dollar value of the index, plus the short-term interest cost and less the dividend yield received.

Suppose we have the market information given in Table 9–4. The T-bill rate exceeds the dividend yield on the S&P 500, so there is a relative advantage to buying the futures contract over the cash index. We can find whether the actual futures price is too high or too low by calculating the **fair premium** for the time remaining in the futures contract. Equation 9–1 shows the relationship. This assumes that both dividends and interest occur in a continuous stream.[3]

$$F = S \, e^{(R - D)T} \qquad (9\text{–}1)$$

Using Equation 9–1 and Table 9–4, the fair value of the futures on this day is

$$F = 1484.43 e^{(0.0607 - 0.0106)(121/365)} = 1509.29$$

Table 9–5 shows the S&P 500 stock index futures prices from August 15, 2000. The calculated fair value of 1509.29 is less than the December futures settlement

---

[3] Actually, dividends on the stocks in the S&P 500 index do not arrive uniformly. Most companies pay their dividends in early February, May, August, and November. This introduces periodic minor error in Equation 9-1.

TABLE 9–5 S&P 500 Stock Index Futures Contract			
SETTLEMENT PRICES **AUGUST 15, 2000**			
MONTH	**HIGH**	**LOW**	**SETTLE**
SEP00	1501.00	1491.00	1494.80
DEC00	1522.10	1513.60	1517.20
MAR01	1545.40	1536.90	1540.50
JUN01	1569.10	1560.60	1564.20
SEP01	1594.10	1585.60	1589.20
DEC01	1619.10	1610.60	1614.20
MAR02	1644.10	1635.60	1639.20
JUN02	1669.10	1660.60	1664.20
CASH INDEX = 1484.43			

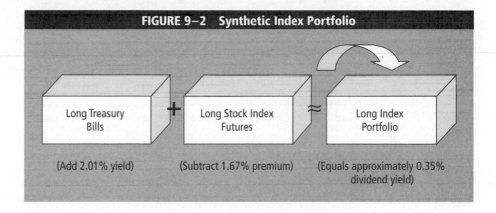

FIGURE 9–2   Synthetic Index Portfolio

Long Treasury Bills (Add 2.01% yield) + Long Stock Index Futures (Subtract 1.67% premium) ≈ Long Index Portfolio (Equals approximately 0.35% dividend yield)

value of 1517.20, suggesting that futures are expensive relative to their theoretical value given the level of the underlying stocks.

Figure 9–2 shows the essence of pricing relationship. The theoretical futures price is (1509.29 – 1484.43)/1484.43, or 1.67% more than the current level of the S&P 500 index. The T-bill yield of 6.07% is per *year*; for *121 days*, the equivalent is 6.07% × (121/365) = 2.01%. The dividend yield on the index was 1.06% on August 15, 2000. For 121 days, this translates to 1.06% × (121/365) = 0.35%.

The concept of a **synthetic index portfolio** is important. It means that large institutional investors such as life insurance companies and pension funds can replicate a well-diversified portfolio of common stock by simply holding a long position in the stock index futures contract and satisfying the good faith deposit, or *margining*,[4] the position with T-bills. Added benefits of the futures approach

[4] Providing collateral for an investment position is sometimes called *margining*.

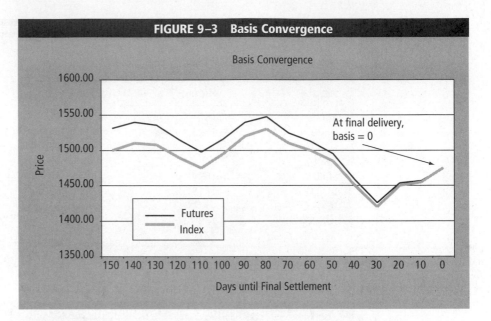

FIGURE 9–3   Basis Convergence

are (1) transaction costs will be much lower on the futures contracts than on 500 separate stock issues, and (2) the portfolio will be much easier to follow and manage. There are still some fiduciary restrictions (many clearly outdated) that preclude widespread use of futures as a substitute for stock ownership, but the number of futures users grows daily.

BASIS CONVERGENCE

Recall that basis is the cash price minus the future price. Equation 9–1 indicates that as time goes by, the difference between the cash index and the futures price will narrow. At the end of the futures contract, when T = 0, the futures price will equal the index. We refer to this phenomenon as **basis convergence**. Figure 9–3 illustrates how the two values converge as time passes.

USES OF STOCK INDEX FUTURES

There are three main uses of stock index futures contracts: speculative purposes, arbitrage-related activities, and hedging risk.

SPECULATION

A person who anticipated that the stock market was about to advance could obtain substantial leverage by buying S&P futures contracts. Each one-point movement in the index translates into $250. Similarly, a bearish speculator could short futures, hoping to see their value decline in the future. Looking at this another way, if the S&P 500 index is 1500.00, the speculative margin of $23,438 controls an investment worth $375,000.

SPREADING

Just as in the options market, some speculators are fond of spreads as a way to speculate with reduced risk. As explained in Chapter Eight, there are various types of spreads with futures. A stock index speculator might believe that the tech-heavy Nasdaq will outperform the Dow Jones Industrial Average in the next few months. He or she might logically employ an *intermarket spread*, buying the Nasdaq 100 futures (ND) and selling the DJIA futures (DJ). Regardless of whether the overall market advances or declines, the spreader will make a profit as long as the ND index outperforms the DJ. The spread dramatically reduces risk because one position is bullish while the other is bearish.[5]

ARBITRAGE

Arbitrageurs are important players in the financial marketplace. Their activities help keep the market efficient and functioning well. Sometimes the market price of a futures contract temporarily deviates upward from the price predicted by pricing theory. Expecting that the futures contract and the value of cash index will soon return to their "normal" relationship, an arbitrageur might *short* the futures contracts and *buy* stock. As the gap between the two prices narrows, the arbitrageur earns a profit.

Suppose an arbitrageur, determining the fair value of the DEC 00 S&P 500 futures contract to be 1509.29, sells a contract at the Table 9–5 settlement price of 1517.20. The arbitrageur then buys the 500 stocks underlying the index at their current value of 1484.30. In practice, this latter transaction would likely come about via **program trading**, which is the computerized submission of multiple trades to the New York Stock Exchange via the SuperDot system.[6] The point is that regardless of what the market does in the future, at settlement of the futures contract in December, its price will equal the S&P 500 index because of basis convergence.

Table 9–6 shows various possible closing levels of the S&P 500 index. If the index closes at 1500, the arbitrageur will make 15.70 points on the stock and make 17.20 points on the futures position. The table indicates that regardless of the ultimate index level, the arbitrageur earns 32.90 index points. This is a riskless return of 32.90/1484.43, or 2.22% for 121 days. This is 20 basis points more than the prevailing T-bill rate for the same period, a situation the market will not allow to persist for long. As people sell futures and buy stock, the gap will narrow

---

[5] When a trader bases a spread on two different indexes, there is always the possibility both legs of the spread could move against him. In the latter part of the year 2000 there were frequent periods when the Nasdaq would move in one direction while the Dow Jones Industrial Average moved in another.

[6] There is more on this subject later in the book.

			S&P 500 INDEX				
	1400	**1425**	**1450**	**1475**	**1500**	**1525**	**1550**
FUTURES	117.20	92.20	67.20	42.20	17.20	−7.80	−32.80
STOCK	−84.30	−59.30	−34.30	−9.30	15.70	40.70	65.70
TOTAL	32.90	32.90	32.90	32.90	32.90	32.90	32.90

TABLE 9–6 Basis Arbitrage

until it returns to the no-arbitrage spread of (1509.29 − 1484.43) = 24.86 points. As always, the arbitrage could go the other way; short the stock and buy futures if the basis was too small.

ANTICIPATION OF STOCK PURCHASE OR SALE

Another use of index futures is to lock in a price in anticipation of a stock purchase or sale. Suppose in mid-August a university endowment fund portfolio manager learns that a wealthy alumnus plans to give $10 million to the university later in the calendar year. The portfolio manager believes the market is going to rally in the fourth quarter of the year, and would prefer to invest the money *now* before the market heads up. Table 9–5 indicates the December 2000, or DEC 00, futures trade for 1517.20. Each DEC contract represents about $250 × 1517.20, or $379,300. Ten million dollars in stock, therefore, corresponds to about 26 futures contracts. Table 9–3 indicates that the initial speculative margin for one futures contract is $23,438, so the margin required for 26 futures contracts is $609,388. The manager can satisfy this performance bond with Treasury bills, which may very well already exist in the endowment fund. The value of the contracts will increase if the market advances as expected. At final settlement the endowment fund will be credited with the gain. Of course, if the market goes down instead of up, the fund will not get back the full amount of the performance bond.

Another portfolio manager might want to get out of the market, but for tax reasons does not want to sell securities until after the first of the year. Selling futures would lock in the current level of the market.

HEDGING

The primary economic purpose of the S&P 500 stock index futures (and all futures contracts) is risk transfer.

As with any futures contract, the primary purpose of S&P futures is to facilitate risk transfer from someone who bears undesired risk to someone else who is willing to bear the risk because of the anticipated profits that might be made. Stock index futures contracts are widely and successfully used for this purpose by most large commercial banks and by many pension funds and foundations. Hedging applications are the subject of the following section.

HEDGING WITH STOCK INDEX FUTURES

A hedger seeks to eliminate price risk; using the S&P 500 futures contract, a portfolio manager can largely eliminate the risk of losses on the portfolio from declining security prices.

SYSTEMATIC AND UNSYSTEMATIC RISK

Stock prices fluctuate because of two sets of factors. Systematic factors are those that influence the stock market as a whole, and include such things as market interest rates, economic indicators, the political climate, regulatory policy, and fiscal or monetary policy. **Systematic risk** is also called **market risk**. Unsystematic factors are unique to a specific company or industry and include earnings reports, technological developments, labor negotiations, cost of materials, and merger or acquisition activity. These effects constitute **unsystematic risk**.

Proper portfolio diversification can virtually eliminate unsystematic risk. In fact, a principal result of capital market theory is the fact that investors are not rewarded for bearing unsystematic risk: the "market" assumes that they are smart enough to reduce risk through diversification as much as possible for a given level of anticipated return.

A well-known study by Evans and Archer[7] shows how portfolio variability declines as the number of securities in the portfolio increases. Figure 9–4 shows these famous results. A portfolio containing 15 or 20 unrelated stocks provides a very high degree of diversification; adding more securities results in only modest additional risk reduction.

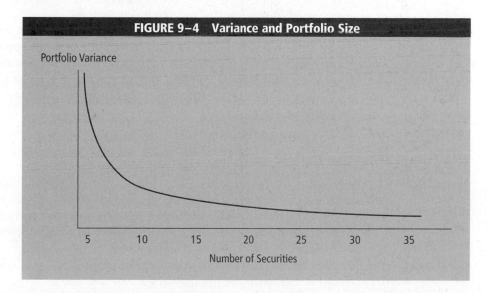

FIGURE 9–4   Variance and Portfolio Size

Portfolio Variance

Number of Securities

[7] Evans, John L., and Stephen H. Archer. "Diversification and the Reduction of Dispersion," *Journal of Finance*, December 1968, 761–767.

Beta is a measure of the relative riskiness of a portfolio compared to a benchmark portfolio like the S&P 500 index; beta measures systematic risk. By definition, the benchmark has a beta of 1.0. Portfolios that are riskier than the benchmark have a beta greater than one, while more conservative portfolios have a beta less than one. Suppose a portfolio has a beta of 0.9. This means that for every 1% change in the value of the S&P 500 index, the portfolio should change in value by 0.9%.

In order for a hedge to be effective, the hedging device one chooses should be similar to the commodity being hedged: farmers do not hedge their wheat crop with corn futures, nor should an equity manager hedge a stock portfolio with a bond index. The wheat farmer will hedge with wheat futures, and the stock portfolio manager will hedge with a stock index. The S&P 500 index is a well-diversified portfolio that is effective in hedging the investment portfolios of endowment funds, mutual funds, and other broad-based portfolios based upon, benchmarked, or highly correlated with the S&P 500.

THE NEED TO HEDGE

Suppose you are the portfolio manager for a $75 million stock fund. You anticipate a downturn in the market soon, but remain bullish for the long term. However, you also know that a declining portfolio value would look bad in the end-of-year report your fund will provide to its investors. What can you do?

One obvious alternative is to sell everything before prices fall. This solution would protect your gains, but would be expensive in terms of transaction costs. Also, you do not want to suffer the embarrassment or illegality of reporting that your "equity" fund contains only cash equivalents.

Another approach is to hedge the stock portfolio. Futures hedging involves taking a position in the futures market that offsets a position you hold in the "cash" market. If you are long stock, logically you should be short futures. Just as the farmer needs to figure out how many contracts to sell, the portfolio manager must calculate the number of contracts necessary to counteract likely changes in the portfolio value.

THE HEDGE RATIO

Portfolios are of different sizes and different risk levels. You must recognize these differences in order to construct a proper hedge. A single S&P 500 stock index futures contract has a value of about $350,000, so a large portfolio requires more contracts than a small one. Similarly, risky portfolios fluctuate more than the market average: thus they require a larger hedge.

The hedge ratio accounts for size and risk differentials.

The **hedge ratio** incorporates the relative value of the stocks and futures and accounts for the relative riskiness of the two "portfolios." One portfolio (the S&P 500 index) has a beta of 1.0 by definition, and the second portfolio (the stocks) may be more risky or less risky than this. If the stock portfolio is less risky, it will be necessary to use fewer futures contracts. If the stock portfolio has a beta greater than one, then more futures contracts are necessary. To hedge a long position, the manager needs to go short the futures contracts. Because futures contracts are not available in fractional amounts, the portfolio manager must also round to a whole number.

You need three pieces of information to determine the hedge ratio:

1. the value of the chosen futures contract;
2. the dollar value of the portfolio to be hedged;
3. the beta of the portfolio.

The first of these pieces is easy to determine. The size of an S&P 500 futures contract is established as $250 times the value of the S&P 500 index. Suppose the manager of a $75 million stock portfolio (beta of 0.9 and dividend yield = 1.0%) studies a possible hedge using the December S&P 500 futures. Table 9–5 shows that the prior day's closing value for the S&P 500 index was 1484.43, and that the DEC 00 S&P 500 futures contract closed at 1517.20. The value of the futures contract is therefore $250 × 1517.20, or $379,300.

The hedge ratio for this example is[8]

$$HR = \frac{\text{Dollar value of the portfolio}}{\text{Dollar value of the S\&P Futures Contract}} \times \text{beta} \qquad (9\text{--}2)$$

$$HR = \frac{\$75,000,000}{1517.20 \times \$250} \times 0.9 = 177.96 \approx 178 \text{ contracts}$$

Consider the consequences of several different market scenarios at the final delivery day for the contract.

The Market Falls.   This is what the portfolio manager expected to happen. There will be a *loss* in the stock portfolio and a *gain* in the futures market. Suppose the S&P 500 index falls 5%, from 1484.43 to 1410.20. Given its beta, the portfolio should have fallen by 5.0% × 0.9 = 4.5%, or *$3,375,000*. This is a portfolio *loss*. (See Figure 9–5.)

In the futures market, there is a *gain*. You sold 178 contracts short at 1517.20. At the expiration of the futures contract, the CME will close them out at 1410.20. (At expiration, the price of the futures contract should exactly equal the index itself.) Your account will benefit by (1517.20 – 1410.20) × $250 × 178 = *$4,761,500*. From mid-August to mid-December is about 1/3 year. Dividends on the portfolio, then, should be about 1% × 0.333 × $75,000,000 = *$250,000*. The combined positions (loss in stock, plus dividends received, plus gains on futures contracts) result in a gain of **$1,636,500**.

[8] In equation 9–2, some reference material will show the spot value of the index in the denominator rather than the value of the futures contract. Which is correct depends on how you define beta. Equation 9–2 as shown above is correct if "beta" is the traditional value from a capital asset pricing model sense. If, however, beta is a parameter that comes from a regression of the stock position on the futures price, then the denominator should be the spot value of the index. In most circumstances the difference in the two methods is modest.

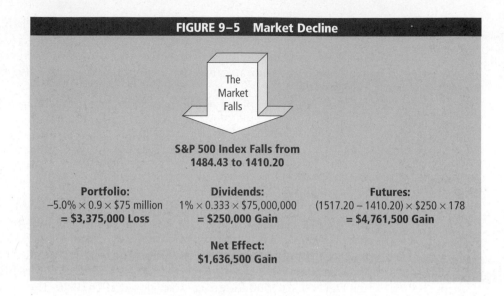

FIGURE 9–5   Market Decline

The Market Falls

**S&P 500 Index Falls from
1484.43 to 1410.20**

Portfolio:
−5.0% × 0.9 × $75 million
= $3,375,000 Loss

Dividends:
1% × 0.333 × $75,000,000
= $250,000 Gain

Futures:
(1517.20 − 1410.20) × $250 × 178
= $4,761,500 Gain

Net Effect:
$1,636,500 Gain

The Market Rises.   Suppose the index rises from 1484.43 to 1558.70. This market rise of 5 percent means the portfolio, with its beta of 0.9, should advance by 4.5%, or *$3,375,000*. Dividends are the same as in the previous scenario, *$250,000*. You will lose money on the futures position, because you sold them short and they rose in price to 1558.70 at expiration. The loss is (1517.20 − 1558.70) × $250 × 178 = *$1,846,750*. The combined positions result in a gain of **$1,778,250**. (See Figure 9–6.)

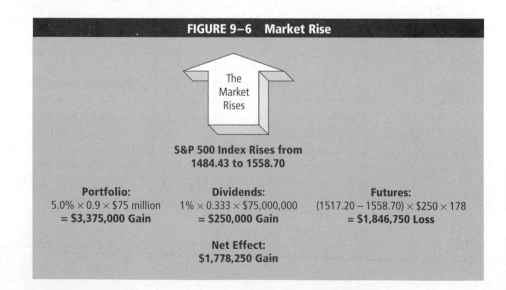

FIGURE 9–6   Market Rise

The Market Rises

**S&P 500 Index Rises from
1484.43 to 1558.70**

Portfolio:
5.0% × 0.9 × $75 million
= $3,375,000 Gain

Dividends:
1% × 0.333 × $75,000,000
= $250,000 Gain

Futures:
(1517.20 − 1558.70) × $250 × 178
= $1,846,750 Loss

Net Effect:
$1,778,250 Gain

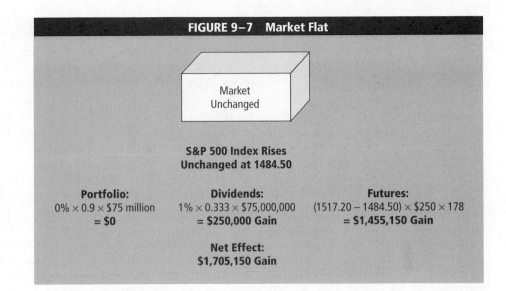

FIGURE 9–7 Market Flat

Market
Unchanged

**S&P 500 Index Rises
Unchanged at 1484.50**

Portfolio:
0% × 0.9 × $75 million
= $0

Dividends:
1% × 0.333 × $75,000,000
= $250,000 Gain

Futures:
(1517.20 – 1484.50) × $250 × 178
= $1,455,150 Gain

Net Effect:
$1,705,150 Gain

The Market is Unchanged.   There is no gain on the stock portfolio. There is, however, a gain in the futures. The basis will deteriorate to zero at expiration, so the short hedger has a gain of (1517.20 – 1484.50) × $250 × 178 = *$1,455,150.* Including dividends, the net gain is **$1,705,150**. (See Figure 9–7.)

It is important to remember that the "gains" in these three scenarios are not speculative gains. Rather, they reflect the fact that the portfolio earns the risk free rate. Borrowing costs associated with posting the performance bond will also affect the net result.

HEDGING IN RETROSPECT

In practice, a hedge of this type will never be perfect; there is usually some relatively small profit or loss at termination of the hedge. There are four reasons for this. First, it is usually not possible to hedge exactly because the futures contracts are only available in integer quantities. This means the portfolio manager must round to the nearest whole number. Second, stock portfolios seldom behave exactly as their beta says they should. In the example above, the portfolio *should* change by 90 percent as much as the general market. Betas are estimated, and the portfolio may change by more or less than this amount. Also, some stocks have a beta with little statistical significance. In such a case, they don't have much predictive power. Third, the futures price does not move in lockstep with the underlying index. This phenomenon is called **basis risk**. Finally, the dividends on the S&P 500 index do not occur uniformly over time, and depending on the date of the calculation, this can make Equation 9–1 slightly inaccurate.

If you examine the results in each of these scenarios carefully, you will note that basis convergence works to the advantage of the short hedger. Even if the

Convergence of the futures contract with the cash index works to the advantage of the short hedger.

DERIVATIVES TODAY

SINGLE STOCK FUTURES

A single stock futures contract is a promise to exchange a quantity of stock at a set price by a certain delivery date. This differs from an option in that the parties agree to the purchase and sale of the stock rather than one party having the "right" to exercise if so desired.

While this notion may be appealing to some investors, the 1982 Shad-Johnson Act made single stock futures illegal in the United States, largely because of the jurisdictional uncertainty. The CFTC governs futures, while the SEC governs stock. Who would govern this futures/stock hybrid?

In September 2000 the London International Financial Futures and Options Exchange announced that it would begin trading single stock futures of U.S., U.K, and other European countries by the end of January 2001. The notion of single stock futures appears in the Commodity Futures Modernization Act of 2000. Institutional trading of single stock futures begins in August 2001, with retail trading beginning in Decem-

ber 2001. The Chicago Mercantile Exchange and the Chicago Board of Trade both are champions of the idea, while the Chicago Board Options Exchange opposes it. Single stock futures will likely mean more business for the futures exchanges and less for the options exchanges.

Rick Redding, Director of Index Products at the CME, says the product "provides everyone, including the institutional investor, another option. It would make the markets more efficient, and that's really what a lot of investors are looking for: efficiency in the market, different ways to trade portfolios and using them to manage risk."[9] Jack Gaine, President of the Managed Futures Association, says, "I don't know for sure if they're going to be successful. But let's at least get it legal to trade them. It's the view that it's another product to trade. Let the market form a judgment."[10]

[9] Clair, Chris. "Single Stock Futures Provision Has Slim Chance," *Pensions and Investments*, November 13, 2000, 56.

[10] Ibid.

market remains unchanged, the value of the futures contracts will decline as the delivery month approaches. On the last day of a future contract's life, its market price should equal the spot price. This means the basis becomes zero. This phenomenon is true for all futures contracts, whether they are agricultural, financial, or precious metals.

The gains earned from the deteriorating basis are modest in percentage terms. In the "market unchanged" scenario, there was combined gain of $1,705,150. On a $75 million portfolio, this is a percentage return of 2.27 percent over four months, or about $6^{3}/_{4}\%$ per year. This represents the return from interest on the good faith deposit (the T-bill rate) plus the dividends on the stock index. Note also that hedging is not a free lunch; in the case in which the market advances, the portfolio would have fared better had the hedge not been used.

The portfolio manager does not need to hedge the entire portfolio. Instead of using 178 contracts as in the examples above, the manager might decide to

TRADING STRATEGY

HEDGING WITH INDEX FLEX OPTIONS

One of the portfolios Robert Alan manages is a $25 million, concentrated collection of technology and Internet issues. While he believes there is still upside potential in this sector of the market, he is nearing the end of his reporting year and does not want to see another big drop in the Nasdaq stock market erode the portfolio's gains. He knows that the Nasdaq 100 index tracks his portfolio pretty well and that he could use the Nasdaq 100 futures contract to largely eliminate market risk, but he hates to give up the upside potential: hedging with futures essentially gets him out of the market.

Instead, Robert is thinking about using Nasdaq 100 FLEX options from the CBOE. He knows these options can be customized with regard to striking price, size, and expiration, and can be either American or European exercise style. He especially likes the fact that he can set the expiration date exactly equal to the end of his performance evaluation period rather than being stuck with the third Friday of the expiration month. The disadvantage of using protective puts is the fact that you have to pay the option premium, so Robert is also thinking about writing an out-of-the-money FLEX call to bring in some income to at least partially offset the cost of the puts. (He remembers that people often call a package of stock, long puts, and short calls a collar.) While writing the call would reduce the position cost, it would also limit the upside potential that he wanted to keep in play.

In this circumstance Robert decides that the FLEX option approach is better than outright hedging with futures. The tricky thing he still needs to decide is how to select the striking prices of the put and call FLEX options he wants to use.

hedge only 80 percent of the portfolio, using 142 contracts. This allows greater upside appreciation if the portfolio manager is wrong about a forthcoming downturn, but would still provide substantial protection against a declining market.

ADJUSTING MARKET RISK

A variation on the hedging theme is using futures to adjust the level of market risk in a portfolio. Consider the manager of the $75 million portfolio in the previous example. This portfolio has a beta of 0.90. Suppose the manager becomes excited about the market and wants to increase market exposure, perhaps to the equivalent of a beta of 1.4. He or she can do this by going *long* futures contracts and holding them with the stock portfolio. The necessary number of contracts needed comes from Equation 9–3.

$$\# \text{ contracts} = \frac{\text{portfolio value} \times (\beta_{\text{desired}} - \beta_{\text{current}})}{\text{futures level} \times \$250} \qquad (9\text{–}3)$$

This manager would want to buy 99 contracts to effectively raise the portfolio beta to 1.4:

$$\# \text{ contracts} = \frac{\$75 \text{ million} \times (1.40 - 0.90)}{1517.30 \times \$250} \approx 99$$

While this does not directly put more dollars into the market, it increases the sensitivity of the aggregate portfolio to market changes so that the dollar gains or losses will mimic those of a larger portfolio.

SUMMARY

Financial futures are a rapidly growing segment of the investment field. These contracts are popular with both speculators and hedgers. They allow the speculator to use substantial leverage and enable the portfolio manager to reduce systematic risk.

The price of a stock index futures contract is a function of the underlying index level, the dividend yield on that index, the current short-term interest rate, and the time remaining in the contract's life. Arbitrageurs help ensure that the difference between the index level and the futures price, known as the basis, remains in line with its equilibrium value.

As time passes the futures price and the underlying index value converge. This means the basis approaches zero as delivery nears. Stock index futures contracts are cash settled; no actual stock certificates change hands.

Accurate hedge ratios are essential to proper hedging. With stock index futures, the hedge ratio depends on the size of the portfolio, its beta, and the value of the chosen futures contract. A portfolio manager can create a synthetic treasury bill by combining short futures with a stock portfolio.

SELF TEST

T ___ F ___   1. Most stock index futures contracts trade at the New York Stock Exchange.

T ___ F ___   2. The S&P 500 stock index is capitalization weighted.

T ___ F ___   3. Delivery of stock certificates on the S&P 500 stock index futures contract occurs via wire transfer of the shares rather than physical delivery.

T ___ F ___   4. The SPX futures contract size is $250 times the index level.

T ___ F ___   5. Changes in the Treasury bill rate do not usually affect the basis in a stock index futures contract.

T ___ F ___   6. The futures price for a stock index futures contract is usually greater than the cash index.

T ___ F ___   7. As time passes the SPX basis approaches zero.

T ___ F ___   8. Program trading relies on computerized trades via the Super-DOT system.

T ___ F ___   9. An SPX hedge ratio accounts for both risk and size differentials.

T ___ F ___   10. A portfolio of stock combined with a long position in futures can become a Treasury bill equivalent.

PROBLEMS & QUESTIONS

1. Suppose you manage a $25 million insurance company stock portfolio. Do you see any advantage in the S&P 500 future contract as a hedging device over the Nasdaq 100 index?

2. Comment on the following statement: "Because the basis works to the benefit of the short hedger with stock index futures, a calendar spread where you are long the near month and short the far month (where the basis is higher) is usually a winner."

3. Suppose that, instead of holding a diversified portfolio of common stock, a mutual fund announces its intent to hold stock index futures and T-bills. Give arguments for and against this practice as a substitute for more conventional equity investing.

4. Comment on the following statement: "Over the long term, people who are long stock index futures contracts are going to be net losers."

5. Why does convergence of a stock index futures contract with the cash index work to the advantage of a short seller?

6. Under what circumstances do you think stock index futures could trade in an inverted market?

7. Should the S&P 500 stock index futures contract be used to hedge a portfolio of only five stocks?

8. What role does beta play in the construction of a hedge ratio for a stock portfolio?

9. In hedging a portfolio, is there anything philosophically wrong with only hedging part of it?

10. Suppose a number of companies in the S&P 500 index simultaneously increase their dividends. What influence would this likely have on the value of an S&P 500 futures contract?

11. Suppose that the current level of the S&P 500 index is 340.00, the dividend yield on the index is 1.55%, and Treasury bills yield 5.88%. What is the theoretical price of an S&P 500 futures contract with delivery in 63 days?

12. In problem 11, suppose the T-bill rate falls to 5.63%. What is the theoretical price of an S&P 500 futures contract with 120 days until final delivery?

13. As the manager of a $200 million stock portfolio with a beta of 0.8, you have decided to hedge 80 percent of the value of your portfolio using the S&P 500 futures. Refer to the prices for September delivery in Table 9–5. What is the appropriate hedge ratio, and how many contracts will you buy or sell?

14. Refer to the data in problem 13. Suppose you want to hedge the portfolio using the DEC 00 S&P 500 stock index futures contracts shown in Table 9–5. How many of these contracts do you need to buy or sell?

15. As the manager of a $750 million stock portfolio with a beta of 1.1, you have decided to hedge 40 percent of the value of your portfolio using the S&P 500 futures. Refer to the prices for September 2000 delivery in Table 9–5. What is the appropriate hedge ratio, and how many contracts will you buy or sell?

16. The SPX index stands at 1475.50. An S&P 500 futures contract with delivery in 85 days sells for 1499.00. If the dividend yield on the SPX is 2.2%, what T-bill rate is implied in these prices?

17. Consider this stock index futures information:
    - cash index = 329.83
    - T-bill yield = 6.02%
    - index dividend yield = 2.65%
    - futures price = 334.30
    - days until futures delivery = 121

    How could an arbitrageur take advantage of this information?

10

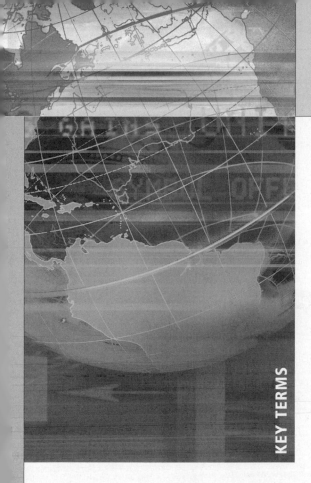

Foreign Exchange Futures

KEY TERMS you will find in this chapter:

accounting exposure	inflation premium
covering the risk	interest rate parity
deflation	nominal interest rate
direct quotation	purchasing power parity
economic exposure	real rate
exposure	risk premium
foreign exchange risk	spot exchange rate
forward exchange rate	transaction exposure
indirect quotation	translation exposure

The inventory of this market is uncertainty.

E. B. Harris
Former Chairman
Chicago Mercantile Exchange

In the world of finance, the capital markets across the globe have become one giant playing field. In fact, about half the world's stock market opportunities are outside the United States. While the United States is home to about 5% of the global population and about 37% of the world market capitalization, the latter figure is steadily declining as world markets develop. Investors sometimes buy stock in companies such as Nokia (*NOK, NYSE*), Ericsson (*ERICY, NASDAQ*), or BP Amoco (*BP, NYSE*) without even realizing they are non-U.S. firms.[1]

Overseas investments or international business dealings usually involve foreign exchange risk. The primary objective of this chapter is to show how forward contracts and foreign currency futures can reduce this risk. A survey of corporate treasurers indicates that *the primary corporate use of derivative assets is hedging foreign*

---

[1] These companies are from Finland, Sweden, and the United Kingdom, respectively.

WHAT COUNTRY OWNS THIS COMPANY/BRAND?

Nokia ___	Nivea ___	Coca Cola ___
Bass ___	Shell Oil ___	Poland Springs ___
Norelco ___	Brooks Brothers ___	IKEA ___
Volvo Cars___	Maybelline ___	Gillette ___
7 Up ___	Dannon ___	Hannaford Brothers ___
Nestle ___	Shaw's ___	Burberry ___
Bayer ___	Virgin Records ___	Dunkin Donuts ___
SAKS ___	Magnavox ___	

(Answers are in the Summary at the end of the chapter.)

	TABLE 10–1 Corporate Use of Derivatives[2]
77%	TO HEDGE FOREIGN EXCHANGE RISK EXPOSURE
56%	TO HEDGE FLOATING RATE DEBT
54%	TO CREATE SYNTHETIC FLOATING RATE DEBT AT A LOWER COST
43%	TO HEDGE INCOME/PROFITS
41%	TO CREATE SYNTHETIC FIXED RATE DEBT AT A LOWER COST
40%	TO ACHIEVE STRATEGIC LIABILITY MANAGEMENT
24%	TO HEDGE OVERSEAS INVESTMENT
19%	TO HEDGE COMMERCIAL PAPER ISSUANCE
10%	TO ACCESS GLOBAL CAPITAL MARKETS
10%	OTHER USES
3%	TO ACCESS FOREIGN EQUITY MARKETS.

exchange exposure (see Table 10–1). In the next section we look at the sources and different dimensions of the foreign exchange risk that corporate treasurers seek to reduce.

FOREIGN EXCHANGE RISK

Foreign exchange risk is the chance of loss due to changes in the relative value of world currencies.

We have seen that with the appropriate hedging strategy, farmers can reduce price risk and portfolio managers can minimize market risk. In the world of international business, **foreign exchange risk** is significant. This is the chance of loss due to changes in the relative value of world currencies. You often see foreign exchange abbreviated as *FX*.

When a U.S. investor buys a foreign security in a foreign country, there are really *two* relevant purchases. The actual purchase of the security is one of them, but before you can do this you must exchange U.S. dollars for the necessary for-

---

[2] Reported in "The Way It Is," *Treasury and Risk Management* (Spring 1993): 19–20.

eign currency. In essence, you are buying the FX, and its price can change daily. To an investor, the changing relationships among currencies of interest introduce additional risk. Modest changes in exchange rates can result in significant dollar differences. On a holding of 1 million units of foreign exchange, for instance, a price change of 1 cent per unit amounts to $10,000.

FX RISK AND INTEREST RATES

It is said that when the United States sneezes, the world catches a cold. While this may be a little parochial, the point is that events in one industrial country affect the rest of the world. When a big player, like the United States government, changes its economic policy, suffers a recession, or experiences high unemployment, these events have significant economic consequences elsewhere in the world. Interest rates are often a good barometer of these events. They are particularly relevant to an understanding of foreign exchange risk.

Students of finance learn that the **nominal interest rate** (the stated rate) can be expressed as the sum of three components: the *real rate*, an *inflation premium*, and a *risk premium*.

The nominal rate of interest is the aggregate of the real rate, an inflation premium, and a risk premium.

The Real Rate of Interest
The **real rate** is an economic abstraction that we cannot directly observe. Theoretically, it reflects the rate of return investors demand for giving up the current use of funds. In a world of no risk and no inflation, the real rate indicates people's willingness to postpone spending their money. This rate often hovers in the 3% to 4% range.

The Inflation Premium
The **inflation premium** reflects how the general price level is changing. Inflation is normally positive (negative inflation is called **deflation**), and it therefore measures how rapidly the money standard is losing its purchasing power. If inflation is 5% per year, an average $100 purchase today will cost $105 in one year. In the past 75 years, U.S. inflation has averaged about 3.2% annually.

The Risk Premium
The **risk premium** is the component of interest rates that is toughest to measure; security analysts earn their pay by their efforts to decipher it. Risk-averse investors will not take unnecessary risks, and they expect to be compensated over the long term for any risks they choose to take. This is why the average return on common stocks (which are risky) is higher than the average return on U.S. Treasury bills (which are assumed to have no risk). Investors will not purchase risky securities offering the same return as a riskless security. The price of a risky security must reflect a risk premium to entice someone to buy it; the magnitude of the risk premium depends on how much risk the security carries. The more risk, the higher the risk premium, and therefore the lower the price.[3] With a real rate of, say, 3.1%

[3] Anything can become an attractive investment if its price falls low enough.

and an inflation premium of 3.2%, a U.S. Treasury bill should yield 6.3%. A corporate bond would have a yield somewhat higher because investors would demand a risk premium.

THE CONCEPT OF EXPOSURE

Exposure is the extent to which you face foreign exchange risk. Unfortunately, there is not always a quick and convenient way to measure that. Accountants have fussed over this problem for years, have rewritten the rules several times, and still it remains a thorny issue. In general, there are two types of exposure: *accounting* and *economic*. An investment manager is primarily concerned with the latter type, but should know something about the former, too.

ACCOUNTING EXPOSURE

Accounting exposure is of greatest concern to multinational corporations that have subsidiaries abroad. It is also of concern to the person who holds foreign securities and must prepare dollar-based financial reports on the portfolio's composition and performance.

The parent company is normally required to prepare consolidated financial statements "reflecting fairly" the current state of affairs of the company. The financial statements, however, must be prepared in a single currency (the U.S. dollar for an American firm). Turning foreign currencies into a dollar equivalent involves two other accounting concepts: *transaction exposure* and *translation exposure*.

According to accounting rules, transactions involving the purchase or sale of goods and services with the price stated in foreign currency are incomplete until you know the amount in dollars necessary to liquidate the related payable or receivable. This is **transaction exposure**. A U.S. importer who promises to pay a European supplier in Swiss francs has a transaction exposure until the importer exchanges U.S. dollars for enough Swiss francs to pay the bill.

The holding of foreign assets and liabilities that are denominated in currencies other than U.S. dollars leads to **translation exposure**. The values of foreign real estate holdings and foreign mortgages, for instance, must be "translated" into U.S. dollars before they are incorporated into a U.S. balance sheet. There is a precise set of rules for how this translation is done, but they are for the accountants to worry about and are not a routine investment management activity.

ECONOMIC EXPOSURE

The portfolio manager is most concerned with foreign exchange economic exposure.

Economic exposure measures the risk that the value of a security or a firm will decline due to an unexpected change in relative foreign exchange rates, thereby reducing the value of the security or firm. This is the type of exposure with which security investors are most concerned.

In determining the value of a financial asset, the security analyst seeks to measure the present value of all the cash flows that will accrue to the security holder.

TABLE 10–2 Cross Currency Exchange Rates									
4 SEPTEMBER 2000 9:18 AM EDT									
DOLLARS PER FOREIGN CURRENCY									
	USD	**GBP**	**CHF**	**JPY**	**CAD**	**AUD**	**EUR**	**NZD**	**DKK**	**SEK**
USD	1.0	1.4627	0.5788	0.9467	0.6789	0.5755	0.8989	0.4295	0.1205	0.1071
GBP	0.6837	1.0	0.3957	0.6472	0.4641	0.3934	0.6146	0.2936	0.0824	0.0733
CHF	1.7276	2.5270	1.0	1.6354	1.1729	0.9942	1.5529	0.7419	0.2082	0.1851
JPY	105.64	154.51	61.15	1.0	71.71	60.79	94.96	45.36	12.73	11.32
CAD	1.4730	2.1546	0.8526	1.3944	1.0	0.8476	1.3241	0.6326	0.1775	0.1578
AUD	1.7378	2.5418	1.0059	1.6451	1.1798	1.0	1.5621	0.7463	0.2094	0.1862
EUR	1.1125	1.6272	0.6439	1.0531	0.7552	0.6402	1.0	0.4778	0.1341	0.1192
NZD	2.3286	3.4060	1.3479	2.2044	1.5808	1.3400	2.0931	1.0	0.2806	0.2495
DKK	8.2991	12.14	4.8038	7.8564	5.6341	4.7757	7.4600	3.5640	1.0	0.8891
SEK	9.3339	13.65	5.4028	8.8360	6.3367	5.3712	8.3902	4.0084	1.1247	1.0

FOREIGN CURRENCY PER DOLLAR

AUD	Australian Dollar	CAD	Canadian Dollar
NZD	New Zealand Dollar	JPY	Japanese Yen
DKK	Danish Krone	GBP	British Pound
USD	United States Dollar	CHF	Swiss Franc
EUR	Euro	SEK	Swedish Krona

(Exchange rates for the Japanese Yen are times 100)

Source: www.Bloomberg.com

The present value of these future cash flows is determined by discounting them, using a well-conceived discount factor. Expected changes in exchange rates should be included in this discount rate. Determination of the discount rate is largely a subjective matter, as is the business of forecasting future exchange rates.

For the security investor, the importance of economic exposure is clear. When it comes time to sell a foreign security, an adverse foreign exchange movement since the security was purchased will attenuate a gain, or even turn it into a loss. Let's consider two examples of FX risk, one from the perspective of a business and another from the perspective of an investor.

FX RISK FROM A BUSINESS PERSPECTIVE

Suppose an American importer agrees to purchase four hundred Swiss overcoats at a price of CHF1,200 apiece, for a total of CHF480,000.[4] The coats will take approximately three months to produce, and the agreement calls for the importer to pay for them upon delivery. Table 10–2 shows currency exchange rates from September 4, 2000.

[4] CHF is the abbreviation for the Swiss Franc. See Table 10–2 for other common abbreviations.

The table shows both *direct* and *indirect* foreign exchange quotations. From the perspective of someone in the United States, a **direct quotation** shows the exchange rate in dollars per unit of foreign currency: that is, the dollar cost of one unit of foreign currency. Again from a U.S. perspective, an **indirect quotation** tells you how many units of the foreign currency you get for each dollar.

There is nothing magic about the U.S. perspective, or any perspective, for that matter. Any exchange rate involves two currencies. Therefore, a direct quote in one currency is equivalent to an indirect quote in the other. It is like saying, "These are fifty cents each or two for a dollar." Both prices express the same notion.

Also, the notion of direct versus indirect quotes need not have anything to do with your "home" currency. You might be based in Chicago, employed as a security analyst for a British investment house, currently analyzing a pending deal between a Thai firm and a South Korean firm. The baht/won exchange rate still involves how much of one you get for one of the other. Sitting in Chicago, you will choose either *baht per won* or *won per baht*, but the terms *direct* and *indirect* don't have much meaning to you in that context.

In the U.S., a direct currency quotation is dollars per unit of foreign currency.

Anyway, Table 10–2 shows that on this day the spot exchange rate for the Swiss franc is CHF1.7276 per U.S. dollar, or $0.5788/CHF. To the U.S. importer, this means that each coat costs CHF1,200 × $0.5788/CHF, or $694.56. The importer has arranged with a local specialty shop to sell the coats wholesale at $900 apiece; the shop owner, in turn, is confident they can be sold at retail for $1,100.

A currency weakens against another when it buys less of the foreign currency.

The importer is concerned that the U.S. dollar might weaken between the time being and coat delivery time. This would mean the "cost of goods sold" went up. A currency *weakens* against another when it buys less of the foreign currency. Suppose, however, the dollar has been *strengthening* for months (buying more of the foreign currency), and the importer remembers the investment saying, "The trend is your friend." If the dollar continues to strengthen, the importer's profit will increase.

To show the effect of modest exchange rate changes, we can calculate the impact of two different scenarios. If the dollar strengthens and the value of the Swiss franc falls to $0.5100, the cost of a coat becomes CHF1,200 × $0.5100/CHF = $612. On the other hand, if the dollar falls to $0.6800/CHF, the cost of a coat increases to CHF1,200 × $0.6800/CHF, or $816. This is about $17\frac{1}{2}$% more than the original price and would seriously erode the importer's anticipated profit margin. The important thing to note here is that the coat manufacturer's agreed-upon price does not change with international exchange rates. A coat still costs CHF1,200. In this example, the price of the Swiss franc with respect to the U.S. dollar has changed. The price of the coat in Swiss francs did not.

Unexpected changes in the exchange rate for foreign currencies are the essence of foreign exchange risk. Before someone can buy a foreign good, they must first buy the appropriate foreign currency. If an American sells goods abroad and receives payment in the local currency, the proceeds cannot be spent at home until the foreign currency is converted into the American "currency of account," the U.S. dollar.

THOSE STRANGE INDIAN NUMBERS[5]

It is impossible to be in India more than ten minutes or to read domestically oriented reports without coming across the terms *lakh* and *crore*. As in "there were almost two lakh people at the Madonna concert last night" or "Nick Leeson lost over 100 crore dollars for Barings." When Americans count, they go hundreds, thousands, millions, billions. When Indians count, they go hundreds, thousands, lakhs, crores. And no, a lakh is not a million and a crore is not a billion. That would be too simple. A lakh is 100,000. A crore is 100 lakh, or to an American, 10 million. So the March on Washington a few years back would have been the 10 Lakh Man March, and Regis Philbin in Bombay would ask, "Do you want to have 10 lakh rupees."

One other thing. Indians do commas a little differently. Americans put commas between every three digits, starting from the right. Indians do put a comma in front of the first three digits starting from the right, just as we do, but after that they put commas between every two digits. For example, one crore, or ten million rupees, would be expressed as Rs. 1,00,00,000. You're now ready to do numbers in India.

The fact that volatility might work in your favor does not reduce the risk.

Also, note that the coats can become more expensive or they can become cheaper. This is price volatility, and price volatility constitutes risk. The fact that the volatility might work in your favor does not reduce the risk.

FX RISK FROM AN INVESTMENT PERSPECTIVE

Through your broker you might place a market order to buy 10,000 shares of Kangaroo Lager, trading on the Sydney Stock Exchange. Assume you get the shares at 1.45 Australian dollars (AUD) apiece. Your brokerage statement will show the value of this purchase in U.S. dollars. The exchange rate might have been $0.5755/AUD at the time you bought the stock. This means the shares cost you $10,000 \times AUD1.45 \times \$0.5755/AUD = \$8,344.75$.

If the shares appreciate to AUD1.95, the result is a holding period return of

$$\frac{AUD1.95 - AUD1.45}{AUD1.45} = 34.5\%$$

Over this period, however, the value of the Australian dollar might fall from $0.5755 to $0.5500. If you were to sell the shares, you would receive $10,000 \times AUD1.95 \times \$0.5500/AUD$, or $10,725.00. From your perspective, the holding period return was *not* 34.5 percent. Rather, it was ($10,725.00 – $8,344.75)/ $8,344.75 = 28.52 percent. This is still a good return, but you were obviously hurt by the foreign exchange risk.

---

[5] Gorham, Mike. "India Does Futures," *Futures Industry*, June/July 2000, 24.

FORWARD RATES

The spot rate is the current price of a foreign currency.

The forward rate is a contractual rate between a commercial bank and a client for future delivery of foreign exchange.

If a traveler cashes a U.S. dollar traveler's check while abroad, the exchange occurs at the **spot exchange rate**. This is the current exchange rate for two currencies, and it is the rate that is posted on signs at international airports and in banking centers. The spot rate changes daily and can increase or decrease.

The **forward exchange rate** is a contractual rate between a commercial bank and a client for the future delivery of a specified quantity of foreign currency. Forward rates are normally quoted on the basis of one, two, three, six, and twelve months, but other terms can be arranged. Widely traded currencies can have a forward market as much as five years ahead. Table 10–3 shows forward rates on six major currencies from September 6, 2000.

TABLE 10–3 Forward Currency Rates					
		SEPTEMBER 6, 2000			
		US $ EQUIVALENT		**CURRENCY PER US $**	
COUNTRY	**CURRENCY**	**WEDNESDAY**	**TUESDAY**	**WEDNESDAY**	**TUESDAY**
BRITAIN	POUND	1.4388	1.455	0.695	0.6873
1 MONTH FWD		1.4396	1.4558	0.6946	0.6869
3 MONTHS FWD		1.4408	1.4569	0.6941	0.6864
6 MONTHS FWD		1.4428	1.4587	0.6931	0.6855
CANADA	DOLLAR	0.6748	0.6772	1.4819	1.4766
1 MONTH FWD		0.6753	0.6777	1.4808	1.4756
3 MONTHS FWD		0.6762	0.6786	1.4789	1.4736
6 MONTHS FWD		0.6777	0.6802	1.4755	1.4702
FRANCE	FRANC	0.1327	0.1357	7.538	7.3666
1 MONTH FWD		0.1329	0.136	7.5254	7.3537
3 MONTHS FWD		0.1333	0.1364	7.5046	7.3332
6 MONTHS FWD		0.1338	0.1369	7.4765	7.3047
GERMANY	MARK	0.4449	0.4553	2.2476	2.1965
1 MONTH FWD		0.4457	0.4561	2.2438	2.1926
3 MONTHS FWD		0.4469	0.4574	2.2376	2.1865
6 MONTHS FWD		0.4486	0.4591	2.2292	2.178
JAPAN	YEN	0.009439	0.00945	105.94	105.82
1 MONTH FWD		0.009491	0.009504	105.36	105.22
3 MONTHS FWD		0.009588	0.009599	104.3	104.18
6 MONTHS FWD		0.009738	0.00975	102.7	102.56
SWITZERLAND	FRANC	0.5623	0.5736	1.7785	1.7433
1 MONTH FWD		0.5639	0.5754	1.7735	1.7380
3 MONTHS FWD		0.5667	0.5782	1.7646	1.7294
6 MONTHS FWD		0.5708	0.5825	1.7518	1.7168

Source: http://interactive.wsj.com

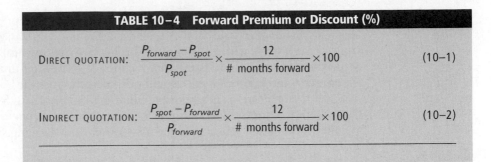

TABLE 10–4   Forward Premium or Discount (%)

$$\text{DIRECT QUOTATION:} \quad \frac{P_{forward} - P_{spot}}{P_{spot}} \times \frac{12}{\# \text{ months forward}} \times 100 \qquad (10\text{–}1)$$

$$\text{INDIRECT QUOTATION:} \quad \frac{P_{spot} - P_{forward}}{P_{forward}} \times \frac{12}{\# \text{ months forward}} \times 100 \qquad (10\text{–}2)$$

We know from academic research[6] that the forward foreign exchange rate is an unbiased estimate of the future spot rate for foreign exchange. The foreign exchange section of the financial pages can provide information on the direction "the market" feels relative currency values will move in the months ahead. If forward rates show that the dollar is expected to strengthen, it would make sense to delay paying Swiss francs as long as possible. If the dollar is expected to weaken, then you should lock in a rate now before your cost goes up.

Table 10–3 shows the Swiss franc spot exchange rate is $0.5623/CHF and the three-month forward rate is $0.5667/CHF. Note that under the forward contract the future dollar price is more than the prevailing spot rate. This means that the marketplace expects the value of the U.S. dollar to *decline* relative to the Swiss franc in the next 90 days. The difference between the two rates can be quoted as an annual premium or discount using the formulas in Table 10–4.

For the Swiss franc, using Equation 10–1 for direct quotations,[7] we find a forward premium of 3.13%:

$$\frac{\$0.5667 - \$0.5623}{\$0.5623} \times \frac{12}{3} \times 100 = 3.13\%$$

Having discussed this, let's now examine the dual notions of *purchasing power parity* and *interest rate parity* and see why we get this result.

PURCHASING POWER PARITY

The concept of **purchasing power parity** is an arbitrage-based idea stating that in a world of perfect markets, the same good should sell for the same price in

---

[6] See, for instance, Bradford Cornell's article, "Spot Rates, Forward Rates, and Exchange Market Efficiency," *Journal of Financial Economics* (August 1977): 55–65.

[7] We get essentially the same answer if we use indirect quotations. Using Equation 10–2,

$$\frac{1.7785 - 1.7646}{1.7646} \times \frac{12}{3} \times 100 = 3.15\%.$$

Rounding causes the difference.

different countries. If there are no barriers to trade, no taxes, or other "costs," for instance, an ounce of gold should be worth just as much in Vancouver as in Paris.

We can see this with an example. Consider two hypothetical countries, A and B, whose currencies are in equilibrium: currency A equals 2 units of currency B. Countries A and B are contiguous, and people freely cross the border to purchase goods from their foreign neighbors. If inflation in country A suddenly rises by 2% more than in country B, country A's currency will depreciate by 2% relative to country B's currency. This means the new equilibrium exchange rate will become 1.02A = 2B, or A = 1.9608B.

Unexpected inflation causes the value of the home currency to fall.

The reason for this change stems from the behavior of the international trading partners. People naturally want to buy a particular good for the least cost. In country A, the higher level of domestic inflation causes the prices of goods to increase, making them less desirable to people in both country A and country B. Fewer people are now going to buy goods in country A; it is cheaper to get them in B. The end result is that country A will export fewer goods, while country B will sell more. This can cause country A to develop a trade deficit with country B. Less international trade means people in country B will have less demand for country A's currency because they are not buying as much in country A. This reduced demand will cause the price of the currency to fall to a new equilibrium level, where residents of country B are again motivated to cross the border to buy goods in country A.

There are other relevant economic issues that complicate this simple example substantially. The important point is the fact that differentials in international inflation rates can be a source of foreign exchange risk.

INTEREST RATE PARITY

Forward rates reflect differences in national interest rates.

The **interest rate parity** theorem states that differences in national interest rates will be reflected in the currency forward market. If there are no transaction cost differentials, two securities of similar risk and maturity will show a difference in their interest rates equal to the forward premium or discount, but with the opposite sign.

Using the example above, if 90-day U.S. Treasury bills yield 6.30%, the interest rate parity theorem requires that 3-month Swiss bills yield 3.13% less, or 3.17%. (This assumes that the world considers the two securities equally risky. If this is not so, there will be a risk premium reflected in the riskier security's interest rate.) Table 10–5 shows the equation for interest rate parity.

Let's investigate equation 10–3 using the Table 10–3 figures for Germany. The 6-month forward rate for the deutsche mark is DM2.2292/\$; the spot rate is DM 2.2476/\$. We can solve for the implied German 6-month interest rate:

$$\frac{DM2.2292}{DM2.2476} = \frac{1 + R_{Germany}}{1 + \dfrac{0.063}{2}}$$

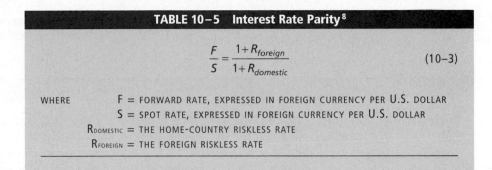

TABLE 10–5   Interest Rate Parity[8]

$$\frac{F}{S} = \frac{1 + R_{foreign}}{1 + R_{domestic}} \qquad\qquad (10-3)$$

WHERE F = FORWARD RATE, EXPRESSED IN FOREIGN CURRENCY PER U.S. DOLLAR
               S = SPOT RATE, EXPRESSED IN FOREIGN CURRENCY PER U.S. DOLLAR
     $R_{DOMESTIC}$ = THE HOME-COUNTRY RISKLESS RATE
     $R_{FOREIGN}$ = THE FOREIGN RISKLESS RATE

We find $R_{Germany}$ = 2.31%. This corresponds to an annual rate of 2.31% × 2 = 4.62%.

It may be interesting and instructive to repeat this using the figures for Japan. In September 2000 interest rates in Japan were close to zero as they had been for several years. The 6-month forward rate for the yen is ¥102.7/$; the spot rate is ¥105.94/$. We can solve for the implied Japanese 6-month interest rate, R_{Japan}:

$$\frac{¥102.7}{¥105.94} = \frac{1 + R_{Japan}}{1 + \dfrac{0.063}{2}}$$

(We divide the interest rate by two because we are looking at only one-half of a year in the forward premium.) Rearranging, and solving, we find

$$1 + R_{Japan} = (1.0315)(102.7)/105.94 = 1.0$$

This implied a Japanese 6-month interest rate of zero, which, while historically very unusual, is what we expected.[9]

A Treasury bill rate for any country is a nominal rate. Recall that the nominal rate is the aggregation of the real rate, the inflation premium, and a risk premium. If some economic event happens that causes interest rates in the United States or in Canada to change, the relative value of the two currencies will change. This, by definition, is foreign exchange risk.

When applied to currency, purchasing power parity is essentially an extension of the interest rate parity theorem, stating that, for two currencies that are initially

---

[8] This is also sometimes shown in continuous time as $F = Se^{(R_{domestic} - R_{foreign})T}$.

[9] On September 8, 2000 the actual Japanese 6-month government rate was 0.39%. The difference comes largely from bid-ask spread effects in selecting the currency rates.

in equilibrium, a relative change in the prevailing inflation rate in one country will be reflected as an equal but opposite change in the value of its currency.

FOREIGN CURRENCY FUTURES

If you understand basic principles of hedging and speculating, you will have no trouble applying those ideas to futures contracts on foreign currencies. Foreign currency futures contracts were the first financial futures traded on exchanges in the United States. They began trading at the Chicago Mercantile Exchange in 1972, about the time that currencies began to float relative to each other. Prior to this time the value of the U.S. dollar was pegged to the price of gold, with most world currencies related to the value of the dollar. Once the U.S. went off the gold standard and exchange rates moved with market forces rather than because of government fiat, international financiers faced a new type of risk. As people in Chicago are fond of saying, "Risk creates need, need creates traders, and the rest is just sophistication." FX futures were quickly recognized as a very effective way to deal with the risk.

"Risk creates need, need creates traders, and the rest is just sophistication."

PRICING OF FOREIGN EXCHANGE FUTURES CONTRACTS

Foreign currency futures call for delivery of the foreign currency in the *country of issuance* to a bank of the clearinghouse's choosing.

Futures prices are simply a function of the spot price and the cost of carrying the particular asset or financial instrument. With foreign currency, the "cost" of holding one currency rather than another is really an opportunity cost measured by differences in the interest rates prevailing in the two countries. Table 10–6 presents a basic pricing model for foreign currency futures contracts.

The local currency rate is the "risk-free" interest rate prevailing in the country of concern. Suppose that in the Land of Leptonia interest rates are 10% and that the current dollar price of a Lepton is $0.4817. Also suppose that the current Eurodollar deposit rate is 7.50%. This is the interest rate earned on a U.S. dollar

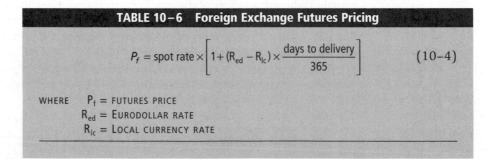

TABLE 10–6   Foreign Exchange Futures Pricing

$$P_f = \text{spot rate} \times \left[1 + (R_{ed} - R_{lc}) \times \frac{\text{days to delivery}}{365}\right] \qquad (10\text{–}4)$$

WHERE P_f = FUTURES PRICE
         R_{ed} = EURODOLLAR RATE
         R_{lc} = LOCAL CURRENCY RATE

on deposit outside the United States. For how much should a 90-day futures contract sell? Using the formula, we find that the equilibrium price is

$$\$0.4817 \times [1 + (0.075 - 0.100) \times 90/365] = \$0.4787$$

This means that the futures price for Leptons should be *less* than their cost in the spot market.

As in the currency forward market, foreign exchange futures are priced this way because of the theory of interest rate parity. This states that securities with similar risk and maturity should differ in price by an amount equal to (but opposite in sign) from the difference between national interest rates in the two countries. In this example, Leptonia's interest rates are 2.5% (on an annual basis) higher than the U.S. rate. For 90 days, or one fourth of a year, Leptonia's rates are 0.625% higher. Therefore, Leptons for delivery in 90 days should sell at a 0.625% discount from their spot value, and this is exactly what we find.

Consider one more example. Suppose I sell a Country X foreign currency futures contract to someone residing in Country X. By selling a contract as an opening transaction, I promise to deliver a certain quantity of foreign currency. Assume the contract calls for delivery in six months, and that the interest rates in

Any futures price is a function of the cash price and the carrying cost associated with holding the commodity or financial instrument.

FOREIGN EXCHANGE RISK AND FOREIGN BONDS

TRADING STRATEGY

In one of her managed portfolios, Kirsten Joy holds $25 million worth of foreign bonds, mostly from Germany, Switzerland, and France. Some of the bonds mature about five months from today, with the others maturing within eighteen months. The average coupon rate for this portfolio is 4.40%.

Kirsten believes the European currencies are all likely to depreciate against the dollar in the next few months, and she wants to preserve the yield from this portfolio. She has historically done this with futures contracts on each of the currencies involved. As Europe moves toward a standardized currency, however, she has noticed that some of the futures, especially the deutsche mark contract, have little trading volume or open interest, and this concerns her.

She decides to try a different type of hedge, using the new Euro FX futures contract at the Chicago Mercantile Exchange. This contract covers €125,000 and works the same way as other currency futures. She sees that a Euro is currently worth $0.9430, so her $25 million portfolio is equivalent to about €26,511,135. With €125,000 per futures contract, she calculates that 212 Euro futures contracts will hedge almost all of the risk. She picks up the phone and goes short 212 contracts. From previous activity she knows that this trade qualifies for the hedger's margin, and she satisfies the reduced good faith deposit with Treasury bills also held in this portfolio. She also knows that she will sleep better with the FX risk largely removed.

my country are higher than the interest rates in Country X. I can invest the currency until I must deliver it. Similarly, the buyer of the futures contract can invest the funds that will be used to pay for the foreign exchange. Because my interest rates are somewhat higher than those of the Country X resident, I have an advantage: I will earn more interest. This differential is reflected in "compensation" to the Country X futures contract buyer via a discounted futures contract price.

DEALING WITH THE RISK

DEALING WITH THE EXPOSURE

Having identified foreign exchange exposure, a decision needs to be made about what to do about it. In general, the portfolio manager faces three choices: *ignore* the exposure, *eliminate* it, or *hedge* it.

Ignore the Exposure

People often select this choice by default. An investor might be aware of the foreign exchange risk associated with a non-U.S. security, but considers that risk to be a fact of life of global investing. This strategy is also appropriate if you expect foreign exchange movements to be modest or if the dollar amount of the exposure is small relative to the cost of doing something about it.

Doing nothing also would be an appropriate action if the U.S. dollar was expected to depreciate relative to the country of the foreign security. This is because the depreciation of the dollar would result in a gain to the U.S. holder of a security denominated in a foreign currency.

Reduce or Eliminate the Exposure

This alternative amounts to getting rid of the foreign security, or at least reducing the size of your position in it. Certainly this is a way to deal with the problem, but a rather extreme one. Still, if the dollar is expected to appreciate dramatically, this is an approach to consider.

Hedge the Exposure

Hedging involves taking a position in the market that offsets another position. (Hedging foreign exchange risk is also called **covering the risk**.) There are various ways in which foreign exchange exposure can be hedged. The most common methods are via the forward market or the futures market.[10]

A BUSINESS EXAMPLE

Let's return to the earlier example of a U.S. importer with an obligation to pay Swiss francs for a delivery of coats. The 400 coats cost a total of CHF480,000, with

---

[10] People also hedge via the foreign currency options market, discussed in Chapter 13.

DERIVATIVES TODAY

50% HEDGING[11]

The foreign currency hedging decision is a complicated one. An article in *Institutional Investor* states,

An emerging consensus in the money management industry holds that currency risk may be safely ignored when it's a small part of a portfolio. Once international exposure passes a threshold of 10 to 20 percent, however, the currency risk becomes substantial and ought to be hedged in some form (depending on the firm's asset mix, time horizon, and tolerance for volatility).[12]

In one of his research papers, Fischer Black reports that the appropriate degree of currency exposure is somewhere between zero and 100%, and not at either extreme.[13] When you think about it, 100 percent hedging amounts to a bet the foreign currency will depreciate, while zero percent hedging amounts to a bet the foreign currency will appreciate.

A number of firms, including Unisys, GTE, and General Motors, have settled on a 50% currency hedge in their portfolios. A portfolio manager at GM stated he does not believe in currency forecasting and that "anything but a 50% hedged policy implicitly states a view of currency direction." When investment performance is judged against an "average benchmark," 50 percent hedging may be the safest and most prudent option.

[11] This material comes from Robert A. Strong, *Practical Investment Management*, 2nd edition, 304–305.

[12] Miriam Bensman, "Hedging on the Hedges," *Institutional Investor* (June 1996), 73–79.

[13] Fischer Black, "Universal Hedging: Optimizing Currency Risk and Reward in International Equity Portfolios," *Financial Analysts Journal* (July/August 1989), 16–22.

payment due in three months. The importer can hedge this risk using either the currency forward market or the futures market.[14]

Hedging with the Forward Market

Hedging with a forward contract is simple and easy. The importer will visit his or her commercial bank and enter into a forward contract to buy Swiss francs in 90 days. Table 10–3 shows the 3-month forward rate for the Swiss franc to be $0.5667. The importer will agree to exchange CHF480,000 at this price 90 days from today.

Regardless of what happens to exchange rates in the next three months, the importer knows the final purchase price of the coats. At the end of the forward contract, the importer will pay the bank CHF480,000 × $0.5667/CHF, or $272,016, and receive the 480,000 Swiss francs in return.[15]

[14] A three-month forward price will usually differ slightly from a three-month futures price. The primary reason for this is that a futures contract is marked to market daily, while a forward contract is not. Because of the marking to market we *do not know*, in advance, the exact cash flows associated with the futures contract; we *do* know them with the forward contract. Depending on someone's outlook on future interest rates, this difference may show up in a preference for a forward over a futures contract, or vice versa.

[15] In practice, the importer will probably never see the Swiss francs. Instead, his bank will generate a wire transfer to the other party's bank account.

TABLE 10–7   Swiss Franc Futures Prices

SEPTEMBER 6, 2000
CHF125,000; $ PER CHF

	DAILY						PRIOR DAY		
MONTH	OPEN	HIGH	LOW	SETTLE	CHANGE	EST. VOLUME	SETTLE	VOLUME	OPEN INTEREST
SEP00	0.5742	0.5753	0.5621	0.5629	−105	20000	0.5734	18339	55525
DEC00	0.5784	0.5784	0.5664	0.5673	−106	4846	0.5779	884	5256
MAR01	0.5712	0.5720	0.5712	0.5716	−106	3	0.5822		9
JUN01	0.5810	0.5810	0.5810	0.5759	−106	2	0.5865		
					TOTALS	EST. VOLUME 25133		VOLUME 19223	OPEN INTEREST 60790

Source: www.cme.com

Hedging with the Futures Market

Alternately, the importer could use the futures market. There are CHF125,000 in a futures contract, so it would not be possible to hedge exactly. Four contracts would cover CHF500,000, slightly more than needed. Table 10–7 shows sample Swiss franc futures prices.

Using the futures market, the importer might buy 4 December contracts at $0.5673. This obligates him to pay CHF500,000 × $0.5673/CHF, or $283,650. Regardless of how the Swiss franc changes value, the importer knows the ultimate exchange rate for the coat purchase.

AN INVESTMENT EXAMPLE

Let's now consider another example from the perspective of the manager of an international bond portfolio. Suppose Britta Katrina, CFA, manages a portfolio containing CHF1,200,000 par value in 8.33%, semi-annual pay Swiss corporate bonds. These bonds come due next March, when the issuing firm will mail the bondholders their final check. In Britta's case, this will be a check for CHF1,250,000: CHF1,200,000 principal amount plus the final interest check of CHF50,000. These funds will most likely have to be converted into dollars before they can be reinvested, unless the proceeds will be used to buy new Swiss securities.

Using the values in Table 10–3, the spot rate for the Swiss franc is $0.5623. This means that CHF1,250,000 are currently worth $702,875. Between now and next March, this value can go up or down as the dollar depreciates or strengthens. Britta does not know for certain the dollar value of the Swiss franc check to be received next March.

If she is uncomfortable with this uncertainty and wants to hedge the foreign exchange exposure, she can do so using either the currency forward market or the Swiss franc futures contract. From Table 10–3, the six-month forward rate is $0.5708. She might decide to deliver CHF1,250,000 at this forward exchange rate six months from now, anticipating receipt of $713,500.

If, instead, she wants to hedge using the futures market, the appropriate transaction is to short futures: promise to deliver the Swiss francs. Britta might sell ten contracts at $0.5716, the March settlement price in Table 10–7. The contraparty promises to pay $0.5716/CHF × CHF125,000/contract × 10 contracts = $714,500.

In March, there will be a gain or a loss in the futures market that will largely offset the gain or loss experienced when the Swiss francs are converted to dollars. Suppose the spot exchange rate in March is $0.5600. The check the manager receives from the bonds would be worth CHF1,250,000 × $0.56/CHF, or $700,000. This is $14,500 less than the value locked in with the hedge. Britta can now close out her futures position at the new spot price of $0.5600 by buying ten contracts. Having bought at $0.5600 contracts that were initially sold at $0.5716, there is a gain of $0.0116 on each unit of the 1,250,000 Swiss francs for a total of $14,500. The gain in the futures market exactly cancels the loss in the spot market.

If the dollar had depreciated by March, and the spot exchange rate became $0.6000, then the CHF check would be worth $750,000. The price locked in was $714,500; the check is worth $35,500 more than that. In the futures market, Britta sold at $0.5716 and bought at $0.6000; this is a loss of $35,500 that exactly cancels the reduced value of the final check on the bond.

Financial managers know that a hedge of this sort only works exactly if the change in the spot price and the change in the futures price are equal. If the futures contract has a life different than the investment or transaction horizon, it is possible that the two price changes may not be the same, although they will probably still be close.

KEYS ISSUES IN FOREIGN EXCHANGE RISK MANAGEMENT

For many portfolio managers, foreign exchange risk is a very modest component of total risk, and often one that is for all practical purposes immaterial. Still, if foreign exchange risk is ignored, it should be ignored on purpose rather than through ignorance. The steps in good foreign exchange risk management are these:

1. define and measure foreign exchange exposure;
2. organize a system that monitors this exposure and exchange rate changes;
3. assign responsibility for hedging;
4. formulate a strategy for hedging.

SUMMARY

Foreign exchange risk is increasingly important to portfolio managers and corporate treasurers. Hedging this risk, in fact, is the primary use of derivatives by corporate treasurers. There is a strong connection between relative exchange rates and the respective level of interest rates between the two countries.

The presence of foreign exchange risk is called exposure. This arrives from business transactions that are incomplete or from the holding of assets denominated in a foreign currency.

Foreign exchange futures and the currency forward market can be used to reduce foreign exchange risk. Both forward contracts and futures contracts are priced according to the theory of interest rate parity, which is really just another version of the cost-of-carry pricing model.

ANSWERS TO DERIVATIVES TODAY QUESTIONS

Nokia — Finland

Bass — U.K.

Norelco — Netherlands

Volvo Cars — U.S.

7 Up — U.K.

Nestle — Switzerland

Bayer — Germany

SAKS — U.K.

Nivea — Germany

Shell Oil — Netherlands

Brooks Brothers — U.K.

Maybelline — France

Dannon — France

Shaw's — U.K.

Virgin Records — U.K.

Magnavox — Netherlands

Coca Cola — U.S.

Poland Springs — France

IKEA — Sweden

Gillette — U.S.

Hannaford Brothers — Netherlands

Burberry — U.S.

Dunkin Donuts — U.K.

SELF TEST

T ___ F ___ 1. Nearly 65% of global stock market capitalization comes from the United States.

T ___ F ___ 2. Foreign exchange risk represents the chance of default by a foreign lender.

T ___ F ___ 3. The nominal rate equals the real rate plus a risk premium plus an inflation premium.

T ___ F ___ 4. A portfolio manager is more concerned with economic for-eign exchange exposure than with accounting foreign exchange exposure.

T ___ F ___ 5. A direct foreign exchange quotation is the inverse of an indirect foreign exchange quotation.

T ___ F ___ 6. If a currency weakens relative to another, it buys more of the foreign currency.

T ___ F ___   7. A forward exchange rate may be more or less than the spot exchange rate.

T ___ F ___   8. A change in a country's interest rates usually results in a change in the forward discount or premium of that country's currency on the global market.

T ___ F ___   9. Forward rates reflect differences in national interest rates.

T ___ F ___   10. Unexpected inflation causes the value of the home currency to fall.

T ___ F ___   11. Purchasing power parity states that in a world of perfect markets the same good should sell for the same price in different countries.

T ___ F ___   12. The interest rate parity theorem states that differences in national interest rates will be reflected in the currency forward market.

T ___ F ___   13. Forward contracts are marked to market in the same manner as a futures contract.

T ___ F ___   14. According to one market survey, the most common corporate use of derivatives is to access foreign equity markets.

T ___ F ___   15. The spot price is the same as the cash price for a foreign currency.

PROBLEMS & QUESTIONS

1. Comment on the following statement: "If you have a lot of foreign holdings scattered around the world, foreign exchange risk is not much of a problem, because the various translation gains and losses all average out to zero long term."

2. If a person anticipated receiving a quantity of a foreign currency in 90 days, why not hedge this transaction by using a 30-day forward contract and replacing it twice? Wouldn't this give you greater flexibility than you would have by locking in the 90-day rate?

3. At present, one unit of currency X equals three units of currency Y. Interest rates are 6% in X and 8% in Y. Inflation in both countries suddenly rises by 3%. What effect would you expect this to have (a) on the respective interest rates, and (b) on the relative exchange rates?

4. Why is economic exposure more important to a portfolio manager than either type of accounting exposure?

5. Comment on the following statement: "I've never made any money in the currency forward market."

6. How might someone use foreign exchange futures in a *short hedge*?

7. Suppose you are a speculator in deutsche mark futures, and you are currently long three contracts. You hear a rumor about interest rates rising in Germany. Is this good news for you?

8. Why might overhedging be considered speculation?

9. The current exchange rate is one U.S. dollar equal to 1.4456 units of currency G. In the United States, the T-bill rate is 8.68%. The 60-day forward rate for currency G is $0.7100/G. What country G interest rate is implied in these prices?

10. Check the *Wall Street Journal* for 90-day forward prices on the German mark.
   a. What is the forward premium or discount?

CHAPTER 10 REVIEW

b. Does the market anticipate the US dollar appreciating (strengthening) or depreciating (weakening) relative to the German mark?

11. Using your answer on Problem 10, and assuming 90-day T-bills yield 9%, what should a 90-day German T-bill yield if both governments are considered equally risky?

12. Suppose a Canadian dollar costs seventy-five cents in U.S. dollars. If the market begins in equilibrium, what should the new exchange rate be if U.S. inflation is one percent greater than the Canadian rate?

13. Using data from a recent edition of the *Wall Street Journal*, find the U.S. and Canadian prime interest rates. Based on those values, what changes does the market expect in the value of the Canadian dollar relative to the U.S. dollar during the next year?

14. You have CHF1,000,000 in bonds that will mature in 90 days. Using current data from the *Wall Street Journal*, show how you can hedge the foreign exchange risk by (a) using the forward market, and (b) using the futures market.

15. Refer to Table 10–7. You hold equity securities in Switzerland valued at CHF58 million. How many DEC CHF futures should be bought or sold to hedge the foreign exchange risk?

16. In Problem 15, would your answer be different if the securities were bonds?

17. Based on your answer to Problem 15, suppose the value of the Swiss securities rises to CHF60 million, but the Table 10–7 information remains unchanged. How should you adjust the hedge from problem 15?

11

Fundamentals of Interest Rate Futures

KEY TERMS you will find in this chapter:

KEY TERMS

The most expensive real estate in Chicago is the top step of the bond pit.

Dale Lorenzo
Former Vice Chairman, CBOT

We saw in the previous chapters that an investor can remove much of the worry about adverse stock market fluctuations or foreign exchange movements by hedging that risk away with stock index futures or foreign exchange futures.

Many portfolios contain securities that are **interest rate sensitive**. As it is used here, the term means that changes in the general level of market interest rates can adversely affect their value. Corporate and government bonds, for instance, are interest rate sensitive; their prices move inversely with interest rates. This means that the market value of a bond portfolio will decline if market interest rates increase.

A passbook savings account, on the other hand, is not interest rate sensitive. There is no way that the principal value of such an account can decline, regardless of what happens to interest rates. The rate of interest paid on the account can change, but the value of the account will never decline because of market forces unless the bank defaults and there is no FDIC deposit insurance.

In this chapter we look at the fundamentals of interest rate futures. In the next chapter we look at several methods of using these and other derivatives to reduce a portfolio's interest rate risk.

INTEREST RATE FUTURES

Interest rate futures contracts exist across the yield curve and on many different types of interest rates. The T-bond contract, introduced by the Chicago Board of Trade in 1975, is one of the most successful futures contracts in the world. Daily volume is often over 500,000 contracts, representing $50 billion in face value, of which between 4% and 5% will ultimately be settled by delivery. There are short-term, intermediate-term, and long-term interest rate futures contracts.

The best-known short-term interest rate contract is the **Eurodollar (ED)** futures contract. Eurodollars are simply American dollars on deposit in a bank outside the United States. Other short-term contracts include U.S. Treasury bills, federal funds, and LIBOR. **LIBOR** is the London InterBank Offered Rate.[1] (There is more discussion on this interest rate later in the chapter.) The federal funds contract trades at the Chicago Board of Trade, with the others trading at the Chicago Mercantile Exchange. The Chicago Board of Trade cites its 2-, 5-, 10-, and 30-year treasury contracts as targeting "the most actively traded points along the Treasury yield curve."[2]

Various other short-term contracts trade around the world. There is also a Euroyen contract at the CME, short sterling, Euroswiss, and Euro contracts at the London International Financial Futures and Options Exchange (LIFFE), and a three-month Euribor contract at the French MATIF. (Euribor stands for Euro Inter Bank Offer Rate.) More such contracts are very likely to develop on other exchanges.

The contract on 10-year U.S. Treasury notes is the principal member of the intermediate-term category, with 30-year Treasury bonds predominant in the long-term category.

TREASURY BILLS, EURODOLLARS, AND THEIR FUTURES CONTRACTS

The pricing and characteristics of T-bills and Eurodollars are similar. Despite the fact that Eurodollars are the most widely traded futures contracts in the world, the following section will focus on T-bills due to their familiarity.

CHARACTERISTICS OF U.S. TREASURY BILLS

Unlike most long-term fixed income instruments, U.S. Treasury bills sell at a discount from their par, or face value. The government sells 91-day (13-week) and

---

[1] LIBOR varies according to currency. LIBOR associated with Eurodollars is dollar LIBOR. LIBOR on Euroyen is Yen LIBOR, etc.

[2] "Practical Uses of Treasury Futures," Chicago Board of Trade, 1999.

TERM	ISSUE DATE	MATURITY DATE	DISCOUNT RATE %	INVESTMENT RATE %	PRICE PER $100	CUSIP
91-DAY	09-21-2000	12-21-2000	5.960	6.137	98.493	912795FLO
182-DAY	09-21-2000	03-22-2001	5.935	6.203	97.000	912795FY2
91-DAY	09-14-2000	12-14-2000	5.945	6.121	98.497	912795FK2
182-DAY	09-14-2000	03-15-2001	5.955	6.226	96.989	912795FX4
14-DAY	09-01-2000	09-15-2000	6.440	6.530	99.750	912795GZ8
364-DAY	08-31-2000	08-30-2001	5.880	6.338	94.055	912795HL8
92-DAY	08-24-2000	11-24-2000	6.110	6.291	98.439	912795FH9
182-DAY	08-24-2000	02-22-2001	6.090	6.371	96.921	912795FU0
91-DAY	08-17-2000	11-16-2000	6.090	6.269	98.461	912795FG1

TABLE 11–1   Treasury Bill Auction Results (selected issues)

182-day (26-week) T-bills at a weekly auction in which all trades occur at a single, market-clearing price. The more you pay for them, the lower the yield to you, and the less interest the government must pay.

Table 11–1 shows a sample of T-bill auction results from the year 2000. Consider the 91-day T-bill issued on September 21st. An investor who bought $10,000 par value of this T-bill paid 98.493% of par, or $9,849.30. At maturity, the investor receives $10,000, earning $150.70 in interest. Treasury bills do not carry a stated interest rate. The calculated interest rate earned depends on the time until maturity and the price paid for the bill.

The market typically quotes T-bill prices on a *discount basis* using a 360-day year and twelve 30-day months. This is the "discount rate %" column in Table 11–1. For this T-bill, we get a discount rate (usually called a **discount yield**) from Equation 11–1:

$$\text{Discount Yield} = \frac{\text{Par Value} - \text{Market Price}}{\text{Par Value}} \times \frac{360}{\text{Days}} \qquad (11\text{-}1)$$

Substituting,

$$\frac{\$10,000 - \$9,849.30}{\$10,000} \times \frac{360}{91} = 5.96\%$$

The financial press usually reports T-bill prices based on the **ask discount**, which is the discount rate associated with paying the ask price for the security. The discount yield is not directly comparable to other investments because it relates the income to the *par value* rather than to the *price paid* and uses 360 days rather than a true 365-day year. To fix this we can calculate the **bond equivalent yield**:

$$\text{bond equivalent yield} = \frac{\text{discount amount}}{\text{discount price}} \times \frac{365}{\text{days to maturity}} \qquad (11\text{-}2)$$

If the T-bill sells for $9,849.30, the bond equivalent yield is

$$\text{bond equivalent yield} = \frac{\$10,000 - \$9,849.30}{\$9,849.30} \times \frac{365}{91} = 6.137\%$$

This is the value in the Table 11–1 column labeled "Investment Rate %." The bond equivalent yield adjusts for two things: (1) the fact that there are 365 days (not 360) in a year, and (2) the actual investment required is the discounted price, not the face value. The value of this measure is that it enables you to compare more directly the yield on T-bills with competing investment alternatives.

THE TREASURY BILL FUTURES CONTRACT

Treasury bill futures contracts call for the delivery of $1 million par value of 91-day T-bills on the delivery date of the futures contract. This means that on the day the Treasury bills are delivered, they mature in 91 days (Figure 11–1).

Table 11–2 is an extract of futures prices from the financial pages. Note that prices for the contract appear as both a percentage of par and as a discount from par. The settlement price of 93.97 for the December futures represents 93.97% of

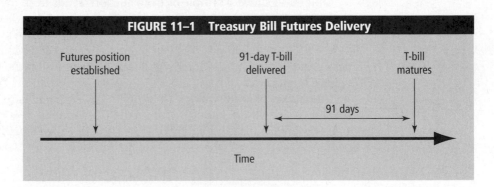

FIGURE 11–1   Treasury Bill Futures Delivery

Futures position established · 91-day T-bill delivered · T-bill matures · 91 days · Time

TABLE 11–2   Treasury Bill Futures

SEPTEMBER 15, 2000
$1 MILLION; PTS. OF 100%

	OPEN	HIGH	LOW	SETTLE	CHANGE	DISCOUNT SETTLE	DISCOUNT CHANGE	OPEN INTEREST
SEPT	94.03	94.03	94.02	94.02	−.01	5.98	+.01	1,311
DEC	94.00	94.00	93.96	93.97	−.02	6.03	+.02	1,083

100, or a discount of 100% – 93.97% = 6.03% *from* par. This figure of 6.03% is the futures *discount yield* and is the market's best estimate of what the three-month T-bill annual yield will be near the end of December.[3]

Remember that 6.03% for 91 days is different than 6.03% for one year. The rate published in the *Wall Street Journal* or on the Internet is an annual rate; we need to use Equation 11-1 to convert the price in the paper to our actual cost in dollars. (We would have $\frac{10,000 - X}{10,000} \times \frac{360}{91} = 6.03\%$. Solving, X = \$9,847.58.)

CHARACTERISTICS OF EURODOLLARS

The term "Eurodollar" refers to any dollar-denominated account outside the U.S.

Eurodollars came about in the Cold War days of the 1950s. The Soviet Union, Eastern Europe, and China feared the evolution of circumstances that might cause the U.S. government to freeze or confiscate their deposits in New York's money center banks. (This did happen to Iranian bank accounts following the hostage crisis in 1979.) To avoid this possibility, Communist countries transferred their dollar balances to banks in Europe.

Today, the term Eurodollars applies to any U.S. dollar deposited in a commercial bank outside the jurisdiction of the U.S. Federal Reserve Board. Banks often prefer Eurodollar deposits to domestic deposits because EDs are not subject to reserve requirement restrictions. This means that every ED received by a bank can be reinvested somewhere else. This bank preference for EDs usually results in a slightly higher interest rate on ED deposits.

Although EDs have this important advantage, they also carry more risk than a domestic deposit. They could be confiscated or frozen by the government of the country in which they are located, and there is not necessarily any deposit insurance outside the United States. Note that a Eurodollar is not a security that can be bought or sold; rather, it is a bank deposit that is non-transferable.

Eurodollars are time deposits rather than securities.

Most Eurodollar activity is in London, and as a consequence Eurodollar deposit rates are usually based on the London InterBank Offered Rate, or LIBOR.[4] For futures contract purposes, LIBOR is determined the way Olympic gymnastics is scored. The clearinghouse surveys 12 large banks to find their LIBOR rate, eliminates the two highest and two lowest values, and averages the remaining eight.

THE EURODOLLAR FUTURES CONTRACT

The Chicago Mercantile Exchange Eurodollar contract began trading in December 1981, and is extremely popular with corporate treasurers and other hedgers. On November 1, 1991, open interest in ED futures topped the 1 million mark for the first time, representing more than \$1 trillion Eurodollars. By September 2000 open interest had tripled, to about 3 million contracts.

[3] This is another instance in which the price discovery function of the futures markets is shown.

[4] As we will see later in the book, this rate is especially important in the interest rate swaps market.

TABLE 11–3 Treasury Bill vs. Eurodollar Futures	
TREASURY BILLS	**EURODOLLARS**
DELIVERABLE UNDERLYING COMMODITY	UNDELIVERABLE UNDERLYING COMMODITY
SETTLED BY DELIVERY	SETTLED BY CASH
TRANSFERABLE	NON-TRANSFERABLE
YIELD QUOTED ON DISCOUNT BASIS	YIELD QUOTED ON ADD-ON BASIS
MATURITIES OUT TO ONE YEAR	MATURITIES OUT TO 10 YEARS
ONE TICK[5] IS $25	ONE TICK IS $25

Like T-bill futures, the underlying asset with the Eurodollar futures contract is a three-month, $1 million face value instrument. The instrument is a non-transferable time deposit rather than a security, though, so the ED futures contract is cash settled with no actual delivery procedure. Table 11–3 highlights differences and similarities with Treasury bill and Eurodollar futures.

Table 11–4 shows sample ED futures prices. The prices shown are **IMM index** prices, which equal 100 – LIBOR, where LIBOR is an annualized three-month rate. IMM stands for the International Monetary Market division of the Chicago Mercantile Exchange. The December 2000 settlement price of 93.26, for instance, corresponds to an annualized LIBOR rate of 6.74%. A person long the futures contract would receive a three-month time deposit at this rate in approximately two months.

TABLE 11–4 Eurodollar Futures (partial listing)

OCTOBER 3, 2000
$1 MILLION; PTS. OF 100%

	OPEN	HIGH	LOW	SETTLE	CHANGE	YIELD	CHANGE	OPEN INTEREST
OCT	93.21	93.22	93.21	93.22	....	6.78	....	37,312
NOV	93.24	93.24	93.24	93.24	....	6.76	....	7,374
DEC	93.26	93.27	93.26	93.26	....	6.74	....	589,493
JAN01	93.41	93.43	93.41	93.43	....	6.57	....	2,340
MAR	93.45	93.47	93.44	93.46	....	6.54	....	537,276
JUN	93.51	93.53	93.49	93.51	....	6.49	....	328,272
SEP	93.53	93.55	93.51	93.54	....	6.46	....	309,547
DEC	93.45	93.47	93.44	93.47	+.01	6.53	−.01	206,910
MAR02	93.51	93.53	93.49	93.52	+.01	6.48	−.01	177,991
JUN	93.46	93.49	93.46	93.48	+.01	6.52	−.01	128,587

[5] A *tick* is the smallest permissible price change.

The format of the listing and the information contained therein are similar to the T-bill futures listing. An important difference is that the quoted yield with Eurodollars is an **add-on yield**, while the yield with T-bills is a *discount* yield. LIBOR is an add-on yield determined by Equation 11–3:

$$\text{Add-on Yield} = \frac{\text{Discount}}{\text{Price}} \times \frac{360}{\text{days to maturity}} \qquad (11\text{--}3)$$

An add-on yield of 6.74% corresponds to a discount of $16,751.82.

$$.0674 = \frac{\text{discount}}{\$1,000,000 - \text{discount}} \times \frac{360}{91}$$

$$\text{discount} = \$16,751.82$$

If a $1 million Treasury bill sold for a discount of $16,751.82 we would determine a discount yield of 6.63%:

$$\frac{\$16,751.82}{\$1,000,000} \times \frac{360}{91} = 6.63\%$$

An add-on yield exceeds the corresponding discount yield.

What this shows is that for a given discount, an add-on yield will exceed the corresponding discount yield.

SPECULATING WITH T-BILL FUTURES

Suppose a speculator buys a DEC T-bill futures contract at a price of 93.97. The T-bill futures contract has a face value of $1 million. Industry practice is to compute futures price changes by using 90 days until expiration. Rearranging equation 11-1, the price the speculator is promising to pay for $1 million face value in T-bills is

$$\text{Price} = \text{Face Value} \left[1 - \frac{\text{Discount Yield} \times 90}{360} \right]$$

Substituting our values,

$$\text{Price} = \$1 \text{ million} \left[1 - \frac{.0603 \times 90}{360} \right] = \$984,925$$

Now imagine that by the middle of December interest rates have risen to 7%. The new *WSJ* price will be 93.00. What specifically does this mean in dollars and cents? To find out, we determine the new T-bill price:

$$\text{Price} = \$1 \text{ million} \left[1 - \frac{0.0700 \times 90}{360} \right] = \$982,500$$

The speculator lost money:

$982,500.00   final value
$984,925.00   initial value
$2,425.00   net loss

Speculators buy T-bills
contracts when they
expect short-term rates
to fall and sell con-
tracts when rates are
expected to rise.

It is an obvious point, but worth stressing: The price of a fixed income security moves inversely with market rates. In this example, our speculator was long
a T-bill contract and interest rates rose. Consequently, he lost money.[6]

Using 90 days rather than 91 in the calculation of futures prices is convenient
because it means a change of one basis point (0.01%) in the price of a T-bill
futures contract equals a $25 change in the value of the contract. In the example,
the discount yield rose by 97 basis points. At $25 apiece, the contract should have
changed in value of $25 × 97 = $2,425, which is exactly what we found.

HEDGING WITH T-BILL FUTURES

Let's look at another example, this time as a hedger. Suppose you learn that a university foundation whose assets you manage will receive $10 million from an
estate in three months. As the portfolio manager, you would like to invest the
money in T-bills *now* because you believe that interest rates are going to fall soon.
If you had the money, you would buy them now; however, you will not receive
the money for another three months.

To lock in a current
interest rate, buy T-bill
futures.

Using the futures market, you can lock in the current interest rate that you
find attractive. Because you *want* the T-bills you establish a long hedge in T-bill
futures. We saw in the example above that you are promising to pay $984,925
for $1 million in T-bills if you buy a futures contract at 93.97. You will receive
$10 million from the estate, so perhaps you decide to buy 10 DEC T-bill futures
contracts, promising to pay 10 contracts × $984,925/contract = $9,849,250.

Three months later the gift arrives as expected. Now you can remove your
hedge by selling the futures contracts. Suppose that interest rates did fall, and that
90-day T-bills now yield 5.50%. This is a decline of 53 basis points from the original 6.03% rate. $10 million in T-bills would then cost

$$\$10 \text{ million} \left[1 - \frac{0.055 \times 90}{360} \right] = \$9,862,500$$

This is $13,250 more than the price at the time you established the hedge.
In the futures market, however, you have a gain that will offset the increased pur-

---

[6] The question is not necessarily whether rates will fall, but whether the T-bill rate at contract expiration will be higher or
lower than that implied by the futures contract price. For instance, the speculator may buy contracts if he or she expects a
smaller drop in rates than the market seems to expect.

chase price. A yield of 5.50% means the futures contracts will be quoted in the paper as 94.50. When you close out these futures positions, you will sell your contracts for more than you paid for them. In fact, your gain in the futures market will be

$$10 \text{ contracts} \times \frac{53 \text{ basis points}}{\text{contract}} \times \frac{\$25}{\text{basis point}} = \$13,250$$

This is exactly equal to your "opportunity cost" from the decline in interest rates.

TREASURY BONDS AND THEIR FUTURE CONTRACTS

Some commodity traders consider the T-bond pit to be the most sophisticated arena of any futures exchange. It is one of the largest and most difficult for an observer to follow; at the CBOT, there are sometimes over 700 people in the pit at the opening bell. The depth and efficiency of this market help explain why this contract is so popular with institutional investors.

CHARACTERISTICS OF U.S. TREASURY BONDS

Some Treasury bonds may be callable after 15 years.

Treasury bonds are similar to corporate bonds in almost every respect. They pay semi-annual interest, have a maturity date of up to 30 years from time of issuance, and are readily traded in the capital markets. The two differences between a Treasury *bond* and a Treasury *note* are (1) notes, by definition, have a life of less than ten years at the time they are initially offered, and (2) some T-bonds may be callable fifteen years after issuance. (The U.S. Treasury has not issued callable T-notes since 1984.)

The Treasury seldom calls bonds, but it does happen. On January 14, 2000, the Treasury called the $8\frac{1}{4}$% serial bond issue of 2000–2005 effective May 15, 2000. (Treasury rules require a 4-month call notice.) After May 15th, these bonds ceased to accrue any interest. The bonds were selling at a slight premium before the call, but were retired at par. The loss in market value due to the call illustrates why investors should be aware of call provisions.

All new Treasury bonds and notes are issued in book entry form only; the U.S. Treasury no longer issues actual bond certificates. Despite the fact that book-entry bonds do not require the bondholder to clip a coupon, we still refer to a bond's *coupon rate*. This is the stated interest rate that determines the dollar amount of interest the bond pays. If a $1,000 par bond has a coupon rate of $8\frac{1}{2}$%, this means the bond will pay $8\frac{1}{2}$% of par value per year, or $85. In actual practice, this would be paid in two $42.50 installments, six months apart.

Bonds are identified by the issuer, the coupon, and the year of maturity. We might refer, for instance, to the U.S. government "six and a quarters of 23." This means the Treasury bonds with a $6\frac{1}{4}$% coupon rate that come due in 2023.

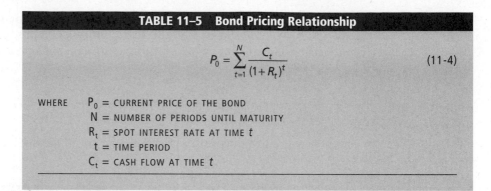

TABLE 11–5   Bond Pricing Relationship

$$P_0 = \sum_{t=1}^{N} \frac{C_t}{(1+R_t)^t} \qquad (11\text{-}4)$$

WHERE P_0 = CURRENT PRICE OF THE BOND
         N = NUMBER OF PERIODS UNTIL MATURITY
         R_t = SPOT INTEREST RATE AT TIME t
         t = TIME PERIOD
         C_t = CASH FLOW AT TIME t

TABLE 11–6   Treasury Spot Rates

MATURITY	SPOT RATE
6 MONTHS	5.73%
12 MONTHS	5.80%
18 MONTHS	5.82%
24 MONTHS	6.03%
30 MONTHS	6.10%
36 MONTHS	6.14%

PRICING OF TREASURY BONDS

Pricing of Treasury bonds is a straightforward process, although many people misunderstand how the market does this. We know the bond's maturity date and par value, and the timing and magnitude of the interest payments. Table 11–5 outlines the pricing relationship.

Suppose we have a two-year government bond[7] with a 6% coupon and the Treasury spot rates shown in Table 11–6. For what price should this bond sell? To find out, we discount each of the bond's cash flows at the appropriate spot rate:

$$P_0 = \frac{\$30}{(1.0573)^{0.5}} + \frac{\$30}{(1.0580)^{1.0}} + \frac{\$30}{(1.0582)^{1.5}} + \frac{\$1,030}{(1.0603)^{2.0}} = \$1,001.28$$

This corresponds to a newspaper price of about 100:04 (100 4/32nds). Knowing the price of the bond, if we wish we could now solve for the yield to maturity by finding the single discount rate (R) that makes the pricing equation hold.

$$\$1,001.28 = \frac{\$30}{(1+R)^{0.5}} + \frac{\$30}{(1+R)^{1.0}} + \frac{\$30}{(1+R)^{1.5}} + \frac{\$1,030}{(1+R)^{2.0}}$$

[7] This example is to illustrate bond pricing. A two-year bond is not eligible for delivery against a T-bond futures contract.

To do this, we can either look at a "bond book," use a spreadsheet package like Microsoft Excel, or use a trial and error approach in which we estimate R and search for the value that makes the equation hold. Because the bond sells at a premium to its par value of $1000, the yield to maturity will be slightly less than its coupon rate of 6%. We find the yield to maturity (R) is 5.93%.[8]

A bond's yield to maturity is determined by the market price, not the other way around.

Note that we did not find the value of the bond by plugging in the yield to maturity and solving. The yield to maturity is an "after-the-fact" calculation that you can only make if you already know the bond price. In the next chapter we will see that some interest rate risk hedging techniques employ the yield to maturity statistic, so it is something portfolio managers may need to determine.

A callable bond is a portfolio of expected future cash flows plus a short call option on the bond.

Also, remember from the early part of this book that a callable bond is really a package of two sets of securities: a long position in a non-callable bond (which itself is a portfolio of cash flows) and a short call option on the bond. The value of a callable bond, then, equals the value of a comparable non-callable bond minus the value of the "written" call.

THE TREASURY BOND FUTURES CONTRACT

This contract calls for the delivery of $100,000 face value of U.S. Treasury bonds that have a minimum of 15 years until maturity (and, if callable, have a minimum of 15 years of call protection.) Bonds that meet these criteria are **deliverable bonds**.

Defining the underlying commodity for the T-bond futures contract, however, is trickier than with other commodities. An important feature of all commodity contracts is fungibility. Hedgers and speculators both want to be able to trade out of their contracts without having to go through the delivery process.

DEALING WITH COUPON DIFFERENCES

As with the T-bill contract, speculators buy T-bond contracts when they expect interest rates to fall, and go short when they expect them to rise. While an exchange-inspected bushel of wheat is the same as any other such bushel, a Treasury bond with a 9% coupon, and twelve years until maturity is not the same as another bond with an 11% coupon and 23 years to maturity. Unlike stock index futures, delivery does actually occur with Treasury bill, bond, and note futures, although most contracts are closed via an offsetting trade. Only about 4% of Treasury bond contracts, for instance, are settled by delivery.

Conversion factors are used to "standardize" bonds for futures delivery.

To "standardize" the $100,000 face value T-bond contract traded on the Chicago Board of Trade, a **conversion factor** is used to convert all deliverable bonds to bonds yielding 6% (see Table 11-7).

---

[8] The yield to maturity is sensitive to the bond coupon. If instead of a 6% coupon this two-year bond had a 20% coupon (deliberately high to magnify the point), its price would be $1,262.08. This results in a yield to maturity of 5.91%, less than the 5.93% YTM associated with the 6% bond. The longer the term of the bond, the more sensitive YTM is to the coupon rate.

[9] These are also called *adjustment* or *correction* factors. Prior to 1999 the benchmark was 8% rather than 6%.

TABLE 11–7   Chicago Board of Trade T-Bond Conversion Factors

Coupon	Issue Date	Maturity Date	6% Conversion Factors					
			Sep. 2000	Dec. 2000	Mar. 2001	Jun. 2001	Sep. 2001	Dec. 2001
5¼	11/16/98	11/15/28	0.8989	0.8991	0.8996	0.8999	0.9003	0.9006
5¼	02/16/99	02/15/29	0.8984	0.8989	0.8991	0.8996	0.8999	0.9003
5½	08/17/98	08/15/28	0.9327	0.9331	0.9332	0.9336	0.9337	0.9341
6	02/15/96	02/15/26	0.9999	1.0000	0.9999	1.0000	0.9999	1.0000
6⅛	11/17/97	11/15/27	1.0166	1.0164	1.0165	1.0163	1.0164	1.0162
6⅛	02/17/98	11/15/27	1.0166	1.0164	1.0165	1.0163	1.0164	1.0162
6⅛	08/16/99	08/15/29	1.0169	1.0170	1.0168	1.0169	1.0167	1.0167
6¼	08/16/93	08/15/23	1.0307	1.0306	1.0304	1.0303	1.0300	1.0300
6¼	02/15/94	08/15/23	1.0307	1.0306	1.0304	1.0303	1.0300	1.0300
6¼	02/15/00	05/15/30	1.0344	1.0342	1.0342	1.0339	1.0339	1.0337
6¼	08/15/00	05/15/30	1.0344	1.0342	1.0342	1.0339	1.0339	1.0337
6⅜	08/15/97	08/15/27	1.0495	1.0495	1.0491	1.0491	1.0487	1.0487
6½	11/15/96	11/15/26	1.0654	1.0650	1.0649	1.0645	1.0643	1.0639
6⅝	02/18/97	02/15/27	1.0820	1.0818	1.0813	1.0811	1.0806	1.0804
6¾	08/15/96	08/15/26	1.0976	1.0973	1.0968	1.0965	1.0959	1.0956
6⅞	08/15/95	08/15/25	1.1119	1.1116	1.1109	1.1105	1.1099	1.1095
7⅛	02/16/93	02/15/23	1.1370	1.1364	1.1355	1.1349	1.1340	1.1333
7⅛	05/17/93	02/15/23	1.1370	1.1364	1.1355	1.1349	1.1340	1.1333
7¼	05/15/86	05/15/16	1.1250	1.1236	1.1225	—	—	—
7¼	08/17/92	08/15/22	1.1506	1.1499	1.1489	1.1481	1.1471	1.1463

TABLE 11–7 (Continued)

Coupon	Issue Date	Maturity Date	6% Conversion Factors					
			Sep. 2000	Dec. 2000	Mar. 2001	Jun. 2001	Sep. 2001	Dec. 2001
$7\frac{1}{2}$	11/15/86	11/15/16	1.1529	1.1513	1.1500	1.1484	1.1470	—
$7\frac{1}{2}$	08/15/94	11/15/24	1.1895	1.1885	1.1877	1.1866	1.1858	1.1847
$7\frac{5}{8}$	11/15/92	11/15/22	1.1971	1.1958	1.1949	1.1936	1.1926	1.1913
$7\frac{5}{8}$	02/15/95	02/15/25	1.2061	1.2053	1.2042	1.2033	1.2022	1.2013
$7\frac{7}{8}$	02/15/91	02/15/21	1.2180	1.2167	1.2151	1.2138	1.2122	1.2109
8	11/15/91	11/15/21	1.2370	1.2354	1.2341	1.2325	1.2311	1.2295
$8\frac{1}{8}$	08/15/89	08/15/19	1.2371	1.2355	1.2336	1.2320	1.2300	1.2283
$8\frac{1}{8}$	05/15/91	05/15/21	1.2488	1.2470	1.2456	1.2438	1.2423	1.2405
$8\frac{1}{8}$	08/15/91	08/15/21	1.2502	1.2488	1.2470	1.2456	1.2438	1.2423
$8\frac{1}{2}$	02/15/90	02/15/20	1.2830	1.2812	1.2790	1.2771	1.2749	1.2729
$8\frac{3}{4}$	05/15/87	05/15/17	1.2855	1.2828	1.2803	1.2775	1.2750	1.2721
$8\frac{3}{4}$	05/15/90	05/15/20	1.3136	1.3113	1.3093	1.3069	1.3048	1.3024
$8\frac{3}{4}$	08/15/90	08/15/20	1.3156	1.3136	1.3113	1.3093	1.3069	1.3048
$8\frac{7}{8}$	08/15/87	08/15/17	1.3010	1.2985	1.2957	1.2931	1.2902	1.2875
$8\frac{7}{8}$	02/15/89	02/15/19	1.3161	1.3138	1.3112	1.3089	1.3062	1.3038
9	11/22/88	11/15/18	1.3275	1.3247	1.3223	1.3195	1.3170	1.3141
$9\frac{1}{8}$	05/15/88	05/15/18	1.3357	1.3328	1.3302	1.3272	1.3245	1.3214
$9\frac{1}{4}$	02/15/86	02/15/16	1.3216	1.3185	—	—	—	—
$9\frac{7}{8}$	11/29/85	11/15/15	1.3798					

Source: Chicago Board of Trade.

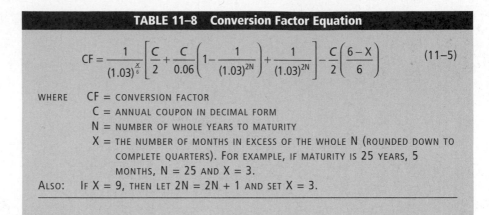

TABLE 11–8   Conversion Factor Equation

$$CF = \frac{1}{(1.03)^{\frac{X}{6}}}\left[\frac{C}{2} + \frac{C}{0.06}\left(1 - \frac{1}{(1.03)^{2N}}\right) + \frac{1}{(1.03)^{2N}}\right] - \frac{C}{2}\left(\frac{6-X}{6}\right) \qquad (11\text{–}5)$$

WHERE   CF = CONVERSION FACTOR

C = ANNUAL COUPON IN DECIMAL FORM

N = NUMBER OF WHOLE YEARS TO MATURITY

X = THE NUMBER OF MONTHS IN EXCESS OF THE WHOLE N (ROUNDED DOWN TO COMPLETE QUARTERS). FOR EXAMPLE, IF MATURITY IS 25 YEARS, 5 MONTHS, N = 25 AND X = 3.

ALSO: IF X = 9, THEN LET 2N = 2N + 1 AND SET X = 3.

Source: Chicago Board of Trade.

The Chicago Board of Trade publishes these conversion factors on their website (*http://www.cbot.com*) and in a pamphlet. They are a function of the remaining life of a particular bond and its coupon rate. Bonds that have coupons higher than 6% are more valuable than bonds with lower yields, so these bonds "count extra" if delivered. Similarly, bonds with yields less than 6% have adjustment factors less than one. Table 11–7 shows some example conversion factors. Table 11–8 shows the formula that produces them.

In words, the conversion factor equation in Table 11–8 shows the price of the bond at a yield of 6% where the maturity has been rounded down to the nearest quarterly futures contract month. The futures price multiplied by the conversion factor is sometimes called the *cash equivalent price.*

Consider, for instance, the 9s of 18 in Table 11–7. Let's confirm the correction factor for this bond in September 2000. Using Equation 11–5, we have C = 0.09 and N = 18. The bond matures in November 2018, so there are two months in excess of the whole N. However, we round this down to the complete quarter, which means X = 0 at present. Inputting the variables,

$$CF = \frac{1}{(1.03)^{0/6}}\left[\frac{0.09}{2} + \frac{0.09}{0.06}\left(1 - \frac{1}{(1.03)^{36}}\right) + \frac{1}{(1.03)^{36}}\right] - \frac{0.09}{2}\left(\frac{6-0}{6}\right) = 1.3275$$

This confirms the value in Table 11–7. Note that in December 2000, the factor will fall to 1.3247 and steadily decline as time passes.

THE MATTER OF ACCRUED INTEREST

Bondholders earn interest each calendar day they hold a bond. This is unlike the situation with common stock, where the dividend is an "all-or-nothing" item.[10]

---

[10] If you buy stock before an ex-dividend date, you get the entire forthcoming dividend. If you buy it on the ex-dividend date or later, you are not entitled to the next dividend.

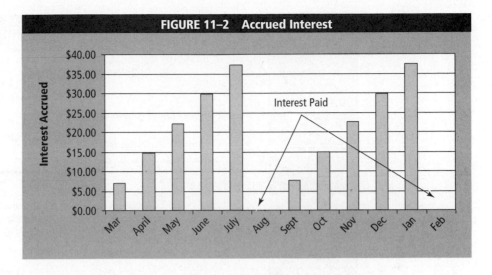

FIGURE 11–2   Accrued Interest

Despite this, the Treasury only mails interest payment checks twice a year. Someone might buy a bond today and receive a check for six months' interest two weeks later. This would be a substantial return in two weeks' time. However, no seller would agree to give up his accrued coupon without compensation.

When someone buys a bond, they pay the **accrued interest** to the seller of the bond. Similarly, the bond seller receives accrued interest from the new bond owner. One day's interest accrues for each day the bond is held. At the end of the interest payment period, the bond issuer sends one check for the entire six months' interest to the current T-bond holder.

Figure 11–2 shows how bond interest accrues over the calendar year. With U.S. government securities, the accrued interest comes from a 365-day year.[11] This example is for a T-bond with 9% coupon that pays interest on the first day of February and of August. A 9% bond pays $90 in interest each year. This amounts to $0.246575 per day. A person who buys one of these bonds on May 5th, for instance, gets the bond 94 days into the interest cycle. The buyer must pay $0.246575 / day × 94 days = $23.18 in accrued interest to the seller of the bond. If this bond were purchased at a price of 95, the buyer would pay $950 (the principal) plus $23.18 (the accrued interest) for a total of $973.18.

DELIVERY PROCEDURES

Unlike stock index futures delivery actually occurs with Treasury securities. There is a precise set of events that participants follow to ensure the orderly transfer of securities. **First position day** is two business days before the first business day of the delivery month. On this day everyone with a long position in T-bond futures must report to the Clearing Corporation a list of their long positions by trade date.

---

[11] This is unlike the practice with corporate bonds, where accrued interest is based on twelve 30-day months.

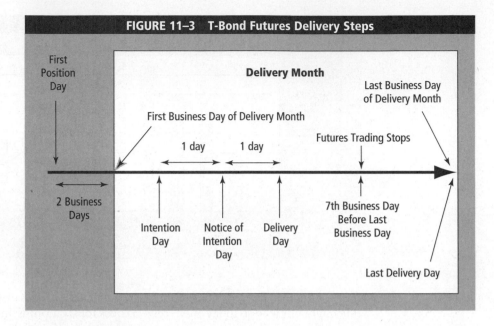

FIGURE 11–3   T-Bond Futures Delivery Steps

Anytime during the delivery month persons with a short position in futures may begin the three-day process ultimately resulting in delivery of the bonds. The first of these days is **intention day**, when a short seller notifies the Clearing Corporation of intent to deliver. The Clearing Corporation matches the oldest long position (as determined by the trade date) with the short position intending to deliver. The day following intention day is **notice of intention day**; on this day the Clearing Corporation notifies both parties of the other's identity, and the short seller prepares an invoice identifying the precise securities to be delivered and the associated invoice price. The third day in the sequence, **delivery day**, is when the financial instrument actually changes hands. Delivery and funds transfer occurs via wire transfer between accounts and must be completed by 1 P.M. on delivery day. Figure 11–3 shows the steps in the process.

THE INVOICE PRICE

The actual cash that changes hands at futures settlement equals the futures settlement price multiplied by the conversion factor, plus any accrued interest. The **invoice price** is the amount that the deliverer of the bond receives from the purchaser. Equation 11–6 summarizes.

$$\text{Invoice price} = (\text{settlement price on position day} \times \\ \text{conversion factor}) + \text{accrued interest} \qquad (11\text{--}6)$$

Suppose someone delivers the 7¼s of May 15, 2016 (from Table 11–7) on September 3, 2000 with a futures settlement price of 98:00 on position day. Using a Texas Instruments BAII+ calculator,[12] the accrued interest on $100,000 par value of this bond is $2,186.82.[13] The invoice price is then

	0.9800	futures settlement price
×	$100,000	contract size
×	1.1250	correction factor
	$110,250.00	
+	$2,186.82	accrued interest
	$112,436.82	**invoice price**

CHEAPEST TO DELIVER

At any given time, there are usually several dozen bonds that are eligible for delivery on the T-bond futures contract. Normally, only one of these bonds will be **cheapest to deliver**.

As we have seen, the yield on a bond depends on the bond price, the coupon, and the time until maturity. Bonds with coupons of 6%, for instance, may yield more or less than 6%, depending on their price. Only if they sell for par will they yield 6% exactly. Five percent bonds yielding 6% necessarily sell for less than par, while seven percent bonds yielding 6% sell for more than par. The conversion factors make all bonds equally attractive for delivery only when the bonds under consideration yield 6%. If they yield more or less than this, one bond is going to have the lowest adjusted price, and hence be cheapest to deliver.[14]

Consider the information in Table 11–9. If I have to buy bonds to deliver against a futures contract, I want to get these bonds as cheaply as possible. Table 11–9 shows that if I use the 8s of 2021, they would cost me $98,650.92. The other bond (the 5¼s of 29) would cost more: $99,725.90. The former are cheaper to deliver and would be preferred over their counterpart. A hedger will collect information on all the deliverable bonds and select the one most advantageous to deliver.

The way the delivery system actually works is slightly different from this example. If I am short 10 T-bond futures contracts, I promise to deliver $1,000,000 face value of bonds. I will deliver 1,000 bonds; I cannot deliver fractional bonds. Consequently, the "correction factor" adjustment influences the *amount I receive* from the person who receives the bonds I deliver. The lower the coupon on the bond I deliver, the less I receive for it. The buyer pays an "invoice price," calculated as we saw in Equation 11–6.

---

[12] Do this using the "bond" register. Get into this by typing 2nd bond. Then enter the following: SDT = 9-03-2000, CPN = 7.25, RDT = 5-15-2016, RV = 100, ACT, and 2/Y. The calculator automatically gives accrued interest (AI) of 2.1868. This is percent of par, so on $100,000 par this is $2,186.80.

[13] You can also get this without a calculator. There are 184 days between May 15, 2000 (date of the last coupon) and November 15, 2000 (date of the next coupon). There are 111 days between May 15 and the settlement date of September 3. The accrued interest is $(111/184) \times (7.25/2) = \$2.18682$ percent of par, or $2,186.82 on a $100,000 bond.

[14] Another reasonably quick way to find the cheapest to deliver bond is to divide the deliverable bonds' market prices by their respective conversion factors. Whichever bond has the lowest ratio is the cheapest to deliver.

TABLE 11–9   Cost of Delivery

BOND	PRICE	CONVERSION FACTOR
8s OF NOVEMBER 2021	122:01	1.2370
5¼s OF FEBRUARY 2029	89:19	0.8984

8s OF NOVEMBER 2021
COST OF BUYING 100 BONDS TO DELIVER:
100 BONDS/1.2370 = 80.8407
80.8407 × $1,220.3125 = $98,650.92

5¼s OF FEBRUARY 2029
COST OF BUYING 100 BONDS TO DELIVER:
100 BONDS/0.8984 = 111.3090
111.3090 × $895.9375 = $99,725.90

DERIVATIVES TODAY

CORPORATE BOND FUTURES?

In mid-summer 2000 the Bond Market Association formed a working group to explore the feasibility of a futures contract on corporate bonds. Corporate bonds are much more varied than Treasury bonds, so defining the underlying asset is extremely important.

According to Michel de Konkoly Thege, vice-president and associate general counsel of the Bond Market Association, the group is considering an index made from about 100 different corporate bonds with maturities of 8 to 12 years. Fixed income managers find the 10-year portion of the yield curve especially popular, plus there is considerable liquidity in this portion of the yield curve.

The exchanges have introduced many products over the years that have been unsuccessful, either because of faulty product design, unexpected regulatory hurdles, or inability to attract both hedgers and speculators. According to de Konkoly Thege, "There has been a lot of investment of time and effort in this. We want a product that has a reasonable shot at working in the market."[15]

[15] "Bond Future Update," *Risk*, October 2000, 15.

PRICING INTEREST RATE FUTURES CONTRACTS

As with all futures contracts, interest rate futures prices come from the implications of *cost of carry*. Symbolically,

$$F_t = S(1 + C_{0,t}) \qquad (11\text{–}7)$$

Where F_t = futures price for delivery at time t
       S = spot commodity price
       $C_{0,t}$ = cost of carry from time zero to time t

TABLE 11–10 T-Bill Prices		
INSTRUMENT	**MATURITY**	**PRICING INFO**
T-Bill Futures Contract	45 days	IMM Index = 93.98
T-Bill	45 days	Discount yield = 5.75%
T-Bill	136 days	Discount yield = 5.90%

The cost of carry is the net cost of carrying the commodity forward in time. In other words, the carry *return* minus the carry *charges*. If you can borrow money at the same rate that a Treasury bond pays, your cost of carry is zero. Most of us cannot borrow at the same rate as the U.S. government, so we face a cost of carry that is non-zero. With interest rate futures we know the spot price of the T-bills or T-bonds as well as the price of the futures contracts. When we use these known values to solve for C in equation 11-7, the result is the **implied repo rate**, also called the **implied financing rate**.

"Repo" is short for repurchase agreement. This is a contract in which one party sells a security and promises to buy it back at a predetermined price on some future date. With futures, this is the rate of return (before accounting for financing costs) that should prevail in the absence of arbitrage.[16] You can think of this as the riskless return you get from buying the underlying asset and simultaneously selling a futures contract against the underlying asset.[17]

Suppose a pension fund owns $10 million in T-bills with a current market value of $9,887,455. Because of a short-term cash crunch the fund investigates a repurchase agreement with a commercial bank. The bank proposes to advance $9,887,455 to the fund with the fund promising to pay $9,889,975 to buy the bills back in three days. The repo rate is

$$\frac{\$9,889,975 - \$9,887,455}{\$9,887,455} \times \frac{365}{3} = 3.10\%$$

The implied repo rate is the riskless return you get from buying the underlying asset and simultaneously selling a futures contract "against it."

If the T-bill itself yields more than 3.10% the bank's repo rate constitutes an arbitrage opportunity. The fund could benefit by borrowing from the bank at this low rate, buying more T-bills, and doing another repo. Such a situation would not last for long in a well-functioning, efficient market.

Now let's return to the T-bill futures market. Consider the data in Table 11–10. Someone could buy the 136-day T-bill and earn the riskless return implied in the discount yield. Alternatively, someone could buy the futures contract. The one in this example matures in 45 days.

---

[16] The concept is probably easiest to see with stock index futures. Suppose someone buys stock and simultaneously sells index futures. They will earn dividends and benefit by the deterioration of the futures basis. This would be a winner if the person could borrow the money to buy the stock and pay less interest than the amount received from dividends and the basis. The borrowing rate that exactly offsets these gains is the implied repo rate.

[17] The implied repo rate is also instrumental in determining the bond cheapest to deliver against the T-bond futures contract.

Recall that at maturity the futures contract calls for the delivery of a 91-day T-bill. Buying the futures today, then, is equivalent to buying the 136-day T-bill; the person long the futures will receive a 91-day T-bill in 45 days. Stated another way, a T-bill futures contract is really a forward contract on a 91-day Treasury bill. The law of one price states that equivalent assets should sell for the same price, so it seems likely that the price of the futures contract should be related to the discount yield of the contemporaneous T-bills.

We can check the data in Table 11–10 to see if this is the case. Table 11–11 shows one way to do so. For the 45-day T-bill, the discount yield translates into a price of 99.2813% of par and a 45-day return of 0.7239%. The 136-day return on the other T-bill is 2.22797%. Buying the futures contract is equivalent to buying the 45-day T-bill followed by a 91-day T-bill when the first 45-day bill matures. Because we know the rate of return on both the 45-day and 136-day T-bills, we can solve for the implied yield on the 91-day T-bill that will be delivered on the futures contract. The notation $_{45}R_{136}$ is shorthand for the forward interest rate from day 45 to day 136. From this yield we can back out the IMM index, which is 93.98 in this case. This is the same value as in Table 11–10, so the figures in that table are logically consistent and provide no arbitrage opportunity.

TABLE 11–11   Reconciling Futures and T-bill Prices

45-DAY T-BILL

$$P_{45} = 1 - \frac{(0.0575)(45)}{360} = 0.992813$$

Unannualized yield for 45 days $= \dfrac{1 - 0.992813}{0.992813} = 0.007239$

136-DAY T-BILL

$$P_{136} = 1 - \frac{(0.0590)(136)}{360} = 0.977711$$

Unannualized yield for 136 days $= \dfrac{1 - 0.977711}{0.977711} = 0.022797$

FUTURES CONTRACT

$(1.022797) = (1.007239)(1 + {}_{45}R_{136})$
${}_{45}R_{136} = 0.015446$

Futures price $= \dfrac{1}{1.015446} = 0.984789$

Futures discount yield $= \dfrac{1 - 0.98479}{1} \times \dfrac{360}{91} = 0.060175 = 6.02\%$

IMM INDEX $= 100 - 6.02 = 93.98$

ARBITRAGE WITH T-BILL FUTURES

Continuing with the above example, if an arbitrageur were to discover a disparity between the implied financing rate and the available repo rate, there is an opportunity for riskless profit. If the implied financing rate from the T-bill futures market was greater than his or her own borrowing rate, the appropriate steps would be to borrow for 45 days, buy 136-day T-bills, and sell futures due in 45 days. If the implied financing rate were lower than the borrowing rate, the arbitrageur would borrow for 136 days, buy the 45-day T-bill, and buy futures due in 45 days.

Suppose instead of selling for 93.98 T-bill futures sell for 94.10, and that an arbitrageur can borrow at a 45-day repo rate of 15 basis points more than treasuries, or 5.90% given a 45-day T-bill rate of 5.75%. This repo rate and futures price result in "free money" for someone who knows how to collect it. The IMM index of 94.10 translates into a dollar cost of $985,086:

$$\text{Discount yield} = 100 - 94.10 = 5.90\%$$

$$(1 - \text{futures price}) \times \frac{360}{91} = 0.0590$$

$$\text{Solving, futures price} = 0.985086$$

Table 11–12 shows the steps the arbitrageur would follow. Anytime you begin with no cash requirement and end up with money in hand something is out of line in the financial system. Either the repo rate is too low or the futures price is too high (or both). Most likely futures have drifted away from their equilibrium price and would move back toward it. Given the repo rate of 5.90%, the no-arbitrage futures price would be 94.04. At this price, the proceeds from the futures

TABLE 11–12 T-Bill Futures Arbitrage	
TODAY:	
BUY 136-DAY T-BILL	($977,711.11)
BORROW $977,711.11 @ 5.90% FOR 45 DAYS	$977,711.11
SELL 1 FUTURES CONTRACT @ 94.10	—
NET CASH REQUIREMENT	$0
45 DAYS LATER:	
DELIVER T-BILL ON SHORT FUTURES CONTRACT; COLLECT	$985,086.00
REPAY REPO PRINCIPAL:	(977,711.11)
PAY REPO INTEREST: $0.0590 \times 977,711.11 \times \dfrac{45}{360} =$	(7,210.62)
NET CASH RECEIPT	$164.27

TABLE 11–13   T-Bill Futures Equilibrium

TODAY:

BUY 136-DAY T-BILL	($977,711.11)
BORROW $977,711.11 @ 5.90% FOR 45 DAYS	$977,711.11
SELL 1 FUTURES CONTRACT @ 94.04	—
NET CASH REQUIREMENT	$0

CALCULATE FUTURES PRICE:
DISCOUNT YIELD = 100 − 94.04 = 5.96%

$$(1 - \text{futures price}) \times \frac{360}{91} = 0.0596$$

SOLVING, FUTURES PRICE = 0.984934

45 DAYS LATER:

DELIVER T-BILL ON SHORT FUTURES CONTRACT; COLLECT	$984,934.00
REPAY REPO PRINCIPAL:	(977,711.11)
PAY REPO INTEREST: $0.0590 \times 977,711.11x\dfrac{45}{360}$	(7,210.62)
NET CASH RECEIPT	$12.27

short sale would be very close to the cost of borrowing the money to buy the 136-day T-bill, as Table 11–13 shows.[18]

DELIVERY OPTIONS[19]

Some of the most sophisticated research in finance deals with the Treasury bond futures contract. There are some modest but tricky aspects of T-bond and T-note futures pricing that occur during the last few weeks of the futures contract. In particular, there are *delivery options* associated with fulfillment of the futures promise, and these options have value.

1. *The Quality Option.* A person with a short futures position has the prerogative to deliver any T-bond that satisfies the delivery requirements. This is called the **quality option**. The essence of this is that the person who is long a T-bond futures contract does not know which particular Treasury security they will receive, while the person short the futures can deliver whichever is cheapest to deliver. This is an advantage to the person short futures and potentially a disadvantage to

---

[18] With each basis point of the IMM index equaling $25, the steps might not net to exactly zero.

[19] See Hugh Cohen, "Evaluating Embedded Options," *Economic Review* (Nov/Dec 91): 9–16, for a good discussion of embedded options. See also Gerald Gay and Steven Manaster, "Implicit Delivery Options and Optimal Delivery Strategies for Financial Futures Contracts," *Journal of Financial Economics* (1986), Vol. 16, no. 1, 41–72.

the person with the long position. Some traders estimate the quality option is worth $25–$50 per futures contract.

2. *The Timing Option.* The holder of a short position can initiate the delivery process anytime the exchange is open during the delivery month. This is the **timing option**. This option is valuable to the arbitrageur who seeks to take advantage of minor price discrepancies. Also, the final invoice price for delivery is set at the final trading day of the contract, which is eight business days before the end of the month. The person short futures can announce delivery up to seven business days *after* this, however, and potentially benefit from the time gap depending on what happens to the price of the bond during this period. It is conceivable, for instance, that the cheapest-to-deliver bond might change subsequent to the final invoice price.

Another consideration making the timing option valuable is the relationship between the rate at which interest is accruing on the bond and the cost of financing the position. If someone holds a bond on which they are accruing interest faster than the rate at which they are paying it, they want to delay delivery as long as possible. Alternately, if the financing rate is higher it might make sense to deliver the bond as soon as feasible.

3. *The Wild Card Option.* Treasury bonds cease trading at 3 P.M. eastern standard time. A person may choose to initiate delivery anytime between the 3 P.M. settlement and 9 P.M. (EST) that evening. Changes in market conditions may change the desirability of delivery. In essence, the short hedger may make a transaction and receive cash based on a price determined up to six hours earlier. This important, and valuable, option is called the **wild card option**. If T-bond prices were to decline late in the day, one could buy at the new, lower price and deliver at the previous, higher price.

SPREADING WITH INTEREST RATE FUTURES

Many traders actively employ sophisticated strategies simultaneously using more than one of the financial futures traded on the financial futures trading floor. This brief section focuses on two especially popular strategies of this kind: The *TED spread* and the *NOB spread*. Others of lesser importance are also mentioned.

TED SPREAD

At the International Monetary Market of the Chicago Mercantile Exchange, a popular strategy is "TED spreading," which involves the T-bill futures contract and the Eurodollar futures contract. Traders who use this spread are anticipating changes in the relative riskiness of Eurodollar deposits.

The futures contracts on these short-term assets are very popular, even more so than that of the T-bill contract. The daily trading volume for Eurodollar futures is much more than that of T-bill futures. Open interest is over 1.5 million contracts, with a dollar value more than $1 trillion. Eurodollar rates tend to change

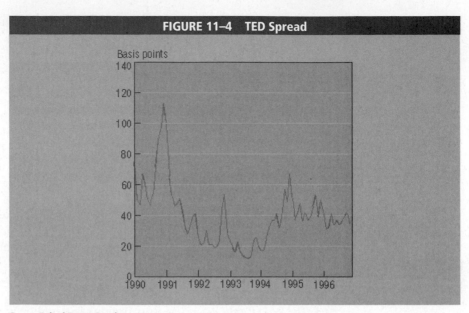

FIGURE 11–4   TED Spread

Source: Federal Reserve Board

more rapidly than U.S. T-bill rates, although the two rates usually move up or down together. This is one reason the TED spread is popular. (See Figure 11–4.)

In a nutshell, the **TED spread** is the difference between the price of the U.S. T-bill futures contract and the Eurodollar futures contract, in which both futures contracts have the same delivery month.

The trading pits for the T-bills (ticker symbol TB) and the Eurodollars (ticker symbol ED) are only a few feet apart, thus facilitating spreading. Traders who employ this spread anticipate some change in the TB/ED price relationship. This differential frequently changes in response to developments in the world economy.

Suppose you feel that the gap between the TB and ED yields will widen because of increasing tension in Europe. The T-bill yield has always been less than the ED yield,[20] and conversely the T-bill price is always more than the ED price. By convention, a person who buys the TED spread buys the T-bill and sells the ED. When you sell the TED spread, you sell the T-bill and buy the ED. If you think the spread will widen, you want to buy the spread. You really do not care if interest rates rise or fall; all that matters is that the spread widens. If this happens, you will make a profit.

Suppose the settlement price of a March 03 ED is 92.00, while the March 03 TB is 93.41. These prices translate into yields of 8.00% for the ED and 6.59% for the TB. This is a difference of 141 basis points. Suppose a speculator can buy a ten-contract TED spread at these prices. Two weeks later, as anticipated, the spread

The TED spread is the price difference between a three-month T-bill futures contract and a three-month Eurodollar futures contract, in which the two contracts have the same delivery month.

---

[20] This is because of the bank preference for Eurodollars.

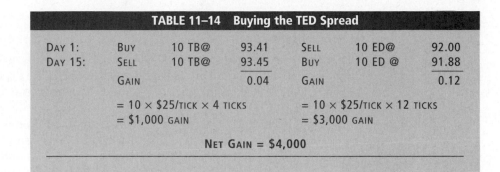

TABLE 11–14 Buying the TED Spread						
DAY 1:	BUY	10 TB@	93.41	SELL	10 ED@	92.00
DAY 15:	SELL	10 TB@	93.45	BUY	10 ED @	91.88
	GAIN		0.04	GAIN		0.12
	= 10 × $25/TICK × 4 TICKS			= 10 × $25/TICK × 12 TICKS		
	= $1,000 GAIN			= $3,000 GAIN		
		NET GAIN = $4,000				

has widened. Current prices become 93.45 for the TB, and 91.88 for the ED; the spread is therefore 157 basis points. If the speculator is able to close out the positions at these prices, there is a profit as calculated in Table 11–14. Each tick (0.01%) is worth $25 per contract.[21]

THE NOB SPREAD

Another popular strategy is "notes over bonds," or the **NOB spread**. A spreader might buy T-bond futures and simultaneously sell T-note futures. Traders who use these spreads are speculating on shifts in the yield curve. Treasury notes are intermediate-term securities, while Treasury bonds are long term. Normally, long-term interest rates are higher than shorter-term rates, but the magnitude of the difference frequently changes. A speculator who anticipates such a change can construct a spread using T-note futures and T-bond futures in precisely the same fashion as with the TED spread.

The T-note futures contract calls for the delivery of $100,000 face value of Treasury notes, just like the T-bond contract. Securities deliverable against T-note futures have a maturity of no less than $6\frac{1}{2}$ years and no more than 10 years from the date of delivery: deliverable T-bonds must have remaining life of at least fifteen years.

Suppose I feel that the gap between the long-term rates and short-term rates is going to narrow. Stated another way, I think that the price of T-notes is going to rise relative to the price of T-bonds. To take advantage of this belief, I would buy T-note futures contracts and sell T-bond futures. Conversely, if I felt the spread was going to widen, I would sell T-note futures contracts and buy T-bonds. My aggregate profit/loss would be determined in the same manner as in Table 11-14.[22]

[21] 0.01% of $1 million is $100. The T-bill futures contract calls for the delivery of T-bills with 90 days until maturity, or one-fourth of a year. T-bills yields are quoted on an annual basis, but if they are three-month bills, their actual yield is one-fourth the annual rate. Hence, a tick is $100/4, or $25.

[22] Note that both T-note and T-bond futures trade in 32nds of a point rather than in decimals; do not forget to convert to decimal prices.

OTHER SPREADS WITH FINANCIAL FUTURES

LED Spread

LED spread is trader talk for the LIBOR-Eurodollar spread. As we saw earlier, LIBOR is the London InterBank Offered Rate; this rate is the deposit rate associated with inter-bank loans in London. It is much like the federal funds rate in the United States.

The futures contract on LIBOR implies a one-month Eurodollar time deposit rate. The Eurodollar futures contract is similar to the U.S. Treasury bill futures contract and implies a three-month rate. Normally, the three-month rate is higher than the one-month rate, as the yield curve is usually upward sloping. LED spreaders usually adopt this strategy because of a belief about a change in the slope of the yield curve or because of apparent arbitrage in the forward rates associated with the implied yields.

MOB Spread

The **MOB Spread** is "municipals over bonds." In essence, it is a play on the taxable bond market (Treasury bonds) versus the tax-exempt bond market (municipal bonds). Tax-exempt yields are much less than taxable yields on securities of comparable risk, but the gap between them can vary significantly. Regardless, interest rates tend to move together, so there is high correlation between the yields (and therefore the prices) of Treasury bonds and municipal bonds. As with all spreads, the MOB spreader buys the futures contract that is expected to outperform the other and sells (promises to deliver against) the weaker contract. The size of the MOB spread depends on many economic and psychological factors, including tax laws, the general quality and availability of credit in the marketplace, and the shape of the yield curve.

SUMMARY

Interest rate futures are divided into short-term, intermediate-term, and long-term. Eurodollars are the most popular short-term futures contract. Treasury notes and Treasury bonds are the most popular in the latter two categories, respectively. These contracts can be used to hedge interest rate risk such as that faced by financial institutions.

Conversion factors are used to turn eligible T-bonds into "equivalents" for futures delivery. Bonds with coupons above 6% count extra, while bonds with lower coupons do not count as much. While there can be several dozen Treasury bonds eligible for delivery at a given time, one may be cheapest to deliver.

Like other futures, the cost of carry determines the price of an interest rate futures contract. The net cost of carry is the difference between the return earned on a security and the financing cost associated with holding it. A particular financing rate, or implied repo rate, is implied in the futures price.

T-bond futures contain a number of embedded options available to the short hedger. The quality option allows choice of which bond to deliver; the timing option permits selection of which day to deliver; and the wild card option permits the delivery decision to be made up to six hours after the close of futures trading.

SELF TEST

T ___ F ___   1. A Eurodollar is the formal term for the new currency called the Euro.

T ___ F ___   2. The financial press reports Treasury bill prices on an *ask discount* basis.

T ___ F ___   3. A T-bill futures contract calls for the delivery of 30-day T-bills at the delivery date of the contract.

T ___ F ___   4. Open interest and trading volume are much higher for Eurodollar futures than for T-bill futures.

T ___ F ___   5. A speculator who believes that short-term interest rates are going to fall might logically buy T-bill futures.

T ___ F ___   6. A banker can lock in a current interest rate by buying T-bill futures.

T ___ F ___   7. Treasury notes, by definition, have a longer initial life than Treasury bonds.

T ___ F ___   8. The market determines a bond's price before it determines the bond's yield to maturity.

T ___ F ___   9. A bond deliverable against the T-bond futures contract must have at least 15 years until maturity.

T ___ F ___   10. Conversion factors are used to compensate for the fact that T-bonds have different coupons and maturities.

T ___ F ___   11. The conversion factor seeks to reduce all bonds to 7% equivalents.

T ___ F ___   12. A person who buys a Treasury bond receives accrued interest from the seller.

CHAPTER 11 REVIEW

T ___ F ___ 13. Of the dozens of deliverable T-bonds, usually only the three bonds most recently issued are cheapest to deliver.

T ___ F ___ 14. If someone can borrow money at the same rate that a Treasury bond pays, the person's cost of carry on a T-bond futures contract is essentially zero.

T ___ F ___ 15. Delivery options with T-bond futures are the quality option, the timing option, the wild card option, and the spread option.

PROBLEMS & QUESTIONS

1. Briefly explain why it is necessary to translate all bonds into "6 percent equivalents" in the delivery process for Treasury bond futures.

2. What is the purpose of calculating the "bond equivalent yield" with Treasury bills?

3. Suppose you are the manager of a money-market mutual fund. Would it matter if you hedged interest rate risk using Treasury bond futures instead of T-bill futures?

4. Why is it necessary to include the provision about call protection in the definition of bonds eligible for delivery against the T-bond futures contract?

5. Who might logically use T-bills or Eurodollars in a hedge designed to reduce interest rate risk?

6. Do you feel that the need to hedge short-term interest rates is as important as the need to hedge long-term rates?

7. Explain why the cheapest to deliver bond has the lowest ratio of market price to conversion factor.

8. Look at a current *Wall Street Journal*. Compare the settlement prices of the different Treasury bill futures contracts. Why do you think they are different?

9. In hedging a portfolio, is there anything philosophically wrong with only hedging part of it?

10. Why might overhedging be considered speculation?

11. How can there be a "quality option" if all U.S. Treasury bonds are of equal default risk?

12. What is the difference between the "timing option" and the "wild card option?"

13. The newspaper price for a T-bill futures contract is 92.33. What is the value of the T-bills promised at delivery based on this price?

14. A speculator goes long 4 T-bill contracts at 93.34 and closes them out three weeks later at 93.40. Calculate this person's gain or loss in dollar terms.

15. A $10,000 T-bill comes due in 88 days and sells for $9,800. Calculate
    (a) the ask discount
    (b) the bond equivalent yield

16. Zero coupon bonds are securities that pay no periodic interest. They have one cash flow: the return of principal at maturity. What is the duration of a zero-coupon bond?

17. You deliver 16-year T-bonds with a 7% coupon on an interest payment date against a futures contract position. If the T-bond settlement price on position day is 92, what is the invoice price?

18. A Treasury bond matures in 21 years and has a coupon of $7\frac{5}{8}\%$. What is its conversion factor?

19. A Treasury bond matures in 21 years and has a coupon of 9%. What is its conversion factor?

20. A T-bond futures contract was purchased at 92. The hedger chooses to deliver bonds with a $6\frac{1}{2}\%$ coupon that mature in 24 years, 5 months. If delivery occurs exactly halfway through an interest payment cycle, what is the invoice price?

21. A 10% bond sells for 110% of par, and matures in exactly 16 years. Calculate its conversion factor.

22. You expect to receive $4.5 million to invest in Treasury bills in one month. Using current price information from the *Wall Street Journal*, show specifically how to lock in a current interest rate using Treasury bill futures.

23. Refer to problem 20. Suppose, instead, the bond chosen for delivery is a 9%, 20-year bond. Other conditions remain the same. What is the invoice price?

24. What is the TED spread?

25. Give an example of a situation in which someone might consider using the TED spread.

26. What is the NOB spread?

27. Suppose the slope of the yield curve is expected to flatten. How would a NOB spreader take advantage of this?

28. Why might someone consider using the LED spread?

29. What is the motive of the MOB spreader?

CHAPTER 11 REVIEW

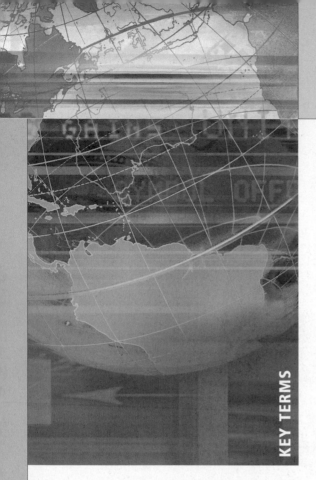

12

Futures Contracts and Portfolio Management

Interest rate hedging is a bit like air conditioning. For eons humans have generally survived heat and humidity without electronic chilling, just as corporate treasurers survived the ravages of interest rate risk before hedge instruments were invented. Nevertheless, few of us today would consider going on without either invention.

Chuck Epstein
Treasury and Risk Management

There are two main topics in this chapter: using futures for *immunization* against interest rate risk and using futures to *shift asset allocation* between stocks and bonds. The ease of managing interest rate risk with Treasury bond futures is one of the single most compelling attractions in the world of financial futures. An earlier chapter showed how stock index futures make it easy to alter market risk. Using T-bond and stock index futures in tandem, a portfolio manager can quickly alter portfolio asset allocation without having to make wholesale changes in the portfolio components.

THE CONCEPT OF IMMUNIZATION

It is seldom possible to completely eliminate interest rate risk.

Immunization means precisely what the name suggests. An immunized bond portfolio is largely protected from "catching a disease" from fluctuations in market interest rates. Nonetheless, it is seldom possible to eliminate interest rate risk completely. Just as with childhood vaccinations, there is always a possibility that someone will develop a disease against which they were immunized.[1] Continuing with the medical analogy, some immunizations are not permanent. The patient requires booster shots. Similarly, under some circumstances a portfolio's immunization can wear out, requiring managerial action to reinstate the protection.

Continually immunizing a fixed-income portfolio is a time-consuming and technical chore. With very large portfolios where precision is critical, there are technical points of hedging with Treasury bonds that can complicate the process. People involved in fixed income security management should continue their education by learning about the assumptions, shortcomings, and popularity of the various ways interest rate futures facilitate immunization strategies, asset allocation, and other portfolio adjustments.

BOND RISKS

A fixed income investor faces three primary sources of price risk:[2] *credit risk, interest rate risk,* and *reinvestment rate risk.* **Credit risk** is the likelihood that a borrower will be unable or unwilling to repay a loan as agreed. Rating agencies such as Standard & Poor's and Moody's measure this risk with their published bond ratings. Investors choose the level of credit risk that they wish to assume by selecting bonds with the appropriate bond rating. Lower bond ratings mean higher expected return, but with more risk of default.

The two other sources of risk stem from changes in the general level of interest rates over time rather than changes in the fortunes of the borrower. **Interest rate risk** is a consequence of the fundamental fact that the present value of a bond's cash flows moves inversely with the discount rate. That is, as market interest rates climb, prevailing bond prices will be lower, and vice versa. **Duration** is the most widely used measure of a bond's interest rate risk.

Reinvestment rate risk is the uncertainty associated with not knowing at what rate money can be put back to work after the receipt of an interest check. An investor who receives an interest check may fully intend to reinvest the check, but the reinvestment rate will be the prevailing interest rate at the time of reinvestment, not some rate determined in the past. This rate can be more or less than the original rate.

---

[1] Sometimes the marketplace does not behave like it is "supposed to," as evidenced by the widespread apparent arbitrage during the Crash of 1987.

[2] Bonds may also carry *call risk,* reflecting the possibility that the debt will be retired early. This is a *convenience* risk rather than a *price* risk.

CREDIT DERIVATIVES

The **credit derivatives** market is important, but still obscure even to those familiar with basic futures and options contracts. The British Bankers Association estimates that there was nearly $900 billion in credit derivatives globally at the end of calendar year 2000. While international treasurers are among the only people familiar with them, the rest of us are likely to hear more about them in the years ahead.

A credit derivative is a legal contract between two parties that provides for the transfer of risk on some extension of credit (such as a bond or other loan). A lender anticipates receiving interest and principal from the borrower. Credit risk stems from the fact that sometimes the borrower is unable (or unwilling) to comply with the terms of the loan. With the creation of the credit derivative, one party (the *protection seller*) essentially sells credit risk protection to the other party (the *originator* or *protection buyer*).

A credit derivative is an over-the-counter derivative, so the parties involved determine mutually agreeable terms.

The simplest form of credit derivative is a *guarantee*: the protection seller agrees to step in and make good on a contract in the event of default by a borrower. The guarantee often takes the form of a *total return swap* in which the protection seller guarantees a certain return to the protection buyer in exchange for some premium. Another form is a *default swap* that might provide a payment from the guarantor in the event a borrower's credit rating is downgraded or the firm runs afoul of a loan covenant.

As with other unusual derivatives, these do not come about because of a slick marketing campaign by investment bankers. They deal with an identified need facing corporate treasurers and investors, and represent a market response to that need.

DURATION MATCHING

Duration matching is a term for the general process of selecting a level of duration that minimizes the combined effects of reinvestment rate risk and interest rate risk.

There are two versions of duration matching: *bullet immunization* and *bank immunization*. **Bullet immunization** seeks to ensure that a predetermined sum of money is available at a specific time in the future regardless of the path interest rates take. The objective is to get the effects of interest rate risk and reinvestment rate risk to offset. If market interest rates rise, coupon proceeds can be reinvested at a higher rate (which is good), but the increase in interest rates will reduce the value of bonds (which is bad). Proper immunization will make sure that the dollars and cents effects of these two sources of risk net to zero.

Bullet immunization is concerned with getting the effects of interest rate risk and reinvestment rate risk to cancel.

An example will help. Suppose a portfolio manager receives $93,600 to invest in bonds and needs to ensure that the money will grow at a 10% compound rate over the next six years, at which time the funds will be withdrawn. This means in six years the fund needs to be worth $165,818.[3]

---

[3] $93,600 \times (1.10)^6 = 165,818$.

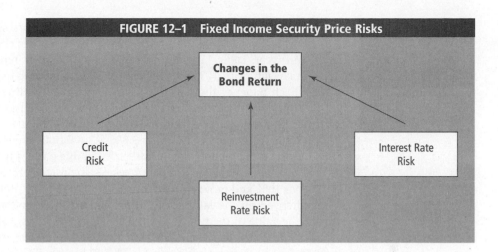

FIGURE 12–1   Fixed Income Security Price Risks

Over the six-year period, interest rates will most likely change. If they go up, the reinvested coupons will earn more interest, but the market value of the bonds will go down. The account will be liquidated after six years, so there is a possibility of a capital loss on the bonds, causing the account to end with a value below the target.

A manager can reduce this risk by judicious selection of the bonds. The task is to invest $93,600 in some asset or portfolio of assets such that its yield to maturity is 10% (the target rate of return) and its duration is 6.00 years (the investment horizon). This is the essence of bullet immunization: *investing the present value of the payout(s) and matching the durations of the deposits and the withdrawals.*

Suppose the manager buys $100,000 par value of a bond selling for 93.6% with a coupon of 8.8%, maturity in eight years, and a yield to maturity of 10%;

The essence of immunization: investing the present value of the payouts and matching the durations of the deposits and the withdrawals.

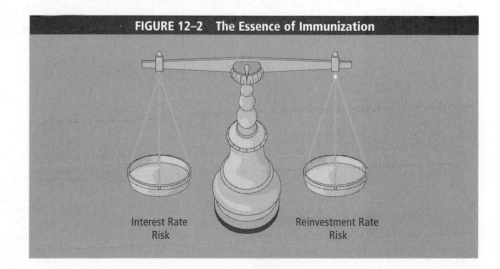

FIGURE 12–2   The Essence of Immunization

we would find its duration[4] to be 6.00 years. For simplicity's sake, assume the bond pays its interest annually, and that market interest rates change only once, after the third year. Table 12–1 shows three scenarios: rates remain unchanged (Panel A), rates fall from 10% to 9% (Panel B), and rates rise from 10% to 11% (Panel C). Each panel of the table shows the annual interest received from the bond, plus the value of any previously earned interest after it has been reinvested. For instance, in Panel A we see that the bond pays $8,800 after one year. This is the coupon rate times the par value, or 8.8% × $100,000. We immediately reinvest this money at the prevailing rate (still 10% in this panel.) In the second year we receive another $8,800 check and reinvest it. The interest from year one earns an additional 10% and grows to $8,800 × 1.10 = $9,680. If interest rates remain constant, after year six the value or the accumulated (and reinvested) interest proceeds plus the value of the bond[5] approximately equals the targeted amount.

If rates fall to 9% the interest accumulated is $1,329 less than in the "constant rate" scenario, but the bond value is $1,730 higher. Rising rates increase the interest received by $1,350, but the bond price is lower by $1,690.

The terminal values in each of the three scenarios represent compound rates of return of 10.10%, 10.04%, and 9.96%, respectively. They differ slightly from the target rate of 10% because of rounding and the inaccuracy of duration for non-trivial changes in interest rates.[6] Still, the immunized portfolio comes very close to the investor's stated return objective regardless of the change in interest rates.

BANK IMMUNIZATION

The example above showed how an independent bond portfolio can have its interest rate risk reduced by lowering the average duration of the portfolio. The problem is different if the portfolio also holds interest-sensitive *liabilities*. This kind of problem is dubbed the **bank immunization** case.

Besides managing portfolios like anyone else, a bank CFO is also concerned with the balance sheet effects associated with market value changes in the bank's assets *and* its liabilities. Assume that a bank holds the bonds in Table 12–2 and that these are part of the balance sheet shown in Table 12–3.

Some assets are **rate sensitive**; their values change as the level of interest rates changes. A bank's **funds gap** is the dollar value of its interest rate sensitive assets (hereafter RSA) minus its interest rate sensitive liabilities (RSL). To immunize itself

---

[4] You can confirm this with the DURATION.xls file.

[5] We must solve for the hypothetical bond value. For example, given an 8.8% coupon, a 10% yield to maturity, and 2 years of remaining life, a $1,000 par annual pay bond would sell for $979.20. With a 9% or 11% yield to maturity, the bond price is $996.50 and $962.30, respectively.

[6] More precise immunization would consider the effects of convexity, which is a measure of how duration changes with changes in the interest rate. Duration is a first-derivative statistic, and it only works well for small changes in Interest rates. Larger changes result in a divergence between actual price changes and those predicted by duration.

TABLE 12–1   Effects of Immunization

PANEL A: INTEREST RATES REMAIN CONSTANT
REINVESTMENT RATE AT END OF YEAR

10%	10%	10%	10%	10%	10%
YEAR 1	YEAR 2	YEAR 3	YEAR 4	YEAR 5	YEAR 6
$8,800	$9,680	$10,648	$11,713	$12,884	$14,172
	$8,800	$ 9,680	$10,648	$11,713	$12,884
		$ 8,800	$ 9,680	$10,648	$11,713
			$ 8,800	$ 9,680	$10,648
				$ 8,800	$ 9,680
					$ 8,800
				TOTAL INTEREST	$ 67,897
				BOND VALUE	$ 97,920
				TOTAL VALUE	$165,817

PANEL B: INTEREST RATES FALL 1 POINT IN YEAR 3
REINVESTMENT RATE AT END OF YEAR

10%	10%	9%	9%	9%	9%
YEAR 1	YEAR 2	YEAR 3	YEAR 4	YEAR 5	YEAR 6
$8,800	$9,680	$10,648	$11,606	$12,651	$13,789
	$8,800	$ 9,680	$10,551	$11,501	$12,536
		$ 8,800	$ 9,592	$10,455	$11,396
			$ 8,800	$ 9,592	$10,455
				$ 8,800	$ 9,592
					$ 8,800
				TOTAL INTEREST	$ 66,568
				BOND VALUE	$ 99,650
				TOTAL VALUE	$166,218

PANEL C: INTEREST RATES RISE 1 POINT IN YEAR 3
REINVESTMENT RATE AT END OF YEAR

10%	10%	11%	11%	11%	11%
YEAR 1	YEAR 2	YEAR 3	YEAR 4	YEAR 5	YEAR 6
$8,800	$9,680	$10,648	$11,819	$13,119	$14,563
	$8,800	$ 9,680	$10,745	$11,927	$13,239
		$ 8,800	$ 9,768	$10,842	$12,035
			$ 8,800	$ 9,768	$10,842
				$ 8,800	$ 9,768
					$ 8,800
				TOTAL INTEREST	$ 69,247
				BOND VALUE	$ 96,230
				TOTAL VALUE	$165,477

TABLE 12–2	Bond Portfolio					
PAR VALUE	COMPANY	COUPON	MATURITY	MARKET VALUE	YIELD TO MATURITY	DURATION
$50,000	XYZ	$10\frac{1}{8}$	2008	$ 50,860	9.78%	5.20
75,000	DEF	8	2013	63,728	10.20%	7.55
40,000	ALQ	$9\frac{1}{2}$	2009	40,376	9.33%	5.79
60,000	LLG	$7\frac{7}{8}$	2016	48,810	10.35%	8.38
70,000	FFQ	$8\frac{1}{2}$	2003	69,972	8.52%	1.88
$295,000				$273,746		5.55*

*Value-weighted

TABLE 12–3	Simple Bank Balance Sheet		
INTEREST SENSITIVE BOND PORTFOLIO	$273,746	NON-INTEREST SENSITIVE LIABILITIES	$26,000
		INTEREST-SENSITIVE LIABILITIES	400,000
NON-INTEREST SENSITIVE ASSETS	500,000	NET WORTH	347,746
TOTAL ASSETS	$773,746	TOTAL LIABILITIES AND NET WORTH	$773,746

from the effect of interest rate fluctuations, the bank must reorganize its balance sheet such that the following condition holds:

$$\$_A \times D_A = \$_L \times D_L \qquad (12\text{–}1)$$

where $\$_{A,L}$ = dollar value of interest sensitive assets or liabilities
   $D_{A,L}$ = dollar-weighted average duration of assets or liabilities

Assume that the bank's interest sensitive assets are limited to the bonds in Table 12–2; the duration of this bond portfolio is 5.55 years.[7] Assume also that the rate sensitive liabilities have a duration of 1.00 year.[8] At the moment the bank is not immunized because Equation 12–1 does not hold:

Assets: $273,746 × 5.55 years = 1,519,290.30 $-years

Liabilities: $400,000 × 1.00 years = 400,000 $-years

$1,519,290.30 ≠ $400,000

[7] Portfolio duration is an interesting concept. While most people calculate this value as a weighted average of the component durations, you can also view the portfolio as a single security with its own cash flows. The two methods yield slightly different measures of duration. For more information on this point see "Portfolio Duration," by Strong and Borgman, *Journal of Business and Economic Studies*, Fall 1999, 67–81.

[8] These might be the bank's own bonds, previously issued in the capital market.

A bank that is asset
sensitive may be hurt
by rising interest rates.

Instead, the bank is *asset sensitive* and will see its net worth decline if interest rates rise. It is important to understand the implications of this. The $-duration value of the asset side of the portfolio exceeds that of the liability side. If market interest rates rise, the value of the rate sensitive assets and rate sensitive liabilities will both fall. However, because there are more rate sensitive securities on the asset side of the balance sheet, the decline in value of the RSA will exceed the decline in the RSL. The balance sheet must balance, and this means that net worth must decline. Net worth helps determine the value of a firm's stock, and management clearly wants to take action to keep share price from falling. Declining net worth also will cause problems with capital adequacy ratios of the type that bank examiners watch.

To immunize the portfolio, the bank needs to do some combination of the following: eliminate a portion of the RSA, reduce the duration of the RSA, issue more RSL, or raise the duration of the RSL. Practical considerations make certain of these alternatives more attractive than others. Banks do not generally have the ability to alter the liability side of the balance sheet quickly. Floating a new bond issue takes time and involves flotation costs.

Banks usually make
duration adjustments
by altering the left side
of the balance sheet.

This reduces the choices to the left-hand side of the balance sheet. One option would be to sell some bonds and put the proceeds into non-RSA. The remaining alternative is to replace high-duration bonds with lower duration bonds.

With one equation and two unknowns (the dollar amount of RSA and their duration), there are theoretically an infinite number of solutions to the problem. Looking carefully at the existing bond portfolio, it is apparent that the ultimate solution will require a reduction in RSA. The lowest duration bond is the FFQ 8½s03, with a duration of 1.88 years. If the manager were to sell all the other bonds and invest the proceeds in more FFQ bonds, the '$-years' value would be $273,746 × 1.88 years = 514,642 $-years, still above the target value of 400,000 $-years. This means the manager must reduce the RSA.

Note that reducing the RSA does not imply that the bank CFO is throwing anything away. The bank has plenty of other assets (like cash, overnight federal funds, and non-negotiable certificates of deposit) that are not rate sensitive. The bank can simply replace some rate sensitive assets with others that are non-rate sensitive.

Someone skilled in operations research can prepare a simple algorithm to search the possible ways of rearranging the portfolio. From this list the CFO can choose the most desirable option. Even without computational help the problem can still be solved reasonably quickly.

One feasible solution to the problem is to sell all the bonds except XYZ and FFQ. These are the bonds with the lowest durations. This changes the portfolio to Table 12–4. This portfolio has a dollar-duration level of $120,832 × 3.28 years = 396,328 $-years, not too far from the target figure of 400,000 $-years.

DURATION SHIFTING

Duration is a measure of interest rate risk. The higher the duration, the higher the level of interest rate risk. Faced with the prospect of rising interest rates, the bond

	TABLE 12–4	**Modified Bond Portfolio**				
PAR	COMPANY	COUPON	MATURITY	PRICE	YIELD	DURATION
$50,000	XYZ	10¹⁄₈	2008	$50,860	9.78%	5.20
70,000	FFQ	8¹⁄₂	2003	69,972	8.52%	1.88
			TOTAL RSA	120,832		
			CASH EQUIV.			
			(NON-RSA)	152,914		0
			TOTAL	$273,746	AVERAGE	3.28

portfolio manager may choose to continue to bear interest rate risk but to reduce its level. This is **duration shifting**.

Reducing maturities and raising coupons lowers duration. This means the portfolio manager could sell long-term bonds and replace them with short-term bonds, and/or sell bonds with low coupons, replacing them with higher coupon bonds. Either option would reduce duration.

> If interest rates are expected to rise, bond portfolio managers can reduce the anticipated damage to the portfolio by lowering duration.

Table 12–5 shows the relationship among duration, coupon rate, and maturity. Simultaneously reducing maturity and increasing coupon will unambiguously reduce duration, and vice versa. The effect of reducing maturity and lowering coupon, however, is inconclusive, because it is not clear which effect will predominate. A portfolio manager may experiment with various combinations of alternate securities to find the best new package. If you know the bonds' durations, the task can be accomplished in one step: Sell bonds with high durations and replace them with bonds of lower duration.

Returning to Table 12–2, this portfolio has a market value of $273,746, and, based on this market value, its average duration is 5.55 years. An extreme approach to reducing duration would be to sell all these bonds and replace them with the shortest duration securities we can find. Thirty-day Treasury bills would be one solution, as would bank repurchase agreements or short-term certificates of deposit.

Another manager might have a different view about future interest rates and choose to increase exposure to interest rate risk by increasing duration. He or she

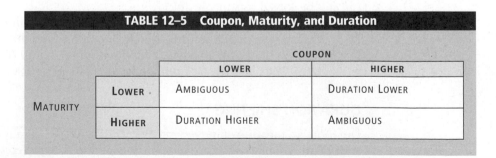

		TABLE 12–5	**Coupon, Maturity, and Duration**	
			COUPON	
			LOWER	HIGHER
MATURITY	LOWER		AMBIGUOUS	DURATION LOWER
	HIGHER		DURATION HIGHER	AMBIGUOUS

might replace high coupon bonds with lower coupon bonds or replace bonds approaching maturity with longer-term bonds.

HEDGING WITH INTEREST RATE FUTURES

A commercial bank usually holds a portion of its investment portfolio in government securities like Treasury bonds. If interest rates rise, the market value of these bonds will fall, and so will the firm's net worth. As we saw in the previous chapter, the institution can use T-bond futures contracts to hedge the risk.

Suppose a bank portfolio manager holds $10 million face value in government bonds, and that they have a market value of $9.7 million, and an average yield to maturity of 7.8%. Assume also that the weighted average duration of the portfolio is 9.0 years, and that the cheapest to deliver bond has a duration[9] of 11.14 years, a yield to maturity of 7.1%, and a CBOT correction factor of 1.1529. Perhaps the manager is afraid that interest rates are going to rise, causing the value of the bond portfolio to decline. Equation 12–2 shows one popular version of the hedge ratio:[10]

$$HR = CF_{ctd} \times \frac{P_b \times D_b \times (1 + YTM_{ctd})}{P_f \times D_f \times (1 + YTM_b)} \tag{12-2}$$

where P_b = price of the bond portfolio as a percentage of par
$\quad\quad$ D_b = duration of the bond portfolio
$\quad\quad$ P_f = price of the futures contract as a percentage of 100%
$\quad\quad$ D_f = duration of the cheapest to deliver bond eligible for delivery
$\quad\quad\quad$ against the futures contract
$\quad$ CF_{ctd} = correction factor for the cheapest to deliver bond
$\quad$ YTM_{ctd} = yield to maturity of the cheapest to deliver bond
$\quad$ YTM_b = yield to maturity of the bond portfolio

The ratio $\dfrac{1 + YTM_{ctd}}{1 + YTM_b}$ is usually approximately equal to one, and for small portfolios it does not materially change the hedge ratio. Some managers routinely omit this term in the calculation.

The hedger wants to select a quantity of futures contracts with characteristics such that

$$P_{b2} - P_{b1} + HR\left(P_{f2} - P_{f1}\right) = 0 \tag{12-3}$$

where P_{bt} = price of the bond portfolio at time t
$\quad\quad$ P_{ft} = price of the futures contract at time t
$\quad\quad$ HR = hedge ratio

---

[9] There are many different strategies for hedging interest rate risk. This duration-based example is just one of them. It assumes that if interest rates change, the shift in the yield curve will be parallel. That is, all maturities will change yields by the same amount.

[10] A good overview of some of the theoretical issues regarding interest rate hedge ratios is in Kolb and Chiang, "Improving Hedging Performance Using Interest Rate Futures," *Financial Management* (Autumn 1981): 72–79.

In other words, we want the portfolio price change due to interest rate movements $(P_{b2} - P_{b1})$ to be equal and opposite in sign to the change in the value of the futures position. This is the goal of immunization: getting the change in value of one set of securities to offset the change in value of another set.

Suppose the portfolio manager chooses to hedge using a futures contract with a market price of 90 22/32 of par, or 0.906875. The hedge ratio is

$$HR = 1.1529 \times \frac{0.97 \times 9.0 \times 1.071}{0.906875 \times 11.14 \times 1.078} = 0.9898$$

The number of contracts necessary depends on both the portfolio size and the hedge ratio. Recall that a T-bond futures contract calls for the delivery of $100,000 par value of T-bonds. Equation 12–4 shows how to include a size adjustment with the hedge ratio to determine the necessary number of futures.

$$\# \text{ contracts} = \frac{\text{portfolio par value}}{\$100,000} \times \text{hedge ratio} \tag{12–4}$$

In this situation 99 contracts would do the trick:

$$\frac{\$10 \text{ million}}{\$100,000} \times 0.9898 = 98.98 \text{ contracts} \rightarrow 99 \text{ contracts}$$

This procedure is very similar to the computations used with stock index futures.

A word of caution is in order. Financial futures are sophisticated financial instruments. There are many nuances in their pricing, including assumptions about such things as yield curve behavior and delivery procedures that have not been covered here. There are, for instance, at least five other ways of calculating the appropriate hedge ratio with financial futures. With "small" portfolios they produce similar results, but with large portfolios more powerful hedge calculations are appropriate.

INCREASING DURATION WITH FUTURES

While immunization activities are customarily oriented toward reducing the duration of a portfolio, it is sometimes appropriate to increase the duration. An active manager who believed rates were about to fall would earn a greater return by extending duration. Adding long futures positions to a bond portfolio will increase duration, just as adding short futures will reduce it.

One method for achieving a target duration is via the **basis point value** (BPV) method. The basis point value is the change in the price of a bond for a one basis point change in the yield to maturity of the bond. Consider a $1,000, ten year, semi-annual pay bond with an 8% coupon that sells for par. Such a bond would have a yield to maturity equal to the coupon rate, or 8.00%. If its yield to maturity were 8.01% instead of 8.00%, its price would be 99.93% of par, or $999.30. This is a decline of 70 cents from the par value of $1,000. If its yield were 7.99%, the bond price would be $1,000.70, an increase of 70 cents.[11] For a thousand dollars par value of this bond, a one basis point change in yield to maturity results in a $0.70 change in value. This difference is called the bond's *price value of a basis point*. As time passes or the general level of interest rates changes this value may change.

Changing the duration of a portfolio by this method requires the calculation of three basis point values: one for the current portfolio, one for the target portfolio, and one for the cheapest to deliver bond. Equation 12–5 shows how to determine the number of futures contracts to buy.

A basis point value is the change in the price of a bond associated with a one basis point change in the yield to maturity of the bond.

$$\# \ \text{contracts} = \frac{BPV_{target} - BPV_{current}}{BPV_{futures}} \qquad (12\text{--}5)$$

For the current and target portfolios, basis point value depends on duration, yield to maturity, and portfolio size, as Equation 12–6 shows:

$$BPV_{current,target} = \frac{\text{duration} \times \text{portfolio size} \times 0.0001}{\left(1 + {}^{R}\!/_{2}\right)} \qquad (12\text{--}6)$$

where R = the portfolio yield to maturity[12]

The *BPV* of the cheapest to deliver bond is also a function of the relevant Chicago Board of Trade conversation factor:

$$BPV_{ctd} = \frac{\text{duration} \times \text{portfolio size} \times 0.0001}{\left(1 + {}^{R}\!/_{2}\right) \times \text{conversion factor}} \qquad (12\text{--}7)$$

Suppose a portfolio has a market value of $10 million, an average yield to maturity of 8.5%, and duration of 4.85. A forecast of declining interest rates causes a bond manager to decide to double the portfolio's interest rate risk exposure by increasing the portfolio duration to 9.70. Assume also that the cheapest to deliver Treasury bond sells for 98% of par, has a yield to maturity of 7.22%, duration of 9.7, and a conversion factor of 1.1223. Table 12–6 shows the relevant BPVs.

Applying Equation 12–5, the number of futures contracts that will double the portfolio duration is then

$$\frac{\$9,304.56 - \$4,652.28}{\$83.42} = 55.77 \ \text{contracts}$$

---

[11] The new prices come from a Texas Instruments BA II+ calculator.

[12] Portfolio yield to maturity is an ambiguous concept. Seldom do all portfolio components mature at the same time, so there are actually numerous relevant maturity dates. The portfolio yield to maturity can be calculated as a weighted average of the components' yields to maturity, but it is important to remember the implicit assumption that all intervening cash flows are reinvested at the average portfolio YTM.

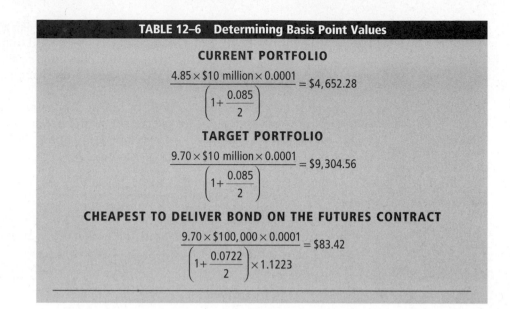

TABLE 12–6 Determining Basis Point Values

CURRENT PORTFOLIO

$$\frac{4.85 \times \$10 \text{ million} \times 0.0001}{\left(1 + \dfrac{0.085}{2}\right)} = \$4,652.28$$

TARGET PORTFOLIO

$$\frac{9.70 \times \$10 \text{ million} \times 0.0001}{\left(1 + \dfrac{0.085}{2}\right)} = \$9,304.56$$

CHEAPEST TO DELIVER BOND ON THE FUTURES CONTRACT

$$\frac{9.70 \times \$100,000 \times 0.0001}{\left(1 + \dfrac{0.0722}{2}\right) \times 1.1223} = \$83.42$$

By buying 56 contracts, the bond manager will effectively double the portfolio duration, resulting in capital gains should the market interest rates fall as expected. At the same time, by increasing portfolio risk, the adverse consequences of an interest rate rise also increase.

DISADVANTAGES OF IMMUNIZING

If immunization is a good idea, why doesn't everyone do it?[13] For one thing, there are potential disadvantages. It is probably not a good idea to immunize continuously for the reasons discussed below.

Opportunity Cost of Being Wrong

Immunization strategies may be based on certain assumptions about the future direction of interest rates, or they may simply be based on the assumption that future rates will be volatile. If the market is efficient, it is very difficult to forecast changes in interest rates. With an incorrect forecast, immunized portfolios can suffer an opportunity loss.

Consider the sample bank balance sheet in Table 12–3. This bank has more $-years in RSA than in RSL. We went through an exercise to get these two figures approximately equal, because if interest rates rise the bank will suffer a decline in its net worth.

Suppose, however, that contrary to expectation interest rates *declined*. Then, if the balance sheet had been left alone, the value of the RSA would have risen by more than the rise in value of the RSL. This would have resulted in an increase in the bank's net worth.

---

[13] Ignorance is a prime reason.

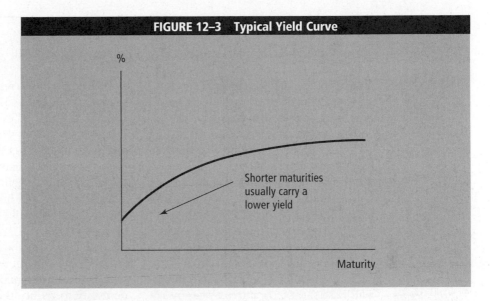

FIGURE 12–3   Typical Yield Curve

Immunization usually reduces the portfolio yield.

Lower Yield

Another consideration is that immunization usually results in a lower level of income generated by the funds under management. The typical yield curve is upward sloping. This means that everything else being equal, the longer the term of a fixed income security, the higher its yield. (See Figure 12–3.)

By reducing the portfolio duration, the portfolio return will shift to the left on the yield curve, resulting in a lower level of income for the fund beneficiary. It is a fundamental of finance that lower risk means a lower expected return. This principle holds for immunization strategies, just as with other investment activities.

Transaction Costs

Immunization is also not a costless activity. Selling one set of bonds and buying another involves trading fees, including brokerage commissions, the bid-ask spread, and possibly tax liabilities.

There are also commissions associated with the futures market, but these will be much lower than those resulting from wholesale replacement of bonds. This, in fact, is a primary reason why the futures market is the method of choice for immunization strategies among many portfolio managers.

Immunization: Instantaneous Only

A final consideration is the fact that a portfolio may be only temporarily immunized. With each day that passes, durations change, yields to maturity change, and market interest rates change. Unless the portfolio is adjusted periodically, minor changes in duration will result in an increasing divergence between what

TRADING STRATEGY

STRIPPING OUT ALPHA

Kirsten Joy is the Chief Investment Officer at a large investment firm. One of her fixed income analysts, Jessica, has consistently shown unusual skill in bond selection. Jessica seems to have a real knack for identifying bonds that are about to be upgraded by Standard & Poor's. An improvement in a bond's credit rating invariably results in an immediate upward pop in the bond price. Because of this skill, over the past three years Jessica has outperformed her benchmarks by 200 basis points.

The economist at Kirsten's firm believes that the Federal Reserve Board will raise short-term interest rates by 75 basis points in the next year and that the yield on the 30-year bond will rise by 125 basis points. A general upward shift in the yield curve will obviously hurt her firm's bond funds.

Kirsten wants to retain Jessica's bond selection skill but wants to remove the interest rate risk. The investment community uses the term "alpha" to refer to returns that are better than predicted by financial theory. Kirsten wants to keep Jessica's ability to generate alpha while simultaneously avoiding the loss in portfolio value that would come from a rise in interest rates.

She knows this is a straightforward task with T-bond futures. Kirsten simply sells the number of futures contracts necessary to reduce the portfolio duration to zero. In theory, this enables her to capture alpha while avoiding interest rate risk.

Immunization is neither a costless nor a permanent portfolio adjustment, and continuous immunization is probably not an optimum strategy.

was expected to happen and what actually occurred. Minor changes will also occur in the hedge ratio (for futures) or the funds gap (for bank immunization).

It is not practical for any but the largest portfolios to make daily adjustments to account for changing immunization needs. Smaller portfolios may be initially immunized, and revised only after weeks have passed or when conditions change enough to make revision cost-effective.

ALTERING ASSET ALLOCATION WITH FUTURES

TACTICAL CHANGES

Statements of investment policy usually give the portfolio manager some latitude in how to split the portfolio between equities and fixed income securities. A policy might, for instance, specify a normal range of 70% stock, 30% bonds, but permit the manager to invest anywhere between 50% and 85% in stock. The manager might choose to increase the allocation to equity when things seem particularly promising for the stock market or when interest rates are unattractive.

In Chapter Nine we saw that an equity manager can reduce market risk by selling stock index futures. The manager, in fact, can turn the stock portfolio into a synthetic Treasury bill by selling the appropriate number of contracts. Similarly,

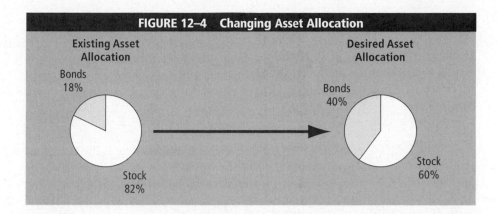

FIGURE 12–4   Changing Asset Allocation

Existing Asset Allocation — Bonds 18%, Stock 82%

Desired Asset Allocation — Bonds 40%, Stock 60%

we have seen that you can use T-bond futures to remove all or part of a portfolio's sensitivity to changing interest rates. In this section we will see how the portfolio manager can mix *both* T-bond and S&P 500 futures into the portfolio to quickly adjust asset allocation without having to buy or sell any of the existing portfolio components.

INITIAL SITUATION

Suppose a portfolio has a market value of $175 million. (See Figure 12–4.) It is currently invested 82% in common stock (average beta = 1.10) and 18% in bonds (average duration = 8.7; average yield to maturity = 8.00%.) The manager decides to reduce the equity exposure and move the portfolio to a 60% stock/40% bonds mix.

We have the futures information in Table 12-7. The steps to follow are logical. We will determine how many contracts will remove 100% of each type of risk (interest rate and market), and then use a percentage of this 100% hedge that matches the proportion of the risk we wish to retain.

TABLE 12–7   Futures Information

STOCK INDEX FUTURES

SEPTEMBER SETTLEMENT = 1020.00

TREASURY BOND FUTURES

SEPTEMBER SETTLEMENT = 91.05
CHEAPEST TO DELIVER BOND:
    PRICE = 95%
    MATURITY = 18 YEARS
    COUPON = 9 %
    DURATION = 10.83
    CONVERSION FACTOR = 1.3275

BOND ADJUSTMENT

We will use the basis point value technique from earlier in this chapter. The basis point value of the existing bond portfolio is

$$BPV_{current} = \frac{8.7 \times (\$175,000,000 \times 18\%) \times 0.0001}{\left(1 \times \dfrac{0.08}{2}\right)} = 26,351$$

Note that the portfolio size that matters here is the size of the *bond* portion of the portfolio; this is 18% of $175 million.

For the target portfolio, the basis point value is

$$BPV_{target} = \frac{8.7 \times (\$175,000,000 \times 40\%) \times 0.0001}{\left(1 \times \dfrac{0.08}{2}\right)} = 58,558$$

The only difference in the formula is that we want a bigger proportion in bonds, so we increase the 18% to 40%. The basis point value for the chosen futures contract is

$$BPV_{futures} = \frac{10.83 \times \$100,000 \times 0.0001}{\left(1 \times \dfrac{0.0748}{2}\right) \times 1.3275} = 78.64$$

The number of contracts to completely hedge the bond portion of the portfolio is then

$$\frac{58,558 - 26,351}{78.64} = 409.55$$

Buying 410 T-bond futures and adding them to the portfolio would give the portfolio the same sensitivity to interest rates as a $175 million portfolio invested 40% in bonds.

STOCK ADJUSTMENT

Buying 410 T-bond futures will give us the desired exposure in fixed income. We follow a similar procedure to get the stock position we want. In Chapter Nine we saw that the 100% hedge ratio is the portfolio beta multiplied by the ratio of the portfolio size to the value of the stock index futures contract. For the portfolio in this example,

$$HR = \frac{\$175 \text{ million} \times 82\%}{\$250 \times 1020.00} \times 1.10 = 619.02$$

Selling 619 stock index futures contracts would turn the stock into a synthetic Treasury bill.

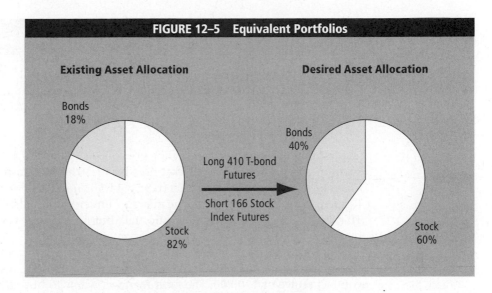

FIGURE 12–5   Equivalent Portfolios

At present the stock investment is $175,000,000 × 82% = $143,500,000. The desired exposure is $175,000,000 × 60% = $105,000,000. This is 26.83% less than the current level. If we want to reduce the stock holding by 26.83%, it seems logical that we can use 26.83% of the stock index futures hedge ratio. This is 26.83% × 619.02 = 166.08, so selling 166 stock index futures contracts would do the trick. (See Figure 12–5.)

These results tell us that the portfolio manager can move the asset allocation from the present 82% stock, 18% bonds to the desired 60/40 mix by buying 410 T-bond futures and selling 166 stock index futures. Making the adjustment this way does not disrupt the underlying portfolio and thereby avoids the inconvenience of tax consequences, trading fees, and the cost of managerial time.

NEUTRALIZING CASH

Stock portfolios suffer from "cash drag" if they are not fully invested.

Money managers know that their performance is periodically judged relative to some market index. They also know that if they appear to underperform they will lose clients and find it difficult to get new ones.

Consider the case of an all-equity mutual fund manager whose benchmark is the S&P 500 index. Suppose the fund's assets total $500 million, with 5% routinely held in cash equivalents. (See Figure 12–6.) A mutual fund needs to keep a certain amount of cash on hand to accommodate investor share redemption requests, something that occurs daily. The fund receives additional deposits from existing customers and checks from new accounts on a daily basis as well. Over long periods of time the evidence is clear that equity securities earn a higher return than cash. It is hard enough for a money manager to "beat the market" without having a downward bias in relative fund performance because of part of the portfolio being invested in an asset likely to earn a below-market rate.

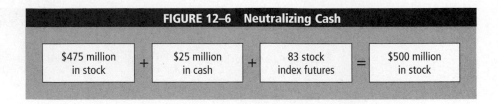

FIGURE 12–6   Neutralizing Cash

$475 million in stock $+$ $25 million in cash $+$ 83 stock index futures $=$ $500 million in stock

Suppose the equity portion of the portfolio has a beta of 1.0 and that over a six-month period the broad market rises by 11.50%, with cash earning 2.50%. The return on this portfolio is then $(0.95 \times 11.50\%) + (0.05 \times 2.50\%) = 11.05\%$. Relative to the S&P benchmark, the manager underperformed by 45 basis points. This may not seem like much of a shortfall, but no manager wants to face comments of the "didn't even match the market average" sort.

Many fund managers deal with this situation by holding a long position in stock index futures that will offset the cash position. Suppose a distant SPX futures contract settled at 1200.00. The fund manager wants to buy enough of these to bring up the market exposure of the fund assets from 95% to 100%. The hedge ratio from Chapter 9 is an easy way to find the appropriate quantity.

$$HR = \frac{\text{Portfolio size}}{\text{Futures size}} \times \text{beta}$$

The "portfolio size" we want to add is 5% of $500 million:

$$HR = \frac{0.05 \times \$500 \text{ million}}{1200.00 \times \$250} \times 1.0 = 83.33$$

If the portfolio manager buys 83 SPX futures and mixes them with the existing stock/cash portfolio, it should behave very much like a 100% equity index fund.

The same procedure works with a bond fund. The manager can offset the "cash drag" on fund performance by holding a long position in interest rate futures.

SUMMARY

Immunization is a technique designed to eliminate much of the interest rate risk inherent in a bond portfolio or the net interest rate risk on a balance sheet. The essence of immunization is structuring the portfolio so that the effects of interest rate risk and reinvestment rate risk cancel.

Immunization is not a costless activity. It usually lowers the expected return of a portfolio, results in an opportunity loss if you incorrectly forecast the direction of interest rates, and results in higher transaction costs. It also is an instantaneous strategy that requires frequent revision.

Portfolio managers can combine futures contracts with their equity or fixed income holdings to synthetically alter the portfolio's asset allocation. This is attractive because it allows shifting the portfolio between stocks and bonds without having to disrupt the underlying portfolio. Fund managers who must routinely keep part of their portfolio in cash can reduce the "cash drag" on their performance by holding sufficient long futures contracts to offset the effect of the cash holding.

SELF TEST

T ___ F ___   1. Immunization is the process of removing interest rate risk from a portfolio.

T ___ F ___   2. An immunization strategy usually seeks to get interest rate risk and reinvestment rate risk to cancel.

T ___ F ___   3. The dollar value of a bank's interest rate liabilities is called its funds gap.

T ___ F ___   4. Banks usually make duration adjustments by altering the left side of the balance sheet.

T ___ F ___   5. Duration is a combined measure of both market risk and interest rate risk.

T ___ F ___   6. Everything else being equal, the higher a bond's coupon the higher its duration.

T ___ F ___   7. Interest rate hedging techniques using futures contracts involve a bond known as the *cheapest to deliver* bond.

T ___ F ___   8. A treasurer who wanted to increase the duration of a bond portfolio could do so by selling T-bond futures contracts.

T ___ F ___   9. A basis point value is the change in the price of a bond associated with a one point change in the yield to maturity of a bond.

T ___ F ___ 10. Immunization usually reduces portfolio yield.

T ___ F ___ 11. Futures contracts can be used to alter asset allocation without disrupting the underlying portfolio.

T ___ F ___ 12. A stock portfolio manager can neutralize the effects of having to hold cash by selling stock index futures.

T ___ F ___ 13. A disadvantage of hedging with any kind of financial futures contract is the fact that if you are short the futures you must carry the contract until its final delivery date.

T ___ F ___ 14. The simplest form of credit derivative is a guarantee.

T ___ F ___ 15. Duration matching is the general process of minimizing the combined effects of reinvestment rate risk and interest rate risk.

PROBLEMS & QUESTIONS

1. What does "immunization" mean?
2. Explain the difference between bullet immunization and bank immunization.
3. Explain the relationship between interest rate risk and reinvestment rate risk in a bullet immunization strategy.
4. Explain the concept of "funds gap."
5. Which side of the balance sheet do banks generally alter as part of their immunization strategies? Why?
6. Give examples of assets that are "rate sensitive" and others that are not.
7. List several ways the duration of a portfolio can be changed.
8. Why are some bonds cheaper to deliver than others?
9. Explain the idea of "basis point value."
10. What are the disadvantages of immunizing?
11. Why is immunization "instantaneous only"?
12. Briefly explain why it is necessary to translate bonds into "6% equivalents" in the delivery process for Treasury bond futures.
13. Refer to Table 12–1 in this chapter. Suppose the interest rate changed instantaneously to 8% after two years. Show the resulting portfolio value, as with the rest of the table.
14. Refer to Table 12–2. Suppose the portfolio manager sold all the XYZ bonds and put the money into 90-day T-bills. What is the new portfolio duration? (Ignore commissions and accrued interest.)
15. Make up a bullet immunization example, using two of the bonds in Table 12–2. Show the cash flow, and so forth, as in Table 12–1. Assume the bonds pay interest annually.

16. Suppose a bank has rate sensitive assets of $450 million, rate sensitive liabilities of $23 million, total assets of $1 billion, and equity of $500 million. The duration of the RSA is 3.3, while the duration of the RSL is 13.5. What is the bank's funds gap?
17. If the cheapest to deliver bond has a duration of 7.5, a price of 100, and a conversion factor of 0.9150, how many futures contracts (selling for 98) must be used to hedge a $10 million portfolio with a duration of 14.6? Assume the bond portfolio sells at par.
18. If the cheapest to deliver bond has a duration of 9.5, a price of 90, and a conversion factor of 0.8450, how many future contracts (selling for 99) must be used to hedge a $130 million portfolio with a duration of 8.6? Assume the bond portfolio sells at par.
19. What is the conversion factor for a $7\tfrac{5}{8}\%$ coupon bond that matures in 21 years, 4 months?
20. What is the conversion factor for a 9% coupon bond that matures in 16 years, 11 months?
21. A bond portfolio has a market value of $56 million, a yield to maturity of 8.7%, and a duration of 6.44. What is its basis point value?
22. Assume the cheapest to deliver T-bond sells for 97, has a yield of maturity of 6.6%, a duration of 5.5, and a conversion factor of .8124. What is the basis point value of the associated futures contract?

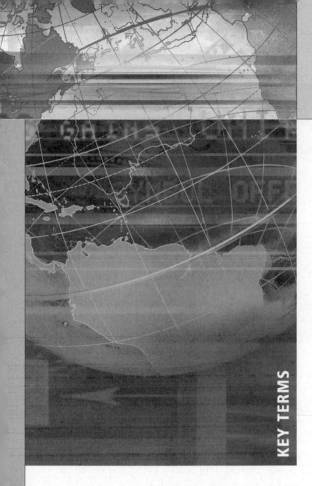

13

Swaps and Interest Rate Options

I must tell you that I take terrible risks. Because my playing is very clear, when I make a mistake you hear it. If you want me to play only the notes without any specific dynamics, I will never make one mistake. Never be afraid to dare.

Vladimir Horowitz (1903–1989)
Pianist

This chapter looks at the swaps market and the interest rate options market. While relatively new, both markets are huge. Currency swaps are older, but the interest rate swap market involves many more dollars. In mid-2000 there was over $60 trillion outstanding in interest rate swaps, foreign currency swaps, and various forms of interest rate options, as Figure 13–1 shows.

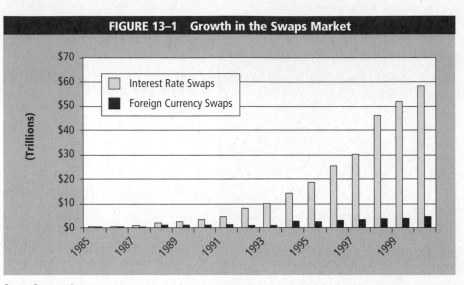

FIGURE 13–1 Growth in the Swaps Market

Source: Swapsmonitor.com

The most common swap is the fixed for floating interest rate swap.

The most common form of an interest rate swap involves one party making a fixed interest rate payment to another party who, in turn, makes a floating interest rate payment to the first party. Such a swap is a fixed for floating rate swap. Only the net payment changes hands, so the firm obliged to pay the higher rate remits funds to the other with a **difference check**. The firm paying the floating rate is the swap seller, while the firm paying the fixed rate is the swap buyer.[1]

In a currency swap, two parties exchange currencies at the prevailing exchange rate, and then make periodic interest payments to each other based on a predetermined pair of interest rates. At the conclusion of the swap they re-exchange the original currencies. This arrangement is an exchange of borrowings.

Interest rate options take many forms, but they all have familiar option characteristics. Caps and floors serve the same purpose as calls and puts in portfolio management, with swaptions being an option to enter into a swap contract. We will look at all of these in detail.

INTEREST RATE SWAPS

An *interest rate swap*[2] is a popular tool with bankers, corporate treasurers, and portfolio managers who need to manage interest rate risk. As with other derivatives,

---

[1] The firm paying the floating rate is also sometimes said to be *short* the swap; the firm paying the fixed rate is *long* the swap.

[2] Don't confuse an interest rate swap with a *bond* swap. The latter is a physical trade of one bond for another. For instance, an investor might own one particular bond whose value has fallen because of rising interest rates. The investor might engage in a tax swap by selling the original bond for a tax loss and then purchasing another bond with similar characteristics. This is not an interest rate swap; it is a bond swap.

a swap enables you to alter the level of risk without disrupting the underlying portfolio. The Student Loan Marketing Association (Sallie Mae) engaged in the first such contract in 1982.

Some interest-bearing assets carry a **fixed rate**; the level of income they produce does not vary with changes in the general level of interest rates. Other assets have a **floating**, or variable, rate. Typically, the floating rate is linked to a market rate such as the London InterBank Offered Rate (LIBOR) or the U.S. Treasury bill rate. Most often the floating rate is for a six-month period.

The firm paying the fixed rate "buys" the swap.

There are two principal participants in the swap, one of whom pays a fixed rate that does not change, with the other paying a floating rate that varies according to the benchmark rate. When someone pays the fixed rate, we say they *buy the swap*. If you pay the floating rate, you *sell the swap*. Let's look at an example of how two corporations might engage in a plain vanilla interest rate swap. The term **plain vanilla** is common in derivatives. It refers to a standard contract with no unusual features or bells and whistles added.

As the swaps market grew, it became apparent that some standardization would be helpful and would reduce the legal fees associated with contract preparation. Institutions using swaps realized that it was not necessary to start the paperwork from scratch each time they contemplated a new swap arrangement.

This led to the formation of the International Swap Dealers Association, now known as the **International Swaps and Derivatives Association**, or ISDA,[3] to more accurately reflect its involvement in the broader derivatives market. The ISDA substantially contributed to the development of a standardized terminology and set of swap conditions, including procedures for calculation of interest. These ISDA provisions are known as **master agreements** and have been associated with most swaps since 1987.

Figure 13–2 shows a plain vanilla interest rate swap between two corporations. The larger firm pays a fixed interest rate of 8.05% to its bondholders, while the smaller firm pays its bondholders a floating rate of LIBOR + 100 bp. The two firms engage in a swap transaction that results in just the reverse: the larger firm pays floating and the smaller firm pays fixed.

Sometimes there is an intermediary, or **swap facilitator**, involved. For a fee, the facilitator finds a counterparty to a desired swap, or perhaps takes the other side itself. When the facilitator acts as an agent and does not take any position in the swap, the facilitator is called a **swap broker**. If the swap facilitator does take the other side of the swap, the firm is functioning as a **swap dealer**, also called a **swap bank**. Over time a swap bank accumulates a portfolio of swap positions that comprise its **swap book**. The swap bank may choose to hedge all or part of its swap book in the futures market, as we will see in Chapter 14. Life is simplest for the swap bank when the swap book is *matched*, meaning that the floating and fixed rate obligations from the various swaps "match up" so that the swap bank has no market position, but just collects the fee from making the trade. The fee shows up as an increased borrowing rate for one or both of the parties involved.

---

[3] Pronounced "Is' duh."

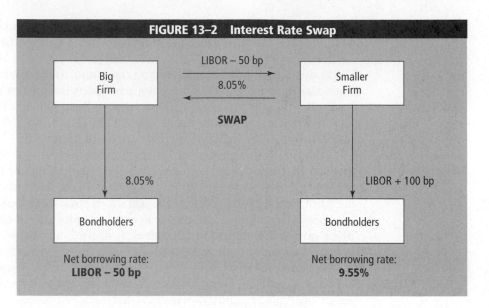

FIGURE 13–2   Interest Rate Swap

Figure 13–3 shows how the previous example might look if the facilitator took a 15 bp fee for the service.

By following the relatively simple steps shown in this example, a swap can transform a fixed rate liability into a variable rate liability, and vice versa. The same is true on the other side of the balance sheet: a swap can change a variable rate investment into a fixed rate investment, and vice versa.

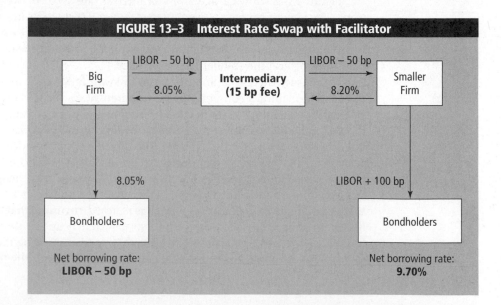

FIGURE 13–3   Interest Rate Swap with Facilitator

Let's now look at a more detailed example with actual interest calculations. Suppose the Third National Bank currently owns variable rate loans totaling $100 million. These are assets on its balance sheet. Elsewhere, the Trekkers Insurance Company holds $100 million in corporate bonds, with an average fixed rate coupon of 7.00%. The investment manager at Trekkers believes that interest rates are going to rise soon, causing the value of its bond investments to fall. To deal with this, the manager decides to reduce the duration of the interest sensitive assets.

The people at Third National do not share the interest rate outlook of the folks at Trekkers: in fact, they believe rates are going down. These two institutions are good candidates for an interest rate swap.

The essence of the arrangement is simple: Trekkers agrees to pay a fixed rate on $100 million to Third National in exchange for receiving a variable rate on $100 million. Figure 13–4 shows the net effect of the cash flows from the perspectives of the two institutions. Initially, Trekkers receives a fixed rate and is subject to interest rate risk. After the swap, the fixed rate Trekkers receives from its bonds is passed on to Third National. Trekkers is left receiving a variable rate and has essentially eliminated the interest rate risk.

The **swap price** is the fixed rate that the two parties agree upon.[4] The term *swap coupon* is synonymous with swap price, although it is less common. Suppose in this example that the agreed-upon fixed rate (the swap price) is 8.50%. The variable rate is set as LIBOR plus 100 basis points. The life, or term, of the swap is the swap **tenor**. The swap's **notional value** determines the size of the interest rate payments. Figure 13–5 shows the cash flows the two parties exchange based on hypothetical changes in interest rates. In an interest rate swap like this, only the net cash flow changes hands; there is no need for both parties to deliver cash. The party owing the larger amount pays the excess over what they are owed by remitting a difference check.[5] Note that neither party has borrowed money from the other; this is why the term *notional* is appropriate with a swap contract. The fact that a firm is party to a $100 million interest rate swap does not mean that this is a loan requiring eventual repayment.

There is a new type of risk introduced by using a swap. This is **counterparty risk**. Because there is no clearinghouse guaranteeing the trade, there is a possibility that one party to the swap will not honor its part of the agreement. The consequences of this are not as severe as they might initially seem, however. If Third National fails to pay Trekkers, it is not likely that Trekkers will choose to pay Third National. The amount at risk is just the net amount owed plus the opportunity cost of not completing the swap arrangement. (Presumably the party *receiving* the net cash flow will not default on the agreement. It is the *payer* who might do so.) We see in Figure 13–5 that the actual cash flows are much less than $100 mil-

---

[4] The chosen fixed rate will be the interest rate that causes the swap to have a net present value of zero from the perspective of both parties. It is easy to solve for this rate from the spot rate curve, and both parties will determine the same fixed rate value. The next chapter illustrates this. Because the swap initially has no value to either party, it is not an asset and does not appear on either firm's balance sheet except as a footnote. Consequently, a swap is an off-balance sheet item.

[5] The master agreement spells out exactly how to calculate and pay the interest.

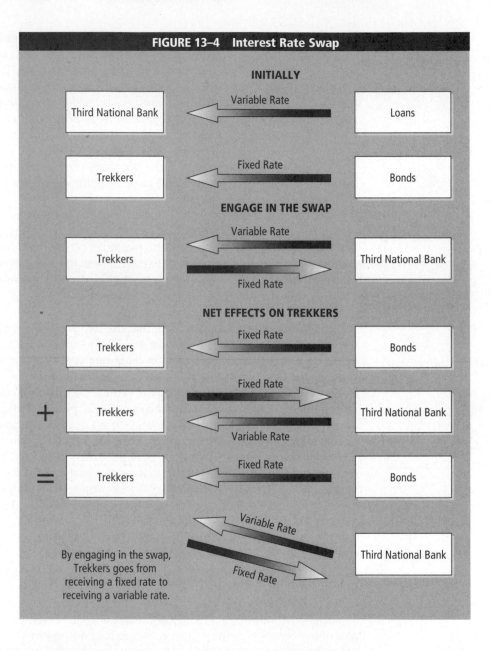

FIGURE 13–4   Interest Rate Swap

INITIALLY

Third National Bank ← Variable Rate — Loans

Trekkers ← Fixed Rate — Bonds

ENGAGE IN THE SWAP

Trekkers ← Variable Rate — Third National Bank
Trekkers → Fixed Rate → Third National Bank

NET EFFECTS ON TREKKERS

Trekkers ← Fixed Rate — Bonds

+

Trekkers → Fixed Rate → Third National Bank
Trekkers ← Variable Rate — Third National Bank

=

Trekkers ← Fixed Rate — Bonds

Trekkers ← Variable Rate — Third National Bank
Trekkers → Fixed Rate → Third National Bank

By engaging in the swap, Trekkers goes from receiving a fixed rate to receiving a variable rate.

lion. It would not be reasonable to interpret this swap as putting $100 million at risk. This is the reason the size of the swap is referred to as the *notional* amount. It is just the reference point for determining how much interest is to be paid; the principal amount never changes hands.[6]

---

[6] Foreign currency swaps are different; the principal amount *does* change hands in such a swap.

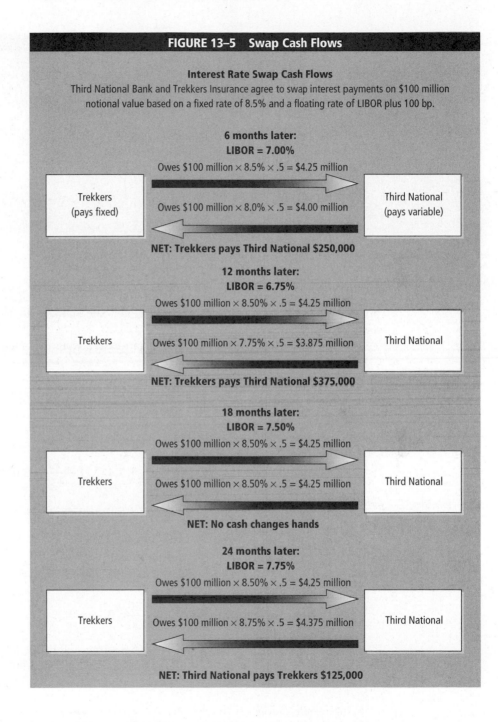

FIGURE 13–5   Swap Cash Flows

Interest Rate Swap Cash Flows

Third National Bank and Trekkers Insurance agree to swap interest payments on $100 million notional value based on a fixed rate of 8.5% and a floating rate of LIBOR plus 100 bp.

6 months later:
LIBOR = 7.00%

Owes $100 million × 8.5% × .5 = $4.25 million

Trekkers (pays fixed) → Third National (pays variable)

Owes $100 million × 8.0% × .5 = $4.00 million

NET: Trekkers pays Third National $250,000

12 months later:
LIBOR = 6.75%

Owes $100 million × 8.50% × .5 = $4.25 million

Trekkers → Third National

Owes $100 million × 7.75% × .5 = $3.875 million

NET: Trekkers pays Third National $375,000

18 months later:
LIBOR = 7.50%

Owes $100 million × 8.50% × .5 = $4.25 million

Trekkers → Third National

Owes $100 million × 8.50% × .5 = $4.25 million

NET: No cash changes hands

24 months later:
LIBOR = 7.75%

Owes $100 million × 8.50% × .5 = $4.25 million

Trekkers → Third National

Owes $100 million × 8.75% × .5 = $4.375 million

NET: Third National pays Trekkers $125,000

FIGURE 13–6	Bank Balance Sheet	
ASSETS	**LIABILITIES & NET WORTH**	
CASH $200 (D = 0.00)	3 YEAR FLOATING RATE	
3 YEAR LOANS @ 7% 600 (D = 2.43)	LOAN @ LIBOR + 10 bp	
7 YEAR LOANS @ 8% 1,100 (D = 4.43)	(ANNUAL RESET)	$ 700 (D = 1.00)
TOTAL ASSETS $1,900	5 YEAR LOAN @ 6%	200 (D = 3.41)
	8 YEAR ZERO COUPON	550 (D = 8.00)
	TOTAL LIABILITIES	$ 1,450
	NET WORTH	450
	TOTAL LIABILITIES & NET WORTH	**$ 1,900**

IMMUNIZING WITH INTEREST RATE SWAPS

Interest rate swaps are a very handy way for corporate treasurers to adjust their exposure to interest rate risk. Suppose at a later date Trekkers has the balance sheet shown in Figure 13–6.[7]

The treasurer calculates portfolio duration as a weighted average of the component durations. For the asset side,

$$D_{asset} = \left(\frac{200}{1,900} \times 0\right) + \left(\frac{600}{1,900} \times 2.43\right) + \left(\frac{1,100}{1,900} \times 4.43\right) = 3.33$$

For the liabilities,

$$D_{liabilities} = \left(\frac{700}{1,450} \times 1.0\right) + \left(\frac{200}{1,450} \times 3.41\right) + \left(\frac{550}{1,450} \times 8.00\right) = 3.99$$

Banks define their **duration gap** according to Equation 13–1:

$$D_{gap} = D_{asset} - \frac{\text{Total liabilities}}{\text{Total assets}} \times D_{liabilities} \qquad (13-1)$$

Substituting,

$$D_{gap} = 3.33 - \frac{1,450}{1,900} \times 3.99 = 0.29$$

A positive duration gap means the bank's net worth will suffer if interest rates rise. The treasurer may choose to deal with this risk by making adjustments to move the duration gap to zero.[8]

---

[7] The intuition for this example comes from an excellent tutorial published by the Research Foundation of the Institute of Chartered Financial Analysts entitled "Interest Rate and Currency Swaps: A Tutorial," by Keith C. Brown and Donald J. Smith, Charlottesville, VA, 1995.

[8] Pension funds and insurance companies often use swaps to accomplish similar ends.

One way to accomplish this would be to sell some of the bank's loans (on the asset side of the balance sheet) and hold cash equivalent securities instead. To figure out the dollar volume of loans to sell, the treasurer solves the algebra problem below where x_{cash} represents the proportion of the firm's assets to be held in cash:

$$D_{gap} = \left[\left(x_{cash} \times 0.00\right) + \left(1 - x_{cash}\right)\left(\text{average loan asset duration}\right)\right] - \quad (13\text{--}2)$$

$$\left(\frac{\text{Total Liabilities}}{\text{Total Assets}} \times D_{liabilities}\right) = 0$$

What we want to solve for is the proportion of the portfolio that should be in cash so that the duration of the portfolio is zero after accounting for the liabilities. The average duration of the loans on the asset side of the balance sheet is

$$\left(\frac{600}{600+1,100}\right)(2.43) + \left(\frac{1,100}{600+1,100}\right)(4.43) = 3.72$$

Putting in the values for the bank,

$$D_{gap} = \left[(1 - x_{cash})(3.72)\right] - \left(\frac{1,450}{1,900} \times 3.99\right) = 0$$

Solving, we find x_{cash} is 18.15%. This means 18.15% × $1,900, or $344.85, should be in cash to bring the gap to zero. Selling $144.85 of the loan portfolio, however, would substantially reduce the bank's income producing assets and likely reduce its profitability. Using an interest rate swap is a better way to close the duration gap.

The treasurer could enter into a fixed for floating swap on a portion of the liability portfolio. The most direct way to do this would be to swap part of the 3-year floating rate stream for a 3-year fixed rate stream. Suppose the swap price is 7.25%. The duration[9] of the fixed rate side of the swap would be 2.57. To find the size of the swap we use equation 13–3, a slightly modified version of Equation 13–1:

$$D_{assets} = \frac{\text{Total Liabilities}}{\text{Total Assets}} \times D_{liabilities} \quad (13\text{--}3)$$

The duration of both the assets and the liabilities are dollar-weighted averages. Substituting,

$$3.33 = \left(\frac{1,450}{1,900}\right) \times \left[\left(\frac{700 - \text{swap}}{1,450}\right)(1.0) + \left(\frac{\text{swap}}{1,450} \times 2.57\right) + \left(\frac{200}{1,450} \times 3.41\right) + \left(\frac{550}{1,450} \times 8.00\right)\right]$$

---

[9] This is the duration of a three-year, annual payment loan with a 7.25% coupon rate.

Solving, we find the swap notional principal to close the duration gap is $338.32. Such a swap would maintain the existing assets while removing the risk to the bank's net worth because of the positive duration gap. In other words, if the treasurer swaps $338.32 of the 3-year floating rate debt for 3-year fixed @ 7.25% the duration gap would go to zero and the interest rate risk largely disappears.

EXPLOITING COMPARATIVE ADVANTAGE IN THE CREDIT MARKET

Another common use of an interest rate swap is to exploit differentials in the credit market. Imagine that there are two companies, AAA bank and BBB bank, with S&P credit ratings corresponding to their names. Both firms currently face the borrowing possibilities shown in Table 13–1.

The **quality spread** is the difference in borrowing rates the two firms must pay for otherwise similar loans. AAA bank has an **absolute advantage** over BBB in both the fixed and the floating rate markets; its borrowing rate is lower in both instances. AAA has a **comparative advantage** in the fixed rate market. It pays 60 basis points less than BBB in the fixed rate market, and only 30 basis points less in the floating rate market. The total gain available to be shared among the swap participants is the differential in the fixed rate market minus the differential in the variable rate market, or 60 bp – 30 bp = 30 bp.

Now suppose AAA wants to issue a floating rate bond, while BBB wants to borrow at a fixed rate. Both banks will borrow at lower cost if their CFOs get together and agree to engage in an interest rate swap. In so doing, AAA issues a fixed rate bond because it has a comparative advantage in this market. BBB borrows at a floating rate and the two firms then swap the payments. Suppose they set the swap up such that they split the rate savings 50-50 and that the current 5-year T-bond rate is 4.50%. Figure 13–7 shows the resulting cash flows.

Both firms face counterparty risk, and each can argue that because of this new source of risk the borrowing cost *should* be lower. A firm can argue that if it takes on more risk of any type it should be compensated for it. If you take on counterparty risk, you can be compensated for it by a lower borrowing rate.

In practice, both firms can make the argument, but because AAA is the higher-rated firm, its CFO will likely hold out for a greater share of the interest rate savings. An alternate arrangement, for instance, might result in AAA paying a net rate of LIBOR – 20 bp while BBB pays Treasury + 75 bp. In this setup AAA saves 20

TABLE 13–1 Borrowing Possibilities		
FIRM	FIXED RATE	FLOATING RATE
AAA	CURRENT 5 YR T-BOND + 25 bp	LIBOR
BBB	CURRENT 5 YR T-BOND + 85 bp	LIBOR + 30 bp
QUALITY SPREAD	60 bp	30 bp

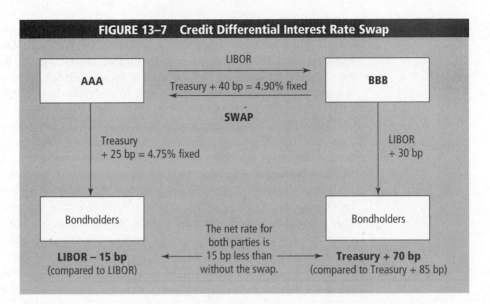

FIGURE 13–7   Credit Differential Interest Rate Swap

An Interest rate swap enables firms to exploit their comparative rate advantage in the marketplace.

basis points while BBB saves only 10. Regardless, both companies pay less interest with the swap in place and are able to borrow in the market (fixed or floating) they prefer.

In this example the two firms have different credit ratings, but this is not a necessary condition for a swap of this type. One firm might be lesser known than the other, with a higher cost of funds as a consequence. The presence of a comparative advantage for one firm might stem from market inefficiencies that have nothing to do with credit rating.

FOREIGN CURRENCY SWAPS

Currency swaps predate interest rate swaps. Historically, these were short-term arrangements between two central banks. In the 1960s, for instance, there are examples of one country finding itself short of dollars and choosing to borrow them from another country's central bank by pledging its own currency as collateral and paying interest. Later, the borrower would return the dollars and the lender would release the collateral. The modern currency swap arrangement is not too different.

Foreign exchange risk made a dramatic entrance into the enterprise risk equation in August of 1971 when global monetary leaders suspended the Bretton Woods agreement. Prior to the suspension, the world faced fixed exchange rates that were pegged to the price of gold, which itself was priced in U.S. dollars.

After the suspension of the agreement, currencies were free to float until they found a market equilibrium price. Floating rates translated into volatility in the foreign exchange market. Volatility means risk, and where there is risk people will look for a way to measure and manage it. In 1972 the Chicago Mercantile Exchange introduced foreign currency futures contracts on its International Monetary Market division. As we saw earlier, these continue to be popular, although the futures contract on the Euro is likely to divert much of the trading in the individual currency contracts.

In 1981 Salomon Brothers brokered the first currency swap. This was a deal between IBM and the World Bank in which they agreed to trade a stream of Swiss franc cash flows for another stream denominated in German deutsche marks. This innovation attracted attention, and the volume of currency involved with swaps skyrocketed in the following years. Today, currency swaps are one of an international financial manager's favorite risk management tools. They provide a convenient mechanism for fixing an exchange rate over a long period of time, thereby providing a significant hedge against foreign currency risk.

Figure 13–8 shows the cash flows with a foreign currency swap. At origination, the two parties exchange principal amounts, perhaps dollars for yen. Each party owes an interest payment on each payment date, although the swap con-

DERIVATIVES TODAY

LIBOR

The London InterBank Offered Rate is an important benchmark rate in international finance. It is established by the British Bankers Association and represents the average of rates quoted by about 16 multinational banks.

Dollar LIBOR is the interest rate paid on European deposits denominated in U.S. dollars. Yen LIBOR is the rate paid on European deposits on yen, and so on. These rates change daily and depend on the time period for the deposit. Table 13–2 shows representative U.S. $ LIBOR rates[10] for the first week of February 2001.

TABLE 13-2 $ LIBOR				
	1 MONTH	**3** MONTHS	**6** MONTHS	**12** MONTHS
FEB 1, 2001	5.48%	5.32%	5.16%	5.11%
FEB 2, 2001	5.48%	5.31%	5.16%	5.17%
FEB 5, 2001	5.47%	5.34%	5.18%	5.13%
FEB 6, 2001	5.52%	5.34%	5.17%	5.10%
FEB 7, 2001	5.52%	5.35%	5.20%	5.13%

Source: Reuters

While London is the center of non-US banking activity, similar interest rate quotations come from other parts of the world. PIBOR, for instance, is the Paris Interbank Offered Rate. SIBOR is the Singapore Interbank Offered Rate.

[10] Note the atypical share of the yield curve, with longer maturities carrying lower rates. It is more common for the yield curve to have a positive slope.

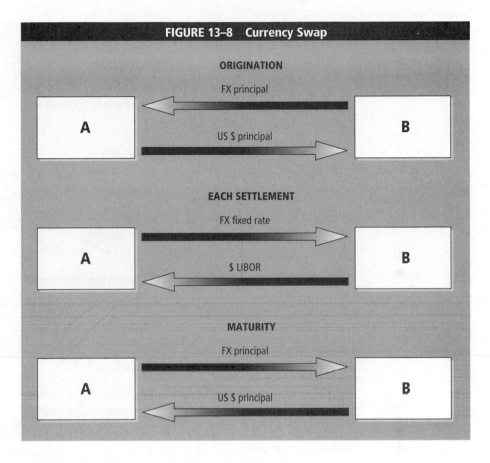

FIGURE 13–8 Currency Swap

ORIGINATION

FX principal

A ← B

US $ principal

A → B

EACH SETTLEMENT

FX fixed rate

A → B

$ LIBOR

A ← B

MATURITY

FX principal

A → B

US $ principal

A ← B

tract may provide for netting the two payments with only the party owing the larger amount actually remitting anything (i.e., a difference check). The floating rate on a currency swap is normally $ LIBOR when the dollar is the floating currency, although the swap participants can set the swap up anyway they wish. Finally, at the maturity of the swap the original principal amounts are returned.

To see how a currency swap can help manage foreign exchange risk, consider the following example. Suppose a US multinational corporation has a subsidiary in Germany and just signed a three-year contract with a local firm. The local firm will provide raw materials on site in Germany, with the US firm paying 1 million Euros every six months for the three-year period. Assume that currently the exchange rate is €1.00 = $0.90. While the contract is fixed in Euro terms, from the perspective of the US corporate treasurer there is the risk that the dollar might depreciate against the Euro, increasing the account payable in dollar terms, and adversely affecting the firm's financial statements. Suppose also that the firm currently has $250 million in US Treasury bills in its investment portfolio.

To mitigate the foreign exchange risk, the treasurer can enter into a foreign currency swap as follows: tenor of three years, notional value of €25 million (or,

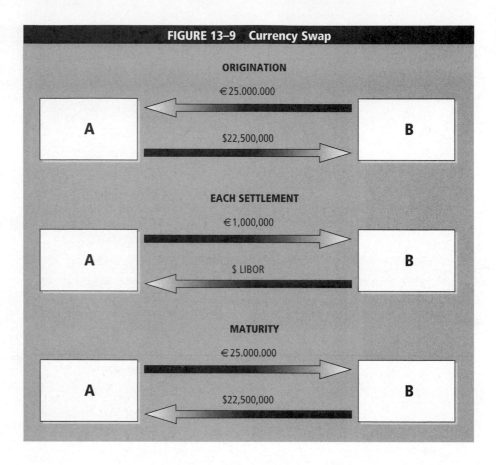

FIGURE 13–9   Currency Swap

ORIGINATION

€25.000.000

A   B

$22,500,000

EACH SETTLEMENT

€1,000,000

A   B

$ LIBOR

MATURITY

€25.000.000

A   B

$22,500,000

equivalently, $22.5 million), floating rate = $ LIBOR, fixed rate = 8% on Euros. The treasurer will begin things by cashing in $22.5 million of the T-bills and remitting them to the swap counterparty, who, in turn, will send €25 million to the treasurer. The treasurer will invest these at the Euro LIBOR rate.

The fixed rate payment on the Euros will be €25,000,000 × 8% × 0.5 = €1,000,000. The floating rate payment every six months will be 0.5 times the LIBOR rate multiplied by $22.5 million. Figure 13–9 shows the cash flows.[11]

At each payment period the treasurer uses the $ LIBOR earned from the LIBOR deposit to make the cash flow required by the swap, and uses the €1 million swap receipt to satisfy the account payable due the vendor. In essence, the foreign exchange risk associated with the account payable stream disappears.

---

[11] Actually, the interest calculation is slightly more complicated than this example shows. On most swaps the interest is calculated on the basis of the actual number of days in the payment period. On a semi-annual pay swap, this might be 182 or 183 days. The precise amount of interest will differ depending on the number used. Also, the interest might be paid in *advance* or *in arrears*. This will also affect the size of the interest payment required.

CIRCUS SWAP

A circus swap is the combination of a fixed for floating interest rate swap and a currency swap.

In the above example firm A receives a floating US dollar rate. Suppose that after a few months pass conditions change and the firm would now prefer to receive a fixed US dollar rate. A *combined interest rate and currency swap*, or **circus swap**, will do the trick. As the name implies, this means you are a joint party to two swaps, one a plain vanilla interest rate swap and the other an ordinary foreign currency swap. Both swaps might be with the same counterparty or they might be done with different counterparties.

Figure 13–10 shows the net effect, from firm A's perspective, of adding an interest rate swap with counterparty C. By exchanging the $ LIBOR cash flows for a fixed US dollar rate, the firm is effectively paying 8% on Euros and receiving 6.5% in U.S. dollars.

SWAP VARIATIONS

Because a swap is non-exchange traded and non-marketable, the parties involved can make the terms of the swap just about anything they wish. There are several especially noteworthy variations.

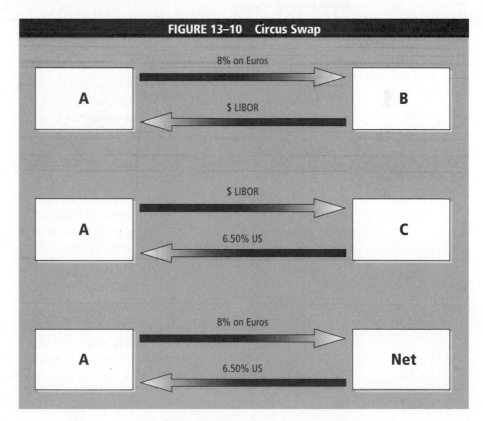

FIGURE 13–10   Circus Swap

Deferred Swap

One such variation is a **deferred swap**, also called a **forward start swap**. As the name suggests, this is a swap in which the cash flows do not begin until sometime after the initiation of the swap agreement. Normally, the swap begins now, which is why the plain vanilla version is sometimes called a **spot start swap**.

As an example, a corporate treasurer might anticipate receiving ¥10 million in 120 days and having to pay ¥10 million in 360 days. The treasurer might not want to bear the foreign exchange risk of holding the Japanese yen for the intervening 240 days. There are various ways in which the treasurer might deal with the situation. One way would be to enter a swap agreement in which he would exchange ¥10 million for U.S. dollars in 120 days and reverse the exchange in 360 days, with some provision for interest rate payments along the way. This would be a deferred foreign currency swap.

Floating for Floating Swap

Normally one party to a swap receives a floating rate. While not common, a swap might be structured with both parties paying a floating rate, but with different benchmark indices such as the three-month Treasury bill rate and $ LIBOR.

Amortizing Swap

An **amortizing swap** is one in which the notional value declines over time according to some schedule. The notional value might begin at $100 million and decline by $20 million for each of the next four years after which it terminates.

Accreting Swap

An **accreting swap** is the opposite of an amortizing swap. The notional value increases through time according to some schedule.

INTEREST RATE OPTIONS

Like the swaps market, the interest rate options market is huge. While most of this trading is done off the exchange floors, it is highly efficient, liquid, and easy to use. Figure 13–11 shows the steady growth in the notional value outstanding in the past decade. The most popular tools in this market are interest rate *caps* and *floors*. A slightly different but equally versatile product is a *swaption*.

INTEREST RATE CAP

An interest rate **cap** is much like a portfolio of European call options on an interest rate. To see how a cap might be useful, suppose a firm currently has a floating rate liability that requires semi-annual interest payments. This firm could buy a cap with a notional amount equal to the liability principal to ensure that regardless of how high interest rates might rise, the firm will not have to pay more than the "capped" amount. On each interest payment date over the life of the cap, one

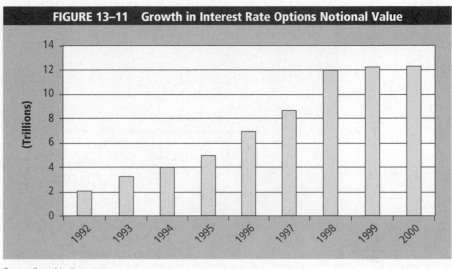

FIGURE 13–11   Growth in Interest Rate Options Notional Value

Source: SwapsMonitor.com

An interest rate cap is like a series of call options on an interest rate.

option in the portfolio expires. The individual options making up the cap are known as **caplets**. If, at the expiration of a caplet, the floating rate obligation is above the exercise price on the cap, the cap writer makes a payment to the cap buyer, thereby making the cap buyer's effective rate equal to the exercise price.[12] If the floating rate is below the exercise price, the expiring option is out-of-the-money and expires worthless.

Figure 13–12 shows a payoff diagram for a cap with a 7% exercise price. At any market rate below 7%, the cap will be out-of-the-money and will expire worthless. Figure 13–13 shows the payoffs from the perspective of the cap writer.

Citibank usually gets credit for having sold the first interest rate cap, which occurred in 1983. This was a 10-year, $100 million transaction for a real estate firm.

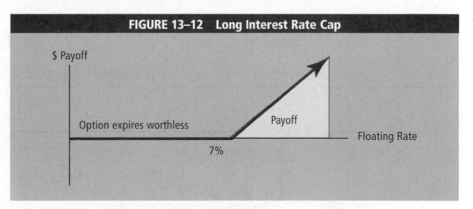

FIGURE 13–12   Long Interest Rate Cap

[12] The cap buyer must pay a premium to acquire the cap, so after accounting for the premium the effective interest rate is somewhat higher than the exercise price.

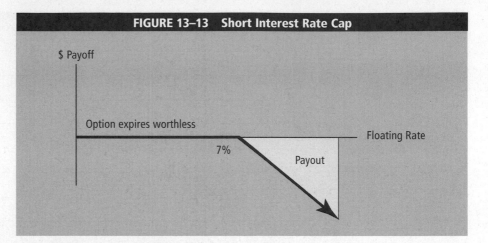

FIGURE 13–13   Short Interest Rate Cap

INTEREST RATE FLOOR

An interest rate floor is a portfolio of European put options on an interest rate.

An interest rate **floor** is related to a cap in the same way that a put is related to a call. A floor is a portfolio of European put options on an interest rate. Each individual put option making up the floor is a **floorlet**.

A bank might have a floating rate mortgage portfolio in which the average mortgage rate is 7.25%. The bank will earn less interest if the mortgage benchmark rate declines. It could protect against this risk by acquiring an interest rate floor in much the same way that a stock investor might purchase a protective put.

Figure 13–14 shows a payoff diagram for an interest rate floor with an exercise price of 6.5%. If the benchmark rate falls below 6.5% the put writer must remit a cash payment to the owner of the floor. Figure 13–15 shows payoffs as the floor writer sees them.

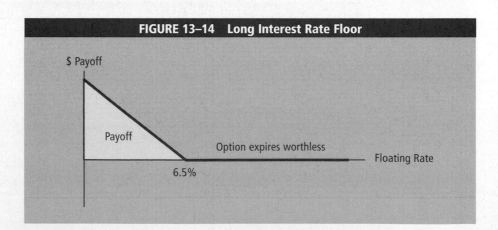

FIGURE 13–14   Long Interest Rate Floor

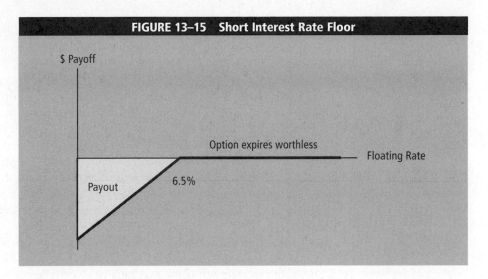

FIGURE 13–15   Short Interest Rate Floor

CALCULATING CAP AND FLOOR PAYOFFS

As with most off-exchange derivatives, the parties involved can set the terms of a cap and floor however they wish. Frequently, however, the terms provide for the cash payment on an in-the-money caplet or floorlet to be based on a 360-day year and the actual number of days in the payment period.

Suppose a $10 million cap has a 7.00% exercise price with the caplets expiring approximately six months apart. At the expiration of the first caplet the benchmark rate is 7.13%, with 182 days in the payment period. When the option is in-the-money, the cap writer's financial obligation comes from Equation 13–4:

$$\text{cap payout} = (\text{notional value}) \times \frac{\text{days in payment period}}{360} \times$$
$$(\text{benchmark rate} - \text{striking price}) \tag{13-4}$$

As with any option, intrinsic value cannot be less than zero, so the payout on the cap is zero if the benchmark rate is less than the exercise price. Substituting,

$$\text{cap payout} = \$10 \text{ million} \times \frac{182}{360} \times (0.0713 - 0.0700) = \$6{,}572.22$$

The formula to calculate the payout on an in-the-money floor is the same except that the intrinsic value of the option is the exercise price minus the benchmark rate:

$$\text{floor payout} = (\text{notional value}) \times \frac{\text{days in payment period}}{360} \times$$
$$(\text{striking price} - \text{benchmark rate}) \tag{13-5}$$

INTEREST RATE COLLAR

Clearly, buying a cap or a floor can provide risk reduction to a financial institution. However, options are *not free;* you must pay the option premium to acquire the protection. As with other options, the premium is the option writer's to keep no matter what happens in the future. Sometimes a firm chooses to reduce this cost by sacrificing some upside potential in exchange for a lower position cost. Recall how a stock investor who wants to buy a call option can lower the position cost by writing another call option at a higher exercise price, thereby constructing a bullspread. Other investors may want to purchase a protective put, and decide to simultaneously write a covered call to help pay for the put. Users of interest rate options are sometimes similarly motivated and elect to construct an interest rate **collar**. This is a position that is simultaneously long an interest rate cap and short an interest rate floor. Figure 13–16 illustrates.

Suppose a firm constructs the collar. Writing the floor will offset part of the cost of the long cap. If the benchmark rate rises above the higher exercise price (K_2), the long cap pays off. If the rate falls below the lower exercise price (K_1), the firm has a cash obligation to the holder of the floor in accordance with Equation 13–5. At each caplet and floorlet expiration date there is no payout to either party if the benchmark rate remains between the two exercise prices.

SWAPTION

A **swaption** is an option on a swap.[14] This market dates back to about 1987. Comprehending the underlying asset is the key to understanding a swaption. When the swaption is on an interest rate swap there are two types. A *payer* swaption gives

---

DERIVATIVES TODAY

LESLIE RAHL

Leslie Rahl, a pioneer in the development of interest rate derivative products, was trading a proprietary options portfolio for Citibank when the bank sold the first cap in 1983. She recalls a business conversation at a cocktail reception:

"It was a sizable and long-term deal even by today's standards. Caps had been around for a couple of months. But the concept of the collar, of a 'floor/ceiling' as it was called at the time, evolved when we learned that some clients didn't want to pay premiums. The collar was a way to eliminate the premium fee or at least to reduce significantly

the upfront cash that needed to change hands. The client said, 'I love the idea of buying a cap, but I don't want to write a cheque. Is there something you can do?'"[13]

Today, of course, we are quite accustomed to the notion of buying one option and writing another to offset the premium cost. As we will see in the next chapter, the notion of a "zero cost collar," where the premium on a written call equals the premium on a long put, is fundamental to pricing a plain vanilla interest rate swap.

[13] "Derivatives Pioneers," *Risk*, December 1997.

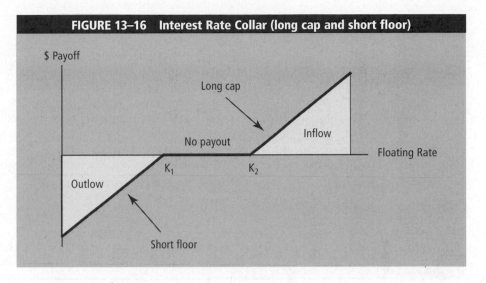

FIGURE 13–16   Interest Rate Collar (long cap and short floor)

$ Payoff

Long cap

No payout

Inflow

Floating Rate

K_1 K_2

Outlow

Short floor

A payer swaption is like an interest rate call; a receiver swaption is like an interest rate put.

its owner the right to pay the fixed interest rate on a swap. A payer swaption is also called a *put* swaption. A *receiver* swaption, also called a *call* swaption, gives its owner the right to receive the fixed rate (and therefore to pay the floating rate). As with other option-like instruments, the swaption can be either American or European exercise style.

Suppose a firm pays a $25,000 premium for a three-year, American style, payer swaption on a five-year plain vanilla interest rate swap, where the swap price is 6.450% (in exchange for LIBOR) and the notional value is $10 million. Two years pass, and the firm owning the swaption decides it makes sense to exercise the swaption and enter into the swap agreement. It is important to note that upon exercise the swap has a tenor of five years, not (5 *minus* 2) because the option is two years old. Upon exercise the swaption disappears and the swap runs its course like any other.

Like a cap, a payer swaption is related to an interest rate call. Thinking back to equity options, if a stock price goes up, it is attractive to buy the stock at a lower exercise price. Similarly, if interest rates (the underlying asset) go up, it becomes attractive to pay a fixed, lower interest rate. In the same way, if stock prices go down, puts become valuable. If interest rates fall, receiver swaptions become valuable and will be exercised before they expire. The swap owner would like to receive a higher-than-market fixed interest rate in exchange for a lower floating rate.

If the owner of the swaption chooses not to exercise, the parties do not enter into a swap agreement, and the swaption expires worthless. In general, one party to a swaption cannot close out the contract with another party in the secondary market because of differences in counterparty risk.

---

[14] You can think of a swaption as an entry or exit option on a swap.

TRADING STRATEGY

SWAPTIONS FOR INCOME

Kirsten Joy has a professional colleague named Jessica who is the CFO of a global travel agency, specializing in exotic trips such as treks in Nepal, rock climbing in Viet Nam, and Amazon River canoe trips. Six months ago she entered into an interest rate swap in which she pays a floating rate in exchange for a fixed rate on a 2.5-year, $2 million swap. She now expects rates to remain relatively constant for the remaining life of the swap.

It occurs to Jessica that she could add a few bucks to the corporate coffers by writing a two-year receiver swaption. Her firm would keep the premium from writing the swaption, and if it were to be exercised it would effectively cancel her existing interest rate swap. Because she anticipates little interest rate movement, this would not be much of an inconvenience.

Jessica decides to write the swaption. She earns the premium and currently keeps her existing swap in place, but wouldn't mind having to remove it.

One corporate use of a swaption is to give a treasurer a convenient way to terminate an existing swap. A firm might have in place an eight-year swap on which it is paying the fixed rate. The firm believes that it may wish to terminate this arrangement in two years. While it could try to negotiate out of the deal with the swap counterparty, a receiver swaption would enable the treasurer to effectively cancel the deal. The firm would be paying fixed (and receiving floating) on the original swap and receiving fixed (and paying floating) on the new swap, for a net position of zero. There is a cost to the swaption, but it facilitates terminating the trade without further negotiation.

SUMMARY

While relatively new, the market for interest rate swaps and for currency swaps is quite large, with an outstanding notional value over $60 trillion. Such a notional value, however, does not mean that this much money is at risk because most swaps involve a net payment via a difference check rather than a loan that must be eventually repaid.

The most common swap is a fixed for floating interest rate swap, often called a plain vanilla swap. The International Swaps and Derivatives Association publishes standardized master agreements that make it convenient to enter into swaps quickly without extensive legal work. The fixed rate on an interest rate swap is called the swap price.

Corporate treasurers find interest rate swaps especially useful for managing interest rate risk and for taking advantage of differences in quality spreads in the fixed versus floating rate markets. While swaps can reduce interest rate risk or foreign currency risk, they introduce counterparty risk because the swap agreement does not come with a guarantee like that provided by the Options Clearing Corporation.

Foreign currency swaps differ from interest rate swaps in that they do involve an exchange of principal at the beginning and the end of the swap term. The swap term is called the swap tenor. Still, if one party defaults and will not return their principal the counterparty is not likely to do so either. The combination of an interest rate swap and a currency swap is a circus swap. These usually result in the firm paying a fixed rate on foreign exchange and receiving a fixed rate in U.S. dollars.

An interest rate cap is much like a portfolio of call options on an interest rate, in which the individual options have sequential expirations. Each component call option within the cap is called a caplet. An interest rate floor is like a portfolio of put options, with each put known as a floorlet. An institution can buy or write caps or floors in the same way that they can use calls and puts. A long cap combined with a short floor is an interest rate collar.

A swaption is an option to enter into an interest rate swap. With a payer swaption, the swaption owner has the right to enter into a swap and pay the fixed rate. In a receiver swap, the owner has the right to enter into a swap and pay the floating rate.

SELF TEST

T ___ F ___   1. The modern swaps market is less than thirty years old.

T ___ F ___   2. A plain vanilla interest rate swap is sometimes called a fixed for floating rate swap.

T ___ F ___   3. The swap buyer pays the floating rate.

T ___ F ___   4. The term "exchange of borrowings" normally refers to a currency swap rather than an interest rate swap.

T ___ F ___   5. The swap *tenor* refers to the fixed interest rate.

T ___ F ___   6. The first payment on an interest rate swap is based on the principal amount, while the last payment is based on the notional amount.

T ___ F ___   7. A bank's duration gap equals the duration of its assets minus the duration of its liabilities.

CHAPTER 13 REVIEW

T ___ F ___ 8. To take advantage of differentials in the credit market, a firm should borrow in the market in which it has an absolute advantage rather than a comparative advantage.

T ___ F ___ 9. A major difference between a currency swap and an interest rate swap is that principal is exchanged in a currency swap while it is not in an interest rate swap.

T ___ F ___ 10. A combined interest rate and currency swap is known as a clown swap.

T ___ F ___ 11. A deferred swap is also called a European swap.

T ___ F ___ 12. An interest rate cap is more similar to a put option than to a call option.

T ___ F ___ 13. An interest rate cap contains one or more caplets and at least one floorlet.

T ___ F ___ 14. A firm that writes a floor will probably have to pay out cash if interest rates decline sharply.

T ___ F ___ 15. A payer swaption gives its owner the right to pay the fixed rate.

T ___ F ___ 16. An interest rate collar is the simultaneous holding of a long cap and a long floor.

T ___ F ___ 17. The swap clearinghouse serves the same purpose as the Option Clearing Corporation with listed options.

PROBLEMS & QUESTIONS

1. Explain the term *swap seller*.
2. For an interest rate swap, explain the difference between the swap *tenor* and the swap *price*.
3. In Figure 13–2, suppose the big bank paid a floating rate of LIBOR minus 20 basis points. What is the net borrowing rate for the two parties?
4. Figure 13–3 shows an interest rate swap with a facilitator. Why do you think the net borrowing rate might be higher for the smaller bank but no different from Figure 13–2 for the big bank?
5. Firm A has two financial agreements with Firm B. One is an interest rate swap with a notional value of $10 million. The other is a commercial loan with a principal value of $10 million. Firm A considers the swap much less risky than the loan. Why is that?
6. Explain why a firm remitting a difference check on an interest rate swap has little counterparty risk.

7. A bank has the balance sheet below.

BANK BALANCE SHEET

ASSETS

CASH	$300 (D = 0.00)
7% LOANS	1,200 (D = 3.47)
8% LOANS	1,400 (D = 8.43)

TOTAL ASSETS $2,900

LIABILITIES AND NET WORTH

3 YEAR FLOATING RATE LOAN @ LIBOR (ANNUAL RESET)	$900	(D = 1.00)
5 YEAR LOAN @ 6%	600	(D = 3.41)
10 YEAR ZERO COUPON	400	(D = 10.00)
TOTAL LIABILITIES	$1,900	
NET WORTH	1,000	
TOTAL LIABILITIES & NET WORTH	$2,900	

a. Determine its duration gap.

b. Will the bank's net worth increase or decrease if the general level of interest rates rises?

8. In Problem 7, show how the bank treasurer could move the duration gap to zero using an interest rate swap.

9. Two firms have the borrowing rates shown below. As the CFO of firm AAA, you always consider an interest rate swap before borrowing money. Explain how, if at all, a swap with BBB could be advantageous to you if
   a. you wanted to borrow at a fixed rate.
   b. you wanted to borrow at a floating rate.

FIRM	FIXED RATE	FLOATING RATE
AAA	5 YR T-BOND + 60 bp	LIBOR
BBB	5 YR T-BOND + 85 bp	LIBOR + 40 bp

10. In Problem 9, explain firm AAA's comparative and absolute advantages in the fixed and floating rate markets relative to firm BBB.

11. State whether you agree or disagree with the following statement, and explain your answer:

   "A currency swap is inherently riskier than an interest rate swap because a currency swap involves the actual exchange of principal amounts while an interest rate swap uses a notional amount that does not change hands."

12. Make up an example showing how the manager of an international fixed income mutual fund might logically use a foreign currency swap.

13. A firm is committed to paying LIBOR + 100 bp on $5 million for the next four years, with payments made quarterly. The firm is considering buying a cap to reduce the risk of an upward jump in interest rates. LIBOR is currently 5.52%. Explain the relative advantages and disadvantages of
   a. a two-year, 6% cap;
   b. a four-year, 5.52% cap;
   c. a four-year, 6.25% cap;
   d. a five-year, 7% cap.

14. In Problem 13, instead of buying a cap, explain the relative advantages and disadvantages of writing a floor.

15. Make up an example showing how a firm might use a swaption to terminate an existing swap.

16. Suppose a financial institution is a currently paying the fixed rate on a four-year swap with three years of payments remaining. How might the firm logically engage in a swaption transaction given that they are already involved in a swap *and have no intention of terminating it?*

CHAPTER 13 REVIEW

14

Swap Pricing

It is not necessary to change. Survival is not mandatory.

W. Edwards Deming

The previous chapter showed how swaps are useful in risk management. The fixed interest rate (e.g., the *swap price* in an interest rate swap) plays a crucial role in determining the merits of a swap arrangement. In this chapter we first get some intuition into the origin of the swap price and then look at an analytical procedure to precisely determine it. Next, we look at ways in which a swap dealer might hedge the swap using Eurodollar futures contracts. Finally, we see how the principles of interest rate swap pricing help in understanding the pricing of currency swaps.

INTUITION INTO SWAP PRICING

In their excellent tutorial[1] on swaps, Keith Brown and Donald Smith propose three ways in which you can view a swap: as a pair of *bond* transactions, as a series

[1] "Interest Rate and Currency Swaps: A Tutorial," The Research Foundation of the Institute of Chartered Financial Analysts, Charlottesville, VA, 1995. This monograph is part of the reading material in the Chartered Financial Analyst program.

TABLE 14–1   Ways to View a Swap
(1) A PAIR OF BOND TRANSACTIONS;
(2) A SERIES OF FORWARD RATE TRANSACTIONS;
(3) A PAIR OF OPTION CONTRACTS.

of *forward rate* transactions, or as a pair of *option* contracts. Let's apply each of these perspectives to a plain vanilla interest rate swap.

SWAPS AS A PAIR OF BONDS

If you buy a bond you *receive* interest. If you issue a bond you *pay* interest. In a plain vanilla interest rate swap, you actually are doing both: you pay a fixed rate and receive floating, or you pay floating and receive fixed. If you both issue and buy a bond, logically you want to receive as much interest as you can and pay as little as you can.

> An interest rate swap is analogous to a portfolio comprised of a purchased bond and an issued bond with a different coupon rate.

A bond with a floating interest rate will normally sell for close to its par value. This is because the cashflows on the bond adjust to market conditions such that the bond's appeal remains relatively constant. Because the floating rate moves with market conditions, the attractiveness of the swap depends on the fixed rate. A bond with a fixed interest rate of 7% will sell at a *premium* if this is above the current market rate or at a *discount* if this is below the prevailing rate.

The implication of this to the swap participant is easy to see. If a firm is involved in a swap and pays a fixed rate of 7% at a time when they would otherwise have to pay 8%, the swap clearly is saving them money and therefore has value. On the other hand, if because of the swap you are obliged to pay more than the current rate, the swap is beneficial to the other party, but not to you.

SWAPS AS A SERIES OF FORWARD CONTRACTS

As we have seen, a forward contract is an agreement to exchange assets at a particular date in the future, with no marking-to-market along the way. In an interest rate swap, there are known payment dates evenly spaced throughout the tenor of the swap. On each of those dates one party pays the fixed rate and receives the current floating rate, with the counterparty doing just the opposite.

> An interest rate swap is analogous to a series of forward transactions.

A swap with a single payment date six months hence is no different than an ordinary six-month forward contract. At that payment date, the party owing the greater amount remits a difference check to the other party and the contract ends. A one-year swap with semi-annual payments is just a package of two forward contracts, one with a six-month maturity and another with a twelve-month maturity. Cash changes hands at each maturity depending on the behavior of the floating rate. The same logic holds regardless of the swap tenor.

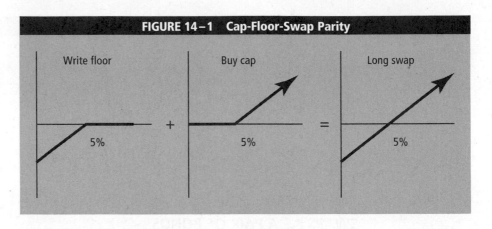

FIGURE 14–1   Cap-Floor-Swap Parity

SWAPS AS A PAIR OF OPTION CONTRACTS

For a student of the derivative markets seeking to understand swap pricing, viewing a swap as a pair of option contracts is an especially interesting way to look at the arrangement.

Suppose a firm buys a cap and writes a floor, both with a 5% striking price and identical payment dates. At the next payment date (i.e., the expiration of the next caplet and floorlet) the firm will receive a check if the benchmark rate is *above* 5% because of the long cap. They will have to remit a check because of the short floor if the benchmark rate is *below* 5%. If the benchmark rate is exactly 5% both options expire at-the-money and there is no payout on either one.

An interest rate swap is analogous to a zero cost collar in which you buy a cap and write a floor.

The cash flows associated with these two options are identical to the cash flows associated with a 5% fixed rate swap. Think of the swap fixed rate as the option striking price. If the floating rate is above the swap "striking price" the cap is in-the-money and the party paying the fixed rate receives a check. If the floating rate is below the fixed rate, the fixed rate payer must remit a check to the other party. In simple terms and from the perspective of the fixed rate payer, if interest rates rise above a certain level, we receive a payoff. If, instead, they are below the magic number, we must pay someone else. This relationship is called **cap-floor-swap parity** and appears in Figure 14–1.

SOLVING FOR THE SWAP PRICE

The swaps material we have looked at make it clear that the fixed interest rate is a very important number in the analysis of an interest rate swap. As we are about to see, the market uses a logical procedure to solve for this value. The swap price is not an arbitrary value determined by someone behind a desk. Rather, it comes from fundamental arbitrage arguments with all swap dealers in close agreement on what this rate should be.

SWAPPING TO AVOID PREPAYMENT PENALTIES

Unlike individuals, corporate borrowers usually face penalties and/or fees if they choose to repay a loan ahead of schedule. When the general level of market interest rates falls, however, the corporation has the same incentive as anyone else to refinance at a lower interest rate. The presence of the refinancing fees may make refinancing uneconomic, however.

In a climate with interest rates at historically low levels, a corporate borrower that currently is paying on a floating rate loan may well find that there are interest savings associated with a "floating for fixed" interest rate swap. Engaging in the swap effectively converts the floating rate obligation to a fixed rate obligation that is locked in for the duration of the swap. This reduces the volatility of the stream of interest payment obligations. It also takes advantage of the currently low level of interest rates. Also, the swap amounts to refinancing of the floating rate loan without the need to pay refinancing fees.

THE ROLE OF THE FORWARD CURVE FOR LIBOR

Earlier, we saw that there is a term structure to interest rates; the borrowing rate differs according to the life of the loan. The same is true for LIBOR; the interest rate depends on when you want to begin the loan and how long it will last.

There is a useful notation associated with forward rate agreements that will be helpful in this discussion. If we borrow at LIBOR today for three months this is called "spot" LIBOR. We might also enter into an agreement to borrow *for* three months *in* three months. This is called a 3×6 Forward Rate Agreement (FRA) with the associated interest rate shown as $_3f_6$. A 6×12 FRA is a forward contract to enter into a six-month loan six months from today. In other words, the loan begins at month 6 and lasts until month 12 with the associated interest rate $_6f_{12}$. A 3×9 FRA is a six-month contract that begins in three months, and so on. Suppose that we have the LIBOR interest rate information shown in Table 14–2 and Figure 14–2. The table shows an upward sloping yield curve for loan terms of 3, 6, 9, and 12 months.

TABLE 14–2 LIBOR	
SPOT ($_0f_3$)	5.42%
SIX MONTH ($_0f_6$)	5.50%
NINE MONTH ($_0f_9$)	5.57%
TWELVE MONTH ($_0f_{12}$)	5.62%

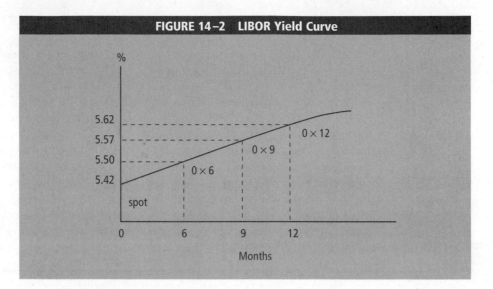

FIGURE 14–2   LIBOR Yield Curve

IMPLIED FORWARD RATES

There is other information contained within Table 14–2. This is the set of values known as **implied forward rates**. From these data we can determine the three-month rate that the market anticipates will prevail in three months ($_3f_6$), six months ($_6f_9$), and nine months ($_9f_{12}$). We use a process known as **bootstrapping** to solve for these values.[2]

The logic of bootstrapping is simple. Today, an investor could invest in six month LIBOR and earn 5.50% according to Table 14–2. Alternatively, the investor could invest in spot, three-month LIBOR at 5.42% and, upon maturity of this deposit, re-invest for another three months. If either of these choices were clearly preferable to the other the interest rate associated with the lesser choice would have to rise until it provided a comparable return. If the market expects both choices to provide the same return (as it does if neither is preferable to the other), then we can solve for the implied forward rate[3] on the 3 × 6 FRA using equation 14–1[4]:

$$\left(1+\frac{_0f_3}{4}\right)\left(1+\frac{_3f_6}{4}\right)=\left(1+\frac{_0f_6}{4}\right)^2 \tag{14-1}$$

---

[2] This is the same procedure used to solve for forward rates with any other base interest rate.

[3] In this section the examples all are based on quarterly compounding of LIBOR.

[4] The right side of this equation could also be written as

$$\left(1+\frac{_0f_6}{2}\right).$$

This notation reflects half the annual rate as opposed to the quarterly rate squared.

The rates quoted in Table 14–2 are annual rates. In this initial example we will assume that each three-month period has an equal number of days,[5] so each of the annual rates gets divided by four to show them as quarterly (three-month) rates. The term on the right hand side of the equation is squared because there are two three-month periods associated with the six-month rate of 5.50% per year. Plugging in the values we know,

$$\left(1+\frac{0.0542}{4}\right)\left(1+\frac{_3f_6}{4}\right)=\left(1+\frac{0.0550}{4}\right)^2$$

Solving, we find the 3×6 implied FRA rate is 5.58%.

We can use the same procedure to find the implied 6×9 FRA:

$$\left(1+\frac{_0f_6}{4}\right)^2\left(1+\frac{_6f_9}{4}\right)=\left(1+\frac{_0f_9}{4}\right)^3$$

$$\left(1+\frac{0.0550}{4}\right)^2\left(1+\frac{_6f_9}{4}\right)=\left(1+\frac{0.0557}{4}\right)^3$$

The term on the right side has the exponent "3" because there are three quarters in nine months. Solving, the 6×9 FRA rate is 5.71%. Finally, we can get the 9×12 FRA:

$$\left(1+\frac{_0f_9}{4}\right)^3\left(1+\frac{_9f_{12}}{4}\right)=\left(1+\frac{_0f_{12}}{4}\right)^4$$

$$\left(1+\frac{0.0557}{4}\right)^3\left(1+\frac{_9f_{12}}{4}\right)=\left(1+\frac{0.0562}{4}\right)^4$$

The 9×12 FRA rate is 5.77%. The same procedure can be used to find the implied forward rate at any point on the yield curve. Table 14–3 and Figure 14–3 show the implied forward rates just determined.

TABLE 14–3 Implied Forward LIBOR Rates	
TERM	IMPLIED RATE
3×6	5.58%
6×9	5.71%
9×12	5.77%

[5] In determining the difference payment, swaps commonly use the actual number of days in a payment period relative to a 360-day year, as we will see.

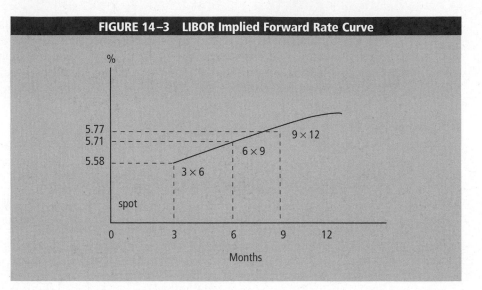

FIGURE 14–3   LIBOR Implied Forward Rate Curve

INITIAL CONDITION PRICING

At the origination of a swap, we know the cash flows that are associated with the fixed rate payments, but we do not know the cash flows stemming from the floating rate payments because they are a function of an unobservable future rate. The initial terms of an interest rate swap are usually such that they are priced *at-the-market*. An **at-the-market swap** is one in which the swap price is set such that the present value of the floating rate side of the swap equals the present value of the fixed rate side.

An at-the-market swap is one in which the swap price is set such that the present value of the floating rate side of the swap equals the present value of the fixed rate side.

A logical question is "How do we know the present value of the floating rate side if we do not know the future cash flows?" The answer is that the market uses its best estimate of the future cash flows, and this comes from the spot rate yield curve and the implied forward rate curve. There will be one single interest rate that will cause the fixed rate side of the swap to have a present value equal to the floating rate side of the swap.

Suppose we have a one-year, quarterly payment swap based on actual days in the quarter and a 360-day year on both the fixed and floating sides. Going to the calendar, we find 91, 90, 92, and 92 days in the next four quarters. Figure 14-3 shows the forward LIBOR curve. The notional principal of the swap is irrelevant in the calculation of the swap price because it is merely a dollar multiplier; it does not influence the interest rate itself. Let's assume the notional principal is $1. We convert future values into present values by discounting at the appropriate zero coupon rate contained in the forward rate curve.

Table 14-2 shows that the three-month spot rate is 5.42%. There are 91 days until the first swap payment, so the discount factor associated with the first swap payment (three months from now) is

$$1 + R_3 = 1 + \left(\frac{91}{360} \times 0.0542 \right) = 1.013701$$

The second payment occurs further in the future (six months from now), so it should be more heavily discounted. The second discount factor comes from this equation, where 5.50% is the six-month spot rate:

$$1 + R_6 = 1 + \left(\frac{91 + 90}{360} \times 0.0550 \right) = 1.027653$$

We get the last two discount factors in similar fashion.

$$1 + R_9 = 1 + \left(\frac{91 + 90 + 92}{360} \times 0.0557 \right) = 1.042239$$

$$1 + R_{12} = 1 + \left(\frac{91 + 90 + 92 + 92}{360} \times 0.0562 \right) = 1.056981$$

We can now apply these discount factors to both the fixed and floating rate sides of the swap to solve for the swap fixed rate that will make the value of the two sides equal.

In this example, the present value of the floating rate side is

$$PV_{floating} = \frac{5.42\% \times \dfrac{91}{360}}{1.013701} + \frac{5.58\% \times \dfrac{90}{360}}{1.027653} + \frac{5.71\% \times \dfrac{92}{360}}{1.042239} + \frac{5.77\% \times \dfrac{92}{360}}{1.056981}$$

$$= 0.013515 + 0.013575 + 0.014001 + 0.013951$$

$$= \mathbf{0.055042}$$

The expression to find the present value of the fixed rate side is similar except that we have a single unknown interest rate in the numerator of the expression.

$$PV_{fixed} = \frac{X\% \times \dfrac{91}{360}}{1.013701} + \frac{X\% \times \dfrac{90}{360}}{1.027653} + \frac{X\% \times \dfrac{92}{360}}{1.042239} + \frac{X\% \times \dfrac{92}{360}}{1.056981}$$

$$= 0.249361X + 0.243273X + 0.245199X + 0.241779X$$

$$= \mathbf{0.979612X}$$

Setting these two expressions for present value equal, we have one equation and one unknown, leaving an algebraic exercise to find the equilibrium fixed rate X. We find $X = \mathbf{5.62\%}$. This is the equilibrium swap fixed rate, or swap price.[6]

You can think of the swap fixed rate in the same way that you think of a bond's yield to maturity. The marketplace values a bond by discounting each of

---

[6] More precisely, the rate is 5.6188%. We normally express rates to the nearest basis point, but as we will see in a forthcoming example, the rounding causes slight differences in subsequent calculations.

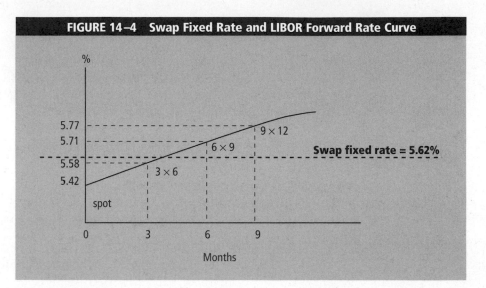

FIGURE 14–4   Swap Fixed Rate and LIBOR Forward Rate Curve

the bond's future cash flows at the corresponding spot rate. The sum of these present values is the bond price. Once you have the bond price, you can find the one *single* interest rate that *also* makes the present value of the future cash flows equal to the bond's market price. This interest rate is the yield to maturity. In some respects the yield to maturity is like an "average" of the spot rates over the bond's life. Stated another way, the swap price is the weighted average of the forward rates discounted by when they occur in the future. (See Figure 14–4.)

The swap price is to forward rates as a bond's yield to maturity is to spot rates.

Similarly, swap dealers price a swap based on the forward rate curve over the life of the swap. Once again, the swap price is the single interest rate over all the various forward rate terms that causes the valuation equation to hold.

QUOTING THE SWAP PRICE

The previous discussion showed the importance of the forward rate curve in determining the swap price. Interest rates change continuously in the market place, and as a consequence so do the associated forward rates. Because of the dynamic nature of interest rates it is common practice to quote the swap price relative to the U.S. Treasury yield curve, and to use the yield on the most recently issued, or *on-the-run*, Treasury security with a maturity matching the tenor of the swap. For instance, we would quote a five-year swap relative to the yield on a new five-year U.S. Treasury note.

As with most other financial instruments, at any given time there is both a *bid* and an *ask* associated with the swap price. The dealer adds a **swap spread** to the appropriate Treasury yield.[7] This increment compensates the dealer for ser-

---

[7] Remember that the swap price is analogous to a bond's yield to maturity. The dealer adds a "static spread" across the term structure to arrive at the swap price.

vice in providing the swap and potentially for assuming some counterparty risk. A dealer might currently quote a five-year plain vanilla interest rate swap as 26 bp bid, 28 bp ask. If the prevailing five-year treasury yield is 5.95%, this translates into 6.21% bid, 6.23% ask. A firm that wants to *pay* the fixed rate would be quoted a fixed rate of 6.23%. A firm that wants to pay the floating rate and *receive* a fixed rate would be quoted the lower rate of 6.21%. The two basis point differential is the dealer's gross profit. The swap spread tends to be larger the longer the tenor of the swap.

COUNTERPARTY RISK IMPLICATIONS

The relationship between the yield curve and the swap price has important implications for the assessment of counterparty risk. Consider the term structure in Figure 14–5. As interest rates currently stand, in the front part of the swap the fixed rate exceeds the forward LIBOR, or floating, rate. After a certain period, the market expects the floating rate to move ahead of the fixed rate. If you are the party paying the floating rate, it is highly unlikely that you would choose to default on the swap in its early stages because you will be receiving a difference check. If you default, you won't receive anything. From the perspective of the party paying the fixed rate, this means there is little counterparty risk in the front "half" of an interest rate swap when the yield curve is upward sloping. The counterparty risk appears in the latter part of the swap's life.

   Just the opposite is true when you pay the floating rate. The counterparty risk is in the front half of the swap because the other party must initially remit a difference check. Once the cash flow changes direction, however, there is little counterparty risk (arguably none at all because default would in some respects be advantageous to you).

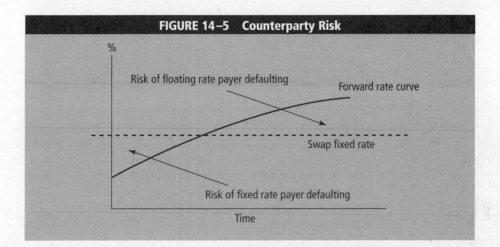

FIGURE 14–5   Counterparty Risk

VALUING AN OFF-MARKET SWAP

We have seen that most swaps have a fixed rate, or swap price, such that the swap has no initial value. If interest rates subsequently change, as they almost certainly will, one side or the other of the swap becomes an asset. The **swap value** reflects the difference between the swap price and the interest rate that would make the swap have zero value. In other words, at the time the two parties enter into the swap, it has no "balance sheet" value to either of them. As soon as market interest rates change, however, one of the two parties is glad they entered into the swap. An **off-market swap** is one in which the fixed rate is such that the fixed rate and floating rate sides of the swap do not have equal value, and therefore the swap *does* have value to one of the counterparties.

In our example we found an equilibrium swap price of 5.62%. At this rate the present value of the floating rate side equals the present value of the fixed rate side. If we assume a notional principal of $1.00,

$$PV_{floating} = \frac{5.42\% \times \dfrac{91}{360}}{1.013701} + \frac{5.58\% \times \dfrac{90}{360}}{1.027653} + \frac{5.71\% \times \dfrac{92}{360}}{1.042239} + \frac{5.77\% \times \dfrac{92}{360}}{1.056981}$$

$$= 0.013515 + 0.013575 + 0.014001 + 0.013951$$

$$= \mathbf{0.055042}$$

$$PV_{fixed} = \frac{0.0562 \times \dfrac{91}{360}}{1.013701} + \frac{0.0562 \times \dfrac{90}{360}}{1.027653} + \frac{0.0562 \times \dfrac{92}{360}}{1.042239} + \frac{0.0562 \times \dfrac{92}{360}}{1.056981}$$

$$= 0.014014 + 0.013648 + 0.013780 + 0.013588$$

$$= \mathbf{0.055030}$$

Rounding causes the values to differ slightly, but they are equal to the fourth decimal place. Suppose that instead of having a 5.62% swap price the rate were 5.75%. The value of the floating rate side will not change, but the value of the fixed rate side will. Doing the numbers with the new rate,

$$PV_{fixed} = \frac{0.0575 \times \dfrac{91}{360}}{1.013701} + \frac{0.0575 \times \dfrac{90}{360}}{1.027653} + \frac{0.0575 \times \dfrac{92}{360}}{1.042239} + \frac{0.0575 \times \dfrac{92}{360}}{1.056981}$$

$$= 0.014338 + 0.013988 + 0.014099 + 0.013902$$

$$= \mathbf{0.056327}$$

On a $1 notional principal swap, the value of the fixed rate side changed from 0.0550 to 0.0563. On $10 million notional principal, this amounts to (.056327 − .055030)($10 million) = $12,970. From the perspective of the floating rate payer, the swap value is $12,970. The floating rate payer is receiving a 5.75% fixed rate when the equilibrium fixed rate is only 5.62%. This is clearly a good situation for the fixed rate receiver.

HEDGING THE SWAP

As we saw above, the swap dealer charges a differential on the swap price depending on whether a firm pays or receives the fixed rate. While the differential is revenue to the swap dealer, it is relatively small compared to the interest rate risk the dealer might be taking. If the swap dealer's counterparties are about evenly split between wanting to pay fixed and wanting to pay floating, then the dealer's risk is modest. If, however, the demand is predominately in one direction, such as everyone wanting to pay the fixed rate, then the dealer stands to suffer a considerable loss if interest rates move sharply. To deal with an unacceptably high level of this risk, the dealer may choose to hedge the risk, or "lay it off," in the Eurodollar futures market.

Suppose a customer approaches a swap dealer and wants to enter into a one-year, $10 million swap with quarterly payments on which the customer pays the fixed rate. The dealer agrees to be the counterparty. In so doing, the dealer will receive a fixed rate and pay a floating rate at each quarterly settlement.

In this example the risk to the dealer is that rates rise. The dealer would be receiving a below-market fixed rate. The best way to hedge the swap would be to find another firm that wanted to do precisely the opposite: pay floating and receive fixed on the same notional principal for the same time period. The dealer could be the counterparty for both swaps. The cash flow streams on the two swaps would service each other, with the dealer earning a spread on the fixed rate differential. The dealer would retain counterparty risk, but the interest rate risk would be gone. A perfect situation like this seldom appears, however.

More commonly the dealer will need to hedge in another fashion. Because an interest rate swap is equivalent to a series of LIBOR-based forward rate transactions, the dealer can use Eurodollar futures (also based on LIBOR) to hedge the interest rate risk. Because the dealer's risk is that swap fixed rates rise, the dealer will sell futures. Rising rates cause them to fall in value (to the benefit of the seller), thereby offsetting the below-market fixed rate associated with the floating rate payment on the swap. Figuring out the quantity and maturity of the futures is a bit of a mathematical exercise, but the logic behind the procedure is relatively straightforward.

> A swap dealer can use Eurodollar futures to hedge an interest rate swap obligation.

The first step is to remember the fundamental rule that with an at-the-market swap, the fixed rate is set such that the present value of the fixed rate side equals the present value of the floating rate side. This means the present value of the fixed rate side minus the present value of the floating rate side equals zero. In a fashion similar to that which we saw earlier in hedging with interest rate futures, the key is to relate the basis point values of the swap to the fact that a one basis point change in the yield of a Eurodollar futures contract equals $25 as we saw in Chapter 11.

There are two forms of swap hedging one might use. One method assumes any change in interest rates will be a parallel shift. The other, more accurate method, considers changes in the swap value for a change in interest rates at each point on the relevant yield curve. Let's look at an example of swap hedging using each method.

HEDGING AGAINST A PARALLEL SHIFT IN THE YIELD CURVE

We previously saw that you can view a swap as a pair of bond transactions. Equivalently, you can think of the swap as having two parts. To hedge a swap against a parallel shift in the yield curve, the first step is to see how the value of each part of the swap changes if interest rates change by one basis point.

Think of the fixed rate side of the swap in our example as a 5.62% coupon bond selling for par with four quarterly payments. Because it sells for par, its yield to maturity equals its coupon rate. Now let the yield to maturity increase by one basis point. We find that the bond price changes by –0.0097%:

$$\text{New bond price} = \frac{1.405}{\left(1+\frac{.0563}{4}\right)} + \frac{1.405}{\left(1+\frac{.0563}{4}\right)^2} + \frac{1.405}{\left(1+\frac{.0563}{4}\right)^3} + \frac{101.405}{\left(1+\frac{.0563}{4}\right)^4}$$

$$= 99.9903\%$$

On $10 million notional value, this is a change of –$970.

Payments on the floating rate side are usually determined in advance and paid in arrears. This means the next payment is "fixed" while future cash flows will adjust to any change in interest rates. Consequently, on every payment date the floating rate side is worth par. If interest rates change just after a payment date, the value of a floating rate note, as a percentage of par, is shown in Equation 14–2.

$$PV_{floating} = \frac{1+\dfrac{\text{prior rate}}{\text{\# periods per year}}}{1+\dfrac{\text{new rate}}{\text{\# periods per year}}} \tag{14-2}$$

In this example,

$$PV_{floating} = \frac{1+\dfrac{5.62\%}{4}}{1+\dfrac{5.63\%}{4}} = 99.9975\%$$

This is a change of 0.0025%, or $250 on $10 million notional principal. A change in interest rates affects each side of the swap in the opposite direction, so one side of the swap increases in value because of the increase in rates and the other side decreases in value. In this example, the net change in the swap value is $970 – $250 = $720. A rise in interest rates hurts the floating rate payer. To hedge this risk, the swap dealer, who is paying the floating rate, wants to short Eurodollar futures to offset the loss. In an earlier chapter we saw that a one basis point change in yield translates into a $25 change in value of a Eurodollar futures contract. Therefore, hedging this $10 million swap requires $720 divided by $25, or 28.8 ED futures contracts. Fractional contracts are not available, so the swap dealer would likely sell **29** Eurodollar futures contracts.

There is still another decision to make, however. As Table 14–4 shows, there are a variety of ED futures from which to choose. Which Eurodollar futures should we select? There are two widely used techniques for putting the hedge in place. With a **stack hedge**, the hedger places all the futures contracts at a single point on the yield curve, usually selecting a futures contract with a nearby delivery date because of the exceptionally good liquidity with near-term contracts. In the current example, the hedger might choose to sell 29 three-month ED futures. Remember that the swap dealer in this example will be paying the floating rate. By shorting ED futures, the dealer will effectively be receiving the floating rate from the futures market, and it can then be "passed on" to the counterparty with no interest rate risk to the hedger.

With a **strip hedge**, the hedger distributes the futures contracts along the relevant portion of the yield curve depending on the tenor of the swap. Here, the dealer might sell 9 or 10 contracts each for delivery in 6, 9, and 12 months. These contracts would comprise a **Eurodollar strip**. Both the stack hedge and the strip hedge work equally well if the yield curve shifts in parallel fashion.

HEDGING AGAINST ANY SHIFT IN THE YIELD CURVE

The yield curve seldom undergoes a parallel shift. To hedge the swap against *any* change in the yield curve we need to see how its value changes with changes at

TABLE 14–4 Eurodollar Futures								
20 FEBRUARY 2001								
MATURITY	OPEN	HIGH	LOW	SETTLE	CHANGE	YIELD	CHANGE	OPEN INTEREST
JUN 01	95.01	95.05	94.99	95.04	+.01	4.96	−.01	567,620
SEP 01	95.02	95.08	95.01	95.07	+.02	4.93	−.02	606,243
DEC 01	94.83	94.89	94.82	94.88	+.02	5.12	−.02	330,996
MAR 02	94.77	94.83	94.76	94.82	+.02	5.18	−.02	297,270
JUN 02	94.61	94.67	94.60	94.66	+.02	5.34	−.02	250,291
SEP 02	94.48	94.53	94.47	94.52	+.01	5.48	−.01	239,396
DEC 02	94.31	94.36	94.30	94.35	+.01	5.65	−.01	157,462
MAR 03	94.29	94.33	94.28	94.33	+.01	5.67	−.01	110,303
JUN 03	94.22	94.26	94.21	94.26	+.01	5.75	−.01	91,795
SEP 03	94.15	94.19	94.15	94.19	+.01	5.81	−.01	90,262
DEC 03	94.03	94.07	94.03	94.07	+.01	5.93	−.01	73,719

Source: Wall Street Journal.

each point along the yield curve. We want to let each spot rate vary by one basis point, determine the new value for the swap, and translate the value change into an equivalent number of ED futures contracts. The precise procedure for doing this can get rather technical, but there is a heuristic that works quite well in most circumstances.

Using the values from the earlier example and assuming a notional principal of $1, we have these two expressions for the present values of the floating and fixed rate sides of the swap:

$$PV_{floating} = \frac{5.42\% \times \dfrac{91}{360}}{1.013701} + \frac{5.58\% \times \dfrac{90}{360}}{1.027653} + \frac{5.71\% \times \dfrac{92}{360}}{1.042239} + \frac{5.77\% \times \dfrac{92}{360}}{1.056981}$$

$$= 0.013515 + 0.013575 + 0.014001 + 0.013951$$

$$= \mathbf{0.055042}$$

$$PV_{fixed} = \frac{0.0562 \times \dfrac{91}{360}}{1.013701} + \frac{0.0562 \times \dfrac{90}{360}}{1.027653} + \frac{0.0562 \times \dfrac{92}{360}}{1.042239} + \frac{0.0562 \times \dfrac{92}{360}}{1.056981}$$

$$= 0.014014 + 0.013648 + 0.013780 + 0.013588$$

$$= \mathbf{0.055030}$$

Again, rounding causes a slight difference, but the values are equal to the fourth decimal. As we determined previously, the 5.62% fixed rate causes the swap to have zero value because the present value of the cash inflows are exactly equal to the present value of the cash outflows.

The steps are as follows. First, determine LIBOR for the tenor of the swap, such as two-year LIBOR for a two-year swap. Use Equation 14–3 to convert the annual rate into effective rates using compounding periods equal to the payment intervals of the swap.

$$Z_T = \left[\left(1 + \frac{R}{N} \right)^T - 1 \right] \times \frac{N}{T} \qquad (14\text{-}3)$$

where Z_T = effective interest rate for payment T
   R = LIBOR over the tenor of the swap
   N = number of swap payments per year
   T = payment number

Once you have these rates, use Equation 14–4 to find the number of futures needed at each payment date.

$$F_T = \frac{\text{swap notional principal}}{1 + \left(Z_T \times \dfrac{T}{N} \right)} \frac{\$1,000,000}{} \qquad (14\text{-}4)$$

Let's figure out how to build a strip hedge on the $10 million swap in this example. From Table 14–2 we see that one year LIBOR is 5.62%. Using equation 14–3 to determine the effective interest rates corresponding to 6, 9, and 12 months from now, we have

$$\text{Payment in 6 months: } Z_2 = \left[\left(1 + \frac{0.0562}{4} \right)^2 - 1 \right] \times \frac{4}{2} = 5.66\%$$

$$\text{Payment in 9 months: } Z_3 = \left[\left(1 + \frac{0.0562}{4} \right)^3 - 1 \right] \times \frac{4}{3} = 5.70\%$$

$$\text{Payment in 12 months: } Z_4 = \left[\left(1 + \frac{0.0562}{4} \right)^4 - 1 \right] \times \frac{4}{4} = 5.74\%$$

Now we use these values and Equation 14–4 to solve for the number of futures contracts we need at each payment date.

$$F_2 = \frac{\dfrac{\$10 \text{ million}}{\$1,000,000}}{1 + (0.0566 \times \frac{2}{4})} = 9.72 \quad F_3 = \frac{\dfrac{\$10 \text{ million}}{\$1,000,000}}{1 + (0.0570 \times \frac{3}{4})} = 9.59 \quad F_4 = \frac{\dfrac{\$10 \text{ million}}{\$1,000,000}}{1 + (0.0574 \times \frac{4}{4})} = 9.46$$

This analysis suggests that we buy 10 futures for delivery in six months, 10 futures for delivery in nine months, and 9 futures for delivery in one year. Note that we have a total of 29 contracts just like we did using the stack hedge.

TAILING THE HEDGE

Unfortunately, there is a further complication that arises with the hedging of a large or long-tenor swap. This stems from the fact that futures contracts are marked to market daily, while forward contracts are not. You have to wait until the end of a forward contract's life to receive its outcome, whether it is good or bad. With a futures contract, cash flows move into and out of the account on a daily basis.

This introduces a time value of money differential. If we ignore it, we will overhedge by using the equations shown above. The way to deal with the situation, however, is easy. We simply reduce the size of the hedge by the appropriate time value of money adjustment. This is called **tailing the hedge**. For instance, if we determine that we need 100 ED futures contracts for delivery two years from now and the two-year interest rate is 6%, to tail the hedge we would reduce the number of contracts to $100/(1.06)^2 = 89$.

$$\text{Hedge}_{\text{tailed}} = \frac{\text{Hedge}_{\text{untailed}}}{(1+R)^T} \qquad (14\text{-}5)$$

In the example just completed, before rounding we found a need for 9.72, 9.59, and 9.46 contracts six, nine, and twelve months out, respectively. Tailing these, the figures adjust to

$$\frac{9.72}{\left(1+0.0550\right)^{.5}}=9.46 \quad \frac{9.59}{\left(1+0.0557\right)^{.75}}=9.21 \quad \frac{9.46}{\left(1+0.0562\right)^{1}}=8.96$$

Including the tailing adjustment, the swap dealer needs only 9 futures contracts at each payment date (a total of 27 rather than 29) to properly hedge the swap. Tailing is especially important with large swaps, in which the dollar value necessarily involves a large number of futures, and with long tenor swaps, in which the time value of money adjustment makes a significant difference.

PRICING A CURRENCY SWAP

Knowing how to price an interest rate swap is helpful in understanding how the market prices a foreign currency swap. For the sake of simplicity assume that two firms, one U.S. and one British, are able to borrow in the floating rate market at their respective LIBOR rates or at the fixed rates shown in Table 14–5.

Suppose we want to determine the relevant interest rates on a two-year dollars for sterling swap with annual payments. The first step in valuing the currency swap is to solve for the equilibrium fixed rate on a plain vanilla interest rate swap in *each* of the two countries. We do this in the same fashion as previously. We need to find the implied forward rates, and to do this we first need to determine the relevant spot rates over the tenor of the swap.

Looking at the U.S. rates, we know the one-year spot rate: 5%. To get the two-year spot rate, we solve the equation below.

$$100=\frac{6}{1.05}+\frac{106}{\left(1+R\right)^2}$$

This equation applies to a two-year, 6% annual coupon bond selling for par (which means its yield to maturity equals the two-year rate of 6%). The two-year

TABLE 14–5 Fixed Borrowing Rates		
	US	**BRITAIN**
1 YEAR	5%	4.50%
2 YEARS	6%	5%

spot rate is the only unknown, and we find it to be 6.03%. We can quickly find the US implied forward rate $_1f_2$ from this equation:

$$(1.05)(1+_1f_2) = (1.0603)^2$$

We find the implied forward rate is 7.07%.

To find the British two-year spot rate, we can look at a two-year, 5% annual coupon bond, also selling for par. The valuation equation is

$$100 = \frac{5}{1.045} + \frac{105}{(1+R)^2}$$

We find the British two-year spot rate is 5.01%. We get the implied forward rate $_1f_2$ in similar fashion, $(1.045)(1 + _1f_2)^2 = (1.0501)^2$, and find it to be 5.52%:

With the forward rates in hand, we now find the equilibrium swap price for a two-year interest rate swap in both the United States and in Britain. As we saw earlier, this involves setting the present value of the floating rate side equal to the present value of the fixed rate side and finding the fixed rate that makes the equation hold. In the U.S. market,

$$\frac{0.0500}{1.0500} + \frac{0.0707}{(1.0603)^2} = \frac{X}{(1.0500)} + \frac{X}{(1.0603)^2}$$

and the fixed rate X is 6.00%. In the British market,

$$\frac{0.0450}{1.0450} + \frac{0.0552}{(1.0501)^2} = \frac{X}{(1.0450)} + \frac{X}{(1.0501)^2}$$

and the fixed rate is 5.00%.

Note that the swap fixed rate in each country is exactly equal to the two-year borrowing rate that each firm faces. This is a necessary result, because in the absence of arbitrage the borrowing rates, the spot rate curve, and the implied forward rates form an interrelated interest rate complex. If you know two sets of rates you can solve for the third.

The way to interpret these results is simple. The floating side of the currency swap will be the appropriate LIBOR. The fixed rate side will be the equilibrium interest rate swap fixed rate. For instance, if the U.S. firm wanted to receive a floating rate in British pounds and pay a fixed rate in U.S. dollars, the equilibrium swap would have them receiving £ LIBOR and paying 6.00% U.S. If, instead, the firm wanted to receive a fixed British rate, the terms would be $ LIBOR, 5.00% sterling. Two other possibilities, while uncommon, would be for the firms to exchange $ LIBOR and £ LIBOR, or for them to exchange 5.00% in sterling and 6.00% in dollars.

SUMMARY

The swap price plays a crucial role in determining the merits of a swap arrangement. You can view an interest rate swap in one of three ways: as a pair of bonds, as a series of forward rate transactions, or as a pair of option contracts. The fact that a long swap (where you pay the fixed rate) is equivalent to a zero cost collar (long cap and short floor) gives rise to the notion of cap/floor/swap parity.

To solve for the equilibrium swap price we must know periodic interest rates, the associated spot rates, and the implied forward rates. The bootstrapping technique helps us find the implied forward rates. Given the implied forward rates, the swap price is the swap fixed rate that makes the present value of the fixed rate side of the swap equal to the present value of the floating rate side. Once we solve for the swap fixed rate, you can think of this value relative to the forward rates in the same way you think of a bond's yield to maturity relative to the spot rate curve.

When the yield curve is upward sloping, from the perspective of the party paying the fixed rate there is little counterparty risk in the front part of the swap. The floating rate payer has little counterparty risk in the latter part of the swap. This is because the party receiving a difference check is unlikely to default.

A swap dealer can effectively hedge a swap using Eurodollar futures contracts. A stack hedge, in which the futures have a common delivery date, can be used to hedge against a parallel shift in the yield curve. A strip hedge, with multiple delivery dates, can be used to hedge against any change in the yield curve. Because a futures contract involves marking to market while a forward contract does not, it is necessary to tail the hedge to account for the time value of money differential associated with having to wait for the forward contract settlement.

To value a currency hedge we must first find the equilibrium fixed rate for the corresponding interest rate swaps in the two countries involved. Having done this, the equilibrium fixed rate for the interest rate swap becomes the equilibrium fixed rate on the currency swap when the other party pays their respective LIBOR rate.

SELF TEST

T ___ F ___ 1. An interest rate swap is like a position that is both long a cap and long a floor.

T ___ F ___ 2. An interest rate swap is similar to a series of forward rate transactions.

T ___ F ___ 3. The swap price is identical to the swap fixed rate.

T ___ F ___ 4. The equilibrium swap price will increase if the yield curve shifts downward.

T ___ F ___ 5. A 3×6 forward rate agreement is a six-month deposit that begins in three months.

T ___ F ___ 6. Bootstrapping is the technique used to find spot LIBOR.

T ___ F ___ 7. If the three-month and six-month spot rates are both 5.00%, the 3×6 implied forward rate is also 5.00%.

T ___ F ___ 8. In an off-market interest rate swap, the present value of the fixed rate side always exceeds the present value of the floating rate side.

T ___ F ___   9. The swap fixed rate is analogous to an average of the forward rates over the life of the swap.

T ___ F ___   10. The swap value equals the swap price multiplied by the notional value.

T ___ F ___   11. The swap spread is an increment above the U.S. Treasury yield that reflects profit to the swap dealer.

T ___ F ___   12. A swap dealer can effectively hedge an interest rate swap using the Eurodollar futures market.

T ___ F ___   13. In a stack hedge, the swap hedger usually uses the most distant futures delivery date that falls within the swap tenor.

T ___ F ___   14. In a strip hedge, the swap dealer uses a variety of futures delivery months.

T ___ F ___   15. If a swap dealer fails to tail the swap hedge, he will tend to overhedge.

T ___ F ___   16. A tailed hedge is the present value of an untailed hedge.

T ___ F ___   17. In pricing a currency swap, it is important to first solve for the equilibrium swap price for an interest rate swap in each of the two countries involved.

T ___ F ___   18. If one side of a currency swap pays its domestic LIBOR, the equilibrium fixed rate for the other currency will equal the equilibrium fixed rate on an interest rate swap in that country.

PROBLEMS & QUESTIONS

1. Having learned that you can view a swap as a pair of option contracts, you are looking at the equity options market and see that a particular non-dividend paying stock sells for $28.55 while a six-month Treasury bill yields 5.50%. You are wondering about the characteristics of a six-month, zero cost collar in which you write the put and buy a call. At what striking price would the net cost of the collar be zero?

2. Explain the difference between the swap *price* and the swap *value*.

3. Why is the value of an at-the-market swap initially zero?

4. Explain how a *short* swap (that is, one in which you pay the floating rate) can be viewed as a pair of options.

5. Suppose the interest rates in Table 14–2 all increase by 35 basis points. Solve for the new implied forward rates.

6. Given your answer to Question 5, find the equilibrium fixed rate on a one-year, quarterly payment swap where there are 90, 91, 92, and 92 days in the four quarters.

7. Having increased the interest rates in Table 14–2 by 35 basis points, determine the value of a $100 million, one-year, quarterly payment swap if the fixed rate is 5.70%.

8. The three-year Treasury yield is 5.57%. A swap dealer quotes a three-year swap as 24–27 bp. What interest rate would a floating rate payer receive on an interest rate swap?

9. Suppose the yield curve is downward sloping. From the perspective of the fixed rate payer, explain how counterparty risk changes over the life of a swap.

10. A swap dealer notes the following spot interest rates: six months, 5.45%; twelve

CHAPTER 14 REVIEW

months, 5.65%; eighteen months, 5.90%; and twenty-four months, 6.15%.

a. Determine the equilibrium swap price on a semi-annual payment, two-year swap.

b. The swap dealer enters into a $75 million two-year swap with a fixed rate equal to the solution in part a of this problem. He chooses to hedge this via a stack hedge. Determine the number of Eurodollar futures contracts necessary to do so.

11. In Problem 10, suppose instead the swap dealer chooses to hedge this swap via a strip hedge. Calculate the number of Eurodollar futures necessary at each payment date
   a. without a tailing adjustment;
   b. with a tailing adjustment.

12. Consider the rates in Table 14–5. Suppose an annual pay, two year currency swap has one party paying £ LIBOR + 50 bp and receiving a fixed rate in US dollars. Solve for the equilibrium fixed rate.

Other Derivative Assets

KEY TERMS you will find in this chapter:

foreign currency option	warrant
futures option	warrant hedge
serial expiration	when-issued stock

You may not get rich by using all the available information, but you surely will get poor if you don't.

Jack Treynor

This chapter covers futures options and other well-established derivative securities; warrants, when-issued stock, and foreign currency options. In recent years, the rocket scientists of finance have spawned new derivative products faster than theoretical physicists have proposed new subatomic particles. We will look at a few other derivative products in the later chapter on financial engineering.

FUTURES OPTIONS

I once heard these securities described as "uniquely worthless." This is wrong. Futures options are versatile financial instruments that can efficiently modify a portfolio's risk exposure or enhance its income stream.

CHARACTERISTICS

Futures options give users of the futures market an enhanced ability to tailor their risk/return exposure to specific needs.

The initial proposal for listed options on futures contracts were met with cries that these securities served no economic purpose and were simply gambling instruments. Few informed people continue to share this view, however. Futures options give users of the futures market an enhanced ability to tailor their risk/return exposure to individual needs. They also provide an opportunity for the speculator to avoid the unlimited losses that are theoretically possible with futures contracts.

Options on futures contracts are relatively new. Non-agricultural futures options began trading in 1982, with agricultural futures options following two years later. The Commodity Futures Trading Commission Act of 1974 provides that futures contract markets must be "not contrary to the public interest," and such products as might be traded on the exchanges must serve legitimate hedging purposes.

In principle, these options are no different from listed options on stocks or stock indexes. Futures calls give you the right to go long, and futures puts give you the right to go short. It is important to recognize that *the underlying security is the futures contract, not the physical commodity or security represented by the futures contract.* In other words, the owner of a call option on soybean futures has the right to assume a long position in a soybean futures contract. The owner of a soybean futures *put* has the right to go *short* a soybean futures contract. As with other options, the option holder decides if and when to exercise.

Futures calls give their owner the right to go long a futures contract; a put gives its owner the right to go short.

Exercise of a futures call does not result in delivery of the underlying commodity. Instead, the exerciser's account will be credited with a long position in the futures contract that he or she must eventually settle in normal fashion.

Writing an equity call and buying an equity put (or vice versa) are not equivalent strategies. They are not equivalent with futures options, either. Someone who buys a futures put has the *right* to go short a futures contract. Someone who writes a futures call has the *obligation* to go short if the call holder chooses to exercise. Similarly, if I buy a futures option call, I have the right to go long, while a futures put writer has the obligation to go long if exercise occurs.

Tables 15–1 and 15–2 show selected futures and futures option prices. The format of the futures option listing is like the traditional option quotations. Expiration dates are from left to right, striking prices are listed vertically, and the prices (premiums) for puts and calls are side by side. In Table 15–2, the price listed for a NOV 575 call option on soybeans, for instance, is 3 cents per bushel. A future option corresponds to a single commodity futures contract, which for soybeans is 5,000 bushels.

The person who buys this call pays the premium of $0.03 on each of 5,000 bushels, for a total of $150.00. The option writer receives this sum and keeps it, regardless of what happens to soybean prices between now and the expiration date of the option.

Like other puts and calls, futures options have both *intrinsic value* and *time value.* Table 15–1 shows a settlement price for November soybeans of $5.05 per bushel. A call option with a striking price of 575 ($5.75 per bushel) is out-of-the-money if the underlying commodity sells for less than this. Therefore, there is no

TABLE 15–1 Futures Prices					
SEPTEMBER 8, 2000					

SOYBEANS (CBT)

5,000 BU; CENTS PER BUSHEL	OPEN	HIGH	LOW	SETTLE	CHANGE
SEP	488½	495	487	495	+15
NOV	490	505½	489½	505	+15
JAN01	501	515	501	514½	+14½
MAR	515½	523½	515½	523	+13¾
MAY	522½	530½	522	530	+13¾

SWISS FRANC (CME)

125,000 FRANCS; $ PER FRANC	OPEN	HIGH	LOW	SETTLE	CHANGE
SEP	.5642	.5650	.5585	.5624	−.0020
DEC	.5709	.5709	.5630	.5668	−.0020

S&P 500 INDEX (CME)

$250 TIMES INDEX	OPEN	HIGH	LOW	SETTLE	CHANGE
SEP	150000	150150	149100	149660	−980
DEC	152860	152950	151350	151900	−1000
MAR01	153800	154610	153800	154230	−980
JUN	...	...	...	156610	−980
SEP	...	...	...	159060	−980

Note: The prices for the S&P 500 contract omit the decimal. A price of 150000, for instance, actually represents an index level of 1500.00.

Some futures options expire in the month prior to the futures delivery month.

intrinsic value with the NOV 575 call. A NOV 575 *put*, however, has intrinsic value of $5.75 – $5.05 = $0.70. Table 15–2 shows that the premium for a NOV 575 put on soybean futures is $0.7275 cents. Because the intrinsic value is 70 cents, its time value must be $0.7275 – $0.70 = $0.0275, or 2¾ cents.

One major difference between futures options and equity or index options has to do with their expiration. Generally, the option month refers to the futures contract delivery month. Depending on the commodity, though, the option may expire on a specific date in the *preceding* month. The actual expiration date varies by commodity. Expiration is not necessarily the third Friday of the stated month, as with equity or index options. You should carefully check the exercise and expiration terms of any future option you are considering.

Some futures options, like those on soybeans and the S&P 500, have a **serial expiration** feature. S&P 500 stock index futures contracts, for instance, have delivery months of March, June, September, and December. A March, June, September, or December S&P 500 option expires on the *Thursday* prior to the third Friday of the expiration month. An option with any other expiration month expires on the *third Friday*. With serial expiration the option exerciser takes a posi-

TABLE 15–2   Futures Options Prices

SEPTEMBER 8, 2000

SOYBEANS (CBOT)	5000 BU (CENTS/BU)	CALLS			PUTS		
STRIKE PRICE	OCT	NOV	JAN	OCT	NOV	JAN
450	55	56 1/2	...	1/8	1 1/2	...
475	31 1/2	35 5/8	...	1 1/2	5 3/8	...
500	13 1/4	20	31 1/4	8 1/4	15	17 1/4
525	4	10 1/2	...	24	30 1/2	...
550	1 1/4	5	...	...	50	...
575	...	3	...	...	72 3/4	...

SWISS FRANC (CME)	125,000 FRANCS (CENTS PER FRANC)	CALLS			PUTS		
STRIKE PRICE	SEP	OCT	NOV	SEP	OCT	NOV
5500	...	...	...	0.00	0.28	0.52
5550	...	...	...	0.00	0.38	...
5600	0.24	...	...	0.00	0.54	0.88
5650	0.00	0.94	...	0.26	0.76	1.10
5700	0.00	0.94	...	0.76	1.04	1.37
5750	0.00	0.53	...	1.26	1.35	...

S&P 500 STOCK INDEX (CME)	($250 TIMES PREMIUM)	CALLS			PUTS		
STRIKE PRICE	SEP	OCT	NOV	SEP	OCT	NOV
1485	20.40	...	...	8.80	22.50	32.80
1490	17.10	52.90	...	10.50	24.10	...
1495	14.00	...	...	12.40	25.70	...
1500	11.20	46.40	...	14.60	27.50	38.20
1505	8.80	43.20	...	17.20	29.30	40.10
1510	6.70	40.10	51.10	20.10	31.20	42.20

A futures option holder who exercises his or her option takes a position in the next futures delivery.

tion in the *next* futures contract. If, for instance, someone exercises an October or a November S&P call, they would assume a long position in the December futures contract. Someone who exercises a December call would also momentarily assume a long position in the December contract, but because its last delivery date is at hand the option would be settled in cash.

SPECULATING WITH FUTURES OPTIONS

The principles of speculation with futures options are similar to those with equity or index options. Suppose in early September a speculator anticipates a better-than-expected crop of soybeans and is confident that the price of soybeans is going to drop. He could write naked calls, but might be uneasy about the unlimited risk and predetermined maximum gain characteristic of this strategy. Instead, he decides to buy a put option on the soybean futures, facing the same decisions regarding expiration and striking price as any options user. The longer the time until option expiration, the greater the likelihood of a favorable price movement, but the more the option costs. The more favorable the striking price, the higher the option premium as well.

After considering these factors the speculator buys 3 NOV 500 puts at the listed price of 15 cents. The money at risk is

$$3 \text{ contracts} \times \frac{5,000 \text{ bu}}{\text{contract}} \times \frac{\$0.15}{\text{bu}} = \$2,250.00$$

This is the most that the option buyer can lose.

By mid-October the price of soybeans falls, as predicted. If the settlement price of the futures contract falls to $4.85, the 500 put has intrinsic value of fifteen cents. There is still time value, and the option premium might be twenty-five cents. Selling the three puts results in a profit of $0.25 (sale price) − $0.15 (purchase price) on each of 15,000 bushels, for a total gain of $1,500. On the other hand, if soybean prices remained above $5, the value of the puts would approach zero as the expiration date approached.

SPREADING WITH FUTURES OPTIONS

It is common for speculators in futures options to reduce their money at risk by setting up various types of spreads. An investor who was bullish on soybeans, for instance, might construct a bullspread by buying calls with one striking price and writing other calls with a higher striking price.

Consider the NOV 500 and 525 calls on soybeans from Table 15–2. These show settlement prices of 20 cents and 10½ cents per bushel, respectively. Table 15–3 is a profit and loss summary for the associated bullspread.

The maximum loss is 9½ cents per bushel, or $475 for the 5,000 bushels covered by one option. The maximum gain is $775. Because the multiplier with a futures option is often something other than 100 you have to be careful to interpret the "net" figure properly.

BASIS RISK WITH SPREADS

Remember the Chapter 8 discussion on the implications of changing basis with agricultural commodities. Someone who buys a January soybean contract and

> Buying futures options involves a predetermined, known, and limited maximum loss, just as with options on other assets.

TABLE 15–3 Soybean Bullspread							
FUTURES SETTLEMENT PRICE (CENTS PER BUSHEL)							
495	**500**	**505**	**510**	**515**	**520**	**525**	**530**
Buy 500 call @ 20 −20	−20	−15	−10	−5	0	+5	+10
Write 525 call @ 10½ +10½	+10½	+10½	+10½	+10½	+10½	+10½	+5½
Net −9½	−9½	−4½	+ ½	+5½	+10½	+15½	+15½

sells a November contract runs a basis risk, because these two contracts have a *different* basis, and it is possible that both contracts could move against you.[1]

The same warning is appropriate with futures options. Consider a calendar spread with soybean calls, constructed by buying the JAN 550 and writing the NOV 550 using the Table 15–2 prices. Also suppose that on this day the cash price for soybeans is 490.

There is basis risk with such a spread. The JAN 550 call gives its owner the right to go long a January futures contract. The short position in the November call gives someone else the right to go long a November futures contract. If the owner of the November call exercises it, the call writer assumes a short position in futures. The pricing of the January and November futures contracts can be quite different.

The spreader buys the JAN 500 call for 31¼ cents, and writes the NOV 500 call, receiving 20 cents. The net cost of the spread is 11¼ cents per bushel. There are 5,000 bushels covered by one contract, so the spread requires a cash outlay of 5,000 bu × $0.1125 / bu = $562.50.

Over the next month there is a major increase in the price of soybeans because of concern about a newly discovered crop disease with unknown implications. The cash price increases to 540, and the futures contracts rise to 550 for the November contracts and 555 for the January contracts. The prices of the options change to 67 cents for the November calls, and 72 cents for the January calls. Table 15–4 shows the net effect. Because the January contract basis change is more than the November contract basis change, this results in a loss for the spreader.

HEDGING WITH FUTURES OPTIONS

There are as many ways to hedge with futures options as there are with equity or index options. Any hedge serves to limit risk with some tradeoff in potential return. In the commodities market, there are sometimes several levels of hedging going on when futures options get involved.

---

[1] Under most circumstances the various delivery months of an agricultural commodity futures contract will move together. Unusual storage circumstances or demand patterns could cause some deviation from this, however.

TABLE 15-4	Effect of Changing Basis on Futures Option Spread						
	NOVEMBER DELIVERY				JANUARY DELIVERY		
	CASH PRICE	FUTURES PRICE	BASIS	OPTION VALUE	FUTURES PRICE	BASIS	OPTION VALUE
SEPT 8TH	490	505	+15	20	514 ½	+24 ½	31 ¼
SOMETIME IN OCTOBER	540	550	+10	67	555	+15	72
CHANGE		+45	−5	+47	+40 ½	−9 ½	+40 ¾

Loss on short November call: Gain on long January call:
$0.47 × 5,000 = $2,350 $0.4075 × 5,000 = $2,037.50

Net loss = $2,037.50 − $2,350 = −$312.50

Suppose a Midwest family operates a 1,500-acre farm and knows from experience that they can expect to harvest between 30 and 40 bushels of soybeans per acre. The family plans on an expected harvest of 50,000 bushels. The family routinely uses the futures market to hedge the price risk. They could logically go short 10 soybean futures contracts, covering 50,000 bushels.[2]

Unexpected problems with the crop (weather, bugs, tornadoes, etc.) sometimes make it impractical (or impossible) to deliver the full 50,000 bushels called for by the futures contracts. They hedge this risk by going short 9 contracts only. This is to reduce the inconvenience and cost of having to either close out some contracts at a financial loss or acquire soybeans in the cash market to deliver against the short contracts.

Finally, the family might feel that there is a substantial chance that this year's soybean prices will be higher than in the past. Hedging in the futures or futures options market locks in a price, and this price might well be less than the one that prevails at harvest time. To deal with this possibility they buy a few soybean calls. This way, if prices advance sharply, they will recover some of what would have otherwise been an opportunity loss. The cost of the call options is analogous to insurance against missing out on a good market price at harvest time.

SPECULATORS AND HEDGING

Futures options are particularly useful to the individual investor who speculates with interest rate or stock index futures. If someone buys an S&P 500 index futures contract, for instance, a market decline results in their account balance dwindling as it is marked to market each day. Puts on the S&P futures would provide some protection against the potentially large losses. (You also could write call options, but this would provide less protection.) Similarly, the person who is short S&P 500 futures might buy calls or write puts as a hedge.

[2] In practice, most farms only hedge between 25% and 50% of their overall potential crop.

EARLY EXERCISE OF FUTURES OPTIONS

Listed call options on equity securities or indexes will not normally be exercised early, because doing so results in an abandonment of the remaining time value of the option. With futures options, there are circumstances in which it *is* optimal to exercise a call early. This can be explained by intuition alone without any mathematics.

Someone who buys a call option has a net cash outlay. This money is the option writer's to keep no matter what happens. When I buy (go long) a futures contract, I put up a good faith deposit that is still my money; in fact, I can satisfy the good faith deposit with interest-bearing Treasury bills.

Suppose that the value of a futures contract rises dramatically, leaving certain call options deep-in-the-money. The deeper in the money any option goes, the more it behaves like the underlying security itself. A deep-in-the-money futures call is a valuable asset, and it could be sold to generate cash; it earns no interest, however. Because this option will behave very much like the futures contract itself, there is little reason to prefer the call to the futures contract.

> Early exercise of futures options is sometimes optimal when they become deep-in-the-money.

In fact, there is a good reason to prefer the futures contract to the call. The investment characteristics of the two assets are similar. If I exercise the call, though, I get to go long the futures contract, and my cash investment begins to earn interest, whereas if I keep the call I earn no interest. Of course, you also could sell the call, but this would get you out of the market entirely.

PRICING FUTURES OPTIONS

Fisher Black (of Black-Scholes fame) extended the principles of the BSOPM to futures pricing. Although this model is limited to European options, it is a useful starting point for determining a theoretical futures option premium. Table 15–5 shows the model.

Suppose (1) a two-month (0.1667 year) call option is available on a new dot.com index futures contract, (2) T-bills yield 6%, (3) the dot.com futures contract currently sells for 270.00, (4) the option has a striking price of 275.00, and (5) volatility[3] is 35 percent. What is the theoretical value of the call?

First, solve for the arguments a and b:

$$a = \frac{\ln\left(\frac{270}{275}\right) + \frac{0.35^2}{2}\,0.1667}{0.35\sqrt{0.1667}} = -0.05698$$

$$b = -0.05698 - 0.35\sqrt{0.1667} = -0.19987$$

Next, find the N($\bullet$) values:[4]

[3] We assume "volatility" means sigma.

[4] As with Black-Scholes values, accuracy is important in calculating N ($\bullet$) values. Depending on the circumstances, rounding N(a) and N(b) to two decimals can sometimes make a difference of a dollar in the predicted call value!

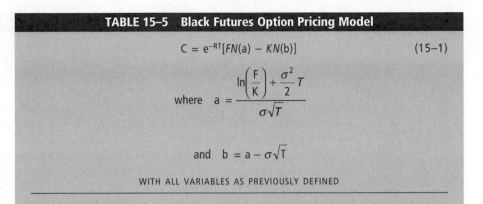

TABLE 15–5   Black Futures Option Pricing Model

$$C = e^{-RT}[FN(a) - KN(b)] \tag{15-1}$$

$$\text{where} \quad a = \frac{\ln\left(\dfrac{F}{K}\right) + \dfrac{\sigma^2}{2}T}{\sigma\sqrt{T}}$$

$$\text{and} \quad b = a - \sigma\sqrt{T}$$

WITH ALL VARIABLES AS PREVIOUSLY DEFINED

$$N(a) = N(-0.05698) = 0.4773$$
$$N(b) = N(-0.19987) = 0.4208$$

Now substitute values:

$$C = e^{-.06(.1667)}[270(0.4773) - 275(0.4208)] = \$13.02$$

These calls should sell for about $13.

The futures call option pricing model can be readily adapted to a futures put option-pricing model. See Table 15–6.

Inputting the pertinent data into equation 15–2, we have

$$P = e^{-(.06)(.1667)}[275\, N(0.19987) - 270\, N(0.05698)]$$
$$= 0.990048[275(0.579209) - 270(0.522720)] = \mathbf{\$17.97}$$

It is also possible to use the principles of put/call parity to value a put option once you know the value of the associated call. Table 15–7 shows how.

Let's solve for equilibrium value of a put on the dot.com index futures using the put/call parity version of the model. We have already solved for the value of the call: $13.02. Therefore, $P = \$13.02 - e^{-.06(.1667)}(270 - 275) = \$17.97$. This is the same value we determined with the Black model.

DISPOSING OF VALUABLE OPTIONS

As with other options, the holder of a futures option has three alternatives: (1) keep the option, (2) exercise it, or (3) sell it. The risk of holding onto the

TABLE 15–6   Black Futures Put Option Pricing Model

$$P = e^{-RT}[KN(-b) - FN(-a)] \tag{15-2}$$

WITH ALL VARIABLES AS PREVIOUSLY DEFINED

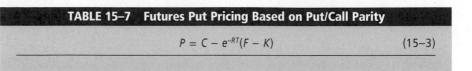

TABLE 15–7 Futures Put Pricing Based on Put/Call Parity

$$P = C - e^{-RT}(F - K) \qquad (15\text{–}3)$$

option is that prices may move adversely, resulting in a decline in the value of the option. Conversely, of course, prices may move in your favor and the value of the option could increase.

The early exercise of options is normally sub optimal. The exerciser would abandon any remaining time value. Options that are deep-in-the-money have little time value; they sell for very close to their intrinsic value. It is often advantageous to exercise these early as discussed above.

Selling the option has the merit of capturing the remaining time value (and converting the intrinsic value to cash). This alternative also gets you out of the market. (Remember that when you exercise a futures option, you are still in the market. If you exercise a call, you acquire a long futures position; if you exercise a put, you acquire a short futures position.) This means that when the holder of a valuable futures option decides to leave the market, the option will normally be sold rather than exercised.

FUTURES OPTION DELTAS

The delta for futures options is slightly different from delta for equity or index options. The call delta is $e^{-RT}N(a)$, while the put delta is $e^{-RT}N(-b)$.

IMPLIED VOLATILITY

Implied volatility is an important idea with futures option pricing, just as with the pricing of other options. Implied volatility is the standard deviation of returns that will cause the pricing model to predict the actual option premium.

Calculating implied volatility must be done via a trial and error process as with other options, because it is not possible to isolate sigma in the valuation equation.

WARRANTS

Warrants are long-term call options issued by the underlying company.

A **warrant** is a non-dividend paying security giving its owner the right to buy a certain number of shares at a set price directly from the issuing company.[5] Warrants are relatively rare; the New York Stock Exchange usually has several dozen listed, with a smaller number on the American Stock Exchange. You can find many more in the Nasdaq market, but most of these seldom trade. In January

---

[5] A warrant is very much like a long-term call option issued by the underlying company. The warrant holder has the right, but not the obligation, to buy shares at a set price during the life of the warrant. Warrants provide leverage in the same fashion as an option.

1995, the Irwin *Yearbook of Convertible Securities*[6] reported 476 warrants, with 406 traded via Nasdaq.

CHARACTERISTICS

Warrants are really long-term call options issued by a corporation. They give the owner the right to purchase a set number of shares of stock directly from the company issuing the warrant. There is a predetermined exercise price and expiration date that might be as far as twenty years in the future.

Corporations sometimes issue warrants in conjunction with a new bond issue; the potential benefits of these securities allow the company to sell the bonds at a slightly higher price or lower interest rate than would otherwise be necessary. The higher price reflects the warrant option premium. Warrants pay no dividends and their owners have no voting rights, but investors like them because of the leverage they provide. Like a call option, warrants let you assume a bullish position on a stock but with a lower investment than would be necessary if you bought the stock outright. Warrant holders can make enormous profits during bull markets or merger waves, but their downside risk is limited.

You have to do a little homework to get details about the trading terms of a warrant. One convenient source of information is the Standard and Poors' *Stock Guide*. Other sources are the Standard and Poors' *Stock Report* or the *Value Line Investment Survey*.

> Warrants give their owner the right to buy shares of stock at a set price directly from the company.

Warrants can have very unusual exercise terms and conditions. The Standard & Poor's *Stock Guide* listing for many warrants indicates "terms and trading basis should be checked in detail." The vast majority of U. S. warrants are from small, relatively risky firms, often originating in conjunction with an initial public offering.

PRICING

The most important factor influencing the market price of a warrant is the relationship between the price of the underlying common stock and the price at which the investor may buy shares, called the exercise price. As with a call, when the stock price rises above the exercise price, the warrant is in-the-money.

Figure 15–1 shows the minimum, maximum, and actual market values of a warrant. This figure assumes that one warrant is required to buy one share of stock. Sometimes this is not the case, and, as Standard and Poor's warns, "trading terms and basis should be checked in detail."

> The maximum price of a warrant is the stock value.

It would not make sense for the warrant to ever sell for more than the value of the underlying asset. For instance, if one share of the stock sells for $25, no rational person would be willing to pay more than $25 for the right to buy a share, even if the warrant exercise price were zero. The theoretical maximum price of a warrant is therefore equal to the stock value.

The theoretical *minimum* value is the warrant's intrinsic value, which is the greater of zero and the amount by which the stock price exceeds the exercise price.

---

[6] Noddings Investment Group, *The Irwin Yearbook of Convertible Securities: Warrants, Bonds, and Preferred Stock (1995)*. Irwin Professional Publishing, Chicago, 1995.

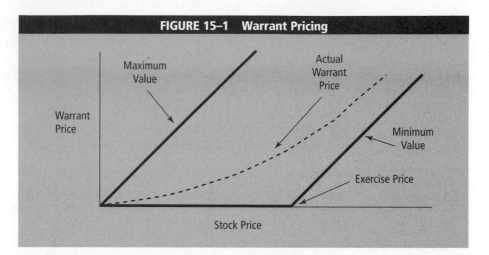

FIGURE 15–1 Warrant Pricing

TABLE 15–8 New York Stock Exchange Warrants

Issuer	Symbol	# Warrants to Buy One Share	Exercise Price	Expiration	Warrant Price	Stock Price
Bentley Pharmaceuticals	BNT	2.0	$5.00	2-14-01	$0.375	$3.00
Careside, Inc.	CSA	1.0	9.00	6-16-04	1.25	5.1875
Hemisphere BioPharma	HEB	1.0	4.00	11-2-00	2.625	6.25
NTN Communications	NTN	1.0	0.96	2-18-01	2.25	1.1875
Titan Pharmaceuticals	TTP	1.0	6.02	1-18-01	2.75	8.50

Source: Standard & Poor's September 1999 Stock Guide.

Given a stock price of $25 and an exercise price of $20, this warrant should always sell for at least $5. If this were not so, arbitrage would be present.

Actual warrant prices fall between these two extremes. The gap between the market price of the warrant and its minimum value is largest when the stock price equals the exercise price. As the stock price rises or falls from this point, the gap narrows.[7] Table 15–8 is a representative sample of warrants from the New York Stock Exchange.

Consider, for instance, the Titan Pharmaceuticals warrant. With an exercise price of $6.02 and a current stock price of $8.50, this warrant is in-the-money. It must sell for at least its intrinsic value of ($8.50 – 6.02) = $2.48, which it does. The market price of $2.75 contains a time value premium over the warrant's intrinsic value. Investors are willing to pay this extra amount because the warrant enables them to risk less money and enjoy leveraged performance if the stock advances.

[7] This is consistent with option pricing theory.

The Careside warrant is out-of-the-money. The stock must rise by over 70% to reach the exercise price. Still, the warrant has several years until expiration, and it provides a convenient means of speculating on the company's fortunes.

Companies sometimes extend the life of an out-of-the-money warrant as it nears expiration. Doing so increases the likelihood that the warrant will eventually move into the money and the warrant holders will exercise. The exercise of warrants is a relatively inexpensive source of new capital for the firm. Management may not want to let the opportunity pass. Extending the life of a warrant will immediately add value to it. A nearly worthless expiring warrant would likely jump in value by several dollars if the firm extends its life a few years. The actual price change would depend on the stock/exercise price relationship, the added term of the warrant, and the anticipated volatility of the stock over the extension period.

HEDGING WITH STOCK WARRANTS[8]

The strategy of using a **warrant hedge** is similar to a covered call writing strategy. The outcome to the hedger is the same, but warrant hedging involves an extra player—the warrant lender. Under this strategy, an investor buys shares of stock and simultaneously sells short warrants on the same company. To sell short, the investor borrows the warrants and then sells them.

If, at warrant expiration, the stock price is below the exercise price of the warrants, the warrants are worthless. This effectively means that the person who sold the warrants short owes the lender nothing and can pocket the full proceeds from the short sale. The loss in value of the underlying stock is cushioned by the proceeds from the warrant sale.

If, however, the stock price rises, at expiration the warrant holder will exercise the warrants. Because the warrants are valuable, the investor must repay *the lender* that which was borrowed, although he still pockets the proceeds from the short sale. The obligation is to return the warrants—or the equivalent—and, in general, this is fulfilled by the investor selling the shares at the exercise price to the warrant lender. The investor's profit on the deal is limited to the exercise price at which it was necessary to sell the shares, plus the proceeds from the short sale. The outcome is the same as in a covered call writing strategy, except that the investor now owes stock to the warrant lender, whereas in call writing he would owe stock to the call holder.

Let's look at a hypothetical example of a warrant hedge. Suppose the common stock of company XYZ pays a 40 cent dividend, sells for $21, and that there are warrants trading for $5 allowing the purchase of one share of XYZ common stock at $24.25 anytime between the time of purchase and January 1, 2005. An investor buys 1,000 shares of XYZ, and simultaneously sells short 1,000 warrants. No further action is taken until the expiration of the warrants.

---

[8] Much of the material in this section is from Robert A. Strong and Steven V. Fischetti, "Hedging with Stock Warrants: A Free Lunch?" *American Association of Individual Investors Journal* (November 1984): 9–13.

TABLE 15–9 Warrant Hedge						
	STOCK PRICE AT WARRANT EXPIRATION					
	5	**10**	**15**	**20**	**25**	**30**
STOCK	−16	−11	−6	−1	+4	+9
WARRANT	+5	+5	+5	+5	+4.25	−0.75
DIVIDENDS	+2.50	+2.50	+2.50	+2.50	+2.50	+2.50
TOTAL PROFIT OR LOSS	−8.50	−3.50	+1.50	+6.50	+10.75	+10.75

Values are "per share."

If, at expiration, the stock price is $24.25 or less, the warrants will expire worthless and the investor makes $5,000 on the short position: 1,000 warrants were sold at $5 and were "reacquired" at $0. In addition, the investor is still long 1,000 shares of stock and would have received dividends along the way.

If the stock rises above $24.25, the warrants will be valuable. Warrant holders will exercise them, and the short seller will have to cover the short position by buying warrants on the open market, or by delivering shares of stock at $24.25 despite the higher market price. In this example, the investor's maximum gain is $8.25 per share plus any dividends paid over the period. This maximum profit occurs at any stock price of $24.25 or more. At this price, the investor will make $3.25 on the stock ($24.25 − $21) and $5 on the warrant. Profit is limited even if stock prices move higher, because the shares must be delivered at $24.25.

If the stock price declines, losses are offset by the $5,000 proceeds from the short sale and any dividends received. In this example, share prices could actually fall to $16 before the investor began to lose money.

If the stock price is unchanged at expiration of the warrant, there is no capital gain on the stock, but there is still a $5,000 gain from the short side of the warrants. Table 15–9 shows the results, assuming a total of $2.50 in dividends on the stock over the period of the warrant's life.

In a study of profitability of this strategy, Strong and Fischetti found that over the period 1968–81 warrant hedges showed above-average risk-adjusted performance. This means that after considering the volatility of the warrant hedge relative to the overall market, the returns from warrant hedges were higher than predicted by financial theory. More research is necessary to understand precisely how the marketplace determines a price for these securities.

OTHER DERIVATIVE ASSETS

Foreign currency options began trading at the Philadelphia Stock Exchange in 1982. Today options trade on the Australian dollar, the British pound, the Canadian dollar, the German mark, the Euro, the Japanese yen, and the Swiss franc.

While these still trade at the PHLX, commercial banks arrange most currency option trading today.

CHARACTERISTICS

Foreign currency options are not the same as foreign currency futures options.

Like equity and index options, the Options Clearing Corporation guarantees these contracts. There are a variety of expirations for these options, including mid-month, month-end, and long-term versions. They can be either American or European exercise style.

Foreign currency *options* are different from options on foreign currency *futures*. It is important to be precise with your terminology here. A foreign currency call option gives you the right to buy a certain quantity of the foreign currency; a foreign currency *futures* call gives you the right to go long the futures contract.

A foreign currency call is the same as a dollar put.

It is useful to note the phenomenon of put/call equivalence with certain foreign currency options. If an American buys a Swiss franc call denominated in dollars, this gives him or her the right to exchange U.S. dollars for Swiss francs. This is no different from a U.S. dollar put denominated in Swiss francs. Such a security would give its owner the right to deliver U.S. dollars and receive Swiss francs. A foreign currency call requiring payment in U.S. dollars is equivalent to a U.S. dollar put on the foreign currency.

The contract size for foreign currency options is currently set at one half the size of the futures contract for the same currency. The primary purpose for this is to keep the option premium at a relatively modest level. Unlike futures, in which only a good faith deposit is required, options must be paid for in full (if purchased) or a significant margin posted (if the option is written). The futures contract for the German deutsche mark, for instance, covers 125,000 marks; the DM option covers 62,500 marks.

A NOTE ON THE PRICING OF FOREIGN CURRENCY OPTIONS

The Black-Scholes model does not work well with foreign currency options.

You might expect that the Black-Scholes Option Pricing Model would work with these options just like it does with equity options. The fact that we have two interest rates, one on the domestic currency and one on the foreign currency, complicates the arbitrage arguments behind option pricing and means that the Black-Scholes model needs a modification to account for this. One popular way of doing so is via the Garman and Kohlhagen model.[9] This is very similar to the Black-Scholes model except that the current exchange rate substitutes for the price of the underlying asset and is discounted by the foreign interest rate. Table 15–10 shows the model. All variables are as previously defined except there are two interest rates, one foreign ($R_{foreign}$) and one domestic ($R_{domestic}$), and S_0 represents the spot exchange rate.

To illustrate the model, suppose we have the following data.

[9] Garman, Mark B., and Steven W. Kohlhagen. "Foreign Currency Option Values," *Journal of International Money and Finance* 2 (1983): 231–237.

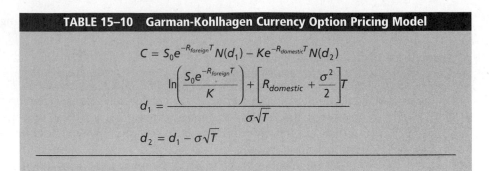

TABLE 15–10   Garman-Kohlhagen Currency Option Pricing Model

$$C = S_0 e^{-R_{foreign}T} N(d_1) - K e^{-R_{domestic}T} N(d_2)$$

$$d_1 = \frac{\ln\left(\dfrac{S_0 e^{-R_{foreign}T}}{K}\right) + \left[R_{domestic} + \dfrac{\sigma^2}{2}\right]T}{\sigma\sqrt{T}}$$

$$d_2 = d_1 - \sigma\sqrt{T}$$

Current exchange rate = $0.5050 per unit of foreign currency

U.S. interest rate = 4.45%

Foreign interest rate = 5.50%

Time until option expiration = 113 days = 0.31 years

Sigma = 0.10

Option striking price = $0.50

As with a Black-Scholes problem, we must first solve for the standard normal arguments d_1 and d_2:

$$d_1 = \frac{\ln\left(\dfrac{0.505 e^{-(0.055)(.31)}}{0.50}\right) + \left[0.0445 + \dfrac{.10^2}{2}\right]0.31}{.10\sqrt{.31}}$$

$$= \frac{-0.007100 + 0.015345}{0.055678} = 0.148084$$

$$N(0.148084) = 0.558862$$

$$d_2 = 0.148084 - 0.10\sqrt{0.31} = 0.092406$$

$$N(0.092406) = 0.536812$$

$$C = 0.505 e^{-(0.0550)(.31)}(0.558862) - 0.50 e^{-(0.0445)(.31)}(0.536812)$$

$$= \mathbf{\$0.012725}$$

The call is worth about 1.3 cents per unit of foreign currency.

WHEN-ISSUED STOCK

A good case could be made for the claim that *when-issued stock* is the least understood financial asset. Few stockbrokers, finance professors, or investors are familiar with these curious securities, yet their prices appear in the financial pages every day. In the stock listings you can usually find a few stocks apparently double listed with the code *wi* following the second entry. The *wi* indicates these are when-issued shares. Don't confuse the *wi* with the *wt* abbreviation for warrants. The two securities are quite different.

COMMON STOCK TRADING ON A WHEN-ISSUED BASIS[10]

When a firm splits its stock, the post-split price of shares will reflect the change in the number of outstanding shares. In a two for one split, for instance, an investor who owns 300 shares will receive a new stock certificate for another 300 shares, making a total of 600. But the investor's wealth does not double, because the price of the post-split shares will be approximately one half the pre-split price.

The New York Stock Exchange permits investors to trade shares of stock issued in conjunction with a stock split even before these new shares are distributed to existing shareholders. The motivation for this policy is unclear, but the NYSE *Company Manual* indicates that it is considered desirable, from the standpoint of public interest, to provide when-issued trading to investors.

The specialist on the floor of the exchange begins to make a market in the lower-price split shares shortly after the recapitalization has been approved by the shareholders, and *both the new shares and the old shares trade simultaneously*. The period of simultaneous trading is short, generally ranging from 4 days to 35 days.

As with a cash dividend, the old shares will go ex-distribution on the second business day before the date of record established for the stock split. Anyone purchasing the old shares after this date will purchase them with a *due bill* for the additional shares. This due bill will be noted on the investor's purchase confirmation. Holders of the due bill are entitled to the new shares when they are issued.

Although both the old shares and the new shares are proportional claims on the same cash income stream, their adjusted prices may logically differ due to the manner in which trades in when-issued shares are settled. Investors who buy or sell the old shares have their accounts debited or credited for the net amount of the transaction on the third business day following the trade. Trades in the when-issued securities, on the other hand, do not settle until after the date of distribution. Thus, the purchase of when-issued shares is analogous to buying the stock on 100 percent margin with no interest changed on the debit balance.

We would expect the price of the when-issued shares to exceed that of the old shares by the value of this interest concession. In a study by Choi and Strong, they found that even after adjusting prices for the time value of money, the when-issued shares consistently sell for a slight premium over their theoretical value. This seems to show that if you are interested in selling shares of a stock that recently declared a stock split, and you are in no hurry for your money, it may make sense to sell them on a when-issued basis.

In any event, further research is necessary to discover how the market assigns value to these curious securities.

---

[10] Much of the material in this section comes from Dosoung Choi and Robert A. Strong, "The Pricing of When-Issued Common Stock: A Note," *Journal of Finance* (September 1983): 1293–98.

SUMMARY

Futures options are options on futures contracts; futures calls give the call holder the right to *go long* a futures contract at predetermined price, while futures puts give the put holder the right to *go short*. Buying a futures call is not the same as writing a futures put. Speculators can spread these options in the same fashion as equity options, although a futures option spread carries basis risk.

Warrants are like long-term call options issued *by the company* rather than another investor. Determining the intrinsic value of a warrant is complicated by the fact that warrants often have unique exercise features, such as conversion ratios other than one to one. Certain hedging strategies using warrants appear to be unusually profitable.

Foreign currency options are not futures contracts. They are options that give you the right to buy or to sell a given quantity of foreign exchange. These options cannot be accurately priced with the BSOPM or its futures counterpart because the behavior of foreign currencies violates an important assumption of the OPM. Today, most foreign currency trading is facilitated by banks rather than at an options exchange.

When-issued stock usually comes about because of a stock split. These new shares and the old shares trade simultaneously for a brief period, and at some brokerage firms when-issued shares can be purchased without any cash outlay.

SELF TEST

T ___ F ___   1. Futures options are not legal in the United States; they only trade in Europe.

T ___ F ___   2. With a futures option, the underlying security is the futures contract, not the physical commodity represented by the futures contract.

T ___ F ___   3. A futures put gives its owner the right to go short a futures contract.

T ___ F ___   4. Unlike most other options, a futures option involves no premium.

T ___ F ___   5. A futures option may have intrinsic value or time value, but not both.

T ___ F ___   6. Some futures options expire in the month prior to the futures delivery month.

T ___ F ___   7. Buying futures options involves a predetermined, known, and limited maximum loss.

T ___ F ___   8. A futures option call spread has basis risk, while a call spread with common stock does not.

T ___ F ___   9. Early exercise of a futures call is sometimes economically optimal.

T ___ F ___   10. The Black-Scholes model is widely used to value futures options.

T ___ F ___   11. Unlike other options, the owner of a futures option does not have the choice of abandoning the option.

T ___ F ___   12. Individual investors may write warrants in the same manner as they write covered calls.

T ___ F ___   13. A warrant is similar to a long-term call option.

T ___ F ___ 14. The maximum price of a warrant is the underlying stock value.

T ___ F ___ 15. There is no substantive difference between an option on Japanese yen and a yen futures option.

T ___ F ___ 16. A yen put denominated in dollars is identical to a dollar call denominated in yen.

T ___ F ___ 17. When-issued stock normally originates in conjunction with a stock split.

PROBLEMS & QUESTIONS

1. Remembering that the purchase of a futures contract requires only a good faith deposit (which can be satisfied by the deposit of interest-bearing Treasury bills), and the formula for put-call parity from Chapter 5, what relationship would you expect between the prices of *at-the-money* futures puts and calls on the same underlying commodity?

2. Refer to Figure 15–1. At what stock price do warrants sell for their greatest premium over intrinsic value? Is this what you would expect from the Black-Scholes OPM?

3. What do you consider to be the advantages and disadvantages of buying *when-issued* stock rather than "regular way" shares?

4. The issuing firm sometimes extends the life of a warrant that is about to expire.
   (a) Why do you think the firm might do this?
   (b) What effect, if any, would this have on the warrant hedging strategy described in the chapter?

5. Suppose someone is interested in speculating on an increase in the value of the U.S. dollar relative to the German deutsche mark. What are the relative advantages of using foreign currency options rather than foreign currency futures options?

6. Warrants are like-term call options issued by a company. Would it make sense for a firm to create a new type of security that was essentially a long term *put* option? Such a security could conceivably provide a floor value to shares of common stock, because the shareholder could exercise the "put" and sell them back to the company at this price.

7. Explain how a farmer who normally used a short hedge on his crop could logically use futures options on his crop, too.

8. Explain how a farmer can eliminate price risk using futures puts.

9. How is buying a futures call different than writing a futures put?

10. Explain the following statement: "From the perspective of a U.S. investor, a deutsche mark call option is the same as a U.S. dollar put option on deutsche marks."

11. Explain why basis is especially important to a futures option spreader.

12. Why is early exercise of futures options sometimes appropriate?

13. Would you expect an at-the-money futures option ever to be exercised early?

14. Using the S&P 500 futures option prices from Table 15–2,
    (a) Calculate the breakeven price for a person who buys an OCT 1505 call;
    (b) Determine this person's gain or loss in dollars if, at option expiration, the S&P 500 index is 1530.25.

15. Draw a profit and loss diagram for an S&P 500 SEP 1500/1510 call option bullspread.

16. Do Problem 15 by using put options.

CHAPTER 15 REVIEW

17. Refer to Table 15–2. Suppose there are 15 days until expiration of the September options, and the September S&P 500 futures settled at 1496.60. Using the 1500 calls and a T-bill rate of 5.7%, what is the implied volatility of the option?

18. Using your answer to Problem 17, what is the theoretical value of an S&P 500 SEP 1515 call?

19. A futures call has a striking price of 55. The underlying asset sells for 53, has a volatility of 0.25, and the option has 110 days of life remaining. If interest rates are 3.3%, what is the delta of this option?

20. A speculator is long 5 contracts of SEP S&P 500 futures, with initial conditions as listed in Problem 17. If the speculator writes 3 SEP 1510 calls,
    (a) How much money will be received?
    (b) What will the position delta become?

21. A warrant has an exercise price of $20, a market value of $7, with an underlying stock price of $18. You decide to set up a warrant hedge by buying 100 shares of the stock and selling 100 warrants short; assume each trade occurs at the prices listed above. Each warrant covers 1.12 shares of stock. Calculate your profit or loss if the stock price is $21 at warrant expiration.

22. Refer to Table 15–2. Suppose a speculator buys three NOV 525 soybean puts.
    (a) Calculate the gain or loss in dollars if, at option expiration, the futures contract sells for 502.
    (b) Prepare a profit/loss worksheet for the purchase of one of these put options.

23. Using current data for the U.S. and Canada estimate the value of a six-month, at-the-money call option on the Canadian dollar if the volatility is 0.05.

16

Financial Engineering and Risk Management

The most complicated risk management structure can be broken down into components that any high school graduate should be able to understand thoroughly. Ph.D.'s with various specialties—the "rocket scientists" described in the press—play an important role in financial risk management. But a Ph.D. is not necessary to understand any single aspect of financial risk or to evaluate the overall effectiveness of risk control.

Gary L. Gastineau
Swiss Bank Corporation

Although the world has had a century to react to Senator Washburn's comments (see the opening quotation for Chapter 8), futures and options continue to generate controversy, partly because of the rapid pace of market change and the difficulty outsiders have in understanding the products. This chapter provides an introduction to financial engineering and further exploration of risk management. Financial engineering is a relatively new derivatives endeavor, with Wall Street's rocket scientists mixing up products like chemists in a lab. Developments with financial engineering have led directly to improvements in the process of risk management. According to the Chief Financial Engineer of one firm, "Risk management has become a hot topic. The road to risk management awareness is paved with phrases like Asian flu, global contagion, Russian default, the Mexican peso crisis, derivatives scandals, the fall of Barings Bank, rogue traders, Orange County, Tiger Management, fear of a global meltdown, and the rescue of Long-Term Capital Management. No wonder there is a growing interest in measuring and managing risk."[1]

In one of its advertisements, the money management firm Barra states, "There are bold risk takers. And old risk takers. But very few bold, old risk takers."[2] There is much to be said for playing the odds.

Risk management is not just a Wall Street phenomenon. Professional golfers know the merits of playing the "smart shot" even though going for the green would be more fun. Poker players know that drawing to inside straights is a losing strategy in the long run. Football coaches punt on fourth down despite the crowd's exhortations to "go for it."

Many of the good things in life are not risk-free. We take the risks because of the potential reward. The stunt motorcyclist Evel Knievel sums things up nicely when he says, "Risk is good. Not properly managing your risk is a dangerous leap." Whatever your profession, hobby, or family situation, there are elements of risk. Recognizing them and effectively managing them will make you a happier person.

FINANCIAL ENGINEERING

Financial engineering is the popular name for constructing asset portfolios that have precise technical characteristics, particularly when those characteristics are not conveniently available in an existing exchange product.

In the early days of the CBOE there were no puts; only calls traded.

While this is a relatively new term, the notion of creating one security from a mixture of others is not new. When the Chicago Board Options Exchange opened in 1973, trading was only in call options. You could not buy or write an exchange-traded put option. Some regulators thought that puts would be disruptive to the market and that they were not in the best interest of the economy.

Even then, however, people familiar with options knew that you can *construct* a put if one is not conveniently available on the exchange. The profit and loss diagrams from Chapter Two show that all you have to do is combine a short position in the underlying asset with a long call option. The result is identical to the diagram for a long put. You could argue that these **synthetic puts** were the first widespread use of financial engineering. (See Figure 16–1.)

Synthetic puts were probably the first widespread application of financial engineering.

While people who used options knew that restrictions against puts could be circumvented, the first one didn't get listed until 1975 when each of the five

---

[1] Don Goldman, "The Strengths and Weaknesses of Risk Management Tools," *Risk Management for the Investment Community* supplement, *Risk Magazine*, December 1999, 16–17.

[2] *Pensions and Investments*, March 5, 2001, 15.

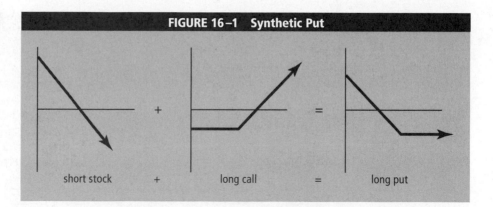

FIGURE 16–1 Synthetic Put

short stock + long call = long put

exchanges,[3] as a test case, was able to list puts on five stocks. Trading in these 25 puts was active, it did not turn the market upside down, and within a few years more puts were listed. Today every stock on which calls are available also has listed puts.

ENGINEERING AN OPTION

Suppose we consider a scenario from the perspective of an equity portfolio manager somewhere in the Pacific Rim. The manager's performance benchmark is the local XPS index on which both futures contracts and futures options trade, all modeled after the US S&P 500 stock index. Currently, the XPS is 326.00. Imagine now that tensions in the region heat up and the manager decides it makes sense to acquire some long-term downside protection even if it means giving up some portfolio return. Perhaps the manager wants insurance against a market decline over the next two years, but also wants to retain the potential for upside appreciation. There is a variety of tactics by which wealth can be protected without disturbing the underlying portfolio.

Normal hedging by shorting XPS futures would provide the downside peace of mind, but at the opportunity cost of future gains in the portfolio. A futures hedge "locks in" a price level, precluding further price appreciation.

Writing a call option provides only limited downside protection. Receiving a premium of $1 provides exactly $1 in downside protection and has the further disadvantage of attenuating gains at the striking price. This is not an appropriate tactic when the objective is keeping the road to profits open while defeating most of the downside risk.

Buying a put is probably the most appropriate tactic. For a cost, puts provide reliable protection without prejudice to the upside potential of the portfolio. Table 16–1 reviews these alternatives.

---

[3] CBOE, AMEX, Philadelphia Stock Exchange, Pacific Stock Exchange, and the Midwest Stock Exchange.

TABLE 16–1 Portfolio Protection Alternatives		
STRATEGY	**ADVANTAGES**	**DISADVANTAGES**
SHORT FUTURES	LOW TRADING FEES; EASY TO DO	LOSE UPSIDE POTENTIAL; POSSIBLE TRACKING ERROR
WRITE CALLS	GENERATE INCOME	LOSE MOST UPSIDE POTENTIAL; INCONVENIENCE IF EXERCISED; LIMITED PROTECTION
BUY PUTS	RELIABLE PROTECTION	PREMIUM MUST BE PAID; HEDGE MAY REQUIRE PERIODIC ADJUSTMENT

Extensive purchase of individual equity puts is inefficient in a large portfolio.

Having decided to use puts, the equity manager still faces choices, because the available puts arsenal includes options on at least three different types of underlying assets: individual equities, index options, and index futures contracts.

Extensive purchase of individual equity puts is inefficient in a large portfolio. Because a portfolio may contain dozens of stocks, buying equity puts involves numerous trading fees, managerial time, and a significant premium cost. Either index options or futures options are best suited to this mission, and in many applications the two categories are interchangeable.

Suppose the decision is to use options on XPS futures. These options have lives of less than a year. Consequently, it is not possible to purchase a 2-year put directly. However, knowing something about financial engineering, the portfolio manager intends to construct one via a judicious combination of the available options. The greater the range of striking prices and expirations from which to choose, the easier the task.

We know from option pricing theory that an option is reasonably well defined by its pricing model derivatives. Assuming Treasury bills yield 8% and market volatility is 15%, the Black options pricing model predicts the theoretical variables for a 2-year XPS futures put option with a 325.00 striking price as shown in Table 16–2.

TABLE 16–2 2-Year Put Theoretical Values	
GIVEN: STRIKING PRICE =	325.00
INDEX LEVEL =	326.00
THEORETICAL VALUES:	
OPTION PREMIUM =	$23.15
DELTA =	−0.388
THETA =	−0.011
GAMMA =	0.016
VEGA =	1.566

		CALLS		PUTS	
STRIKING PRICE		**JAN**	**MAR**	**JAN**	**MAR**
320	PREMIUM	$9.97	$13.25	$4.02	$7.38
	DELTA	0.645	0.595	−0.346	−0.384
	THETA	−0.069	−0.045	−0.071	−0.046
	GAMMA	0.071	0.047	0.071	0.047
	VEGA	0.411	0.651	0.411	0.651
330	PREMIUM	$4.88	$8.36	$8.84	$12.28
	DELTA	0.413	0.445	−0.578	−0.533
	THETA	−0.074	−0.047	−0.074	−0.047
	GAMMA	0.075	0.049	0.075	0.049
	VEGA	0.433	0.672	0.433	0.672

TABLE 16–3   Theoretical Option Values

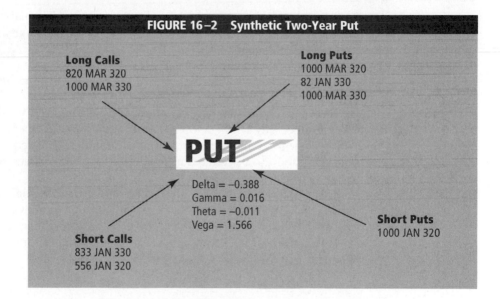

FIGURE 16–2   Synthetic Two-Year Put

Now assume that the eight options shown in Table 16–3 are available. The chore is assembling these options in the right combination to get position derivatives that match the theoretical values of the desired put.

Figure 16–2 shows one solution generated from a linear program.[4] The synthetic two-year put includes two long call positions (820 March 320s and 1000

----

[4] Linear programming is a mathematical technique to minimize or maximize some function given a set of constraints. Here, we want to find the least-cost combination of the available options giving the required position derivatives.

TABLE 16–4 Portfolio Summary				
POSITION	**DELTA**	**GAMMA**	**THETA**	**VEGA**
LONG 820 MAR 320 CALLS	487.90	38.54	−36.90	533.82
LONG 1000 MAR 330 CALLS	445.00	49.00	−47.00	672.00
SHORT 556 JAN 320 CALLS	−358.62	−39.48	38.36	−228.52
SHORT 833 JAN 330 CALLS	−344.03	−62.48	61.64	−360.69
SHORT 1000 JAN 320 PUTS	346.00	−71.00	71.00	−411.00
LONG 82 JAN 330 PUTS	−47.40	6.15	−6.07	35.51
LONG 1000 MAR 320 PUTS	−384.00	47.00	−46.00	651.00
LONG 1000 MAR 330 PUTS	−533.00	49.00	−47.00	672.00
TOTAL	−388.15	16.73	−11.97	1564.12
SCALED DOWN BY 1000:	−0.388	0.017	−0.012	1.564
NET COST = $25.99				

March 330s), three long put positions (1000 Mar 320s, 82 January 330s, and 1000 March 330s), two short calls (833 January 330s and 556 January 320s), and one short put (1000 January 320s).

"Smaller" puts can be constructed by scaling down each of the above positions proportionately. Table 16–4 shows the calculations; the slight error in the totals is due to rounding.

The tough part of engineering an option is dealing with the dynamic nature of the product. Any synthetic option portfolio requires frequent adjustment if it is to continue to mimic the desired theoretical option. This requires adjustments to the long and short positions in the portfolio as time passes and the value of the underlying asset changes.

After two days, for instance, the level of the cash index might have fallen one point to 325.00. The passage of time and the change in the value of the underlying asset will cause the pricing model derivatives to change also. Table 16–5 shows the new position characteristics compared to those of the theoretical put we seek to replicate.

Table 16–5 Position Derivatives After Two Days		
	TARGET	**ACTUAL**
DELTA	−0.388	−0.394
THETA	−0.011	−0.006
GAMMA	0.016	0.013
VEGA	1.566	1.555

PRIMES AND SCORES

PRIMES and SCORES were arguably the first of the engineered hybrid securities. Although they are now out of existence, they provide a good case study. **PRIME** is the acronym for "Prescribed Right to Income and Maximum Equity"; **SCORE** stands for "Special Claim on Residual Equity." Rather than being issued by an underlying company, these were issued by a separate legal entity called the **Americus Trust**. There were 24 separate companies on which an Americus Trust unit was issued in 1986. Each unit contained one PRIME and one SCORE. These securities provided investors a means of separating a stock's income and capital appreciation potential. Both types of securities had a five-year initial life and were marketable.

A person who bought a PRIME obtained all the rights of ordinary equity ownership except unlimited upside potential.[5] Above a certain price level, the PRIME owner received no further capital gains. This is analogous to the profit/loss characteristics associated with the writing of a covered call.

Owning a SCORE was like owning a long-term European call option.[6] The SCORE owner received nothing other than the intrinsic value of the option at its "expiration." Rather than a striking price, the SCORE had a *termination claim*. If the stock price was above the termination claim at the dissolution of the trust, the SCORE was valuable.

The holder of Americus Trust securities could become an ordinary stockholder by redeeming a PRIME and a SCORE, receiving a share of common stock in exchange. Figure 16–3 shows the relationship. A *unit* contained both a PRIME and a SCORE; a unit could be exchanged for a share of stock. A share of stock, however, could not be exchanged for a unit.

[5] The PRIME holder received the same dividends as the underlying shareholder minus a small fee associated with the administration of the trust. This was about a penny per share per quarter.

[6] SCORES resembled long-term call options more than warrants. Warrants are issued directly by the company and can dilute earnings per share. SCORES and listed options are issued by an entity other than the underlying company.

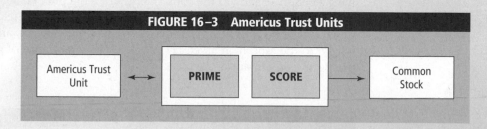

FIGURE 16–3   Americus Trust Units

Americus Trust Unit ↔ PRIME   SCORE → Common Stock

To keep the engineered put behaving like a "real" one, it is necessary to adjust the option positions that comprise it. This is an example of **dynamic hedging**, in which the manager continually adjusts a derivatives position as market variables change. Using updated pricing model derivatives and new option premiums, the linear program can be modified slightly to find a new basket of options that will have the desired characteristics. Table 16–6 shows a new solution.

TABLE 16–6 Adjustments to Replicate the Put			
OPTION	**ORIGINAL POSITION**	**NEW MIX**	**ACTION**
JAN 320 CALL	SHORT 556	SHORT 1000	SELL 444
MAR 320 CALL	LONG 820	LONG 793	SELL 27
JAN 330 CALL	SHORT 833	SHORT 408	BUY 425
MAR 330 CALL	LONG 1000	LONG 1000	—
JAN 320 PUT	SHORT 1000	SHORT 248	BUY 752
MAR 320 PUT	LONG 1000	LONG 1000	—
JAN 330 PUT	LONG 82	SHORT 589	SELL 671
MAR 330 PUT	LONG 1000	LONG 1000	—

These extensive adjustments are necessary in order to replicate the two-year put option exactly. The money manager is probably most interested in the position delta as time passes, and the new position delta of –0.394 is not so different from the original target of –0.388. Many managers would not choose to adjust the portfolio merely because of this slight deviation from the target figure. How frequently you should reconstruct the portfolio to fine-tune delta depends on the rest of your market positions and the magnitude of the trading fees you pay, in addition to how rapidly the market has moved since you first built the put.

GAMMA RISK

There is usually a variety of ways to engineer a derivatives product. Not all solutions are equally desirable, as they differ with regard to their cost and their robustness. One especially important characteristic is the product's **gamma risk**. This measures two things: (1) how sensitive the position is to changes in the underlying asset price, and (2) the consequences of a big price change.

Earlier, we saw that gamma is a measure of how delta (related to the directional market) changes as the underlying asset price changes, and that gamma is related to the "speed" market. Let's look at the importance of gamma from the perspective of a financial engineer.

TABLE 16–7 Options Data						
	CALLS			**PUTS**		
STRIKE	**PREMIUM**	**DELTA**	**GAMMA**	**PREMIUM**	**DELTA**	**GAMMA**
50	$11.24	0.880	0.019	$ 0.63	–0.121	0.019
60	$ 4.51	0.565	0.037	$ 3.84	–0.445	0.038
70	$ 1.31	0.244	0.029	$10.71	–0.787	0.033

TABLE 16-8   Alternative Solutions

SOLUTION A

POSITION	QUANTITY	DELTA	GAMMA	PREMIUM
STOCK	+10,000	+10,000	—	—
60 CALL	−100	−5,650	−370	+$45,100
60 PUT	+98	−4,361	+372	−$37,632
		−11	+2	+$7,468

SOLUTION B

POSITION	QUANTITY	DELTA	GAMMA	PREMIUM
STOCK	+10,000	+10,000	—	—
50 CALL	−114	−10,032	−217	+ $128,136
		−32	−217	+ $128,136

Suppose we hold 10,000 shares of a $60 stock and want to temporarily move to a position delta of zero. We have the options data in Table 16-7 and two possible solutions in Table 16-8.

Both solutions have an initial position delta close to zero. While both solutions bring in option premium, Solution B has the attraction of bringing in a great deal more than Solution A. Note, however, that there is a considerable difference in the position gammas. As we saw in Chapter 7, Solution B, with its negative gamma, may be hurt by a fast market. Suppose that the underlying stock price rises by 5%, from $60 to $63. Table 16-9 shows new option values.

Table 16-10 shows the effect on each solution. After this shock in the stock price, Solution A is preferable for two reasons. For one thing, its position delta remains near the target figure of zero. This means the financial engineer does not need to make any adjustments to keep the portfolio on track. A second positive characteristic of Solution A is that its value changed by only $68, while the other portfolio declined by over $1,000.

TABLE 16-9   Options Data

	CALLS			PUTS		
STRIKE	PREMIUM	DELTA	GAMMA	PREMIUM	DELTA	GAMMA
50	$13.96	0.927	0.012	$0.36	−0.074	0.013
60	$ 6.38	0.668	0.032	$2.68	−0.339	0.033
70	$ 2.14	0.336	0.033	$8.47	−0.687	0.035

TABLE 16–10	Impact of 5% Increase in Stock Price			

SOLUTION A

POSITION	QUANTITY	DELTA	CHANGE IN OPTION VALUE	GAIN OR LOSS
STOCK	+10,000	+10,000	—	+$30,000
60 CALL	−100	−6,680	+$1.87	−18,700
60 PUT	+98	−3,322	−1.16	−11,368
TOTAL		−2		−$68

SOLUTION B

POSITION	QUANTITY	DELTA	CHANGE IN OPTION VALUE	GAIN OR LOSS
STOCK	+10,000	+10,000	—	+$30,000
50 CALL	−114	−10,568	+ $2.72	− 31,008
TOTAL		−568		− $1,008

Gamma risk is analogous to construction quality.

In some respects gamma risk is analogous to construction quality. A Florida building contractor can cut corners when erecting a house, and as long as the weather is calm there may not be any problems. After every hurricane, though, the television cameras show whole subdivisions of houses that lost their roofs, while homes a mile away that were built by someone else remain intact. You can pay for quality, or you can accept poorer design. An options portfolio with a gamma far from zero will rattle apart when the market experiences stormy weather.

RISK MANAGEMENT

Risk management is the primary reason the derivatives markets exist.

It is difficult to write about the derivatives markets without incorporating risk management into almost every example. Risk management is the primary reason these markets exist. Each previous chapter discussed at least a small aspect of the topic. Any strategy using derivatives assets, such as covered calls, protective puts, or futures hedges, alters the risk/expected return characteristics of a portfolio.

A clairvoyant equity manager will be either 100 percent in the market or completely out of it at any point in time. For the rest of us, changing market conditions cause our stock market optimism to periodically refashion itself. Consequently, the proportion of our portfolios held in stock is subject to frequent change. This section provides additional perspective on the power of derivative assets as tools to the financial risk manager.

MANAGED FUTURES

The term **managed futures** refers to investment management in which futures contracts are used as an asset class, especially for their profit potential rather than for their risk reduction benefits. Money managers who deal in futures are formally called **commodity trading advisors**, or CTAs.

There is some evidence that futures as a group have low or even negative return correlation with stock and bond markets. If this is the case, it makes them excellent portfolio components. The managed futures industry got a significant shot in the arm in 1983 when a Harvard professor, John Lintner, reported on his research showing that futures have an important role to play in investment management. At the 1983 Annual Conference of the Financial Analysts Federation in Toronto, Canada, Professor Lintner presented a paper entitled "The Potential Role of Managed Commodity-Financial Futures Accounts (and/or Funds) in Portfolios of Stocks and Bonds."

The paper reported that "the improvements from holding an efficiently-selected portfolio of managed accounts or funds are so large—and the correlation between returns on the futures portfolios and those on the stock and bond portfolio are so surprisingly low (sometimes even negative)—that the return/risk tradeoffs provided by augmented portfolios . . . clearly dominate the tradeoffs available from portfolio of stocks alone or from portfolios of stocks and bonds."

By mid-2001 there was probably about $50 billion invested in managed futures accounts. As with investment managers in any asset class, the performance of the CTAs varies. Some have lost most of their capital, while others have made their clients very happy. For many large institutional investors, especially endowments and foundations, managed futures have become an important part of the portfolio.

MANAGING COMPANY RISK

Options pricing theory and its offspring have turned modern portfolio management on its nose during the last two decades. Few option traders can talk shop for more than a minute without paying homage to the delta god. Many modern portfolio managers actively practice some form of **delta management**, which refers to any investment practice that monitors position delta and seeks to maintain it within a certain range. Delta is an extremely useful idea for many reasons, one of which is particularly material here: It is a direct measure of the "degree of bullishness" represented in a particular security position or portfolio.

Delta management seeks to maintain position delta in an acceptable range.

We have seen that delta is the first derivative of the option-pricing model with respect to the price of the underlying asset, and ranges from −1.0 to 1.0. A call option might have a delta of 0.70; this means for every $1 change in the value of the underlying asset, the value of the option will increase by 70 cents.

If someone owns 10,000 shares of AVP (*AVP, NYSE*) that person's position delta in AVP is 10,000 × 1.0, or 10,000: each share of stock counts one "delta

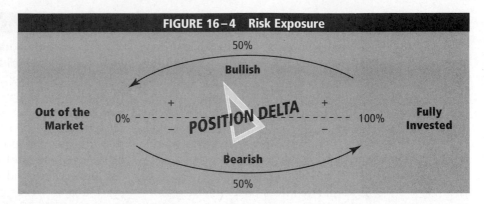

FIGURE 16–4   Risk Exposure

point." The AVP position delta is simply the sum of the deltas contained therein from AVP stock and the related options position.

Figure 16–4 shows how you can think of position delta as a position on a dial. In this AVP example we begin fully invested with a position delta of 10,000. Reducing position delta to 5,000 is analogous to turning the dial counter clockwise halfway toward zero. If we were really bearish we could go past zero and assume a *negative* position delta.[7] By adding positions or closing out existing ones, the portfolio manager can assume any desired degree of risk.

A CASE STUDY

This example shows how a portfolio manager can use options to alter temporarily the risk exposure in a position, generate income in the process, and restore the portfolio to its original state with little disruption.

Initial Conditions
Suppose that on January 26 a portfolio manager holds 10,000 shares of AVP, currently selling for $33. Recent events cause the portfolio manager to become slightly less optimistic regarding the AVP position, and she decides to turn the dial down to 90%. Viewing the initial 10,000-share block as a 100% bullish position, there are several ways to reduce the risk in the stock.

−100%   +100%

At first, the AVP position delta is 10,000. The objective is to reduce the position delta to 90 percent of this, or 9,000. There are three choices:

1. sell 1,000 shares of AVP and hold cash;

2. buy put options;

3. write call options.

---

[7] This would be equivalent to a short position in the stock.

An obvious way is to sell shares and hold cash. Selling 1,000 shares, for instance, would reduce the position delta to 9,000 (90% of the original value). Relative to the starting point, the portfolio manager is now "90% bullish." A problem with this method of adjusting the portfolio is the potential for cries of churning[8] if the shares are bought back after the economic smoke clears.

Another alternative is to buy AVP puts, which would add *negative* deltas to the portfolio and consequently reduce the total. Buying puts requires cash, however, and you may not want to make the expenditure. You can also write AVP calls (adding negative deltas), or you could do some combination of the various methods. Considering all this, suppose the decision is to write calls.

Perhaps the AVP MAR 35 call sells for $2 and has a delta of 0.441. The manager determines that writing 23 of these contracts will reduce the position delta appropriately:

$10,000 - (N \times 0.441 \times 100) = 9,000$

$1,000 = 44.1\ N$

$N = 22.68$, rounded to 23

This brings $4,600 in premium income into the portfolio. The position delta is now 8,986:

$$(10,000\ \text{shares} \times 1.0) - (2,300\ \text{calls} \times 0.441) = \mathbf{8,986}$$

Relative to the starting position delta of 10,000, the portfolio is at about the 90% bullish mark as the portfolio manager desired.

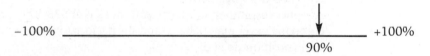

-100% _____ $+100\%$

90%

One Week Passes

After one week, AVP stock sells for $32^{1}/_{2}$. The MAR 35 calls now have a delta of 0.404. The position delta changes to 9,071:

$$(10,000\ \text{shares} \times 1.0) - (2,300\ \text{calls} \times 0.404) = \mathbf{9,071}$$

The manager decides to reduce the AVP exposure further, to 50% of the original level. Again, there are three methods for doing this:

1. sell 4,071 shares of AVP and hold cash;

2. buy put options;

3. write more call options.

---

[8] Churning is generating trading fees for the broker through unwarranted trades.

The manager selects the latter. According to Black-Scholes, the MAR 35 calls should now sell for $1⅝. The manager can write 77 more of these and they will still be covered by the stock. This would generate $12,513 in premium income. The position delta becomes 5,960:

$$(10,000 \text{ shares} \times 1.0) - (10,000 \text{ calls} \times 0.404) = \textbf{5,960}$$

This position, 59.6% bullish relative to the starting position, is higher than the manager wants. Writing any additional calls would leave them uncovered, and the manager does not want to do this. Unless she sells some stock, she has to buy puts.

Buying Puts

The APR 30 puts would sell for $1.95 and have a delta of –0.310. The manager figures out that the purchase of 31 contracts will adjust the position delta to the desired level as Table 16–11 shows.

At March Expiration

At option expiration in March, AVP stock is at $33. The manager's fears about the company never materialized, and she decides to return to the original 100% position (position delta of 10,000).

The MAR 35 calls expire worthless. The APR 30 puts can be sold for $0.96 according to Black-Scholes. Table 16–12 summarizes the total option income associated with this risk management case study.

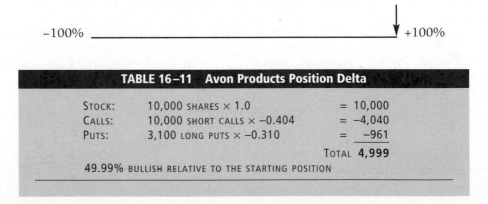

TABLE 16–11 Avon Products Position Delta		
Stock:	10,000 shares × 1.0	= 10,000
Calls:	10,000 short calls × –0.404	= –4,040
Puts:	3,100 long puts × –0.310	= –961
		Total **4,999**
49.99% bullish relative to the starting position		

TABLE 16–12 Total Option Income	
23 CALLS SOLD ON JAN 26:	+ $4,600
77 CALLS SOLD A WEEK LATER:	+ 12,513
31 PUTS BOUGHT @ $1.95:	– 6,045
31 PUTS SOLD @ $0.96:	+ 2,976
NET INCOME FROM OPTIONS:	**$14,044**

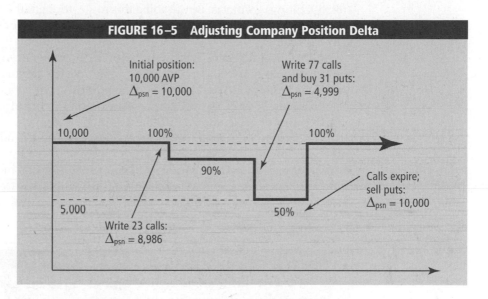

FIGURE 16–5   Adjusting Company Position Delta

Figure 16–5 shows how the portfolio manager used options to alter the risk exposure of an individual security position without disturbing the equity portfolio.

MANAGING MARKET RISK

In practice, most institutional use of stock index futures is to reduce risk rather than to eliminate it.

William Schreyer, former Chairman and CEO of Merrill Lynch, once said, "Life wasn't designed to be risk-free. The key is not to eliminate risk, but to estimate it accurately and manage it wisely." Earlier in this book we saw how stock index futures like those on the S&P 500 can alter the market risk of a stock portfolio. In practice, most institutional use of SPX futures is to *reduce* risk rather than *eliminate* it. A principle of finance is that risk and expected return are directly related. If you completely reduce risk, returns should be modest in a well-functioning marketplace.

Puts and calls are an essential part of delta management with individual equities. The same discussion applies to delta management of market risk using *futures* puts and calls. A long futures contract has a delta of +1.0; a position that is short

100 futures has a delta of –100.00. Call options have deltas near 1.0 if they are deep-in-the-money and near zero if they are far out-of-the-money. Puts have deltas near –1.0 when deep-in-the-money and near zero if far out-of-the-money. When the option striking price is near the price of the underlying asset, the option delta will be near 0.5 (for calls) or –0.5 (for puts). We get the exact value of delta using the Black futures option-pricing model.

Suppose that an equity portfolio manager determines that his portfolio can be completely hedged by selling 300 SPX futures contracts. He decides to hedge one third of the portfolio. Obviously, the quickest way to do so would be to sell 100 SPX futures contracts. Before going this route, though, the manager wants to investigate possibilities in the futures options market. He finds the market data in Table 16–13.

The hedging objective is to subtract 100 delta points from the portfolio, or, equivalently, to add 100 *negative* delta points. We get negative delta by selling futures, by writing calls, or by buying puts. While there is a variety of ways to get the desired result, suppose the manager uses a combination of short futures, short calls, and short puts as shown in Table 16–14.

This package has the desired position delta and has the added advantage of gathering almost $2\frac{1}{2}$ million in premium income. As with equity options, this money belongs to the portfolio regardless of what happens in the future, which is the next logical question: What might happen? Table 16–15 shows the consequences of market movements.

TABLE 16–13 Futures Options Data		
S&P 500 STOCK INDEX = 1235.00		
	PREMIUM	**DELTA**
1225 PUT	$50.56	–0.45
1250 CALL	$49.18	0.47

Values from the Black option pricing model with T = 100 days, σ = 22%, R = 5%.

TABLE 16–14 Three-part Futures Hedge		
POSITION	**INCOME**	**DELTA**
SHORT 100 FUTURES	0	–100
WRITE 96 CALLS	96 × 250 × $49.18 = $1,180,320	–45
WRITE 100 PUTS	100 × 250 × $50.56 = $1,264,000	+45
TOTAL	$2,444,320	–100

TABLE 16–15 Market Scenarios		
AT EXPIRATION:		
S&P 500 < 1225	**1225 < S&P 500 < 1250**	**S&P 500 > 1250**
THE PUTS ARE EXERCISED; GOING LONG THE 100 CONTRACTS ESSENTIALLY REMOVES THE HEDGE PREVIOUSLY IN PLACE.	THE OPTIONS EXPIRE WORTHLESS.	THE CALLS ARE EXERCISED; THE FUTURES HEDGE BECOMES LARGER BY 96 CONTRACTS.

If the S&P 500 index falls below the put striking price of 1225, the put holder will exercise them. When you exercise a futures put you assume a short position in futures, with the other side of the trade obligated to take a long position. In this example, the portfolio was already short 100 futures, so if you simultaneously take a long position in 100 futures the Clearinghouse will close you out. You still have the stock portfolio, but the hedge is gone.

If the index lies between the two striking prices, both the puts and the calls expire worthless, the portfolio remains intact, and you keep the two option premiums.

If the index rises above the call striking price, the call owner will exercise them, and you will have an obligation to take a short position in the futures. Your hedge becomes larger by 96 contracts in this example, meaning that you have a larger hedge than you want.

With derivatives available, we have many more tools to use in the practice of investment management. Remember that derivatives are neutral products; their risk and utility depends on what you do with them. They may not be appropriate in every situation, but a money manager who takes his or her job seriously should consider ways in which they might improve a portfolio or facilitate risk management.

SUMMARY

Financial engineering is a rapidly growing sub-field of the derivative assets business. It is the popular name for the construction of asset portfolios that have precise technical characteristics, particularly when those characteristics are not available in an existing exchange-traded product.

One of the first instances of financial engineering was the construction of synthetic put options before puts were available on the exchanges. Another important instance was the Americus Trust units with their PRIMES and SCORES.

Because the characteristics of a particular option are easily determined, it is often possible to create an option portfolio with a particular set of position "Greeks" so that it mimics a desired, but unlisted, option. The financial engineer mixes the existing option products in the right proportion much as a cook follows a recipe.

Because the characteristics of an option change as the underlying variables change, in many option applications it is necessary to periodically adjust the components of the option position in order to keep it on track. This process is called dynamic hedging.

Delta management is the practice of maintaining a portfolio's position delta within a desired range. This can be done on individual securities (to deal with company risk) or on the aggregate portfolio (to deal with market risk).

SELF TEST

T ___ F ___   1. It is good practice to eliminate investment risk.

T ___ F ___   2. The first widespread use of financial engineering was the creation of synthetic call options at the CBOE.

T ___ F ___   3. Extensive purchase of individual equity puts is inefficient in a large portfolio.

T ___ F ___   4. Unless there are LEAPS available, it is not possible to engineer an option with a life of more than one year.

T ___ F ___   5. Dynamic hedging is the practice of adjusting portfolio components with the passage of time.

T ___ F ___   6. The closer position gamma is to zero, the more frequent the adjustments necessary to keep it near this level.

T ___ F ___   7. If the underlying asset price does not change, theta and delta will change with the passage of time, but gamma will not.

T ___ F ___   8. PRIMES and SCORES no longer trade.

T ___ F ___   9. A negative position gamma means that a fast market will always help you.

T ___ F ___   10. If position delta is near zero, the portfolio value will not change much with normal changes in the price of the underlying asset.

T ___ F ___   11. Gamma risk is analogous to the quality of building construction.

T ___ F ___ 12. Risk management is the primary reason the derivatives markets exist.

T ___ F ___ 13. Delta management refers to any investment practice that tries to keep position delta within a particular range.

T ___ F ___ 14. A stock position can be made less bullish by selling shares, by writing calls, or by writing puts.

T ___ F ___ 15. Most institutional use of stock index futures is to completely remove market risk from an equity portfolio.

PROBLEMS & QUESTIONS

Use the following data as needed: stock price = $55, interest rates = 4%, volatility = .25, time until MAY expiration = 45 days, time until JUN expiration = 74 days, European style.

1. Someone once said, "Finance is the study of arbitrage." What does this statement mean?
2. Explain the term "financial engineering."
3. Why is buying a put better portfolio protection than writing a covered call?
4. Why does selling stock index futures eliminate upside profit potential on a diversified portfolio?
5. Suppose a portfolio contains options on twenty different underlying securities. Explain why the portfolio's aggregate position *theta* is probably more meaningful than the aggregate position *delta*.
6. How does the options concept of position risk affect financial engineering applications?
7. In engineering a put for downside protection, why is gamma important?
8. Why do engineered options need periodic adjustment?
9. You hold 5 JUN 45 calls, 5 JUN 55 calls, and are short 5 JUN 60 calls.
   a. What is the position delta?
   b. What is the position theta?
   c. What is the position gamma?
10. In Problem 9, suppose that 10 days pass and the stock price retreats to $54. What are the new position derivatives?

11. In Problem 9, suppose all the options were *puts* instead of calls. Do you need to recalculate values to determine
    a. position delta?
    b. position theta?
    c. position gamma?
12. Refer to the data at the beginning of this section. What is the theoretical Black-Scholes value for a 3-year put with a striking price of 55?
13. How many days could you keep the put option in the previous problem before it lost 10% of its initial value?
14. According to Black-Scholes, the premium for a one-year option is less than the sum of the premiums for two successive six-month options. Show that this is true, and explain why this is.
15. Select a LEAP from the *Wall Street Journal* listing. Calculate its implied volatility. Do the same for an ordinary equity option on the same company. Why do you think the implied volatility values might be different?
16. Prepare a plot showing time value decay of a 3-year call option. Use the data at the start of this section and a striking price of $60.
17. Refer to Table 16–4. Determine the position derivatives of this synthetic put if
    a. The XPS index fell suddenly to 200;
    b. The XPS index rose suddenly to 500.

CHAPTER 16 REVIEW

18. You write an out-of-the-money covered call. What happens to your position delta as time passes if the option remains out-of-the-money?

19. You buy an at-the-money protective put. Subsequently, the stock price falls. What happens to your position delta as expiration approaches?

20. You write an out-of-the-money covered call and buy an out-of-the-money protective put. As expiration approaches, what happens to your
    a. position delta?
    b. position gamma?
    c. position theta?

17

Contemporary Issues

The question . . . is whether the LTCM disaster was merely a unique and isolated event, a bad drawing from nature's urn; or whether such disasters are the inevitable consequence of the Black-Scholes formula itself and the illusion it may give that all market participants can hedge away all their risk at the same time.

> Merton Miller
> Nobel Prize winner in Economics

This concluding chapter looks at some of the contemporary issues that are newsworthy in the derivatives world today. The collapse of *Long-Term Capital Management* (LTCM) has become a case study for what can go wrong when you rely on historical data and couple the data with high leverage. *Value at risk* (VAR) represents the industry's efforts to find a way to meaningfully measure the risk of a derivatives position. *New products* continue to appear in response to new risks, or old ones that were previously unhedgable. Weather derivatives are an especially interesting innovation. While not a new topic, financial news services still routinely mention *program trading* in their reports. Finally, there are substantial risk management implications stemming from the new accounting rule known as *FAS 133*.

LONG-TERM CAPITAL MANAGEMENT[1]

The rise and fall of Long-Term Capital Management (LTCM) is already a case study at Harvard Business School. Founded by some of Wall Street's brightest minds and best traders, this hedge fund's stature was further enhanced by two big names from academics, Robert Merton and Myron Scholes. These two finance professors received the Nobel Prize in economics for their work in the area of option pricing. *Institutional Investor* called them the best finance faculty in the world.

John Meriwether was the driving force behind the fund. He is a well-respected former Salomon Brothers partner who made a fortune for the firm (and himself) in the bond arbitrage group, which he formed in 1977. A variety of events led him to leave Salomon, and in 1993 he began to seriously promote the idea of the LTCM hedge fund among his many acquaintances on Wall Street.

A **hedge fund** is a largely unregulated investment portfolio, usually with a substantial minimum investment. Typically the fund engages in esoteric investment activities that would be unavailable to an individual or small institutional investor. A shroud of secrecy with regard to trading strategy and specific activities often surrounds a hedge fund. Such was clearly the case at LTCM. Meriwether and his colleagues kept their investment strategies close to their vests and relied on their reputations to raise money.

LTCM's traders believed that money management was a quantifiable science rather than an art. In particular, their computer models suggested long-term global bond price relationships that should prevail. When actual market prices departed from these values, LTCM would "play the spread," anticipating a "return to normal" in the bond prices.

Early in 1998 LTCM began to place bets that market volatility would decline, back to its historical average level. The firm's traders wrote options at an implied volatility of 19%, did so on a huge scale, and employed substantial leverage in placing their bets. In his account of LTCM, Roger Lowenstein writes that "Eventually, they had a staggering $40 million riding on each volatility point change in equity volatility in the United States and an equivalent amount in Europe—perhaps a fourth of the overall market. Morgan Stanley coined a nickname for the fund: the Central Bank of Volatility."[2] By August the fund's capital totaled $3.6 billion. Five weeks later it would all be gone.

Part of the problem was that LTCM's positions were so huge it was unable to move out of them. Again citing Lowenstein: "Despite the ballyhooed growth in derivatives, there was no liquidity in credit markets. There never is when everyone wants out at the same time. This is what the models had missed. When losses mount, leveraged investors such as Long-Term are *forced* to sell, lest their losses

A hedge fund is a largely unregulated investment portfolio.

---

[1] The facts in this section come from "When Genius Failed: The Rise and Fall of Long-Term Capital Management" by Roger Lowenstein. New York: Random House, 2000.

[2] Ibid, page 126.

If you owe $100 and cannot pay **you** are in trouble. But if you owe $100 million and cannot pay, **they** are in trouble.

overwhelm them. When a firm has to sell in a market without buyers, prices run to the extremes beyond the bell curve."[3]

By mid-September equity volatility was up to 33%. This was a 19-point increase from a month earlier, with each point costing the fund $40 million. Prices still had not returned to where they were "supposed" to be. "In every class of asset and all over the world, the market moved against the hedge fund in Greenwich. . . . Every roll was turning up snake eyes. The mathematicians had not foreseen this. Random markets, they had thought, would lead to standard distributions—to a normal pattern of black sheep and white sheep, heads and tails, and jacks and deuces, not to staggering losses in every trade, day after day after day."[4]

On September 21st, the fund lost $553 million, leaving it with under $1 billion in equity. That means the *fund lost one third of its equity in a single day*! Although its equity was $1 billion, the fund's total assets were over *$100 billion* (not counting the positions in derivatives). In other words, the fund was leveraged more than 100 to 1. If the fund were to lose an additional 1%, its net worth would be entirely gone.

There is an old saying that if you owe $100 and cannot pay you are in trouble. But if you owe $100 million and cannot pay, *they* are in trouble. LTCM's looming collapse led a consortium of Wall Street banks, facilitated by the Federal Reserve Bank of New York, to arrange a bailout of the fund. If LTCM had failed, it would have had catastrophic consequences on markets across the globe. While no taxpayer dollars were involved, there were the inevitable headlines about the "government coming to the rescue of multimillionaires." In testimony before the U.S. Senate, Patrick Parkinson of the Federal Reserve Board stated

LTCM appears to have received very generous credit terms, even though it took an exceptional degree of risk. . . . counter parties obtained information from LTCM that indicated that it had securities and derivatives positions that were very large relative to its capital. However, few, if any, seem to have really understood LTCM's risk profile.[5]

"Markets can remain irrational longer than you can remain solvent."
—John Maynard Keynes

The famous economist John Maynard Keynes made many memorable statements about the market. In retrospect, one of his proverbs is especially poignant in armchair quarterbacking LTCM: "Markets can remain irrational longer than you can remain solvent." LTCM fully believed that prices would return to where the computer models said they should be, but the firm ran out of money before prices decided to go there.

Value at Risk

As we saw in Chapter 7, those who use derivatives are very interested in what can go *really* wrong. A small adverse price movement normally generates a small loss,

---

[3] Ibid, page 151.

[4] Ibid, p. 173.

[5] Patrick M. Parkinson, "Progress report by the President's Working Group on Financial Markets," testimony before Committee on Agriculture, Nutrition, and Forestry, U.S. Senate, December 16, 1998.

one that won't break the bank. It is important to understand the consequences of an *unusually large* price change, even if such a change is unlikely. This is why options traders look at position risk and doomsday scenarios.

While we are interested in abnormal behavior in the marketplace, we also like to know something about *normal* behavior and what we can reasonably expect in ordinary times. If we can draw some statistical inference about changes in market prices, we can draw similar inferences about future values of a portfolio. This is the motivation behind the emergence of a concept known as *value at risk*.

Value at risk seeks to measure the maximum loss that a portfolio might sustain over a period of time given a set probability level.

Value at risk seeks to measure the maximum loss that a portfolio might sustain over a period of time given a set probability level. Typically, value at risk (often abbreviated VAR) looks at a 95% probability range over 1 day. For instance, a portfolio manager might report that the portfolio has a one-day VAR of $25,000. This means that based on historical data and/or mathematical modeling, 95% of the days the portfolio did not decline in value by more than $25,000. VAR can be reported either as a dollar amount or as a percentage of fund assets.

Pensions and Investments[6] reported that in early 2000 the median value at risk for the 200 largest corporate defined benefit pension plans in the United States was 17% of the portfolio value over a one-year period, based on the 95% probability level. The range of fund VARs was 9.5% to 28%.

Credit Suisse Asset Management assembled the report with these results, and also found a few thought-provoking relationships. The pension funds that were underfunded tended to have the lowest VAR, meaning they were the most conservative. Overfunded funds tended to have the highest VAR, meaning they were the most aggressive in their risk taking.

As yet there is no absolute industry standard for the calculation of VAR. While most calculations use the 95% confidence interval for one day, some firms do otherwise. There is some debate among theoreticians regarding the best way to model VAR over more than one day. Logically, you can envision a large loss in the next two weeks more easily than a large loss in the next ten minutes. There is more dispersion of results over longer periods. As Long-Term Capital Management learned, relying on past data to predict market behavior in the future can be a treacherous practice. It seems, however, that no one has yet discovered a better way of expressing VAR over time than relating standard deviation to the square root of time, or $\sigma\sqrt{T}$. This is a familiar expression from the Black-Scholes option-pricing model.

"Planning for crises is more important than VAR analysis."
—Myron Scholes

Myron Scholes commented[7] on the LTCM experience and the dangers of using historical data in VAR calculations in an address to the European Derivatives and Risk Management Conference in Paris on April 12, 2000:

---

[6] Phyllis Feinberg, "Companies' Median VAR 17%," *Pensions and Investments*, January 24, 2000, 93.

[7] Reported in Myron Scholes, "Crisis and Risk," *Risk*, May 2000, 50–53.

Correlation patterns and variances, however, are not stationary, especially when market prices move dramatically. Factors that might exhibit low levels of correlation or association most of the time appear to be highly correlated in volatile times. When the value of nearly all asset classes are moving in step, diversification is not helpful in reducing risk. The actual realized correlation patterns appear to be close to one. In these times, the volatility of profit and losses will be far greater than VAR would predict. In addition, liquidity and risk premiums change dramatically, resulting in far greater measured underlying asset volatility.

VAR CALCULATION

To get some insight into the VAR calculation, suppose we have a six-month call option on a $100 stock. The call is at the money, with volatility equal to 35%, no dividends, and a 4% riskless interest rate. According to the Black-Scholes model, such a call is worth $10.77. Probability theory tells us that in a normal distribution 95% of the observations lie within 1.96 standard deviations of the mean. We can apply this information to our stock to calculate VAR.

There are about 252 trading days in a year, so an annual sigma of 35% corresponds to a daily sigma of

$$\frac{0.35}{\sqrt{252}} = 0.220 = 2.20\%$$

Multiplying the daily sigma by 1.96, we get 4.31%. If the stock were to fall by 4.31%, its price would be $95.69. If it were to rise by 4.31% its price would be $104.31. We can then say there is a 95% chance that tomorrow the stock price will be between $95.69 and $104.31.

Suppose someone has 100 of these call contracts. The current value of this position is $107,700. There are two elements of risk to the position. One comes from time value decay. Time is going to pass regardless of what else happens, and the option will lose money with the passage of time. (Theta for this option is three cents per day.) The second element of risk comes from a decline in the stock price. If the stock drops, the call value will drop, too.

If the stock drops by $4.31 and one day passes, the new Black-Scholes value is $8.41. The 100-contract position would be worth $84,100. This is a decline of $23,600 from the previous value, so the one-day, 95% VAR for this long call position is $23,600.

Calculating VAR for a portfolio involves multiple calculations of this sort. The procedure becomes complicated when some of the components are clearly correlated. For instance, in calculating the VAR for a long straddle it would not make sense to simply add the VAR for the call to the VAR for the put. If the stock moves sharply you do not lose on both sides of the position. This simple example helps make it apparent why the calculation can be involved and why there is a good market for software to do the calculations for you.

NEW PRODUCT DEVELOPMENT

The exchanges are perpetually on the lookout for changing risk management needs in the marketplace. They do not create new products willy-nilly and then try to sell them. Rather, the exchange's institutional marketing people find out what money managers, corporate treasurers, and other financial professionals *need* and then see if they can construct a product to meet that need. This concluding chapter looks at several of these innovations.

WEATHER DERIVATIVES

Most existing weather derivatives are temperature-based options or swaps.

Mark Twain said, "Everybody talks about the weather, but nobody does anything about it." A savvy financial manager whose bottom line can be hurt by adverse weather conditions *may*, in fact, be able to do something about it. This is the purpose of weather derivatives. Most existing weather derivatives are temperature-based options or swaps.

There are a variety of institutions that face some weather-related risk. An electric utility, for instance, experiences dramatic changes in energy demand during an unusually cold winter (more electric heat) or an unusually hot summer (more air conditioning). Depending on its power supply arrangements, a utility may find that it must purchase power on the open market in order to satisfy demand. These shortfalls are likely to occur when the spot rate for electricity is at its highest. This is clearly not a good situation for the power company whose rates have already been set by the state public utilities commission.

Numerous other types of businesses worry about the weather. A ski resort can make some of its own snow, but business is a lot better with a substantial natural snowfall. There are both psychological and scientific reasons for this. It is easy to imagine how a firm like American Skiing Company could be interested in a product that would let it hedge against the adverse effects of a mild winter.

DERIVATIVES TODAY

RAIN AND CHEESE PRICES

Kraft Foods, a division of Philip Morris, is a significant seller of cheese products. Milk is the principal raw material in the manufacture of cheese. As with most other goods, when there is less of a supply of milk, prices tend to be higher. Agricultural experts have discovered that cows produce less milk when they stand in mud for long periods. An unusually rainy period makes the ground very muddy, a condition that may persist for weeks. Lots of rain means lots of mud and a higher price for milk. Kraft's raw materials costs are going up. From the corporate perspective, rainfall is potentially a risky phenomenon. A financial product that permits hedging rainfall above a certain level could be useful to Kraft.

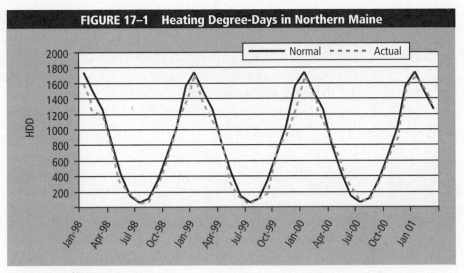

FIGURE 17–1   Heating Degree-Days in Northern Maine

Source: Maine Public Service Company.

Property and casualty insurance companies are swamped with claims after a hurricane or an ice storm. Lots of rain also keeps people away from Disney World, racetracks, and many other outdoor activities. All of these are examples of businesses in which extreme weather impacts corporate profitability, a risk that the corporation might like to hedge.

Weather Swaps

A *temperature swap* might be set up with the floating rate side based on the sum of the **heating degree-days** (HDD)[8] from the effective date of the swap through its termination. The swap fixed rate might be 200 HDDs. The "notional principal" might be $5,000 per HDD, and there may be a cap on the total payout. As with most off-exchange derivatives, a product can usually be custom-built depending on the needs of the client. Figure 17–1 shows the seasonal pattern of heating degree-days in northern Maine.

Weather Options

There is a variety of ways these might be structured. With a plain vanilla temperature *put*, there is a payoff to the option holder if the heating degree-days or cooling degree-days fall below a set level over a period of time at a specific location. With a temperature *call*, we have just the opposite; there is a payoff if the HDD or CDD count is above a set figure.

---

[8] A heating degree-day is a measure of the extent to which temperatures deviate from some norm, usually 65°F. A common measure is 65°F minus the average of the daily high and low temperature over a specific period at some location, with a floor of zero. The flipside of HDD is the cooling degree-day (CDD), calculated the same way except it is the average minus 65°F.

RETAIL WEATHER DERIVATIVES

In early 2000 an Internet company known as RainDay.com (owned by Worldwide Weather Insurance Agency, Inc. in New York) began offering a variety of weather derivatives to the public. The firm's arsenal of products included contracts on fog, lightning, cloud cover, and rain. Someone could get a quotation for a weather product online, send in a premium payment, and receive a weather insurance policy by mail. The policy paid the notional amount once the closest National Weather Service station con-firmed the risk event. The maximum notional amount for a single day was $50,000, and $100,000 for a vacation.

As an example[9] of one product designed to appeal to a certain type of customer, if you had a 2 P.M. tee time on January 30th at Pebble Beach Golf Club you could purchase $10,000 worth of insurance against 1/100 of an inch of rain from 2 to 3 P.M. for a mere $1,203.20.

[9] Nina Mehta, "Get Wet . . . It Pays! Retail Weather Derivatives Via the Internet," *Derivatives Strategy*, January 2000, 8.

Alternatively, the option may be an exotic version, with lookback characteristics, a variable striking price, or it might be a collar that provides potential payoffs in both directions.

ZERO COST WEATHER COLLAR

Britta Katrina's real job (when she isn't trading options) is in a large office building that her firm owns. Knowing of her prowess with derivatives, the CFO of her company asks if she can propose a way in which the firm might protect itself against an unusually cold winter without giving away the store. After doing some research, Britta proposes a zero cost collar.

She discovers that the firm can purchase a local 4,900 HDD call for December, January, and February at a cost of $220,000. She also learns that the firm could write a 4,500 HDD put for the same premium, $220,000. The options provide that each HDD above the strike (with the call) or below the strike (with the put) require the writer to pay $5,000. The proceeds from writing the put offset the cost of the call.

Figure 17–2 shows the implications of various actual HDD experiences. If the local HDD total is between the striking prices (4,500 to 4,900), both options expire worthless and there is no payout. If the HDD level is above 4,900 the call is valuable, and the firm will receive a cash inflow from the call writer. If, however, the winter is unusually warm and the HDD level is below 4,500, the firm would have to pay $5,000 per HDD to the put owner.

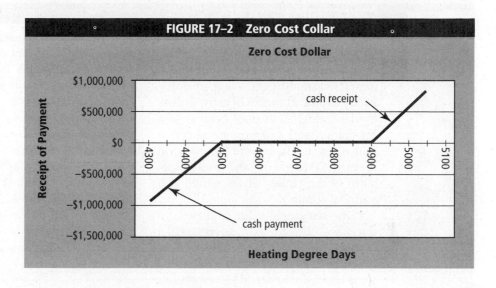

FIGURE 17–2   Zero Cost Collar

TELECOM CAPACITY

Beginning in early 1999 bankers and telecommunication companies began looking at the possibility of risk transfer relating to bandwidth constraints, Internet congestion, and similar matters. There was generally a shortage of telecom capacity in mid-2001. As new players enter the market, capacity will increase and prices will likely fall. Some telecom companies would like to lock in current prices, and if there were a futures contract or other derivative enabling them to do so they would seriously consider it.

Some industry officials anticipate the emergence of a forward market in international telecommunications traffic within a short time. Growing use of the Internet spawns risks of various sorts for those in this industry, and where there is risk there is a need for hedging instruments.

RENTAL CAPS

Another derivative innovation is the **rental cap**, especially as applied to interest rates. Suppose a corporate treasurer is concerned about rising interest rates, but that the concern is short-term pending the forthcoming announcement of certain economic news. The treasurer could buy an ordinary interest rate cap, but this could be expensive. An alternative would be to rent one. Instead of paying an upfront premium, the buyer of a rental cap would make a quarterly premium payment, with the ability to terminate the agreement whenever desired by simply not making a scheduled payment. As an example, in January 1994, a 3-year

CATASTROPHE FUTURES

The Chicago Board of Trade introduced catastrophe futures, called CAT futures, in December 1992. This product was geared toward insurance companies that have periodic instances of many policy-holder claims all at once because of a hurricane, flood, riot, or some other natural disaster. There were contracts on eastern, Midwestern, and western regions of the United States as well as a national contract.

The settlement value of these contracts was linked to a governmental "measure of loss ratio" multiplied by $25,000. The loss ratio was a calculated value based on the actual loss experience of a group of insurance companies.

While the product has intuitive ap-peal, it was not successful for various reasons. Those who went short the contract took substantial risk in the event of a major disaster. Marking to market was problematic because many disasters occur all at once rather than developing over time. There were also complicated regulatory issues that were never completely resolved. Perhaps most important, reinsurance[10] was a well-understood and established alternative. Many insurance companies did not see the advantage of the CBOT product over the traditional method of hedging via reinsurance.

[10] Reinsurance is the practice of an insurance company itself buying insurance against an unusually large dollar amount of claims.

4.50% cap would have cost 175 basis points. A rental cap with similar terms would have cost 25 basis points per quarter.[11]

EQUITY SWAPS

Equity swaps are a popular way to circum-vent local restrictions on the purchase of stock by foreigners.

An **equity swap** is an arrangement in which one party buys stock on behalf of another, receives interest from the other party, with the two parties periodically settling up paper gains/losses on the stock. Equity swaps are a popular way to circumvent local restrictions on the purchase of stock by foreigners.

India, for instance, has restrictive rules on global access to its markets. A U.S. customer (firm A) could enter into an arrangement with another firm (B) that *did* have the ability to buy Indian shares. The swap might involve B buying shares for a set period of time on A's behalf, with B borrowing the money to acquire them. Firm A would pay LIBOR plus a spread to B to cover the borrowing costs. Every three or six months there would be a periodic settlement, with B paying A if the stock went up, or A paying B if the stock went down. The payment between the two parties might simply be the gain or loss on the stock. At the conclusion of the swap B sells the stock, pays off the loan, with a final remittance check between A and B. Firm A has effectively bought the stock and borrowed the money to pay for it.

[11] Reported in "Rent-a-Caps and Other Innovations," *Derivatives Strategy*, 30 January 1994, 5.

ESOPS, INTERNET STOCKS, AND THE IRS

During the dot.com craze the news was full of stories of start-up firms staffed by new millionaires who got rich when their firm went public. In an effort to retain key employees, the majority of these firms provided hefty employment incentives in the form of **employee stock option plans**, or ESOPs. While these made many people extremely rich, they also sent some folks to the poorhouse or into a new line of work.

With an ESOP an employee acquires call options to buy the company's shares, often a substantial quantity, at an attractive striking price. These options are not marketable and do not trade on an exchange. They are private transactions between the company and the employee.

The *Industry Standard*, a widely read E-Commerce publication, relates the tale of one of the founders of E-Toys.[12] In January 2000, the man exercised options on 250,000 shares for between $0.01 and $0.14 apiece. With E-Toy selling for $19¾ at the time, he had nearly

a $5 million gain from the exercise. Because of the Alternative Minimum Tax provision of the Internal Revenue Code, he also acquired a tax liability of 28% of his paper gains from the options.

The dot.coms were hit hard in the last part of 2000, and near the end of the year the company's stock was down to 25 cents per share. He could avoid the AMT assessment by selling the shares and reporting the actual loss on the sale of the stock in addition to the paper gain on the option exercise, but as an officer of the company his shares were restricted meaning that he could only sell a portion of his holdings unless he resigned his position.

This is what he decided he had to do. He left his job at E-Toys, sold more than 1.4 million shares for about $266,000, and avoided the tax bill. Accountants say this is an extreme situation, but that there are similar stories elsewhere in Silicon Valley.

[12] Miguel Helft, "Out of Options," *The Industry Standard*, February 12, 2001, 49.

The periodic settlement feature of an equity swap is important because it substantially reduces the credit risk involved. If there were only a single payment from the stock gain or loss at the end of the swap there could be a substantial incentive for the losing party to default.

PROGRAM TRADING

One fundamental principle of finance is that arbitrage opportunities will be short-lived. When security prices deviate from their "true" value such that riskless profits can be made, some market observers will find the arbitrage, exploit it, and quickly eliminate it. This was LTCM's basic game plan.

One method of exploiting arbitrage is via **program trading**. This is "any computer-aided buying or selling activity in the stock market." Other people view program trading as synonymous with "stock index futures arbitrage." Hans Stoll and Robert Whaley, two well-known market researchers, propose that program trading has three key characteristics.[13]

1. It is *portfolio trading*, meaning that an entire portfolio of stocks is traded via a single order;

2. It is *computerized trading* done with small individual lots of stock rather than large blocks;

3. It is *computer decision making*, in which the decisions are triggered by the existence of mispricing (arbitrage).

Arbitrageurs in the marketplace perform a useful function, helping keep the market efficient and ensuring that prices do not deviate from their proper values for very long. As a group, they are not hurting for pocket change, particularly in markets that are popular with the investing public.

IMPLEMENTATION

Computers have made the life of both the arbitrageur and the institutional investor simpler and more profitable. Using the New York Stock Exchange's *Designated Order Turnaround system*, called **DOT**, market orders for less than 2100 shares of a stock may be placed with the stock specialist electronically rather than going through a floor broker. We have seen previously certain relationships that should prevail among security prices, such as the theory of put/call parity and the fair value of stock index futures contracts. With high-speed, continuously on-line computers, it is much easier to identify those instances when arbitrage is present.

A perception that is not accurate is the notion that these watchful computers call the shots on which way stock prices are to move next. The computer identifies situations in which arbitrage is present but does not cause the situation.

Groups of arbitrageurs often identify profitable opportunities almost simultaneously, and they take advantage of these computer-identified opportunities on a grand scale by collectively buying or selling hundreds of thousands of shares in a matter of minutes. Contrary to popular belief, however, this extra volume is mostly from many small institutional trades rather than massive 100,000-share transactions.

Because the arbitrage situation will normally work in only a single direction (e.g., everyone buys or everyone sells), this large influx of orders can cause prices to change drastically. Some people use the term program trading to refer to any strategy that instantaneously recommends buy or sell orders because of arbitrage.

At present, program traders normally fall into one of two groups: (1) institutions that buy stock index futures and Treasury bills to create the equivalent of an index portfolio (long stock index futures + long T-bills = long index portfo-

---

[13] Hans Stoll and Robert Whaley, "Program Trading and the Monday Massacre." Unpublished paper; November 4, 1987.

lio), or (2) institutions that combine a well-diversified stock portfolio with short positions in stock index futures to create synthetic Treasury bills (long index portfolio + short index futures = long T-bills.) If these traders find that they can synthetically create an index fund that yields more than the actual T-bills, they are going to jump on the chance. In doing so, they may collectively buy or sell thousands of shares in the blink of an eye.

Program trading suffers from a bad name because of the alleged impact these programs have on security prices. If the market takes a real tumble or if it is unusually volatile, someone will certainly put the blame on program trading. The stock specialist needs to match buy and sell orders as they arrive, and if program trading leads to the rapid arrival of many DOT orders at once, the specialist can have difficulty maintaining a "fair and orderly market." This situation can lead to increased volatility, which is not desirable.

On September 11, 1986, for instance, the Dow Jones Industrial Average fell 86.61 points (4.61%); the following day it continued to decline, and the total drop was 120 points in two days. On January 12, 1987, there was an intraday swing of 114 points in the DJIA. Program trading was blamed for this market behavior on both occasions. While these changes seem modest by the volatile standard of today, they were a subject of great concern in the pre-dot.com days. There were many fingers pointed at program trading as the culprit behind the crash of 1987.

Many professional traders and investment managers believe that program trading benefits the public. W. Gordon Binns, vice-president and chief investment funds officer of General Motors, told a congressional panel that the use of program trading enabled GM to reduce average commission costs for the company pension fund from between 7 and 10 cents per share to between 2 and 3 cents per share. This is clearly to the benefit of the many retirees receiving checks from the fund.

To study the impact that futures and options may have on the cash (stock) markets, the Federal Reserve Board, the Commodity Futures Trading Commission, and the Securities Exchange Commission jointly commissioned a study. The report concludes "futures and options markets do not destabilize cash market prices, and indeed, may work to stabilize them."[14]

THE OPEN OUTCRY AND SPECIALIST SYSTEMS

A discussion of program trading often leads into a discussion of the merits and demerits of the two trading systems used in the United States, the specialist system and the marketmaker system. The *specialist system* is used on the American and Philadelphia Stock Exchanges; *marketmakers* are used on the Pacific Stock Exchange and at the Chicago Board Options Exchange. Trading pits, of course,

---

[14] "A Study of the Effects on the Economy of Trading in Futures and Options," Board of Governors of the Federal Reserve System, Commodity Futures Trading Commission, and Securities and Exchange Commission (December 1984), pp. 1–18 and 1–19.

are used at the commodities exchanges. Each system has its own apologists and critics.

Andrew Schwarz, a specialist at the American Stock Exchange, says, "The specialist acts at all times to maintain a fair and orderly market." As specialists buy and sell against the prevailing trend of the market, they incur substantial risks while helping to promote continuous, fair pricing. In exchange for this role, option specialists receive a modest commission of a half-dollar or so for each option contract they handle from the public. Because specialists are in a position to make substantial profits from their "book," it is in their interest to make a good market with heavy trading activity.

Gary Lahey, former vice chairman of the CBOE, expresses a different view. He states, "If a multitude of people [i.e., marketmakers] in a trading crowd are all trying to do different things, the interaction provides a better market than one individual."

While representatives of the various exchanges logically want to argue the respective merits of their system, there is one area in which consensus is building. High-volume markets seem to lend themselves to the marketmaker system, while low-volume or recently listed securities are best traded via the specialist system. The successful OEX contract is traded at the CBOE via marketmakers, and Schwartz calls the OEX arena "the most efficient marketplace" he has ever seen.

FAS 133

In 1996 the Financial Accounting Standards Board (FASB) issued a proposal for derivatives accounting. This proposal, known as **FAS 133**, started a substantial debate that continues to this day, with very few people liking the proposal. Even the Securities and Exchange Commission is opposed to it. The FASB remains convinced that the standard is a good idea, and it is now part of the accounting rules all firms must follow.

FASB states that the purpose of the rule is to disclose the market risk potential of derivative contracts. Prior to the rule two firms might logically account for the same derivatives transaction differently, or even not report it at all. FASB strongly believes that there should be consistency in reporting to maximize the value of financial statements to the user.

REQUIREMENTS

FAS 133 requires firms to report the "fair value" of any derivatives (assets or liabilities) on the firm's balance sheet.

FAS 133 requires firms to report the "fair value" of any derivatives (assets or liabilities) on the firm's balance sheet. In a nutshell, derivatives represent rights or obligations that should be disclosed. This essentially requires a derivatives user to mark to market all derivative transactions when preparing periodic financial statements.

The rule also limits the use of "hedge accounting" to certain designated transactions that are matched with a particular derivative. There is an additional reporting and disclosure requirement associated with these hedges. FAS 133 is not friendly toward the use of options as a hedging tool. Some hybrid instruments, in fact, must be dissected into their component parts, with each part separately valued.

Firms must show evidence of the effectiveness of the derivative as a hedge by measuring the fair value of the derivative against the fair value of the asset being hedged, with the assessment made at least quarterly. Firms must classify derivatives use as (1) a fair value hedge, when used with an asset or liability; (2) a cash flow hedge, when associated with an anticipated transaction; or (3) a foreign currency value hedge, when associated with an investment denominated in a foreign currency.

FAS 133 classifies certain items as derivatives that historically have not been so. For instance, a commercial bank makes mortgage loan commitments on a daily basis to its commercial customers. This is essentially a statement by the bank that "We will lend you this much money at these terms, and you have until next Friday to come in and sign the papers." If the bank intends to sell this mortgage to a third party, FASB considers the loan commitment a derivative that must be accounted for under the terms of FAS 133.[15] However, if the bank intends to keep the mortgage, then it does not apply.

CRITICISM

The criticisms of FAS 133 largely fall into three groups. The first criticism is that the marking to market rules will tend to increase a firm's earnings volatility. This is something security analysts and shareholders do not like. Increased volatility means more risk, and more risk often means a lower stock price. The treasurer of Eastman Chemical Company states that "If you hedge anticipated revenue a year from now, you must mark to market all positive or negative earnings in every quarter. This introduces volatility to the income statement. The assumption among many companies like us is that shareholders won't fully understand this volatility, and we won't be able to explain it."[16]

A primary criticism of FAS 133 is that the rule increases earnings volatility.

The second criticism is that it is not possible to accurately estimate the value of every derivative before the end of its life. Exchange traded products are easy to value, but private, over-the-counter transactions can be much more complicated (and expensive) to value. Some likely derivatives users will choose not to use them at all if they have to go through what they consider an unacceptable inconvenience.

Finally, firms may choose no longer to use derivatives because they fear the consequences of non-compliance with the accounting rules. A partner at PricewaterhouseCoopers says, "Many companies are not prepared to deal with the cost and complexity that FAS 133 imposes."[17] When a firm has to restate results it usually gets bad press, with the stock price suffering. A treasurer might decide it is "too risky" to use a risk-reducing strategy.

[15] FASB, Statement 133 Implementation Issues No. E13, "Scope Exceptions: When a Loan Commitment is Included in the Scope of Statement 133."

[16] Simon Boughey, "That Darned Euro!," *Treasury and Risk Management*, 6–7.

[17] Steve Bergsman, "133 Help on the Web," *Treasury and Risk Management*, 15–16.

IMPLICATIONS

The most thought-provoking implication of FAS 133 is an unintended conse-quence. *Risk* magazine reports that a survey of corporate derivative users suggests around a third of them would "seriously reduce their use of derivatives as a result of the new standard."[18]

---

[18] Lisa Cooper, "Rewriting the Rules," FAS 133 special report, *Risk*, May 2000, 1.

SUMMARY

The market learned some lessons from the collapse of the Long-Term Capital Management hedge fund. Prices do not always move the way they are "supposed to," and high degrees of leverage can be very dangerous. Keynes said "Markets can remain irrational longer than you can remain solvent."

Value at risk is a statistic designed to give an estimate of what can reasonably be expected to be a normal worst-case scenario. As yet there is no precise industry standard for the calculation, but it is often expressed as the largest loss you would expect 95% of the time over a one-day period.

There are new derivatives products continuously coming to the marketplace. One especially noteworthy product category gaining popularity is weather derivatives. These can be options or swaps and often involve a payout based on heating or cooling degree-days over a period of time.

Program trading is a practice at least 15 years old that involves computerized trading of baskets of stocks in order to take advantage of price differences between stocks in New York and futures contracts in Chicago. Computers instantaneously place trades when prices deviate from equilibrium levels.

FAS 133 is a new accounting standard requiring derivatives users to mark these products to market. This standard has not been well received and may cause some people to cease using derivative products because of the managerial inconvenience the standard imposes.

SELF TEST

T ___ F ___ 1. A hedge fund is another name for a mutual fund.

T ___ F ___ 2. Long-Term Capital Management's extraordinary profitability when it closed has led to the development of numerous other hedge funds.

T ___ F ___ 3. Value at Risk refers to the net worth of a portfolio after accounting for any derivative positions.

T ___ F ___ 4. A VAR calculation usually covers one day and 95% probability.

T ___ F ___ 5. The most popular weather derivative product trades at the CBOE.

T ___ F ___ 6. Over a period of time, in a particular location the sum of the heating degree-days and the cooling degree-days equals 1.0.

T ___ F ___ 7. With a zero cost weather collar, the greatest payout is likely to occur if average temperatures are equal to their long-term average.

T ___ F ___ 8. A rental cap is a cancelable interest rate cap.

T ___ F ___ 9. A substantial benefit of an employee stock option plan (ESOP) is the tax-exempt nature of the exercise procedure.

T ___ F ___ 10. An equity swap is an attractive way to invest in some emerging markets.

T ___ F ___ 11. Program trading is illegal although many firms still engage in it.

CHAPTER 17 REVIEW

T ___ F ___ 12. FAS 133 compliance is optional until the year 2005.

T ___ F ___ 13. FAS 133 requires firms to mark to market all derivative positions at least annually.

PROBLEMS & QUESTIONS

1. Why did the Long-Term Capital Management hedge fund collapse?
2. Suppose you own 100 shares of Microsoft common stock. Explain how you could estimate your value at risk.
3. Suppose you own 100 shares of Microsoft common stock and wrote a near-the-money call option against it. Explain how you could estimate your value at risk.
4. Select a Microsoft option and perform the calculation in Problem 3 based on a one-week period and a 95% confidence interval.
5. Explain how a large university system might use a weather derivative to reduce its energy bill.
6. Give a reason why an industrial user might prefer a weather collar to a single weather option.

7. Explain how employee stock options can result in a disastrous tax bill when the underlying firm's stock falls.
8. Briefly explain the structure of an equity swap.
9. What was the Financial Accounting Standards Board's motivation in establishing FAS 133?
10. What are the business community's criticisms of FAS 133?
11. Select two call options on Microsoft that have about three months to expiration, one just in-the-money and one just out-of-the-money. Calculate the VAR of
   a. The in-the-money call;
   b. The out-of-the-money call;
   c. A bullspread using both calls.

Glossary

Derivatives are like NFL quarterbacks. They get too much of the credit and too much of the blame.

Gerald Corrigan
Former President, Federal Reserve Bank of New York

A

absolute advantage: The ability to supply something or acquire something at a rate preferable to that facing your competitor.

Acapulco trade: An unusually large trade by someone who normally trades just a few contracts at a time.

accounting exposure: The chance of loss associated with having to convert a foreign-currency denominated asset into the home currency.

accured interest: Interest that has been earned on a bond, but that has not yet been paid.

add-on yield: The yield convention with Eurodollars, equal to the ratio of the discount to the price, multiplied by the ratio of 360 to the number of days until maturity.

American option: An option that can be exercised anytime prior to its expiration.

Americus Trust: A legal entity that held a portfolio of stock and divided the shares into units composed of PRIMES and SCORES that could be sold separately.

arbitrage: This term has evolved into a generic word for the existence of a riskless profit. In the International Encyclopedia of the Social Sciences, Paul Cootner defines arbitrage as the "simultaneous purchase and sale of equivalent assets at prices which guarantee a fixed profit at the time of the transactions, although the life of the assets, and, hence, the consummation of the profit may be delayed until some future date."

arbitrageur: A person who actively seeks arbitrage situations, and by exploiting them helps keep the marketplace efficient.

Asian option: See *average rate option.*

ask discount: The discount from par value associated with the current asking price for a U.S. Treasury bill.

ask price: The lowest price at which anyone has expressed a willingness to sell a security.

asset allocation: The manner in which funds are divided between various broad classes of investments such as stocks, bonds, and cash.

assignment: The notice received by an option writer that the option holder exercised the option.

as-you-like-it option: An option in which the owner can elect to change from one type of option (such as a call) to another type of option (such as a put) during a certain period of time. Also called a *chooser option.*

at-the-market swap: A swap in which the swap price is such that the swap has a value of zero.

at-the-money: An option in which the striking price equals the current market price of the underlying asset.

average rate option: An option with a payout equal to the difference between a stated striking price and an average price for the underlying security over a period of time. Also called an *Asian option.*

away from the market: A price that is far away from the current trading range.

B

backspread: A vertical option spread in which extra options are written such that the spread often generates a credit to your account.

backwardation: The situation in the futures market in which the futures price is less than the cash price. Also called an *inverted market.*

bank immunization: A risk-reduction technique used by financial institutions in which the dollar-weighted duration of its rate-sensitive assets is made equal to the dollar-weighted duration of its rate-sensitive liabilities.

barrier option: A class of path-dependent options in which the payout depends on whether or not the underlying asset price rose or fell sufficiently to hit a predetermined barrier price.

basis: The difference between a futures price for a commodity and the current cash price at a specific location.

basis convergence: The phenomenon with stock index futures contracts that causes the futures price to equal the stock index itself at a delivery date. At this point, the basis equals zero.

basis point: One one-hundredth of one percent.

basis point value: The change in the price of a bond for a one basis point change in the yield to maturity of the bond.

basis risk: The risk stemming from the fact that a futures price does not always move in lockstep with the underlying asset.

bearish: The belief that the price of a particular asset will move lower.

bearspread: A spread that becomes valuable as prices of the underlying asset decline.

beta: A measure of the systematic risk of an asset. The average beta is one; securities with a beta more than this are more risky than average, and vice-versa.

bid price: The highest price at which anyone has expressed a willingness to buy.

binomial pricing: A method of option pricing based on arbitrage arguments in which the underlying asset moves to one of only two prices during each period.

Black Monday: The colloquial term given to October 19, 1987 (the day the stock market crashed).

Black-Scholes options pricing model: One of the most significant developments in the history of finance. This model provides an analytical framework for the evaluation of securities that provide a claim on other assets.

bond equivalent yield: A method of determining the yield on a U.S. Treasury bill so as to account for a 365-day year and for the fact that the security is purchased at a discount.

bootstrapping: A recursive technique for extracting implied forward interest rates or spot rates from other interest rate data.

Brady Report: A study conducted following Black Monday to determine the cause and implications of the Crash of 1987.

broker: A person at an exchange who works for a member of the exchange.

bucket trading: A fraudulent practice in which a client is charged more than necessary for a trade and two brokers split the difference.

bullet immunization: A technique appropriate for a client who has an initial sum of money to invest and wants to accumulate a predetermined sum by a specific future date; the technique involves assembling a basket of bonds whose collective holding period returns will match that of a hypothetical zero coupon bond.

bullion: Unworked gold, usually in bar form.

bullish: The belief that the price of an asset will increase.

bullspread: An option spread that becomes valuable as the price of the underlying asset rises.

butterfly spread: A spread involving three option positions. There are various ways to construct such a spread, but all involve writing two options and then buying one with a higher-striking price and one with a lower striking price.

buying hedge: When a hedger goes long to protect some economic interest; also known as a *long hedge*.

buy/write: Buying stock and writing a covered call.

C

calendar spread: A simultaneous long and short position in options, in which the options are chosen horizontally from the financial listing. Also called a *time spread* or *horizontal spread*.

call a stock: The act of exercising one's prerogative as the owner of a call option. If you buy a call option and subsequently "call the stock," it means you want the writer of the call option to deliver the stock to you in exchange for your payment of the striking price.

call option: The owner of a call option has the right to buy a quantity of an asset at a set price (the striking, or exercise, price) from a specified person (the option writer) by a specified date (expiration date).

call ratio spread: A call bullspread is transformed into a call ratio spread by writing more than one call at the higher-striking price.

cap: A portfolio of call options, with successive expiration dates, on an interest rate.

cap/floor/swap parity: The no-arbitrage relationship between an interest rate swap, a cap, and a floor in which the cap and floor constitute a zero-cost collar.

capitalization weighting: A method of constructing a market index in which each component is assigned weight according to the aggregate value of its outstanding shares.

caplet: A component option within an interest rate cap.

carrying cost: The cost of actually holding a commodity, including insurance costs, storage costs, interest charges, and so forth.

cash dividend: A payment to shareholders of a portion of the firm's earnings.

cash market: Any market in which cash is exchanged for current delivery of an asset.

cash price: The current price of an asset, particularly an asset on which futures contracts trade. Also called the *spot price*.

cash secured put: See *fiduciary put*.

cash settlement: The settlement procedure used with stock index futures and options. No delivery of the underlying asset occurs with these securities.

cheapest to deliver: The specific financial instrument that is most advantageous to use in delivery against a Treasury bond or Treasury note futures contract. The term originated with the now-inactive GNMA futures contract.

chooser option: See *as-you-like-it option*.

churning: An illegal activity in which a broker makes, or advises a client to make unnecessary trades in an account for the purpose of generating excess commissions.

circuit breaker: A system to temporarily halt trading in the markets in the event of a major change in price levels.

circus swap: A combined interest rate and currency swap. This term applies to the simultaneous entry into an interest rate swap and a foreign currency swap, usually in order to receive a fixed U.S. dollar rate while paying a fixed foreign currency rate.

class: All options on the same underlying asset.

Clearing Corporation: A mechanism designed to eliminate uncertainty in the futures and options markets. It does this by interposing itself between buyers and sellers. All trades are actually sales to or purchases from the clearing corporation.

clearinghouse: An agency associated with a futures or options exchange where trade reports are matched and out trades are identified.

closing price: The price that is actually paid when a previously established option position is eliminated, or closed. Also the last price of the day (or the settlement price) for a particular commodity.

closing transaction: An option trade in which an investor eliminates a previously established option position. For the purchaser of an option, a closing transaction would be a sale or exercise of the option. For an option writer, a closing transaction is a purchase of the option or receipt of an exercise notice from the option holder.

collar: A position that is simultaneously long an interest rate cap and short an interest rate floor. The term may also be applied to any option position in which you are long (or short) a call and short (or long) a put.

combination: An option strategy in which you are simultaneously long or short puts and calls.

combined call writing: Writing calls at more than one striking price.

commission: A fee paid to a broker for executing a trade.

Commodity Futures Trading Commission: A five-member U.S. government agency charged with supervising and regulating the futures exchanges.

commodity trading advisor: An investment manager who advises other people on futures trading.

comparative advantage: The ability of one party to provide or acquire something relatively more cheaply than another party.

compound option: An option on an option

condor: A less risky version of the strangle that involves four different striking prices.

contango market: The typical relationship with most futures contracts, in which the futures price exceeds the cash price.

contingent immunization: The essence of contingent immunization is the provision of a floor value below which the value of the portfolio will not fall or the establishment of a minimum rate of return for the portfolio; it leaves the upside open while limiting downside risk.

continuous compounding: The most advantageous form of calculating interest for a saver. Continuous compounding uses natural logarithms and continuous time rather than discrete time intervals.

contract: The unit of trading for a futures transaction.

contract month: See *delivery month.*

conversion factor: An adjustment factor used to convert U.S. Treasury bonds into 6 percent equivalents.

convexity: For a given interest rate change, convexity is the difference between the actual price change in a bond and that predicted by the duration statistic.

corner: Any system for interrupting the supply of a commodity in the marketplace in an attempt to manipulate prices.

counterparty risk: The chance of loss due to default by the other party to a derivatives contract.

coupon rate: The stated interest rate that determines the dollar amount of interest a bond pays.

cover: The process of eliminating an existing investment position by taking an offsetting trade.

cover a short: The elimination of a short position by buying securities identical to those sold short.

covered call: A call option that an investor has written against common stock that he or she owns. A call option is also considered covered if it is held in the same portfolio as a call option with the same expiration date but a lower striking price, or with a call of the same striking price but a later expiration date.

covered futures option: A written futures option in which the writer holds a corresponding futures position on the other side of the market.

covered put: An ambiguous term that usually refers to a fiduciary put. Also sometimes used to refer to a combination of a short put and a short stock position.

covered write: See *covered call.*

covering the risk: Any method of reducing or eliminating a particular type of risk.

crack: A crude oil/heating oil/gasoline counterpart to the soybean/soybean meal/ soybean oil "crush."

credit: An option transaction that results in a cash inflow into the investor's account.

credit derivative: A legal contract between two parties that provides for the transfer of risk on some extension of credit.

credit risk: See *default risk.*

credit spread: Buying one option and writing another with a higher premium.

cross company spread: A non-standard spread using securities on more than one company.

cross trading: The illegal practice of switching customer orders and those for one's personal account.

crowd: The colloquial term used for the people in a trading pit.

crush: A hedging activity used by soybean processors in which soybean futures are purchased and soybean oil and meal futures are sold. By "putting on a crush," the processor can lock in a certain profit margin.

current yield: The annual income generated by a security divided by its current price.

D

daily price limit: An exchange-imposed restriction on how much the price of a particular futures contract is allowed to move in a single trading day. Contracts are said to be "limit up" or "limit down" when the daily price limit is reached.

day trader: A person who opens security positions or futures contracts and closes them on the same day.

debit: An option position that requires a cash outflow from an investor's brokerage account.

debit spread: Buying one option and writing another with a lower premium.

deck: The collection of order cards on which a futures or options trader has recorded the day's transactions.

deep-in-the-money: This subjective description applies to any option that has "substantial" intrinsic value.

default risk: A measure of the likelihood that a borrower will be unable to repay principal and interest as agreed. Also called *credit risk.*

deferred swap: An agreement to enter into a swap beginning at some future date. Also called a *forward start swap*.

deflation: The situation in which the general price level is declining; negative inflation.

deliverable bond: A bond that satisfies the delivery requirements of the U.S. Treasury bond futures contract. A deliverable bond has at least 15 years until maturity, and if callable, at least 15 years of call protection.

delivery day: The day that a commodity or financial instrument is actually delivered against a futures contract.

delivery month: The month during which a commodity is due to be delivered in a futures contract.

delivery notice: The written notice that a futures seller gives, indicating a desire to make delivery of the commodity underlying the futures contract.

delta: The change in option premium expected from a small change in the stock price.

delta exposure: The sum of deltas in a portfolio.

delta management: A method of risk management in which the manager seeks to maintain position delta within a certain range.

delta neutrality: The situation in which the delta exposure of a position is zero.

derivative: An asset whose value is primarily determined by the value of another asset.

diagonal spread: A spread in which the options are selected from different expiration months and in which the options have different striking prices.

difference check: The net payment on a swap, equal to the larger payment minus the smaller payment.

directional market: One's outlook for the overall market: bullish, bearish, or neutral.

direct quotation: An exchange rate stated in dollars per unit of foreign currency.

discount factor: The interest rate used to equate present values and futures values. The discount factor may include a risk factor in addition to a pure interest rate.

discount yield: A method of quoting Treasury bill yields equal to the annualized difference between the par value and the market value, divided by the par value.

discrete compounding: The periodic computation of interest. Periods are defined in finite time intervals.

divisor: An adjustment made to a market index to account for changes in the composition of the index, or for stock splits.

DOT: The Designated Order Turnaround system at the New York Stock Exchange; also called *SuperDOT*. This system allows trades of less than 2100 shares to be placed directly with the specialist via electronic means.

Dow Jones Industrial Average: A popular measure of stock market activity based on the closing prices of the common stock of 30 large firms.

down and in option: An option position automatically created if the underlying asset falls below a specified level.

down and out option: An option that becomes worthless if the underlying asset falls below a specified price.

dual trading: The situation in which a futures or options contract trades simultaneously on two or more exchanges, and in which the contracts are fungible across the exchanges.

due bill: A document received during the processing of a stock split. Holders of due bills are entitled to new shares when the shares are issued.

duration: A measure of interest rate risk. Duration is a weighted average of the length of time required for cash flows to be received from a fixed-income security.

duration gap: A bank measurement reflecting the interest rate sensitivity of its assets and liabilities.

duration matching: A form of portfolio dedication or immunization in which a basket of assets is assembled such that its present value and its duration match that of a liability or stream of liabilities.

duration shifting: An interest rate reduction strategy in which the duration of a portfolio is altered in anticipation of changing market interest rates.

dynamic hedging: A portfolio insurance technique that requires frequent revision of a hedge using stock index futures or options.

E

economic exposure: This type of exposure measures the risk that the value of a security will decline due to an unexpected change in relative foreign exchange rates.

effective rate: The realized compound yield on an investment. The effective rate considers the effects of compounding.

efficient market hypothesis: The theory that publicly available information is rapidly and accurately reflected in the price of securities, and that over the long run realized returns will be consistent with their level of undiversifiable risk.

employee stock option plan (ESOP): A corporate arrangement in which, as part of the firm's total compensation plan, the company awards certain employees non-marketable options to purchase the company's shares directly from treasury stock.

equity option: An option in which common stock is the underlying security.

equity swap: A contract between two parties in which they agree to exchange cash flows, one of which depends on the level of an equity index or portfolio, with the other depending on an interest rate.

Eurodollar: A U.S. dollar-denominated account located outside the United States.

Eurodollar strip: A sequence of Eurodollar futures contracts used by a swap dealer to hedge an interest rate swap.

European option: An option that can be exercised only at expiration.

ex-dividend date: The date established by the brokerage community to eliminate uncertainty about who is entitled to dividends when trades are made near the date of record. The ex-dividend date is two business days prior to the date of record. Investors must buy stock before the ex-dividend date to be entitled to the next dividend.

exercise: The act by which an option holder expresses an interest to sell shares to the option writer at the specified price (with puts) or to buy shares from the option writer at the specified price (with calls).

exercise price: The agreed-upon price for the exchange of common stock (or the other appropriate underlying asset) in the terms of a put or call option; synonymous with the term *striking price*.

exotic option: Any option-like contract with unusual terms.

expectations hypothesis: The theory that the futures price for a commodity is what the marketplace expects the cash price to be when the delivery month arrives.

expected value: The weighted average of all possible outcomes from a distribution, in which the weights reflect the probability of the various outcomes.

expiration date: The last day of an option's life.

exposure: The extent to which a loss is possible because of adverse changes in foreign exchange rates.

F

fair premium: A term used with stock index futures to reflect the value that the index futures contract should sell for in the absence of arbitrage.

FAS 133: A controversial Financial Accounting Standards Board requirement that firms preparing public financial statements show the fair market value of their derivative positions.

fiat value: Value arbitrarily established by a government authority. Currency has value because the government says it does, not because of intrinsic value.

fiduciary: A person or institution responsible for the management of someone else's money.

fiduciary put: A short put option in which the put writer deposits the striking price of the put into an interest bearing account. Also called a *cash-secured put*.

financial asset: An asset for which there is a corresponding liability somewhere.

financial engineering: The construction of asset portfolios with predetermined technical characteristics, particularly when those characteristics are not available in an exchange-traded product.

financial futures: A generic term for futures contracts on debt instruments, stock indexes, and foreign currencies.

financial risk: The variation of returns that are a function of the extent to which borrowed funds are used in the generation of the returns.

First Notice Day: Generally, the first business day prior to the first day of the delivery month.

first position day: With U.S. Treasury bond futures, two business days before the first business day of the futures delivery month.

fixed rate: On a swap, an interest rate that does not change over its tenor.

FLEX option: A customized, exchange-traded option in which the user can specify expiration, striking price, and quantity.

floating rate: On a swap, an interest rate that is variable, periodically changing as some reference rate changes.

floor: A portfolio of put options, with successive expiration dates, on an interest rate.

floor broker: A member of an exchange who, for a fee, executes orders for other members.

floorlet: A component option within an interest rate floor.

floor trader: See *local*.

foreign currency option: A listed option giving the holder the right to buy or sell a specified quantity of foreign currency. These are distinct from foreign currency futures options.

foreign currency swap: An agreement between two parties to exchange foreign currencies, subsequent interest payments on these currencies, and ultimately to re-exchange the original currencies.

foreign exchange risk: The chance of loss due to adverse fluctuations in exchange rates between national currencies.

forward contract: A non-marketable agreement to exchange certain assets at a set date in the future.

forward exchange rate: A contractual rate between a commercial bank and a client for the future delivery of a specified quantity of foreign currency; normally quoted on the basis of one, two, three, six, and twelve months.

forward split: A stock split in which shareholders receive additional shares and are left with a greater number of shares than before the split.

forward start swap: See *deferred swap*.

full carrying charge market: A futures market for a particular commodity in which the basis for successive delivery months reflects the cost of storing (or holding, in the case of financial futures) the commodity or financial instrument.

fundamental analyst: A person who studies earn-ings and relative value in determining the intrinsic value of a security.

funds gap: The difference between a bank's rate sensitive assets and its rate sensitive liabilities.

fungibility: The ability of participants in the futures and options markets to reverse their position by making an offsetting trade. This occurs because the individual contracts are standardized and interchangeable.

futures commission merchant (FCM): A broker in commodity futures.

futures contract: A legal, transferable, standardized contract that represents a promise to buy or sell a quantity of a standardized commodity by a predetermined delivery date.

futures option: A type of option that gives the holder of a call the right to assume a long position in a futures contract, while the holder of a futures put has the right to go short a futures contract.

G

gamma: The sensitivity of delta to changes in the stock price.

gamma risk: The chance of loss in an options portfolio due to large movements in the underlying asset causing large changes in the aggregate position delta.

Globex: An after-hours screen-based worldwide trading system developed by the Chicago Mercantile Exchange, the Chicago Board of Trade, and Reuters Limited.

good delivery bar: A 400-troy ounce bar of gold that is at least 99.6 percent pure. Good delivery bars may be delivered against a short futures position.

good faith deposit: The initial equity requirement that must be deposited with an opening transaction in a futures contract. This is often called *margin*, although no money is borrowed.

H

heating degree day: A statistic calculated as 65 degrees Fahrenheit minus the average of the high and low temperature for the day in a specific location.

hedge: The purchase and sale of two assets whose values are expected to move in opposite directions

hedge fund: A largely unregulated private investment company that often invests in arbitrage-related activities.

hedger: A person who faces some type of economic risk and chooses to eliminate or reduce it by some type of offsetting transaction.

hedge ratio: A calculated value that indicates the quantity of an asset that must be acquired or sold to completely eliminate a certain type of risk with an investment position.

hedge wrapper: The simultaneous writing of a covered call and buying a protective put.

historical volatility: The volatility that is determined from a past series of prices.

holding period return: A comparison of the ending value of an investment with its original cost. The holding period return is insensitive to the length of the period.

horizontal spread: See *calendar spread.*

house out: An out trade in which the clearing members do not match.

I

IMM index: The value 100% minus LIBOR.

immunization: The process of removing interest rate risk by adjusting the duration of assets and liabilities via the futures market or with portfolio rebalancing.

implied financing rate: The indicated interest rate from the futures contract cost of carry relationship.

implied forward rate: The forward interest rate expected to prevail in the future given the current yield curve.

implied repo rate: See *implied financing rate.*

implied volatility: The annual volatility that, when input into an option-pricing model, will cause the model to predict the current market price with no error. Implied volatility is sometimes thought to be the market's estimate of future volatility.

improve on the market: The practice of writing deep-in-the-money covered calls to sell stock at a slightly above-market price, or writing in-the-money puts to acquire stock at a below-market price.

index: A calculated measure of market activity, such as the S&P 500 stock index.

indexing: The practice of continually adjusting a portfolio so that its characteristics match as nearly as possible those of a market index.

index option: An option to buy or sell a hypothetical basket of securities whose value is determined by a market index. Index options are settled in cash; there is no delivery mechanism.

indirect quotation: A foreign currency exchange rate stated in units of foreign currency per U.S. dollar.

inflation premium: Reflects the rapidity with which prices are rising; it measures how rapidly the money standard is losing its purchasing power.

informational efficiency: The aspect of the market considered by the efficient market hypothesis. Informational efficiency means that the market quickly and accurately reacts to the arrival of new information.

inside information: Privately held news which, when released to the public, is likely to have an impact on security prices. Trading on the basis of inside information is illegal.

intention day: The first day in the three-day process resulting in the delivery of U.S. Treasury bonds against a futures contract.

intercommodity spread: This type of spread involves a long and short position in two related commodities.

interest rate parity: The fact that differences in national interest rates are reflected in the currency forward market.

interest rate risk: The chance of loss due to changes in the level of interest rates.

interest rate sensitive: An asset whose price may change if the level of interest rates changes.

interest rate swap: An agreement between two parties to exchange a fixed interest rate for a floating interest rate on a principal sum.

intermarket spread: Two simultaneous positions, one long and one short, in different but potentially related underlying assets.

internal rate of return: This discount rate that will cause a series of future cash flows to have a present value equal to the cost of acquiring the future cash flows.

International Swaps and Derivatives Association (ISDA):   A trade association facilitating the use of swaps and derivatives by the creation of master agreements outlining the terms of common contracts.

in-the-money: An option is in-the-money if it has intrinsic value based on the stock price and striking price. Calls are in-the-money when the striking price is less than the stock price; the opposite is true for puts.

intracommodity spread: Also called an *intermonth spread;* involves taking different positions in different delivery months.

intrinsic value: An option has intrinsic value determined by the degree to which it is in-the-money.

inverted market: When a futures price is less than the cash price. Also called *backwardation.*

investment grade: Bonds related BBB or higher by Standard & Poor's.

investment horizon: The period of time a particular investment is expected to be held.

invoice price: The amount that the buyer of an interest rate futures contract must pay when the securities underlying the futures contract are delivered.

issuer: The organization that created a particular debt or equity security.

J

junk bond: Historically, a junk bond is any bond rated below BBB by Standard and Poor's.

K

kappa: See *vega.*

karat: A measure of the purity of gold. 24 karat gold is 99.9 percent pure.

L

lambda: See *vega.*

last trading day: The final day in which trading occurs for a particular futures or options contract.

law of one price: The fundamental economic principle that requires equivalent assets to sell for the same price.

LED spread: An interest rate spread involving the LIBOR and Eurodollar futures contract.

LIBOR: The London InterBank Offered Rate, an important money market interest rate.

limit order: An order to buy or sell securities or other assets in which the client has specified the time for which the order is to be kept open and the minimum price acceptable for the trade.

limit price: On a standing order, the highest price the buyer will pay or the lowest price a seller will accept.

liquidity: The extent to which something can be quickly converted into cash at approximately its market value.

liquidity risk: The potential for loss because of an inability to convert an asset to cash at a reasonable price.

listed derivative: A futures or options contract that trades on an organized exchange.

listed option: An option that trades on an exchange.

locals: Members of an exchange who trade for their own account. They are not employees of another firm.

London fix: The price of gold determined twice a day in London by a group of bankers who seek to match buy and sell orders until equilibrium is found.

long hedge: A transaction in which an asset is purchased as a hedge.

long position: The common investment position in which an asset is held as opposed to borrowed or written.

Long Position Report: This document provides a summary of all clearing members' long positions and their dates of purchase.

Long Term Capital Management: A hedge fund, organized by some of Wall Street's brightest traders and academicians, that made headlines in 1998 when its bankruptcy because of high leverage nearly caused a major financial collapse elsewhere in the market.

Long-term Equity AnticiPation Security (LEAP): An exchange traded long-term option.

lookback option: An option with a payout equal to the highest intrinsic value of the option at any time over its life.

M

Macauley duration: The traditional measure of duration. Duration is a measure of interest rate risk and a weighted average of the time it takes to recover the cost of a security.

maintenance margin: The minimum equity requirement that must be maintained with a particular investment position before a margin call is received and more money must be deposited into your account.

managed futures: The practice of using futures contracts as a separate asset class in investment management.

margin: A deposit of funds required to provide collateral for an investment position.

margin call: The requirement to add equity to an investment account because of adverse price movements or new transactions.

margin requirement: See *margin*.

marketmaker: One of a number of people who compete against one another for the public's business, thereby helping to ensure that the public receives a market-determined price for their trades.

marketmaker system: The trading system used at the futures exchanges, at the Chicago Board Options Exchange, and at the Pacific Stock Exchange.

market order: The simplest type of order. It instructs a broker to execute a client's order at the best possible price at the earliest opportunity.

market risk: The chance of loss due to adverse movements in the level of the stock market.

market variation call: A Clearing Corporation directive to a member to deposit more funds into his account during the day because of adverse price movements. Market variation calls must be met within one hour of the time they are received.

marking to market: The practice in the futures markets of transferring funds from one account to another each day on the basis of unrealized (or paper) gains and losses.

master agreement: A legal document issued by the International Swaps and Derivatives Association outlining the terms of a swap or interest rate options contract.

matching trades: The act of processing one's deck through a clearing corporation.

Merton model: A modification to the Black-Scholes option-pricing model that accounts for the underlying asset paying dividends.

MOB spread: An interest rate spread using municipal bonds and U.S. Treasury bonds.

N

naked call: A short call option in which the writer does not own or have a claim to the underlying security or asset.

naked option: This term properly is given only to the writing of an uncovered call option. To the writer of an uncovered call, potential losses are theoretically unlimited.

naked put: Usually means a short put by itself.

near-the-money: An option in which the striking price and the price of the underlying asset are approximately equal.

NOB spread: An interest rate futures spread in which opposite positions are established using U.S. Treasury bond futures and U.S. Treasury note futures.

nominal interest rate: Stated interest rate.

normal backwardation: The theory of futures pricing that predicts the futures price is downward biased in order to provide a risk premium to the speculators, who normally have a net long position.

notice of intention day: The day following intention day in the U.S. Treasury bond futures contract delivery process.

notional value: The principal value upon which interest rate payments are based in a swap contract.

O

odd-lot: A quantity of stock that is not evenly divisible by 100 shares.

odd-lot generating split: A stock split that is not in a whole number ratio like two- or four-to-one. For instance in a three-for-two split, the holder of 100 shares would have 150 shares after the split. One hundred fifty shares is an odd lot.

OEX: The Standard & Poor's 100 stock index. This term is particularly used with options on this index.

offer price: See *asked price.*

off-market swap: A swap whose price is not equal to the equilibrium rate and, consequently, has value to one of the participants.

opening transaction: The establishment of an investment position. This position may be long or short.

open interest: A measure of how many futures contracts in a given commodity exist at a particular point in time.

open outcry: The trading method used at the futures exchanges and at some of the options exchanges. Trades are made verbally among members of a trading "crowd," rather than through a single specialist.

option: A contract that gives the holder the right to buy (with a call) or sell (with a put) a certain security at a set price, on or before a given date.

option elasticity: An option's delta multiplied by the ratio of the underlying asset price and the option premium.

Options Clearing Corporation (OCC): An organization that acts as a guarantor of all option trades between buyers and sellers. The OCC also regulates the trading activities of members of option exchanges.

order book: A book that is kept by a specialist in which he or she keeps standing orders from all over the country to ensure that the market in these securities is maintained in a fair or orderly fashion.

Order Book Official: The exchange employee responsible for maintaining the order book at an options exchange.

out-of-the-money: An option that has no intrinsic value.

out trade: When a Clearing Corporation's computer is not able to exactly match all trades, the mismatches are called "out trades."

overriding: See *overwriting.*

Over the Counter (OTC) derivative: A futures contract, option, or swap that is not traded on an organized exchange.

over the counter option: An options contract that is not traded on an organized exchange.

overwriting: The practice of writing options against an existing portfolio.

P

percent of par: The pricing convention for debt instruments. If a security has a par value of $100,000, a price of 78 6/32 means the price is 78 6/32 "percent of par" or $78,187.50.

pit: Refers to the sunken trading arena of a futures or options exchange where members of that exchange engage in trades.

plain vanilla: A generic term for any standard derivatives contract that does not contain unusual provisions.

portfolio insurance: A quasi-insurance activity that seeks to provide a floor value below which a portfolio will not fall, or a minimum level of income.

position day: The date that the exchange requires a Long Position Report.

position delta: The sum of the deltas in a portfolio.

position gamma: The sum of the gammas in a portfolio.

position limit: In the futures or options market, the maximum number of contracts a party may legally have open at a given time.

position risk: The possible loss associated with extreme market movements.

position theta: The sum of the thetas in a portfolio.

position trader: A speculator who routinely maintains futures positions overnight and sometimes keeps a contract open for weeks.

precious metals: The term is applied to the platinum group metals, to gold, and to silver.

premium: With options, the actual amount that is paid for an option. With futures, the situation in which a particular futures price is higher than some other price.

price discovery: The function of the futures markets that produces a "best estimate" of the future spot price of a commodity; a function of the futures market which helps indicate the market's consensus about likely future prices for a commodity.

price out: An out trade in which the prices differ.

price risk: The chance of loss due to a change in the price of an asset.

PRIME: "Prescribed Right to Income and Maximum Equity"; one part of an Americus Trust unit. PRIMES are like covered call positions.

priority trading rule: An exchange's policy that ensures that public orders of ten options or less are quickly executed at a fair price.

processor: A participant in the soybean market who buys soybeans and crushes them into soy oil and soy meal.

program trading: A generic term used for any activity that involves the trading of portfolios via computers, in which the decision to make a trade is also computer generated.

protective put: A long position in a put option held simultaneously with a long position in the same common stock. A protective put is a hedge.

purchasing power parity: The phenomenon in international finance whereby relative exchange rates reflect differences in the relative purchasing power of a currency in the two countries.

put/call parity: The theory that call prices should exceed put prices by about the riskless rate of interest when the options are at-the-money and the stock pays no dividends.

put option: The owner of a put option has purchased the right to sell a set number of shares of common stock (normally 100) for a set price (the striking, or exercise price) to a specified person (the option writer) anytime prior to a specified date (the expiration date).

put overwriting: The practice of writing put options while simultaneously owning the underlying stock.

put ratio spread: A bear spread with puts becomes a put ratio backspread by the addition of extra short put positions.

putting on a crush: The activity of a soybean oil and soybean meal processor that enables him to lock in an acceptable profit margin.

Q

quality option: The right of the holder of a short position in Treasury bond futures contracts to deliver any eligible bond against the contract.

quality spread: The difference in interest rates on loans of differing levels of credit risk.

quantity out: An out trade in which the number of contracts in a particular trade is in dispute.

R

rate sensitive: The extent to which an asset's value is affected by changing interest rates.

ratio backspread: The opposite of ratio spreads. Backspreads generate a credit to one's account.

ratio spread: A spread with an unequal number of long and short options.

real asset: An asset for which there is no corresponding liability.

realized compound yield: The effective rate of interest actually earned on an investment over a period of time, including the reinvestment of intermediate cash flows.

real option: Any of various types of options that are embedded in other assets, such as the right to abandon a project, the right to expand, the right to choose, and the right to postpone.

real rate: The interest rate that reflects the market's willingness to postpone spending until a later time.

reinvestment rate risk: The chance of loss associated with reinvesting cash flows at a lower rate than previously available.

rental cap: A derivative interest rate product similar to an interest rate cap except that the purchaser can abandon the cap by ceasing to make payments on it.

Retail Automatic Execution System (RAES): An automated trading system used at the Chicago Board Options Exchange for the rapid filling of market orders for ten contracts or less.

rho: The sensitivity of an option premium to changes in the interest rate.

riskless rate of interest: A theoretical value representing the price of deferring consumption from one period to the next. The riskless interest rate is usually proxied by the rate on a 30-day U.S. Treasury bill.

risk premium: The component of interest rates that is toughest to measure; the magnitude of the risk premium is a function of how much risk the security carries.

round lot: The purchase or sale of shares of stock in multiples of 100 shares.

round-turn: The convention for commissions on commodity futures. A single commission provides for both the establishment of a position and its subsequent closing by delivery or an offsetting trade.

S

S&P 500 Stock Index: A standard against which portfolio managers and investment advisors might be judged. It is currently one of the Commerce Department's leading indicators.

scalper: See *local.*

SCORE: A "Special Claim on Residual Equity"; one part of an Americus Trust unit. Owning a SCORE is like owning a long-term call option.

serial expiration: Options on a particular futures contract that have multiple expiration months.

settlement price: Analogous to the closing price with stock, the settlement price represents the "ending" price for a futures contract at the close of trading. The settlement price may be an average of prices during the last few minutes of trading.

short call: A written call.

short hedge: A hedge using futures contracts in which the hedger promises to deliver the underlying commodity.

short position: 1. In the futures market, a promise to deliver; 2. in the options market, writing an option; 3. in the stock market, borrowing shares and selling them in the hope of buying them back later at a lower price.

short put: A written put.

short sale: Short sellers borrow stock from their broker, sell it, and hope to buy similar shares in the future at a lower price to replace those borrowed.

sides out: An out trade in which both cards indicate the same side of the market, i.e., both indicate buy, or both indicate sell.

sigma: The annualized volatility of an option as measured by its standard deviation.

specialist: An individual at the American and New York Stock Exchanges through whom all orders to buy or sell a particular security must pass. The specialist is charged with maintaining a fair and orderly market.

specialist system: A market trading system in which all orders pass through one individual who is charged by the exchange with the duty to maintain a fair and orderly market in the assigned security.

speculator: In the futures market a speculator is a person who, for a price, is willing to bear the risk that the hedger does not want.

speed market: The aspect of the market measured by gamma; the extent to which a position benefits from rapid or slow changes in market prices.

spot exchange rate: 1. The current exchange rate for two currencies; 2. the cash price for a commodity.

spot market: See *cash market.*

spot price: See *cash price.*

spread: The simultaneous purchase and sale of futures or options contracts, in which there is an anticipated relation between the assets underlying the futures or options.

stack hedge: A Eurodollar futures hedge in which the required quantity of futures contracts all have the same delivery month.

stock index: A measure of the general level of stock market prices.

stock index arbitrage: A type of program trading that seeks to take advantage of discrepancies in the relative pricing of stock index futures contracts and the level of the stock index itself.

stock split: Recapitalization of a firm's equity by increasing or decreasing the number of shares outstanding.

stop loss order: A special type of limit order that becomes a market order if the stop price is touched.

stop order: See *stop loss order.*

stop price: The "trigger" price with a stop order, causing the order to be executed.

straddle: Holding a put and a call with the same striking price, expiration date, and on the same underlying security, is being long a straddle. If one is short these options, they have written a straddle.

strangle: Similar to a straddle, except that the puts and calls have different striking prices.

striking price: Synonymous with exercise price, but striking price is generally used when describing options.

strip hedge: A Eurodollar futures hedge in which the required quantity of futures contracts are distributed throughout a time period rather than concentrated at one point.

swap: An agreement to exchange interest rate payments on a notional value for a period of time, usually with one party paying a fixed rate and the other party paying a floating rate.

swap facilitator: An institution that finds and arranges for two parties to engage in a swap transaction.

swap price: The fixed interest rate on a swap that causes the present value of the floating rate payments to equal the present value of the fixed rate payments.

swap spread: An increment added to the swap price to compensate the swap dealer for providing the service.

swaption: An option giving its owner the right to enter into a swap agreement.

swap value: The difference between the present value of the payments one party to a swap agrees to make and the present value of the payments to be received.

synthetic index portfolio: A combination of futures contracts and Treasury bills that yields a position equivalent to an equity portfolio.

synthetic option: A portfolio of security positions that is equivalent to a particular option position.

synthetic purchase: The combination of a short position in a put option, a long position in a call option, and a long position in Treasury bills, such that the resulting portfolio has investment characteristics nearly identical to a long position in the common stock of the same company.

synthetic put: The combination of a short stock position with a long call position.

systematic factors: Factors that influence the stock market as a whole, including market interest rates, economic indicators, the political climate, regulatory policy, and fiscal or monetary policy.

systematic risk: The risk associated with owning equity securities due to their tendency to move in tandem.

T

tailing the hedge: A time value of money adjustment to the size of an interest rate hedge reflecting the fact that futures are marked to market while forward contracts are not.

Tapioca City: A colloquial name for the destination of traders who lose their trading capital.

TED spread: An interest rate futures spread using U.S. Treasury bill futures and Eurodollar futures.

tenor: The period of time associated with a swap agreement.

termination claim: The "strike price" of an Americus Trust PRIME or SCORE.

Terrible Tuesday: October 20, 1987, the day after the Crash of 1987.

theta: A measure of the sensitivity of a call option to the time remaining until its expiration.

thin trading: Sparse volume.

tick: The minimum allowable price change in a futures or options position.

time decay: The phenomenon whereby the value of an option declines as time passes if the price of the underlying asset does not change.

time out: An out trade in which the delivery month or expiration is in dispute.

time spread: See *calendar spread.*

time value: The amount by which the market price of an option exceeds its intrinsic value.

timing option: The right of someone with a short position in T-bond futures to choose when to deliver.

transaction exposure: According to the Financial Accounting Standards Board: "A transaction involving purchase or sale of goods or services with the price stated in foreign currency is incomplete until the amount in dollars necessary to liquidate the related payable or receivable is determined."

translation exposure: This type of exposure stems from the holding of foreign assets and liabilities that are denominated in currencies other than U.S. dollars.

trend: The general direction of the market for a particular commodity.

triple witching hour: Occurs on four days each year in which stock index futures, stock index options, and equity options all expire. These dates are the third Fridays of March, June, September, and December.

troy ounce: The standard for gold weight. A troy ounce weighs 9.7 percent more than the standard ounce.

type of option: There are two types of options: puts and calls.

U

uncovered call: This term is normally used as an alternative to naked call.

underlying asset: The common stock or other asset that an option allows its holder to buy or sell.

underlying security: See *underlying asset*.

unit: The combination of an Americus Trust PRIME and a SCORE.

unmatched trade: Another term for an *out trade*.

Unmatched Trade Notice: A notice informing clearing members of the existence of out trades with their accounts.

unsystematic factors: Factors unique to a specific company or industry, including earnings reports, technological developments, labor negotiations, cost of materials, and merger or acquisition activity.

unsystematic risk: The chance of loss associated with company specific events rather than broad market movements.

up and in option: An option automatically created if the price of the underlying asset rises to a specified level.

up and out option: An option that becomes worthless if the price of the underlying asset rises to a specified level.

V

value at risk: A measure of the largest loss expected on a position within a certain level of statistical certainty over a particular period of time (usually one day).

vega: The sensitivity of an option premium to changes in the volatility of the underlying asset.

vertical spread: A spread in which the options have the same expiration but different striking prices.

volatility: The extent to which an asset changes in price with the passage of time. In option pricing, volatility is measured as the annualized standard deviation of returns.

volatility smile: A name given to the characteristic plot of implied volatility values stemming from the different striking prices on a given underlying security.

volatility spread: A broad class of option spreads designed to take advantage of an expected change in the volatility of an underlying asset.

volume: The quantity of futures or options contracts traded during a given period of time.

W

warehouse receipt: A document representing the ownership of a specific quantity and quality of a commodity. Warehouse receipts are sometimes called *depository receipts*, especially with gold.

warrant: Essentially a long-term call option issued by a company rather than written by an individual.

warrant hedge: A strategy that appears unusually profitable, in which shares are purchased and warrants on the same company are sold short.

wasting asset: A property of an option that, when everything else remains equal (i.e., the stock price does not change), the value of the option will decline over time.

weather derivative: A swap or options contract that usually has a payout based on the average temperature in a set location over a period of time.

when-issued stock: A curious, short-lived security that is issued in conjunction with a stock split.

wild card option: The right of someone with a short position in T-bond futures to choose to deliver based upon a settlement price determined earlier in the day.

write an option: The act of selling options as an opening transaction.

Y

yield curve inversion: The phenomenon whereby long-term interest rates are lower than short-term rates.

yield to maturity: The true rate of return that will be earned on a debt instrument if the security is held until its maturity and all interest and principal is repaid as agreed. The calculation of yield to maturity assumes that it is possible to reinvest coupon returns at the yield to maturity.

Chapter Two: Basic Principles of Stock Options

1. F. There are two types: puts and calls.
2. F. The *writer* of the put has an obligation to sell.
3. T.
4. T.
5. F. It is normally 100 shares of stock.
6. T.
7. T.
8. T.
9. F. They normally expire on the Saturday following the third Friday.
10. F. The option premium is the same as the option price.
11. F. There is no necessary relationship between volume and open interest.
12. F. *Selling* an option as an opening transaction is called writing the option.
13. T.
14. F. Exchange traded puts and calls are both fungible.
15. T.
16. F. The NYSE no longer trades options.
17. T.
18. T.
19. T.
20. F. The owner of an option has the *right* to do something, while the writer has an *obligation to perform* if the option owner exercises.

Chapter Three: Basic Option Strategies: Covered Calls and Protective Puts

1. F. You would use a long call.
2. T.
3. T.
4. T.
5. T.
6. T.
7. T.
8. F. Long stock plus a *long* put is approximately equal to a long call.
9. T.
10. T.
11. T.
12. F. Potential losses are unlimited, but gains are limited to the premium received.
13. T.
14. T.
15. F. If you want to sell, you would write calls that are deep *in the money*.
16. F. Insider trading rules also apply to options.
17. F. The short seller is still susceptible to large losses if prices rise.
18. T.
19. F. The maximum gain equals the striking price minus the premium.
20. F. Your maximum gain is theoretically unlimited.

Chapter Four: Option Combinations and Spreads

1. T.
2. F. This is a short straddle.
3. T.
4. F. There are two breakeven points.
5. T.
6. T.
7. T.
8. T.
9. T. However, you seldom hear the phrase "writing a bearspread."
10. T.
11. T.
12. T.
13. T.

14. T.

15. F. The spreader uses options with more than one striking price or expiration.

16. T.

17. T.

18. F. Spreads are popular with both institutional and individual investors.

19. T.

20. T.

Chapter Five: Option Pricing

1. F. Castelli's work appeared in 1877.

2. T.

3. F. Arbitrage frequently appears, although it does not last long.

4. T.

5. F. Option pricing is directly tied to arbitrage arguments.

6. F. Put call parity states that an at-the-money call will sell for more than an at-the-money put.

7. T.

8. T.

9. F. An at-the-money call should sell for more than an at-the-money put.

10. T.

11. T.

12. F. An increase in time until expiration always means more time value, everything else being equal.

13. T.

14. T.

15. F. An increase in interest rates causes a call option to increase in value.

Chapter Six: The Black-Scholes Option Pricing Model

1. T.

2. T.

3. F. Listed options are not adjusted for cash dividends.

4. F. The person will be short twelve call options, but with a striking price half as large.

5. T.

6. T.

7. F. An American option will sell for more than a European option.

8. F. You must know the volatility of the underlying asset to determine the value of an option.

9. T.

10. F. There is no necessary relationship between implied and historical volatility.

11. T.

12. T.

13. T.

14. F. It is probably because the underlying asset recently had a stock split.

15. T.

Chapter Seven: Option Greeks

1. T.

2. T.

3. F. They range from zero to plus one.

4. T.

5. T.

6. T.

7. F. Delta is positive for calls and negative for puts, both of which have a negative theta.

8. F. Vega is also called lambda or kappa.

9. T.

10. F. There is no necessary relationship between the number of calls and the number of puts in a delta neutral portfolio.

11. F. Delta is the measure of the directional market.

12. T.

13. T.

14. T.

15. T. While a positive delta is generally helped by a price increase, the notion of position risk makes it possible for a very large rise to hurt.

Chapter Eight: Fundamentals of the Futures Market

1. F. Futures markets need a great many speculators to function well.

2. T.

3. T.

4. F. The Commodity Futures Trading Commission regulates futures.

5. T.

6. F. The business would use a long hedge.

7. T.

8. T.
9. T.
10. T.
11. T.
12. T.
13. T.
14. F. They are marked to market daily.
15. F. Open interest is a measure of how many contracts exist, not how many traded.
16. T.
17. T.
18. T.
19. T.
20. F. Normally a futures spread is less risky than single futures position.

Chapter Nine: Stock Index Futures

1. F. Most stock index futures trade at the Chicago Mercantile Exchange.
2. T.
3. F. S&P 500 futures are cash settled.
4. T.
5. F. Changes in the T-bill rate will have an immediate impact on the value of a futures contract.
6. T.
7. T.
8. T.
9. T.
10. F. A portfolio of stock combined with a *short* position in futures becomes a T-bill equivalent.

Chapter Ten: Foreign Exchange Futures

1. F. The U.S. is home to about 37% of global capitalization.
2. F. Foreign exchange risk reflects the chance of loss due to changes in exchange rates.
3. T.
4. T.
5. T.
6. F. It buys less if it weakens.
7. T.
8. T.
9. T.
10. T.
11. T.
12. T.

13. F. Forward contracts are not marked to market.
14. F. This is the least common reason.
15. T.

Chapter Eleven: Fundamentals of Interest Rate Futures

1. F. A Eurodollar is not the same as the Euro currency.
2. T.
3. F. It calls for the delivery of 90-day T-bills.
4. T.
5. T.
6. T.
7. F. T-bonds have a longer initial life than T-notes.
8. T.
9. T.
10. T.
11. F. The conversion factors turn bonds into 6% equivalents.
12. F. The person who buys a bond *pays* accrued interest.
13. F. There is no connection between cheapest to deliver and how recently a bond was issued.
14. T.
15. F. There is no spread option.

Chapter Twelve: Futures Contracts and Portfolio Management

1. T.
2. T.
3. F. The funds gap is the difference between the dollar duration of the assets and the dollar duration of the liabilities.
4. T.
5. F. Duration is a measure of interest rate risk only.
6. F. The higher the coupon, the *lower* the duration.
7. T.
8. F. *Buying* T-bond futures would increase duration.
9. F. It refers to a 0.01% change.
10. T.
11. T.
12. F. *Buying* futures will neutralize the cash in the portfolio.

13. F. You can trade out of a futures position at any time.
14. T.
15. T.

Chapter Thirteen: Swaps and Interest Rate Options

1. T.
2. T.
3. F. The swap buyer pays the fixed rate.
4. T.
5. F. The tenor is the life of the swap.
6. F. All payments are based on the notional amount.
7. F. Duration gap is *dollar* duration of the assets minus dollar duration of the liabilities.
8. F. A firm should borrow where it has a comparative advantage.
9. T.
10. F. A combined interest rate and currency swap is a CIRCUS swap.
11. F. A deferred swap is also called a forward stop swap.
12. F. It is more similar to a call option.
13. F. A cap does not contain a floorlet.
14. T.
15. T.
16. F. A collar is a long floor and a short cap.
17. F. There is no swap clearinghouse.

Chapter Fourteen: Swap Pricing

1. F. A swap is like a position that is both long a cap and short a floor.
2. T.
3. T.
4. F. It will decrease.
5. F. A 3 x 6 FRA is a three-month agreement that begins in three months.
6. F. Bootstrapping is used to find forward or implied rates.
7. F. The 3×6 implied FRA would be 4.94%.

$$(1 + \frac{0.05}{4})(1 + \frac{X}{4}) = (1 + \frac{0.05}{2})$$

8. F. In an off-market swap, either the fixed rate or the floating rate side can be more valuable.
9. T.

10. F. The swap value is the difference between the value of the floating rate side and the fixed rate side.
11. F. The swap spread is an amount over the Treasury curve, but it does not relate directly to profit for the swap dealer.
12. T.
13. F. With a stack hedge, the dealer usually uses the near term futures.
14. T.
15. T.
16. T.
17. T.
18. T.

Chapter Fifteen: Other Derivative Assets

1. F. Futures options do trade in the United States and are perfectly legal.
2. T.
3. T.
4. F. There *is* a premium with a futures option.
5. F. A futures option may have both intrinsic and time value.
6. T.
7. T.
8. T.
9. T.
10. F. A variation of Black-Scholes, the Black model, is for futures options.
11. F. The owner of a futures option may allow it to expire unexercised.
12. F. They may sell warrants short, but they may not create them.
13. T.
14. T.
15. F. A foreign currency option is different than a foreign currency futures option.
16. T.
17. T.

Chapter Sixteen: Financial Engineering and Risk Management

1. F. Eliminating investment risk will reduce your long-term return.
2. F. It was synthetic put options.
3. T.
4. F. By properly mixing puts and calls, you can create a synthetic long-term option.

5. T.
6. F. The closer gamma is to zero, the *less* often adjustments are necessary.
7. F. All position derivatives change with the passage of time.
8. T.
9. F. A fast market can hurt a position with a negative gamma.
10. T.
11. T.
12. T.
13. T.
14. F. Writing puts would make the position more bullish.
15. F. Most institutional use of index futures is to alter risk, but not to completely eliminate it.

Chapter Seventeen: Contemporary Issues

1. F. A hedge fund is a private investment portfolio, while a mutual fund is generally available to the public.

2. F. LTCM was in serious financial trouble when it closed.
3. F. Value at Risk measures the riskiness of a portfolio, not the net worth.
4. T.
5. F. Most weather derivatives are over-the-counter.
6. F. There is no obvious relation between heating degree days and cooling degree days.
7. F. There is likely to be no payout if temperature is near average.
8. T.
9. F. Employee stock options are taxable.
10. T.
11. F. There is nothing illegal about program trading.
12. F. FAS 133 is currently in force.
13. F. FAS 133 requires marking to market whenever accounting statements are prepared.

Index